The Roman History of Ammianus Marcellinus

During the Reigns of the Emperors

by
Ammianus Marcellinus

Contents

PREFACE

Of Ammianus Marcellinus, the writer of the following History, we know very little more than what can be collected from that portion of it which remains to us. From that source we learn that he was a native of Antioch, and a soldier; being one of the *prefectores domestici*—the body-guard of the emperor, into which none but men of noble birth were admitted. He was on the staff of Ursicinus, whom he attended in several of his expeditions; and he bore a share in the campaigns which Julian made against the Persians. After that time he never mentions himself, and we are ignorant when he quitted the service and retired to Rome, in which city he composed his History. We know not when he was born, or when he died, except that from one or two incidental passages in his work it is plain that he lived nearly to the end of the fourth century: and it is even uncertain whether he was a Christian or a Pagan; though the general belief is, that he adhered to the religion of the ancient Romans, without, however, permitting it to lead him even to speak disrespectfully of Christians or Christianity.

His History, which he divided into thirty-one books (of which the first thirteen are lost, while the text of those which remain is in some places imperfect), began with the accession of Nerva, A.D. 96, where Tacitus and Suetonius end, and was continued to the death of Valens, A.D. 378, a period of 282 years. And there is probably no work as to the intrinsic value of which there is so little difference of opinion. Gibbon bears repeated testimony to his accuracy, fidelity, and impartiality, and quotes him extensively. In losing his aid after A.D. 378, he says, "It is not without sincere regret that I must now take leave of an accurate and faithful guide, who has composed the history of his own times without indulging the prejudices and passions which usually affect the mind of a contemporary." Professor Ramsay (in Smith's Dictionary of Greek and Roman Biography) says, "We are indebted to him for a knowledge of many important facts not elsewhere recorded, and for much valuable insight into the modes of thought and the general tone of public feeling prevalent in his day. Nearly all the statements admitted appear to be founded upon his own observations, or upon the information derived from trustworthy eye-witnesses. A considerable number of dissertations and digressions are introduced, many of them highly interesting and valuable. Such are his notices of the institutions and manners of the Saracens (XIV 4), of the Scythians and Sarmatians (XVII 2), of the Huns and Alani (XXXI 2), of the Egyptians and their country (XXII 6, 14–16), and his geographical discussions upon Gaul (XV 9), the Pontus (XXII 8), and Thrace (XXVII. 4). Less legitimate and less judicious are his geological speculations upon earthquakes (XVII 7), his astronomical inquiries into eclipses (XX 3), comets (XXV 10), and the regulation of the calendar (xxvi. 1); his medical researches into the origin of epidemics (XIX 4); his zoological theory on the destruction of lions by mosquitos (XVIII 7), and his horticultural essay on the impregnation of palms (XXIV 3). In addition to industry in research and honesty of purpose, he was gifted with a large measure of strong common sense, which enabled him in many points to rise superior to the prejudices of his day, and with a clear-sighted independence of spirit which prevented him from being dazzled or over-awed by the brilliancy and the terrors which enveloped the imperial throne. But although sufficiently acute in detecting and exposing the follies of others, and especially in ridiculing the absurdities of popular superstition, Ammianus did not entirely escape the contagion. The general and deep-seated belief in magic spells, omens, prodigies, and oracles, which appears to have gained additional strength upon the first introduction of Christianity, evidently exercised no small influence over his mind. The old legends and doctrines of the pagan creed, and the subtle mysticism which philosophers pretended to discover lurking below, when mixed up with the pure and simple but startling tenets of the new faith, formed a confused mass which few intellects could reduce to order and harmony."

The vices of our author's style, and his ambitious affectation of ornament, are condemned by most critics; but some of the points which strike a modern reader as defects evidently arise from the alteration which the Latin language had already undergone since the days of Livy. His great value, however, consists in the facts he has made known to us, and is quite independent of the style or language in which he has conveyed that knowledge, of which without him we should have been nearly destitute.

2

The present translation has been made from Wagner and Erfurdt's edition, published at Leipzig in 1808, and their division of chapters into short paragraphs has been followed.

Feb. 1862.

BOOK XIV

(THE FIRST THIRTEEN BOOKS ARE LOST)

ARGUMENT

I. The cruelty of the Cæsar Gallus.—II. The incursions of the Isaurians.—III. The unsuccessful plans of the Persians.—IV. The invasion of the Saracens, and the manners of that people.—V. The punishment of the adherents of Magnentius.—VI. The vices of the senate and people of Rome.—VII. The ferocity and inhumanity of the Cæsar Gallus.—VIII. A description of the provinces of the East.—IX. About the Cæsar Constantius Gallus.—X. The Emperor Constantius grants the Allemanni peace at their request.—XI. The Cæsar Constantius Gallus is sent for by the Emperor Constantius, and beheaded.

I.

A.D. 353.

§ 1. After the events of an expedition full of almost insuperable difficulties, while the spirits of all parties in the state, broken by the variety of their dangers and toils, were still enfeebled; while the clang of trumpets was ringing in men's ears, and the troops were still distributed in their winter quarters, the storms of angry fortune surrounded the commonwealth with fresh dangers through the manifold and terrible atrocities of Cæsar Gallus:[1] who, when just entering into the prime of life, having been raised with unexpected honour from the lowest depth of misery to the highest rank, exceeded all the legitimate bounds of the power conferred on him, and with preposterous violence threw everything into confusion. For by his near relationship to the royal family, and his connection with the name of Constantine, he was so inflated with pride, that if he had had more power, he would, as it seemed, have ventured to attack even the author of his prosperity.

2. His wife added fuel to his natural ferocity; she was a woman immoderately proud of her sisterly relationship to Augustus, and had been formerly given in marriage by the elder Constantine to King Hannibalianus,[2] his brother's son. She was an incarnate fury: never weary of inflaming his savage temper, thirsting for human blood as insatiably as her husband. The pair, in process of time, becoming more skilful in the infliction of suffering, employed a gang of underhand and crafty talebearers, accustomed in their wickedness to make random additions to their discoveries, which consisted in general of such falsehoods as they themselves delighted in; and these men loaded the innocent with calumnies, charging them with aiming at kingly power, or with practising infamous acts of magic.

3. And among his less remarkable atrocities, when his power had gone beyond the bounds of moderate crimes, was conspicuous the horrible and sudden death of a certain noble citizen of Alexandria, named Clematius. His mother-in-law, having conceived a passion for him, could not prevail on him to gratify it; and in consequence, as was reported, she, having obtained an introduction by a secret door into the palace, won over the queen by the present of a costly necklace, and procured a fatal warrant to be sent to Honoratus, at that time count-governor of the East, in compliance with which Clematius was put to death, a man wholly innocent of any kind of wickedness, without being permitted to say a word in his defence.

4. After this iniquitous transaction, which struck others also with fear lest they should meet with similar treatment, as if cruelty had now obtained a licence, many were condemned on mere vague suspicion; of whom some were put to death, others were punished by the confiscation of their property, and driven forth as exiles from their homes, so that having nothing left but their tears and complaints, they were reduced to live on the contributions of their friends; and many opulent and famous houses were shut up, the old constitutional and just authority being changed into a government at the will of a bloodthirsty tyrant.

5. Nor amid these manifold atrocities was any testimony of an accuser, not even of a suborned one, sought for, in order to give at least an appearance of these crimes being committed according to law and statute, as very commonly even the most cruel princes have done: but whatever suited the implacable temper of Cæsar was instantly accomplished in haste, as if its accordance with human and divine law had been well considered.

6. After these deeds a fresh device was adopted, and a body of obscure men, such as, by reason of the meanness of their condition, were little likely to excite suspicion, were sent through all the districts of Antioch, to collect reports, and to bring news of whatever they might hear. They, travelling about, and concealing their object, joined clandestinely in the conversational circles of honourable men, and also in disguise obtained entrance into the houses of the rich. When they returned they were secretly admitted by back doors into the palace, and then reported all that they had been able to hear or to collect; taking care with an unanimous kind of conspiracy to invent many things, and to exaggerate for the worse all they really knew; at the same time suppressing any praises of Cæsar which had come to their ears, although these were wrung from many, against their consciences, by the dread of impending evils.

7. And it had happened sometimes that, if in his secret chamber, when no domestic servant was by, the master of the house had whispered anything into his wife's ear, the very next day, as if those renowned seers of old, Amphiaraus or Marcius, had been at hand to report it, the emperor was informed of what had been said; so that even the walls of a man's secret chamber, the only witnesses to his language, were viewed with apprehension.

8. And Cæsar's fixed resolution to inquire into these and other similar occurrences was increased by the queen, who constantly stimulated his desire, and was driving on the fortunes of her husband to headlong destruction, while she ought rather, by giving him useful advice, to have led him back into the paths of truth and mercy, by feminine gentleness, as, in recounting the acts of the Gordiani, we have related to have been done by the wife of that truculent emperor Maximinus.

9. At last, by an unsurpassed and most pernicious baseness, Gallus ventured on adopting a course of fearful wickedness, which indeed Gallienus, to his own exceeding infamy, is said formerly to have tried at Rome; and, taking with him a few followers secretly armed, he used to rove in the evening through the streets and among the shops, making inquiries in the Greek language, in which he was well skilled, what were the feelings of individuals towards Cæsar. And he used to do this boldly in the city, where the brillancy of the lamps at night often equalled the light of day. At last, being often recognized, and considering that if he went out in this way he should be known, he took care never to go out except openly in broad daylight, to transact whatever

business which he thought of serious importance. And these things caused bitter though secret lamentation, and discontent to many.

10. But at that time Thalassius was the present prefect³ of the palace, a man of an arrogant temper; and he, perceiving that the hasty fury of Gallus gradually increased to the danger of many of the citizens, did not mollify it by either delay or wise counsels, as men in high office have very often pacified the anger of their princes; but by untimely opposition and reproof, did often excite him the more to frenzy; often also informing Augustus of his actions, and that too with exaggeration, and taking care, I know not with what intention, that what he did should not be unknown to the emperor. And at this Cæsar soon became more vehemently exasperated, and, as if raising more on high than ever the standard of his contumacy, without any regard to the safety of others or of himself, he bore himself onwards like a rapid torrent, with an impetuosity which would listen to no reason, to sweep away all the obstacles which opposed his will.

II.

§ 1. Nor indeed was the East the only quarter which this plague affected with its various disasters. For the Isaurians also, a people who were accustomed to frequent alternations of peace, and of turbulence which threw everything into confusion with sudden outbreaks— impunity having fostered their growing audacity and encouraged it to evil—broke out in a formidable war. Being especially excited, as they gave out by this indignity, that some of their allies, having been taken prisoners, were in an unprecedented manner exposed to wild beasts, and in the games of the amphitheatre, at Iconium, a town of Pisidia.

2. And as Cicero⁴ says, that "even wild beasts, when reminded by hunger, generally return to that place where they have been before." So they all, descending like a whirlwind from their high and pathless mountains, came into the districts bordering on the sea: in which hiding themselves in roads full of lurking-places, and in defiles, when the long nights were approaching, the moon being at that time new, and so not yet giving her full light, they lay wait for the sailors; and when they perceived that they were wrapped in sleep, they, crawling on their hands and feet along the cables which held the anchors, and raising themselves up by them, swung themselves into the boats, and so came upon the crews unexpectedly, and, their natural ferocity being inflamed by covetousness, they spared not even those who of-

fered no resistance, but slew them all, and carried off a splendid booty with no more trouble than if it had been valueless.

3. This conduct did not last long, for when the deaths of the crews thus plundered and slaughtered became known, no one afterwards brought a vessel to the stations on that coast; but, avoiding them as they would have avoided the deadly precipices of Sciron,[5] they sailed on, without halting, to the shores of Cyprus, which lie opposite to the rocks of Isauria.

4. Therefore as time went on, and no foreign vessels went there any more, they quitted the sea-coast, and betook themselves to Lycaonia, a country which lies on the borders of Isauria. And there, occupying the roads with thick barricades, they sought a living by plundering the inhabitants of the district, as well as travellers. These outrages aroused the soldiers who were dispersed among the many municipal towns and forts which lie on the borders. And they, endeavouring to the utmost of their strength to repel these banditti, who were spreading every day more widely, sometimes in solid bodies, at others in small straggling parties, were overcome by their vast numbers.

5. Since the Isaurians, having been born and brought up amid the entangled defiles of lofty mountains, could bound over them as over plain and easy paths, and attacked all who came in their way with missiles from a distance, terrifying them at the same time with savage yells.

6. And very often our infantry were compelled in pursuit of them to climb lofty crags, and, when their feet slipped, to catch hold of the shrubs and briars to raise themselves to the summits; without ever being able to deploy into battle array, by reason of the narrow and difficult nature of the ground, nor even to stand firm; while their enemy running round in every direction hurled down upon them fragments of rock from above till they retired down the declivities with great danger. Or else, sometimes, in the last necessity fighting bravely, they were overwhelmed with fragments of immense bulk and weight.

7. On this account they subsequently were forced to observe more caution, and whenever the plunderers began to retire to the high ground, our soldiers yielded to the unfavourable character of the country and retired. But whenever they could be met with in the plain, which often happened, then charging them without giving them time to combine their strength, or even to brandish the javelins of which they always carried two or three, they slaughtered them like defenceless sheep.

8. So that these banditti, conceiving a fear of Lycaonia, which is for the most part a champaign country, since they had learnt by repeated proofs that they were unequal to our troops in a pitched battle, betook themselves by unfrequented tracks to Pamphylia. This district had long been free from the evils of war, but nevertheless had been fortified in all quarters by strong forts and garrisons, from the dread entertained by the people of rapine and slaughter, since soldiers were scattered over all the neighbouring districts.

9. Therefore hastening with all speed, in order by their exceeding celerity of movement to anticipate all rumour of their motions, trusting to their strength and activity of body, they travelled by winding roads until they reached the high ground on the tops of the mountains, the steepness of which delayed their march more than they had expected. And when at last, having surmounted all the difficulties of the mountains, they came to the precipitous banks of the Melas, a deep river and one full of dangerous currents, which winds round the district, protecting the inhabitants like a wall, the night which had overtaken them increased their fears, so that they halted for a while awaiting the daylight. For they expected to be able to cross without hindrance, and then, in consequence of the suddenness of their inroad, to be able to ravage all the country around; but they had incurred great toil to no purpose.

10. For when the sun rose they were prevented from crossing by the size of the river, which though narrow was very deep. And while they were searching for some fishing-boats, or preparing to commit themselves to the stream on rafts hastily put together, the legions which at that time were wintering about Side, came down upon them with great speed and impetuosity; and having pitched their standards close to the bank with a view to an immediate battle, they packed their shields together before them in a most skilful manner, and without any difficulty slew some of the banditti, who either trusted to their swimming, or who tried to cross the river unperceived in barks made of the trunks of trees hollowed out.

11. And the Isaurians having tried many devices to obtain success in a regular battle, and having failed in everything, being repulsed in great consternation, and with great vigour on the part of the legions, and being uncertain which way to go, came near the town of Laranda. And there, after they had refreshed themselves with food and rest, and recovered from their fears, they attacked several wealthy towns; but being presently scared by the support given to the citizens by some squadrons of horse which happened to be at hand, and which they

would not venture to resist in the extensive plains, they retreated, and retracing their steps summoned all the flower of their youth which had been left at home to join them.

12. And as they were oppressed with severe famine, they made for a place called Palea, standing on the sea-shore, and fortified with a strong wall; where even to this day supplies are usually kept in store, to be distributed to the armies which defend the frontier of Isauria.

13. Therefore they encamped around this fortress for three days and three nights, and as the steepness of the ground on which it stood prevented any attempt to storm it without the most deadly peril, and as it was impossible to effect anything by mines, and no other manœuvres such as are employed in sieges availed anything, they retired much dejected, being compelled by the necessities of their situation to undertake some enterprise, even if it should be greater than their strength was equal to.

14. Then giving way to greater fury than ever, being inflamed both by despair and hunger, and their strength increased by their unrestrainable ardour, they directed their efforts to destroy the city of Seleucia, the metropolis of the province, which was defended by Count Castucius, whose legions were inured to every kind of military service.

15. The commanders of the garrison being forewarned of their approach by their own trusty scouts, having, according to custom, given, out the watchword to the troops, led forth all their forces in a rapid sally, and having with great activity passed the bridge over the river Calicadnus, the mighty waters of which wash the turrets of the walls, they drew out their men as if prepared for battle. But as yet no man left the ranks, and the army was not allowed to engage; for the band of the Isaurians was dreaded, inasmuch as they were desperate with rage, and superior in number, and likely to rush upon the arms of the legions without any regard to their lives. Therefore as soon as the army was beheld at a distance, and the music of the trumpeters was heard, the banditti halted and stood still for a while, brandishing their threatening swords, and after a time they marched on slowly. And when the steady Roman soldiery began to deploy, preparing to encounter them, beating their shields with their spears (a custom which rouses the fury of the combatants, and strikes terror into their enemies), they filled the front ranks of the Isaurians with consternation. But as the troops were pressing forward eagerly to the combat their generals recalled them, thinking it inopportune to enter upon a contest of doubtful issue, when their walls were not far distant, under protec-

tion of which the safety of the whole army could be placed on a solid foundation.

16. Therefore the soldiers were brought back inside the walls in accordance with this resolution, and all the approaches and gates were strongly barred; and the men were placed on the battlements and bulwarks, having vast stones and weapons of all kinds piled close at hand, so that if any one forced his way inside he might be overwhelmed with a multitude of missiles and stones.

17. But those who were shut up in the walls were at the same time greatly afflicted, because the Isaurians having taken some vessels which were conveying grain down the river, were well provided with abundance of food, while they themselves, having almost consumed the usual stores of food, were in a state of alarm dreading the fatal agonies of approaching famine. When the news of this distress got abroad, and when repeated messages to this effect had moved Gallus Cæsar, because the master of the horse was kept away longer than usual at that season, Nebridius the count of the East was ordered to collect a military force from all quarters, and hastened forward with exceeding zeal to deliver the city, so wealthy and important, from such a peril. And when this was known the banditti retired, without having performed any memorable exploit, and dispersing, according to their wont, they sought the trackless recesses of the lofty mountains.

III.

§ 1. While affairs were in this state in Isauria, and while the king of Persia was involved in wars upon his frontier, repulsing from his borders a set of ferocious tribes which, being full of fickleness, were continually either attacking him in a hostile manner, or, as often happens, aiding him when he turned his arms against us, a certain noble, by name Nohodares, having been appointed to invade Mesopotamia, whenever occasion might serve, was anxiously exploring our territories with a view to some sudden incursion, if he could anywhere find an opportunity.

2. And because since every part of Mesopotamia is accustomed to be disturbed continually, the lands were protected by frequent barriers, and military stations in the rural districts, Nohodares, having directed his march to the left, had occupied the most remote parts of the Osdroene, having devised a novel plan of operations which had never hitherto been tried. And if he had succeeded he would have laid waste the whole country like a thunderbolt.

3. Now the plan which he had conceived was of this kind. There is a town in Anthemusia called Batne, built by the ancient Macedonians, a short distance from the river Euphrates, thickly peopled by wealthy merchants. To this city, about the beginning of the month of September, a great multitude of all ranks throng to a fair, in order to buy the wares which the Indians and Chinese send thither, and many other articles which are usually brought to this fair by land and sea.

4. The leader before named, preparing to invade this district on the days set apart for this solemnity, marching through the deserts and along the grassy banks of the river Abora, was betrayed by information given by some of his own men, who being alarmed at the discovery of certain crimes which they had committed, deserted to the Roman garrisons, and accordingly he retired again without having accomplished anything; and after that remained quiet without undertaking any further enterprise.

IV.

§ 1. At this time also the Saracens, a race whom it is never desirable to have either for friends or enemies, ranging up and down the country, if ever they found anything, plundered it in a moment, like rapacious hawks who, if from on high they behold any prey, carry it off with rapid swoop, or, if they fail in their attempt, do not tarry.

2. And although, in recounting the career of the Prince Marcus, and once or twice subsequently, I remember having discussed the manners of this people, nevertheless I will now briefly enumerate a few more particulars concerning them.

3. Among these tribes, whose primary origin is derived from the cataracts of the Nile and the borders of the Blemmyæ, all the men are warriors of equal rank; half naked, clad in coloured cloaks down to the waist, overrunning different countries, with the aid of swift and active horses and speedy camels, alike in times of peace and war. Nor does any member of their tribes ever take plough in hand or cultivate a tree, or seek food by the tillage of the land; but they are perpetually wandering over various and extensive districts, having no home, no fixed abode or laws; nor can they endure to remain long in the same climate, no one district or country pleasing them for a continuance.

4. Their life is one continued wandering; their wives are hired, on special covenant, for a fixed time; and that there may be some appearance of marriage in the business, the intended wife, under the name of a dowry, offers a spear and a tent to her husband, with a right to quit him after a fixed day, if she should choose to do so. And it is

inconceivable with what eagerness the individuals of both sexes give themselves up to matrimonial pleasures.

5. But as long as they live they wander about with such extensive and perpetual migrations, that the woman is married in one place, brings forth her children in another, and rears them at a distance from either place, no opportunity of remaining quiet being ever granted to her.

6. They all live on venison, and are further supported on a great abundance of milk, and on many kinds of herbs, and on whatever birds they can catch by fowling. And we have seen a great many of them wholly ignorant of the use of either corn or wine.

7. So much for this most mischievous nation. Now let us return to the subject we originally proposed to ourselves.

V.

§ 1. While these events were taking place in the East, Constantius was passing the winter at Arles; and after an exhibition of games in the theatre and in the circus, which were displayed with most sumptuous magnificence, on the tenth of October, the day which completed the thirtieth year of his reign, he began to give the reins more freely to his insolence, believing every information which was laid before him as proved, however doubtful or false it might be; and among other acts of cruelty, he put Gerontius, a count of the party of Magnentius, to the torture, and then condemned him to banishment.

2. And as the body of a sick man is apt to be agitated by even trifling grievances, so his narrow and sensitive mind, thinking every sound that stirred something either done or planned to the injury of his safety, made his victory[6] mournful by the slaughter of innocent men.

3. For if any one of his military officers, or of those who had ever received marks of honour, or if any one of high rank was accused, on the barest rumour, of having favoured the faction of his enemy, he was loaded with chains and dragged about like a beast. And whether any enemy of the accused man pressed him or not, as if the mere fact that his name had been mentioned was sufficient, every one who was informed against or in any way called in question, was condemned either to death, or to confiscation of his property, or to confinement in a desert island.

4. For his ferocity was excited to a still further degree when any mention was made of treason or sedition; and the bloodthirsty insinuations of those around him, exaggerating everything that happened, and pretending great concern at any danger which might threaten the life of

the emperor, on whose safety, as on a thread, they hypocritically exclaimed the whole world depended, added daily to his suspicions and watchful anger.

5. And therefore it is reported he gave orders that no one who was at any time sentenced to punishment for these or similar offences should be readmitted to his presence for the purpose of offering the usual testimonies to his character, a thing which the most implacable princes have been wont to permit. And thus deadly cruelty, which in all other men at times grows cool, in him only became more violent as he advanced in years, because the court of flatterers which attended on him added continual fuel to his stern obstinacy.

6. Of this court a most conspicuous member was Paulus, the secretary, a native of Spain, a man keeping his objects hidden beneath a smooth countenance, and acute beyond all men in smelling out secret ways to bring others into danger. He, having been sent into Britain to arrest some military officers who had dared to favour the conspiracy of Magnentius, as they could not resist, licentiously exceeded his commands, and like a flood poured with sudden violence upon the fortunes of a great number of people, making his path through manifold slaughter and destruction, loading the bodies of free-born men with chains, and crushing some with fetters, while patching up all kinds of accusations far removed from the truth. And to this man is owing one especial atrocity which has branded the time of Constantius with indelible infamy.

7. Martinus, who at that time governed these provinces as deputy, being greatly concerned for the sufferings inflicted on innocent men, and making frequent entreaties that those who were free from all guilt might be spared, when he found that he could not prevail, threatened to withdraw from the province, in the hope that this malevolent inquisitor, Paulus, might be afraid of his doing so, and so give over exposing to open danger men who had combined only in a wish for tranquillity.

8. Paulus, thinking that this conduct of Martinus was a hindrance to his own zeal, being, as he was, a formidable artist in involving matters, from which people gave him the nickname of "the Chain," attacked the deputy himself while still engaged in defending the people whom he was set to govern, and involved him in the dangers which surrounded every one else, threatening that he would carry him, with his tribunes and many other persons, as a prisoner to the emperor's court. Martinus, alarmed at this threat, and seeing the imminent danger in which his life was, drew his sword and attacked Paulus. But because

14

from want of strength in his hand he was unable to give him a mortal wound, he then plunged his drawn sword into his own side. And by this unseemly kind of death that most just man departed from life, merely for having dared to interpose some delay to the miserable calamities of many citizens.

9. And when these wicked deeds had been perpetrated, Paulus, covered with blood, returned to the emperor's camp, bringing with him a crowd of prisoners almost covered with chains, in the lowest condition of squalor and misery; on whose arrival the racks were prepared, and the executioner began to prepare his hooks and other engines of torture. Of these prisoners, many of them had their property confiscated, others were sentenced to banishment, some were given over to the sword of the executioner. Nor is it easy to cite the acquittal of a single person in the time of Constantius, where the slightest whisper of accusation had been brought against him.

VI.

§ 1. At this time Orfitus was the governor of the Eternal City, with the rank of prefect; and he behaved with a degree of insolence beyond the proper limits of the dignity thus conferred upon him. A man of prudence indeed, and well skilled in all the forensic business of the city, but less accomplished in general literature and in the fine arts than was becoming in a nobleman. Under his administration some very formidable seditions broke out in consequence of the scarcity of wine, as the people, being exceedingly eager for an abundant use of that article, were easily excited to frequent and violent disorders.

2. And since I think it likely that foreigners who may read this account (if, indeed, any such should meet with it) are likely to wonder how it is that, when my history has reached the point of narrating what was done at Rome, nothing is spoken of but seditions, and shops, and cheapness, and other similarly inconsiderable matters, I will briefly touch upon the causes of this, never intentionally departing from the strict truth.

3. At the time when Rome first rose into mundane brilliancy— that Rome which was fated to last as long as mankind shall endure, and to be increased with a sublime progress and growth—virtue and fortune, though commonly at variance, agreed upon a treaty of eternal peace, as far as she was concerned. For if either of them had been wanting to her, she would never have reached her perfect and complete supremacy.

4. Her people, from its very earliest infancy to the latest moment of its youth, a period which extends over about three hundred years, carried on a variety of wars with the natives around its walls. Then, when it arrived at its full-grown manhood, after many and various labours in war, it crossed the Alps and the sea, till, as youth and man, it had carried the triumphs of victory into every country in the world.

5. And now that it is declining into old age, and often owes its victories to its mere name, it has come to a more tranquil time of life. Therefore the venerable city, after having bowed down the haughty necks of fierce nations, and given laws to the world, to be the foundations and eternal anchors of liberty, like a thrifty parent, prudent and rich, intrusted to the Cæsars, as to its own children, the right of governing their ancestral inheritance.

6. And although the tribes are indolent, and the countries peaceful, and although there are no contests for votes, but the tranquillity of the age of Numa has returned, nevertheless, in every quarter of the world Rome is still looked up to as the mistress and the queen of the earth, and the name of the Roman people is respected and venerated.

7. But this magnificent splendour of the assemblies and councils of the Roman people is defaced by the inconsiderate levity of a few, who never recollect where they have been born, but who fall away into error and licentiousness, as if a perfect impunity were granted to vice. For as the lyric poet Simonides teaches us, the man who would live happily in accordance with perfect reason, ought above all things to have a glorious country.

8. Of these men, some thinking that they can be handed down to immortality by means of statues, are eagerly desirous of them, as if they would obtain a higher reward from brazen figures unendowed with sense than from a consciousness of upright and honourable actions; and they even are anxious to have them plated over with gold, a thing which is reported to have been first done in the instance of Acilius Glabrio, who by his wisdom and valour had subdued King Antiochus. But how really noble a thing it is to despise all these inconsiderable and trifling things, and to bend one's attention to the long and toilsome steps of true glory, as the poet of Ascrea[7] has sung, and Cato the Censor has shown by his example. For when he was asked how it was that while many other nobles had statues he had none, replied: "I had rather that good men should marvel how it was that I did not earn one, than (what would be a much heavier misfortune) inquire how it was that I had obtained one."

9. Others place the height of glory in having a coach higher than usual, or splendid apparel; and so toil and sweat under a vast burden of cloaks, which are fastened to their necks by many clasps, and blow about from the excessive fineness of the material; showing a desire, by the continual wriggling of their bodies, and especially by the waving of the left hand, to make their long fringes and tunics, embroidered in multiform figures of animals with threads of various colours, more conspicuous.

10. Others, with not any one asking them, put on a feigned severity of countenance, and extol their patrimonial estates in a boundless degree, exaggerating the yearly produce of their fruitful fields, which they boast of possessing in numbers from east to west, being forsooth ignorant that their ancestors, by whom the greatness of Rome was so widely extended, were not eminent for riches; but through a course of dreadful wars overpowered by their valour all who were opposed to them, though differing but little from the common soldiers either in riches, or in their mode of life, or in the costliness of their garments.

11. This is how it happened that Valerius Publicola was buried by the contributions of his friends, and that the destitute wife of Regulus was, with her children, supported by the aid of the friends of her husband, and that the daughter of Scipio had a dowry provided for her out of the public treasury, the other nobles being ashamed to see the beauty of this full-grown maiden, while her moneyless father was so long absent on the service of his country.

12. But now if you, as an honourable stranger, should enter the house of any one well off, and on that account full of pride, for the purpose of saluting him, at first, indeed, you will be hospitably received, as though your presence had been desired; and after having had many questions put to you, and having been forced to tell a number of lies, you will wonder, since the man had never seen you before, that one of high rank should pay such attention to you who are but an unimportant individual; so that by reason of this as a principal source of happiness, you begin to repent of not having come to Rome ten years ago.

13. And when relying on this affability you do the same thing the next day, you will stand waiting as one utterly unknown and unexpected, while he who yesterday encouraged you to repeat your visit, counts upon his fingers who you can be, marvelling, for a long time, whence you come, and what you want. But when at length you are recognized and admitted to his acquaintance, if you should devote yourself to the attention of saluting him for three years consecutively,

and after this intermit your visits for an equal length of time, then if you return to repeat a similar course, you will never be questioned about your absence any more than if you had been dead, and you will waste your whole life in submitting to court the humours of this blockhead.

14. But when those long and unwholesome banquets, which are indulged in at certain intervals, begin to be prepared, or the distribution of the usual dole-baskets takes place, then it is discussed with anxious deliberation whether when those to whom a return is due are to be entertained, it is proper to invite also a stranger; and if, after the matter has been thoroughly sifted, it is determined that it may be done, that person is preferred who waits all night before the houses of charioteers, or who professes a skill in dice, or pretends to be acquainted with some peculiar secrets.

15. For such entertainers avoid all learned and sober men as unprofitable and useless; with this addition, that the nomenclators[8] also, who are accustomed to make a market of these invitations and of similar favours, selling them for bribes, do for gain thrust in mean and obscure men at these dinners.

16. The whirlpools of banquets, and the various allurements of luxury, I omit, that I may not be too prolix, and with the object of passing on to this fact, that some people, hastening on without fear of danger, drive their horses, as if they were post-horses, with a regular licence, as the saying is, through the wide streets of the city, over the roads paved with flint, dragging behind them large bodies of slaves like bands of robbers; not leaving at home even Sannio,[9] as the comic poet says.

17. And many matrons, imitating these men, gallop over every quarter of the city with their heads covered, and in close carriages. And as skilful conductors of battles place in the van their densest and strongest battalions, then their light-armed troops, behind them the darters, and in the extreme rear troops of reserve, ready to join in the attack if necessity should arise; so, according to the careful arrangements of the stewards of these city households, who are conspicuous by wands fastened to their right hands, as if a regular watchword had been issued from the camp, first of all, near the front of the carriage march all the slaves concerned in spinning and working; next to them come the blackened crew employed in the kitchen; then the whole body of slaves promiscuously mixed up with a gang of idle plebeians from the neighbourhood; last of all, the multitude of eunuchs, beginning with the old men and ending with the boys, pale and unsightly

from the distorted deformity of their features; so that whichever way any one goes, seeing troops of mutilated men, he will detest the memory of Semiramis, that ancient queen who was the first person to castrate male youths of tender age; doing as it were a violence to nature, and forcing it back from its appointed course, which at the very first beginning and birth of the child, by a kind of secret law revealing the primitive fountains of seed, points out the way of propagating posterity.

18. And as this is the case, those few houses which were formerly celebrated for the serious cultivation of becoming studies, are now filled with the ridiculous amusements of torpid indolence, re-echoing with the sound of vocal music and the tinkle of flutes and lyres. Lastly, instead of a philosopher, you find a singer; instead of an orator, some teacher of ridiculous arts is summoned; and the libraries closed for ever, like so many graves; organs to be played by water-power are made; and lyres of so vast a size, that they look like waggons; and flutes, and ponderous machines suited for the exhibitions of actors.

19. Last of all, they have arrived at such a depth of unworthiness, that when, no very long time ago, on account of an apprehended scarcity of food, the foreigners were driven in haste from the city; those who practised liberal accomplishments, the number of whom was exceedingly small, were expelled without a moment's breathing-time; yet the followers of actresses, and all who at that time pretended to be of such a class, were allowed to remain; and three thousand dancing-girls had not even a question put to them, but stayed unmolested with the members of their choruses, and a corresponding number of dancing masters.

20. And wherever you turn your eyes, you may see a multitude of women with their hair curled, who, as far as their age goes, might, if they had married, been by this time the mothers of three children, sweeping the pavements with their feet till they are weary, whirling round in rapid gyrations, while representing innumerable groups and figures which the theatrical plays contain.

21. It is a truth beyond all question, that, when at one time Rome was the abode of all the virtues, many of the nobles, like the Lotophagi, celebrated in Homer, who detained men by the deliciousness of their fruit, allured foreigners of free birth by manifold attentions of courtesy and kindness.

22. But now, in their empty arrogance, some persons look upon everything as worthless which is born outside of the walls of the city,

except only the childless and the unmarried. Nor can it be conceived with what a variety of obsequious observance men without children are courted at Rome.

23. And since among them, as is natural in a city so great as to be the metropolis of the world, diseases attain to such an insurmountable degree of violence, that all the skill of the physician is ineffectual even to mitigate them; a certain assistance and means of safety has been devised, in the rule that no one should go to see a friend in such a condition, and to a few precautionary measures a further remedy of sufficient potency has been added, that men should not readmit into their houses servants who have been sent to inquire how a man's friends who may have been seized with an illness of this kind are, until they have cleansed and purified their persons in the bath. So that a taint is feared, even when it has only been seen with the eyes of another.

24. But nevertheless, when these rules are observed thus stringently, some persons, if they be invited to a wedding, though the vigour of their limbs be much diminished, yet, when gold is offered[10] in the hollow palm of the right hand, will go actively as far as Spoletum. These are the customs of the nobles.

25. But of the lower and most indigent class of the populace some spend the whole night in the wine shops. Some lie concealed in the shady arcades of the theatres; which Catulus was in his ædileship the first person to raise, in imitation of the lascivious manners of Campania, or else they play at dice so eagerly as to quarrel over them; snuffing up their nostrils and making unseemly noises by drawing back their breath into their noses; or (and this is their favourite pursuit of all others) from sunrise to evening they stay gaping through sunshine or rain, examining in the most careful manner the most sterling good or bad qualities of the charioteers and horses.

26. And it is very wonderful to see an innumerable multitude of people with great eagerness of mind intent upon the event of the contests in the chariot race. These pursuits, and others of like character, prevent anything worth mentioning or important from being done at Rome. Therefore we must return to our original subject.

VII.

§ 1. His licentiousness having now become more unbounded, the Cæsar began to be burdensome to all virtuous men; and discarding all moderation, he harassed every part of the East, sparing neither those who had received public honours, nor the chief citizens of the different cities; nor the common people.

2. At last by one single sentence he ordered all the principal persons at Antioch to be put to death; being exasperated because when he recommended that a low price should be established in the market at an unseasonable time, when the city was threatened with a scarcity, they answered him with objections, urged with more force than he approved; and they would all have been put to death to a man, if Honoratus, who was at that time count of the East, had not resisted him with pertinacious constancy.

3. This circumstance was also a proof, and that no doubtful or concealed one, of the cruelty of his nature, that he took delight in cruel sports, and in the circus he would rejoice as if he had made some great gain, to see six or seven gladiators killing one another in combats which have often been forbidden.

4. In addition to these things a certain worthless woman inflamed his purpose of inflicting misery; for she, having obtained admission to the palace, as she had requested, gave him information that a plot was secretly laid against him by a few soldiers of the lowest rank. And Constantina, in her exultation, thinking that her husband's safety was now fully secured, rewarded and placed this woman, in a carriage, and in this way sent her out into the public street through the great gate of the palace, in order, by such a temptation, to allure others also to give similar or more important information.

5. After these events, Gallus being about to set out for Hierapolis, in order, as far as appearance went, to take part in the expedition, the common people of Antioch entreated him in a suppliant manner to remove their fear of a famine which for many reasons (some of them difficult to explain) it was believed was impending; Gallus, however, did not, as is the custom of princes whose power, by the great extent of country over which it is diffused, is able continually to remedy local distresses, order any distribution of food to be made, or any supplies to be brought from the neighbouring countries; but he pointed out to them a man of consular rank, named Theophilus, the governor of Syria, who happened to be standing by, replying to the repeated appeals of the multitude, who were trembling with apprehensions of the last extremities, that no one could possibly want food if the governor were not willing that they should be in want of it.

6. These words increased the audacity of the lower classes, and when the scarcity of provisions became more severe, urged by hunger and frenzy, they set fire to and burnt down the splendid house of a man

of the name of Eubulus, a man of great reputation among his fellow-citizens; and they attacked the governor himself with blows and kicks as one especially made over to them by the judgment of the emperor, kicking him till he was half dead, and then tearing him to pieces in a miserable manner. And after his wretched death every one saw in the destruction of this single individual a type of the danger to which he was himself exposed, and, taught by this recent example, feared a similar fate.

7. About the same time Serenianus, who had previously been duke[11] of Phœnicia, to whose inactivity it was owing, as we have already related, that Celse in Phœnicia was laid waste, was deservedly and legally accused of treason and no one saw how he could possibly be acquitted. He was also manifestly proved to have sent an intimate friend with a cap (with which he used to cover his own head) which had been enchanted by forbidden acts to the temple of prophecy,[12] on purpose to ask expressly whether, according to his wish, a firm enjoyment of the whole empire was portended for him.

8. And in these days a twofold misfortune occurred: first, that a heavy penalty had fallen upon Theophilus who was innocent; and, secondly, that Serenianus who deserved universal execration, was acquitted without the general feeling being able to offer any effectual remonstrance.

9. Constantius then hearing from time to time of these transactions, and having been further informed of some particular occurrences by Thalassius, who however had now died by the ordinary course of nature, wrote courteous letters to the Cæsar, but at the same time gradually withdrew from him his support, pretending to be uneasy, least as the leisure of soldiers is usually a disorderly time, the troops might be conspiring to his injury: and he desired him to content himself with the schools of the Palatine,[13] and with those of the Protectors, with the Scutarii, and Gentiles. And he ordered Domitianus, who had formerly been the Superintendent of the Treasury, but who was now promoted to be a prefect, as soon as he arrived in Syria, to address Gallus in persuasive and respectful language, exhorting him to repair with all speed to Italy, to which province the emperor had repeatedly summoned him.

10. And when, with this object, Domitianus had reached Antioch, having travelled express, he passed by the gates of the palace, in contempt of the Cæsar, whom, however, he ought to have visited, and proceeded to the general's camp with ostentatious pomp, and there pretended to be sick; he neither visited the palace, nor ever appeared in

public, but keeping himself private, he devised many things to bring about the destruction of the Cæsar, adding many superfluous circumstances to the relations which he was continually sending to the emperor.

11. At last, being expressly invited by the Cæsar, and being admitted into the prince's council-chamber, without making the slightest preface he began in this inconsiderate and light-minded manner: "Depart," said he, "as you have been commanded, O Cæsar, and know this, that if you make any delay I shall at once order all the provisions allotted for the support of yourself and your court to be carried away." And then, having said nothing more than these insolent words, he departed with every appearance of rage; and would never afterwards come into his sight though frequently sent for.

12. The Cæsar being indignant at this, as thinking he had been unworthily and unjustly treated, ordered his faithful protectors to take the prefect into custody; and when this became known, Montius, who at that time was quæstor, a man of deep craft indeed, but still inclined to moderate measures,[14] taking counsel for the common good, sent for the principal members of the Palatine schools and addressed them in pacific words, pointing out that it was neither proper nor expedient that such things should be done; and adding also in a reproving tone of voice, that if such conduct as this were approved of, then, after throwing down the statues of Constantius the prefect would begin to think how he might also with the greater security take his life also.

13. When this was known Gallus, like a serpent attacked with stones or darts, being now reduced to the extremity of despair, and eager to insure his safety by any possible means, ordered all his troops to be collected in arms, and when they stood around him in amazement he gnashed his teeth, and hissing with rage, said,—

14. "You are present here as brave men, come to the aid of me who am in one common danger with you. Montius, with a novel and unprecedented arrogance, accuses us of rebellion and resistance to the majesty of the emperor, by roaring out all these charges against us. Being offended forsooth that, as a matter of precaution, I ordered a contumacious prefect, who pretended not to know what the state of affairs required, to be arrested and kept in custody."

15. On hearing these words the soldiers immediately, being always on the watch to raise disturbances, first of all attacked Montius, who happened to be living close at hand, an old man of no great bodily strength, and enfeebled by disease; and having bound his legs with

coarse ropes, they dragged him straddling, without giving him a moment to take breath, as far as the general's camp.

16. And with the same violence they also bound Domitianus, dragging him head first down the stairs; and then having fastened the two men together, they dragged them through all the spacious streets of the city at full speed. And, all their limbs and joints being thus dislocated, they trampled on their corpses after they were dead, and mutilated them in the most unseemly manner; and at last, having glutted their rage, they threw them into the river.

17. But there was a certain man named Luscus, the governor of the city, who, suddenly appearing among the soldiers, had inflamed them, always ready for mischief, to the nefarious actions which they had thus committed; exciting them with repeated cries, like the musician who gives the tune to the mourners at funerals, to finish what they had begun: and for this deed he was, not long after, burnt alive.

18. And because Montius, when just about to expire under the hands of those who were tearing him to pieces, repeatedly named Epigonius and Eusebius, without indicating either their rank or their profession, a great deal of trouble was taken to find out who they were; and, lest the search should have time to cool, they sent for a philosopher named Epigonius, from Lycia, and for Eusebius the orator, surnamed Pittacos, from Emissa; though they were not those whom Montius had meant, but some tribunes, superintendents of the manufactures of arms, who had promised him information if they heard of any revolutionary measures being agitated.

19. About the same time Apollinaris, the son-in-law of Domitianus, who a short time before had been the chief steward of the Cæsar's palace, being sent to Mesopotamia by his father-in-law, took exceeding pains to inquire among the soldiers whether they had received any secret despatches from the Cæsar, indicating his having meditated any deeper designs than usual. And as soon as he heard of the events which had taken place at Antioch, he passed through the lesser Armenia and took the road to Constantinople; but he was seized on his journey by the Protectors, and brought back to Antioch, and there kept in close confinement.

20. And while these things were taking place there was discovered at Tyre a royal robe, which had been secretly made, though it was quite uncertain who had placed it where it was, or for whose use it had been made. And on that account the governor of the province, who was at that time the father of Apollinaris, and bore the same name, was arrested as an accomplice in his guilt; and great numbers of other per-

sons were collected from different cities, who were all involved in serious accusations.

21. And now, when the trumpets of internal war and slaughter began to sound, the turbulent disposition of the Cæsar, indifferent to any consideration of the truth, began also to break forth, and that not secretly as before. And without making any solemn investigation into the truth of the charges brought against the citizens, and without separating the innocent from the guilty, he discarded all ideas of right or justice, as if they had been expelled from the seat of judgment. And while all lawful defence on trials was silent, the torturer, and plunderer, and the executioner, and every kind of confiscation of property, raged unrestrained throughout the eastern provinces of the empire, which I think it now a favourable moment to enumerate, with the exception of Mesopotamia, which I have already described when I was relating the Parthian wars; and also with the exception of Egypt, which I am forced to postpone to another opportunity.

VIII.

§ 1. After passing over the summit of Mount Taurus, which towards the east rises up to a vast height, Cilicia spreads itself out for a very great distance—a land rich in all valuable productions. It is bordered on its right by Isauria, which is equally fertile in vines and in many kinds of grain. The Calycadnus, a navigable river, flows through the middle of Isaurus.

2. This province, besides other towns, is particularly adorned by two cities, Seleucia, founded by King Seleucus, and Claudiopolis, which the Emperor Claudius Cæsar established as a colony. For the city of Isauria, which was formerly too powerful, was in ancient times overthrown as an incurable and dangerous rebel, and so completely destroyed that it is not easy to discover any traces of its pristine splendour.

3. The province of Cilicia, which exults in the river Cydnus, is ornamented by Tarsus, a city of great magnificence. This city is said to have been founded by Perseus, the son of Jupiter and Danaë; or else, and more probably, by a certain emigrant who came from Ethiopia, by name Sandan, a man of great wealth and of noble birth. It is also adorned by the city of Anazarbus, which bears the name of its founder; and by Mopsuestia, the abode of the celebrated seer Mopsus, who wandered from his comrades the Argonauts when they were returning after having carried off the Golden Fleece, and strayed to the African coast, where he died a sudden death. His heroic remains, though cov-

ered by Punic turf, have ever since that time cured a great variety of diseases, and have generally restored men to sound health.

4. These two provinces being full of banditti were formerly subdued by the proconsul Servilius, in a piratical war, and were passed under the yoke, and made tributary to the empire. These districts being placed, as it were, on a prominent tongue of land, are cut off from the main continent by Mount Amanus.

5. The frontier of the East stretching straight forward for a great distance, reached from the banks of the river Euphrates to those of the Nile, being bounded on the left by the tribes of the Saracens and on the right by the sea.

6. Nicator Seleucus, after he had occupied that district, increased its prosperity to a wonderful degree, when, after the death of Alexander, king of Macedonia, he took possession of the kingdom of Persia by right of succession; being a mighty and victorious king, as his surname indicates. And making free use of his numerous subjects, whom he governed for a long time in tranquillity, he changed groups of rustic habitations into regular cities, important for their great wealth and power, the greater part of which at the present day, although they are called by Greek names which were given them by the choice of their founder, have nevertheless not lost their original appellations which the original settlers of the villages gave them in the Assyrian language.

7. After Osdroene, which, as I have already said, I intend to omit from this description, the first province to be mentioned is Commagena, now called Euphratensis, which has arisen into importance by slow degrees, and is remarkable for the splendid cities of Hierapolis, the ancient Ninus, and Samosata.

8. The next province is Syria, which is spread over a beautiful champaign country. This province is ennobled by Antioch, a city known over the whole world, with which no other can vie in respect of its riches, whether imported or natural: and by Laodicea and Apameia, and also by Seleucia, all cities which have ever been most prosperous from their earliest foundation.

9. After this comes Phœnicia, a province lying under Mount Lebanon, full of beauty and elegance, and decorated with cities of great size and splendour, among which Tyre excels all in the beauty of its situation and in its renown. And next come Sidon and Berytus, and on a par with them Emissa and Damascus, cities founded in remote ages.

10. These provinces, which the river Orontes borders, a river which passes by the foot of the celebrated and lofty mountain Cassius,

and at last falls into the Levant near the Gulf of Issus, were added to the Roman dominion by Cnæus Pompey, who, after he had conquered Tigranes, separated them from the kingdom of Armenia.

11. The last province of the Syrias is Palestine, a district of great extent, abounding in well-cultivated and beautiful land, and having several magnificent cities, all of equal importance, and rivalling one another as it were, in parallel lines. For instance, Cæsarea, which Herod built in honour of the Prince Octavianus, and Eleutheropolis, and Neapolis, and also Ascalon, and Gaza, cities built in bygone ages.

12. In these districts no navigable river is seen: in many places, too, waters naturally hot rise out of the ground well suited for the cure of various diseases. These regions also Pompey formed into a Roman province after he had subdued the Jews and taken Jerusalem: and he made over their government to a local governor.

13. Contiguous to Palestine is Arabia, a country which on its other side joins the Nabathæi—a land full of the most plenteous variety of merchandize, and studded with strong forts and castles, which the watchful solicitude of its ancient inhabitants has erected in suitable defiles, in order to repress the inroads of the neighbouring nations. This province, too, besides several towns, has some mighty cities, such as Bostra, Gerasa, and Philadelphia, fortified with very strong walls. It was the Emperor Trajan who first gave this country the name of a Roman province, and appointed a governor over it, and compelled it to obey our laws, after having by repeated victories crushed the arrogance of the inhabitants, when he was carrying his glorious arms into Media and Parthia.

14. There is also the island of Cyprus, not very far from the continent, and abounding in excellent harbours, which, besides its many municipal towns, is especially famous for two renowned cities, Salamis and Paphos, the one celebrated for its temple of Jupiter, the other for its temple of Venus. This same Cyprus is so fertile, and so abounding in riches of every kind, that without requiring any external assistance, it can by its own native resources build a merchant ship from the very foundation of the keel up to the top sails, and send it to sea fully equipped with stores.

15. It is not to be denied that the Roman people invaded this island with more covetousness than justice. For when Ptolemy, the king, who was connected with us by treaty, and was also our ally, was without any fault of his own proscribed, merely on account of the necessities of our treasury, and slew himself by taking poison, the island was made tributary to us, and its spoils placed on board our fleet,

as if taken from an enemy, and carried to Rome by Cato. We will now return to the actions of Constantius in their due order.

IX.

§ 1. Amid all these various disasters, Ursicinus, who was the governor of Nisibis, an officer to whom the command of the emperor had particularly attached me as a servant, was summoned from that city, and in spite of his reluctance, and of the opposition which he made to the clamorous bands of flatterers, was forced to investigate the origin of the pernicious strife which had arisen. He was indeed a soldier of great skill in war, and an approved leader of troops; but a man who had always kept himself aloof from the strife of the forum. He, alarmed at his own danger when he saw the corrupt accusers and judges who were associated with him, all emerging out of the same lurking-places, wrote secret letters to Constantius informing him of what was going on, both publicly and in secret; and imploring such assistance as, by striking fear into Gallus, should somewhat curb his notorious arrogance.

2. But through excessive caution he had fallen into a worse snare, as we shall relate hereafter, since his enemies got the opportunity of laying numerous snares for him, to poison the mind of Constantius against him; Constantius, in other respects a prince of moderation, was severe and implacable if any person, however mean and unknown, whispered suspicion of danger into his ears, and in such matters was wholly unlike himself.

3. On the day appointed for this fatal examination, the master of the horse took his seat under the pretence of being the judge; others being also set as his assessors, who were instructed beforehand what was to be done: and there were present also notaries on each side of him, who kept the Cæsar rapidly and continually informed of all the questions which were put and all the answers which were given; and by his pitiless orders, urged as he was by the persuasions of the queen, who kept her ear at the curtain, many were put to death without being permitted to soften the accusations brought against them, or to say a word in their own defence.

4. The first persons who were brought before them were Epigonius and Eusebius, who were ruined because of the similarity of their names to those of other people; for we have already mentioned that Montius, when just at the point of death, had intended to inculpate the tribunes of manufactures, who were called by these names, as men who had promised to be his supports in some future enterprise.

5. Epigonius was only a philosopher as far as his dress went, as was evident, when, having tried entreaties in vain, his sides having been torn with blows, and the fear of instant death being presented to him, he affirmed by a base confession that his companion was privy to his plans, though in fact he had no plans; nor had he ever seen or heard anything, being wholly unconnected with forensic affairs. But Eusebius, confidently denying what he was accused of, continued firm in unshaken constancy, loudly declaring that it was a band of robbers before whom he was brought, and not a court of justice.

6. And when, like a man well acquainted with the law, he demanded that his accuser should be produced, and claimed the usual rights of a prisoner; the Cæsar, having heard of his conduct, and looking on his freedom as pride, ordered him to be put to the torture as an audacious calumniator; and when Eusebius had been tortured so severely that he had no longer any limbs left for torments, imploring heaven for justice, and still smiling disdainfully, he remained immovable, with a firm heart, not permitting his tongue to accuse himself or any one else. And so at length, without having either made any confession, or being convicted of anything, he was condemned to death with the spiritless partner of his sufferings. He was then led away to death, protesting against the iniquity of the times; imitating in his conduct the celebrated Stoic of old, Zeno, who, after he had been long subjected to torture in order to extract from him some false confession, tore out his tongue by the roots and threw it, bloody as it was, into the face of the king of Cyprus, who was examining him.

7. After these events the affair of the royal robe was examined into. And when those who were employed in dyeing purple had been put to the torture, and had confessed that they had woven a short tunic to cover the chest, without sleeves, a certain person, by name Maras, was brought in, a deacon, as the Christians call him; letters from whom were produced, written in the Greek language to the superintendent of the weaving manufactory at Tyre, which pressed him to have the beautiful work finished speedily; of which work, however, these letters gave no further description. And at last this man also was tortured, to the danger of his life, but could not be made to confess anything.

8. After the investigation had been carried on with the examination, under torture of many persons, when some things appeared doubtful, and others it was plain were of a very unimportant character, and after many persons had been put to death, the two Apollinares, father and son, were condemned to banishment; and when they had

come to a place which is called Crateræ, a country house of their own, which is four-and-twenty miles from Antioch, there, according to the order which had been given, their legs were broken, and they were put to death.

9. After their death Gallus was not at all less ferocious than before, but rather like a lion which has once tasted blood, he made many similar investigations, all of which it is not worth while to relate, lest I should exceed the bounds which I have laid down for myself; an error which is to be avoided.

X.

§ 1. While the East was thus for a long time suffering under these calamities, at the first approach of open weather, Constantius being in his seventh consulship, and the Cæsar in his third, the emperor quitted Arles and went to Valentia, with the intention of making war upon the brothers Gundomadus and Vadomarius, chiefs of the Allemanni; by whose repeated inroads the territories of the Gauls, which lay upon their frontier, were continually laid waste.

2. And while he was staying in that district, as he did for some time while waiting for supplies, the importation of which from Aquitania was prevented by the spring rains which were this year more severe than usual, so that the rivers were flooded by them, Herculanus arrived, a principal officer of the guard, son of Hermogenes, who had formerly been master of the horse at Constantinople, and had been torn to pieces in a popular tumult as we have mentioned before. And as he brought a faithful account of what Gallus had done, the emperor, sorrowing over the miseries that were passed, and full of anxious fear for the future, for a time stilled the grief of his mind as well as he could.

3. But in the mean time all the soldiery being assembled at Cabillon,[15] began to be impatient of delay, and to get furious, being so much the more exasperated because they had not sufficient means of living, the usual supplies not yet having arrived.

4. And in consequence of this state of things, Rufinus, at that time prefect of the camp, was exposed to the most imminent danger. For he himself was compelled to go among the soldiers, whose natural ferocity was inflamed by their want of food, and who on other occasions are by nature generally inclined to be savage and bitter against men of civil dignities. He was compelled, I say, to go among them to appease them and explain on what account the arrival of their corn was delayed.

5. And the task thus imposed on him was very cunningly contrived, in order that he, the uncle of Gallus, might perish in the snare; lest he, being a man of great power and energy, should rouse his nephew to confidence, and lead him to undertake enterprises which might be mischievous. Great caution, however, was used to escape this; and, when the danger was got rid of for a while, Eusebius, the high chamberlain, was sent to Cabillon with a large sum of money, which he distributed secretly among the chief leaders of sedition: and so the turbulent and arrogant disposition of the soldiers was pacified, and the safety of the prefect secured. Afterwards food having arrived in abundance the camp was struck on the day appointed.

6. After great difficulties had been surmounted, many of the roads being buried in snow, the army came near to Rauracum[16] on the banks of the Rhine, where the multitude of the Allemanni offered great resistance, so that by their fierceness the Romans were prevented from fixing their bridge of boats, darts being poured upon them from all sides like hail; and, when it seemed impossible to succeed in that attempt, the emperor being taken by surprise, and full of anxious thoughts, began to consider what to do.

7. When suddenly a guide well acquainted with the country arrived, and for a reward pointed out a ford by night, where the river could be crossed; and the army crossing at that point, while the enemy had their attention directed elsewhere, might without any one expecting such a step, have and waste the whole country, if a few men of the same nation to whom the higher posts in the Roman army were intrusted had not (as some people believe) informed their fellow-countrymen of the design by secret messengers.

8. The disgrace of this suspicion fell chiefly on Latinus, a commander of the domestic guard, and on Agilo, an equerry, and on Scudilo, the commander of the Scutarii, men who at that time were looked up to as those who supported the republic with their right hands.

9. But the barbarians, though taking instant counsel on such an emergency, yet either because the auspices turned out unfavourable, or because the authority of the sacrifices prohibited an instant engagement, abated their energy, and the confidence with which they had hitherto resisted; and sent some of their chiefs to beg pardon for their offences, and sue for peace.

10. Therefore, having detained for some time the envoys of both the kings, and having long deliberated over the affair in secret, the emperor, when he had decided that it was expedient to grant peace on

the terms proposed, summoned his army to an assembly with the intention of making them a short speech, and mounting the tribunal, surrounded with a staff of officers of high rank, spoke in the following manner:

11. "I hope no one will wonder, after the long and toilsome marches we have made, and the vast supplies and magazines which have been provided, from the confidence which I felt in you, that now although we are close to the villages of the barbarians, I have, as if I had suddenly changed my plans, adopted more peaceful counsels.

12. "For if every one of you, having regard to his own position and his own feelings, considers the case, he will find this to be the truth: that the individual soldier in all cases, however strong and vigorous he may be, regards and defends nothing but himself and his own life; while the general, looking on all with impartiality as the guardian of their general safety, is aware that the common interest of the people cannot be separated from his own safety; and he is bound to seize with alacrity every remedy of which the condition of affairs admits, as being put into his hand by the favour of the gods.

13. "That therefore I may in a few words set before you and explain on what account I wished all of you, my most faithful comrades, to assemble here, I entreat you to listen attentively to what I will state with all the brevity possible. For the language of truth is always concise and simple.

14. "The kings and people of the Allemanni, viewing with apprehension the lofty steps of your glory (which fame, increasing in magnificence, has diffused throughout the most distant countries), now by their ambassadors humbly implore pardon for their past offences, and peace. And this indulgence I, as a cautious and prudent adviser of what is useful, think expedient to grant them, if your consent be not wanting: being led to this opinion by many considerations, in the first place that so we may avoid the doubtful issues of war; in the second place, that instead of enemies we may have allies, as they promise we shall find them; further, that without bloodshed we may pacify their haughty ferocity, a feeling which is often mischievous in our provinces; and last of all, recollecting that the man who falls in battle, overwhelmed by superior weapons or strength, is not the only enemy who has to be subdued; and that with much greater safety to the state, even while the trumpet of war is silent, he is subdued who makes voluntary submission, having learnt by experience that we lack neither courage against rebels, nor mercy towards suppliants.

15. "To sum up, making you as it were the arbitrators, I wait to see what you determine: having no doubt myself, as an emperor always desirous of peace, that it is best to employ moderation while prosperity descends upon us. For, believe me, this conduct which I recommend, and which is wisely chosen, will not be imputed to want of courage on your part, but to your moderation and humanity."

16. As soon as he had finished speaking, the whole assembly being ready to agree to what the emperor desired, and praising his advice, gave their votes for peace; being principally influenced by this consideration, that they had already learnt by frequent expeditions that the fortune of the emperor was only propitious in times of civil troubles; but that when foreign wars were undertaken they had often proved disastrous. On this, therefore, a treaty being made according to the customs of the Allemanni, and all the solemnities being completed, the emperor retired to Milan for the winter.

XI.

§ 1. At Milan, having discarded the weight of other cares, the emperor took into his consideration that most difficult gordian knot, how by a mighty effort to uproot the Cæsar. And while he was deliberating on this matter with his friends in secret conference by night, and considering what force, and what contrivances might be employed for the purpose, before Gallus in his audacity should more resolutely set himself to plunging affairs into confusion, it seemed best that Gallus should be invited by civil letters, under pretence of some public affairs of an urgent nature requiring his advice, so that, being deprived of all support, he might be put to death without any hindrance.

2. But as several knots of light-minded flatterers opposed this opinion, among whom was Arbetio, a man of keen wit and always inclined to treachery, and Eusebius, a man always disposed to mischief, at that time the principal chamberlain, they suggested that if the Cæsar were to quit those countries it would be dangerous to leave Ursicinus in the East, with no one to check his designs, if he should cherish ambitious notions.

3. And these counsels were supported by the rest of the royal eunuchs, whose avarice and covetousness at that period had risen to excess. These men, while performing their private duties about the court, by secret whispers supplied food for false accusations; and by raising bitter suspicions of Ursicinus, ruined a most gallant man, creating by underhand means a belief that his grown-up sons began to aim at supreme power; intimating that they were youths in the flower of

33

their age and of admirable personal beauty, skilful in the use of every kind of weapon, well trained in all athletic and military exercises, and favourably known for prudence and wisdom. They insinuated also that Gallus himself, being by nature fierce and unmanageable, had been excited to acts of additional cruelty and ferocity by persons placed about him for that purpose, to the end that, when he had brought upon himself universal detestation, the ensigns of power might be transferred to the children of the master of the horse.

4. When these and similar suspicions were poured into the ears of Constantius, which were always open to reports of this kind, the emperor, revolving different plans in his mind, at last chose the following as the most advisable course. He commanded Ursicinus in a most complimentary manner to come to him, on the pretence that the urgent state of certain affairs required to be arranged by the aid of his counsel and concurrence, and that he had need of such additional support in order to crush the power of the Parthian tribes, who were threatening war.

5. And that he who was thus invited might not suspect anything unfriendly, the Count Prosper was sent to act as his deputy till he returned. Accordingly, when Ursicinus had received the letters, and had obtained a sufficient supply of carriages, and means of travelling, we[17] hastened to Milan with all speed.

6. The next thing was to contrive to summon the Cæsar, and to induce him to make the like haste. And to remove all suspicion in his mind, Constantius used many hypocritical endearments to persuade his own sister, Gallus's wife, whom he pretended he had long been wishing to see, to accompany him. And although she hesitated from fear of her brother's habitual cruelty, yet, from a hope that, as he was her brother, she might be able to pacify him, she set out; but when she reached Bithynia, at the station named Cæni Gallici, she was seized with a sudden fever and died. And after her death, her husband, considering that he had lost his greatest security and the chief support on which he relied, hesitated, taking anxious thought what he should do.

7. For amid the multiplicity of embarrassing affairs which distracted his attention, this point especially filled his mind with apprehension, that Constantius, determining everything according to his own sole judgment, was not a man to admit of any excuse, or to pardon any error; but being, as he was, more inclined to severity towards his kinsmen than towards others, would be sure to put him to death if he could get him into his power.

8. Being therefore in this critical situation, and feeling that he had to expect the worst unless he took vigilant care, he embraced the idea of seizing on the supreme power if he could find any opportunity: but for two reasons he distrusted the good faith of his most intimate councillors; both because they dreaded him as at once cruel and fickle, and also because amid civil dissensions they looked with awe upon the loftier fortune of Constantius.

9. While perplexed with these vast and weighty anxieties he received continual letters from the emperor, advising and entreating him to come to him; and giving him hints that the republic neither could nor ought to be divided; but that every one was bound to the utmost of his power to bring aid to it when it was tottering; alluding in this to the devastations of the Gauls.

10. And to this suggestion he added an example of no great antiquity, that in the time of Diocletian and his colleague,[18] the Cæsars obeyed them as their officers, not remaining stationary, but hastening to execute their orders in every direction. And that even Galerius went in his purple robe on foot for nearly a mile before the chariot of Augustus[19] when he was offended with him.

11. After many other messengers had been despatched to him, Scudilo the tribune of the Scutarii arrived, a very cunning master of persuasion under the cloak of a rude, blunt disposition. He, by mixing flattering language with his serious conversation, induced him to proceed, when no one else could do so, continually assuring him, with a hypocritical countenance, that his cousin was extremely desirous to see him; that, like a clement and merciful prince, he would pardon whatever errors had been committed through thoughtlessness; that he would make him a partner in his own royal rank, and take him for his associate in those toils which the northern provinces, long in a disturbed state, imposed upon him.

12. And as when the Fates lay their hand upon a man his senses are wont to be blunted and dimmed, so Gallus, being led on by these alluring persuasions to the expectation of a better fortune, quitted Antioch under the guidance of an unfriendly star, and hurried, as the old proverb has it, out of the smoke into the flame;[20] and having arrived at Constantinople as if in great prosperity and security, at the celebration of the equestrian games, he with his own hand placed the crown on the head of the charioteer Corax, when he obtained the victory.

13. When Constantius heard this he became exasperated beyond all bounds of moderation; and lest by any chance Gallus, feeling uncertain of the future, should attempt to consult his safety by flight, all

the garrisons stationed in the towns which lay in his road were carefully removed.

14. And at the same time Taurus, who was sent as quæstor into Armenia, passed by without visiting or seeing him. Some persons, however, by the command of the emperor, arrived under the pretence of one duty or another, in order to take care that he should not be able to move, or make any secret attempt of any kind. Among whom was Leontius, afterwards prefect of the city, who was sent as quæstor; and Lucillianus, as count of the domestic guards, and a tribune of the Scutarii named Bainobaudes.

15. Therefore after a long journey through the level country, when he had reached Hadrianopolis, a city in the district of Mount Hæmus, which had been formerly called Uscudama, where he stayed twelve days to recover from his fatigue, he found that the Theban legions, who were in winter quarters in the neighbouring towns of those parts, had sent some of their comrades to exhort him by trustworthy and sure promises to remain there relying upon them, since they were posted in great force among the neighbouring stations; but those about him watched him with such diligent care that he could get no opportunity of seeing them, or of hearing their message.

16. Then, as letter after letter from the emperor urged him to quit that city, he took ten public carriages, as he was desired to do, and leaving behind him all his retinue, except a few of his chamberlains and domestic officers, whom he had brought with him, he was in this poor manner compelled to hasten his journey, his guards forcing him to use all speed; while he from time to time, with many regrets, bewailed the rashness which had placed him in a mean and despised condition at the mercy of men of the lowest class.

17. And amid all these circumstances, in moments when exhausted nature sought repose in sleep, his senses were kept in a state of agitation by dreadful spectres making unseemly noises about him; and crowds of those whom he had slain, led on by Domitianus and Montius, seemed to seize and torture him with all the torments of the Furies.

18. For the mind, when freed by sleep from its connection with the body, is nevertheless active, and being full of the thoughts and anxieties of mortal pursuits, engenders mighty visions which we call phantoms.

19. Therefore his melancholy fate, by which it was destined he should be deprived of empire and life, leading the way, he proceeded on his journey by continual relays of horses, till he arrived at Peto-

bio,[21] a town in Noricum. Here all disguise was thrown off, and the Count Barbatio suddenly made his appearance, with Apodemius, the secretary for the provinces, and an escort of soldiers whom the emperor had picked out as men bound to him by especial favours, feeling sure that they could not be turned from their obedience either by bribes or pity.

20. And now the affair was conducted to its conclusion without further disguise or deceit, and the whole portion of the palace which is outside the walls was surrounded by armed men. Barbatio, entering the palace before daybreak, stripped the Cæsar of his royal robes, and clothed him with a tunic and an ordinary soldier's garment, assuring him with many protestations, as if by the especial command of the emperor, that he should be exposed to no further suffering; and then said to him, "Stand up at once." And having suddenly placed him in a private carriage, he conducted him into Istria, near to the town of Pola, where it is reported that Crispus, the son of Constantine, was formerly put to death.

21. And while he was there kept in strict confinement, being already terrified with apprehensions of his approaching destruction, Eusebius, at that time the high chamberlain, arrived in haste, and with him Pentadius the secretary, and Mallobaudes the tribune of the guard, who had the emperor's orders to compel him to explain, case by case, on what accounts he had ordered each of the individuals whom he had executed at Antioch to be put to death.

22. He being struck with a paleness like that of Adrastus[22] at these questions, was only able to reply that he had put most of them to death at the instigation of his wife Constantina; being forsooth ignorant that when the mother of Alexander the Great urged him to put to death some one who was innocent, and in the hope of prevailing with him, repeated to him over and over again that she had borne him nine months in her womb, and was his mother, that emperor made her this prudent answer, "My excellent mother, ask for some other reward; for the life of a man cannot be put in the balance with any kind of service."

23. When this was known, the emperor, giving way to unchangeable indignation and anger, saw that his only hope of establishing security firmly lay in putting the Cæsar to death. And having sent Serenianus, whom we have already spoken of as having been accused of treason, but acquitted by intrigue, and Pentadius the secretary, and Apodemius the secretary for the provinces, he commanded that they should put him to death. And accordingly his hands were bound like

those of some convicted thief, and he was beheaded, and his carcass, which but a little while ago had been the object of dread to cities and provinces, deprived of head and defaced: it was then left on the ground.

24. In this the supervision of the supreme Deity manifested itself to be everywhere vigilant. For not only did the cruelties of Gallus bring about his own destruction, but they also who, by their pernicious flattery and instigation, and charges supported by perjury, had led him to the perpetration of many murders, not long afterwards died miserably. Scudilo, being afflicted with a liver complaint which penetrated to his lungs, died vomiting; while Barbatio, who had long busied himself in inventing false accusations against Gallus, was accused by secret information of aiming at some post higher than his command of infantry, and being condemned, though unjustly, was put to death, and so by his melancholy end made atonement to the shade of the Cæsar.

25. These, and innumerable other actions of the same kind, Adrastea, who is also called Nemesis, the avenger of wicked and the rewarder of good deeds, is continually bringing to pass: would that she could always do so! She is a kind of sublime agent of the powerful Deity, dwelling, according to common belief, above the human circle; or, as others define her, she is a substantial protection, presiding over the particular destinies of individuals, and feigned by the ancient theologians to be the daughter of Justice, looking down from a certain inscrutable eternity upon all terrestrial and mundane affairs.

26. She, as queen of all causes of events, and arbitress and umpire in all affairs of life, regulates the urn which contains the lots of men, and directs the alternations of fortune which we behold in the world, frequently bringing our undertakings to an issue different from what we intended, and involving and changing great numbers of actions. She also, binding the vainly swelling pride of mankind by the indissoluble fetters of necessity, and swaying the inclination of progress and decay according to her will, sometimes bows down and enfeebles the stiff neck of arrogance, and sometimes raises virtuous men from the lowest depth, leading them to a prosperous and happy life. And it is on this account that the fables of antiquity have represented her with wings, that she may be supposed to be present at all events with prompt celerity. And they have also placed a rudder in her hand and given her a wheel under her feet, that mankind may be aware that she governs the universe, running at will through all the elements.[23]

27. In this untimely manner did the Cæsar, being himself also already weary of life, die, in the twenty-ninth year of his age, having reigned four years. He was born in the country of the Etrurians, in the district of Veternum,[24] being the son of Constantius, the brother of the Emperor Constantine; his mother was Galla, the sister of Rufinus and Cerealis, men who had been ennobled by the offices of consul and prefect.

28. He was a man of splendid stature and great beauty of person and figure, with soft hair of a golden colour, his newly sprouting beard covering his cheeks with a tender down, and in spite of his youth his countenance showed dignity and authority. He differed as much from the temperate habits of his brother Julian, as the sons of Vespasian, Domitian and Titus, differed from each other.

29. After he had been taken by the emperor as his colleague, and raised to the highest eminence of power, he experienced the fickle changeableness of fortune which mocks mortality, sometimes raising individuals to the stars, at others sinking them to the lowest depths of hell.

30. And though the examples of such vicissitudes are beyond number, nevertheless I will only enumerable a few in a cursory manner. This changeable and fickle fortune made Agathocles, the Sicilian, a king from being a potter, and reduced Dionysius, formerly the terror of all nations, to be the master of a grammar school. This same fortune emboldened Andriscus of Adramyttium, who had been born in a fuller's shop, to assume the name of Philip, and compelled the legitimate son of Perseus[25] to descend to the trade of a blacksmith to obtain a livelihood. Again, fortune surrendered Mancinus[26] to the people of Numantia, after he had enjoyed the supreme command, exposed Veturius[27] to the cruelty of the Samnites, Claudius[28] to that of the Corsicans, and made Regulus[29] a victim to the ferocity of the Carthaginians. Through the injustice of fortune, Pompey,[30] after he had acquired the surname of the Great by the grandeur of his exploits, was murdered in Ægypt at the pleasure of some eunuchs, while a fellow named Eunus, a slave who had escaped from a house of correction, commanded an army of runaway slaves in Sicily. How many men of the highest birth, through the connivance of this same fortune, submitted to the authority of Viriathus and of Spartacus![31] How many heads at which nations once trembled have fallen under the deadly hand of the executioner! One man is thrown into prison, another is promoted to unexpected power, a third is hurled down from

the highest rank and dignity. But he who would endeavour to enumerate all the various and frequent instances of the caprice of fortune, might as well undertake to number the sands or ascertain the weight of mountains.

Notes

[1] Gallus and his brother Julian were the nephews of the great Constantine, sons of his brother Julius. When Constantius, who succeeded Constantine on the throne, murdered his uncles and most of his cousins, he spared these two, probably on account of their tender age.

[2] Hannibalianus was another nephew of Constantine. That emperor raised his own three sons, Constantine, Constantius, and Constans, to the dignity of Cæsar; and of his two favourite nephews, Dalmacius and Hannibalianus, he raised the first, by the title of Cæsar, to an equality with his cousins; "in favour of the latter he invented the new and singular appellation of Fortitissimus, to which he annexed the flattering distinction of a robe of purple and gold. But of the whole series of Roman princes in any age of the empire Hannibalianus alone was distinguished by the title of *king*, a name which the subjects of Tiberius would have detested as the profane and cruel insult of capricious tyranny."—Gibbon, cxviii. The editor of Bohn's edition adds in a note: "The title given to Hannibalianus did not apply to him as a *Roman* prince, but as king of a territory assigned to him in Asia. This territory consisted of Pontus, Cappadocia, and the lesser Armenia, the city of Cæsarea being chosen for his residence."—Gibbon, Bohn's edition, vol. ii. pp. 256, 257.

[3] "There was among the commanders of the soldiery one prefect who was especially entitled Præsens, or Præsentalis, because his office was to be always in the court or about the person of the prince, and because the emperor's body-guard was under his particular orders."—H. Valesius.

[4] The passage is found in Cicero's Oration pro Cluentio, c. 25.

[5] Sciron was a pirate slain by Theseus, v. Ov. Metam. vii. 44 and the Epistle of Ariadne to Theseus.
"Cum fuerit Sciron lectus, torvusque Procrustes."

[6] His victory over Magnentius, whom he defeated at Mursa, on the Doave, in the year 351. Magnentius fled to Aquileia, but was pursued, and again defeated the next year, at a place called Mons Seleuci, in the neighbourhood of Gap, and threw himself on his own sword to avoid falling into the hands of Constantius.

[7] Hesiod. Ammianus refers to the passage in Hesiod's Op. et Dies, 289, beginning—τῆς δ' ἀρεῆς ἱδρῶτα θεοὶ προπάροιθεν ἔθησαν.

8 A nomenclator was a slave who attended a great noble in his walk through the city to remind him of the names of those whom he met. See Cicero pro Muræna, c. 36.

9 The name of a slave in the Eunuch, of Terence, who says, act. iv sc. 8— Sannio alone stays at home.

10 It was customary on such solemnities, as also on the occasion of assuming the toga virilis, or entering on any important magistracy, to make small presents of money to the guests who were invited to celebrate the occasion. Cf. Plin. Epist. x. 117.

11 The Latin is Dux. It is about this period that the title Duke and Count, which we have already had, arose, indicating however at first not territorial possessions, but military commands; and it is worth noticing that the rank of Count was the higher of the two.

12 Constantine, on his conversion to Christianity, had issued an edict forbidding the consultation of oracles; but the practice was not wholly abandoned till the time of Theodosius.

13 Schools was the name given at Rome to buildings where men were wont to meet for any purpose, whether of study, of traffic, or of the practice of any art. The schools of the Palatine were the station of the cohorts of the guard. The "Protectors or Guards" were a body of soldiers of higher rank, receiving also higher pay; called also "Domestici or household troops," as especially set apart for the protection of the imperial palace and person. The "Scutarii" (shield-bearers) belonged to the Palatine schools; and the Gentiles were troops enlisted from among those nations which were still accounted barbarous.

14 Gibbon here proposes for lenitatem to read levitatem, fickleness; himself describing Montius as "a statesman whose art and experience were frequently betrayed by the levity of his disposition."—Cap. xix., p. 298, vol. iii., Bohn's edition.

15 Châlons sur Saône.

16 Near Basle.

17 It will be observed that Ammianus here speaks of himself as in attendance upon Ursicinus.

18 Maximianus Herculius.

19 Diocletian.

20 As we say, Out of the frying-pan into the fire.

21 The town of Pettau, on the Drave.

22 A paleness such as overspread the countenance of Adrastus when he saw his two sons-in-law, Pydeus and Polynices, slain at Thebes. Virgil speaks of Adrasti pallentis imago, Æn. vi. 480.

23 Ammianus here confounds Nemesis with Fortuna. Compare Horace's description of the latter goddess, Lib. i. Od. 34:—

" ... Valet ima summis
Mutare, et insignia attenuat deus
Obscura promens: hinc apicem rapax
Fortuna cum stridore acuto
Sustulit; hic posuisse gaudet."

Or, as it is translated by Dr. Francis:—

"The hand of Jove can crush the proud
Down to the meanness of the crowd:
And raise the lowest in his stead:
But rapid Fortune pulls him down,
And snatches his imperial crown,
To place, not fix it, on another's head."

[24] Near the modern city of Sienna.

[25] See Plutarch's Life of Æmilius, c. 37. The name of the young prince was Alexander.

[26] Called also Hostilius; cf. Vell. Paterc. ii. 1.

[27] Cf. Liv. ix. c. x.; Cicero de Officiis, iii. 30.

[28] Cf. Val. Max. vi. 3.

[29] Cf. Horace, Od. iv. ult.; Florus, ii. 1. The story of the cruelties inflicted on Regulus is now, however, generally disbelieved.

[30] The fate of Pompey served also as an instance to Juvenal in his satire on the vanity of human wishes.

Provida Pompeio diderat Campania febres
Optandas, sed multæ urbes et publica vota
Vicerunt; igitur Fortuna ipsius et urbis
Servatum victo caput abstulit.

Sat. X. 283, &c.

[31] Spartacus was the celebrated leader of the slaves in the Servile War.

BOOK XV

I.

A.D. 354.

§ 1. Having investigated the truth to the best of our power we have hitherto related all the transactions which either our age permitted us to witness, or which we could learn from careful examination of those who were concerned in them, in the order in which the several events took place. The remaining facts, which the succeeding books will set forth, we will, as far as our talent permits, explain with the greatest accuracy, without fearing those who may be inclined to cavil at our work as too long; for brevity is only to be praised when, while it puts an end to unseasonable delays, it suppresses nothing which is well authenticated.

2. Gallus had hardly breathed his last in Noricum, when Apodemius, who as long as he lived had been a fiery instigator of disturbances, caught up his shoes and carried them off, journeying, with frequent relays of horses, so rapidly as even to kill some of them by excess of speed, and so brought the first news of what had occurred to Milan. And having made his way into the palace, he threw down the shoes before the feet of Constantius, as if he were bringing the spoils of a king of the Parthians who had been slain. And when this sudden news arrived that an affair so unexpected and difficult had been executed with entire facility in complete accordance with the wish of the emperor, the principal courtiers, according to their custom, exerting all their zeal in the path of flattery, extolled to the skies the virtue and good fortune of the emperor, at whose nod, as if they had been mere common soldiers, two princes had thus been deprived of their power, namely, Veteranio and Gallus.

3. And Constantius being exceedingly elated at the exquisite taste of this adulation, and thinking that he himself for the future should be free from all the ordinary inconveniences of mortality, now began to depart from the path of justice so evidently that he even at times laid claim to immortality; and in writing letters with his own hand, would style himself lord of the whole world; a thing which, if others had said, any one ought to have been indignant at, who laboured with proper diligence to form his life and habits in emulation of the constitutional princes who had preceded him, as he professed to do.

4. For even if he had under his power the infinities of worlds fancied by Democritus, as Alexander the Great, under the promptings of Anaxarchus, did fancy, yet either by reading, or by hearing others speak, he might have considered that (as mathematicians unanimously agree) the circumference of the whole earth, immense as it seems to us, is nevertheless not bigger than a pin's point as compared with the greatness of the universe.

II.

§ 1. And now, after the pitiable death of the Cæsar, the trumpet of judicial dangers sounded the alarm, and Ursicinus was impeached of treason, envy gaining more and more strength every day to attack his safety; envy which is inimical to all powerful men.

2. For he was overcome by this difficulty, that, while the ears of the emperor were shut against all defences which were reasonable and easy of proof, they were open to all the secret whispers of calumniators, who pretended that his name was almost disused among all the

districts of the East, and that Ursicinus was urged by them both privately and publicly to be their commander, as one who could be formidable to the Persian nation.

3. But this magnanimous man stood his ground immovably against whatever might happen, only taking care not to throw himself away in an abject manner, and grieving from his heart that innocence had no safe foundation on which to stand. And the more sad also for this consideration, that before these events took place many of his friends had gone over to other more powerful persons, as in cases of official dignity the lictors go over to the successors of former officers.

4. His colleague Arbetio was attacking him by cajoling words of feigned good-will, often publicly speaking of him as a virtuous and brave man; Arbetio being a man of great cunning in laying snares for men of simple life, and one who at that season enjoyed too much power. For as a serpent that has its hole underground and hidden from the sight of man observes the different passers-by, and attacks whom it will with a sudden spring, so this man, having been raised from being a common soldier of the lowest class to the highest military dignities, without having received any injury or any provocation, polluted his conscience from an insatiable desire of doing mischief.

5. Therefore, having a few partners in his secrets for accomplices, he had secretly arranged with the emperor when he asked his opinion, that on the next night Ursicinus should be seized and carried away from the sight of the soldiers, and so be put to death uncondemned, just as formerly Domitius Corbulo, that faithful and wise defender of our provinces, is said to have been slain in the miserable period of Nero's cruelty.

6. And after the matter had been thus arranged, while the men destined for the service of seizing Ursicinus were waiting for the appointed time, the emperor's mind changed to mercy, and so this impious deed was put off for further consideration.

7. Then the engine of calumny was directed against Julian, who had lately been brought to court; a prince who afterwards became memorable, but who was now attacked with a twofold accusation, as the iniquity of his enemies thought requisite. First, that he had gone from the Park of Macellum, which lies in Cappadocia, into Asia, from a desire of acquiring polite learning. Secondly, that he had seen his brother as he passed through Constantinople.

8. And when he had explained away the charges thus brought against him, and had proved that he had not done either of these things without being ordered, he would still have perished through the in-

trigues of the abandoned court of flatterers, if he had not been saved by the favour of the supreme Deity, with the assistance of Queen Eusebia. By her intercession he obtained leave to be conducted to the town of Como, in the neighbourhood of Milan; and after he had remained there a short time he was permitted to go to Greece for the purpose of cultivating his literary tastes, as he was very eager to do.

9. Nor were there wanting other incidents arising out of these occurrences, which might be looked upon as events under the direction of Providence, as some of them were rightly punished, while others failed of their design, proving vain and ineffective. But it occasionally happened that rich men, relying on the protection of those in office, and clinging to them as the ivy clings to lofty trees, bought acquittals at immense prices; and that poor men who had little or no means of purchasing safety were condemned out of hand. And therefore truth was overshadowed by falsehood, and sometimes falsehood obtained the authority of truth.

10. In these days Gorgonius also was summoned to court, the man who had been the Cæsar's principal chamberlain. And though it was made plain by his own confession that he had been a partner in his undertakings, and sometimes a chief instigator of them, yet through the conspiracy of the eunuchs justice was overpowered by dexterously arranged falsehoods, and he was acquitted and so escaped the danger.

III.

§ 1. While these events were taking place at Milan, battalions of soldiers were brought from the East to Aquileia, with a number of members of the court, who, being broken in spirit, while their limbs were enfeebled by the weight of their chains, cursed the protraction of their lives which were surrounded with every variety of misery. For they were accused of having been the ministers of the ferocity of Gallus, and it was believed to be owing to them that Domitian had been torn to pieces, and that Montius and others had been brought to destruction.

2. Arboreus, and Eusebius, at that time high chamberlain, both men of insane arrogance, and equally unjust and cruel, were appointed to try these men. And they, without any careful examination, or making any distinction between the innocent and the guilty, condemned some to scourgings, others to torture and exile, some they adjudged to serve in the lowest ranks of the army, and the rest they condemned to death. And when they had thus filled the sepulchres with dead bodies, they returned as if in triumph, and brought an account of their exploits

to the emperor, who was notoriously severe and implacable against all offences of the kind.

3. After this, throughout the rest of his reign, Constantius, as if resolved to reverse the prescribed arrangement of the Fates, behaved with greater violence than ever, and opened his heart to numbers of designing plotters. And owing to this conduct, many men arose who watched for all kinds of reports, at first attacking, as with the appetite of wild beasts, those in the enjoyment of the highest honours and rank, and afterwards both poor and rich indiscriminately. Not like those Cibyratæ in the time of Verres,[32] fawning on the tribunal of a single lieutenant, but harassing the limbs of the whole republic by means of all the evils that arose anywhere.

4. Among these men Paulus and Mercurius were especially conspicuous, the first a Dacian born, the latter a Persian. Mercurius was a notary, and Paulus had been promoted from being a steward of the emperor's table to a receivership in the provinces. Paulus, as I have already mentioned, had been nicknamed The Chain, because in weaving knots of calumnies he was invincible, scattering around foul poisons and destroying people by various means, as some skilful wrestlers are wont in their contests to catch hold of their antagonists by the heel.

5. Mercurius was nicknamed Count of Dreams, because (as a dog fond of biting secretly fawns and wags his tail while full of inward spite) he forced his way into feasts and companies, and if any one in his sleep (when nature roves about with an extraordinary degree of freedom) communicated to a friend that he had seen anything, exaggerated it, colouring it for the most part with envenomed arts, and bore it to the open ears of the emperor. And for such speeches men were attacked with formidable accusations, as if they had committed inexpiable crimes.

6. The news of these events having got abroad, men were so cautious of even relating nocturnal dreams, that, in the presence of a stranger, they would scarcely confess they had slept at all. And some accomplished men lamented that they had not been born in the country of Mount Atlas,[33] where it is said that dreams never occur, though what the cause of such a fact is, we must leave to those who are learned in such matters to decide.

7. Amid all these terrible investigations and punishments, another disaster took place in Illyricum, which from some empty words involved many in danger. At an entertainment given by Africanus, the governor of the second Pannonia, at Sirmium, some men having drunk

rather too much, and thinking there was no witness of their proceedings, spoke freely of the existing imperial government, accusing it as most vexatious to the people. And some of them expressed a hope that a change, such as was wished for by all, might be at hand, affirming that this was portended by omens, while some, with incredible rashness, affirmed that the auguries of their ancestral house promised the same thing.

8. Among those present at the banquet was Gaudentius, one of the secretaries, a stupid man, and of a hasty disposition. And he looking upon the matter as serious, reported it to Rufinus, who was at that time the chief commander of the guard of the prætorian prefecture, a man always eager for the most cruel measures, and infamous for every kind of wickedness.

9. He immediately, as if borne on wings, flew to the court of the emperor, and so bitterly inflamed him, always easy of access and susceptible of impressions from suspicious circumstances of this kind, that without a moment's deliberation he ordered Africanus and all who had been partakers of his fatal banquet to be seized. And when this was done, the wicked informer, always fond of whatever is contrary to popular manners, obtained what he most coveted, a continuation of his existing office for two years.

10. To arrest these men, Teutomeres, the chief of the Protectores, was sent with his colleague; and he loaded them all with chains, and conducted them, as he had been ordered, to the emperor's court. But when they arrived at Aquileia, Marinus, who from having been a drillmaster had been promoted to a tribuneship, but who at that time had had no particular duty, being a man who had held dangerous language, and who was in other respects of an intemperate disposition, being left in an inn while things necessary for the journey were being prepared, stabbed himself with a knife which he accidentally found, and his bowels gushed out, so that he died. The rest were conducted to Milan, and subjected to torture; and having been forced by their agony to confess that while at the banquet they had used some petulant expressions, were ordered to be kept in penal confinement, with some hope, though an uncertain one, of eventual release. But Teutomeres and his colleague, being accused of having allowed Marinus to kill himself, were condemned to banishment, though they were afterwards pardoned through the intercession of Arbetio.

IV.

§ 1. Soon after this transaction had been thus terminated, war was declared against the tribes of the Allemanni around Lentia,[34] who had often made extensive incursions into the contiguous Roman territories. The emperor himself set out on the expedition, and went as far as Rhætia, and the district of the Canini.[35] And there, after long and careful deliberation, it was decided to be both honourable and expedient that Arbetio, the master of the horse, should march with a division of the troops, in fact with the greater part of the army, along the borders of the lake of Brigantia, with the object of coming to an immediate engagement with the barbarians. And I will here describe the character of the ground briefly, as well as I can.

2. The Rhine rising among the defiles of lofty mountains, and forcing its way with immense violence through steep rocks, stretches its onward course without receiving any foreign waters, in the same manner as the Nile pours down with headlong descent through the cataracts. And it is so abundantly full by its own natural riches that it would be navigable up to its very source were it not like a torrent rather than a stream.

3. And soon after it has disentangled itself from its defiles, rolling onward between high banks, it enters a vast lake of circular form, which the Rhætian natives call Brigantia,[36] being four hundred and sixty furlongs in length, and of nearly equal extent in breadth, unapproachable on account of a vast mass of dark woods, except where the energy of the Romans has made a wide road through them, in spite of the hostility of the barbarians, and the unfavourable character both of the ground and the climate.

4. The Rhine forcing its way into this pool, and roaring with its foaming eddies, pierces the sluggish quiet of the waters, and rushes through the middle from one end to the other. And like an element separated from some other element by eternal discord, without any increase or diminution of the volume of water which it has brought into the lake, it comes forth from it again with its old name and its unalloyed power, never having suffered from the contact, and so proceeds till it mingles with the waves of the sea.

5. And what is exceedingly strange, the lake is not moved at all by this rapid passage of the river through it, nor is it affected by the muddy soil beneath the waters of the lake; the two bodies of water being incapable of mingling with each other. A thing which would be supposed impossible, did not the very sight of the lake prove the fact.

6. In a similar manner, the Alpheus, rising in Arcadia, being seized with a love for the fountain Arethusa,[37] passing through the Ionian sea, as is related by the poets, proceeds onward till it arrives at the neighbourhood of its beloved fountain.

7. Arbetio not choosing to wait till messengers arrived to announce the approach of the barbarians, although he knew the fierce way in which they begin their wars, allowed himself to be betrayed into a hidden ambush, where he stood without the power of moving, being bewildered by the suddenness of his disaster.

8. In the mean time the enemy, showing themselves, sprang forth from their hiding-places and spared not one who came in their way, but overwhelmed them with every kind of weapon. For none of our men could offer the smallest resistance, nor was there any hope of any of them being able to save their lives except by a speedy flight. Therefore, being intent only on avoiding wounds, our soldiers, losing all order, ran almost at random in every direction, exposing their backs to the blows of the enemy. Nevertheless the greater part of them, scattering themselves among narrow paths, were saved from danger by the protecting darkness of the night, and at the return of day recovered their courage and rejoined their different legions. But still by this sad and unexpected disaster a vast number of common soldiers and ten tribunes were slain.

9. The Allemanni were greatly elated at this event, and advanced with increased boldness, every day coming up to the fortifications of the Romans while the morning mists obscured the light; and drawing their swords roamed about in every direction, gnashing their teeth, and threatening us with haughty shouts. Then with a sudden sally our Scutarii would rush forth, and after being stopped for a moment by the resistance of the hostile squadrons, would call out all their comrades to join them in the engagement.

10. But the greater part of our men were alarmed by the recollection of their recent disaster, and Arbetio hesitated, thinking everything pregnant with danger. Upon this three tribunes at once sallied forth, Arintheus who was a lieutenant commander of the heavy troops, Seniauchus who commanded the cavalry of the Comites,[38] and Bappo who had the command of the Promoti[39] and of those troops who had been particularly intrusted to his charge by the emperor.

11. These men, looking on the common cause as their own, resolved to repel the violence of the enemy according to the example of their ancient comrades. And pouring down upon the foe like a torrent, not in a regular line of battle, but in desultory attacks like those of

banditti, they put them all to flight in a disgraceful manner. Since they, being in loose order and straggling, and hampered by their endeavours to escape, exposed their unprotected bodies to our weapons, and were slain by repeated blows of sword and spear.

12. Many too were slain with their horses, and seemed as they lay on their backs to be so entangled as still to be sitting on them. And when this was seen, all our men who had previously hesitated to engage in battle with their comrades, poured forth out of the camp; and now, forgetful of all precautions, they drove before them the mob of barbarians, except such as flight had saved from destruction, trampling on the heaps of slain, and covered with gore.

13. When the battle was thus terminated the emperor in triumph and joy returned to Milan to winter quarters.

V.

A.D. 355.

§ 1. After these unhappy circumstances, accompanied as they were with equal calamities in the provinces, a whirlwind of new misfortunes arose which seemed likely to destroy the whole state at once, if Fortune, which regulates the events of human life, had not terminated a state of affairs which all regarded with great apprehension, by bringing the dangers to a speedy issue.

2. From the long neglect with which these provinces had been treated, the Gauls, having no assistance on which to rely, had borne cruel massacres, with plunder and conflagration, from barbarians who raged throughout their land with impunity. Silvanus, the commander of the infantry, being a man well suited to correct these evils, went thither at the command of the emperor, Arbetio at the same time urging with all his power that this task should be undertaken without delay, with the object of imposing the dangerous burden of this duty on his absent rival, whom he was vexed to see still in prosperity....

3. There was a certain man named Dynamius, the superintendent of the emperor's beasts of burden, who had begged of Silvanus recommendatory letters to his friends as of one who was admitted to his most intimate friendship. Having obtained this favour, as Silvanus, having no suspicion of any evil intention, had with great simplicity granted what he was asked, Dynamius kept the letters, in order at a future time to plan something to his injury.

4. Therefore, when the aforesaid commander had gone to the Gauls in the service of the republic, and while he was engaged in repelling the barbarians, who already began to distrust their own power,

51

and to be filled with alarm, Dynamius, being restless, like a man of cunning and practised deceitfulness, devised a wicked plot; and in this it is said he had for his accomplices Lampadius, the prefect of the prætorian guard, Eusebius, who had been the superintendent of the emperor's privy purse, and was known by the nickname of Mattyo-copa,[40] and Ædesius, formerly keeper of the records, whom this prefect had contrived to have elected consul, as being his dearest friend. He then with a sponge effaced the contents of the letters, leaving nothing but the address, and inserted a text materially differing from the original writing, as if Silvanus had asked, by indirect hints, and entreated his friends who were within the palace, and those who had no office (among whom was Albinus of Etruria, and many others), to aid him in projects of loftier ambition, as one who would soon attain the imperial throne. This bundle of letters he thus made up, inventing at his leisure, in order with them to endanger the life of this innocent man.

5. Dynamius was appointed to investigate these charges on behalf of the emperor; and while he was artfully weaving these and similar plans, he contrived to enter alone into the imperial chamber, choosing his opportunity, and hoping to entangle firmly in his meshes the most vigilant guardian of the emperor's safety. And being full of wicked cunning, after he had read the forged packet of letters in the council chamber, the tribunes were ordered to be committed to custody, and also several private individuals were commanded to be arrested and brought up from the provinces, whose names were mentioned in those letters.

6. But presently Malarichus, the commander of the Gentiles, being struck with the iniquity of the business, and taking his colleagues to his counsel, spoke out loudly that men devoted to the preservation of the emperor ought not to be circumvented by factions and treachery. He accordingly demanded that he himself, his nearest relations being left as hostages, and Mallobaudes, the tribune of the heavy-armed soldiers, giving bail that he would return, might be commissioned to go with speed to bring back Silvanus, who he was certain had never entertained the idea of any such attempt as these bitter plotters had imputed to him. Or, as an alternative, he entreated that he might become security for Mallobaudes, and that their officers might be permitted to go and do what he had proposed to take upon himself.

7. For he affirmed that he knew beyond all question that, if any stranger were sent, Silvanus, who was inclined to be somewhat appre-

hensive of danger, even when no circumstances were really calculated to alarm him, would very likely throw matters into confusion.

8. But, although the advice which he gave was useful and necessary, he spoke as to the winds, to no purpose. For by the counsels of Arbetio, Apodemius, who was a persevering and bitter enemy to all good men, was sent with letters to summon Silvanus to the presence. When he had arrived in Gaul, taking no heed of the commission with which he was charged, and caring but little for anything that might happen, he remained inactive, without either seeing Silvanus, or delivering the letters which commanded him to appear at court. And having taken the receiver of the province into his counsels, he began with arrogance and malevolence to harass the clients and servants of the master of the horse, as if that officer had been already condemned and was on the point of being executed.

9. In the mean time, while the arrival of Silvanus was looked for, and while Apodemius was throwing everything, though quiet before, into commotion, Dynamius, that he might by still more convincing proofs establish belief in his wicked plots, had sent other forged letters (agreeing with the previous ones which he had brought under the emperor's notice by the agency of the prefect) to the tribune of the factory at Cremona: these were written in the names of Silvanus and Malarichus, in which the tribune, as one privy to their secrets, was warned to lose no time in having everything in readiness.

10. But when this tribune had read the whole of the letters, he was for some time in doubt and perplexity as to what they could mean (for he did not recollect that those persons whose letters he had thus received had ever spoken with him upon private transactions of any kind); and accordingly he sent the letters themselves, by the courier who had brought them, to Malarichus, sending a soldier also with him; and entreated Malarichus to explain in intelligible language what he wanted, and not to use such obscure terms. For he declared that he, being but a plain and somewhat rude man, had not in the least understood what was intimated so obscurely.

11. Malarichus the moment he received the letters, being already in sorrow and anxiety, and alarmed for his own fate and that of his countryman Silvanus, called around him the Franks, of whom at that time there was a great multitude in the palace, and in resolute language laid open and proved the falsehood of the machinations by which their lives were threatened, and was loud in his complaints.

12. When these things became known to the emperor, he appointed the members of his secret council and the chief officers of his

army to make further investigation of the matter. And when the judges appeared to make light of it, Florentius the son of Nigridianus, who at that time filled the post of master of the offices,[41] having examined the writings carefully, and detecting beneath them some vestiges of the tops of the former words which had been effaced, perceived, as was indeed the case, that by interpolations of the original letter, matters very different from any of which Silvanus was author had been written over them, according to the fancy of the contriver of this forgery.

13. On this the cloud of treachery was dispersed, and the emperor, informed of the truth by a faithful report, recalled the powers granted to the prefect, and ordered him to be submitted to an examination. Nevertheless he was acquitted through the active combination of many of his friends; while Eusebius, the former treasurer of the emperor's secret purse, being put to the torture, confessed that these things had been done with his privity.

14. Ædesius, affirming with obstinate denial that he had never known anything which had been done in the matter, escaped, being adjudged innocent. And thus the transaction was brought to an end, and all those who had been accused in the original information were acquitted; and Dynamius, as a man of exceeding accomplishments and prudence, was appointed to govern Etruria with the rank of corrector.

15. While these affairs were proceeding, Silvanus was living at Agrippina,[42] and having learnt by continual information sent to him by his friends what Apodemius was doing with the hope of effecting his ruin; and knowing also how impressible the mind of the feeble emperor was; began to fear lest in his absence, and without being convicted of any crime, he might still be treated as a criminal. And so, being placed in a situation of the greatest difficulty, he began to think of trusting himself to the good faith of the barbarians.

16. But being dissuaded from this by Laniogaisus, at that time a tribune, whom we have already spoken of as the only person who was present with Constans when he was dying, himself serving at that time as a volunteer; and being assured by Laniogaisus that the Franks, of whom he himself was a countryman, would put him to death, or else betray him for a bribe, he saw no safety anywhere in the present emergency, and so was driven to extreme counsels. And by degrees, having secretly conferred with the chiefs of the principal legions, and having excited them by the magnitude of promised rewards, he tore for use on this occasion the purple silk from the insignia of the dragons[43] and standards, and so assumed the title of emperor.

17. And while these events are passing in Gaul, one day, a little before sunset, an unexpected messenger arrived at Milan, relating fully that Silvanus, being ambitious to rise above his place as commander of the infantry, had tampered with the army, and assumed the imperial dignity.

18. Constantius, at this amazing and unexpected event, seemed as if struck by a thunderbolt of fate, and having at once summoned a council to meet at the second watch, all the nobles hastened to the palace. No one had either mind to conceive or tongue to recommend what was best to be done; but in suppressed tones they mentioned the name of Ursicinus as a man eminent for skill in affairs of war, and one who had been undeservedly exposed to most injurious treatment. He was immediately sent for by the principal chamberlain, which is the most honourable kind of summons, and as soon as he entered the council-chamber was offered the purple to salute much more graciously than at any former time. Diocletian was the first who introduced the custom of offering reverence to the emperor after this foreign manner and royal pretension; whereas all former princes, as we read, had been saluted like judges.

19. And so the man who a little while before, through the malevolent persecution of certain of the courtiers, had been termed the whirlpool of the East, and who had been accused of a design to aim at the supreme power for his sons, was now recommended as one who was a most skilful general, who had been the comrade of the great Constantine, and as the only man capable of extinguishing the threatened conflagration. And though the reasons for which he was sent for were honest, they were not wholly free from underhand motives. For while great anxiety was felt that Silvanus should be destroyed as a most formidable rebel, yet, if that object miscarried, it was thought that Ursicinus, being damaged by the failure, would himself easily be ruined; so that no scruple, which else was to be feared, would interpose to save him from destruction.

20. While arrangements were being made for accelerating his journey, the general was preparing to repel the charges which had been brought against him; but the emperor prevented him, forbidding him in conciliatory language, saying that this was not an opportunity suitable for undertaking any controversy in defence of his cause, when the imminent necessity of affairs rather prompted that no delay should be interposed to the restoration of parties to their pristine concord before the disunion got worse.

21. Therefore, after a long deliberation about many things, the first and most important matter in which consultation was held, was by what means Silvanus could be led to think the emperor still ignorant of his conduct. And the most likely manner to confirm him in his confidence appeared to be that he should be informed, in a complimentary despatch, that Ursicinus was appointed his successor, and that he was invited to return to court with undiminished power.

22. After this affair was arranged, the officer who had brought the news to Milan was ordered to depart with some tribunes and ten of the Protectores and domestic guard as an escort, given to him at his own request, to aid him in the discharge of his public duty. And of these I myself was one, with my colleague Verrinianus; and all the rest were either friends or relations of mine.

23. And now all of us, fearing mainly for ourselves, accompanied him a long distance on his journey; and although we seemed as exposed to danger as gladiators about to fight with wild beasts, yet considering in our minds that evils are often the forerunners of good, we recollected with admiration that expression of Cicero's, uttered by him in accordance with the eternal maxims of truth, which runs in these words:[44]—"And although it is a thing most desirable that one's fortune should always continue in a most flourishing condition; still that general level state of life brings not so much sensation of joy as we feel when, after having been surrounded by disasters or by dangers, fortune returns into a happier condition."

24. Accordingly we hastened onwards by forced journeys, in order that the master of the horse, who was eager to acquire the honour of suppressing the revolt, might make his appearance in the suspected district before any rumour of the usurpation of Silvanus had spread among the Italians. But rapidly as we hastened, fame, like the wind, had outstripped us, and had revealed some part of the facts; and when we reached Agrippina we found matters quite out of the reach of our attempts.

25. For a vast multitude of people, assembled from all quarters, were, with a mixture of haste and alarm, strengthening the foundations of Silvanus's enterprise, and a numerous military force was collected; so that it seemed more advisable, on the existing emergency, for our unfortunate general to await the intentions and pleasure of the new emperor, who was assuring himself by ridiculous omens and signs that he was gaining accessions of strength. By permitting his feelings of security to increase, by different pretences of agreement and flattery,

Silvanus, it was thought, might be relieved from all fear of hostility, and so be the more easily deceived.

26. But the accomplishment of such a design appeared difficult. For it was necessary to use great care and watchfulness to make our desires subordinate to our opportunities, and to prevent their either outrunning them, or falling behind them; since if our wishes were allowed to become known unseasonably, it was plain we should all be involved in one sentence of death.

27. However our general was kindly received, and (the very business itself forcing us to bend our necks), having been compelled to prostrate himself with all solemnity before the newly robed prince, still aiming at higher power, was treated as a highly favoured and eminent friend; having freedom of access and the honour of a seat at the royal table granted to him in preference to every one else, in order that he might be consulted with the more secrecy about the principal affairs of state.

28. Silvanus expressed his indignation that, while unworthy persons had been raised to the consulship and to other high dignities, he and Ursicinus alone, after the frequent and great toils which they had endured for the sake of the republic, had been so despised that he himself had been accused of treason in consequence of the examination of some slaves, and had been exposed to an ignoble trial; while Ursicinus had been brought over from the East, and placed at the mercy of his enemies; and these were the subjects of his incessant complaints both in public and in private.

29. While, however, he was holding this kind of language, we were alarmed at the murmurs of our soldiers who were now suffering from want, which surrounded us on all sides; the troops showing every eagerness to make a rapid march, through the defiles of the Cottian Alps.

30. In this state of anxiety and agitation, we occupied ourselves in secretly deliberating on the means of arriving at our object; and at length, after our plans had been repeatedly changed out of fear, it was determined to use great industry in seeking out prudent agents, binding them to secrecy by solemn oaths, in order to tamper with the Gallic soldiers whom we knew to be men of doubtful fidelity, and at any time open to change for a sufficient reward.

31. Therefore, after we had secured our success by the address of some agents among the common soldiers, men by their very obscurity fitted for the accomplishment of such a task, and now excited by the expectation of reward, at sunrise, as soon as the east began to redden, a

band of armed men suddenly sallied forth, and, as is common in critical moments, behaving with more than usual audacity. They slew the sentinels and penetrated into the palace, and so having dragged Silvanus out of a little chapel in which, in his terror, he had taken refuge on his way to a conventicle devoted to the ceremonies of the Christian worship, they slew him with repeated strokes of their swords.

32. In this way did a general of no slight merit perish, through fear of false accusations heaped on him in his absence by a faction of wicked men, and which drove him to the utmost extremities in order to preserve his safety.

33. For although he had acquired strong claims on the gratitude of Constantius by his seasonable sally with his troops before the battle of Mursa, and although he could boast the valorous exploits of his father Bonitus, a man of Frankish extraction, but who had espoused the party of Constantine, and often in the civil war had exhibited great prowess against the troops of Licinius, still he always feared him as a prince of wavering and fickle character.

34. Now before any of these events had taken place in Gaul, it happened that one day in the Circus Maximus at Rome, the populace cried out with a loud voice, "Silvanus is conquered." Whether influenced by instinct or by some prophetic spirit, cannot be decided.

35. Silvanus having been slain, as I have narrated, at Agrippina, the emperor was seized with inconceivable joy when he heard the news, and gave way to exceeding insolence and arrogance, attributing this event also to the prosperous course of his good fortune; giving the reins to his habitual disposition which always led him to hate men of brave conduct, as Domitian in former times had done, and desiring at all times to destroy them by every act of opposition.

36. And he was so far from praising even his act of diligence and fidelity, that he recorded in writing a charge that Ursicinus had embezzled a part of the Gallic treasures, which no one had ever touched. And he ordered strict inquiry to be made into the fact, by an examination of Remigius, who was at that time accountant-general to Ursicinus in his capacity of commander of the heavy troops. And long afterwards, in the time of Valentinian, this Remigius hung himself on account of the trouble into which he fell in the matter of his appointment as legate in Tripolis.

37. And after this business was terminated, Constantius, thinking his prosperity had now raised him to an equality with the gods, and had bestowed on him entire sovereignty over human affairs, gave himself up to elation at the praises of his flatterers, whom he himself

encouraged, despising and trampling under foot all who were unskilled in that kind of court. As we read that Crœsus, when he was king, drove Solon headlong from his court because he would not fawn on him; and that Dionysius threatened the poet Philoxenus with death because, when the king recited his absurd and unrhythmical verses, he alone refused to fall into an ecstasy while all the rest of the courtiers praised them.

38. And this mischievous taste is the nurse of vices; for praise ought only to be acceptable in high places, where blame also is permitted when things are not sufficiently performed.

VI.

§ 1. And now, after the re-establishment of security, investigations as usual were set on foot, and many persons were put in prison as guilty. For that infernal informer Paulus, boiling over with delight, arose to exercise his poisonous employment with increased freedom, and while the members of the emperor's council and the military officers were employed in the investigation of these affairs, as they were commanded, Proculus was put to the torture, who had been a servant of Silvanus, a man of weak body and of ill health; so that every one was afraid lest the exceeding violence of his torture should prove too much for his feeble limbs, so that he would expose numbers to be implicated in the accusations of atrocious crimes. But the result proved quite different to what had been expected.

2. For remembering a dream in which he had been forbidden, while asleep, as he affirmed, to accuse any innocent person, though he should be tortured till he was brought to the very point of death, he neither informed against, nor even named any one; but, with reference to the usurpation of Silvanus, he invariably asserted that he had been driven to contemplate that act, not out of ambition, but from sheer necessity; and he proved this assertion by evident arguments.

3. For he adduced one important excuse, which was established by the testimony of many persons, that, five days before he assumed the ensigns of imperial authority, he addressed the soldiers, while distributing their pay to them, in the name of Constantius, exhorting them to prove always brave and loyal. From which it was plain that if he had then been thinking of seizing on a loftier fortune, he would have given them this money as if it had proceeded from himself.

4. After Proculus, Pœmenius was condemned and put to death: he who, as we have mentioned before,[45] when the Treveri had shut their gates against Cæsar Decentius, was chosen to defend that people.

After him, Asclepiodotus, and Luto, and Maudio, all Counts, were put to death, and many others also, the obdurate cruelty of the times seeking for these and similar punishments with avidity.

VII.

§ 1. While the fatal disturbances of the state multiplied these general slaughters, Leontius, who was the governor of Rome itself, gave many proofs of his deserving the character of an admirable judge; being prompt in hearing cases, rigidly just in deciding them, and merciful by nature, although, for the sake of maintaining lawful authority, he appeared to some people to be severe. He was also of a somewhat amorous temperament.

2. The first pretext for exciting any sedition against him was a most slight and trumpery one. For when an order had been issued to arrest a charioteer, named Philoromus, the whole populace followed him, as if resolved to defend something of their own, and with terrible violence assailed the prefect, presuming him to be timorous. But he remained unmoved and upright, and sending his officers among the crowd, arrested some and punished them, and then, without any one venturing to oppose him, or even to murmur, condemned them to banishment.

3. A few days later the populace again became excited to its customary frenzy, and alleging as a grievance the scarcity of wine, assembled at the well-known place called Septemzodium, where the Emperor Marcus built the Nymphæum,[46] an edifice of great magnificence. To that place the prefect went forthwith, although he was earnestly entreated by all his household and civil officers not to trust himself among an arrogant and threatening multitude, now in a state of fury equal to any of their former commotions; but he, unsusceptible of fear, went right onwards, though many of his attendants deserted him, when they saw him hastening into imminent danger.

4. Therefore, sitting in a carriage, with every appearance of confidence, he looked with fierce eyes at the countenance of the tumultuous mobs thronging towards him from all quarters, and agitating themselves like serpents. And after suffering many bitter insults, at last, when he had recognized one man who was conspicuous among all the rest by his vast size and red hair, he asked him whether his name was Petrus Valvomeres, as he had heard it was; and when the man replied in a defiant tone that it was so, Leontius, in spite of the outcries of many around, ordered him to be seized as one who had long since

been a notorious ringleader of the disaffected, and having his hands bound behind him, commanded him to be suspended on a rack.

5. And when he was seen in the air, in vain imploring the aid of his fellow-tribesmen, the whole mob, which a little while before was so closely packed, dispersed at once over the different quarters of the city, so as to offer no hindrance to the punishment of this seditious leader, who after having been thus tortured—with as little resistance as if he been in a secret dungeon of the court—was transported to Picenum, where, on a subsequent occasion, having offered violence to a virgin of high rank, he was condemned to death by the judgment of Patruinus, a noble of consular dignity.

6. While Leontius governed the city in this manner, Liberius, a priest of the Christian law, was ordered by Constantius to be brought before the council, as one who had resisted the commands of the emperor, and the decrees of many of his own colleagues, in an affair which I will explain briefly.

7. Athanasius was at that time bishop of Alexandria; and as he was a man who sought to magnify himself above his profession, and to mix himself up with affairs which did not belong to his province, as continual reports made known, an assembly of many of his sect met together—a synod, as they call it—and deprived him of the right of administering the sacraments, which he previously enjoyed.

8. For it was said that he, being very deeply skilled in the arts of prophecy and the interpretation of auguries and omens, had very often predicted coming events. And to these charges were added others very inconsistent with the laws of the religion over which he presided.

9. So Liberius, being of the same opinion with those who condemned these practices, was ordered, by the sentence of the emperor, to expel Athanasius from his priestly seat; but this he firmly refused to do, reiterating the assertion that it was the extremity of wickedness to condemn a man who had neither been brought before any court nor been heard in his defence, in this openly resisting the commands of the emperor.

10. For that prince, being always unfavourable to Athanasius, although he knew that what he ordered had in fact taken effect, yet was exceedingly desirous that it should be confirmed by that authority which the bishops of the Eternal City enjoy, as being of higher rank. And as he did not succeed in this, Liberius was removed by night; a measure which was not effected without great difficulty, through the fear which his enemies had of the people, among whom he was exceedingly popular.

VIII.

§ 1. These events, then, took place at Rome, as I have already mentioned. But Constantius was agitated by frequent intelligence which assured him that the Gauls were in a lamentable condition, since no adequate resistance could be made to the barbarians who were now carrying their devastations with fire and sword over the whole country. And after deliberating a long time, in great anxiety, what force he could employ to repel these dangers (himself remaining in Italy, as he thought it very dangerous to remove into so remote a country), he at last determined on a wise plan, which was this: to associate with himself in the cares of the empire his cousin Julian, whom he had some time before summoned to court, and who still retained the robe he had worn in the Greek schools.

2. And when, oppressed by the heavy weight of impending calamities, he had confessed to his dearest friends that by himself he was unequal to the burden of such weighty and numerous difficulties—a thing which he had never felt before—they, being trained to excessive flattery, tried to fill him with foolish ideas, affirming that there was nothing in the world so difficult but what his pre-eminent virtue and his good fortune, equal to that of the gods, would be able to overcome, as it always hitherto had done. And many of them added further, being stung by their consciousness of guilt, that henceforth he ought to beware of conferring the title of Cæsar on any one, enumerating the deeds which had been done in the time of Gallus.

3. They therefore opposed his design resolutely, and it was supported by no one but the queen, who, whether it was that she feared a journey to a distant country, or that, from her own natural wisdom, she saw the best course for the common good, urged him that a relation like Julian ought to be preferred to every one else. Accordingly, after many undecided deliberations and long discussions, his resolution was at last taken decidedly, and having discarded all further vain debate, he resolved on associating Julian with him in the empire.

4. He was therefore summoned; and when he had arrived, on a fixed day, the whole of his fellow-comrades who were in the city were ordered to attend, and a tribunal was erected on a lofty scaffolding, surrounded by the eagles and standards. And Augustus, mounting it, and holding Julian by the right hand, made this conciliatory speech:—

5. "We stand here before you, most excellent defenders of the republic, to avenge with one unanimous spirit the common dangers of

the state. And how I propose to provide for it I will briefly explain to you, as impartial judges.

6. "After the death of those rebellious tyrants whom rage and madness prompted to engage in the enterprises which they undertook, the barbarians, as if they meant to sacrifice unto their wicked manes with Roman blood, having violated the peace and invaded the territories of the Gauls, are encouraged by this consideration, that our empire, being spread over very remote countries, causes us to be beset with great difficulties.

7. "If, then, your decision and mine are mutual to encounter this evil, already progressing beyond the barriers which were opposed to it, while there is still time to check it, the necks of these haughty nations will learn to humble their pride, and the borders of the empire will remain inviolate. It remains for you to give, by your strength, prosperous effect to the hopes which I entertain.

8. "You all know my cousin Julian, whom I here present to you; a youth endeared to us by his modesty as well as by his relationship; a youth of virtue already proved, and of conspicuous industry and energy. Him I have determined to raise to the rank of Cæsar, and hope, if this seems expedient to you, to have my decision confirmed by your consent."

9. He was proceeding to say more, but was prevented by the whole assembly interrupting him with friendly shouts, declaring that his decision was the judgment of the Supreme Deity, and not of any human mind; with such certainty that one might have thought them inspired with the spirit of prophecy.

10. The emperor stood without moving till they resumed silence, and then with greater confidence proceeded to explain what he had to say further.

"Because, therefore, your joyful acclamations show that you look favourably on the design I have announced, let this youth, of tranquil strength, whose temperate disposition it will be better to imitate than merely to praise, rise up now to receive the honours prepared for him. His excellent disposition, increased as it has been by all liberal accomplishments, I will say no more of than is seen in the fact that I have chosen him. Therefore, now, with the manifest consent of the Deity, I will clothe him with the imperial robe."

11. This was his speech. And then, having immediately clothed Julian with the purple robe of his ancestors, and having pronounced him Cæsar, to the great joy of the army, he thus addressed him, though

Julian himself appeared by his grave countenance to be somewhat melancholy.

12. "Most beloved of all my brothers, you thus in early youth have received the splendid honour belonging to your birth, not, I confess, without some addition to my own glory; who thus show myself as just in conferring supreme power on a noble character nearly related to me, as I appear also sublime by virtue of my own power. Come thou, therefore, to be a partner in my labours and dangers, and undertake the defence of the government of the Gauls, devoting thyself with all beneficence to alleviate the calamities of those afflicted countries.

13. "And if it should be necessary to engage with the enemy in battle, do thou take thy place steadily among the standard-bearers themselves, as a prudent encourager of daring at the proper opportunity; exciting the warriors by leading them on with caution, supporting any troops which may be thrown into disorder by reserves, gently reproving those who hang back, and being present as a trustworthy witness of the actions of all, whether brave or timid.

14. "Think that a serious crisis is upon us, and so show yourself a great man, worthy to command brave men. We ourselves will stand by you in the energetic constancy of affection, or will join you in the labours of war, so that we may govern together the whole world in peace, if only God will grant us, as we pray he may, to govern with equal moderation and piety. You will everywhere represent me, and I also will never desert you in whatever task you may be engaged. To sum up: Go forth; go forth supported by the friendly prayers of men of all ranks, to defend with watchful care the station assigned to you, it may be said, by the republic itself."

15. After the emperor had thus ended his speech, no one held his peace, but all the soldiers, with a tremendous crash, rattled their shields against their knees (which is an abundant indication of applause; while on the other hand to strike the shield with the spear is a testimony of anger and indignation), and it was marvellous with what excessive joy they all, except a very few, showed their approbation of the judgment of Augustus: and they received the Cæsar with well-deserved admiration, brilliant as he was with the splendour of the imperial purple.

16. And while they gazed earnestly on his eyes, terrible in their beauty, and his countenance more attractive than ever by reason of his present excitement, they augured from his looks what kind of ruler he was likely to prove, as if they had been searching into those ancient volumes which teach how to judge of a man's moral disposition by the

external signs on his person. And that he might be regarded with the greater reverence, they neither praised him above measure, nor yet below his desert. And so the voices raised in his favour were looked upon as the judgment of censors, not of soldiers.

17. After the ceremony was over, Julian was taken up into the imperial chariot and received into the palace, and was heard to whisper to himself this verse of Homer—

"Now purple death hath seized on me,
And powerful strength of destiny."

These transactions took place on the sixth of November, in the year of the consulship of Arbetio and Lollianus.

18. A few days afterwards, Helen, the maiden sister of Constantius, was also given in marriage to the Cæsar. And everything being got ready which the journey required, he started on the first of December with a small retinue, and having been escorted on his way by Augustus himself as far as the spot, marked by two pillars, which lies between Laumellum and Ticinum, he proceeded straight on to the country of the Taurini, where he received disastrous intelligence, which had recently reached the emperor's court, but still had been intentionally kept back, lest all the preparations made for his journey should be wasted.

19. And this intelligence was that Colonia Agrippina,[47] a city of great renown in lower Germany, had been carried by a vigorous siege of the barbarians, who appeared before it in great force, and had utterly destroyed it.

20. Julian being greatly distressed at this news, looking on it as a kind of omen of misfortunes to come, was often heard to murmur in querulous tones, "that he had gained nothing except the fate of dying amid greater trouble and employment than before."

21. But when he arrived at Vienne, people of every age and class went forth to meet him on his entrance to the city, with a view to do him honour by their reception of him as one who had been long wished for, and was now granted to their prayers. And when he was seen in the distance the whole population of the city and of the adjacent neighbourhood, going before his chariot, celebrated his praises, saluting him as Emperor, clement and prosperous, greeting with eager joy this royal procession in honour of a lawful prince. And they placed all their hopes of a remedy for the evils which affected the whole province on his arrival, thinking that now, when their affairs were in a most desperate condition, some friendly genius had come to shine upon them.

22. And a blind old woman, when in reply to her question "Who was entering the city?" she received for answer "Julian the Cæsar," cried out that "He would restore the temples of the gods."

IX.

§ 1. Now then, since, as the sublime poet of Mantua has sung, "A greater series of incident rises to my view; in a more arduous task I engage,"—I think it a proper opportunity to describe the situation and different countries of the Gauls, lest, among the narration of fiery preparations and the various chances of battles, I should seem, while speaking of matters not understood by every one, to resemble those negligent sailors, who, when tossed about by dangerous waves and storms, begin to repair their sails and ropes which they might have attended to in calm weather.

2. Ancient writers, pursuing their investigations into the earliest origin of the Gauls, left our knowledge of the truth very imperfect; but at a later period, Timagenes, a thorough Greek both in diligence and language, collected, from various writings facts which had been long unknown, and guided by his faithful statements, we, dispelling all obscurity, will now give a plain and intelligible relation of them.

3. Some persons affirm that the first inhabitants ever seen in these regions were called Celts, after the name of their king, who was very popular among them, and sometimes also Galatæ, after the name of his mother. For Galatæ is the Greek translation of the Roman term Galli. Others affirm that they are Dorians, who, following a more ancient Hercules, selected for their home the districts bordering on the ocean.

4. The Druids affirm that a portion of the people was really indigenous to the soil, but that other inhabitants poured in from the islands on the coast, and from the districts across the Rhine, having been driven from their former abodes by frequent wars, and sometimes by inroads of the tempestuous sea.

5. Some again maintain that after the destruction of Troy, a few Trojans fleeing from the Greeks, who were then scattered over the whole world, occupied these districts, which at that time had no inhabitants at all.

6. But the natives of these countries affirm this more positively than any other fact (and, indeed, we ourselves have read it engraved on their monuments), that Hercules, the son of Amphitryon, hastening to the destruction of those cruel tyrants, Geryon and Tauriscus, one of whom was oppressing the Gauls, and the other Spain, after he had

conquered both of them, took to wife some women of noble birth in those countries, and became the father of many children; and that his sons called the districts of which they became the kings after their own names.

7. Also an Asiatic tribe coming from Phocæa in order to escape the cruelty of Harpalus, the lieutenant of Cyrus the king, sought to sail to Italy.[48] And a part of them founded Velia, in Lucania, others settled a colony at Marseilles, in the territory of Vienne; and then, in subsequent ages, these towns increasing in strength and importance, founded other cities. But we must avoid a variety of details which are commonly apt to weary.

8. Throughout these provinces, the people gradually becoming civilized, the study of liberal accomplishments flourished, having been first introduced by the Bards, the Eubages,[49] and the Druids. The Bards were accustomed to employ themselves in celebrating the brave achievements of their illustrious men, in epic verse, accompanied with sweet airs on the lyre. The Eubages investigated the system and sublime secrets of nature, and sought to explain them to their followers. Between these two came the Druids, men of loftier genius, bound in brotherhoods according to the precepts and example of Pythagoras; and their minds were elevated by investigations into secret and sublime matters, and from the contempt which they entertained for human affairs they pronounced the soul immortal.

X.

§ 1. This country then of the Gauls was by reason of its lofty mountain ranges perpetually covered with terrible snows, almost unknown to the inhabitants of the rest of the world, except where it borders on the ocean; vast fortresses raised by nature, in the place of art, surrounding it on all sides.

2. On the southern side it is washed by the Etruscan and Gallic sea: where it looks towards the north it is separated from the tribes of the barbarians by the river Rhine; where it is placed under the western star it is bounded by the ocean, and the lofty chain of the Pyrenees; where it has an eastern aspect it is bounded by the Cottian[50] Alps. In these mountains King Cottius, after the Gauls had been subdued, lying by himself in their defiles, and relying on the rugged and pathless character of the country, long maintained his independence; though afterwards he abated his pride, and was admitted to the friendship of the Emperor Octavianus. And subsequently he constructed immense

works to serve as a splendid gift to the emperor, making roads over them, short, and convenient for travellers, between other ancient passes of the Alps; on which subject we will presently set forth what discoveries have been made.

3. In these Cottian Alps, which begin at the town of Susa, one vast ridge rises up, scarcely passable by any one without danger.

4. For to travellers who reach it from the side of Gaul it descends with a steepness almost precipitous, being terrible to behold, in consequence of the bulk of its overhanging rocks. In the spring, when the ice is melting, and the snow beginning to give way from the warm spring breezes, if any one seeks to descend along the mountain, men and beasts and wagons all fall together through the fissures and clefts in the rocks, which yawn in every direction, though previously hidden by the frost. And the only remedy ever found to ward off entire destruction is to have many vehicles bound together with enormous ropes, with men or oxen hanging on behind, to hold them back with great efforts; and so with a crouching step they get down with some degree of safety. And this, as I have said, is what happens in the spring.

5. But in winter, the ground being covered over with a smooth crust of ice, and therefore slippery under foot, the traveller is often plunged headlong; and the valleys, which seem to open here and there into wide plains, which are merely a covering of treacherous ice, sometimes swallow up those who try to pass over them. On account of which danger those who are acquainted with the country fix projecting wooden piles over the safest spots, in order that a series of them may conduct the traveller unhurt to his destination; though if these piles get covered with snow and hidden, or thrown down by melting torrents descending from the mountains, then it is difficult for any one to pass, even if natives of the district lead the way.

6. But on the summit of this Italian mountain there is a plain, seven miles in extent, reaching as far as the station known by the name of Mars; and after that comes another ridge, still more steep, and scarcely possible to be climbed, which stretches on to the summit of Mons Matrona, named so from an event which happened to a noble lady.

7. From this point a path, steep indeed, but easily passable, leads to the fortress of Virgantia.[51] The sepulchre of this petty prince whom we have spoken of as the maker of these roads is at Susa, close to the walls; and his remains are honoured with religious veneration for two reasons: first of all, because he governed his people with equitable

moderation; and secondly, because, by becoming an ally of the Roman republic, he procured lasting tranquillity for his subjects.

8. And although this road which I have been speaking of runs through the centre of the district, and is shorter and more frequented now than any other, yet other roads also were made at much earlier periods, on different occasions.

9. The first of them, near the maritime alps, was made by the Theban Hercules, when he was proceeding in a leisurely manner to destroy Geryon and Tauriscus, as has already been mentioned; and he it was who gave to these alps the name of the Grecian Alps.[52] In the same way he consecrated the citadel and port of Monæcus to keep alive the recollection of his name for ever. And this was the reason why, many ages afterwards, those alps were called the Penine Alps.[53]

10. Publius Cornelius Scipio, the father of the elder Africanus, when about to go to the assistance of the citizens of Saguntum—celebrated for the distresses which they endured, and for their loyalty to Rome, at the time when they were besieged with great resolution by the Carthaginians—led to the Spanish coast a fleet having on board a numerous army. But after the city had been destroyed by the valour of the Carthaginians, he, being unable to overtake Hannibal, who had crossed the Rhone, and had obtained three days' start of him in the march towards Italy, crossed the sea, which at that point was not wide, making a rapid voyage; and taking his station near Genoa, a town of the Ligures, awaited his descent from the mountains, so that, if chance should afford him an opportunity, he might attack him in the plain while still fatigued with the ruggedness of the way by which he had come.

11. But still, having regard to the interests of the republic, he ordered Cnæus Scipio, his brother, to go into Spain, to prevent Hasdrubal from making a similar expedition from that country. But Hannibal, having received information of their design by some deserters, being also a man of great shrewdness and readiness of resources, obtained some guides from the Taurini who inhabited those districts, and passing through the Tricastini and through the district of the Vocontii, he thus reached the defiles of the Tricorii.[54] Then starting from this point, he made another march over a line previously impassable. And having cut through a rock of immense height, which he melted by means of mighty fires, and pouring over it a quantity of vinegar, he proceeded along the Druentia, a river full of danger from its eddies and currents, until he reached the district of Etruria. This is enough to say of the Alps; now let us return to our original subject.

XI.

§ 1. In former times, when these provinces were little known, as being barbarous, they were considered to be divided into three races:[55] namely, the Celtæ, the same who are also called Galli; the Aquitani, and the Belgæ: all differing from each other in language, manners, and laws.

2. The Galli, who, as I have said, are the same as the Celtæ, are divided from the Aquitani by the river Garonne, which rises in the mountains of the Pyrenees; and after passing through many towns, loses itself in the ocean.

3. On the other side they are separated from the Belgians by the Marne and the Seine, both rivers of considerable size, which flowing through the tribe of the Lugdunenses, after surrounding the stronghold of the Parisii named Lutetia, so as to make an island of it, proceed onwards together, and fall into the sea near the camp of Constantius.

4. Of all these people the Belgians are said by ancient writers to be the most warlike, because, being more remote from civilization, and not having been rendered effeminate by foreign luxuries, they have been engaged in continual wars with the Germans on the other side of the Rhine.

5. For the Aquitanians, to whose shores, as being nearest and also pacific, foreign merchandise is abundantly imported, were easily brought under the dominion of the Romans, because their character had become enervated.

6. But from the time when the Gauls, after long and repeated wars, submitted to the dictator Julius, all their provinces were governed by Roman officers, the country being divided into four portions; one of which was the province of Narbonne; containing the districts of Vienne and Lyons: a second province comprehended all the tribes of the Aquitanians; upper and lower Germany formed a third jurisdiction, and the Belgians a fourth at that period.

7. But now the whole extent of the country is portioned out into many provinces. The second (or lower) Germany is the first, if you begin on the western side, fortified by Cologne and Tongres, both cities of great wealth and importance.

8. Next comes the first (or high) Germany, in which, besides other municipal towns, there is Mayence, and Worms, and Spiers, and Strasburg, a city celebrated for the defeats sustained by the barbarians in its neighbourhood.

9. After these the first Belgic province stretches as far as Metz and Treves, which city is the splendid abode of the chief governor of the country.

10. Next to that comes the second Belgic province, where we find Amiens, a city of conspicuous magnificence, and Châlons,[56] and Rheims.

11. In the province of the Sequani, the finest cities are Besançon and Basle. The first Lyonnese province contains Lyons, Châlons,[57] Sens, Bourges, and Autun, the walls of which are very extensive and of great antiquity.

12. In the second Lyonnese province are Tours, and Rouen, Evreux, and Troyes. The Grecian and Penine Alps have, besides other towns of less note, Avenche, a city which indeed is now deserted, but which was formerly one of no small importance, as even now is proved by its half-ruinous edifices. These are the most important provinces, and most splendid cities of the Galli.

13. In Aquitania, which looks towards the Pyrenees, and that part of the ocean which belongs to the Spaniards, the first province is Aquitanica, very rich in large and populous cities; passing over others, I may mention as pre-eminent, Bordeaux, Clermont, Saintes, and Poictiers.

14. The province called the Nine Nations is enriched by Ausch and Bazas. In the province of Narbonne, the cities of Narbonne, Euses, and Toulouse are the principal places of importance. The Viennese exults in the magnificence of many cities, the chief of which are Vienne itself, and Arles, and Valence; to which may be added Marseilles, by the alliance with and power of which we read that Rome itself was more than once supported in moments of danger.

15. And near to these cities is also Aix, Nice, Antibes, and the islands of Hieres.

16. And since we have come in the progress of our work to this district, it would be inconsistent and absurd to omit all mention of the Rhone, a river of the greatest celebrity. The Rhone rises in the Penine Alps, from sources of great abundance, and descending with headlong impetuosity into the more champaign districts, it often overruns its banks with its own waters, and then plunges into a lake called Lake Leman, and though it passes through it, yet it never mingles with any foreign waters, but, rushing over the top of those which flow with less rapidity, in its search for an exit, it forces its own way by the violence of its stream.

17. And thus passing through that lake without any damage, it runs through Savoy and the district of Franche Comté; and, after a long course, it forms the boundary between the Viennese on its left, and the Lyonnese on its right. Then after many windings it receives the Saône, a river which rises in the first Germany, and this latter river here merges its name in the Rhone. At this point is the beginning of the Gauls. And from this spot the distances are measured not by miles but by leagues.

18. From this point also, the Rhone, being now enriched by other rivers, becomes navigable for large vessels, which are often tossed about in it by gales of wind; and at last, having finished the course which nature has marked out for it, foaming on it joins the Gallic Sea in the wide gulf which they call the Gulf of Lyons, about eighteen miles from Arles. This is enough to say of the situation of the province; I will now proceed to describe the appearance and character of the inhabitants.

XII.

§ 1. Nearly all the Gauls are of a lofty stature, fair, and of ruddy complexion; terrible from the sternness of their eyes, very quarrelsome, and of great pride and insolence. A whole troop of foreigners would not be able to withstand a single Gaul if he called his wife to his assistance, who is usually very strong, and with blue eyes; especially when, swelling her neck, gnashing her teeth, and brandishing her sallow arms of enormous size, she begins to strike blows mingled with kicks, as if they were so many missiles sent from the string of a catapult.

2. The voices of the generality are formidable and threatening, whether they are in good humour or angry: they are all exceedingly careful of cleanliness and neatness, nor in all the country, and most especially in Aquitania, could any man or woman, however poor, be seen either dirty or ragged.

3. The men of every age are equally inclined to war, and the old man and the man in the prime of life answer with equal zeal the call to arms, their bodies being hardened by their cold weather and by constant exercise so that they are all inclined to despise dangers and terrors. Nor has any one of this nation ever mutilated his thumb from fear of the toils of war, as men have done in Italy, whom in their district are called Murci.

4. The nation is fond of wine, and of several kinds of liquor which resemble wine. And many individuals of the lower orders,

whose senses have become impaired by continual intoxication, which the apophthegm of Cato defined to be a kind of voluntary madness, run about in all directions at random; so that there appears to be some point in that saying which is found in Cicero's oration in defence of Fonteius, "that henceforth the Gauls will drink their wine less strong than formerly," because forsooth they thought there was poison in it.

5. These countries, and especially such parts of them as border on Italy, fell gradually under the dominion of the Romans without much trouble to their conquerors, having been first attacked by Fulvius, afterwards weakened in many trifling combats by Sextius, and at last entirely subdued by Fabius Maximus; who gained an additional surname from the complete accomplishment of this task, after he had brought into subjection the fierce tribe of the Allobroges.

6. Cæsar finally subdued all the Gauls, except where their country was absolutely inaccessible from its morasses, as we learn from Sallust, after a war of ten years, in which both nations suffered many disasters; and at last he united them to us in eternal alliance by formal treaties. I have digressed further than I had intended, but now I will return to my original subject.

XIII.

§ 1. After Domitianus had perished by a cruel death, Musonianus his successor governed the East with the rank of prætorian prefect; a man celebrated for his eloquence and thorough knowledge of both the Greek and Latin languages; from which he reaped a loftier glory than he expected.

2. For when Constantine was desirous of obtaining a more accurate knowledge of the different sects in the empire, the Manicheans and other similar bodies, and no one could be found able sufficiently to explain them, Musonianus was chosen for the task, having been recommended as competent; and when he had discharged this duty with skill, the emperor gave him the name of Musonianus, for he had been previously called Strategius. After that he ran through many degrees of rank and honour, and soon reached the dignity of prefect; being in other matters also a man of wisdom, popular in the provinces, and of a mild and courteous disposition. But at the same time, whenever he could find an opportunity, especially in any controversies or lawsuits (which is most shameful and wicked), he was greatly devoted to sordid gain. Not to mention many other instances, this was especially exemplified in the investigations which were made into the death of Theophilus, the governor of Syria, a man of consular rank,

who gave information against the Cæsar Gallus, and who was torn to pieces in a tumult of the people; for which several poor men were condemned, who, it was clearly proved, were at a distance at the time of the transaction, while certain rich men who were the real authors of the crime were spared from all punishment, except the confiscation of their property.

3. In this he was equalled by Prosper, at that time master of the horse in Gaul; a man of abject spirit and great inactivity; and, as the comic poet has it, despising the acts of secret robbing he plundered openly.[58]

4. And, while these two officers were conniving together, and reciprocally helping each other to many means of acquiring riches, the chiefs of the Persian nation who lived nearest to the river, profiting by the fact that the king was occupied in the most distant parts of his dominions, and that these commanders were occupied in plundering the people placed under their authority, began to harass our territories with predatory bands, making audacious inroads, sometimes into Armenia, often also into Mesopotamia.

Notes

[32] Tlepolemus and Hiero, whom Cicero, Verres iii. 11, calls Cibyratici canes.

[33] Herodotus, iv. 184, records that in Africa, in the country about Mount Atlas, dreams are unknown.

[34] Lintz.

[35] The district around Bellinzona.

[36] The Bodensee, more generally known as the Lake of Constance: at its south-eastern end is the town of Bregenz, the ancient Brigantia.

[37] The Arethusa is in Sicily, near Syracuse.

[38] The Comites were a picked body of troops, divided into several regiments distinguished by separate names, such as Seniores, Juniores, Sagittarii, &c.

[39] The Promoti were also picked men, something like the Comites; the French translator calls them the Veterans.

[40] From κόπτω to cut, and ματτύα any delicate food; meant as equivalent to our cheeseparer, or skinflint.

[41] This was a very important post; it seems to have united the functions of a modern chamberlain, chancellor, and secretary of state. The master presented citizens to the emperor, received foreign ambassadors, recommended men for civil employments, decided civil actions of several kinds, and superintended many of the affairs of the post.

[42] Cologne.

[43] The dragons were the effigies on some of the standards.

[44] There is no such passage in any extant work of Cicero, but a sentence in his speech ad Pontifices resembles it: "For although it be more desirable to end one's life without pain, and without injury, still it tends more to an immortality of glory to be regretted by one's countrymen, than to have been always free from injury." And a still closer likeness to the sentiment is found in his speech ad Quirites post reditum: "Although there is nothing more to be wished for by man than prosperous, equal, continual good-fortune in life, flowing on in a prosperous course, without any misadventure; still, if all my life had been tranquil and peaceful, I should have been deprived of the incredible and almost heavenly delight and happiness which I now enjoy through your kindness."—Orations, v. 2; Bohn, p. 491–2.

[45] In one of the lost books of this history.

[46] The Nymphæum was a temple sacred to the Nymphs, deriving its name of Septemzodium, or Septizonium (which it shared with more than one other building at Rome), from the seven rows of pillars, one above the other, and each row lessening both in circuit and in height, with which the exterior was embellished. Another temple of this kind was built by Septimius Severus.

[47] Cologne.

[48] This story of the Phocæenses is told by Herodotus, i. 166, and alluded to by Horace, Epod. xv. 10.

[49] The Eubages, or Οὐατεῖς, as Strabo calls them, appear to have been a tribe of priests.

[50] The Cottian Alps are Mont Genevre. It is unnecessary to point out how Ammianus mistakes the true bearing of these frontiers of Gaul.

[51] Briançon.

[52] The Graiæ Alps are the Little St. Bernard; and it was over them that Hannibal really passed, as has been conclusively proved by Dr. J.A. Cramer.

[53] From the god Pen, or Peninus, Liv. xxi. 38. The Alpes Peninæ are the Great St. Bernard.

[54] Compare Livy's account of Hannibal's march, from which, wholly erroneous as it is, this description seems to have been taken; not that even Livy has made such a gross mistake about the Druentia, or Durance, which falls into the Rhone.

[55] Cæsar's account of his expedition begins with the statement that "Gaul is divided into three provinces."

[56] Châlons sur Marne.

[57] Châlons sur Saône.

[58] Ammianus refers to Plautus, Epidicus, Act. I., sc. i., line 10:—
Thesprio. I am less of a pilferer now than formerly.

Ep. How so?
Thes. I rob openly.

BOOK XVI

I.

A.D. 356.

§ 1. While the chain of destiny was bringing these events to pass in the Roman world, Julian, being at Vienne, was taken by the emperor, then in his own eighth consulship, as a partner in that dignity; and, under the promptings of his own innate energy, dreamt of nothing but the crash of battles and the slaughter of the barbarians; preparing without delay to re-establish the province, and to reunite the fragments that had been broken from it, if only fortune should be favourable to him.

2. And because the great achievements which by his valour and good fortune Julian performed in the Gauls, surpass many of the most gallant exploits of the ancients, I will relate them in order as they occurred, employing all the resources of my talents, moderate as they are, in the hope that they may suffice for the narrative.

3. But what I am about to relate, though not emblazoned by craftily devised falsehood, and being simply a plain statement of facts, supported by evident proofs, will have all the effect of a studied pane-gyric.

4. For it would seem that some principle of a more than com-monly virtuous life guided this young prince from his very cradle to his last breath. Increasing rapidly in every desirable quality, he soon became so conspicuous both at home and abroad, that in respect to his prudence he was looked upon as a second Titus: in his glorious deeds of war he was accounted equal to Trajan; in mercy he was the proto-type of Antoninus; and in the pursuit and discovery of true and perfect wisdom, he resembled Marcus Aurelius, in imitation of whom he formed all his actions and character.

5. And since, as we are taught by Cicero, that the loftiness of great virtues delights us, as does that of high trees, while we are not equally interested in the roots and trunks; so, also, the first beginnings of his admirable disposition were kept concealed by many circum-stances which threw a cloud over them; though in fact they ought to be preferred to many of his most marvellous actions of later life, in that he, who in his early youth had been brought up like Erectheus in the retirement sacred to Minerva, nevertheless when he was drawn forth from the quiet shades of the academy (and not from any military tent) into the labours of war, subdued Germany, tranquillized the districts of the frozen Rhine, routed the barbarian kings breathing nothing but bloodshed and slaughter, and forced them to submission.

II.

§ 1. Therefore while passing a toilsome winter in the city afore-said, he learnt, among the numerous reports which were flying about, that the ancient city of Autun, the walls of which, though of vast ex-tent, were in a state of great decay from age, was now besieged by the barbarians, who had suddenly appeared before it in great force; and while the garrison remained panic-stricken and inactive, the town was defended by a body of veterans who were behaving with great courage and vigilance; as it often happens that extreme despair repulses dan-gers which appear destructive of all hope or safety.

2. Therefore, without relaxing his anxiety about other matters, and putting aside all the adulation of the courtiers with which they sought to divert his mind towards voluptuousness and luxury, he has-tened his preparations, and when everything was ready he set out, and on the 24th of June arrived at Autun; behaving like a veteran general

conspicuous alike for skill and prowess, and prepared to fall upon the barbarians, who were straggling in every direction over the country, the moment fortune afforded him an opportunity.

3. Therefore having deliberated on his plans, and consulted those who were acquainted with the country as to what would be the safest line of march for him to adopt, after having received much information in favour of different routes, some recommending Arbois, others insisting on it that the best way was by Saulieu and Cure.

4. But as some persons affirmed that Silvanus, in command of a body of infantry, had, a short time before, made his way with 8,000 men by a road shorter than either, but dangerous as lying through many dark woods and defiles suitable for ambuscades, Julian became exceedingly eager to imitate the audacity of this brave man.

5. And to prevent any delay, taking with him only his cuirassiers and archers, who would not have been sufficient to defend his person had he been attacked, he took the same route as Silvanus; and so came to Auxerre.

6. And there, having, according to his custom, devoted a short time to rest, for the purpose of refreshing his men, he proceeded onwards towards Troyes; and strengthened his flanks that he might with the greater effect watch the barbarians, who attacked him in numerous bodies, which he avoided as well as he could, thinking them more numerous than they really were. Presently, however, having occupied some favourable ground, he descended upon one body of them, and routed it, and took some prisoners whom their own fears delivered to him; and then he allowed the rest, who now devoted all their energies to flying with what speed they could, to escape unattacked, as his men could not pursue them by reason of the weight of their armour.

7. This occurrence gave him more hope of being able to resist any attack which they might make, and marching forwards with this confidence, after many dangers he reached Troyes so unexpectedly, that when he arrived at the gates, the inhabitants for some time hesitated to give him entrance into the city, so great was their fear of the straggling multitudes of the barbarians.

8. After a little delay, devoted to again refreshing his weary troops, thinking that there was no time to waste, he proceeded to the city of Rheims, where he had ordered his whole army, carrying[59] ... to assemble, and there to await his presence. The army at Rheims was under the command of Marcellus, the successor of Ursicinus; and Ursicinus himself was ordered to remain there till the termination of the expedition.

9. Again Julian took counsel, and after many opinions of different purport had been delivered, it was determined to attack the host of the Allemanni in the neighbourhood of Dieuse; and to that quarter the army now marched in dense order, and with more than usual alacrity.

10. And because the weather, being damp and misty, prevented even what was near from being seen, the enemy, availing themselves of their knowledge of the country, came by an oblique road upon the Cæsar's rear, and attacked two legions while they were piling their arms; and they would almost have destroyed them if the uproar which suddenly arose had not brought the auxiliary troops of the allies to their support.

11. From this time forth Julian, thinking it impossible to find any roads or any rivers free from ambuscades, proceeded with consummate prudence and caution; qualities which above all others in great generals usually bring safety and success to armies.

12. Hearing therefore that Strasburg, Brumat, Saverne, Spiers, Worms, and Mayence, were all in the hands of the barbarians, who were established in their suburbs, for the barbarians shunned fixing themselves in the towns themselves, looking upon them like graves surrounded with nets, he first of all entered Brumat, and just as he reached that place he was encountered by a body of Germans prepared for battle.

13. Having arranged his own army in the form of a crescent, the engagement began, and the enemy were speedily surrounded and utterly defeated. Some were taken prisoners, others were slain in the heat of the battle, the rest sought safety by rapid flight.

III.

§ 1. After this, meeting with no resistance, he determined to proceed to recover Cologne, which had been destroyed before his arrival in Gaul. In that district there is no city or fortress to be seen except that near Confluentes;[60] a place so named because there the river Moselle becomes mingled with the Rhine; there is also the village of Rheinmagen, and likewise a single tower near Cologne.

2. After having taken possession of Cologne he did not leave it till the Frank kings began, through fear of him, to abate of their fury, when he contracted a peace with them likely to be of future advantage to the republic. In the mean time he put the whole city into a state of complete defence.

3. Then, auguring well from these first-fruits of victory, he departed, passing through the district of Treves, with the intention of

wintering at Sens, which was a town very suitable for that purpose. When bearing, so to say, the weight of a world of wars upon his shoulders, he was occupied by perplexities of various kinds, and among them how to provide for establishing in places most exposed to danger the soldiers who had quitted their former posts; how to defeat the enemies who had conspired together to injure the Roman cause; and further, how to provide supplies for the army while employed in so many different quarters.

IV.

§ 1. While he was anxiously revolving these things in his mind, he was attacked by a numerous force of the enemy, who had conceived a hope of being able to take the town. And they were the more confident of success because, from the information of deserters, they had learnt that he neither had with him his Scutarii nor his Gentiles, both of which bodies of troops had been distributed among the different municipal towns in order that they might be the more easily supplied with provisions.

2. Therefore after the gates of the city had been barricaded, and the weakest portions of the walls carefully strengthened, Julian was seen night and day on the battlements and ramparts, attended by a band of armed men, boiling over with anger and gnashing his teeth, because, often as he wished to sally forth, he was prevented from taking such a step by the scantiness of the force which he had with him.

3. At last, after thirty days, the barbarians retired disappointed, murmuring that they had been so vain and weak as to attempt the siege of such a city. It deserves however to be remarked, as a most unworthy circumstance, that when Julian was in great personal danger, Marcellus, the master of the horse, who was posted in the immediate neighbourhood, omitted to bring him any assistance, though the danger of the city itself, even if the prince had not been there, ought to have excited his endeavours to relieve it from the peril of a siege by so formidable an enemy.

4. Being now delivered from this fear, Julian, ever prudent and active, directed his anxious thoughts incessantly to the care of providing that, after their long labours, his soldiers should have rest, which, however brief, might be sufficient to recruit their strength. In addition to the exhaustion consequent on their toils, they were distressed by the deficiency of crops on the land, which through the frequent devastations to which they had been exposed afforded but little suitable for human food.

5. But these difficulties he likewise surmounted by his ever wakeful diligence, and a more confident hope of future success opening itself to his mind, he rose with higher spirits to accomplish his other designs.

V.

§ 1. In the first place (and this is a most difficult task for every one), he imposed on himself a rigid temperance, and maintained it as if he had been living under the obligation of the sumptuary laws. These were originally brought to Rome from the edicts of Lycurgus and the tables of laws compiled by Solon, and were for a long time strictly observed. When they had become somewhat obsolete, they were re-established by Sylla, who, guided by the apophthegms of Democritus, agreed with him that it is Fortune which spreads an ambitious table, but that Virtue is content with a sparing one.

2. And likewise Cato of Tusculum, who from his pure and temperate way of life obtained the surname of the Censor, said with profound wisdom on the same subject, "When there is great care about food, there is very little care about virtue."

3. Lastly, though he was continually reading the little treatise which Constantius, when sending him as his step-son to prosecute his studies, had written for him with his own hand, in which he made extravagant provision for the dinner-expenses of the Cæsar, Julian now forbade pheasants, or sausages, or even sow's udder to be served up to him, contenting himself with the cheap and ordinary food of the common soldiers.

4. Hereupon arose his custom of dividing his nights into three portions, one of which he allotted to rest, one to the affairs of the state, and one to the study of literature; and we read that Alexander the Great had been accustomed to do the same, though he practised the rule with less self-reliance. For Alexander, having placed a brazen shell on the ground beneath him, used to hold a silver ball in his hand, which he kept stretched outside his bed, so that when sleep pervading his whole body had relaxed the rigour of his muscles, the rattling of the ball falling might banish slumber from his eyes.

5. But Julian, without any instrument, awoke whenever he pleased; and always rising when the night was but half spent, and that not from a bed of feathers, or silken coverlets shining with varied brilliancy, but from a rough blanket or rug, would secretly offer his supplications to Mercury, who, as the theological lessons which he had received had taught him, was the swift intelligence of the world, excit-

ing the different emotions of the mind. And thus removed from all external circumstances calculated to distract his attention, he gave his whole attention to the affairs of the republic.

6. Then, after having ended this arduous and important business, he turned and applied himself to the cultivation of his intellect. And it was marvellous with what excessive ardour he investigated and attained to the sublime knowledge of the loftiest matters, and how, seeking as it were some food for his mind which might give it strength to climb up to the sublimest truths, he ran through every branch of philosophy in profound and subtle discussions.

7. Nevertheless, while engaged in amassing knowledge of this kind in all its fullness and power, he did not despise the humbler accomplishments. He was tolerably fond of poetry and rhetoric, as is shown by the invariable and pure elegance, mingled with dignity, of all his speeches and letters. And he likewise studied the varied history of our own state and of foreign countries. To all these accomplishments was added a very tolerable degree of eloquence in the Latin language.

8. Therefore, if it be true, as many writers affirm, that Cyrus the king, and Simonides the lyric poet, and Hippias of Elis, the most acute of the Sophists, excelled as they did in memory because they had obtained that faculty through drinking a particular medicine, we must also believe that Julian in his early manhood had drunk the whole cask of memory, if such a thing could ever be found. And these are the nocturnal signs of his chastity and virtue.

9. But as for the manner in which he passed his days, whether in conversing with eloquence and wit, or in making preparations for war, or in actual conflict of battle, or in his administration of affairs of the state, correcting all defects with magnanimity and liberality, these things shall all be set forth in their proper place.

10. When he was compelled, as being a prince, to apply himself to the study of military discipline, having been previously confined to lessons of philosophy, and when he was learning the art of marching in time while the pipes were playing the Pyrrhic air, he often, calling upon the name of Plato, ironically quoted that old proverb, "A packsaddle is placed on an ox; this is clearly a burden which does not belong to me."

11. On one occasion, when some secretaries were introduced into the council-chamber, with solemn ceremony, to receive some gold, one of their company did not, as is the usual custom, open his robe to receive it, but took it in the hollow of both his hands joined together;

on which Julian said, secretaries only know how to seize things, not how to accept them.

12. Having been approached by the parents of a virgin who had been ravished, seeking for justice, he gave sentence that the ravisher, on conviction, should be banished; and when the parents complained of this sentence as unequal to the crime, because the criminal had not been condemned to death, he replied, "Let the laws blame my clemency: but it is fitting that an emperor of a most merciful disposition should be superior to all other laws."

13. Once when he was about to set forth on an expedition, he was interrupted by several people complaining of injuries which they had received, whom he referred for a hearing to the governors of their respective provinces. And after he had returned, he inquired what had been done in each case, and with genuine clemency mitigated the punishments which had been assigned to the offences.

14. Last of all, without here making any mention of the victories in which he repeatedly defeated the barbarians, and the vigilance with which he protected his army from all harm, the benefits which he conferred on the Galli, previously exhausted by extreme want, are most especially evident from this fact, that when he first entered the country he found that four-and-twenty pieces of gold were exacted, under the name of tribute, in the way of poll-tax, from each individual. But when he quitted the country seven pieces only were required, which made up all the payments due from them to the state. On which account they rejoiced with festivals and dances, looking upon him as a serene sun which had shone upon them after melancholy darkness.

15. Moreover we know that up to the very end of his reign and of his life, he carefully and with great benefit observed this rule, not to remit the arrears of tribute by edicts which they call indulgences. For he knew that by such conduct he should be giving something to the rich, whilst it is notorious everywhere that, the moment that taxes are imposed, the poor are compelled to pay them all at once without any relief.

16. But while he was thus regulating and governing the country in a manner deserving the imitation of all virtuous princes, the rage of the barbarians again broke out more violently than ever.

17. And as wild beasts, which, owing to the carelessness of the shepherds, have been wont to plunder their flocks, even when these careless keepers are exchanged for more watchful ones, still cling to their habit, and being furious with hunger, will, without any regard for their own safety, again attack the flocks and herds; so also the barbari-

ans, having consumed all their plunder, continued, under the pressure of hunger, repeatedly to make inroads for the sake of booty, though sometimes they died of want before they could obtain any.

VI.

§ 1. These were the events which took place in Gaul during this year; at first of doubtful issue, but in the end successful. Meanwhile in the emperor's court envy constantly assailed Arbetio, accusing him of having already assumed the ensigns of imperial rank, as if designing soon to attain the supreme dignity itself. And especially was he attacked by a count named Verissimus, who with great vehemence brought forth terrible charges against him, openly alleging that although he had been raised from the rank of a common soldier to high military office, he was not contented, thinking little of what he had obtained, and aiming at the highest place.

2. And he was also vigorously attacked by a man named Dorus, who had formerly been surgeon of the Scutarii, and of whom we have spoken, when promoted in the time of Magnentius to be inspector of the works of art at Rome, as having brought accusations against Adelphius, the prefect of the city, as forming ambitious designs.

3. And when the matter was brought forward for judicial inquiry, and all preliminary arrangements were made, proof of the accusations which had been confidently looked for was still delayed; when suddenly, as if the business had been meant as a satire on the administration of justice, through the interposition of the chamberlain as rumour affirmed, the persons who had been imprisoned as accomplices were released from their confinement: Dorus disappeared, and Verissimus kept silence for the future, as if the curtain had dropped and the scene had been suddenly changed.

VII.

§ 1. About the same time, Constantius having learnt, from common report, that Marcellus had omitted to carry assistance to the Cæsar when he was besieged at Sens, cashiered him, and ordered him to retire to his own house. And he, as if he had received a great injury, began to plot against Julian, relying upon the disposition of the emperor to open his ears to every accusation.

2. Therefore, when he departed, Eutherius, the chief chamberlain, was immediately sent after him, that he might convict him before the emperor if he propagated any falsehoods. But Marcellus, unaware

of this, as soon as he arrived at Milan, began talking loudly, and seeking to create alarm, like a vain chatterer half mad as he was. And when he was admitted into the council-chamber, he began to accuse Julian of being insolent, and of preparing for himself stronger wings in order to soar to a greater height. For this was his expression, agitating his body violently as he uttered it.

3. While he was thus uttering his imaginary charges with great freedom, Eutherius being, at his own request, introduced into the presence, and being commanded to say what he wished, speaking with great respect and moderation showed the emperor that the truth was being overlaid with falsehood. For that, while the commander of the heavy-armed troops had, as it was believed, held back on purpose, the Cæsar having been long besieged at Sens, had by his vigilance and energy repelled the barbarians. And he pledged his own life that the Cæsar would, as long as he lived, be faithful to the author of his greatness.

4. The opportunity reminds me here to mention a few facts concerning this same Eutherius, which perhaps will hardly be believed; because if Numa Pompilius or Socrates were to say anything good of a eunuch, and were to confirm what they said by an oath, they would be accused of having departed from the truth. But roses grow up among thorns, and among wild beasts some are of gentle disposition. And therefore I will briefly mention a few of his most important acts which are well ascertained.

5. He was born in Armenia, of a respectable family, and having while a very little child been taken prisoner by the enemies on the border, he was castrated and sold to some Roman merchants, and by them conducted to the palace of Constantine, where, while growing up to manhood, he began to display good principles and good talents, becoming accomplished in literature to a degree quite sufficient for his fortune, displaying extraordinary acuteness in discovering matters of a doubtful and difficult complexion; being remarkable also for a marvellous memory, always eager to do good, and full of wise and honest counsel. A man, in short, who, if the Emperor Constantius had listened to his advice, which, whether he gave it in youth or manhood, was always honourable and upright, would have been prevented from committing any errors, or at least any that were not pardonable.

6. When he became high chamberlain he sometimes also found fault even with Julian, who, as being tainted with Asiatic manners, was apt to be capricious. Finally, when he quitted office for private life, and again when he was recalled to court, he was always sober and

consistent, cultivating those excellent virtues of good faith and constancy to such a degree that he never betrayed any secret, except for the purpose of securing another's safety; nor was he ever accused of covetous or grasping conduct, as the other courtiers were.

7. From which it arose that, when at a late period he retired to Rome, and fixed there the abode of his old age, bearing with him the company of a good conscience, he was loved and respected by men of all ranks, though men of that class generally, after having amassed riches by iniquity, love to seek secret places of retirement, just as owls or moths, and avoid the sight of the multitude whom they have injured.

8. Though I have often ransacked the accounts of antiquity, I do not find any ancient eunuch to whom I can compare him. There were indeed among the ancients some, though very few, faithful and economical, but still they were stained by some vice or other; and among the chief faults which they had either by nature or habit, they were apt to be either rapacious or else boorish, and on that account contemptible; or else ill-natured and mischievous; or fawning too much on the powerful; or too elated with power, and therefore arrogant. But of any one so universally accomplished and prudent, I confess I have neither ever read nor heard, relying for the truth of this judgment on the general testimony of the age.

9. But if any careful reader of ancient histories should oppose to us Menophilus, the eunuch of King Mithridates, I would warn him to recollect that nothing is really known of him except this single fact, that he behaved gloriously in a moment of extreme danger.

10. When the king above mentioned, having been defeated by the Romans under the command of Pompey, and fleeing to his kingdom of Colchis, left a grown-up daughter, named Drypetina, who at the time was dangerously ill, in the castle of Synhorium, under the care of this Menophilus, he completely cured the maiden by a variety of remedies, and preserved her in safety for her father; and when the fortress in which they were enclosed began to be besieged by Manlius Priscus, the lieutenant of the general, and when he became aware that the garrison were proposing to surrender, he, fearing that, to the dishonour of her father, this noble damsel might be made a prisoner and be ravished, slew her, and then fell upon his sword himself. Now I will return to the point from which I digressed.

VIII.

§ 1. After Marcellus had been foiled, as I have mentioned, and had returned to Serdica, which was his native place, many great crimes were perpetrated in the camp of Augustus, under pretence of upholding the majesty of the emperor.

2. For if any one had consulted any cunning soothsayer about the squeak of a mouse, or the appearance of a weasel, or any other similar portent, or had used any old woman's chants to assuage any pain—a practice which the authority of medicine does not always prohibit—such a man was at once informed against, without being able to conceive by whom, and was brought before a court of law, and at once condemned to death.

3. About the same time an individual named Dames was accused by his wife of certain trifling acts, of which, whether he was innocent or not is uncertain; but Rufinus was his enemy, who, as we have mentioned, had given information of some matters which had been communicated to him by Gaudentius, the emperor's secretary, causing Africanus, then governing Pannonia with the rank of a consul, to be put to death, with all his friends. This Rufinus was now, for his devotion to the interests of the emperor, the chief commander of the prætorian guard.

4. He, being given to talking in a boastful manner, after having seduced that easily deluded woman (the wife of Dames) into an illicit connection with him, allured her into a perilous fraud, and persuaded her by an accumulation of lies to accuse her innocent husband of treason, and to invent a story that he had stolen a purple garment from the sepulchre of Diocletian, and, by the help of some accomplices, still kept it concealed.

5. When this story had been thus devised in a way to cause the destruction of many persons, Rufinus himself, full of hopes of some advantage, hastened to the camp of the emperor, to spread his customary calumnies. And when the transaction had been divulged, Manlius, at that time the commander of the prætorian camp, a man of admirable integrity, received orders to make a strict inquiry into the charge, having united to him, as a colleague in the examination, Ursulus, the chief paymaster, a man likewise of praiseworthy equity and strictness.

6. There, after the matter had been rigorously investigated according to the fashion of that period, and when, after many persons had put to the torture, nothing was found out, and the judges were in doubt and perplexity; at length truth, long suppressed, found a respite, and, under the compulsion of a rigorous examination, the woman confessed that Rufinus was the author of the whole plot, nor did she even conceal the fact of her adultery with him. Reference was imme-

diately made to the law, and as order and justice required, the judges condemned them both to death.

7. But as soon as this was known, Constantius became greatly enraged, and lamenting Rufinus as if the champion of his safety had been destroyed, he sent couriers on horseback express, with threatening orders to Ursulus, commanding him to return to court. Ursulus, disregarding the remonstrances of those who advised him to disobey, hastened fearlessly to the presence; and having entered the emperor's council-chambers, with undaunted heart and voice related the whole transaction; and this confident behaviour of his shut the mouths of the flatterers, and delivered both the prefect and himself from serious danger.

8. It was at this time also that an event took place in Aquitania which was more extensively talked about. A certain cunning person being invited to a splendid and sumptuous banquet, which are frequent in that province, having seen a pair of coverlets, with two purple borders of such width, that by the skill of those who waited they seemed to be but one; and beholding the table also covered with a similar cloth, he took up one in each hand, and arranged them so as to resemble the front of a cloak, representing them as having formed the ornament of the imperial robe; and then searching over the whole house in order to find the robe which he affirmed must be hidden there, he thus caused the ruin of a wealthy estate.

9. With similar malignity, a certain secretary in Spain, who was likewise invited to a supper, hearing the servants, while bringing in the evening candles, cry "let us conquer," affixing a malignant interpretation to that common exclamation, in like manner ruined a noble family.

10. These and other evils increasing more and more, because Constantius, being a man of a very timorous disposition, was always thinking that blows were being aimed at him, like the celebrated tyrant of Sicily, Dionysius, who, because of this vice of his, taught his daughters to shave him, in order that he might not have to put his face in a stranger's power; and surrounded the small chamber in which he was accustomed to sleep with a deep ditch, so placed that it could only be entered by a drawbridge; the loose beams and axles of which when he went to bed he removed into his own chamber, replacing them when about to go forth at daybreak.

11. Moreover, those who had influence in the court promoted the spread of these evils, with the hope of joining to their own estates the

forfeited possessions of those who should be condemned; and thus becoming rich by the ruin of their neighbours.

12. For, as clear evidence has shown, if Constantine was the first to excite the appetites of his followers, Constantius was the prince who fattened them on the marrow of the provinces.

13. For under him the principal persons of every rank burnt with an insatiable desire of riches, without any regard for justice or right. And among the ordinary judges, Rufinus, the chief prefect of the prætorium, was conspicuous for this avarice. And among the military officers Arbetio, the master of the horse, and Eusebius, the high chamberlain, ... Ard ... anus, the quæstor, and in the city, the two Anicii, whose posterity, treading in the steps of their fathers, could not be satisfied even with possessions much larger than they themselves had enjoyed.

IX.

§ 1. But in the East, the Persians now practising predatory inroads and forays, in preference to engaging in pitched battles, as they had been wont to do before, carried off continually great numbers of men and cattle: sometimes making great booty, owing to the unexpectedness of their incursions, but at other times being overpowered by superior numbers, they suffered losses. Sometimes, also, the inhabitants of the districts which they had invaded had removed everything which could be carried off.

2. But Musonianus, the prefect of the prætorium, a man, as we have already said, of many liberal accomplishments but corrupt, and a person easily turned from the truth by a bribe, acquired, by means of some emissaries who were skilful in deceiving and obtaining information, a knowledge of the plans of the Persians; taking to his counsels on this subject Cassianus, duke of Mesopotamia, a veteran who had served many campaigns, and had become hardened by all kinds of dangers.

3. And when, by the concurrent report of spies, these officers had become certain that Sapor was occupied in the most remote frontier of his kingdom in repelling the hostilities of the bordering tribes, which he could not accomplish without great difficulty and bloodshed, they sought to tamper with Tamsapor, the general in command in the district nearest our border. Accordingly they sent soldiers of no renown to confer with him secretly, to engage him, if opportunity served, to write to the king to persuade him to make peace with the Roman emperor;

whereby he, being then secure on every side, might be the better able to subdue the rebels who were never weary of exciting disturbances.

4. Tamsapor coincided with these wishes, and, trusting to them, reported to the king that Constantius, being involved in very formidable wars, was a suppliant for peace. But it took a long time for these letters to reach the country of the Chionites and the Euseni, on whose borders Sapor had taken up his winter quarters.

X.

§ 1. While matters were thus proceeding in the eastern regions and in the Gauls, Constantius, as if the temple of Janus were now shut and hostilities everywhere at an end, became desirous of visiting Rome, with the intention of celebrating his triumph over Magnentius, to which he could give no name, since the blood that he had spilt was that of Roman foes.

2. For indeed, neither by his own exertions, nor by those of his generals did he ever conquer any nation that made war upon him; nor did he make any additions to the empire; nor at critical moments was he ever seen to be the foremost or even among the foremost; but still he was eager to exhibit to the people, now in the enjoyment of peace, a vast procession, and standards heavy with gold, and a splendid train of guards and followers, though the citizens themselves neither expected nor desired any such spectacle.

3. He was ignorant, probably, that some of the ancient emperors were, in time of peace, contented with their lictors, and that when the ardour of war forbade all inactivity, one,[61] in a violent storm, had trusted himself to a fisherman's boat; another,[62] following the example of the Decii, had sacrificed his life for the safety of the republic; another[63] had by himself, accompanied by only a few soldiers of the lowest rank, gone as a spy into the camp of the enemy: in short, that many of them had rendered themselves illustrious by splendid exploits, in order to hand down to posterity a glorious memory of themselves, earned by their achievements.

4. Accordingly, after long and sumptuous preparation, ... in the second prefecture of Orfitus, Constantius, elated with his great honours, and escorted by a formidable array of troops, marching in order of battle, passed through Ocricoli, attracting towards himself the astonished gaze of all the citizens.

5. And when he drew near to the city, contemplating the salutations offered him by the senators, and the whole body of fathers

venerable from their likeness to their ancestors, he thought, not like Cineas, the ambassador of Pyrrhus, that a multitude of kings was here assembled together, but that the city was the asylum of the whole world.

6. And when from them he had turned his eyes upon the citizens, he marvelled to think with what rapidity the whole race of mankind upon earth had come from all quarters to Rome; and, as if he would have terrified the Euphrates or the Rhine with a show of armed men, he himself came on, preceded by standards on both sides, sitting alone in a golden chariot, shining with all kinds of brilliant precious stones, which seemed to spread a flickering light all around.

7. Numbers also of the chief officers who went before him were surrounded by dragons embroidered on various kinds of tissue, fastened to the golden or jewelled points of spears, the mouths of the dragons being open so as to catch the wind, which made them hiss as though they were inflamed with anger; while the coils of their tails were also contrived to be agitated by the breeze.

8. After these marched a double row of heavy-armed soldiers, with shields and crested helmets, glittering with brilliant light, and clad in radiant breastplates; and among these were scattered cavalry with cuirasses, whom the Persians call Clibanarii,[64] protected by coverings of iron breastplates, and girdled with belts of iron, so that you would fancy them statues polished by the hand of Praxiteles, rather than men. And the light circular plates of iron which surrounded their bodies, and covered all their limbs, were so well fitted to all their motions, that in whatever direction they had occasion to move, the joints of their iron clothing adapted themselves equally to any position.

9. The emperor as he proceeded was saluted as Augustus by voices of good omen, the mountains and shores re-echoing the shouts of the people, amid which he preserved the same immovable countenance which he was accustomed to display in his provinces.

10. For though he was very short, yet he bowed down when entering high gates, and looking straight before him, as though he had had his neck in a vice, he turned his eyes neither to the right nor to the left, as if he had been a statue: nor when the carriage shook him did he nod his head, or spit, or rub his face or his nose; nor was he ever seen even to move a hand.

11. And although this calmness was affectation, yet these and other portions of his inner life were indicative of a most extraordinary patience, as it may be thought, granted to him alone.

12. I pass over the circumstance that during the whole of his reign he never either took up any one to sit with him in his chariot, or admitted any private person to be his partner in the consulship, as other emperors had done; also many other things which he, being filled with elation and pride, prescribed to himself as the justest of all rules of conduct, recollecting that I mentioned those facts before, as occasion served.

13. As he went on, having entered Rome, that home of sovereignty and of all virtues, when he arrived at the rostra, he gazed with amazed awe on the Forum, the most renowned monument of ancient power; and, being bewildered with the number of wonders on every side to which he turned his eyes, having addressed the nobles in the senate-house, and harangued the populace from the tribune, he retired, with the good-will of all, into his palace, where he enjoyed the luxury he had wished for. And often, when celebrating the equestrian games, was he delighted with the talkativeness of the common people, who were neither proud, nor, on the other hand, inclined to become rebellious from too much liberty, while he himself also reverently observed a proper moderation.

14. For he did not, as was usually done in other cities, allow the length of the gladiatorial contests to depend on his caprice; but left it to be decided by various occurrences. Then, traversing the summits of the seven hills, and the different quarters of the city, whether placed on the slopes of the hills or on the level ground, and visiting, too, the suburban divisions, he was so delighted that whatever he saw first he thought the most excellent of all. Admiring the temple of the Tarpeian Jupiter, which is as much superior to other temples as divine things are superior to those of men; and the baths of the size of provinces; and the vast mass of the amphitheatre, so solidly erected of Tibertine stone, to the top of which human vision can scarcely reach; and the Pantheon with its vast extent, its imposing height, and the solid magnificence of its arches, and the lofty niches rising one above another like stairs, adorned with the images of former emperors; and the temple of the city, and the forum of peace, and the theatre of Pompey, and the odeum, and the racecourse, and the other ornaments of the Eternal City.

15. But when he came to the forum of Trajan, the most exquisite structure, in my opinion, under the canopy of heaven, and admired even by the deities themselves, he stood transfixed with wonder, casting his mind over the gigantic proportions of the place, beyond the power of mortal to describe, and beyond the reasonable desire of mor-

tals to rival. Therefore giving up all hopes of attempting anything of this kind, he contented himself with saying that he should wish to imitate, and could imitate the horse of Trajan, which stands by itself in the middle of the hall, bearing the emperor himself on his back.

16. And the royal prince Hormisdas, whose departure from Persia we have already mentioned, standing by answered, with the refinement of his nature, "But first, O emperor, command such a stable to be built for him, if you can, that the horse which you purpose to make may have as fair a domain as this which we see." And when he was asked what he thought of Rome, he said that "he was particularly delighted with it because he had learnt that men died also there."

17. Now after he had beheld all these various objects with awful admiration, the emperor complained of fame, as either deficient in power, or else spiteful, because, though it usually exaggerates everything, it fell very short in its praises of the things which are at Rome; and having deliberated for some time what he should do, he determined to add to the ornaments of the city by erecting an obelisk in the Circus Maximus, the origin and form of which I will describe when I come to the proper place.

18. At this time Eusebia, the queen, who herself was barren all her life, began to plot against Helena, the sister of Constantius, and wife of the Cæsar Julian, whom she had induced to come to Rome under a pretence of affection, and by wicked machinations she induced her to drink a poison which she had procured, which should have the effect, whenever Helena conceived, of producing abortion.

19. For already, when in Gaul, she had borne a male child, but that also had been dishonestly destroyed because the midwife, having been bribed, killed it as soon as it was born, by cutting through the navel-string too deeply; such exceeding care was taken that this most gallant man should have no offspring.

20. But the emperor, while wishing to remain longer in this most august spot of the whole world, in order to enjoy a purer tranquillity and higher degree of pleasure, was alarmed by repeated intelligence on which he could rely, which informed him that the Suevi were invading the Tyrol, that the Quadi were ravaging Valeria,[65] and that the Sarmatians, a tribe most skilful in plunder, were laying waste the upper Mœsia, and the second Pannonia. And roused by these news, on the thirtieth day after he had entered Rome, he again quitted it, leaving it on the 29th of May, and passing through Trent he proceeded with all haste towards Illyricum.

21. And from that city he sent Severus to succeed Marcellus, a man of great experience and ripe skill in war, and summoned Ursicinus to himself. He, having gladly received the letter of summons, came to Sirmium, with a large retinue, and after a long deliberation on the peace which Musonianus had reported as possible to be made with the Persians, he was sent back to the East with the authority of commander-in-chief, and the older officers of our company having been promoted to commands over the soldiers, we younger men were ordered to follow him to perform whatever he commanded us for the service of the republic.

XI.

A.D. 357.

§ 1. But Julian, having passed his winter at Sens, amid continual disturbance, in the ninth consulship of the emperor, and his own second, while the threats of the Germans were raging on all sides, being roused by favourable omens, marched with speed to Rheims, with the greater alacrity and joy because Severus was in command of the army there; a man inclined to agree with him, void of arrogance, but of proved propriety of conduct and experience in war, and likely to follow his lawful authority, obeying his general like a well-disciplined soldier.

2. In another quarter, Barbatio, who after the death of Silvanus had been promoted to the command of the infantry, came from Italy by the emperor's orders, to Augst, with 25,000 heavy-armed soldiers.

3. For the plan proposed and very anxiously prepared was, that the Allemanni, who were in a state of greater rage than ever, and were extending their incursions more widely, should be caught between our two armies, as if between the arms of a pair of pincers, and so driven into a corner and destroyed.

4. But while these well-devised plans were being pressed forward, the barbarians, in joy at some success which they had obtained, and skilful in seizing every opportunity for plunder, passed secretly between the camps of the armies, and attacked Lyons unexpectedly. And having plundered the district around, they would have stormed and burnt the city itself, if they had not found the gates so strongly defended that they were repulsed; so that they only destroyed all they could find outside the city.

5. When this disaster was known, Cæsar, with great alacrity, despatched three squadrons of light cavalry, of approved valour, to

watch three lines of road, knowing that beyond all question the invaders must quit the district by one of them.

6. Nor was he mistaken; for all who came by these roads were slaughtered by our men, and the whole of the booty which they were carrying off was recovered unhurt. Those alone escaped in safety who passed by the camp of Barbatio, who were suffered to escape in that direction because Bainobaudes the tribune, and Valentinian (afterwards emperor), who had been appointed to watch that pass with the squadrons of cavalry under their orders, were forbidden by Cella (the tribune of the Scutarii, who had been sent as colleague to Barbatio) to occupy that road, though they were sure that by that the Germans would return to their own country.

7. The cowardly master of the horse, being also an obstinate enemy to the glory of Julian, was not contented with this, but being conscious that he had given orders inconsistent with the interests of Rome (for when he was accused of it Cella confessed what he had done), he made a false report to Constantius, and told him that these same tribunes had, under a pretence of the business of the state, came thither for the purpose of tampering with the soldiers whom he commanded. And owing to this statement they were deprived of their commands, and returned home as private individuals.

8. In these days, also, the barbarians, alarmed at the approach of our armies, which had established their stations on the left bank of the Rhine, employed some part of their force in skilfully barricading the roads, naturally difficult of access, and full of hills, by abattis constructed of large trees cut down; others occupied the numerous islands scattered up and down the Rhone, and with horrid howls poured forth constant reproaches against the Romans and the Cæsar; who, being now more than ever resolved to crush some of their armies, demanded from Barbatio seven of those boats which he had collected, for the purpose of constructing a bridge with them, with the intention of crossing the river. But Barbatio, determined that no assistance should be got from him, burnt them all.

9. Julian, therefore, having learnt from the report of some spies whom he had lately taken prisoners, that, when the drought of summer arrived, the river was fordable, addressed a speech of encouragement to his light-armed auxiliary troops, and sent them forward with Bainobaudes, the tribune of the Cornuti, to try and perform some gallant exploit, if they could find an opportunity. And they, entering the shallow of the river, and sometimes, when there was occasion for swimming, putting their shields under them like canoes, reached a

neighbouring island, and having landed, killed every one they found on it, men and women, without distinction of age, like so many sheep. And having found some empty boats, though they were not very safe, they crossed in them, forcing their way into many places of the same land. When they were weary of slaughter, and loaded with a rich booty, some of which, however, they lost through the violence of the river, they returned back to the camp without losing a man.

10. And when this was known, the rest of the Germans, thinking they could no longer trust the garrisons left in the islands, removed their relations, and their magazines, and their barbaric treasures, into the inland parts.

11. After this Julian turned his attention to repair the fortress known by the name of Saverne, which had a little time before been destroyed by a violent attack of the enemy, but which, while it stood, manifestly prevented the Germans from forcing their way into the interior of the Gauls, as they had been accustomed to do; and he executed this work with greater rapidity than he expected, and he laid up for the garrison which he intended to post there sufficient magazines for a whole year's consumption, which his army collected from the crops of the barbarians, not without occasional contests with the owners.

12. Nor indeed was he contented with this, but he also collected provisions for himself and his army sufficient for twenty days. For the soldiers delighted in using the food which they had won with their own right hands, being especially indignant because, out of all the supplies which had been recently sent them, they were not able to obtain anything, inasmuch as Barbatio, when they were passing near his camp, had with great insolence seized on a portion of them, and had collected all the rest into a heap and burnt them. Whether he acted thus out of his own vanity and insane folly, or whether others were really the authors of this wickedness, relying on the command of the emperor himself, has never been known.

13. However, as far as report went, the story commonly was, that Julian had been elected Cæsar, not for the object of relieving the distresses of the Gauls, but rather of being himself destroyed by the formidable wars in which he was sure to be involved; being at that time, as was supposed, inexperienced in war, and not likely to endure even the sound of arms.

14. While the works of the camp were steadily rising, and while a portion of the army was being distributed among the stations in the country districts, Julian occupied himself in other quarters with collecting supplies, operating with great caution, from the fear of

ambuscades. And in the mean time, a vast host of the barbarians, out-stripping all report of their approach by the celerity of their movements, came down with a sudden attack upon Barbatio, and the army which (as I have already mentioned) he had under his command, separated from the Gallic army of Severus only by a rampart; and hav-ing put him to flight, pursued him as far as Augst, and beyond that town too, as far as they could; and, having made booty of the greater part of his baggage and beasts of burden, and having carried off many of the sutlers as prisoners, they returned to their main army.

15. And Barbatio, as if he had brought his expectations to a prosperous issue, now distributed his soldiers into winter quarters, and returned to the emperor's court, to forge new accusations against the Cæsar, according to his custom.

XII.

§ 1. When this disgraceful disaster had become known, Chnodomarius and Vestralpus, the kings of the Allemanni, and Urius and Ursicinus, with Serapion, and Suomarius, and Hortarius, having collected all their forces into one body, encamped near the city of Strasburg, thinking that the Cæsar, from fear of imminent danger, had retreated at the very time that he was wholly occupied with completing a fortress to enable him to make a permanent stand.

2. Their confidence and assurance of success was increased by one of the Scutarii who deserted to them, who fearing punishment for some offence which he had committed, crossed over to them after the departure of Barbatio, and assured them that Julian had now only 13,000 men remaining with him. For that was the number of troops that he had now with him, while the ferocious barbarians were stirring up attacks upon him from all sides.

3. And as he constantly adhered to the same story, they were ex-cited to more haughty attempts by the confidence with which he inspired them, and sent ambassadors in an imperious tone to Cæsar, demanding that he should retire from the territory which they had ac-quired by their own valour in arms. But he, a stranger to fear, and not liable to be swayed either by anger or by disappointment, despised the arrogance of the barbarians, and detaining the ambassadors till he had completed the works of his camp, remained immovable on his ground with admirable constancy.

4. But King Chnodomarius, moving about in every direction, and being always the first to undertake dangerous enterprises, kept every-

thing in continual agitation and confusion, being full of arrogance and pride, as one whose head was turned by repeated success.

5. For he had defeated the Cæsar Decentius in a pitched battle, and he had plundered and destroyed many wealthy cities, and he had long ravaged all Gaul at his own pleasure without meeting with any resistance. And his confidence was now increased by the recent retreat of a general superior to him in the number and strength of his forces.

6. For the Allemanni, beholding the emblems on their shields, saw that a few predatory bands of their men had wrested those districts from those soldiers whom they had formerly never engaged but with fear, and by whom they had often been routed with much loss. And these circumstances made Julian very anxious, because, after the defection of Barbatio, he himself under the pressure of absolute necessity was compelled to encounter very populous tribes, with but very few, though brave troops.

7. And now, the sun being fully risen, the trumpets sounded, and the infantry were led forth from the camp in slow march, and on their flanks were arrayed the squadrons of cavalry, among which were both the cuirassiers and the archers, troops whose equipment was very formidable.

8. And since from the spot from which the Roman standards had first advanced to the rampart of the barbarian camp were fourteen leagues, that is to say one-and-twenty miles, Cæsar, carefully providing for the advantage and safety of his army, called in the skirmishers who had gone out in front, and having ordered silence in his usual voice, while they all stood in battalions around him, addressed them in his natural tranquillity of voice.

9. "The necessity of providing for our common safety, to say the least of it, compels me, and I am no prince of abject spirit, to exhort you, my comrades, to rely so much on your own mature and vigorous valour, as to follow my counsels in adopting a prudent manner of enduring or repelling the evils which we anticipate, rather than resort to an overhasty mode of action which must be doubtful in its issue.

10. "For though amid dangers youth ought to be energetic and bold, so also in cases of necessity it should show itself manageable and prudent. Now what I think best to be done, if your opinion accords with mine, and if your just indignation will endure it, I will briefly explain.

11. "Already noon is approaching, we are weary with our march, and if we advance we shall enter upon rugged paths where we can hardly see our way. As the moon is waning the night will not be

lighted up by any stars. The earth is burnt up with the heat, and will afford us no supplies of water. And even if by any contrivance we could get over these difficulties comfortably, still, when the swarms of the enemy fall upon us, refreshed as they will be with rest, meat, and drink, what will become of us? What strength will there be in our weary limbs, exhausted as we shall be with hunger, thirst, and toil, to encounter them?

12. "Therefore, since the most critical difficulties are often over-come by skilful arrangements, and since, after good counsel has been taken in good part, divine-looking remedies have often re-established affairs which seemed to be tottering; I entreat you to let us here, sur-rounded as we are with fosse and rampart, take our repose, after first parcelling out our regular watches, and then, having refreshed our-selves with sleep and food as well as the time will allow, let us, under the protection of God, with the earliest dawn move forth our conquer-ing eagles and standards to reap a certain triumph."

13. The soldiers would hardly allow him to finish his speech, gnashing their teeth, and showing their eagerness for combat by beat-ing their shields with their spears; and entreating at once to be led against the enemy already in their sight, relying on the favour of the God of heaven, and on their own valour, and on the proved courage of their fortunate general. And, as the result proved, it was a certain kind genius that was present with them thus prompting them to fight while still under his inspiration.

14. And this eagerness of theirs was further stimulated by the full approval of the officers of high rank, and especially of Florentius the prefect of the prætorian guard, who openly gave his opinion for fight-ing at once, while the enemy were in the solid mass in which they were now arranged; admitting the danger indeed, but still thinking it the wisest plan, because, if the enemy once dispersed, it would be im-possible to restrain the soldiers, at all times inclined by their natural vehemence of disposition towards sedition; and they were likely to be, as he thought, so indignant at being denied the victory they sought, as to be easily tempted to the most lawless violence.

15. Two other considerations also added to the confidence of our men. First, because they recollected that in the previous year, when the Romans spread themselves in every direction over the countries on the other side of the Rhine, not one of the barbarians stood to defend his home, nor ventured to encounter them; but they contented themselves with blockading the roads in every direction with vast abattis, throughout the whole winter retiring into the remote districts, and will-

ingly endured the greatest hardships rather than fight; recollecting also that, after the emperor actually invaded their territories, the barbarians neither ventured to make any resistance, nor even to show themselves at all, but implored peace in the most suppliant manner, till they obtained it.

16. But no one considered that the times were changed, because the barbarians were at that time pressed with a threefold danger. The emperor hastening against them through the Tyrol, the Cæsar who was actually in their country cutting off all possibility of retreat, while the neighbouring tribes, whom recent quarrels had converted into enemies, were all but treading on their heels; and thus they were surrounded on all sides. But since that time the emperor, having granted them peace, had returned to Italy, and the neighbouring tribes, having all cause of quarrel removed, were again in alliance with them; and the disgraceful retreat of one of the Roman generals had increased their natural confidence and boldness.

17. Moreover there was another circumstance which at this crisis added weight to the difficulties which pressed upon the Romans. The two royal brothers, who had obtained peace from Constantius in the preceding year, being bound by the obligations of that treaty, neither ventured to raise any disturbance, nor indeed to put themselves in motion at all. But a little after the conclusion of that peace one of them whose name was Gundomadus, and who was the most loyal and the most faithful to his word, was slain by treachery, and then all his tribe joined our enemies; and on this the tribe of Vadomarius also, against his will, as he affirmed, ranged itself on the side of the barbarians who were arming for war.

18. Therefore, since all the soldiers of every rank, from the highest to the lowest, approved of engaging instantly, and would not relax the least from the rigour of their determination, on a sudden the standard-bearer shouted out, "Go forth, O Cæsar, most fortunate of all princes. Go whither thy better fortune leads thee. At least we have learnt by your example the power of valour and military skill. Go on and lead us, as a fortunate and gallant champion. You shall see what a soldier under the eye of a warlike general, a witness of the exploits of each individual, can do, and how little, with the favour of the Deity, any obstacle can avail against him."

19. When these words were heard, without a moment's delay, the whole army advanced and approached a hill of moderate height, covered with ripe corn, at no great distance from the banks of the Rhine. On its summit were posted three cavalry soldiers of the enemy as

scouts, who at once hastened back to their comrades to announce that the Roman army was at hand; but one infantry soldier who was with them, not being able to keep up with them, was taken prisoner by the activity of some of our soldiers, and informed us that the Germans had been passing over the river for three days and three nights.

20. And when our generals beheld them now at no great distance forming their men into solid columns, they halted, and formed all the first ranks of their troops into a similarly solid body, and with equal caution the enemy likewise halted.

21. And when in consequence of this halt, the enemy saw (as the deserter I mentioned above had informed them) that all our cavalry was ranged against them in our right wing, then they posted all their own cavalry in close order on their left wing. And with them they mingled every here and there a few infantry, skirmishers and light-armed soldiers, which indeed was a very wise manœuvre.

22. For they knew that a cavalry soldier, however skilful, if fighting with one of our men in complete armour, while his hands were occupied with shield and bridle, so that he could use no offensive weapon but the spear which he brandished in his right hand, could never injure an enemy wholly covered with iron mail; but that an in-fantry soldier, amid the actual struggles of personal conflict, when nothing is usually guarded against by a combatant except that which is straight before him, may crawl unperceivedly along the ground, and piercing the side of the Roman soldier's horse, throw the rider down headlong, rendering him thus an easy victim.

23. When these dispositions had been thus made, the barbarians also protected their right flank with secret ambuscades and snares. Now the whole of these warlike and savage tribes were on this day under the command of Chnodomarius and Serapio, monarchs of more power than any of their former kings.

24. Chnodomarius was indeed the wicked instigator of the whole war, and bearing on his head a helmet blazing like fire, he led on the left wing with great boldness, confiding much on his vast personal strength. And now with great eagerness for the impending battle he mounted a spirited horse, that by the increased height he might be more conspicuous, leaning upon a spear of most formidable size, and remarkable for the splendour of his arms. Being indeed a prince who had on former occasions shown himself brave as a warrior and a gen-eral, eminent for skill above his fellows.

25. The right wing was led by Serapio, a youth whose beard had hardly grown, but who was beyond his years in courage and strength.

He was the son of Mederichus the brother of Chnodomarius, a man throughout his whole life of the greatest perfidy; and he had received the name of Serapio because his father, having been given as a hostage, had been detained in Gaul for a long time, and had there learnt some of the mysteries of the Greeks, in consequence of which he had changed the name of his son, who at his birth was named Agenarichus, into that of Serapio.

26. These two leaders were followed by five other kings who were but little inferior in power to themselves, by ten petty princes, a vast number of nobles, and thirty-five thousand armed men, collected from various nations partly by pay, and partly by a promise of requiting their service by similar assistance on a future day.

27. The trumpets now gave forth a terrible sound; Severus, the Roman general in command of the left wing, when he came near the ditches filled with armed men, from which the enemy had arranged that those who were there concealed should suddenly rise up, and throw the Roman line into confusion, halted boldly, and suspecting some yet hidden ambuscade, neither attempted to retreat nor advance.

28. Seeing this, Julian, always full of courage at the moment of the greatest difficulty, galloped with an escort of two hundred cavalry through the ranks of the infantry at full speed, addressing them with words of encouragement, as the critical circumstances in which they were placed required.

29. And as the extent of the space over which they were spread and the denseness of the multitude thus collected into one body, would not allow him to address the whole army (and also because on other accounts he wished to avoid exposing himself to malice and envy, as well as not to affect that which Augustus thought belonged exclusively to himself), he, while taking care of himself as he passed within reach of the darts of the enemy, encouraged all whom his voice could reach, whether known or unknown to him, to fight bravely, with these and similar words:—

30. "Now, my comrades, the fit time for fighting has arrived; the time which I, as well as you, have long desired, and which you just now invited when, with gestures of impatience, you demanded to be led on." Again, when he came to those in the rear rank, who were posted in reserve: "Behold," said he, "my comrades, the long-wished-for day is at hand, which incites us all to wash out former stains, and to restore to its proper brightness the Roman majesty. These men before you are barbarians, whom their own rage and intemperate madness

have urged forward to meet with the destruction of their fortunes, defeated as they will now be by our might."

31. Presently, when making better dispositions for the array of some troops who, by long experience in war, had attained to greater skill, he aided his arrangements by these exhortations. "Let us rise up like brave men; let us by our native valour repel the disgrace which has at one time been brought upon our arms, from contemplating which it was that after much delay I consented to take the name of Cæsar."

32. But to any whom he saw inconsiderately demanding the signal to be given for instant battle, and likely by their rash movements to be inattentive to orders, he said, "I entreat you not to be too eager in your pursuit of the flying enemy, so as to risk losing the glory of the victory which awaits us, and also never to retreat, except under the last necessity.

33. "For I shall certainly take no care of those who flee. But among those who press on to the slaughter of the enemy I shall be present, and share with you indiscriminately, provided only that your charge be made with moderation and prudence."

34. While repeatedly addressing these and similar exhortations to the troops, he drew up the principal part of his army opposite to the front rank of the barbarians. And suddenly there arose from the Allemanni a great shout, mingled with indignant cries, all exclaiming with one voice that the princes ought to leave their horses and fight in the ranks on equal terms with their men, lest if any mischance should occur they should avail themselves of the facility of escaping, and leave the mass of the army in miserable plight.

35. When this was known, Chnodomarius immediately leapt down from his horse, and the rest of the princes followed his example without hesitation. For indeed none of them doubted but that their side would be victorious.

36. Then the signal for battle being given as usual by the sound of trumpets, the armies rushed to the combat with all their force. First of all javelins were hurled, and the Germans, hastening on with the utmost impetuosity, brandishing their javelins in their right hands, dashed among the squadrons of our cavalry, uttering fearful cries. They had excited themselves to more than usual rage; their flowing hair bristling with their eagerness, and fury blazing from their eyes. While in opposition to them our soldiers, standing steadily, protecting their heads with the bulwark of their shields, and drawing their swords

or brandishing their javelins, equally threatened death to their assailants.

37. And while in the very conflict of battle, the cavalry kept their gallant squadrons in close order, and the infantry strengthened their flanks, standing shoulder to shoulder with closely-locked shields, clouds of thick dust arose, and the battle rocked to and fro, our men sometimes advancing, sometimes receding. Some of the most powerful warriors among the barbarians pressed upon their antagonists with their knees, trying to throw them down; and in the general excitement men fought hand to hand, shield pressing upon shield; while the heaven resounded with the loud cries of the conquerors and of the dying. Presently, when our left wing, advancing forward, had driven back with superior strength the vast bands of German assailants, and was itself advancing with loud cries against the enemy, our cavalry on the right wing unexpectedly retreated in disorder; but when the leading fugitives came upon those in the rear, they halted, perceiving themselves covered by the legions, and renewed the battle.

38. This disaster had arisen from the cuirassiers seeing their commander slightly wounded, and one of their comrades crushed under the weight of his own arms, and of his horse, which fell upon him while they were changing their position, on which they all fled as each could, and would have trampled down the infantry, and thrown everything into confusion, if the infantry had not steadily kept their ranks and stood immovable, supporting each other. Julian, when from a distance he saw his cavalry thus seeking safety in flight, spurred his horse towards them, and himself stopped them like a barrier.

39. For as he was at once recognized by his purple standard of the dragon, which was fixed to the top of a long spear, waving its fringe as a real dragon sheds its skin, the tribune of one squadron halted, and turning pale with alarm, hastened back to renew the battle.

40. Then, as is customary in critical moments, Julian gently reproached his men: "Whither," said he, "gallant comrades, are ye retreating? Are ye ignorant that flight, which never insures safety, proves the folly of having made a vain attempt? Let us return to our army, to be partakers of their glory, and not rashly desert those who are fighting for the republic."

41. Saying these words in a dignified tone, he led them all back to discharge their duties in the fight, imitating in this the ancient hero Sylla, if we make allowances for the difference of situation. For when Sylla, having led his army against Archelaus, the general of Mithridates, became exhausted by the violence of the conflict, and was

deserted by all his soldiers, he ran to the foremost rank, and seizing a standard he turned it against the enemy, exclaiming, "Go! ye once chosen companions of my dangers; and when you are asked where I, your general, was left, tell them this truth,—alone in Bœotia, fighting for us all, to his own destruction."

42. The Allemanni, when our cavalry had been thus driven back and thrown into confusion, attacked the first line of our infantry, expecting to find their spirit abated, and to be able to rout them without much resistance.

43. But when they came to close quarters with them, they found they had met an equal match. The conflict lasted long; for the Cornuti and Braccati,[66] veterans of great experience in war, frightening even by their gestures, shouted their battle cry, and the uproar, through the heat of the conflict, rising up from a gentle murmur, and becoming gradually louder and louder, grew fierce as that of waves dashing against the rocks; the javelins hissed as they flew hither and thither through the air; the dust rose to the sky in one vast cloud, preventing all possibility of seeing, and causing arms to fall upon arms, man upon man.

44. But the barbarians, in their undisciplined anger and fury, raged like the flames; and with ceaseless blows of their swords sought to pierce through the compact mass of the shields with which our soldiers defended themselves, as with the testudo.[67]

45. And when this was seen, the Batavi, with the royal legion, hastened to the support of their comrades, a formidable band, well able, if fortune aided them, to save even those who were in the extremest danger. And amid the fierce notes of their trumpets, the battle again raged with undiminished ferocity.

46. But the Allemanni, still charging forward impetuously, strove more and more vigorously, hoping to bear down all opposition by the violence of their fury. Darts, spears, and javelins never ceased; arrows pointed with iron were shot; while at the same time, in hand-to-hand conflict, sword struck sword, breastplates were cloven, and even the wounded, if not quite exhausted with loss of blood, rose up still to deeds of greater daring.

47. In some sense it may be said that the combatants were equal. The Allemanni were the stronger and the taller men; our soldiers by great practice were the more skilful. The one were fierce and savage, the others composed and wary; the one trusted to their courage, the others to their physical strength.

48. Often, indeed, the Roman soldier was beaten down by the weight of his enemy's arms, but he constantly rose again; and then, on the other hand, the barbarian, finding his knees fail under him with fatigue, would rest his left knee on the ground, and even in that position attack his enemy, an act of extreme obstinacy.

49. Presently there sprang forward with sudden vigour a fiery band of nobles, among whom also were the princes of the petty tribes, and, as the common soldiers followed them in great numbers, they burst through our lines, and forced a path for themselves up to the principal legion of the reserve, which was stationed in the centre, in a position called the prætorian camp; and there the soldiery, being in closer array, and in densely serried ranks, stood firm as so many towers, and renewed the battle with increased spirit. And intent upon parrying the blows of the enemy, and covering themselves with their shields as the Mirmillos[68] do, with their drawn swords wounded their antagonists in the sides, which their too vehement impetuosity left unprotected.

50. And thus the barbarians threw away their lives in their struggles for victory, while toiling to break the compact array of our battalions. But still, in spite of the ceaseless slaughter made among them by the Romans, whose courage rose with their success, fresh barbarians succeeded those who fell; and as the frequent groans of the dying were heard, many became panic-stricken, and lost all strength.

51. At last, exhausted by their losses, and having no strength for anything but flight, they sought to escape with all speed by different roads, like as sailors and traders, when the sea rages in a storm, are glad to flee wherever the wind carries them. But any one then present will confess that escape was a matter rather to be wished than hoped for.

52. And the merciful protection of a favourable deity was present on our side, so that our soldiers, now slashing at the backs of the fugitives, and finding their swords so battered that they were insufficient to wound, used the enemy's own javelins, and so slew them. Nor could any one of the pursuers satiate himself enough with their blood, nor allow his hand to weary with slaughter, nor did any one spare a suppliant out of pity.

53. Numbers, therefore, lay on the ground, mortally wounded, imploring instant death as a relief; others, half dead with failing breath turned their dying eyes to the last enjoyment of the light. Of some the heads were almost cut off by the huge weapons, and merely hung by small strips to their necks; others, again, who had fallen because the

ground had been rendered slippery by the blood of their comrades, without themselves receiving any wound, were killed by being smothered in the mass of those who fell over them.

54. While these events were proceeding thus prosperously for us, the conquerors pressed on vigorously, though the edges of their weapons were blunted by frequent use, and shining helmets and shields were trampled under foot. At last, in the extremity of their distress, the barbarians, finding the heaps of corpses block up all the paths, sought the aid of the river, which was the only hope left to them, and which they had now reached.

55. And because our soldiers unweariedly and with great speed pressed, with arms in their hands, upon the fleeing bands, many, hoping to be able to deliver themselves from danger by their skill in swimming, trusted their lives to the waves. And Julian, with prompt apprehension, seeing what would be the result, strictly forbade the tribunes and captains to allow any of our men to pursue them so eagerly as to trust themselves to the dangerous currents of the river.

56. In consequence of which order they halted on the brink, and from it wounded the Germans with every kind of missile; while, if any of them escaped from death of that kind by the celerity of their movements, they still sunk to the bottom from the weight of their own arms.

57. And as sometimes in a theatrical spectacle the curtain exhibits marvellous figures, so here one could see many strange things in that danger; some unconsciously clinging to others who were good swimmers, others who were floating were pushed off by those less encumbered as so many logs, others again, as if the violence of the stream itself fought against them, were swallowed up in the eddies. Some supported themselves on their shields avoiding the heaviest attacks of the opposing waves by crossing them in an oblique direction, and so, after many dangers, reached the opposite brink, till at last the foaming river, discoloured with barbarian blood, was itself amazed at the unusual increase it had received.

58. And while this was going on, Chnodomarius, the king, finding an opportunity of escaping, making his way over the heaps of dead with a small escort, hastened with exceeding speed towards the camp which he had made near the two Roman fortresses of Alstatt and Lauterbourg, in the country of the Tribocci, that he might embark in some boats which had already been prepared in case of any emergency, and so escape to some secret hiding-place in which he might conceal himself.

59. And because it was impossible for him to reach his camp without crossing the Rhine, he hid his face that he might not be recognized, and after that retreated slowly. And when he got near the bank of the river, as he was feeling his way round a marsh, partly over-flowed, seeking some path by which to cross it, his horse suddenly stumbled in some soft and sticky place, and he was thrown down, but though he was fat and heavy, he without delay reached the shelter of a hill in the neighbourhood; there he was recognized (for indeed he could not conceal who he was, being betrayed by the greatness of his former fortune): and immediately a squadron of cavalry came up at full gallop with its tribune, and cautiously surrounded the wooded mound; though they feared to enter the thicket lest they should fall into any ambuscade concealed among the trees.

60. But when he saw them he was seized with extreme terror, and of his own accord came forth by himself and surrendered; and his companions, two hundred in number, and his three most intimate friends, thinking it would be a crime in them to survive their king, or not to die for him if occasion required, gave themselves up also as prisoners.

61. And, as barbarians are naturally low spirited in adverse fortune, and very much the reverse in moments of prosperity, so now that he was in the power of another he became pale and confused, his consciousness of guilt closing his mouth; widely different from him who lately, insulting the ashes of the Gauls with ferocious and lamentable violence, poured forth savage threats against the whole empire.

62. Now after these affairs were thus by the favour of the deity brought to an end, the victorious soldiers were recalled at the close of the day to their camp by the signal of the trumpeter, and marched towards the bank of the Rhine, and there erecting a rampart of shields piled together in several rows, they refreshed themselves with food and sleep.

63. There fell in this battle, of Romans 243, and four generals: Bainobaudes, the tribune of the Cornuti, and with him Laipso, and Innocentius, who commanded the cuirassiers and one tribune who had no particular command, and whose name I forget. But of the Allemanni, there were found 6000 corpses on the field, and incalculable numbers were carried down by the waves of the river.

64. Then Julian, as one who was now manifestly approved by fortune, and was also greater in his merit than even in his authority, was by unanimous acclamation hailed as Augustus by the soldiers; but

he sharply reproved them for so doing, affirming with an oath that he neither wished for such an honour, nor would accept it.

65. In order to increase the joy at his recent success, Julian ordered Chnodomarius to be brought before him at his council; who at first bowing, and then like a suppliant, prostrating himself on the ground, and imploring pardon with entreaties framed after the fashion of his nation, was bidden to take courage.

66. A few days afterwards he was conducted to the court of the emperor, and thence he was sent to Rome, where he died of a lethargy in the foreign camp which is stationed on Mons Cælius.

67. Notwithstanding that these numerous and important events were brought to so happy an issue, some persons in the palace of Constantius, disparaging Julian in order to give pleasure to the emperor, in a tone of derision called him Victorinus, because he, modestly relating how often he had been employed in leading the army, at the same time related that the Germans had received many defeats.

68. They at the same time, by loading the emperor with empty praises, of which the extravagance was glaringly conspicuous, so inflated an inherent pride, already beyond all natural bounds, that he was led to believe that, whatever took place in the whole circumference of the earth was owing to his fortunate auspices.

69. So that, being inflated by the pompous language of his flatterers, he then, and at all subsequent periods, became accustomed in all the edicts which he published to advance many unfounded statements; assuming, that he by himself had fought and conquered, when in fact he had not been present at anything that had happened; often also asserting that he had raised up the suppliant kings of conquered nations. For instance, if while he was still in Italy any of his generals had fought a brilliant campaign against the Persians, the emperor would write triumphant letters to the provinces without the slightest mention of the general throughout its whole length, relating with odious self-praise how he himself had fought in the front ranks.

70. Lastly, edicts of his are still extant, laid up among the public records of the empire ... relating ...[69] and extolling himself to the skies. A letter also is to be found, though he was forty days' journey from Strasburg when the battle was fought, describing the engagement, saying that he marshalled the army, stood among the standard-bearers, and put the barbarians to the rout; and with amazing falsehood asserting that Chnodomarius was brought before him, without (oh shameful indignity!) saying a single word about the exploits of Julian; which he would have utterly buried in oblivion if fame had not refused to let

great deeds die, however many people may try to keep them in the shade.

Notes

[59] The text is defective here, as it is wherever these marks occur.

[60] Coblenz.

[61] Julius Cæsar: the story of the frightened fisherman being encouraged by the assurance that he was carrying "Cæsar and his fortunes" is universally known.

[62] Claudius, who devoted himself in the Gothic war.

[63] Galerius Maximianus, who reconnoitred in person the camp of the king of Persia.

[64] The word is derived from κλιβανον, an oven, and seems to mean entirely clothed in iron.

[65] Valeria was a division of Pannonia, so called from Valeria, the daughter of Diocletian, and the wife of Galerius.

[66] Troops named from the fashion of their arms; the Cornuti having projections like horns on their helmets, the Braccati wearing drawers.

[67] The testudo was properly applied to the manner in which they locked their shields over their heads while advancing to storm a walled town.

[68] The Mirmillo was a gladiator opposed to a Retiarius, protecting himself by his oblong shield against the net of the latter.

[69] The text is mutilated here, as in many other passages similarly marked.

BOOK XVII

I.

A.D. 357.

§ 1. After the various affairs which we have described were brought to a conclusion, the warlike young prince, now that the battle of Strasburg had secured him the navigation of the Rhine, felt anxious that the ill-omened birds should not feed on the corpses of the slain, and so ordered them all to be buried without distinction. And having dismissed the ambassadors whom we have mentioned as having come with some arrogant messages before the battle, he returned to Saverne.

2. From this place he ordered all the booty and the prisoners to be brought to Metz, to be left there till his return. Then departing for Mayence, to lay down a bridge at that city and to seek the barbarians in their own territories, since he had left none of them in arms, he was at first met by great opposition on the part of his army; but addressing them with eloquence and persuasion he soon won them to his opinion. For their affection for him, becoming strengthened by repeated experience, induced them to follow one who shared in all their toils, and who, while never surrendering his authority, was still accustomed, as every one saw, to impose more labour on himself than on his men. They soon arrived at the appointed spot, and, crossing the river by a bridge they laid down, occupied the territory of the enemy.

3. The barbarians, amazed at the greatness of his enterprise, inasmuch as they had fancied they were situated in a position in which they could hardly be disturbed, were now led by the destruction of their countrymen to think anxiously of their own future fate, and accordingly, pretending to implore peace that they might escape from the violence of his first invasion, they sent ambassadors to him with a set message, offering a lasting treaty of agreement; but (though it is not known what design or change of circumstances altered their purpose) they immediately afterwards sent off some others with all speed, to threaten our troops with implacable war if they did not at once quit their territories.

4. And when this was known, the Cæsar, as soon as all was quiet, at the beginning of night embarked 800 men in some small swift boats, with the intention that they should row with all their strength up stream for some distance, and then land and destroy all they could find with fire and sword.

5. After he had made this arrangement, the barbarians were seen at daybreak on the tops of the mountains, on which our soldiers were led with speed to the higher ground; and when no enemy was found there (since the barbarians, divining their plan, immediately retreated

to a distance), presently large volumes of smoke were seen, which indicated that our men had broken into the enemy's territory, and were laying it waste.

6. This event broke the spirit of the Germans, who, deserting the ambuscades which they had laid for our men in narrow defiles full of lurking-places, they fled across the river Maine to carry aid to their countrymen.

7. For, as is often the case in times of uncertainty and difficulty, they were panic-stricken by the incursion of our cavalry on the one side, and the sudden attacks of our infantry, conveyed in boats, on the other; and therefore, relying on their knowledge of the country, they sought safety in the rapidity of their flight; and, as their retreat left the motions of our troops free, we plundered the wealthy farms of their crops and their cattle, sparing no one. And having carried off a number of prisoners, we set fire to, and burnt to the ground all their houses, which in that district were built more carefully than usual, in the Roman fashion.

8. And when we had penetrated a distance of ten miles, till we came near a wood terrible from the denseness of its shade, our army halted for a while, and stayed its advance, having learnt from information given by a deserter that a number of enemies were concealed in some subterranean passages and caverns with many entrances in the neighbourhood, ready to sally forth when a favourable opportunity should appear.

9. Nevertheless our men presently ventured to advance in full confidence, and found the roads blockaded by oaks, ashes, and pines, of great size, cut down and laid together. And so they retreated with caution, perceiving that it was impossible to advance except by long and rugged defiles; though they could hardly restrain their indignation at being compelled to do so.

10. The weather too became very severe, so that they were enveloped in all kinds of toil and danger to no purpose (forasmuch as it was now past the autumnal equinox, and the snow, which had already fallen in those regions, covered the mountains and the plains), and so, instead of proceeding, Julian undertook a work worthy of being related.

11. He repaired with great expedition, while there was no one to hinder him, the fortress which Trajan had constructed in the territory of the Allemanni, and to which he had given his own name, and which had lately been attacked with great violence and almost destroyed.

114

And he placed there a temporary garrison, and also some magazines, which he had collected from the barbarians.

12. But when the Allemanni saw these preparations made for their destruction, they assembled rapidly in great consternation at what had already been done, and sent ambassadors to implore peace, with prayers of extreme humility. And the Cæsar, now that he had fully matured and secured the success of all his designs, taking into consideration all probabilities, granted them a truce for ten months. In reality he was especially influenced by this prudent consideration, that the camp which he had thus occupied without hindrance, in a way that could hardly have been hoped for, required, nevertheless, to be fortified with mural engines and other adequate equipments.

13. Trusting to this truce, three of the most ferocious of those kings who had sent reinforcements to their countrymen when defeated at Strasburg, came to him, though still in some degree of alarm, and took the oaths according to the formula in use in their country, that they would create no further disturbance, but that they would keep the truce faithfully up to the appointed day, because that had been the decision of our generals; and that they would not attack the fortress; and that they would even bring supplies to it on their shoulders if the garrison informed them that they were in want; all which they promised, because their fear bridled their treachery.

14. In this memorable war, which deserves to be compared with those against the Carthaginians or the Gauls, yet was accompanied with very little loss to the republic, Julian triumphed as a fortunate and successful leader. The very smallness of his losses might have given some colour to the assertions of his detractors, who declared that he had only fought bravely on all occasions, because he preferred dying gloriously to being put to death like his brother Gallus, as a condemned malefactor, as they had expected he would be, if he had not, after the death of Constantius, continued to distinguish himself equally by splendid exploits.

II.

§ 1. Now when everything was settled in that country as fairly as the case permitted, Julian, returning to his winter quarters, found some trouble still left for him. Severus, the master of the horse, being on the way to Rheims through Cologne and Juliers, fell in with some strong battalions of Franks, consisting of six hundred light-armed soldiers, who were laying waste those places which were not defended by garrisons. They had been encouraged to this audacious wickedness by the opportunity afforded them when the Cæsar was occupied in the remote districts of the Allemanni, thinking to obtain a rich booty without any hindrance. But in fear of the army which had now returned, they occupied two fortresses which had been abandoned for some time, and defended themselves there as long as they could.

2. Julian, amazed at the novelty of such an attempt, and thinking it impossible to say how far such a spirit would spread if he allowed it to pass without a check, halted his soldiers, and gave orders to blockade the forts.... The Meuse passes beneath them; and the blockade was protracted for fifty-four days, through nearly the entire months of December and January, the barbarians resisting with incredible obstinacy and courage.

3. Then the Cæsar, like an experienced general, fearing that the barbarians might take advantage of some moonless night to cross over the river, which was now thoroughly frozen, ordered soldiers to go up and down the stream every day in light boats, from sunset till daybreak, so as to break the crust of ice and prevent any one from escaping in that manner. Owing to this manœuvre, the barbarians were so exhausted by hunger, watching, and the extremity of despair, that at last they voluntarily surrendered, and were immediately sent to the court of the emperor.

4. And a vast multitude of Franks, who had come to their assistance, hearing that they were taken prisoners and sent off, would not venture on any further enterprise, but returned to their own country. And when this affair was finished, the Cæsar retired to Paris to pass the winter there.

III.

§ 1. It was now expected that a number of tribes would unite in greater force, and therefore the prudent Julian, bearing in mind the uncertainties of war, became very anxious and full of care. And as he thought that the truce lately made, though not free from trouble, and not of long duration, still gave him opportunity to remedy some things which were faulty, he began to remodel the arrangements about tribute.

2. And when Florentius, the prefect of the prætorium, having taken an estimate of everything, affirmed that whatever deficiency there might be in the produce of a capitation tax he should be able to make good from what he could levy by force, Julian, deprecating this practice, determined to lose his own life rather than permit it.

3. For he knew that the wounds inflicted by such extortions, or, as I should rather call them, confiscations, are incurable, and have often reduced provinces to extreme destitution. Indeed, such conduct, as will be related hereafter, utterly lost us Illyricum.

4. And when, owing to this resolution of his, the prætorian prefect exclaimed that it could not be endured that he, to whom the emperor had intrusted the chief authority in this matter, should be thus distrusted, Julian attempted to appease him, showing by exact and accurate calculations that the capitation tax was not only enough, but more than enough to provide all the necessary supplies.

5. And when some time afterwards an edict for a supplementary tax was nevertheless presented to him by Florentius, he refused to sign or even to read it; and threw it on the ground; and when warned by letters from the emperor (written on receiving the prefect's report) not to act in so embarrassing a manner, lest he should seem to be diminishing the authority of Florentius, Julian wrote in answer, that it was a matter to be thankful for, if a province that had been devastated in every direction could still pay its regular taxes, without demanding from it any extraordinary contributions, which indeed no punishments could extort from men in a state of destitution: and then, and from that time forward, owing to the firmness of one man, no one ever attempted to extort anything illegal in Gaul beyond the regular taxes.

6. The Cæsar had also in another affair set an example wholly unprecedented, entreating the prefect to intrust to him the government of the second Belgic province, which was oppressed by manifold evils; on the especial and single condition that no officer, either belonging to the prefect or to the garrison, should force any one to pay anything. And the whole people whom he thus took under his care, comforted and relieved by this mildness, paid all the taxes due from them before the appointed day, without any demand being made upon them.

IV.

§ 1. While Julian was thus beginning to put Gaul into a better condition, and while Orfitus was still governor of the second province, an obelisk was erected at Rome, in the Circus Maximus, concerning which, as this seems a convenient opportunity, I will mention a few particulars.

2. The city of Thebes, in Egypt, built in remote ages, with enormous walls, and celebrated also for entrances by a hundred gates, was from this circumstance called by its founders ἑκατόμπυλος (Hecatom-

pylos); and from the name of this city the whole district is known as Thebais.

3. When Carthage began to rise in greatness, the Carthaginian generals conquered and destroyed Thebes by a sudden attack. And after it was rebuilt, Cambyses, the celebrated king of Persia, who throughout his whole life was covetous and ferocious, overran Egypt, and again attacked this city that he might plunder it of its wealth, which was enough to excite his envy; and he spared not even the offerings which had been made to the gods.

4. And while he was in his savage manner moving to and fro among his plunderers, he got entangled in his own flowing robes, and fell on his face, and by the fall his dagger, which he wore close to his thigh, got loose from the scabbard, and he was mortally wounded and died.

5. And long afterwards, Cornelius Gallus, who was governor of Egypt at the time when Octavianus was emperor of Rome, impoverished the city by plundering it of most of its treasuries; and returning to Rome on being accused of theft and of laying waste the province, he, from fear of the nobles, who were bitterly indignant against him, as one to whom the emperor had committed a most honourable task, fell on his own sword and so died. If I mistake not, he is the same person as Gallus the poet, whose loss Virgil deplores at the end of his Bucolics, celebrating his memory in sweet verses.

6. In this city of Thebes, among many works of art and different structures recording the tales relating to the Egyptian deities, we saw several obelisks in their places, and others which had been thrown down and broken; which the ancient kings, when elated at some victory or at the general prosperity of their affairs, had caused to be hewn out of mountains in distant parts of the world, and erected in honour of the gods, to whom they solemnly consecrated them.

7. Now an obelisk is a rough stone, rising to a great height, shaped like a pillar in the stadium; and it tapers upwards in imitation of a sunbeam, keeping its quadrilateral shape, till it rises almost to a point, being made smooth by the hand of a sculptor.

8. On these obelisks the ancient authority of elementary wisdom has caused innumerable marks of strange forms all over them, which are called hieroglyphics.

9. For the workmen, carving many kinds of birds and beasts, some even such as must belong to another world, in order that the recollection of the exploits which the obelisk was designed to

commemorate might reach to subsequent ages, showed by them the accomplishment of vows which the kings had made.

10. For it was not the case then as it is now, that the established number of letters can distinctly express whatever the human mind conceives; nor did the ancient Egyptians write in such a manner; but each separate character served for a separate noun or verb, and sometimes even for an entire sense.

11. Of which fact the two following may for the present be sufficient instances: by the figure of a vulture they indicate the name of nature; because naturalists declare that no males are found in this class of bird. And by the figure of a bee making honey they indicate a king; showing by such a sign that stings as well as sweetness are the characteristics of a ruler; and there are many similar emblems.

12. And because the flatterers, who were continually whispering into the ear of Constantius, kept always affirming that when Augustus Octavianus had brought two obelisks from Heliopolis, a city of Egypt, one of which was placed in the Circus Maximus, and the other in the Campus Martius, he yet did not venture to touch or move this one which has just been brought to Rome, being alarmed at the greatness of such a task; I would have those, who do not know the truth, learn that the ancient emperor, though he moved several obelisks, left this one untouched, because it was especially dedicated to the Sun-god, and was set up within the precincts of his magnificent temple, which it was impious to profane; and of which it was the most conspicuous ornament.

13. But Constantine deeming that a consideration of no importance, had it torn up from its place, and thinking rightly that he should not be offering any insult to religion if he removed a splendid work from some other temple to dedicate it to the gods at Rome, which is the temple of the whole world, let it lie on the ground for some time while arrangements for its removal were being prepared. And when it had been carried down the Nile, and landed at Alexandria, a ship of a burden hitherto unexampled, requiring three hundred rowers to propel it, was built to receive it.

14. And when these preparations were made, and after the aforenamed emperor had died, the enterprise began to cool. However, after a time it was at last put on board ship, and conveyed over sea, and up the stream of the Tiber, which seemed as it were frightened, lest its own winding waters should hardly be equal to conveying a present from the almost unknown Nile to the walls which itself cherished. At last the obelisk reached the village of Alexandria, three miles from the

city; and then it was placed in a cradle, and drawn slowly on, and brought through the Ostran gate and the public fish-market to the Circus Maximus.

15. The only work remaining to be done was to raise it, which was generally believed to be hardly, if at all, practicable. And vast beams having been raised on end in a most dangerous manner, so that they looked like a grove of machines, long ropes of huge size were fastened to them, darkening the very sky with their density, as they formed a web of innumerable threads; and into them the great stone itself, covered over as it was with elements of writing, was bound, and gradually raised into the empty air, and long suspended, many thousands of men turning it round and round like a millstone, till it was at last placed in the middle of the square; and on it was placed a brazen sphere, made brighter with plates of gold: and as that was immediately afterwards struck by lightning, and destroyed, a brazen figure like a torch was placed on it, also plated with gold—to look as if the torch were fully alight.

16. Subsequent ages also removed other obelisks; one of which is in the Vatican, a second in the garden of Sallust; and two in the monument of Augustus.

17. But the writing which is engraven on the old obelisk in the Circus, we have set forth below in Greek characters, following in this the work of Hermapion:—

ΑΡΧΗΝ ΑΠΟ ΤΟΝ ΝΟΤΙΟΝ ΔΙΕΡΜΗΝΕΥΜΕΝΑ ΕΧΕΙ
ΣΤΙΧΟΕ ΠΡΩΤΟΕ ΤΑΔΕ.

18. The first line, beginning on the south side, bears this interpretation—"The Sun to Ramestes the king—I have given to thee to reign with joy over the whole earth; to thee whom the Sun and Apollo love—to thee, the mighty truth-loving son of Heron—the god-born ruler of the habitable earth; whom the Sun has chosen above all men, the valiant warlike King Ramestes. Under whose power, by his valour and might, the whole world is placed. The King Ramestes, the immortal son of the Sun."

19. The second line is—"The mighty Apollo, who takes his stand upon truth, the lord of the diadem, he who has honoured Egypt by becoming its master, adorning Heliopolis, and having created the rest of the world, and having greatly honoured the gods who have their shrines in the city of the Sun; whom the son loves."

20. The third line—"The mighty Apollo, the all-brilliant son of the Sun, whom the Sun chose above all others, and to whom the val-

iant Mars gave gifts. Thou whose good fortune abideth for ever. Thou whom Ammon loves. Thou who hast filled the temple of the Phœnix with good things. Thou to whom the gods have given long life. Apollo the mighty son of Heron, Ramestes the king of the world. Who has defended Egypt, having subdued the foreign enemy. Whom the Sun loves. To whom the gods have given long life—the master of the world—the immortal Ramestes."

21. Another second line—"The Sun, the great God, the master of heaven. I have given unto thee a life free from satiety. Apollo, the mighty master of the diadem; to whom nothing is comparable. To whom the lord of Egypt has erected many statues in this kingdom. And has made the city of Heliopolis as brilliant as the Sun himself, the master of heaven. The son of the Sun, the king living for ever, has co-operated in the completion of this work."

22. A third line—"I, the Sun, the god, the master of heaven, have given to Ramestes the king might and authority over all. Whom Apollo the truth-lover, the master of time, and Vulcan the father of the gods hath chosen above others by reason of his courage. The all-rejoicing king, the son of the Sun, and beloved by the Sun."

23. The first line, looking towards the east—"The great God of Heliopolis, the mighty Apollo who dwelleth in Heaven, the son of Heron whom the Sun hath guided. Whom the gods have honoured. He who ruleth over all the earth: whom the Sun has chosen before all others. The king valiant by the favour of Mars. Whom Ammon loveth, and the all-shining god, who hath chosen him as a king for everlasting." And so on.

V.

A.D. 358.

§ 1. In the consulship of Datianus and Cerealis, when all arrangements in Gaul were made with more careful zeal than before, and while the terror caused by past events still checked the outbreaks of the barbarians, the king of the Persians, being still on the frontiers of those nations which border on his dominions, and having made a treaty of alliance with the Chionitæ and the Gelani, the most warlike and indefatigable of all tribes, being about to return to his own country, received the letters of Tamsapor which announced to him that the Roman emperor was a suppliant for peace.

2. And he, suspecting that Constantius would never have done so if the empire had not been weakened all over, raised his own pretensions, and embracing the name indeed of peace, offered very

unwelcome conditions. And having sent a man of the name of Narses as ambassador with many presents, he gave him letters to Constantius, in which he in no respect abated of his natural pride. The purport of these letters we have understood to be this:—

3. "I, Sapor, king of kings, partner of the stars, brother of the sun and moon, to Constantius Cæsar my brother send much greeting. I am glad and am well pleased that at last thou hast returned to the right way, and hast acknowledged the incorruptible decree of equity, having gained experience by facts, and having learnt what disasters an obstinate covetousness of the property of others has often caused.

4. "Because therefore the language of truth ought to be unrestrained and free, and because men in the highest rank ought only to say what they mean, I will reduce my propositions into a few words; remembering that I have already often repeated what I am now about to say.

5. "Even your own ancient records bear witness that my ancestors possessed all the country up to the Strymon and the frontier of Macedonia. And these lands it is fitting that I who (not to speak arrogantly) am superior to those ancient kings in magnificence, and in all eminent virtues, should now reclaim. But I am at all times thoughtful to remember that, from my earliest youth, I have never done anything to repent of.

6. "And therefore it is a duty in me to recover Armenia and Mesopotamia, which were wrested from my ancestor by deliberate treachery. That principle was never admitted by us which you with exultation assert, that all successes in war deserve praise, without considering whether they were achieved by valour or by treachery.

7. "Lastly, if you are willing to be guided by one who gives you good advice, I would bid you despise a small part of your dominions which is ever the parent of sorrow and bloodshed, in order to reign in safety over the rest. Wisely considering that physicians also sometimes apply cautery or amputation, and cut off portions of the body that the patient may have good use of the rest of his limbs. Nay, that even beasts do the same: since when they observe on what account they are most especially hunted, they will of their own accord deprive themselves of that, in order henceforth to be able to live in security.

8. "This, in short, I declare, that should my present embassy return without having succeeded in its object, after giving the winter season to rest I will gird myself up with all my strength, and while fortune and justice give me a well-founded hope of ultimate success, I will hasten my march as much as Providence will permit."

9. Having given long consideration to this letter, the emperor with upright and wise heart, as the saying is, made answer in this manner:—

10. "Constantius, always august, conqueror by land and sea, to my brother Sapor much health. I congratulate thee on thy safety, as one who is willing to be a friend to thee if thou wilt. But I greatly blame thy insatiable covetousness, now more grasping than ever.

11. "Thou demandest Mesopotamia as thine own, and then Armenia. And thou biddest me cut off some members from my sound body in order to place its health on a sound footing: a demand which is to be rejected at once rather than to be encouraged by any consent. Receive therefore the truth, not covered with any pretences, but clear, and not to be shaken by any threats.

12. "The prefect of my prætorian guard, thinking to undertake an affair which might be beneficial to the state, without my knowledge discoursed about peace with thy generals, by the agency of some low persons. Peace we should neither regret nor refuse—let it only come with credit and honour, in such a way as to impair neither our self-respect nor our dignity.

13. "For it would be an unbecoming and shameful thing when all men's ears are filled with our exploits, so as to have shut even the mouth of envy; when after the destruction of tyrants the whole Roman world obeys us, to give up those territories which even when limited to the narrow boundaries of the east we preserved undiminished.

14. "But I pray thee make an end of the threats which thou utterest against me, in obedience to thy national habit, when it cannot be doubted that it is not from inactivity, but from moderation, that we have at times endured attacks instead of being the assailants ourselves: and know that, whenever we are attacked, we defend our own with bravery and good will: being assured both by thy reading and thy personal experience that in battle it has been rare for Romans to meet with disaster; and that in the final issue of a war we have never come off the worst."

15. The embassy was therefore dismissed without gaining any of its objects; and indeed no other reply could be given to the unbridled covetousness of the king. And a few days afterwards, Count Prosper followed, and Spectatus the tribune and secretary; and also, by the suggestion of Musonianus, Eustathius the philosopher, as one skilful in persuading, bearing a letter from the emperor, and presents, with a view to induce Sapor to suspend his preparations, so that all our atten-

tion might be turned to fortifying the northern provinces in the most effective manner.

VI.

§ 1. Now while these affairs, of so doubtful a complexion, were proceeding, that portion of the Allemanni which borders on the regions of Italy, forgetful of the peace and of the treaties which they only obtained by abject entreaty, laid waste the Tyrol with such fury that they even went beyond their usual habit in undertaking the siege of some walled towns.

2. And when a strong force had been sent to repel them under the command of Barbatio, who had been promoted to the command of the infantry in the room of Silvanus, a man of not much activity, but a fluent talker, he, as his troops were in a high state of indignation at the invaders, gave them so terrible a defeat, that only a very few, who took to flight in their panic, escaped to carry back their tears and lamentations to their homes.

3. In this battle Nevitta, who afterwards became consul, was present as commander of a squadron of cavalry, and displayed great gallantry.

VII.

§ 1. This year also some terrible earthquakes took place in Macedonia, Asia Minor, and Pontus, and their repeated shocks overthrew many towns, and even mountains. But the most remarkable of all the manifold disasters which they caused was the entire ruin of Nicomedia, the metropolis of Bithynia; which I will here relate with truth and brevity.

2. On the 23rd of August, at daybreak, some heavy black clouds suddenly obscured the sky, which just before was quite fair. And the sun was so wholly concealed that it was impossible to see what was near or even quite close, so completely did a thick lurid darkness settle on the ground, preventing the least use of the eyes.

3. Presently, as if the supreme deity were himself letting loose his fatal wrath, and stirring up the winds from their hinges, a violent raging storm descended, by the fury of which the groaning mountains were struck, and the crash of the waves on the shore was heard to a vast distance. And then followed typhoons and whirlwinds with a horrid trembling of the earth, throwing down the whole city and its suburbs.

4. And as most of the houses were built on the slopes of the hills, they now fell down one over the other, while all around resounded with the vast crash of their fall. In the mean time the tops of the hills re-echoed all sorts of noises, as well as outcries of men seeking their wives and children, and other relations.

5. At last, after two hours, or at least within three, the air became again clear and serene, and disclosed the destruction which till then was unseen. Some, overwhelmed by the enormous masses of ruins which had fallen upon them, were crushed to death. Some were buried up to the neck, and might have been saved if there had been any timely help at hand, but perished for want of assistance; others were trans-fixed by the points of beams projecting forth, on which they hung suspended.

6. Here was seen a crowd of persons slain by one blow; there a promiscuous heap of corpses piled in various ways—some were buried beneath the roofs of falling houses, which leant over so as to protect them from any actual blows, but reserved them for an agonizing death by starvation. Among whom was Aristænetus, who, with the authority of deputy, governed Bithynia, which had been recently erected into a province; and to which Constantius had given the name of Piety, in honour of his wife Eusebia, (a Greek word, equivalent to Pietas in Latin); and he perished thus by a lingering death.

7. Others who were overwhelmed by the sudden fall of vast buildings, are still lying entombed beneath the immovable masses. Some with their skulls fractured, or their shoulders or legs cut through, lay between life and death, imploring aid from others suffering equally with themselves; but in spite of their entreaties they were abandoned.

8. Not but what the greater part of the temples and buildings and of the citizens also would have escaped unhurt, if a fire had not sud-denly broken out, which raged with great violence for fifty days and nights, and destroyed all that remained.

9. I think this a good opportunity to enumerate a few of the con-jectures which the ancients have formed about earthquakes. For as to any accurate knowledge of their causes, not only has that never been attained by the ignorance of the common people, but they have equally eluded the long lucubrations and subtle researches of natural philoso-phers.

10. And on this account in all priestly ceremonies, whether ritual or pontifical, care is taken not at such times to name one god more than another, for fear of impiety, since it is quite uncertain which god causes these visitations.

11. But as the various opinions, among which Aristotle wavers and hesitates, suggest, earthquakes are engendered either in small caverns under the earth, which the Greeks call σύριγγες, because of the waters pouring through them with a more rapid motion than usual, or, as Anaxagoras affirms, they arise from the force of the wind penetrating the lower parts of the earth, which, when they have got down to the encrusted solid mass, finding no vent-holes, shake those portions in their solid state, into which they have got entrance when in a state of solution. And this is corroborated by the observation that at such times no breezes of wind are felt by us above ground, because the winds are occupied in the lowest recesses of the earth.

12. Anaximander says that the earth when burnt up by excessive heat and drought, and also after excessive rains, opens larger fissures than usual, which the upper air penetrates with great force and in excessive quantities, and the earth, shaken by the furious blasts which penetrate those fissures, is disturbed to its very foundations; for which reason these fearful events occur either at times of great evaporation or else at those of an extravagant fall of rain from heaven. And therefore the ancient poets and theologians gave Neptune the name of Earth-shaker,[70] as being the power of moist substance.

13. Now earthquakes take place in four manners: either they are *brasmatiæ*,[71] which raise up the ground in a terrible manner, and throw vast masses up to the surface, as in Asia, Delos arose, and Hiera; and also Anaphe and Rhodes, which has at different times been called Ophiusa and Pelagia, and was once watered with a shower of gold;[72] and Eleusis in Bœotia, and the Hellenian islands in the Tyrrhenian sea, and many other islands. Or they are *climatiæ*,[73] which, with a slanting and oblique blow, level cities, edifices, and mountains. Or *chasmatiæ*,[74] which suddenly, by a violent motion, open huge mouths, and so swallow up portions of the earth, as in the Atlantic sea, on the coast of Europe, a large island[75] was swallowed up, and in the Crissæan Gulf, Helice and Bura,[76] and in Italy, in the Ciminian district, the town of Saccumum[77] was swallowed up in a deep gulf and hidden in everlasting darkness. And among these three kinds of earthquakes, *myæmotiæ*[78] are heard with a threatening roar, when the elements either spring apart, their joints being broken, or again resettle in their former places, when the earth also settles back; for then it cannot be but that crashes and roars of the earth should resound with bull-like bellowings. Let us now return to our original subject.

126

VIII.

§ 1. Cæsar, passing his winter among the Parisii, was eagerly preparing to anticipate the Allemanni, who were not yet assembled in one body, but who, since the battle of Strasburg, were working themselves up to a pitch of insane audacity and ferocity. And he was waiting with great impatience for the month of July, when the Gallic campaigns usually begin. For indeed he could not march before the summer had banished the frost and cold, and allowed him to receive supplies from Aquitania.

2. But as diligence overcomes almost all difficulties, he, revolving many plans of all kinds in his mind, at last conceived the idea of not waiting till the crops were ripe, but falling on the barbarians before they expected him. And having resolved on that plan, he caused his men to take corn for twenty days' consumption from what they had in store, and to make it into biscuit, so that it might keep longer; and this enabled the soldiers to carry it, which they did willingly. And relying on this provision, and setting out as before, with favourable auspices, he reckoned that in the course of five or six months he might finish two urgent and indispensable expeditions.

3. And when all his preparations were made, he first marched against the Franks, that is against that tribe of them usually called Salii, who some time before had ventured with great boldness to fix their habitations on the Roman soil near Toxandria.[79] But when he had reached Tongres, he was met by an embassy from this tribe, who expected still to find him in his winter quarters, offering him peace on condition of his leaving them unattacked and unmolested, as if the ground they had seized were rightfully their own. Julian comprehended the whole affair, and having given the ambassadors an ambiguous reply, and also some presents, sent them back again, leaving them to suppose he would remain in the same place till they returned.

4. But the moment they had departed he followed them, sending Severus along the bank of the river, and suddenly came upon the whole settlement like a thunderbolt; and availing himself of his victory to make a reasonable exhibition of clemency, as indeed they met him with entreaties rather than with resistance, he received the submission of them and their children.

5. He then attacked the Chamavi,[80] who had been guilty of similar audacity, and through the same celerity of movement he slew one portion of them, and another who made a vigorous resistance he took prisoners, while others who fled precipitately he allowed to escape

unhurt to their own territories, to avoid exhausting his soldiers with a long campaign. And when ambassadors were afterwards sent by them to implore his pardon, and generally to do what they could for them, when they prostrated themselves before him, he granted them peace on condition of retiring to their own districts without doing any mischief.

IX.

§ 1. Everything thus succeeding according to his wish, Julian, always on the watch to establish by every means in his power the security of the provinces on a solid foundation, determined to put in as good repair as the time permitted those fortresses erected in a line on the banks of the Meuse, which some time before had been destroyed by an attack of the barbarians. And accordingly he desisted for a while from all other operations, and restored them.

2. And that he might by a prudent rapidity insure their safety, he took a part of the seventeen days' provisions, which troops, when going on an expedition, carry on their backs, and stored in those forts, hoping to replace what he thus took from the soldiers by seizing the crops of the Chamavi.

3. But he was greatly disappointed. For as the crops were not yet ripe, the soldiers when they had consumed what they had with them were unable to find food, and began to utter violent threats against Julian, mingled with fierce cries and reproaches, calling him Asiatic, Greek, a cheat, and a fool pretending to be wise. And as it is commonly the case among soldiers that some men are found of remarkable fluency of speech, they poured forth such harangues as this:—

4. "Whither are we being dragged, having lost all hope of good fortune? We formerly, indeed, suffered terrible hardships in the snow, and cruel biting frost; but now (oh, shame!), when we have the fate of the enemy in our hands, we are wasting away with famine, the most miserable of all deaths. Let no one think that we are stirrers up of tumults; we declare that we are speaking for our very lives. We do not ask for gold or silver, which it is long since we have touched or seen, and which are as much denied to us as if we had been convicted of having encountered all our toils and perils in the service of the enemies of the republic."

5. And their complaints were just. For after all his gallant exploits and all his doubtful changes and dangers, the soldiers were exhausted by his Gallic campaigns, without even receiving either donation or pay from the time that Julian was sent to take the command; because he himself had nothing to give, nor would Constantius permit

anything to be drawn for that purpose from the treasury, as had been the custom.

6. And at a later period it was manifest that this was owing more to ill-will than to parsimony, because when Julian had given some small coin to one of the common soldiers, who, as was the custom, had asked for some to get shaved with, he was attacked for it with most insulting calumnies by Gaudentius, the secretary, who had long remained in Gaul as a spy upon his actions, and whom he himself subsequently ordered to be put to death, as will be related in its fitting place.

X.

§ 1. When at length their discontent was appeased by various kinds of caresses, and when the Rhine had been crossed by a bridge of boats, which was thrown over it, Severus, the master of the horse, up to that time a brave and energetic soldier, suddenly lost all his vigour.

2. And he who had frequently been used to exhort the troops, both in bodies and as individuals, to gallant acts, now seemed a base and timid skulker from battle, as if he feared the approach of death. As we read in the books of Tages[81] that those who are fated to be soon struck by lightning, so lose their senses that they cannot hear thunder, or even greater noises. And he marched on in a lazy way, not natural to him, and even threatened with death the guides, who were leading on the army with a brisk step, if they would not agree to say that they were wholly ignorant of the road any further. So they, fearing his power, and being forbidden to show the way any more, advanced no further.

3. But amid this delay, Suomarius, king of the Allemanni, arrived unexpectedly with his suite; and he who had formerly been fierce and eager for any injury to the Romans, was now inclined to regard it as an unexpected gain to be permitted to retain his former possessions. And because his looks and his gait showed him to be a suppliant, he was received as a friend, and desired to be of good cheer. But still he submitted himself to Julian's discretion, and implored peace on his bended knees. And peace was granted him, with pardon for the past, on condition of giving up our prisoners and of supplying our soldiers with food, whenever it was required, receiving, like any ordinary purveyor, security for payment of what he provided. But he was at the same time warned, that if he did not furnish the required supplies in time he would be liable to be called in question for his former hostility.

4. And that which had been discreetly planned was carried out without hindrance. Julian desiring to reach a town belonging to another chieftain, named Hortarius, towards which object nothing seemed wanting but guides, gave orders to Nestica, a tribune of the Scutarii, and to Chariettoa, a man of marvellous courage, to take great pains to capture a prisoner and to bring him to him. A youth of the Allemanni was speedily caught and brought before him, who, on condition of obtaining his freedom, promised to show the road. The army, following him as its guide, was soon obstructed by an abattis of lofty trees, which had been cut down; but by taking long and circuitous paths, they at last came to the desired spot, and the soldiers in their rage laid waste the fields with fire, carried off the cattle and the inhabitants, and slew all who resisted without mercy.

5. The king, bewildered at this disaster, seeing the numerous legions, and the remains of his burnt villages, and looking upon the last calamities of fortune as impending over him, of his own accord implored pardon, promising to do all that should be commanded him, and binding himself on oath to restore all his prisoners. For that was the object about which Julian was the most anxious. But still he restored only a few, and detained the greater part of them.

6. When Julian knew this, he was filled with just indignation, and when the king came to receive the customary presents, the Cæsar refused to release his four companions, on whose support and fidelity the king principally relied, till all the prisoners were restored.

7. But when the king was summoned by the Cæsar to a conference, looking up at him with trembling eyes, he was overcome by the aspect of the conqueror, and overwhelmed by a sense of his own embarrassing condition, and especially by the compulsion under which he was now (since it was reasonable that after so many successes of the Romans that the cities which had been destroyed by the violence of the barbarians should be rebuilt) to supply waggons and materials from his own stores and those of his subjects.

8. And after he had promised to do so, and had bound himself with an oath to consent to die if he were guilty of any treachery, he was permitted to return to his own country. For he could not be compelled to furnish provisions like Suomarius, because his land had been so utterly laid waste that nothing could be found on it for him to give.

9. Thus those kings who were formerly so proud and accustomed to grow rich by the plunder of our citizens, were now brought under the Roman yoke; and as if they had been born and brought up among our tributaries, they submitted to our commands, though with reluc-

tance. And when these events were thus brought to a conclusion, the Cæsar distributed his army among its usual stations, and returned to his winter quarters.

XI.

§ 1. When these transactions presently became known in the court of Constantius—for the knowledge of them could not be concealed, since the Cæsar, as if he had been merely an officer of the emperor's, referred to him on all occasions—those who had the greatest influence in the palace, being skilful professors of flattery, turned all Julian's well-arranged plans and their successful accomplishment into ridicule; continually uttering such malicious sayings as this, "We have had enough of the goat and his victories;" sneering at Julian because of his beard, and calling him a chattering mole, a purple-robed ape, and a Greek pedant. And pouring forth numbers of sneers of the same kind, acceptable to the emperor, who liked to hear them, they endeavoured with shameless speeches to overwhelm Julian's virtues, slandering him as a lazy, timid, carpet-knight, and one whose chief care was to set off his exploits by fine descriptions; it not being the first time that such a thing had been done.

2. For the greatest glory is always exposed to envy. So we read in respect of the illustrious generals of old, that, though no fault could be found in them, still the malignity which found offence in their greatest actions was constantly inventing false charges and accusations against them.

3. In the same manner Cimon the son of Miltiades, who destroyed a vast host of the Persians on the Eurymedon, a river in Pamphylia, and compelled a nation always insolent and arrogant to beg for peace most humbly, was accused of intemperance; and again Scipio Æmilianus, by whose indomitable vigilance two[82] most powerful cities, which had made great efforts to injure Rome, were both destroyed, was disparaged as a mere drone.

4. Moreover, wicked detractors, scrutinizing the character of Pompey, when no pretext for finding fault with him could be discovered, remarked two qualities in which they could raise a laugh against him; one that he had a sort of natural trick of scratching his head with one finger: another that for the purpose of concealing an unsightly sore, he used to bind one of his legs with a white bandage. Of which habits, the first they said showed a dissolute man; the second, one eager for a change of government; contending, with a somewhat meagre argument, that it did not signify what part of his body he clothed with

a badge of royal dignity; so snarling at that man of whom the most glorious proofs show that no braver and truer patriot ever lived.

5. During these transactions, Artemius, the deputy governor of Rome, succeeded Bassus in the prefecture also; for Bassus, who had lately been promoted to be prefect of the city, had since died. His administration had been marked by turbulent sedition, but by no other events sufficiently memorable to deserve mention.

XII.

§ 1. In the mean time, while the emperor was passing the winter quietly at Sirmium, he received frequent and trustworthy intelligence that the Sarmatians and the Quadi, two tribes contiguous to each other, and similar in manners and mode of warfare, were conjointly overrunning Pannonia and the second province of Mœsia, in straggling detachments.

2. These tribes are more suited to predatory incursions than to regular war; they carry long spears, and wear breastplates made of horn scraped and polished, let into linen jackets, so that the layers of horn are like the feathers of a bird. Their horses are chiefly geldings, lest at the sight of mares they should be excited and run away, or, when held back in reserve, should betray their riders by their fierce neighing.

3. They cover vast spaces in their movements, whether in pursuit or in retreat, their horses being swift and very manageable; and they lead with them one or sometimes two spare chargers apiece, in order that the change may keep up the strength of their cattle, and that their vigour may be preserved by alternations of rest.

4. Therefore, after the vernal equinox was past, the emperor, having collected a strong body of soldiers, marched forth under the guidance of propitious fortune. Having arrived at a suitable place, he crossed the Danube, which was now flooded from the melting of the snow, by a bridge of boats, and descended on the lands of the barbarians, which he began to lay waste. They, being taken by surprise through the rapidity of his march, and seeing that the battalions of his warlike army were at their throats, when they had not supposed it possible that such a force could be collected for a year, had no courage to make a stand, but, as the only means of escaping unexpected destruction, took to flight.

5. When many had been slain, fear fettering their steps, those whose speed had saved them from death hid themselves among the secret defiles of the mountains, and from thence beheld their country

destroyed by the sword, which they might have delivered if they had resisted with as much vigour as they fled.

6. These events took place in that part of Sarmatia which looks towards the second Pannonia. Another military expedition, conducted with equal courage, routed the troops of the barbarians in Valeria, who were plundering and destroying everything within their reach.

7. Terrified at the greatness of this disaster, the Sarmatians, under pretext of imploring peace, planned to divide their force into three bodies, and to attack our army while in a state of fancied security; so that they should neither be able to prepare their weapons, nor avoid wounds, nor (which is the last resource in a desperate case) take to flight.

8. There were with the Sarmatians likewise on this occasion, as partners in their danger, the Quadi,[83] who had often before taken part in the injuries inflicted on us; but their prompt boldness did not help them on this occasion, rushing as they did into open danger.

9. For many of them were slain, and the survivors escaped among the hills, with which they were familiar. And as this event raised the spirits and courage of our army, they united in solid columns, and marched with speed into the territories of the Quadi; who, having learnt by the past to dread the evils which impended over them, came boldly into the emperor's presence to implore peace as suppliants, since he was inclined to be merciful in such cases. On the day appointed for settling the conditions, one of their princes named Zizais, a young man of great stature, marshalled the ranks of the Sarmatians to offer their entreaties of peace in the fashion of an army; and as soon as they came within sight, he threw away his arms, and fell like one dead, prostrating himself on his breast before the emperor; his very voice from fear refusing its office, when he ought to have uttered his entreaties, he awakened the more pity, making many attempts, and being scarcely able from the violence of his sobs to give utterance to his wishes.

10. At last, having recovered himself, and being bidden to rise up, he knelt, and having regained the use of his tongue, he implored pardon for his offences. His followers also, whose mouths had been closed by fear while the fate of their leader was still doubtful, were admitted to offer the same petition, and when he, being commanded to rise, gave them the signal which they had been long expecting, to present their petition, they all threw away their javelins and their shields, and held out their hands in an attitude of supplication, striving to surpass their prince in the humility of their entreaties.

11. Among the other Sarmatians the prince had brought with him three chiefs of tribes, Rumo, Zinafer, and Fragiledus, and many nobles who came to offer the same petition with earnest hope of success. And they, being elated at the promise of safety, undertook to make amends for their former deeds of hostility by performing the conditions now imposed on them; giving up willingly into the power of the Romans themselves, their wives and children, and all their possessions. The kindness of the emperor, united with justice, subdued them; and he bidding them be of good cheer and return to their homes, they restored our prisoners. They also brought the hostages who were demanded of them, and promised prompt obedience to all the emperor's commands.

12. Then, encouraged by this example of our clemency, other chieftains came with all their tribe, by name Araharius and Usafer, men of distinction among the nobles, and at the head of a great force of their countrymen; one of them being chief of a portion of the Quadi who dwelt beyond the mountains, and the other of a division of the Sarmatians: the two being united by the proximity of their territories, and their natural ferocity. But the emperor, fearing the number of their followers, lest, while pretending to make a treaty, they should suddenly rise up in arms, separated them; ordering those who were acting for the Sarmatians to retire for a while, while he was examining into the affairs of Araharius and the Quadi.

13. And when they presented themselves before him, bowing according to their national custom, as they were not able to clear themselves of heavy charges, so, fearing extreme punishment, they gave the hostages which were demanded, though they had never before been compelled to give pledges for their fidelity.

14. These matters being thus equitably and successfully settled, Usafer was admitted to offer his petition, though Araharius loudly protested against this, and maintained that the peace ratified with him ought to comprehend Usafer also, as an ally of his though of inferior rank, and subject to his command.

15. But when the question was discussed, the Sarmatians were pronounced independent of any other power, as having been always vassals of the Roman empire; and they willingly embraced the proposal of giving hostages as a pledge of the maintenance of tranquillity.

16. After this there came a vast number of nations and princes, flocking in crowds, when they heard that Araharius had been allowed to depart in safety, imploring us to withdraw the sword which was at their throats; and they also obtained the peace which they requested on similar terms, and without any delay gave as hostages the sons of their

nobles whom they brought from the interior of the country; and they also surrendered, as we insisted, all their prisoners, from whom they parted as unwillingly as from their own relations.

17. When these arrangements were completed, the emperor's anxiety was transferred to the Sarmatians, who were objects of pity rather than of anger. It is incredible how much prosperity our connection with their affairs had brought them, so as to give grounds for really believing, what some persons do imagine, that Fate may be either overcome or created at the will of the emperor.

18. There were formerly many natives of this kingdom, of high birth and great power, but a secret conspiracy armed their slaves against them; and as among barbarians all right consists in might, they, as they were equal to their masters in ferocity, and superior in number, completely overcame them.

19. And these native chiefs, losing all their wisdom in their fear, fled to the Victohali,[84] whose settlements were at a great distance, thinking it better in the choice of evils to become subject to their protectors than slaves to their own slaves. But afterwards, when they had obtained pardon from us, and had been received as faithful allies, they deplored their hard fate, and invoked our direct protection. Moved by the undeserved hardship of their lot, the emperor, when they were assembled before him, addressed them with kind words in the presence of his army, and commanded them for the future to own no master but himself and the Roman generals.

20. And that the restoration of their liberty might carry with it additional dignity, he made Zizais their king, a man, as the event proved, deserving the rewards of eminent fortune, and faithful. After these glorious transactions, none of the Sarmatians were allowed to depart till all our prisoners had returned, as we had before insisted.

21. When these matters had been concluded in the territories of the barbarians, the camp was moved to Szœni,[85] that there also the emperor might, by subjugation or slaughter, terminate the war with the Quadi, who were keeping that district in a state of agitation. Their prince Vitrodorus, the son of king Viduarius, and Agilimundus, an inferior chieftain, with the other nobles and judges who governed the different tribes, as soon as they saw the imperial army in the bosom of their kingdom and of their native land, threw themselves at the feet of the soldiers, and having obtained pardon, promised obedience; and gave their children as hostages for the performance of the conditions imposed upon them; and drawing their swords, which they worship as deities, they swore to remain faithful.

XIII.

§ 1. These matters then, as has been related, having been thus successfully terminated, the public interests required that the army should at once march against the Limigantes, the revolted slaves of the Sarmatians, who had perpetrated many atrocities with impunity. For, as soon as the countrymen of free blood had attacked us, they also, forgetful of their former condition, thinking to take advantage of a favourable opportunity, burst through the Roman frontier, in this wickedness alone agreeing with their masters and enemies.

2. But on deliberation we determined that their offence also should be punished with more moderation than its greatness deserved; and that vengeance should limit itself to removing them to a distance where they could no longer harass our territories. The consciousness of a long series of crimes made them fearful of danger.

3. And therefore, suspecting that the weight of war was about to fall upon them, they were prepared, as exigency might require, to resort to stratagem, arms, or entreaties. But at the first sight of our army they became as it were panic-stricken; and being reduced to despair, they begged their lives, offering a yearly tribute, and a body of their chosen youths for our army, and promising perpetual obedience. But they were prepared to refuse if they were ordered to emigrate (as they showed by their gestures and countenances), trusting to the strength of the place where, after they had expelled their masters, they had fixed their abode.

4. For the Parthiscus[86] waters this land, proceeding with oblique windings till it falls into the Danube. But while it flows unmixed, it passes through a vast extent of country, which, near its junction with the Danube, it narrows into a very small corner, so that over on the side of the Danube those who live in that district are protected from the attack of the Romans, and on the side of the Parthiscus they are secured from any irruptions of the barbarians. Since along its course the greater part of the ground is frequently under water from the floods, and always swampy and full of osiers, so as to be quite impassable to strangers; and besides the mainland there is an island close to the mouth of the river, which the stream itself seems to have separated into its present state.

5. Accordingly, at the desire of the emperor, they came with native arrogance to our bank of the river, not, as the result showed, with the intention of obeying his commands, but that they might not seem

alarmed at the presence of his soldiers. And there they stood, stubbornly showing that they had come bent on resistance.

6. And as the emperor had foreseen that this might happen, he secretly divided his army into several squadrons, and by the rapidity of their movements hemmed in the barbarians between his own lines. And then, standing on a mound, with a few of his officers and a small body-guard, he gently admonished them not to give way to ferocity.

7. But they, wavering and in doubt, were agitated by various feelings, and mingling craft with their fury, they had recourse to arms and to prayers at the same time. And meditating to make a sudden attack on those of our men who were nearest, they threw their shields some distance before them, with the intent that while they made some steps forward to recover them, they might thus steal a little ground without giving any indication of their purpose.

8. And as it was now nearly evening, and the departing light warned us to avoid further delay, our soldiers raised their standards and fell upon them with a fiery onset. And they, in close order, directed all their force against the mound on which (as has been already said) the emperor himself was standing, fixing their eyes on him, and uttering fierce outcries against him.

9. Our army was indignant at such insane audacity, and forming into a triangle, to which military simplicity has given the name of "the boar's head," with a violent charge they scattered the barbarians now pressing vigorously upon the emperor; on the right our infantry slew their infantry, and on the left our cavalry dashed among their squadrons of light horsemen.

10. The prætorian cohort, carefully guarding the emperor, spared neither the breasts of those who attacked nor the backs of those who fled, and the barbarians, yielding in their stubbornness to death alone, showed by their horrid cries that they grieved not so much at their own death as at the triumph of our army. And, beside the dead, many lay with their legs cut off, and so deprived of the resource of flight, others had lost their hands; some who had received no wound were crushed by the weight of those who fell upon them, and bore their torments in profound silence.

11. Nor, amid all their sufferings, did any one of them ask for mercy, or throw away his sword, or implore a speedy death, but clinging resolutely to their arms, wounded as they were, they thought it a lesser evil to be subdued by the strength of another than by their own consciences, and at times they were heard to grumble that what had happened was the work of fortune, not of their deserts. And so this

whole battle was brought to an end in half an hour, in which such numbers of barbarians fell that nothing but the fact of our victory proved that there had been any battle at all.

12. Those in arms had scarcely been routed when the relations of the dead, of every age and sex, were brought forward in crowds, having been dragged from their humble dwellings. And all their former pride being now gone, they descended to the lowest depths of servile obedience, and after a very short time nothing but barrows of the dead and bands of captives were beheld.

13. So, the heat of strife and the excitement of victory stimulating our men, they rose up to destroy all who had escaped the battle, or who were lying hidden in their dwellings. And when, eager for the blood of the barbarians, our soldiers had reached the spot, they tore to pieces the slight straw-thatched huts; nor could even the strongest-built cottages, or the stoutest beams save any one from death.

14. At last, when everything was set on fire, and when no one could be concealed any longer, since every protection for their lives was destroyed, they either perished obstinately in the flames, or else, if they avoided the fire and sallied out, they only escaped that destruction to fall beneath the sword of their enemies.

15. Some, however, did escape from the weapons of the enemy and from the spreading flames, and committed themselves to the stream, trusting to their skill in swimming to enable them to reach the further bank; but many of them were drowned, and others were transfixed by our javelins, so that the winding stream of the vast river was discoloured with blood, and thus, by the agency of both elements, did the indignation and valour of the conquerors destroy the Sarmatians.

16. After these events it was determined to leave the barbarians no hope nor comfort of life; and after burning their houses and carrying off their families, an order was given to collect boats in order to hunt out those who, being on the opposite bank of the river, had escaped the attack of our men.

17. And immediately, that the alacrity of our warriors might have no time to cool, some light-armed troops were embarked in boats, and led by secret paths to occupy the retreats of the Sarmatians. The barbarians at first were deceived by seeing only the boats of their own country, and crews with whom they were acquainted.

18. But when the weapons glittered in the distance, and they perceived that what they feared was upon them, they sought refuge in their accustomed marshes. And our soldiers pursuing them with great animosity, slew numbers of them, and gained a victory in a place

where it had not been supposed that any soldier could find a footing, much less do any bold action.

19. After the Anicenses[87] had thus been routed and almost destroyed, we proceeded at once to attack the Picenses, who are so called from the regions which they inhabit, which border on one another; and these tribes had fancied themselves the more secure from the disasters of their allies, which they had heard of by frequent rumours. To crush them (for it was an arduous task for those who did not know the country to follow men scattered in many directions as they were) the aid of Taifali[88] and of the free-born Sarmatians was sought.

20. And as the nature of the ground separated the auxiliary battalions from each other, our own troops took the ground nearest Mœsia, the Taifali that nearest to their own settlements, while the free Sarmatians occupied that in front of their original position.

21. The Limigantes, alarmed at the still fresh examples of nations subdued and crushed by us, for a long time hesitated and wavered whether they should attack us or ask for peace, having arguments of no small weight for either line of conduct. But at last, through the influence of the council of the elders, the idea of surrender prevailed; and the submission also of those who had dared to attack their free-born masters was added to our numerous victories; and the rest of them, who had previously despised their masters, thinking them unwarlike and easily subdued, now finding them stronger than themselves, submitted to them.

22. Accordingly, having received pledges of their safety, and having quitted the defence of their mountains, the greater portion of them came with speed to the Roman camp, and they spread over a vast extent of ground, bringing with them their parents, their children, their wives, and all the movable treasures which their rapid motions had allowed them to carry off.

23. And those who it had been supposed would rather lose their lives than quit their country, while they mistook their mad licentiousness for liberty, now submitted to obey our orders, and to take up another abode in peace and good faith, so as to be undisturbed for the future by wars or seditions. And having been thus accepted as subjects, in accordance with their own wish as it was believed, they remained quiet for a time; but afterwards they broke out in destructive wickedness, as shall be related at the proper time.

24. While our affairs were thus prospering, Illyricum was put in a state of twofold security, since the emperor, in endeavouring by two means to accomplish this object, succeeded in both. He brought back

and established in their ancient homes the people who had been banished, whom, although they were objects of suspicion from their natural fickleness, he believed would go on more moderately than of old. And to crown this kindness, he set over them as a king, not one of low birth, but the very man whom they themselves had formerly chosen, as eminent for all the virtues of mind and body.

25. After such a wise action, Constantius, being now raised above all fear, and having received from the unanimous consent of his soldiers the title of Sarmaticus, from the name of the nation which he had subdued; and being now about to leave the army, summoned all his cohorts and centuries and maniples, and mounting the tribune, surrounded by the standards and eagles, and by a great number of soldiers of all ranks, he addressed the troops in these words, choosing his topics as usual so as to gain the favour of all.

26. "The recollection of our glorious exploits, the dearest of all feelings to brave men, encourages me to repeat, though with great moderation, what, in our heaven-granted victories, and before battle, and in the very heat of the strife, we, the most faithful champions of the Roman state, have conducted to a deservedly prosperous issue. For what can be so honourable or so justly worthy to be handed down to the recollection of posterity as the exultation of the soldier in his brave deeds, and of the general in his wise plans?

27. "The rage of our enemies, in their arrogant pride thinking to profit by our absence, while we were protecting Italy and Gaul, was overrunning Illyricum, and with continual sallies they were ravaging even the districts beyond our frontiers; crossing the rivers, sometimes in boats made of hollow trees, sometimes on foot; not relying on combats, nor on their arms and strength, but being accustomed to secret forays, and having been from the very earliest era of their nation an object of fear to our ancestors, from their cunning and the variety of their manœuvres, which we indeed, being at a great distance, bore as long as we could, thinking that the vigour of our generals would be able to protect us from even slight injury.

28. "But when their licentiousness led them on to bolder attempts, and to inflict great and frequent injury on our provinces, we, having first fortified the passes of the Tyrol, and having secured the safety of the Gauls by watchful care, leaving no danger behind us, have marched into Pannonia, in order, with the favour of the everlasting deity, to strengthen our tottering interests in that country. And after everything was prepared, we set forth, as you know, at the end of the spring, and undertook a great enterprise; first of all taking care that the

140

countless darts of the enemy should not prevent us from making a bridge. And when, with no great trouble, this had been accomplished, after we had set our foot upon the enemy's territories, we defeated, with very little loss to ourselves, the Sarmatians, who with obstinate courage set themselves to resist us to the death. And we also crushed the Quadi, who were bringing reinforcements to the Sarmatians, and who with similar courage attacked our noble legions.

29. "These tribes, after heavy losses sustained in their attacks, and their stubborn and toilsome resistance, have at length learnt the power of our valour, and throwing away their arms, have allowed their hands, prepared for fighting, to be bound behind their backs; and seeing that their only hope of safety is in prayer, have fallen at the feet of your merciful emperor, whose wars they found are usually successful. Having got rid of these enemies, we with equal courage defeated the Limigantes, and after we had put numbers of them to the sword, the rest found their only means of escaping danger lay in fleeing to their hiding-places in the marshes.

30. "And when these things were successfully terminated, it seemed to be a seasonable opportunity for mercy. So we compelled the Limigantes to remove to very distant lands, that they might not be able any more to move to our injury; and we spared the greatest part of them. And we made Zizais king over the free-born portion of them, sure that he would be faithful to us, and thinking it more honour to create a king for the barbarians than to take one from them, the dignity being increased by this honourable consideration, that the ruler whom we thus gave them had before been elected and accepted by them.

31. "So we and the republic have in one campaign obtained a fourfold reward: first, vengeance on our guilty assailants; next, abundance of captive slaves from the enemy, for valour is entitled to those rewards which it has earned with its toil and prowess.

32. "Thirdly, we have ample resources and great treasures of wealth; our labour and courage having preserved the patrimony of each of us undiminished. This, in the mind of a good sovereign, is the best fruit of prosperity.

33. "Lastly, I myself have the well-won spoil of a surname derived from the enemy—the title of Sarmaticus—which you unanimously have (if I may say so without arrogance) deservedly conferred on me."

34. After he had made an end of speaking, the whole assembly, with more alacrity than usual, since its hope of booty and gain was increased, rose up with joyful voices in praise of the emperor; and, as

usual, calling God to witness that Constantius was invincible, returned with joy to their tents. And the emperor was conducted back to his palace, and having rested two days, re-entered Sirmium with a triumphal procession; and the troops returned to their appointed stations.

XIV.

§ 1. About this time Prosper and Spectatus and Eustathius, who, as has been mentioned above, had been sent as ambassadors to the Persians, found the Persian king at Ctesiphon, on his return from his campaign, and they delivered the emperor's letters and presents, and requested peace while affairs were still in their existing state. And mindful of what had been enjoined them, they never forgot the interests nor the dignity of the Roman empire, maintaining that the peace ought to be made on the condition that no alteration should be made in the state of Armenia or Mesopotamia.

2. And having remained for some time, when they saw that the king was obstinate, and resolute not to admit of peace unless the absolute dominion of those regions was assigned to him, they returned without having completed their business.

3. After which, Lucillianus, a count, and Procopius, at that time secretary, were sent to obtain the same conditions, with equal powers. Procopius being the same man who afterwards, under the pressure of violent necessity, committed himself to a revolutionary movement.

Notes

[70] Ἐνοίχθωη, Σεισίχθων, Ἐννοσίγδαιος, from ἐνίθω and σείω, to shake, and χθὰν and γαῖα, the earth.

[71] From βραζω, to boil over.

[72] Strabo gives Ophiusa as one of the names of Rhodes, and Homer mentions the golden shower:—

καί σφιν Θεσπέσιον πλούτου κατέχευε κρονιὼν.—Il. β. vi. 70.

As also does Pindar, Ol. vii. 63.

[73] From κλίνω, to lay down.

[74] From χάσμα, a chasm, derived from χαίνω, to gape.

[75] This is a tale told by Plato in the Timæus (which is believed to have no foundation).

[76] The destruction of Helice is related in Diodorus Sic. xiv. 48; cf. Ov. Met. xv. 290.

[77] The lake Ciminus was near Centumcellæ, cf. Virg. Æn. vii. 697. The town of Saccumum is not mentioned by any other writer.

[78] From μυκάω, to roar like a bull.

[79] Toxandria was in Belgium, on the Scheldt.

[80] The Chamavi were a tribe at the mouth of the Rhine.

[81] Tages was an Etruscan, the son, it is said, of a genius, Jovialis, and grandson of Jupiter, who rose out of the ground as a man named Tarchon was ploughing near Tarquinii, and instructed the auspices in divination. Cf. Cic. Div. ii. 23.

[82] Carthage and Numantia.

[83] The Quadi occupied a part of Hungary.

[84] The Victohali were a tribe of Goths.

[85] Szœni, called by Ammianus Bregetio, is near Cormorn.

[86] The Theiss.

[87] The Anicenses and Picenses were Dacian tribes.

[88] The Taifali were a tribe of the Western Goths.

BOOK XVIII

I.

A.D. 359.

§ 1. These events took place in the different parts of the world in one and the same year. But while the affairs in Gaul were in a better state; and while titles of consul were ennobling the brothers Eusebius and Hypatius, Julian, illustrious for his uninterrupted successes, now in his winter quarters, being relieved for a while from his warlike anxieties, was devoting equal care to many points connected with the welfare of the provinces. Taking anxious care that no one should be oppressed by the burden of taxation; that the power of the officers should not be stretched into extortion; that those who increase their property by the public distresses, should have no sanction, and that no judge should violate justice with impunity.

2. And he found it easy to correct what was wrong on this head, because he himself decided all causes in which the persons concerned were of any great importance; and showed himself a most impartial discerner of right and wrong.

3. And although there are many acts of his in deciding these disputes worthy of praise, it will be sufficient to mention one, on the model of which all his other words and actions were framed.

4. Numerius, a native of Narbonne, had a little time before been accused before the governor as a thief, and Julian, by an unusual exercise of the censor's power, heard his cause in public; admitting into the court all who sought entrance. And when Numerius denied all that was charged against him, and could not be convicted on any point, Delphidius the orator, who was assailing him with great bitterness, being enraged at the failure of his charges, exclaimed, "But, great Cæsar, will any one ever be found guilty if it be enough to deny the charge?" To whom Julian, with seasonable wisdom, replied, "Can any one be judged innocent if it be enough to make a charge?" And he did many similar actions in his civil capacity.

II.

§ 1. But when he was about to set out on an important expedition against some tribes of the Allemanni whom he considered hostile, and likely to proceed to acts of atrocious daring if they were not defeated in a way to be an example to the rest, he hesitated in great anxiety, since a report of his intentions had gone before him, what force he could employ, and how he could be quick enough to take them by surprise the first moment that circumstances should afford him an opportunity.

2. But after he had meditated on many different plans, he decided on trying one, which the result proved to be good without any one being aware of it. He had sent Hariobaudes, a tribune who at that time had no particular command, a man of honour, loyalty, and courage, under pretext of an embassy, to Hortarius the king who was now in a state of friendship with us; in order that from his court Hariobaudes might easily proceed to the frontiers of the enemy whom he was pro-

posing to attack; and so ascertain what they were about, being thoroughly skilled in the language of the barbarians.

3. And when he had gone boldly on this commission, Julian himself, as it was now a favourable time of the year, assembled his soldiers from all quarters for the expedition, and set out; thinking it above all things desirable, before the war had got warm, to effect his entrance into the cities which had been destroyed some time before, and having recovered them to put them in a state of defence; and also to establish granaries in the place of those which had been burnt, in which to store the corn usually imported from Britain.

4. Both these objects were accomplished, and that more speedily than could have been looked for. For the store-houses were rapidly built, and abundance of provisions laid up in them; and seven cities were occupied. The camp of Hercules, Quadriburgium,[89] Kellen, Nuys, Bonn, Andernach, and Bingen. At which last city, by exceedingly good fortune, Florentius the prefect also arrived unexpectedly, bringing with him a division of soldiers, and a supply of provisions sufficient to last a long time.

5. After this, the next measure of urgent necessity was to repair the walls of the recovered cities, while as yet no one raised any hindrance; and it is abundantly plain that at that time the barbarians did out of fear what was commanded them for the public interests, while the Romans did it for love of their ruler.

6. According to the treaty made in the preceding year, the kings sent their own waggons with many articles useful for building. And the auxiliary soldiers who always hold themselves above employments of this kind being won over by Julian's caresses to diligent obedience, now carried beams fifty feet long and more on their shoulders, and gave the greatest aid to the labours of the architect.

7. And while all this was being done with diligence and speed, Hariobaudes, having learnt all he wanted, returned and related what he had ascertained. And after his arrival the army marched with all speed, and soon reached Mayence, where, though Florentius and Lupicinus, who succeeded Severus, insisted vehemently that they might cross by the bridge laid down at that town, the Cæsar strenuously objected, maintaining that it was not well to trample on the lands of those who were brought into a state of tranquillity and friendship; lest the treaty made with them should be brought to an abrupt end, as had often happened through the discourtesy of the soldiers ravaging everything that came in their way.

8. But all the Allemanni who were the objects of our attack, seeing the danger now on their borders, with many threats urged Surmarius their king, who by a previous treaty was on friendly terms with us, to prevent the Romans from crossing the river. For their villages were on the eastern bank of the Rhine. But when Surmarius affirmed that he by himself was unable to offer effectual resistance, the barbarian host assembled in a body, and came up to Mayence, intending by main force to prevent our army from crossing the river.

9. So that Cæsar's advice now seemed best in two points, both not to ravage the lands of our friends; and also, not in the teeth of the opposition of a most warlike people, to risk the loss of many lives in order to make a bridge, even in a spot the most favourable for such a work.

10. And the enemy, watching his movements with great skill, marched slowly along the opposite bank, and when they saw our men pitching their tents at a distance, they still watched all night, exerting the most sleepless vigilance to prevent the passage of the river from being attempted.

11. But when our men reached the spot intended, they surrounded their camp with a rampart and ditch, and took their rest; and the Cæsar, having taken counsel with Lupicinus, ordered some of the tribunes to get ready three hundred light-armed soldiers with stakes, without letting them know what was to be done, or whither they were going.

12. They being collected, when the night was well advanced, and being all embarked on board of forty light boats, which were all that were at hand, were ordered to go down the stream so silently as not to use even their oars, lest the noise should rouse the barbarians, and then using all activity both of mind and body, to force a landing on the opposite bank, within the frontier of the enemy, while they were still watching the camp-fires of our men.

13. While these orders were being performed with great promptness, King Hortarius, who had been previously bound to us by treaties, and was without any intention of revolting, kept on friendly terms with the bordering tribes, having invited all their kings, princes, and chieftains to a banquet, detained them to the third watch, the banquet being prolonged so late according to the custom of his nation. And as they were departing, our men chanced to come upon them suddenly, but could neither stay nor capture any of them owing to the darkness of the night and the fleetness of their horses, on which they fled at random in all directions. A number of sutlers and slaves, however, who were fol-

lowing them on foot, our men slew; the few who escaped being like-wise protected by the darkness of the hour.

14. When it became known that the Romans had crossed the river (and they then as well as in all former expeditions accounted it a great relief to their labours when they could find the enemy), the kings and their people, who were watching zealously to prevent the bridge from being made, were alarmed, and being panic-stricken fled in all directions, and their violent fury being thus cooled, they hastened to remove their relations and their treasures to a distance. And as all dif-ficulties were now surmounted, the bridge was at once made, and before the barbarians could expect it, the Roman army appeared in their territories, and passed through the dominions of Hortarius with-out doing any injury.

15. But when they reached the lands of those kings who were still hostile, they went on invincibly through the midst of their rebel-lious country, laying waste with fire and sword, and plundering everything. And after their frail houses were destroyed by fire, and a vast number of men had been slain, and the army, having nothing to face but corpses and suppliants, had arrived in the region called Capel-latum, or Palas, where there are boundary stones marking the frontiers of the Allemanni and the Burgundians; the army pitched its camp, in order that Macrianus and Hariobaudus, brothers, and both kings, might be received by us, and delivered from their fears. Since they, thinking their destruction imminent, were coming with great anxiety to sue for peace.

16. And immediately after them King Vadomarius also came, whose abode was opposite Augst: and having produced some letters of the Emperor Constantius, in which he was strictly recommended to the protection of the Romans, he was courteously received, as became one who had been admitted by the emperor as a client of the Roman em-pire.

17. And Macrianus and his brother, being admitted among our eagles and standards, marvelled at the imposing appearance of our arms, and various resources which they had never seen before. And they offered up petitions on behalf of their people. But Vadomarius, who had met us before, since he was close to our frontier, admired indeed the appointments of our daring expedition, but remembered that he had often seen such before, ever since his childhood.

18. At last, after long deliberation, with the unanimous consent of all, peace was granted to Macrianus and Hariobaudus; but an an-swer could not be given to Vadomarius, who had come to secure his

own safety, and also as an ambassador to intercede for the kings Urius, Ursicinus, and Vestralpus, imploring peace for them also; lest, as the barbarians are men of wavering faith, they might recover their spirits when our army was withdrawn, and refuse adherence to conditions procured by the agency of others.

19. But when they also, after their crops and houses had been burnt, and many of their soldiers had been slain or taken prisoners, sent ambassadors of their own, and sued for mercy as if they had been guilty of similar violence to our subjects, they obtained peace on similar terms; of which that most rigorously insisted on was that they should restore all the prisoners which they had taken in their frequent incursions.

III.

§ 1. While the god-like wisdom of the Cæsar was thus successful in Gaul, great disturbances arose in the court of the emperor, which from slight beginnings increased to grief and lamentations. Some bees swarmed on the house of Barbatio, at that time the commander of the infantry. And when he consulted the interpreters of prodigies on this event, he received for an answer, that it was an omen of great danger; the answer being founded on the idea that these animals, after they have fixed their abode, and laid up their stores, are usually expelled by smoke and the noisy din of cymbals.

2. Barbatio's wife was a woman called Assyria, neither silent nor prudent. And when he had gone on an expedition which caused her much alarm, she, because of the predictions which she recollected to have been given her, and being full of female vanity, having summoned a handmaid who was skilful in writing, and of whom she had become possessed by inheritance from her father Silvanus, sent an unseasonable letter to her husband, full of lamentations, and of entreaties that after the approaching death of Constantius, if he himself, as she hoped, was admitted to a share in the empire, he would not despise her, and prefer to marry Eusebia, who was Constantius's empress, and who was of a beauty equalled by few women.

3. She sent this letter as secretly as she could; but the maid, when the troops had returned from their expedition at the beginning of the night, took a copy of the letter which she had written at the dictation of her mistress, to Arbetio, and being eagerly admitted by him, she gave him the paper.

4. He, relying on this evidence, being at all times a man eager to bring forward accusations, conveyed it to the emperor. As was usual,

no delay was allowed, and Barbatio, who confessed that he had received the letter, and his wife, who was distinctly proved to have written it, were both beheaded.

5. After this execution, investigations were carried further, and many persons, innocent as well as guilty, were brought into question. Among whom was Valentinus, who having lately been an officer of the protectores, had been promoted to be a tribune; and he with many others was put to the torture as having been privy to the affair, though he was wholly ignorant of it. But he survived his sufferings; and as some compensation for the injury done to him, and for his danger, he received the rank of duke of Illyricum.

6. This same Barbatio was a man of rude and arrogant manners, and very unpopular, because while captain of the protectores of the household, in the time of Gallus Cæsar, he was a false and treacherous man; and after he had attained the higher rank he became so elated that he invented calumnies against the Cæsar Julian, and, though all good men hated him, whispered many wicked lies into the ever-ready ears of the emperor.

7. Being forsooth ignorant of the wise old saying of Aristotle, who when he sent Callisthenes, his pupil and relation, to the king Alexander, warned him to say as little as he could, and that only of a pleasant kind, before a man who carried the power of life and death on the tip of his tongue.

8. We should not wonder that mankind, whose minds we look upon as akin to those of the gods, can sometimes discern what is likely to be beneficial or hurtful to them, when even animals devoid of reason sometimes secure their own safety by profound silence, of which the following is a notorious instance:—

9. When the wild geese leave the East because of the heat, and seek a western climate, as soon as they reach Mount Taurus, which is full of eagles, fearing those warlike birds, they stop up their own beaks with stones, that not even the hardest necessity may draw a cry from them; they fly more rapidly than usual across that range, and when they have passed it they throw away the stones, and then proceed more securely.

IV.

§ 1. While these investigations were being carried on with great diligence at Sirmium, the fortune of the East sounded the terrible trumpet of danger. For the king of Persia, being strengthened by the aid of the fierce nations whom he had lately subdued, and being above all men ambitious of extending his territories, began to prepare men and arms and supplies, mingling hellish wisdom with his human counsels, and consulting all kinds of soothsayers about futurity. And when he had collected everything, he proposed to invade our territories at the first opening of the spring.

2. And when the emperor learnt this, at first by report, but subsequently by certain intelligence, and while all were in suspense from dread of the impending danger, the dependents of the court, hammering on the same anvil day and night (as the saying is), at the prompting of the eunuchs, held up Ursicinus as a Gorgon's head before the suspicious and timid emperor, continually repeating that, because on the death of Silvanus, in a dearth of better men, he had been sent to defend the eastern districts, he had become ambitious of still greater power.

3. And by this base compliance many tried to purchase the favour of Eusebius, at that time the principal chamberlain, with whom (if we are to say the real truth) Constantius had great influence, and who was now a bitter enemy of the safety of the master of the horse, Ursicinus, on two accounts; first, because he was the only person who did not need his assistance, as others did; and secondly, because he would not give up his house at Antioch, which Eusebius greatly coveted.

4. So this latter, like a snake abounding in poison, and exciting its offspring as soon as they can crawl to do mischief, stirred up the other chamberlains, that they, while performing their more private duties about the prince's person, with their thin and boyish voices, might damage the reputation of a brave man by pouring into the too open ears of the emperor accusations of great odium. And they soon did what they were commanded.

5. Disgust at this and similar events leads one to praise Domitian, who although, by the unalterable detestation he incurred, has ever stained the memory of his father and his brother,[90] still deserved credit for a most excellent law, by which he forbade with severe threats any one to castrate any boy within the limits of the Roman jurisdiction. For if there were no such edict, who could endure the swarms of such creatures as would exist, when it is so difficult to bear even a few of them?

6. However, they proceeded with caution, lest, as Eusebius suggested, if Ursicinus were again sent for, he should take alarm and throw everything into confusion; but it was proposed that on the first casual opportunity he should be put to death.

7. While they were waiting for this chance, and full of doubt and anxiety; and while we[91] were tarrying a short time at Samosata, the greatest city of what had formerly been the kingdom of Commagene,

we suddenly received frequent and consistent reports of some new commotions, which I will now proceed to relate.

V.

§ 1. A certain man named Antoninus, who from having been a wealthy merchant had become superintendent of the accounts of the duke of Mesopotamia, and after that entered the corps of the protectores, a man of experience and wisdom, and very well known in all that country. Being through the avarice of certain persons involved in heavy losses, and perceiving that while defending actions against men of influence he was being sunk lower and lower through injustice, since the judges who had to decide on his affairs sought to gratify people in power, he, not wishing to kick against the pricks, bent himself to obsequious caresses; and confessing that he owed what was claimed of him, the claim, by collusion, was transferred to the treasury. He now, having resolved on a flagitious plan, began secretly to look into the secrets of the whole republic; and being acquainted with both languages, he devoted his attention to the accounts; remarking the amount, quality, and situation of the different divisions of the army, and the employment of them on any expeditions; inquiring also with unwearied diligence into the extent of the supplies of arms and provisions, and other things likely to be needful in war.

2. And when he had made himself acquainted with all the internal circumstances of the East, and had learnt that a great portion of the troops and of the money for their pay was distributed in Illyricum, where the emperor himself was detained by serious business; as the day was now approaching which had been fixed for the payment of the money for which he had been constrained by fear to give an acknowledgment of his bond; and as he saw that he must be overwhelmed by disasters on all sides, since the chief treasurer was devoted to the interests of his adversary; he conceived the audacious design of crossing over to the Persians with his wife and children, and his whole numerous family of relations.

3. And to elude the observation of the soldiers at their different stations, he bought for a small price a farm in Hiaspis, a district on the banks of the Tigris. And, relying on this pretext, since no one would venture to ask why a landed proprietor should go to the extreme frontier of the Roman territory, as many others did the same, by the agency of some trusty friends who were skilful swimmers, he carried on frequent secret negotiations with Tamsapor, who was at that time governing the country on the other side of the river with the rank of

152

duke, and with whom he was already acquainted. And at last, having received from the Persian camp an escort of well-mounted men, he embarked in some boats, and crossed over at night with all his family, in the same manner as Zopyrus, the betrayer of Babylon, had formerly done, only with an opposite object.

4. While affairs in Mesopotamia were in this state, the hangers-on of the palace, always singing the same song for our destruction, at last found a handle to injure the gallant Ursicinus; the gang of eunuchs being still the contrivers and promoters of the plot; since they are always sour tempered and savage, and having no relations, cling to riches as their dearest kindred.

5. The design now adopted was to send Sabinianus, a withered old man of great wealth, but infirm and timid, and from the lowness of his birth far removed from any office of command, to govern the districts of the East; while Ursicinus should be recalled to court, to command the infantry, as successor to Barbatio. And then he, this greedy promoter of revolution, as they called him, being within their reach, could easily be attacked by his bitter and formidable enemies.

6. While these things were going on in the camp of Constantius, as at a festival or a theatre, and while the dispensers of rank which was bought and sold were distributing the price agreed upon among the influential houses, Antoninus, having reached Sapor's winter quarters, was received with gladness; and being ennobled by the grant of a turban, an honour which gives admission to the royal table, and also that of assisting at and delivering one's opinion in the councils of the Persians, went onwards, not with a punt pole or a tar rope, as the proverb is (that is to say, not by any tedious or circuitous path), but with flowing sails into the conduct of state affairs, and stirring up Sapor, as formerly Maharbal roused the sluggish Hannibal, was always telling him that he knew how to conquer, but not how to use a victory.

7. For having been bred up in active life, and being a thorough man of business, he got possession of the feelings of his hearers, who like what tickles their ears, and who do not utter their praises aloud, but, like the Phæacians in Homer, admire in silence,[92] while he recounted the events of the last forty years; urging that, after all these continual wars, and especially the battles of Hileia and Singara,[93] where that fierce combat by night took place, in which we lost a vast number of our men, as if some fecial had interposed to stop them, the Persians, though victorious, had never advanced as far as Edessa or the bridges over the Euphrates. Though with their warlike power and splendid success, they might have pushed their advances especially at

that moment, when in consequence of the protracted troubles of their civil wars the blood of the Romans was being poured out on all sides.

8. By these and similar speeches the deserter, preserving his sobriety at the banquets, where, after the fashion of the ancient Greeks, the Persians deliberate on war and other important affairs, stimulated the fiery monarch, and persuaded him to rely upon the greatness of his fortune, and to take up arms the moment that the winter was over, and he himself boldly promised his assistance in many important matters.

VI.

§ 1. About this time Sabinianus, being elated at the power which he had suddenly acquired, and having arrived in Cilicia, gave his predecessor letters from the emperor, desiring him to hasten to court to be invested with higher dignities. In fact the affairs of Asia were in such a state that, even if Ursicinus had been at Ultima Thule their urgency would have required him to be summoned thence to set them right, since he was a man of the ancient discipline, and from long experience especially skilful in the Persian manner of conducting war.

2. But when the report of this reached the provinces, all ranks of the citizens and agricultural population, by formal edicts and by unanimous outcries, endeavoured to detain him, almost forcibly, as the public defender of their country, remembering that though for ten years he had been left to his own resources with a scanty and unwarlike force, he had yet incurred no loss; and fearing for their safety if at so critical a time he should be removed and a man of utter inactivity assume the rule in his stead.

3. We believe, and indeed there is no doubt of it, that fame flies on wings through the paths of the air; and she it was who now gave information of these events to the Persians while deliberating on the entire aspect of affairs. At last, after many arguments pro and con, they determined, on the advice of Antoninus, that as Ursicinus was removed, and as the new governor was contemptible, they might venture to neglect laying siege to cities, an operation which would cause a mischievous loss of time, and at once cross the Euphrates, and advance further, in order, outstripping all rumour of their march, to occupy those provinces which, throughout all our wars, had always been safe (except in the time of Gallienus), and which, from their long enjoyment of peace, were very wealthy. And in this enterprise, with the favour of God, Antoninus offered himself as a most desirable guide.

4. His advice, therefore, being unanimously praised and adopted, and the attention of the whole nation being directed to the speedy col-

lection of those things which were required, supplies, soldiers, arms, and equipments, the preparation of everything for the coming campaign was continued the whole winter.

5. In the mean time, we, hastening at the emperor's command towards Italy, after having been detained a short time on the western side of Mount Taurus, reached the river Hebrus, which descends from the mountains of the Odrysæ[94], and there we received letters from the emperor, ordering us, without the least delay, to return to Mesopotamia, without any officers, and having, indeed, no important duty to discharge, since all the power had been transferred to another.

6. And this had been arranged by those mischievous meddlers in the government, in order that if the Persians failed and returned to their own country, our success might be attributed to the valour of the new governor; while, if our affairs turned out ill, Ursicinus might be impeached as a traitor to the republic.

7. Accordingly we, being tossed about without any reason, after much time had been lost, returned, and found Sabinianus, a man full of pride, of small stature, and of a petty and narrow mind, scarcely able without fear to encounter the slight noise of a beast, much less to face the crash of battle.

8. Nevertheless, since our spies brought positive and consistent intelligence that all kind of preparations were going on among the enemy, and since their report was confirmed by that of the deserters, while this manikin was in a state of perplexity, we hastened to Nisibis to make such preparation as seemed requisite, lest the Persians, while concealing their intention to besiege it, should come upon it by surprise.

9. And while all things necessary were being pressed forward within the walls, continued fires and columns of smoke being seen on the other side of the Tigris, near the town called the Camp of the Moors, and Sisara, and the other districts on the Persian frontier, and spreading up to the city itself, showed that the predatory bands of the enemy had crossed the river, and entered our territories.

10. And therefore we hastened forwards with a forced march, to prevent the roads from being occupied; and when we had advanced two miles, we saw a fine boy of about eight years old, as we guessed, wearing a necklace, of noble appearance, standing on the top of a small hillock, and crying out, stating himself to be the son of a man of noble birth, whom his mother, while fleeing in her alarm at the approach of the enemy, had left in her panic in order to be less encumbered. We pitied him, and at the command of our general, I put

him on my horse, in front of me, and took him back to the city, while the predatory bands of the enemy, having blockaded the city, were ravaging all around.

11. And because I was alarmed at the difficulties in which we should be placed by a blockade, I put the child in at a half open postern gate, and hastened back with all speed to my troop. And I was very nearly taken prisoner; for a tribune named Abdigidus, accompanied by a groom, was fleeing, pursued by a squadron of cavalry, and though the master escaped the servant was taken. And as I was passing by rapidly, they, examining the servant, inquired of him who was the chief who had advanced against them; and when they heard that Ursicinus had a little while before entered the city, and was on his way to Mount Izala, they put their informant to death, and then, forming into one body, pursued us with ceaseless speed.

12. But I outstripped them by the speed of my horse, and finding my comrades reposing securely under the walls of a slight fort, called Amudis, with their horses dispersed over the grass, I waved my hand, and raising the hem of my cloak: by this usual signal I gave notice that the enemy was at hand, and then joining them we retreated together, though my horse was greatly fatigued.

13. Our alarm was increased by the brightness of the night, as the moon was full, and by the even level of the plain, which, if our danger should become worse, afforded no possible hiding-place, as having neither trees, nor bushes, nor anything but low herbage.

14. Accordingly we adopted the following plan: we lit a lamp and fastened it tightly on a horse, which we turned loose without a rider, and let go where it pleased to our left, while we marched towards the high ground on our right, in order that the Persians might fancy the light a torch held before the general as he proceeded slowly forwards, and so keep on in that direction. And unless we had adopted this precaution we should have been circumvented, and have fallen as prisoners into the power of the enemy.

15. Being delivered from this danger, when we had come to a woody spot, full of vines and fruit-bearing trees, called Meiacarire, a name derived from the cool springs found there, we found that the inhabitants had all fled, and there was only a single soldier remaining behind, concealed in a remote corner. And when he was brought before our general, and through fear told all kinds of different stories, and so became an object of suspicion; at last, under the compulsion of our threats, he told the real truth, that he was a native of Gaul, and had been born among the Parisii, that he had served in our cavalry, but that

fearing punishment for some offence he had deserted to the Persians; that he had since married a wife of excellent character, and had a family, and that having been frequently sent as a spy to our camp, he had always brought the Persians true intelligence. And now he said he had been sent by the nobles Tamsapor and Nohodares, who were in command of the predatory bands, to bring them such intelligence as he could collect. After telling us this, and also that he knew of the operations of the enemy, he was put to death.

16. Afterwards, as our anxiety increased, we proceeded from thence with as much speed as we could make to Amida, a city celebrated at a later period for the disaster which befel it. And when our scouts had rejoined us there we found in one of their scabbards a scrap of parchment written in cipher, which they had been ordered to convey to us by Procopius, whom I have already spoken of as ambassador to the Persians with the Count Lucillianus; its terms were purposely obscure, lest if the bearers should be taken prisoners, and the sense of the writing understood, materials should be found for fatal mischief.

17. The purport was, "The ambassadors of the Greeks, having been rejected, and being perhaps to be put to death, the aged king, not contented with the Hellespont, will throw bridges over the Granicus and the Rhyndacus, and invade Asia Minor with a numerous host, being by his own natural disposition irritable and fierce; and being now prompted and inflamed by him who was formerly the successor of the Roman emperor Hadrian,[95] it is all over with the Greeks if they do not take care."

18. The meaning of this was that the Persian king, having crossed the rivers Anzaba and Tigris, at the prompting of Antoninus was aiming at the sovereignty of the entire East. When it had been interpreted with difficulty, from its great obscurity, a wise plan was decided on.

19. The satrap of Corduena, a province under the authority of the Persians, was a man named Jovinianus, who had grown up to manhood in the Roman territories, and was secretly friendly to us, because he had been detained as a hostage in Syria, and being now allured by the love of liberal studies, he was exceedingly desirous to return among us.

20. To this man I, being sent with a faithful centurion, for the purpose of learning with greater certainty what was being done, reached him by travelling over pathless mountains, and dangerous defiles. And when he saw and recognized me, he received me courteously, and I avowed to him alone the reason of my coming; and

157

having received from him a silent guide, well acquainted with the country, I was sent to some lofty rocks at a distance, from which, if one's eyes did not fail, one could see even the most minute object fifty miles off.

21. There we remained two whole days; and on the morning of the third day we saw all the circuit of the earth, which we call the horizon, filled with countless hosts of men, and the king marching before them glittering with the brilliancy of his robes. And next to him on his left hand marched Grumbates, king of the Chionitæ, a man of middle age, and wrinkled limbs, but of a grand spirit, and already distinguished for many victories. On his right hand was the king of the Albani, of equal rank and splendour. After them came various generals, renowned for their rank and power, who were followed by a multitude of all classes, picked from the flower of the neighbouring nations, and trained by long hardship to endure any toil or danger.

22. How long, O mendacious Greece, wilt thou tell us of Doriscus,[96] the Thracian town, and of the army counted there in battalions in a fenced space, when we careful, or to speak more truly, cautious historians, exaggerate nothing, and merely record what is established by evidence neither doubtful nor uncertain!

VII.

§ 1. After the kings had passed by Nineveh, an important city of the province of Adiabene, they offered a sacrifice in the middle of the bridge over the Anzaba, and as the omens were favourable, they advanced with great joy; while we, calculating that the rest of their host could hardly pass over in three days, returned with speed to the satrap, and rested, refreshing ourselves by his hospitable kindness.

2. And returning from thence through a deserted and solitary country, under the pressure of great necessity, and reaching our army more rapidly than could have been expected, we brought to those who were hesitating the certain intelligence that the kings had crossed over the river by a bridge of boats, and were marching straight towards us.

3. Without delay, therefore, horsemen with horses of picked speed were sent to Cassianus, duke of Mesopotamia, and to Euphronius, at that time the governor of the province, to compel the residents in the country to retire with their families and all their flocks to a safer place; and to quit at once the town of Carræ, which was defended by very slight walls; and further, to burn all the standing crops, that the enemy might get no supplies from the land.

4. And when these orders had been executed, as they were without delay, and when the fire was kindled, the violence of the raging element so completely destroyed all the corn,[97] which was just beginning to swell and turn yellow, and all the young herbage, that from the Euphrates to the Tigris nothing green was to be seen. And many wild beasts were burnt, and especially lions, who infest these districts terribly, but who are often destroyed or blinded in this manner.

5. They wander in countless droves among the beds of rushes on the banks of the rivers of Mesopotamia, and in the jungles; and lie quiet all the winter, which is very mild in that country. But when the warm weather returns, as these regions are exposed to great heat, they are forced out by the vapours, and by the size of the gnats, with swarms of which every part of that country is filled. And these winged insects attack the eyes, as being both moist and sparkling, sitting on and biting the eyelids; the lions, unable to bear the torture, are either drowned in the rivers, to which they flee for refuge, or else by frequent scratchings tear their eyes out themselves with their claws, and then become mad. And if this did not happen the whole of the East would be overrun with beasts of this kind.

6. While the plains were thus being laid waste by fire, as I have described, the tribunes, who were sent with a body of protectores, fortified all the western bank of the Euphrates with castles and sharp palisades and every kind of defence, fixing also large engines for hurling missiles on those spots where the more tranquil condition of the river made it likely that the enemy might attempt to cross.

7. While these things were being expeditiously done, Sabinianus, chosen in the hurried moment of general danger as the fittest conductor of an internecine war, was living luxuriously, according to his custom, at the tombs of Edessa,[98] as if he had established peace with the dead, and had nothing to fear: and he took especial pleasure in breaking the silence of the place with the sounding measures of the martial pyathicari, instead of the usual theatrical exhibitions; a fancy, considering the place, pregnant with omens. Since these and similar gloomy scenes foreshow future commotions, as we learn in the progress of time, all good men ought to avoid them.

8. In the mean time, passing by Nisibis as of no importance, while the conflagration increased through the dryness of the crops, the kings, dreading a scarcity of food, marched through the grassy valleys at the foot of the mountains.

9. When they had arrived at a small place called Bebase (from which place to the town of Constantina, which is one hundred miles

distant, the whole country is an arid desert, except where a little water is found in some wells), they hesitated for some time, doubting what to do; and at last resolving to proceed in reliance on the endurance of their men, they learnt from a trusty spy that the Euphrates was swollen by the melting of the snow, and was now extensively inundating the adjacent lands, and so could not possibly be forded.

10. Therefore they turned to see what opportunities chance might afford them, being now cut off unexpectedly from the hope which they had conceived. And in the present emergency a council was held, at which Antoninus was requested to give his advice: and he counselled them to direct their march to the right, so that by a longer circuit they might reach the two strong forts of Barzala and Laudias, to which he could guide them through a region fertile in everything, and still undestroyed, since the march of the army was expected to be made in a straight line. And the only river on their road was one small and narrow, to be passed near its source, before it was increased by any other streams, and easily fordable.

11. When they had heard this, they praised their adviser, and bidding him lead the way, the whole army turned from its previously appointed line, and followed his guidance.

VIII.

§ 1. When our generals received intelligence of this from their spies, we settled to march in haste to Samosata, in order to cross the river at that point, and destroying the bridges at Zeugma and Capersana, to check the invasion of the enemy if we could find a favourable chance for attacking them.

2. But we met with a sad disaster, worthy to be buried in profound silence. For two squadrons of cavalry, of about seven hundred men, who had just been sent from Illyricum to Mesopotamia as a reinforcement, and who were guarding the passes, becoming enervated and timid, and fearing a surprise by night, withdrew from the public causeways in the evening, a time above all others when they most required watching.

3. And when it was remarked that they were all sunk in wine and sleep, about twenty thousand Persians, under the command of Tamsapor and Nohodares, passed without any one perceiving them, and fully armed as they were, concealed themselves behind the high ground in the neighbourhood of Amida.

4. Presently, when (as has been said) we started before daybreak on our march to Samosata, our advanced guard, on reaching a high

spot which commanded a more distant view, was suddenly alarmed by the glitter of shining arms; and cried out in a hurried manner that the enemy were at hand. Upon this the signal for battle was given, and we halted in a solid column, never thinking of fleeing, since, indeed, those who would have pursued us were in sight; nor to engage in battle with an enemy superior to us in numbers, and especially in cavalry; but seeing the necessity for caution in the danger of certain death which lay before us.

5. At last, when it seemed clear that a battle could not be avoided, and while we were still hesitating what to do, some of our men rashly advanced as skirmishers, and were slain. And then, as each side pressed onwards, Antoninus, ambitiously marching in front of the enemy, was recognized by Ursicinus, and addressed by him in a tone of reproach, and called a traitor and a scoundrel; till at last, taking off the tiara which he wore on his head as a badge of honour, he dismounted from his horse, and bending down till his face nearly touched the ground, he saluted the Roman general, calling him patron and master; and holding his hands behind his back, which among the Assyrians is a gesture of supplication, he said, "Pardon me, most noble count, who have been driven to this guilt by necessity, not by my own will. My creditors, as you know, drove me headlong into it: men whose avarice even your high authority, which tried to support me in my distress, could not overcome." Having said this, he withdrew without turning his back upon him, but retiring backwards in a respectful manner, with his face towards him.

6. And while this was taking place, which did not occupy above half an hour, our second rank, which occupied the higher ground, cried out that another body of cuirassiers appeared behind, and was coming on with great speed.

7. And then, as is often the case at critical moments, doubting which enemy we ought, or even could resist, and being pressed on all sides by an overwhelming mass, we dispersed in every direction, each fleeing where he could. And while every one was trying to extricate himself from the danger, we were brought, without any order, face to face with the enemy.

8. And so struggling vigorously while giving up all desire of saving our lives, we were driven back to the high banks of the Tigris. Some of our men, driven into the water where it was shallow, locked their arms, and so made a stand; others were carried off by the current and drowned; some, still fighting with the enemy, met with various fortune, or, panic-stricken at the numbers of the barbarians, sought the

nearest defiles of Mount Taurus. Among these was the general himself, who was recognized and surrounded by a vast body of the enemy;
but he escaped with the tribune Aiadalthes and one groom, being
saved by the swiftness of his horse.

9. I myself was separated from my comrades, and while looking
round to see what to do, I met with one of the protectores named Verrinianus, whose thigh was pierced through by an arrow, and while at
his entreaty I was trying to pull it out, I found myself surrounded on all
sides by Persians, some of whom had passed beyond me. I therefore
hastened back with all speed towards the city, which, being placed on
high ground, is only accessible by one very narrow path on the side on
which we were attacked; and that path is made narrower still by es-
carpments of the rocks, and barriers built on purpose to make the
approach more difficult.

10. Here we became mingled with the Persians, who were hastening with a run, racing with us, to make themselves masters of the
higher ground: and till the dawn of the next day we stood without
moving, so closely packed, that the bodies of those who were slain
were so propped up by the mass that they could not find room to fall to
the ground; and a soldier in front of me, whose head was cloven asunder into equal portions by a mighty sword-blow, still stood upright like
a log, being pressed upon all sides.

11. And although javelins were incessantly hurled from the battlements by every kind of engine, yet we were protected from that
danger by the proximity of the walls. And at last I got in at the postern
gate, which I found thronged by a multitude of both sexes flocking in
from the neighbouring districts. For it happened by chance on these
very days that it was the time of a great annual fair which was held in
the suburbs, and which was visited by multitudes of the country people.

12. In the mean time all was in disorder with every kind of noise;
some bewailing those whom they had lost; others being mortally
wounded; and many calling on their different relations whom the
crowd prevented them from discovering.

IX.

§ 1. This city had formerly been a very small one, till Constantius while Cæsar, at the same time that he built another town called
Antinopolis, surrounded Amida also with strong towers and stout
walls, that the people in the neighbourhood might have a safe place of

refuge. And he placed there a store of mural engines, making it formidable to the enemy, as he wished it to be called by his own name.

2. On the southern side it is watered by the Tigris, which passes close to it, making a kind of elbow: on the east it looks towards the plains of Mesopotamia, on the north it is close to the river Nymphæus, and is overshadowed by the chain of Mount Taurus, which separates the nations on the other side of the Tigris from Armenia. On the west it borders on the province of Gumathena, a fertile and well-cultivated district, in which is a village known as Abarne, celebrated for the healing properties of its hot springs. But in the very centre of Amida, under the citadel, there rises a rich spring of water, drinkable indeed, but often tainted with hot vapours.

3. In the garrison of this town, the fifth or Parthian legion was always located with a considerable squadron of native cavalry. But at that time six legions, by forced marches, had outstripped the Persian host in its advance, and greatly strengthened the garrison: they were the Magnentian and Decentian legions whom, after the end of the civil war, the emperor had sent as mutinous and discontented to the East, since there the only danger was from foreign wars: the tenth, and the thirteenth legion called the Fretensian:[99] and two legions of light infantry called præventores and superventores,[100] with Ælian, who was now a count. Of these latter, when only new recruits, we have already[101] spoken, as sallying out from Singara at the instigation of this same Ælian, then only one of the guard, and slaying a great number of Persians whom they had surprised in their sleep.

4. There was also the greater part of the force called companion archers, being squadrons of cavalry so named, in which all the freeborn barbarians serve, and who are conspicuous among all others for the splendour of their arms and for their prowess.

X.

§ 1. While the first onset of the Persians was by its unexpected vehemence throwing these troops into disorder, the king, with his native and foreign troops, having after leaving Bebase turned his march to the right, according to the advice of Antoninus, passed by Horre and Meiacarire and Charcha, as if he meant also to pass by Amida. And when he had come near the Roman forts, one of which is called Reman, and the other Busan, he learnt from some deserters that many persons had removed their treasures there for protection, trusting to their lofty and strong walls; and it was also added that there was there, with a great many valuables, a woman of exquisite beauty, the wife of a citizen of Nisibis named Craugasius, of great consideration by birth, character, and influence; with her little daughter.

2. Sapor, eager to seize what belonged to another, hastened on, and attacked the castle with force; and the garrison, being seized with a sudden panic at the variety of arms of the assailants, surrendered themselves, and all who had fled to them for protection; and at the first summons gave up the keys of the gates. Possession being taken, all that was stored there was ransacked; women bewildered with fear were dragged forth; and children clinging to their mothers were taught bitter suffering at the very beginning of their infancy.

3. And when Sapor, by asking each whose wife she was, had found that of Craugasius trembling with fear of violence, he allowed her to come in safety to him, and when he saw her, veiled as she was with a black veil to her lips, he kindly encouraged her with a promise that she should recover her husband, and that her honour should be preserved inviolate. For hearing that her husband was exceedingly devoted to her, he thought that by this bribe he might win him over to betray Nisibis.

4. And he also extended his protection to other virgins who, according to Christian rites, had been formally consecrated to the service of God, ordering that they should be kept uninjured, and be allowed to perform the offices of religion as they had been accustomed. Affecting clemency for a time, in order that those who were alarmed at his former ferocity and cruelty might now discard their fears, and come to him of their own accord, learning from these recent examples that he tempered the greatness of his success with humanity and courtesy.

Notes

[89] It is not known what towns are meant by Castra Herculis and Quadriburgium.

[90] Vespasian and Titus.

[91] Ammianus was still in attendance on Ursicinus.

[92] Homer, Od. xiii. I; translated by Pope—

> *"He ceased, but left, so pleasing on their ear,*
> *His voice, that listening still they seemed to hear."*

And imitated by Milton, Paradise Lost, ix. 1—

"The angel ended, and in Adam's ear
So pleasing left his voice that he awhile
Thought him still speaking, still stood fixed to hear."

[93] The battle of Hileia took place A.D. 348; that of Singara three years earlier.

[94] The Maritza, rising in Mount Hæmus, now the Balkan.

[95] Antoninus is meant, as Hadrian was succeeded by Antoninus Pius.

[96] Doriscus was the town where Xerxes reviewed and counted his army, as is related by Herodotus, vii. 60.

[97] "Ammianus has marked the chronology of this year by three signs which do not perfectly coincide with each other, or with the series of the history:—1. The corn was ripe when Sapor invaded Mesopotamia, 'cum jura stipulâ flavente turgerent'—a circumstance which, in the latitude of Aleppo, would naturally refer us to the month of April or May. 2. The progress of Sapor was checked by the overflowing of the Euphrates, which generally happens in July and August. 3. When Sapor had taken Amida, after a siege of seventy-three days, the autumn was far advanced. 'Autumno præcipiti hædorumque improbo sidere exorto.' To reconcile these apparent contradictions, we must allow for some delay in the Persian king, some inaccuracy in the historian, and some disorder in the seasons."—Gibbon, cap. xix.; ed. Bohn, vol. ii. 320. "Clinton, F.R., i. 442, sees no such difficulty as Gibbon has here supposed; he makes Sapor to have passed the Tigris in May, reached the Euphrates July 8th, arrived before Amida July 27th, and stormed the place October 7th."—Editor of Bohn's ed.

[98] That is, in the suburbs of Edessa, as cemeteries in ancient times were usually outside the walls of cities.

[99] It is not known what this name is derived from: some read Fortensis, instead of Fretensis, and those who prefer this reading derive it either from Fortis, brave; or from Fortia, a small town of Asiatic Sarmatia.

[100] Præventores, or "going before;" superventores, "coming after," as a reserve.

[101] In one of the earlier books which has been lost.

BOOK XIX

I.

§ 1. The king, rejoicing at this our disaster and captivity, and expecting other successes, advanced from this castle, and marching slowly, on the third day came to Amida.

2. And at daybreak, everything, as far as we could see, glittered with shining arms; and an iron cavalry filled the plains and the hills.

3. And he himself, mounted on his charger, and being taller than the rest, led his whole army, wearing instead of a crown a golden figure of a ram's head inlaid with jewels; being also splendid from the retinue of men of high rank and of different nations which followed him. And it was evident that his purpose was merely to try the garrison of the walls with a parley, as, in following out the counsel of Antoninus, he was hastening to another quarter.

4. But the deity of heaven, mercifully limiting the disasters of the empire within the compass of one region, led on this king to such an extravagant degree of elation, that he seemed to believe that the moment he made his appearance the besieged would be suddenly panic-stricken, and have recourse to supplication and entreaty.

5. He rode up to the gates, escorted by the cohort of his royal guard; and while pushing on more boldly, so that his very features might be plainly recognized, his ornaments made him such a mark for arrows and other missiles, that he would have been slain, if the dust had not hindered the sight of those who were shooting at him; so that after a part of his robe had been cut off by a blow of a javelin, he escaped to cause vast slaughter at a future time.

6. After this, raging as if against sacrilegious men who had violated a temple, he cried out that the lord of so many monarchs and nations had been insulted, and resolved to use all his efforts to destroy the city. But at the entreaty of his choicest generals not to break the example of mercy which he had so gloriously set, by indulging in anger, he was pacified, and the next day ordered the garrison to be summoned to surrender.

7. Therefore, at daybreak, Grumbates, king of the Chionitæ, went boldly up to the walls to effect that object, with a brave body of guards; and when a skilful reconnoitrer had noticed him coming within shot, he let fly his balista, and struck down his son in the flower of his youth, who was at his father's side, piercing through his breastplate, breast and all; and he was a prince who in stature and beauty was superior to all his comrades.

8. At his death all his countrymen took to flight, but presently returning in order to prevent his body from being carried off, and having roused with their dissonant clamours various tribes to their aid, a stern conflict arose, the arrows flying on both sides like hail.

9. The deadly struggle having been continued till the close of day, it was nightfall before the corpse of the young prince, which had been so stubbornly defended, was extricated from the heap of dead and streams of blood, amid the thick darkness; as formerly at Troy, the

armies fought in furious combat for the comrade of the Thessalian chieftain.[102]

10. At his death the count was sad, and all the nobles as well as his father were distressed at his sudden loss; and a cessation of arms having been ordered, the youth, so noble and beloved, was mourned after the fashion of his nation. He was carried out in the arms he was wont to wear, and placed on a spacious and lofty pile; around him ten couches were dressed, bearing effigies of dead men, so carefully laid out, that they resembled corpses already buried; and for seven days all the men in the companies and battalions celebrated a funeral feast, dancing, and singing melancholy kinds of dirges in lamentation for the royal youth.

11. And the women, with pitiable wailing, deplored with their customary weepings the hope of their nation thus cut off in the early bloom of youth; as the worshippers of Venus are often seen to do in the solemn festival of Adonis, which the mystical doctrines of religion show to be some sort of image of the ripened fruits of the earth.

II.

§ 1. When the body was burnt and the bones collected in a silver urn, which his father had ordered to be carried back to his native land, to be there buried beneath the earth, Sapor, after taking counsel, determined to propitiate the shade of the deceased prince by making the destroyed city of Amida his monument. Nor indeed was Grumbates willing to move onward while the shade of his only son remained unavenged.

2. And having given two days to rest, and sent out large bodies of troops to ravage the fertile and well-cultivated fields which were as heavy with crops as in the time of peace, the enemy surrounded the city with a line of heavy-armed soldiers five deep; and at the beginning of the third day the brilliant squadrons filled every spot as far as the eye could see in every direction, and the ranks marching slowly, took up the positions appointed to each by lot.

3. All the Persians were employed in surrounding the walls; that part which looked eastward, where that youth so fatal to us was slain, fell to the Chionitæ. The Vertæ were appointed to the south; the Albani watched the north; while opposite to the western gate were posted the Segestani, the fiercest warriors of all, with whom were trains of tall elephants, horrid with their wrinkled skins, which marched on slowly, loaded with armed men, terrible beyond the savageness of any other frightful sight, as we have often said.

4. When we saw these countless hosts thus deliberately collected for the conflagration of the Roman world, and directed to our own immediate destruction, we despaired of safety, and sought only how to end our lives gloriously, as we all desired.

5. From the rising of the sun to its setting, the enemy's lines stood immovable, as if rooted to the ground, without changing a step or uttering a sound; nor was even the neigh of a horse heard; and the men having withdrawn in the same order as they had advanced, after refreshing themselves with food and sleep, even before the dawn, returned, led by the clang of brazen trumpets, to surround the city, as if fated to fall with their terrible ring.

6. And scarcely had Grumbates, like a Roman fecial, hurled at us a spear stained with blood, according to his native fashion, than the whole army, rattling their arms, mounted up to the walls, and instantly the tumult of war grew fierce, while all the squadrons hastened with speed and alacrity to the attack, and our men on their side opposed them with equal fierceness and resolution.

7. Soon many of the enemy fell with their heads crushed by vast stones hurled from scorpions, some were pierced with arrows, others were transfixed with javelins, and strewed the ground with their bodies; others, wounded, fled back in haste to their comrades.

8. Nor was there less grief or less slaughter in the city, where the cloud of arrows obscured the air, and the vast engines, of which the Persians had got possession when they took Singara, scattered wounds everywhere.

9. For the garrison, collecting all their forces, returning in constant reliefs to the combat, in their eagerness to defend the city, fell wounded, to the hindrance of their comrades, or, being sadly torn as they fell, threw down those who stood near them, or if still alive, sought the aid of those skilful in extracting darts which had become fixed in their bodies.

10. So slaughter was met by slaughter, and lasted till the close of day, being scarcely stopped by the darkness of evening, so great was the obstinacy with which both sides fought.

11. And the watches of the night were passed under arms, and the hills resounded with the shouts raised on both sides, while our men extolled the valour of Constantius Cæsar as lord of the empire and of the world, and the Persians styled Sapor Saansas and Pyroses, which appellations mean king of kings, and conqueror in wars.

12. The next morning, before daybreak, the trumpet gave the signal, and countless numbers from all sides flocked like birds to a

contest of similar violence; and in every direction, as far as the eye could reach, nothing could be seen in the plains and valleys but the glittering arms of these savage nations.

13. And presently a shout was raised, and as the enemy rushed forward all at once, they were met by a dense shower of missiles from the walls; and as may be conjectured, none were hurled in vain, falling as they did among so dense a crowd. For while so many evils surrounded us, we fought as I have said before, with the hope, not of procuring safety, but of dying bravely; and from dawn to eventide the battle was evenly balanced, both fighting with more ferocity than method, and there arose the shouts of men striking and falling, so that from the eagerness of both parties there was scarcely any one who did not give or receive wounds.

14. At last, night put an end to the slaughter, and the losses on both sides caused a longer truce. For when the time intended for rest was allowed to us, continual sleepless toil still exhausted our little remaining strength, in spite of the dread caused by the bloodshed and the pallid faces of the dying, whom the scantiness of our room did not permit us even the last solace of burying; since within the circuit of a moderate city there were seven legions, and a vast promiscuous multitude of citizens and strangers of both sexes, and other soldiers, so that at least twenty thousand men were shut up within the walls.

15. So each attended to his own wounds as well as he could, availing himself of whatever assistance or remedies came in his way. While some, being severely wounded, died of loss of blood; and some, pierced through by swords, lay on the ground, and breathed their last in the open air; others who were pierced through and through the skilful refused to touch, in order not to pain them further by inflicting useless sufferings; some, seeking the doubtful remedy of extracting the arrows, only incurred agonies worse than death.

III.

§ 1. While the war was going on in this manner around Amida, Ursicinus, vexed at being dependent on the will of another, gave continual warning to Sabinianus, who had superior authority over the soldiers, and who still remained in the quarter of the tombs, to collect all his light-armed troops, and hasten by secret paths along the foot of the mountain chain, with the idea that by the aid of this light force, if chance should aid them, they might surprise some of the enemy's outposts, and attack with success the night watches of the army, which, with its vast circuit, was surrounding the walls, or else by incessant attacks might harass those who clung resolutely to the blockade.

2. But Sabinianus rejected this proposal as mischievous, and produced some letters from the emperor, expressly enjoining that all that could be done was to be done without exposing the troops to any danger; but his own secret motive he kept in his own bosom, namely, that he had been constantly recommended while at court to refuse his predecessor, who was very eager for glory, every opportunity of acquiring renown, however much it might be for the interest of the republic.

3. Extreme pains were taken, even to the ruin of the provinces, to prevent the gallant Ursicinus from being spoken of as the author of or partner in any memorable exploit. Therefore, bewildered with these misfortunes, Ursicinus, seeing that, though constantly sending spies to us (although from the strict watch that was set it was not easy for any one to enter the city), and proposing many advantageous plans, he did no good, seemed like a lion, terrible for his size and fierceness, but with his claws cut and his teeth drawn, so that he could not dare to save from danger his cubs entangled in the nets of the hunters.

IV.

§ 1. But in the city, where the number of the corpses which lay scattered over the streets was too great for any one to perform the funeral rites over them, a pestilence was soon added to the other calamities of the citizens; the carcases becoming full of worms and corruption, from the evaporation caused by the heat, and the various diseases of the people; and here I will briefly explain whence diseases of this kind arise.

2. Both philosophers and skilful physicians agree that excess of cold, or of heat, or of moisture, or of drought, all cause pestilences; on which account those who dwell in marshy or wet districts are subject to coughs and complaints in the eyes, and other similar maladies: on the other hand, those who dwell in hot climates are liable to fevers and inflammations. But since fire is the most powerful of all elements, so drought is the quickest at killing.

3. On this account it is that when the Greeks were toiling at the ten years' war,[103] to prevent a foreigner from profiting by his violation of a royal marriage, a pestilence broke out among them, and numbers died by the darts of Apollo, who is the same as the Sun.

4. Again, as Thucydides relates, that pestilence which at the beginning of the Peloponnesian war harassed the Athenians with a most

cruel kind of sickness, came by slow steps from the burning plains of Ethiopia to Attica.

5. Others maintain that the air and the water, becoming tainted by the smell of corpses, and similar things, takes away the healthiness of a place, or at all events that the sudden change of temperature brings forth slighter sicknesses.

6. Some again affirm that the air becomes heavier by emanations from the earth, and kills some individuals by checking the perspiration of the body, for which reason we learn from Homer, that, besides men, the other living creatures also died; and we know by many instances, that in such plagues this does occur.

7. Now the first species of pestilence is called pandemic; this causes those who live in dry places to be attacked by frequent heats. The second is called epidemic, which gets gradually more violent, dims the sight of the eyes, and awakens dangerous humours. The third is called lœmodes,[104] which is also temporary, but still often kills with great rapidity.

8. We were attacked by this deadly pestilence from the excessive heat, which our numbers aggravated, though but few died: and at last, on the night after the tenth day from the first attack, the heavy and dense air was softened by a little rain, and the health of the garrison was restored and preserved.

V.

§ 1. In the mean time the restless Persians were surrounding the city with a fence of wicker-work, and mounds were commenced; lofty towers also were constructed with iron fronts, in the top of each of which a balista was placed, in order to drive down the garrison from the battlements; but during the whole time the shower of missiles from the archers and slingers never ceased for a moment.

2. We had with us two of the legions which had served under Magnentius, and which, as we have said, had lately been brought from Gaul, composed of brave and active men well adapted for conflicts in the plain; but not only useless for such a kind of war as that by which we were now pressed, but actually in the way. For as they had no skill either in working the engines, or in constructing works, but were continually making foolish sallies, and fighting bravely, they always returned with diminished numbers; doing just as much good, as the saying is, as a bucket of water brought by a single hand to a general conflagration.

3. At last, when the gates were completely blocked, and they were utterly unable to get out, in spite of the entreaties of their tribunes, they became furious as wild beasts. But on subsequent occasions their services became conspicuous, as we shall show.

4. In a remote part of the walls on the southern side, which looks down on the Tigris, there was a high tower, below which yawned an abrupt precipice, which it was impossible to look over without giddiness. From this by a hollow subterranean passage along the foot of the mountain some steps were cut with great skill, which led up to the level of the city, by which water was secretly obtained from the river, as we have seen to be the case in all the fortresses in that district which are situated on any river.

5. This passage was dark, and because of the precipitous character of the rock was neglected by the besiegers, till, under the guidance of a deserter who went over to them, seventy Persian archers of the royal battalion, men of eminent skill and courage, being protected by the remoteness of the spot which prevented their being heard, climbed up by the steps one by one at midnight, and reached the third story of the tower. There they concealed themselves till daybreak, when they held out a scarlet cloak as a signal for commencing an assault, when they saw that the city was entirely surrounded by the multitude of their comrades; and then they emptied their quivers and threw them down at their feet, and with loud cries shot their arrows among the citizens with prodigious skill.

6. And presently the whole of the mighty host of the enemy assaulted the city with more ferocity than ever. And while we stood hesitating and perplexed to know which danger to oppose first, whether to make head against the foe above us, or against the multitude who were scaling the battlements with ladders, our force was divided; and five of the lighter balistæ were brought round and placed so as to attack our tower. They shot out heavy wooden javelins with great rapidity, sometimes transfixing two of our men at one blow, so that many of them fell to the ground severely wounded, and some jumped down in haste from fear of the creaking engines, and being terribly lacerated by the fall, died.

7. But by measures promptly taken, the walls were again secured on that side, and the engines replaced in their former situation.

8. And since the crime of desertion had increased the labours of our soldiers, they, full of indignation, moved along the battlements as if on level ground, hurling missiles of all kinds, and exerting themselves so strenuously that the Virtæ, who were attacking on the south

side, were repulsed covered by wounds, and retired in consternation to their tents, having to lament the fall of many of their number.

VI.

§ 1. Thus fortune showed us a ray of safety, granting us one day in which we suffered but little, while the enemy sustained a heavy loss; the remainder of the day was given to rest in order to recruit our strength; and at the dawn of the next morning we saw from the citadel an innumerable multitude, which, after the capture of the fort called Ziata, was being led to the enemy's camp. For a promiscuous multitude had taken refuge in Ziata on account of its size and strength; it being a place ten furlongs in circumference.

2. In those days many other fortresses also were stormed and burnt, and many thousands of men and women carried off from them into slavery; among whom were many men and women, enfeebled by age, who, fainting from different causes, broke down under the length of the journey, gave up all desire of life, and were hamstrung and left behind.

3. The Gallic soldiers beholding these wretched crowds, demanded by a natural but unseasonable impulse to be led against the forces of the enemy, threatening their tribunes and principal centurions with death if they refused them leave.

4. And as wild beasts kept in cages, being rendered more savage by the smell of blood, dash themselves against their movable bars in the hope of escaping, so these men smote the gates, which we have already spoken of as being blockaded, with their swords; being very anxious not to be involved in the destruction of the city till they had done some gallant exploit; or, if they ultimately escaped from their dangers, not to be spoken of as having done nothing worth speaking of, or worthy of their Gallic courage. Although when they had sallied out before, as they had often done, and had inflicted some loss on the raisers of the mounds, they had always experienced equal loss themselves.

5. We, at a loss what to do, and not knowing what resistance to oppose to these furious men, at length, having with some difficulty won their consent thereto, decided, since the evil could be endured no longer, to allow them to attack the Persian advanced guard, which was not much beyond bowshot; and then, if they could force their line, they might push their advance further. For it was plain that if they succeeded in this, they would cause a great slaughter of the enemy.

6. And while the preparations for this sally were being made, the walls were still gallantly defended with unmitigated labour and watching, and planting engines for shooting stones and darts in every direction. But two high mounds had been raised by the Persian infantry, and the blockade of the city was still pressed forward by gradual operations; against which our men, exerting themselves still more vigorously, raised also immense structures, topping the highest works of the enemy; and sufficiently strong to support the immense weight of their defenders.

7. In the mean time the Gallic troops, impatient of delay, armed with their axes and swords, went forth from the open postern gate, taking advantage of a dark and moonless night. And imploring the Deity to be propitious, and repressing even their breath when they got near the enemy, they advanced with quick step and in close order, slew some of the watch at the outposts, and the outer sentinels of the camp (who were asleep, fearing no such event), and entertained secret hopes of penetrating even to the king's tent if fortune assisted them.

8. But some noise, though slight, was made by them in their march, and the groans of the slain aroused many from sleep; and while each separately raised the cry "to arms," our soldiers halted and stood firm, not venturing to move any further forward. For it would not have been prudent, now that those whom they sought to surprise were awakened, to hasten into open danger, while the bands of Persians were now heard to be flocking to battle from all quarters.

9. Nevertheless the Gallic troops, with undiminished strength and boldness, continued to hew down their foes with their swords, though some of their own men were also slain, pierced by the arrows which were flying from all quarters; and they still stood firm, when they saw the whole danger collected into one point, and the bands of the enemy coming on with speed; yet no one turned his back: and they withdrew, retiring slowly as if in time to music, and gradually fell behind the pales of the camp, being unable to sustain the weight of the battalions pressing close upon them, and being deafened by the clang of the Persian trumpets.

10. And while many trumpets in turn poured out their clang from the city, the gates were opened to receive our men, if they should be able to reach them: and the engines for missiles creaked, though no javelins were shot from them, in order that the captains of the advanced guard of the Persians, ignorant of the slaughter of their comrades, might be terrified by the noise into falling back, and so allowing our gallant troops to be admitted in safety.

11. And owing to this manœuvre, the Gauls about daybreak entered the gate although with diminished numbers, many of them severely and others slightly wounded. They lost four hundred men this night, when if they had not been hindered by more formidable obstacles, they would have slain in his very tent not Rhesus nor Thracians sleeping before the walls of Troy, but the king of Persia, surrounded by one hundred thousand armed men.

12. To their leaders, as champions of valiant actions, the emperor, after the fall of the city, ordered statues in armour to be erected at Edessa in a frequented spot. And those statues are preserved up to the present time unhurt.

13. When the next day showed the slaughter which had been made, nobles and satraps were found lying amongst the corpses, and all kinds of dissonant cries and tears indicated the changed posture of the Persian host: everywhere was heard wailing; and great indignation was expressed by the princes, who thought that the Romans had forced their way through the sentries in front of the walls. A truce was made for three days by the common consent of both armies, and we gladly accepted a little respite in which to take breath.[105]

VII.

§ 1. Now the nations of the barbarians, being amazed at the novelty of this attempt, and rendered by it more savage than ever, discarding all delay, determined to proceed with their works, since open assaults availed them but little. And with extreme warlike eagerness they all now hastened to die gloriously, or else to propitiate the souls of the dead by the ruin of the city.

2. And now, the necessary preparations having been completed by the universal alacrity, at the rising of the day-star all kinds of structures and iron towers were brought up to the walls; on the lofty summits of which balistæ were fitted, which beat down the garrison who were placed on lower ground.

3. And when day broke the iron coverings of the bodies of the foe darkened the whole heaven, and the dense lines advanced without any skirmishers in front, and not in an irregular manner as before, but to the regular and soft music of trumpets; protected by the roofs of the engines, and holding before them wicker shields.

4. And when they came within reach of our missiles, the Persian infantry, holding their shields in front of them, and even then having difficulty in avoiding the arrows which were shot from the engines on the walls, for scarcely any kind of weapon found an empty space, they

broke their line a little; and even the cuirassiers were checked and began to retreat, which raised the spirits of our men.

5. Still the balistæ of the enemy, placed on their iron towers, and pouring down missiles with great power from their high ground on those in a lower position, spread a great deal of slaughter in our ranks. At last, when evening came on, both sides retired to rest, and the greater part of the night was spent by us in considering what device could be adopted to resist the formidable engines of the enemy.

6. At length, after we had considered many plans, we determined on one which the rapidity with which it could be executed made the safest—to oppose four scorpions to the four balistæ; which were carefully moved (a very difficult operation) from the place in which they were; but before this work was finished, day arrived, bringing us a mournful sight, inasmuch as it showed us the formidable battalions of the Persians, with their trains of elephants, the noise and size of which animals are such that nothing more terrible can be presented to the mind of man.

7. And while we were pressed on all sides with the vast masses of arms, and works, and beasts, still our scorpions were kept at work with their iron slings, hurling huge round stones from the battlements, by which the towers of the enemy were crushed and the balistæ and those who worked them were dashed to the ground, so that many were desperately injured, and many crushed by the weight of the falling structures. And the elephants were driven back with violence, and surrounded by the flames which we poured forth against them, the moment that they were wounded retired, and could not be restrained by their riders. The works were all burnt, but still there was no cessation from the conflict.

8. For the king of the Persians himself, who is never expected to mingle in the fight, being indignant at these disasters, adopting a new and unprecedented mode of action, sprang forth like a common soldier among his own dense columns; and as the very number of his guards made him the more conspicuous to us who looked from afar on the scene, he was assailed by numerous missiles, and was forced to retire after he had lost many of his escort, while his troops fell back by echellons; and at the end of the day, though frightened neither by the sad sight of the slaughter nor of the wounds, he at length allowed a short period to be given to rest.

VIII.

§ 1. Night had put an end to the combat; and when a slight rest had been procured from sleep, the moment that the dawn, looked for as the harbinger of better fortune, appeared, Sapor, full of rage and indignation, and perfectly reckless, called forth his people to attack us. And as his works were all burnt, as we have related, and the attack had to be conducted by means of their lofty mounds raised close to our walls, we also from mounds within the walls, as fast as we could raise them, struggled in spite of all our difficulties, with all our might, and with equal courage, against our assailants.

2. And long did the bloody conflict last, nor was any one of the garrison driven by fear of death from his resolution to defend the city. The conflict was prolonged, till at last, while the fortune of the two sides was still undecided, the structure raised by our men, having been long assailed and shaken, at last fell, as if by an earthquake.

3. And the whole space which was between the wall and the external mound being made level as if by a causeway or a bridge, opened a passage to the enemy, which was no longer embarrassed by any obstacles; and numbers of our men, being crushed or enfeebled by their wounds, gave up the struggle. Still men flocked from all quarters to repel so imminent a danger, but from their eager haste they got in one another's way, while the boldness of the enemy increased with their success.

4. By the command of the king all his troops now hastened into action, and a hand-to-hand engagement ensued. Blood ran down from the vast slaughter on both sides: the ditches were filled with corpses, and thus a wider path was opened for the besiegers. And the city, being now filled with the eager crowd which forced its way in, all hope of defence or of escape was cut off, and armed and unarmed without any distinction of age or sex were slaughtered like sheep.

5. It was full evening, when, though fortune had proved adverse, the bulk of our troops was still fighting in good order; and I, having concealed myself with two companions in an obscure corner of the city, now under cover of darkness, made my escape by a postern gate where there was no guard; and aided by my own knowledge of the country and by the speed of my companions, I at last reached the tenth milestone from the city.

6. Here, having lightly refreshed ourselves, I tried to proceed, but found myself, as a noble unaccustomed to such toil, overcome by fatigue of the march. I happened to fall in, however, with what, though a

most unsightly object, was to me, completely tired out, a most season-able relief.

7. A groom riding a runaway horse, barebacked and without a bridle, in order to prevent his falling had knotted the halter by which he was guiding him tightly to his left hand, and presently, being thrown, and unable to break the knot, he was torn to pieces as he was dragged over the rough ground and through the bushes, till at last the weight of his dead body stopped the tired beast; I caught him, and mounting him, availed myself of his services at a most seasonable moment, and after much suffering arrived with my companions at some sulphurous springs of naturally hot water.

8. On account of the heat we had suffered greatly from thirst, and had been crawling about for some time in search of water; and now when we came to this well it was so deep that we could not descend into it, nor had we any ropes; but, taught by extreme necessity, we tore up the linen clothes which we wore into long rags, which we made into one great rope, and fastened to the end of it a cap which one of us wore beneath his helmet; and letting that down by the rope, and draw-ing up water in it like a sponge, we easily quenched our thirst.

9. From hence we proceeded rapidly to the Euphrates, intending to cross to the other side in the boat which long custom had stationed in that quarter, to convey men and cattle across.

10. When lo! we see at a distance a Roman force with cavalry standards, scattered and pursued by a division of Persians, though we did not know from what quarter it had come so suddenly on them in their march.

11. This example showed us that what men call indigenous peo-ple are not sprung from the bowels of the earth, but merely appear unexpectedly by reason of the speed of their movements: and because they were seen unexpectedly in various places, they got the name of Sparti,[106] and were believed to have sprung from the ground, antiquity exaggerating their renown in a fabulous manner, as it does that of other things.

12. Roused by this sight, since our only hope of safety lay in our speed, we drew off through the thickets and woods to the high moun-tains; and from thence we went to Melitina, a town of the Lesser Armenia, where we found our chief just on the point of setting off, in whose company we went on to Antioch.

IX.

§ 1. In the mean time Sapor and the Persians began to think of returning home, because they feared to penetrate more inland with their prisoners and booty, now that the autumn was nearly over, and the unhealthy star of the Kids had arisen.

2. But amid the massacres and plunder of the destroyed city, Ælian the count, and the tribunes by whose vigour the walls of Amida had been defended, and the losses of the Persians multiplied, were wickedly crucified; and Jacobus and Cæsias, the treasurers of the commander of the cavalry, and others of the band of protectores, were led as prisoners, with their hands bound behind their backs; and the people of the district beyond the Tigris, who were diligently sought for, were all slain without distinction of rank or dignity.

3. But the wife of Craugasius, who, preserving her chastity inviolate, was treated with the respect due to a high-born matron, was mourning as if she were to be carried to another world without her husband, although she had indications afforded her that she might hope for a higher future.

4. Therefore, thinking of her own interests, and having a wise forecast of the future, she was torn with a twofold anxiety, loathing both widowhood and the marriage she saw before her. Accordingly, she secretly sent off a friend of sure fidelity, and well acquainted with Mesopotamia, to pass by Mount Izala, between the two forts called Maride and Lorne, and so to effect his entrance into Nisibis, calling upon her husband, with urgent entreaties and the revelation of many secrets of her own private condition, after hearing what the messenger could tell him, to come to Persia and live happily with her there.

5. The messenger, travelling with great speed through jungle roads and thickets, reached Nisibis, pretending that he had never seen his mistress, and that, as in all likelihood she was slain, he had availed himself of an accidental opportunity to make his escape from the enemy's camp. And so, being neglected as one of no importance, he got access to Craugasius, and told him what had happened. And having received from him an assurance that, as soon as he could do so with safety, he would gladly rejoin his wife, he departed, bearing the wished-for intelligence to the lady. She, when she received it, addressed herself, through the medium of Tamsapor, to the king, entreating him that, if the opportunity offered before he quitted the Roman territories, he would order her husband to be restored to her.

6. But the fact of this stranger having departed thus unexpectedly, without any one suspecting it, after his secret return, raised

suspicions in the mind of Duke Cassianus and the other nobles who had authority in the city, who addressed severe menaces to Craugasius, insisting that the man could neither have come nor have gone without his privity.

7. And he, fearing the charge of treason, and being very anxious lest the flight of the deserter should cause a suspicion that his wife was still alive and was well treated by the enemy, feigned to court a marriage with another virgin of high rank. And having gone out to a villa which he had eight miles from the city, as if with the object of making the necessary preparations for the wedding feast, he mounted a horse, and fled at full speed to a predatory troop of Persians which he had learnt was in the neighbourhood, and being cordially received, when it was seen from what he said who he was, he was delivered over to Tamsapor on the fifth day, and by him he was introduced to the king, and recovered not only his wife, but his family and all his treasures, though he lost his wife only a few months afterwards. And he was esteemed only second to Antoninus, though as a great poet has said,

"Longo proximus intervallo."[107]

8. For Antoninus was eminent both for genius and experience in affairs, and had useful counsels for every enterprise that could be proposed, while Craugasius was of a less subtle nature, though also very celebrated. And all these events took place within a short time after the fall of Amida.

9. But the king, though showing no marks of anxiety on his countenance, and though he appeared full of exultation at the fall of the city, still in the depths of his heart was greatly perplexed, recollecting that in the siege he had frequently sustained severe losses, and that he had lost more men, and those too of more importance than any prisoners whom he had taken from us, or than we had lost in all the battles that had taken place; as indeed had also been the case at Singara, and at Nisibis. In the seventy-three days during which he had been blockading Amida, he had lost thirty thousand soldiers, as was reckoned a few days later by Discenes, a tribune and secretary; the calculation being the more easily made because the corpses of our men very soon shrink and lose their colour, so that their faces can never be recognized after four days; but the bodies of the Persians dry up like the trunks of trees, so that nothing exudes from them, nor do they suffer from any suffusion of blood, which is caused by their more sparing diet, and by the dryness and heat of their native land.

X.

§ 1. While these events and troubles were proceeding rapidly in the remote districts of the East, the Eternal City was fearing distress from an impending scarcity of corn; and the violence of the common people, infuriated by the expectation of that worst of all evils, was vented upon Tertullus, who at that time was prefect of the city. This was unreasonable, since it did not depend upon him that the provisions were embarked in a stormy season in ships which, through the unusually tempestuous state of the sea, and the violence of contrary winds, were driven into any ports they could make, and were unable to reach the port of Augustus, from the greatness of the dangers which threatened them.

2. Nevertheless, Tertullus was continually troubled by the seditious movements of the people, who worked themselves up to great rage, being excited by the imminent danger of a famine; till, having no hope of preserving his own safety, he wisely brought his little boys out to the people, who, though in a state of tumultuous disorder, were often influenced by sudden accidents, and with tears addressed them thus:—

3. "Behold your fellow-citizens, who (may the gods avert the omen), unless fortune should take a more favourable turn, will be exposed to the same sufferings as yourselves. If then you think that by destroying them you will be saved from all suffering, they are in your power." The people, of their own nature inclined to mercy, were propitiated by this sad address, and made no answer, but awaited their impending fate with resignation.

4. And soon, by the favour of the deity who has watched over the growth of Rome from its first origin, and who promised that it should last for ever, while Tertullus was at Ostia, sacrificing in the temple of Castor and Pollux, the sea became calm, the wind changed to a gentle south-east breeze, and the ships in full sail entered the port, laden with corn to fill the granaries.

XI.

§ 1. While these perplexing transactions were taking place, intelligence full of importance and danger reached Constantius who was reposing in winter quarters at Sirmium, informing him (as he had already greatly feared) that the Sarmatian Limigantes, who, as we have before related, had expelled their masters from their hereditary homes, had learnt to despise the lands which had been generously allotted to them in the preceding year, in order to prevent so fickle a class from undertaking any mischievous enterprise, and had seized on the districts over the border; that they were straggling, according to their national custom, with great licence over the whole country, and would throw everything into disorder if they were not put down.

2. The emperor, judging that any delay would increase their insolence, collected from all quarters a strong force of veteran soldiers, and before the spring was much advanced, set forth on an expedition against them, being urged to greater activity by two considerations; first, because the army, having acquired great booty during the last summer, was likely to be encouraged to successful exertion in the hope of similar reward; and secondly, because, as Anatolius was at that time prefect of Illyricum, everything necessary for such an expedition could be readily provided without recourse to any stringent measures.

3. For under no other prefect's government (as is agreed by all), up to the present time, had the northern provinces ever been so flourishing in every point of view; all abuses being corrected with a kind and prudent hand, while the people were relieved from the burden of transporting the public stores (which often caused such losses as to ruin many families), and also from the heavy income tax. So that the natives of those districts would have been free from all damage and cause of complaint, if at a later period some detestable collectors had not come among them, extorting money, and exaggerating accusations, in order to build up wealth and influence for themselves, and to procure their own safety and prosperity by draining the natives; carrying their severities to the proscription and even execution of many of them.

4. To apply a remedy to this insurrection, the emperor set out, as I have said, with a splendid staff, and reached Valeria, which was formerly a part of Pannonia, but which had been established as a separate province, and received its new name in honour of Valeria, the daughter of Diocletian. And having encamped his army on the banks of the Danube, he watched the movements of the barbarians, who, before his arrival, had been proposing, under friendly pretences, to enter Pannonia, meaning to lay it waste during the severity of the winter season, before the snow had been melted by the warmth of spring and the river had become passable, and while our people were unable from the cold to bear bivouacking in the open air.

5. He at once therefore sent two tribunes, each accompanied by an interpreter, to the Limigantes, to inquire mildly why they had quitted the homes which at their own request had been assigned to them

after the conclusion of the treaty of peace, and why they were now straggling in various directions, and passing their boundaries in contempt of his prohibitions.

6. They made vain and frivolous excuses, fear compelling them to have recourse to lies, and implored the emperor's pardon, beseeching him to discard his displeasure, and to allow them to cross the river and come to him to explain the hardships under which they were labouring; alleging their willingness, if required, to retire to remoter lands, only within the Roman frontier, where, enjoying lasting peace and worshipping tranquillity as their tutelary deity, they would submit to the name and discharge the duties of tributary subjects.

7. When the tribunes returned and related this, the emperor, exulting that an affair which appeared full of inextricable difficulties was likely to be brought to a conclusion without any trouble, and being eager to add to his acquisitions, admitted them all to his presence. His eagerness for acquiring territory was fanned by a swarm of flatterers, who were incessantly saying that when all distant districts were at peace, and when tranquillity was established everywhere, he would gain many subjects, and would be able to enlist powerful bodies of recruits, thereby relieving the provinces, which would often rather give money than personal service (though this expectation has more than once proved very mischievous to the state).

8. Presently he pitched his camp near Acimincum,[108] where a lofty mound was raised to serve for a tribune; and some boats, loaded with soldiers of the legions, without their baggage, under command of Innocentius, an engineer who had suggested the measure, were sent to watch the channel of the river, keeping close under the bank; so that, if they perceived the barbarians in disorder, they might come upon them and surprise their rear, while their attention was directed elsewhere.

9. The Limigantes became aware of the measures thus promptly taken, but still employed no other means of defence than humility and entreaty; though secretly they cherished designs very different from those indicated by their words and gestures.

10. But when they saw the emperor on his high mound preparing a mild harangue, and about to address them as men who would prove obedient in future, one of them, seized with a sudden fury, hurled his shoe at the tribune, and cried out, "Marha, Marha!" which in their language is a signal of war; and a disorderly mob following him, suddenly raised their barbaric standard, and with fierce howls rushed upon the emperor himself.

11. And when he, looking down from his high position, saw the whole place filled with thousands of men running to and fro, and their drawn swords and rapiers threatening him with immediate destruction, he descended, and mingling both with the barbarians and his own men, without any one perceiving him or knowing whether he was an officer or a common soldier; and since there was no time for delay or inaction, he mounted a speedy horse, and galloped away, and so escaped.

12. But his few guards, while endeavouring to keep back the mutineers, who rushed on with the fierceness of fire, were all killed, either by wounds, or by being crushed beneath the weight of others who fell upon them; and the royal throne, with its golden cushion, was torn to pieces without any one making an effort to save it.

13. But presently, when it became known that the emperor, after having been in the most imminent danger of his life, was still in peril, the army, feeling it to be the most important of all objects to assist him, for they did not yet think him safe, and confiding in their prowess, though from the suddenness of the attack they were only half formed, threw themselves, with loud and warlike cries upon the bands of the barbarians, fearlessly braving death.

14. And because in their fiery valour our men were resolved to wipe out disgrace by glory, and were full of anger at the treachery of the foe, they slew every one whom they met without mercy, trampling all under foot, living, wounded, and dead alike; so that heaps of dead were piled up before their hands were weary of the slaughter. For the rebels were completely overwhelmed, some being slain, and others fleeing in fear, many of whom implored their lives with various entreaties, but were slaughtered with repeated wounds. And when, after they were all destroyed, the trumpets sounded a retreat, it was found that only a very few of our men were killed, and these had either been trampled down at first, or had perished from the insufficiency of their armour to resist the violence of the enemy.

15. But the most glorious death was that of Cella, the tribune of the Scutarii, who at the beginning of the uproar set the example of plunging first into the middle of the Sarmatian host.

16. After these blood-stained transactions, Constantius took what precautions prudence suggested for the security of his frontiers, and then returned to Sirmium, having avenged himself on the perfidity of his enemies. And having there settled everything which the occasion required, he quitted Sirmium and went to Constantinople, that by being nearer to the East, he might remedy the disasters which had been sustained at Amida, and having reinforced his army with new levies,

he might check the attempts of the king of Persia with equal vigour; as it was clear that Sapor, if Providence and some more pressing occupation did not prevent him, would leave Mesopotamia and bring the war over the plains on this side of that country.

XII.

§ 1. But amid these causes of anxiety, as if in accordance with old-established custom, instead of the signal for civil war, the trumpet sounded groundless charges of treason, and a secretary, whom we shall often have to speak of, named Paulus, was sent to inquire into these charges. He was a man skilful in all the contrivances of cruelty, making gain and profit of tortures and executions, as a master of gladiators does of his fatal games.

2. For as he was firm and resolute in his purpose of injuring people, he did not abstain even from theft, and invented all kinds of causes for the destruction of innocent men, while engaged in this miserable campaign.

3. A slight and trivial circumstance afforded infinite material for extending his investigations. There is a town called Abydum in the most remote corner of the Egyptian Thebais, where an oracle of the god, known in that region by the name of Besa, had formerly enjoyed some celebrity for its prophecies, and had sacred rites performed at it with all the ceremonies anciently in use in the neighbouring districts.

4. Some used to go themselves to consult this oracle, some to send by others documents containing their wishes, and with prayers couched in explicit language inquired the will of the deities; and the paper or parchment on which their wants were written, after the answer had been given, was sometimes left in the temple.

5. Some of these were spitefully sent to the emperor, and he, narrow minded as he was, though often deaf to other matters of serious consequence, had, as the proverb says, a soft place in his ear for this kind of information; and being of a suspicious and petty temper, became full of gall and fury; and immediately ordered Paulus to repair with all speed to the East, giving him authority, as to a chief of great eminence and experience, to try all the causes as he pleased.

6. And Modestus also, at that time count of the East, a man well suited for such a business, was joined with him in this commission. For Hermogenes of Pontus, at that time prefect of the prætorium, was passed over as of too gentle a disposition.

7. Paulus proceeded, as he was ordered, full of deadly eagerness and rage; inviting all kinds of calumnies, so that numbers from every

part of the empire were brought before him, noble and low born alike; some of whom were condemned to imprisonment, others to instant death.

8. The city which was chosen to witness these fatal scenes was Scythopolis in Palestine, which for two reasons seemed the most suitable of all places; first, because it was little frequented and secondly, because it was half-way between Antioch and Alexandria, from which city many of those brought before this tribunal came.

9. One of the first persons accused was Simplicius, the son of Philip; a man who, after having been prefect and consul, was now impeached on the ground that he was said to have consulted the oracle how to obtain the empire. He was sentenced to the torture by the express command of the emperor, who in these cases never erred on the side of mercy; but by some special fate he was saved from it, and with uninjured body was condemned to distant banishment.

10. The next victim was Parnasius, who had been prefect of Egypt, a man of simple manners, but now in danger of being condemned to death, and glad to escape with exile; because long ago he had been heard to say that when he left Patræ in Achaia, the place of his birth, with the view of procuring some high office, he had in a dream seen himself conducted on his road by several figures in tragic robes.

11. The next was Andronicus, subsequently celebrated for his liberal accomplishments and his poetry; he was brought before the court without having given any real ground for suspicion of any kind, and defended himself so vigorously that he was acquitted.

12. There was also Demetrius, surnamed Chytras, a philosopher, of great age, but still firm in mind and body; he, when charged with having frequently offered sacrifices in the temple of his oracle, could not deny it; but affirmed that, for the sake of propitiating the deity, he had constantly done so from his early youth, and not with any idea of aiming at any higher fortune by his questions; nor had he known any one who had aimed at such. And though he was long on the rack he supported it with great constancy, never varying in his statement, till at length he was acquitted and allowed to retire to Alexandria, where he was born.

13. These and a few others, justice, coming to the aid of truth, delivered from their imminent dangers. But as accusations extended more widely, involving numbers without end in their snares, many perished; some with their bodies mangled on the rack; others were condemned to death and confiscation of their goods; while Paulus kept

on inventing groundless accusations, as if he had a store of lies on which to draw, and suggesting various pretences for injuring people, so that on his nod, it may be said, the safety of every one in the place depended.

14. For if any one wore on his neck a charm against the quartan ague or any other disease, or if by any information laid by his ill-wishers he was accused of having passed by a sepulchre at nightfall, and therefore of being a sorcerer, and one who dealt in the horrors of tombs and the vain mockeries of the shades which haunt them, he was found guilty and condemned to death.

15. And the affairs went on as if people had been consulting Claros, or the oaks at Dodona, or the Delphic oracles of old fame, with a view to the destruction of the emperor.

16. Meantime, the crowd of courtiers, inventing every kind of deceitful flattery, affirmed that he would be free from all common misfortunes, asserting that his fate had always shone forth with vigour and power in destroying all who attempted anything injurious to him.

17. That indeed strict investigation should be made into such matters, no one in his senses will deny; nor do we question that the safety of our lawful prince, the champion and defender of the good, and on whom the safety of all other people depends, ought to be watched over by the combined zeal of all men; and for the sake of in-suring this more completely, when any treasonable enterprise is discovered, the Cornelian laws have provided that no rank shall be exempted even from torture if necessary for the investigation.

18. But it is not decent to exult unrestrainedly in melancholy events, lest the subjects should seem to be governed by tyranny, not by authority. It is better to imitate Cicero, who, when he had it in his power either to spare or to strike, preferred, as he tells us himself, to seek occasions for pardoning rather than for punishing, which is char-acteristic of a prudent and wise judge.

19. At that time a monster, horrible both to see and to describe, was produced at Daphne, a beautiful and celebrated suburb of Antioch; namely, an infant with two mouths, two sets of teeth, two heads, four eyes, and only two very short ears. And such a mis-shapen offspring was an omen that the republic would become deformed.

20. Prodigies of this kind are often produced, presaging events of various kinds; but as they are not now publicly expiated, as they were among the ancients, they are unheard of and unknown to people in general.

XIII.

§ 1. During this period the Isaurians, who had been tranquil for some time after the transactions already mentioned, and the attempt to take the city of Seleucia, gradually reviving, as serpents come out of their holes in the warmth of spring, descended from their rocky and pathless jungles, and forming into large troops, harassed their neighbours with predatory incursions; escaping, from their activity as mountaineers, all attempts of the soldiers to take them, and from long use moving easily over rocks and through thickets.

2. So Lauricius was sent among them as governor, with the additional title of count, to reduce them to order by fair means or foul. He was a man of sound civil wisdom, correcting things in general by threats rather than by severity, so that while he governed the province, which he did for some time, nothing happened deserving of particular notice.

Notes

[102] Patroclus, the companion of Achilles.

[103] The Trojan war. See the account of the pestilence, Homer Il. i. 50.

[104] *i.e.*, λοιμώδης, from λοιμὸς, pestilence. Pandemic means "attacking the whole people." Epidemic, "spreading from individual to individual."

[105] Ammian alludes to the expedition of Ulysses and Diomede related by Homer, Il. viii.

[106] Ammianus is wrong here; it was only the Thebans who were called Σπαρτοὶ, from σπείρω, to sow, because of the fable of the dragon's teeth sown by Cadmus; the Athenians, who claimed to be earthborn, not called Σπαρτοὶ, but αὐτόχθονες.

[107] A quotation from the description of the foot-race in Virgil, Æn. v. 320.

[108] Salankemen, in Hungary.

BOOK XX

I.

A.D. 360.

§ 1. These were the events which took place in Illyricum and in the East. But the next year, that of Constantius's tenth and Julian's third consulship, the affairs of Britain became troubled, in consequence of the incursions of the savage nations of Picts and Scots, who breaking the peace to which they had agreed, were plundering the districts on their borders, and keeping in constant alarm the provinces exhausted by former disasters, Cæsar, who was wintering at Paris, having his mind divided by various cares, feared to go to the aid of his subjects across the channel (as we have related Constans to have done), lest he should leave the Gauls without a governor, while the Allemanni were still full of fierce and warlike inclinations.

2. Therefore, to tranquillize these districts by reason or by force, it was decided to send Lupicinus, who was at that time commander of the forces; a man of talent in war, and especially skilful in all that related to camps, but very haughty, and smelling, as one may say, of the tragic buskin, while parts of his conduct made it a question which predominated—his avarice or his cruelty.

3. Accordingly, an auxiliary force of light-armed troops, Heruli and Batavi, with two legions from Mœsia, were in the very depth of winter put under the command of this general, with which he marched to Boulogne, and having procured some vessels and embarked his soldiers on them, he sailed with a fair wind, and reached Richborough on the opposite coast, from which place he proceeded to London, that he might there deliberate on the aspect of affairs, and take immediate measures for his campaign.

II.

§ 1. In the mean time, after the fall of Amida, and after Ursicinus had returned as commander of the infantry to the emperor's camp (for we have already mentioned that he had been appointed to succeed Barbatio), he was at once attacked by slanderers, who at first tried to whisper his character away, but presently openly brought forward false charges against him.

2. And the emperor, listening to them, since he commonly formed his opinions on vain conjecture, and was always ready to yield his judgment to crafty persons, appointed Arbetio and Florentius, the chief steward, as judges to inquire how it was that the town was destroyed. They rejected the plain and easily proved causes of the disaster, fearing that Eusebius, at that time high chamberlain, would be offended if they admitted proofs which showed undeniably that what had happened was owing to the obstinate inactivity of Sabinianus; and so distorting the truth, they examined only some points of no consequence, and having no bearing on the transaction.

3. Ursicinus felt the iniquity of this proceeding; and said, "Although the emperor despises me, still the importance of this affair is such that it cannot be judged of and punished by any decision lower than that of the emperor. Nevertheless, let him know what I venture to

prophesy, that while he is concerning himself about this disaster at Amida, of which he has received a faithful account; and while he gives himself up to the influence of the eunuchs, he will not in the ensuing spring,[109] even if he himself should come with the entire strength of his army, be able to prevent the dismemberment of Mesopotamia." This speech having been related to the emperor with many additions, and a malignant interpretation, Constantius became enraged beyond measure; and without allowing the affair to be discussed, or those things to be explained to him of which he was ignorant, he believed all the calumnies against Ursicinus, and deposing him from his office, ordered him into retirement; promoting Agilo, by a vast leap, to take his place, he having been before only a tribune of a native troop of Scutarii.

III.

§ 1. At the same time one day the sky in the east was perceived to be covered with a thick darkness, and from daybreak to noon the stars were visible throughout; and, as an addition to these terrors, while the light of heaven was thus withdrawn, and the world almost buried in clouds, men, from the length of the eclipse, began to believe that the sun had wholly disappeared. Presently, however, it was seen again like a new moon, then like a half-moon, and at last it was restored entire.

2. A thing which on other occasions did not happen so visibly except when after several unequal revolutions, the moon returns to exactly the same point at fixed intervals; that is to say, when the moon is found in the same sign of the zodiac, exactly opposite to the rays of the sun, and stops there a few minutes, which in geometry are called parts of parts.

3. And although the changes and motions of both sun and moon, as the inquiries into intelligible causes have remarked, perpetually return to the same conjunction at the end of each lunar month, still the sun is not always eclipsed on these occasions, but only when the moon, as by a kind of balance, is in the exact centre between the sun and our sight.

4. In short, the sun is eclipsed, and his brilliancy removed from our sight, when he and the moon, which of all the constellations of heaven is the lowest, proceeding with equal pace in their orbits, are placed in conjunction in spite of the height which separates them (as Ptolemy learnedly explains it), and afterwards return to the dimensions which are called ascending or descending points of the ecliptic con-

junctions: or, as the Greeks call them, defective conjunctions. And if these great lights find themselves in the neighbourhood of these points or knots, the eclipse is small.

5. But if they are exactly in the knots which form the points of intersection between the ascending and descending path of the moon, then the sky will be covered with denser darkness, and the whole atmosphere becomes so thick that we cannot see what is close to us.

6. Again, the sun is conceived to appear double when a cloud is raised higher than usual, which from its proximity to the eternal fires, shines in such a manner that it forms the brightness of a second orb as from a purer mirror.

7. Now let us come to the moon. The moon sustains a clear and visible eclipse when, being at the full, and exactly opposite to the sun, she is distant from his orb one hundred and eighty degrees, that is, is in the seventh sign; and although this happens at every full moon, still there is not always one eclipse.

8. But since she is always nearest to the earth as it revolves, and the most distant from the rest of the other stars, and sometimes exposes itself to the light which strikes it, and sometimes also is partially obscured by the intervention of the shade of night, which comes over it in the form of a cone; and then she is involved in thick darkness, when the sun, being surrounded by the centre of the lowest sphere, cannot illuminate her with his rays, because the mass of the earth is in the way; for opinions agree that the moon has no light of her own.

9. And when she returns to the same sign of the zodiac which the sun occupies, she is obscured (as has been said), her brightness being wholly dimmed, and this is called a conjunction of the moon.

10. Again the moon is said to be new when she has the sun above her with a slight variation from the perpendicular, and then she appears very thin to mankind, even when leaving the sun she reaches the second sign. Then, when she has advanced further, and shines brilliantly with a sort of horned figure, she is said to be crescent shaped; but when she begins to be a long way distant from the sun, and reaches the fourth sign, she gets a greater light, the sun's rays being turned upon her, and then she is of the shape of a semicircle.

11. As she goes on still further, and reaches the fifth sign, she assumes a convex shape, a sort of hump appearing from each side. And when she is exactly opposite the sun, she shines with a full light, having arrived at the seventh sign; and even while she is there, having advanced but a very little further, she begins to diminish, which we call waning; and as she gets older, she resumes the same shapes that

she had while increasing. But it is established by unanimous consent that she is never seen to be eclipsed except in the middle of her course.

12. But when we said that the sun moves sometimes in the ether, sometimes in the lower-world, it must be understood that the starry bodies, considered in relation to the universe, neither set nor rise; but only appear to do so to our sight on earth, which is suspended by the motion of some interior spirit, and compared with the immensity of things is but a little point, which causes the stars in their eternal order to appear sometimes fixed in heaven, and at others, from the imperfection of human vision, moving from their places. Let us now return to our original subject.

IV.

§ 1. Even while he was hastening to lead succours to the East, which, as the concurrent testimony of both spies and deserters assured him, was on the point of being invaded by the Persians, Constantius was greatly disturbed by the virtues of Julian, which were now becoming renowned among all nations, so highly did fame extol his great labours, achievements, and victories, in having conquered several kingdoms of the Allemanni, and recovered several towns in Gaul which had been plundered and destroyed by the barbarians, and having compelled the barbarians themselves to become subjects and tributaries of the empire.

2. Influenced by these considerations, and fearing lest Julian's influence should become greater, at the instigation, as it is said, of the prefect Florentius, he sent Decentius, the tribune and secretary, to bring away at once the auxiliary troops of the Heruli and Batavi, and the Celtæ, and the legion called Petulantes,[110] and three hundred picked men from the other forces; enjoining him to make all speed on the plea that their presence was required with the army which it was intended to march at the beginning of spring against the Parthians.

3. Also, Lupicinus was directed to come as commander of these auxiliary troops with the three hundred picked men and to lose no time, as it was not known that he had crossed over to Britain; and Sintula, at that time the superintendent of Julian's stables, was ordered to select the best men of the Scutarii and Gentiles,[111] and to bring them also to join the emperor.

4. Julian made no remonstrance, but obeyed these orders, yielding in all respects to the will of the emperor. But on one point he could not conceal his feelings nor keep silence: but entreated that those men

might be spared from this hardship who had left their homes on the other side of the Rhine, and had joined his army on condition of never being moved into any country beyond the Alps, urging that if this were known, it might be feared that other volunteers of the barbarian nations, who had often enlisted in our service on similar conditions, would be prevented from doing so in future. But he argued in vain.

5. For the tribune, disregarding his complaints, carried out the commands of the emperor, and having chosen out a band suited for forced marches, of pre-eminent vigour and activity, set out with them full of hope of promotion.

6. And as Julian, being in doubt what to do about the rest of the troops whom he was ordered to send, and revolving all kinds of plans in his mind, considered that the matter ought to be managed with great care, as there was on one side the fierceness of the barbarians, and on the other the authority of the orders he had received (his perplexity being further increased by the absence of the commander of the cavalry), he urged the prefect, who had gone some time before to Vienne under the pretence of procuring corn, but in reality to escape from military troubles, to return to him.

7. For the prefect bore in mind the substance of a report which he was suspected to have sent some time before, and which recommended the withdrawing from the defence of Gaul those troops so renowned for their valour, and already objects of dread to the barbarians.

8. The prefect, as soon as he had received Julian's letters, informing him of what had happened, and entreating him to come speedily to him to aid the republic with his counsels, positively refused, being alarmed because the letters expressly declared that in any crisis of danger the prefect ought never to be absent from the general. And it was added that if he declined to give his aid, Julian himself would, of his own accord, renounce the emblems of authority, thinking it better to die, if so it was fated, than to have the ruin of the provinces attributed to him. But the obstinacy of the prefect prevailed, and he resolutely refused to comply with the wishes thus reasonably expressed and enforced.

9. But during the delay which arose from the absence of Lupicinus and of any military movement on the part of the alarmed prefect, Julian, deprived of all assistance in the way of advice, and being greatly perplexed, thought it best to hasten the departure of all his troops from the stations in which they were passing the winter, and to let them begin their march.

10. When this was known, some one privily threw down a bitter libel near the standard of the Petulantes legion, which, among other things, contained these words,—"We are being driven to the farthest parts of the earth like condemned criminals, and our relations will become slaves to the Allemanni after we have delivered them from that first captivity by desperate battles."

11. When this writing was taken to head-quarters and read, Julian, considering the reasonableness of the complaint, ordered that their families should go to the East with them, and allowed them the use of the public wagons for the purpose of moving them. And as it was for some time doubted which road they should take, he decided, at the suggestion of the secretary Decentius, that they should go by Paris, where he himself still was, not having moved.

12. And so it was done. And when they arrived in the suburbs, the prince, according to his custom, met them, praising those whom he recognized, and reminding individuals of their gallant deeds, he congratulated them with courteous words, encouraging them to go cheerfully to join the emperor, as they would reap the most worthy rewards of their exertions where power was the greatest and most extensive.

13. And to do them the more honour, as they were going to a great distance, he invited their chiefs to a supper, when he bade them ask whatever they desired. And they, having been treated with such liberality, departed, anxious and sorrowful on two accounts, because cruel fortune was separating them at once from so kind a ruler and from their native land. And with this sorrowful feeling they retired to their camp.

14. But when night came on they broke out into open discontent, and their minds being excited, as his own griefs pressed upon each individual, they had recourse to force, and took up arms, and with a great outcry thronged to the palace, and surrounding it so as to prevent any one from escaping, they saluted Julian as emperor with loud vociferations, insisting vehemently on his coming forth to them; and though they were compelled to wait till daylight, still, as they would not depart, at last he did come forth. And when he appeared, they saluted him emperor with redoubled and unanimous cheers.

15. But he steadily resisted them individually and collectively, at one time showing himself indignant, at another holding out his hands and entreating and beseeching them not to sully their numerous victories with anything unbecoming, and not to let unseasonable rashness

and precipitation awaken materials for discord. At last he appeased them, and having addressed them mildly, he added—

16. "I beseech you let your anger depart for a while: without any dissension or attempt at revolution what you wish will easily be obtained. Since you are so strongly bound by love of your country, and fear strange lands to which you are unaccustomed, return now to your homes, certain that you shall not cross the Alps, since you dislike it. And I will explain the matter to the full satisfaction of the emperor, who is a man of great wisdom, and will listen to reason."

17. Nevertheless, after his speech was ended, the cries were repeated with as much vigour and unanimity as ever; and so vehement was the uproar and zeal, which did not even spare reproaches and threats, that Julian was compelled to consent. And being lifted up on the shield of an infantry soldier, and raised up in sight of all, he was saluted as Augustus with one universal acclamation, and was ordered to produce a diadem. And when he said that he had never had one, his wife's coronet or necklace was demanded.

18. And when he protested that it was not fitting for him at his first accession to be adorned with female ornaments, the frontlet of a horse was sought for, so that being crowned therewith, he might have some badge, however obscure, of supreme power. But when he insisted that that also would be unbecoming, a man named Maurus, afterwards a count, the same who was defeated in the defile of the Succi, but who was then only one of the front-rank men of the Petulantes, tore a chain off his own neck, which he wore in his quality of standard-bearer, and placed it boldly on Julian's head, who, being thus brought under extreme compulsion, and seeing that he could not escape the most imminent danger to his life if he persisted in his resistance, consented to their wishes, and promised a largesse of five pieces of gold and a pound of silver to every man.

19. After this Julian felt more anxiety than ever; and, keenly alive to the future consequences, neither wore his diadem or appeared in public, nor would he even transact the serious business which pressed upon his attention, but sought retirement, being full of consternation at the strangeness of the recent events. This continued till one of the decurions of the palace (which is an office of dignity) came in great haste to the standards of the Petulantes and of the Celtic legion, and in a violent manner exclaimed that it was a monstrous thing that he who had the day before been by their will declared emperor should have been privily assassinated.

20. When this was heard, the soldiers, as readily excited by what they did not know as by what they did, began to brandish their javelins, and draw their swords, and (as is usual at times of sudden tumult) to flock from every quarter in haste and disorder to the palace. The sentinels were alarmed at the uproar, as were the tribunes and the captain of the guard, and suspecting some treachery from the fickle soldiery, they fled, fearing sudden death to themselves.

21. When all before them seemed tranquil, the soldiers stood quietly awhile; and on being asked what was the cause of their sudden and precipitate movement, they at first hesitated, and then avowing their alarm for the safety of the emperor, declared they would not retire till they had been admitted into the council-chamber, and had seen him safe in his imperial robes.

V.

§ 1. When the news of these events reached the troops, whom we have spoken of as having already marched under the command of Sintula, they returned with him quietly to Paris. And an order having been issued that the next morning they should all assemble in the open space in front of the camp, Julian advanced among them, and ascended a tribunal more splendid than usual, surrounded with the eagles, standards, and banners, and guarded by a strong band of armed soldiers.

2. And after a moment's quiet, while he looked down from his height on the countenances of those before him, and saw them all full of joy and alacrity, he kindled their loyalty with a few simple words, as with a trumpet.

3. "The difficulty of my situation, O brave and faithful champions of myself and of the republic, who have often with me exposed your lives for the welfare of the provinces, requires that, since you have now by your resolute decision raised me, your Cæsar, to the highest of all dignities, I should briefly set before you the state of affairs, in order that safe and prudent remedies for their new condition may be devised.

4. "While little more than a youth, as you well know, I was for form's sake invested with the purple, and by the decision of the emperor was intrusted to your protection. Since that time I have never forgotten my resolution of a virtuous life: I have been seen with you as the partner of all your labours, when, in consequence of the diminution of the confidence felt in us by the barbarians, terrible disasters fell upon the empire, our cities being stormed, and countless thousands of men being slain, and even the little that was left to us being in a very

tottering condition. I think it superfluous to recapitulate how often, in the depth of winter, beneath a frozen sky, at a season when there is usually a cessation from war both by land and sea, we have defeated with heavy loss the Allemanni, previously unconquered.

5. "One circumstance may neither be passed over nor suppressed. On that glorious day which we saw at Strasburg, which brought perpetual liberty to Gaul, we together, I throwing myself among the thickly falling darts, and you being invincible by your vigour and experience, repelled the enemy who poured upon us like a torrent; slaying them as we did with the sword, or driving them to be drowned in the river, with very little loss of our own men, whose funerals we celebrated with glorious panegyrics rather than with mourning.

6. "It is my belief that after such mighty achievements posterity will not be silent respecting your services to the republic, in every country, if you now, in case of any danger or misfortune, vigorously support with your valour and resolution me whom you have raised to the lofty dignity of emperor.

7. "But to maintain things in their due order, so as to preserve to brave men their well-merited rewards and prevent underhand ambition from forestalling your honours, I make this rule in the honourable presence of your counsel. That no civil or military officer shall be promoted from any other consideration than that of his own merits; and he shall be disgraced who solicits promotion for any one on any other ground."

8. The lower class of soldiers, who had long been deprived of rank or reward, were encouraged by this speech to entertain better hopes, and now rising up with a great noise, and beating their shields with their spears, they with unanimous shouts showed their approbation of his language and purpose.

9. And that no opportunity, however brief, might be afforded to disturb so wise an arrangement, the Petulantes and Celtic legion immediately besought him, on behalf of their commissaries, to give them the government of any provinces he pleased, and when he refused them, they retired without being either offended or out of humour.

10. But the very night before the day on which he was thus proclaimed emperor, Julian had mentioned to his most intimate friends that during his slumbers some one had appeared to him in a dream, in the form and habit of the genius of the empire, who uttered these words in a tone of reproach: "For some time, Julian, have I been secretly watching the door of thy palace, wishing to increase thy dignity,

and I have often retired as one rejected; but if I am not now admitted, when the opinion of the many is unanimous, I shall retire discouraged and sorrowful. But lay this up in the depth of thy heart, that I will dwell with thee no longer."

VI.

§ 1. While these transactions were proceeding in Gaul, to the great anxiety of many, the fierce king of Persia (the advice of Antoninus being now seconded by the arrival of Craugasius), burning with eagerness to obtain Mesopotamia, while Constantius with his army was at a distance, crossed the Tigris in due form with a vast army, and laid siege to Singara with a thoroughly equipped force, sufficient for the siege of a town which, in the opinion of the chief commanders of those regions, was abundantly fortified and supplied.

2. The garrison, as soon as they saw the enemy, while still at a distance, at once closed their gates, and with great spirit thronged to the towers and battlements, collecting on them stones and warlike engines. And then, having made all their preparations, they stood prepared to repel the advancing host if they should venture to approach the walls.

3. Therefore the king, when he arrived and found that, though they would admit some of his nobles near enough to confer with them, he could not, by any conciliatory language, bend the garrison to his wishes, he gave one entire day to rest, and then, at daybreak, on a signal made by the raising of a scarlet flag, the whole city was surrounded by men carrying ladders, while others began to raise engines; all being protected by fences and penthouses while seeking a way to assail the foundation of the walls.

4. Against these attempts the citizens, standing on the lofty battlements, drove back with stones and every kind of missile the assailants who were seeking with great ferocity to find an entrance.

5. For many days the struggle continued without any decided result, many being wounded and killed on both sides. At last, the struggle growing fiercer, one day on the approach of evening a very heavy battering-ram was brought forward among other engines, which battered a round tower with repeated blows, at a point where we mentioned that the city had been laid open in a former siege.

6. The citizens at once repaired to this point, and a violent conflict arose in this small space; torches and firebrands were brought from all quarters to consume this formidable engine, while arrows and bullets were showered down without cessation on the assailants. But

the keenness of the ram prevailed over every means of defence, digging through the mortar of the recently cemented stones, which was still moist and unsettled.

7. And while the contest was thus proceeding with fire and sword, the tower fell, and a path was opened into the city, the place being stripped of its defenders, whom the magnitude of the danger had scattered. The Persian bands raised a wild shout, and without hindrance filled every quarter of the city. A very few of the inhabitants were slain, and all the rest, by command of Sapor, were taken alive and transported to the most distant regions of Persia.

8. There had been assigned for the protection of this city two legions, the first Flavian and the first Parthian, and a great body of native troops, as well as a division of auxiliary cavalry which had been shut up in it through the suddenness of the attack made upon it. All of these, as I have said, were taken prisoners, without receiving any assistance from our armies.

9. For the greater part of our army was in tents taking care of Nisibis, which was at a considerable distance. But even if it had not been so, no one even in ancient times could easily bring aid to Singara when in danger, since the whole country around laboured under a scarcity of water. And although a former generation had placed this fort very advisedly, to check sudden movements of hostility, yet it was a great burden to the state, having been several times taken, and always involving the loss of its garrison.

VII.

§ 1. After Singara had fallen, Sapor prudently avoided Nisibis, recollecting the losses which he had several times sustained before it, and turned to the right by a circuitous path, hoping either to subdue by force or to win by bribes the garrison of Bezabde, which its founders also called Phœnice, and to make himself master of that town, which is an exceedingly strong fortress, placed on a hill of moderate height, and close to the banks of the Tigris, having a double wall, as many places have which from their situation are thought to be especially exposed. For its defence three legions had been assigned; the second Flavian, the second Armenian, and the second Parthian, with a large body of archers of the Zabdiceni, a tribe subject to us, in whose territory this town was situated.

2. At the beginning of the siege, the king, with an escort of glittering cuirassiers, himself taller than any of them, rode entirely round the camp, coming up boldly to the very edge of the fosse, where he

was at once a mark for the unerring bullets of the balistæ, and arrows; but he was so completely covered with thick scale-armour that he retired unhurt.

3. Then laying aside his anger, he sent some heralds with all due solemnity, courteously inviting the besieged to consult the safety of their lives, and seeing the desperateness of their situation, to put an end to the siege by a timely surrender; to open their gates and come forth, presenting themselves as suppliants before the conqueror of nations.

4. When these messengers approached the walls, the garrison spared them because they had with them some men of noble birth, who had been made prisoners at Singara, and were well known to the citizens; and out of pity to them no one shot an arrow, though they would give no reply to the proposal of peace.

5. Then a truce being made for a day and night, before dawn on the second day the entire force of the Persians attacked the palisade with ferocious threats and cries, coming up boldly to the walls, where a fierce contest ensued, the citizens resisting with great vigour.

6. So that many of the Parthians[112] were wounded, because some of them carrying ladders, and others wicker screens, advanced as it were blindfold, and were not spared by our men. For the clouds of arrows flew thickly, piercing the enemy packed in close order. At last, after sunset the two sides separated, having suffered about equal loss: and the next day before dawn the combat was renewed with greater vehemence than before, the trumpets cheering the men on both sides, and again a terrible slaughter of each took place, both armies struggling with the most determined obstinacy.

7. But on the following day both armies by common consent rested from their terrible exertions, the defenders of the walls and the Persians being equally dismayed. When a Christian priest made sign by gestures that he desired to go forth, and having received a promise that he should be allowed to return in safety, he advanced to the king's tent.

8. When he was permitted to speak, he, with gentle language, urged the Persians to depart to their own country, affirming that after the losses each side had sustained they had reason perhaps to fear even greater disasters in future. But these and other similar arguments were uttered to no purpose. The fierce madness of the king robbing them of their effect, as Sapor swore positively that he would never retire till he had destroyed our camp.

9. Nevertheless a groundless suspicion was whispered against the bishop, wholly false in my opinion, though supported by the assertions of many, that he had secretly informed Sapor what part of the wall to attack, as being internally slight and weak. Though the suspicion derived some corroboration from the fact that afterwards the engines of the enemy were carefully and with great exultation directed against the places which were weakest, or most decayed, as if those who worked them were acquainted with what parts were most easily penetrable.

10. And although the narrowness of the causeway made the approach to the walls hard, and though the battering-rams when equipped were brought forward with great difficulty, from fear of the stones and arrows hurled upon the assailants by the besieged, still neither the balistæ nor the scorpions rested a moment, the first shooting javelins, and the latter hurling showers of stones, and baskets on fire, smeared with pitch and tar; and as these were perpetually rolled down, the engines halted as if rooted to the ground, and fiery darts and firebrands well-aimed set them on fire.

11. Still while this was going on, and numbers were falling on both sides, the besiegers were the more eager to destroy a town, strong both by its natural situation and its powerful defences, before the arrival of winter, thinking it impossible to appease the fury of their king if they should fail. Therefore neither abundant bloodshed nor the sight of numbers of their comrades pierced with deadly wounds could deter the rest from similar audacity.

12. But for a long time, fighting with absolute desperation, they exposed themselves to imminent danger; while those who worked the battering-rams were prevented from advancing by the vast weight of millstones, and all kinds of fiery missiles hurled against them.

13. One battering-ram was higher than the rest, and was covered with bull's hides wetted, and being therefore safer from any accident of fire, or from lighted javelins, it led the way in the attacks on the wall with mighty blows, and with its terrible point it dug into the joints of the stones till it overthrew the tower. The tower fell with a mighty crash, and those in it were thrown down with a sudden jerk, and breaking their limbs, or being buried beneath the ruins, perished by various and unexpected kinds of death; then, a safer entrance having been thus found, the multitude of the enemy poured in with their arms.

14. While the war-cry of the Persians sounded in the trembling ears of the defeated garrison, a fierce battle within the narrower bounds raged within the walls, while bands of our men and of the en-

emy fought hand to hand, being jammed together, with swords drawn on both sides, and no quarter given.

15. At last the besieged, after making head with mighty exertion against the destruction which long seemed doubtful, were overwhelmed with the weight of the countless host which pressed upon them. And the swords of the furious foe cut down all they could find; children were torn from their mother's bosom, and the mothers were slain, no one regarding what he did. Among these mournful scenes the Persians, devoted to plunder, loaded with every kind of booty, and driving before them a vast multitude of prisoners, returned in triumph to their tents.

16. But the king, elated with insolence and triumph, having long been desirous to obtain possession of Phœnice, as a most important fortress, did not retire till he had repaired in the strongest manner that portion of the walls which had been shaken, and till he had stocked it with ample magazines of provisions, and placed in it a garrison of men noble by birth and eminent for their skill in war. For he feared (what indeed happened) that the Romans, being indignant at the loss of this their grand camp, would exert themselves with all their might to recover it.

17. Then, being full of exultation, and cherishing greater hopes than ever of gaining whatever he desired, after taking a few forts of small importance, he prepared to attack Victa, a very ancient fortress, believed to have been founded by Alexander, the Macedonian, situated on the most distant border of Mesopotamia, and surrounded with winding walls full of projecting angles, and so well furnished at all points as to be almost unassailable.

18. And when he had tried every expedient against it, at one time trying to bribe the garrison with promises, at another to terrify them with threats of torture, and employing all kinds of engines such as are used in sieges, after sustaining more injury than he inflicted, he at last retired from his unsuccessful enterprise.

VIII.

§ 1. These were the events of this year between the Tigris and the Euphrates. And when frequent intelligence of them had reached Constantius, who was in continual dread of Parthian expeditions, and was passing the winter at Constantinople, he devoted greater care than ever to strengthening his frontiers with every kind of warlike equipment. He collected veterans, and enlisted recruits, and increased the legions with reinforcements of vigorous youths, who had already repeatedly signalized their valour in the battles of the eastern campaigns: and beside these he collected auxiliary forces from among the Scythians by urgent requests and promises of pay, in order to set out from Thrace in the spring, and at once march to the disturbed provinces.

2. During the same time Julian, who was wintering at Paris, alarmed at the prospect of the ultimate issue of the events in that district, became full of anxiety, feeling sure, after deep consideration, that Constantius would never give his consent to what had been done in his case, since he had always disdained him as a person of no importance.

3. Therefore, after much reflection on the somewhat disturbed beginning which the present novel state of affairs showed, he determined to send envoys to him to relate all that had taken place; and he gave them letters setting forth fully what had been done, and what ought to be done next, supporting his recommendations by proofs.

4. Although in reality he believed that the emperor was already informed of all, from the report of Decentius, who had returned to him some time before; and of the chamberlains who had recently gone back from Gaul, after having brought him some formal orders. And although he was not in reality vexed at his promotion, still he avoided all arrogant language in his letters, that he might not appear to have suddenly shaken off his authority. Now the following was the purport of his letters.

5. "I have at all times been of the same mind, and have adhered to my original intentions, not less by my conduct than by my promises, as far as lay in my power, as has been abundantly plain from repeated actions of mine.

6. "And up to this time, since you created me Cæsar, and exposed me to the din of war, contented with the power you conferred on me, as a faithful officer I have sent you continued intelligence of all your affairs proceeding according to your wishes; never speaking of my own dangers; though it can easily be proved, that, while the Germans have been routed in every direction, I have always been the first in all toils and the last to allow myself any rest.

7. "But allow me to say, that if any violent change has taken place, as you think, the soldier who has been passing his life in many terrible wars without reward, has only completed what he has long had under consideration, being indignant and impatient at being only under a chief of the second class, as knowing that from a Cæsar no adequate reward for his continued exertions and frequent victories could possibly be procured.

8. "And while angry at the feeling that he could neither expect promotion nor annual pay, he had this sudden aggravation to his discontent, that he, a man used to cold climates, was ordered to march to the most remote districts of the East, to be separated from his wife and children, and to be dragged away in want and nakedness. This made him fiercer than usual; and so the troops one night collected and laid siege to the palace, saluting with loud and incessant outcries Julian as emperor.

9. "I shuddered at their boldness, I confess, and withdrew myself. And retiring while I could, I sought safety in concealment and disguise—and as they would not desist, armed, so to say, with the shield of my own free heart, I came out before them all, thinking that the tumult might be appeased by authority, or by conciliatory language.

10. "They became wonderfully excited, and proceeded to such lengths that, when I endeavoured to overcome their pertinacity with my entreaties, they came close up to me, threatening me with instant death. At last I was overcome, and arguing with myself that if I were murdered by them some one else would willingly accept the dignity of emperor, I consented, hoping thus to pacify their armed violence.

11. "This is the plain account of what has been done; and I entreat you to listen to it with mildness. Do not believe that anything else is the truth; and do not listen to malignant men who deal in mischievous whispers, always eager to seek their own gain by causing ill will between princes. Banish flattery, which is the nurse of vice, and listen to the voice of that most excellent of all virtues, justice. And receive with good faith the equitable condition which I propose, considering in your mind that such things are for the interest of the Roman state, and of us also who are united by affection of blood, and by an equality of superior fortune.

12. "And pardon me. These reasonable requests of mine I am not so anxious to see carried out, as to see them approved by you as expedient and proper; and I shall with eagerness follow all your instructions.

13. "What requires to be done I will briefly explain. I will provide you some Spanish draught horses, and some youths to mingle with the Gentiles and Scutarii of the Letian tribe, a race of barbarians on the side of the Rhine; or else of those people which have come over to our side. And I promise till the end of my life to do all I can to assist you, not only with gratitude, but with eagerness.

14. "Your clemency will appoint us prefects for our prætorium of known equity and virtue: the appointment of the ordinary judges, and

the promotion of the military officers it is fair should be left to me; as also the selection of my guard. For it would be unreasonable, when it is possible to be guarded against, that those persons should be placed about an emperor of whose manners and inclinations he is ignorant.

15. "These things I can further assure you of positively. The Gauls will neither of their own accord, nor by any amount of compulsion, be brought to send recruits to foreign and distant countries, since they have been long harassed by protracted annoyances and heavy disasters, lest the youth of the nation should be destroyed, and the whole people, while recollecting their past sufferings, should abandon themselves to despair for the future.

16. "Nor is it fit to seek from hence assistance against the Parthians, when even now the attempts of the barbarians against this land are not brought to an end, and while, if you will suffer me to tell the truth, these provinces are still exposed to continual dangers on being deprived of all foreign or adequate assistance.

17. "In speaking thus, I do think I have written to you in a manner suited to the interests of the state, both in my demands and my entreaties. For I well know, not to speak in a lofty tone, though such might not misbecome an emperor, what wretched states of affairs, even when utterly desperate and given up, have been before now retrieved and re-established by the agreement of princes, each yielding reciprocally to one another. While it is also plain from the example of our ancestors, that rulers who acknowledge and act upon such principles do somehow ever find the means of living prosperously and happily, and leave behind them to the latest posterity an enviable fame."

18. To these letters he added others of a more secret purport, to be given privily to Constantius, in which he blamed and reproached him; though their exact tenor was not fit to be known, nor if known, fit to be divulged to the public.

19. For the office of delivering these letters, men of great dignity were chosen; namely, Pentadius, the master of the ceremonies, and Eutherius, at that time the principal chamberlain; who were charged, after they had delivered the letters, to relate what they had seen, without suppressing anything; and to take their own measures boldly on all future emergencies which might arise.

20. In the mean time the flight of Florentius, the prefect, aggravated the envy with which these circumstances were regarded. For he, as if he foresaw the commotion likely to arise, as might be gathered from general conversation, from the act of sending for the troops, had

departed for Vienne (being also desirous to get out of the way of Julian, whom he had often slandered), pretending to be compelled to this journey for the sake of providing supplies for the army.

21. Afterwards, when he had heard of Julian's being raised to the dignity of emperor, being greatly alarmed, and giving up almost all hope of saving his life, he availed himself of his distance from Julian to escape from the evils which he suspected; and leaving behind him all his family, he proceeded by slow journeys to Constantius; and to prove his own innocence he brought forward many charges of rebellion against Julian.

22. And after his departure, Julian, adopting wise measures, and wishing it to be known that, even if he had him in his power, he would have spared him, allowed his relations to take with them all their property, and even granted them the use of the public conveyances to retire with safety to the East.

IX.

§ 1. The envoys whom I have mentioned took equal care to discharge their orders; but while eager to pursue their journey they were unjustly detained by some of the superior magistrates on their road; and having been long and vexatiously delayed in Italy and Illyricum, they at last passed the Bosphorus, and advancing by slow journeys, they found Constantius still staying at Cæsarea in Cappadocia, a town formerly known as Mazaca, admirably situated at the foot of Mount Argæus, and of high reputation.

2. Being admitted to the presence, they received permission to present their letters; but when they were read the emperor became immoderately angry, and looking askance at them so as to make them fear for their lives, he ordered them to be gone without asking them any questions or permitting them to speak.

3. But in spite of his anger he was greatly perplexed to decide whether to move those troops whom he could trust against the Persians, or against Julian; and while he was hesitating, and long balancing between the two plans, he yielded to the useful advice of some of his counsellors, and ordered the army to march to the East.

4. Immediately also he dismissed the envoys, and ordered his quæstor Leonas to go with all speed with letters from him to Julian; in which he asserted that he himself would permit no innovators, and recommended Julian, if he had any regard for his own safety or that of his relations, to lay aside his arrogance, and resume the rank of Cæsar.

5. And, in order to alarm him by the magnitude of his preparations, as if he really was possessed of great power, he appointed Nebridius, who was at that time Julian's quæstor, to succeed Florentius as prefect of the prætorium, and made Felix the secretary, master of the ceremonies, with several other appointments. Gumoharius, the commander of the heavy infantry, he had already appointed to succeed Lupicinus, before any of these events were known.

6. Accordingly Leonas reached Paris, and was there received as an honourable and discreet man; and the next day, when Julian had proceeded into the plain in front of the camp with a great multitude of soldiers and common people, which he had ordered to assemble on purpose, he mounted a tribune, in order from that high position to be more conspicuous, and desired Leonas to present his letters; and when he had opened the edict which had been sent, and began to read it, as soon as he arrived at the passage that Constantius disapproved of all that had been done, and desired Julian to be content with the power of a Cæsar, a terrible shout was raised on all sides,

7. "Julian emperor, as has been decreed by the authority of the province, of the army, and of the republic; which is indeed re-established, but which still dreads the renewed attacks of the barbarians."

8. Leonas heard this, and, after receiving letters from Julian, stating what had occurred, was dismissed in safety: the only one of the emperor's appointments which was allowed to take effect was that of Nebridius, which Julian in his letters had plainly said would be in accordance with his wishes. For he himself had some time before appointed Anatolius to be master of the ceremonies, having been formerly his private secretary; and he had also made such other appointments as seemed useful and safe.

9. And since, while matters were going on in this matter, Lupicinus, as being a proud and arrogant man, was an object of fear, though absent and still in Britain; and since there was a suspicion that if he heard of these occurrences while on the other side of the channel, he might cause disorders in the island, a secretary was sent to Boulogne to take care that no one should be allowed to cross; and as that was contrived, Lupicinus returned without hearing of any of these matters, and so had no opportunity of giving trouble.

X.

§ 1. But Julian, being gratified at his increase of rank, and at the confidence of the soldiers in him, not to let his good fortune cool, or to give any colour for charging him with inactivity or indolence, after he had sent his envoys to Constantius, marched to the frontier of the province of lower Germany; and having with him all the force which the business in hand demanded, he approached the town of Santon.[113]

2. Then crossing the Rhine, he suddenly entered the district belonging to a Frank tribe, called the Attuarii, men of a turbulent character, who at that very moment were licentiously plundering the districts of Gaul. He attacked them unexpectedly while they were apprehensive of no hostile measures, but were reposing in fancied security, relying on the ruggedness and difficulty of the roads which led into their country, and which no prince within their recollection had ever penetrated. He, however, easily surmounted all difficulties, and having put many to the sword and taken many prisoners, he granted the survivors peace at their request, thinking such a course best for their neighbours.

3. Then with equal celerity he repassed the river, and examining carefully the state of the garrisons on the frontier, and putting them in a proper state, he marched towards Basle; and having recovered the places which the barbarians had taken and still retained in their hands, and having carefully strengthened them, he went to Vienne, passing through Besançon, and there took up his winter quarters.

XI.

§ 1. These were the events which took place in Gaul, and while they were thus conducted with prudence and good fortune, Constantius, having summoned Arsaces, king of Armenia, and having received him with great courtesy, advised and exhorted him to continue friendly and faithful to us.

2. For he had heard that the king of Persia had often tried by deceits and threats, and all kinds of stratagems, to induce him to forsake the Roman alliance and join his party.

3. But he, vowing with many oaths that he would rather lose his life than change his opinion, received ample rewards, and returned to his kingdom with the retinue which he brought with him; and never ventured at any subsequent time to break any of his promises, being bound by many ties of gratitude to Constantius. The strongest tie of all being that the emperor had given him for a wife, Olympias, the daughter of Abladius, formerly prefect of the prætorium, who had once been betrothed to his own brother Constans.

4. And when Arsaces had been dismissed, Constantius left Cappadocia, and going by Melitina, a town of the lesser Armenia, and

Lacotene, and Samosata, he crossed the Euphrates and arrived at Edessa. Stopping some time in each town, while waiting for divisions of soldiers who were flocking in from all quarters, and for sufficient supplies of provisions. And after the autumnal equinox, he proceeded onwards on his way to Amida.

5. When he approached the walls of that town, and saw everything buried in ashes, he groaned and wept, recollecting what sufferings the wretched city had suffered. And Ursulus, the treasurer, who happened to be present, was moved with indignation, and exclaimed, "Behold the courage with which cities are defended by our soldiers; men for whose pay the whole wealth of the empire is exhausted." This bitter speech the crowd of soldiers afterwards recollected at Chalcedon, when they rose up and destroyed him.

6. Then proceeding onward in close column, he reached Bezabde, and having fixed his camp there, and fortified it with a rampart and a deep fosse, as he took a long ride round the camp, he satisfied himself, by the account which he received from several persons, that those places in the walls which the carelessness of ancient times had allowed to become decayed, had been repaired so as to be stronger than ever.

7. And, not to omit anything which was necessary to do before the heat of the contest was renewed, he sent prudent men to the garrison to offer them two conditions; either to withdraw to their own country, giving up what did not belong to them, without causing bloodshed by resistance, or else to become subjects of the Romans, in which case they should receive rank and rewards. But when they, with native obstinacy, resisted the demands as became men of noble birth, who had been hardened by dangers and labours, everything was prepared for the siege.

8. Therefore the soldiers with alacrity, in dense order, and cheered by the sound of trumpets, attacked every side of the town; and the legions, being protected by various kinds of defences, advanced in safety, endeavouring by slow degrees to overthrow the walls; and because all kinds of missiles were poured down upon them, which disjoined the union of their shields, they fell back, the signal for a retreat being given.

9. Then a truce was agreed upon for one day; but the day after, having protected themselves more skilfully, they again raised their war-cry, and tried on every side to scale the walls. And although the garrison, having stretched cloths before them not to be distinguished, lay concealed within the walls; still, as often as necessity required,

they boldly put out their arms and hurled down stones and javelins on their assailants below.

10. And while the wicker penthouses were advanced boldly and brought close to the walls, the besieged dropped upon them heavy casks and millstones, and fragments of pillars, by the overpowering weight of which the assailants were crushed, their defences torn to pieces, and wide openings made in them, so that they incurred terrible dangers, and were again forced to retreat.

11. Therefore, on the tenth day from the beginning of the siege, when the confidence of our men began to fill the town with alarm, we determined on bringing up a vast battering-ram, which, after having destroyed Antioch with it sometime before, the Persians had left at Carrhæ; and as soon as that appeared, and was begun to be skilfully set up, it cowed the spirits of the besieged, so that they were almost on the point of surrendering, when they again plucked up courage and prepared means for resisting this engine.

12. From this time neither their courage nor their ingenuity failed; for as the ram was old, and it had been taken to pieces for the facility of transporting it, so while it was being put together again, it was attacked with great exertions and vigour by the garrison, and defended with equal valour and firmness by the besiegers; and engines hurling showers of stones, and slings, and missiles of all sorts, slew numbers on each side. Meantime, high mounds rose up with speedy growth; and the siege grew fiercer and sterner daily; many of our men being slain because, fighting as they were under the eye of the emperor, and eager for reward, they took off their helmets in order to be the more easily recognized, and so with bare heads, were an easy mark for the skilful archers of the enemy.

13. The days and nights being alike spent in watching, made each side the more careful; and the Persians, being alarmed at the vast height to which the mounds were now carried, and at the enormous ram, which was accompanied by others of smaller size, made great exertions to burn them, and kept continually shooting firebrands and incendiary missiles at them; but their labour was vain, because the chief part of them was covered with wet skins and cloths, and some parts also had been steeped in alum, so that the fire might fall harmless upon them.

14. But the Romans, driving these rams on with great courage, although they had difficulty in defending themselves, disregarded danger, however imminent, in the hope of making themselves masters of the town.

15. And on the other hand, when the enormous ram was brought against the tower to which it was applied, as if it could at once throw it down, the garrison, by a clever contrivance, entangled its projecting iron head, which in shape was like that of a ram, with long cords on both sides, to prevent its being drawn back and then driven forward with great force, and to hinder it from making any serious impression on the walls by repeated blows; and meanwhile they poured on it burning pitch, and for a long time these engines were fixed at the point to which they had been advanced, and exposed to all the stones and javelins which were hurled from the walls.

16. By this time the mounds were raised to a considerable height, and the garrison, thinking that unless they used extraordinary vigilance their destruction must be at hand, resorted to extreme audacity; and making an unexpected sally from the gates, they attacked our front rank, and with all their might hurled firebrands and iron braziers loaded with fire against the rams.

17. But after a fierce but undecided conflict, the bulk of them were driven within the walls, without having succeeded in their attempt; and presently the battlements were attacked from the mounds which the Romans had raised, with arrows and slings and lighted javelins, which flew over the roofs of the towers, but did no harm, means having been prepared to extinguish any flames.

18. And as the ranks on both sides became thinner, and the Persians were now reduced to extremities unless some aid could be found, they prepared with redoubled energy a fresh sally from the camp: accordingly, they made a sudden sally, supported by increased numbers, and among the armed men were many bearing torches, and iron baskets full of fire, and faggots; and all kinds of things best adapted for setting fire to the works of the besiegers were hurled against them.

19. And because the dense clouds of smoke obscured the sight, when the trumpet gave the signal for battle, the legions came up with quick step; and as the eagerness of the conflict grew hotter, after they had engaged, suddenly all the engines, except the great ram, caught fire from the flames which were hurled at them; but the ropes which held the chief ram were broken asunder, and that the vigorous efforts of some gallant men saved, when it was half burnt.

20. When the darkness of night terminated the combat, only a short time was allowed to the soldiers for rest; but when they had been refreshed by a little food and sleep, they were awakened by their captains, and ordered to remove their works away from the walls of the town, and prepare to fight at closer quarters from the lofty mounds

which were untouched by the flames, and now commanded the walls. And to drive the defenders from the walls, on the summit of the mounds they stationed two balistæ, in fear of which they thought that none of the enemy would venture even to look out.

21. After having taken these efficacious measures, a triple line of our men, having a more threatening aspect than usual from the nodding cones of their helmets (many of them also bearing ladders), attempted about twilight to scale the walls. Arms clashed and trumpets sounded, and both sides fought with equal boldness and ardour. The Romans, extending their lines more widely, when they saw the Persians hiding from fear of the engines which had been stationed on the mounds, battered the wall with their ram, and with spades, and axes, and levers, and ladders, pressed fiercely on, while missiles from each side flew without ceasing.

22. But the Persians were especially pressed by the various missiles shot from the balistæ, which, from the artificial mounds, came down upon them in torrents; and having become desperate, they rushed on, fearless of death, and distributing their force as if at the last extremity, they left some to guard the walls, while the rest, secretly opening a postern gate, rushed forth valiantly with drawn swords, followed by others who carried concealed fire.

23. And while the Romans at one moment were pressing on those who retreated, at another receiving the assault of those who attacked them, those who carried the fire crept round by a circuitous path, and pushed the burning coals in among the interstices of one of the mounds, which was made up of branches of trees, and rushes, and bundles of reeds. This soon caught fire and was utterly destroyed, the soldiers themselves having great difficulty in escaping and saving their engines.

24. But when the approach of evening broke off the conflict, and the two sides separated to snatch a brief repose, the emperor, after due reflection, resolved to change his plans. Although many reasons of great urgency pressed him to force on the destruction of Phœnice, as of a fortress which would prove an impregnable barrier to the inroads of the enemy, yet the lateness of the season was an objection to persevering any longer. He determined, therefore, while he preserved his position, to carry on the siege for the future by slight skirmishes, thinking that the Persians would be forced to surrender from want of provisions, which, however, turned out very different.

25. For while the conflict was proceeding sharply, the heavens became moist, and watery clouds appeared with threatening darkness;

and presently the ground got so wet from continual rain, that the whole country was changed into an adhesive mud (for the soil is naturally rich), and every plan was thrown into confusion; meantime, thunder with incessant crashes and ceaseless lightning filled men's minds with fear.

26. To these portents were added continual rainbows. A short explanation will serve to show how these appearances are formed. The vapours of the earth becoming warmer, and the watery particles gathering in clouds, and thence being dispersed in spray, and made brilliant by the fusion of rays, turn upwards towards the fiery orb of the sun and form a rainbow, which sweeps round with a large curve because it is spread over our world, which physical investigations place on the moiety of a sphere.

27. Its appearance, as far as mortal sight can discern, is, in the first line yellow, in the second tawny, in the third scarlet, in the fourth purple, and in the last a mixture of blue and green.

28. And it is so tempered with this mixed beauty, as mankind believe, because its first portion is discerned in a thin diluted state, of the same colour as the air which surrounds it; the next line is tawny, that is a somewhat richer colour than yellow; the third is scarlet, because it is opposite to the bright rays of the sun, and so pumps up and appropriates, if one may so say, the most subtle portion of its beams; the fourth is purple, because the density of the spray by which the splendour of the sun's rays is quenched shines between, and so it assumes a colour near that of flame; and as that colour is the more diffused, it shades off into blue and green.

29. Others think that the rainbow is caused by the rays of the sun becoming infused into some dense cloud, and pouring into it a liquid light, which, as it can find no exit, falls back upon itself, and shines the more brilliantly because of a kind of attrition; and receives those hues which are most akin to white from the sun above; its green hues from the cloud under which it lies, as often happens in the sea, where the waters which beat upon the shore are white, and those farther from the land, which, as being so, are more free from any admixture, are blue.

30. And since it is an indication of a change in the atmosphere (as we have already said), when in a clear sky sudden masses of clouds appear, or on the other hand, when the sky changed from a gloomy look to a joyful serenity, therefore we often read in the poets that Iris is sent from heaven when a change is required in the condition of any present affairs. There are various other opinions which it would be

superfluous now to enumerate, since my narration must hasten back to the point from which it digressed.

31. By these and similar events the emperor was kept wavering between hope and fear, as the severity of winter was increasing, and he suspected ambuscades in the country, which was destitute of roads; fearing also, among other things, the discontent of the exasperated soldiers. And it further goaded his unquiet spirit to return balked of his purpose, after, as it were, the door of the rich mansion was opened to him.

32. However, giving up his enterprise as fruitless, he returned into the unwelcome Syria, to winter at Antioch, after having suffered a succession of melancholy disasters. For, as if some unfriendly constellation so governed events, Constantius himself, while warring with the Persians, was always attended by adverse fortune; on which account he hoped at least to gain victories by means of his generals; and this, as we remember, usually happened.

Notes

[109] "The minute interval which may be interposed between the *hyeme adultâ* and the *primo vere* of Ammianus, instead of allowing a sufficient space for a march of three thousand miles, would render the orders of Constantius as extravagant as they were unjust; the troops of Gaul could not have reached Syria till the end of autumn. The memory of Ammianus must have been inaccurate, and his language incorrect."—Gibbon, c. xxii.

[110] According to Erdfurt, this legion was so named from its contumacious and mutinous disposition.

[111] The Gentiles were body-guards of the emperor, or of the Cæsar, of barbarian extraction, whether Scythians, Goths, Franks, Germans, &c.

[112] It may be remarked that Ammianus continually uses the words Persian and Parthian as synonymous.

[113] Santon is near Cleves.

BOOK XXI

war—Constantius, intending to march against Julian, harangues his soldiers.—XIV. Omens of the death of Constantius.—XV. Constantius dies at Mopsucrenæ in Cilicia.—XVI. His virtues and vices.

I.

A.D. 360.

§ 1. While Constantius was detained by this perplexing war beyond the Euphrates, Julian at Vienne devoted his days and nights to forming plans for the future, as far as his limited resources would allow; being in great suspense, and continually doubting whether to try every expedient to win Constantius over to friendship, or to anticipate his attack, with the view of alarming him.

2. And while anxiously considering these points he feared him, as likely to be in the one case a cruel friend, while in the other case he recollected that he had always been successful in civil disturbances. Above all things his anxiety was increased by the example of his brother Gallus, who had been betrayed by his own want of caution and the perjured deceit of certain individuals.

3. Nevertheless he often raised himself to ideas of energetic action, thinking it safest to show himself as an avowed enemy to him whose movements he could, as a prudent man, judge of only from his past actions, in order not to be entrapped by secret snares founded on pretended friendship.

4. Therefore, paying little attention to the letters which Constantius had sent by Leonas, and admitting none of his appointments with the exception of that of Nebridius, he now celebrated the Quinquennalia[114] as emperor, and wore a splendid diadem inlaid with precious stones, though when first entering on that power he had worn but a paltry-looking crown like that of a president of the public games.

5. At this time also he sent the body of his wife Helen, recently deceased, to Rome, to be buried in the suburb on the road to Nomentum, where also Constantina, his sister-in-law, the wife of Gallus, had been buried.

6. His desire to march against Constantius, now that Gaul was tranquillized, was inflamed by the belief which he had adopted from many omens (in the interpretation of which he had great skill), and from dreams that the emperor would soon die.

7. And since malignant people have attributed to this prince, so erudite and so eager to acquire all knowledge, wicked practices for the purpose of learning future events, we may here briefly point out how this important branch of learning may be acquired by a wise man.

8. The spirit which directs all the elements, and which at all times and throughout all places exercises its activity by the movement of these eternal bodies, can communicate to us the capacity of foreseeing the future by the sciences which we attain through various kinds of discipline. And the ruling powers, when properly propitiated, as from everlasting springs, supply mankind with words of prophecy, over which the deity of Themis is said to preside, and which, because she teaches men to know what has been settled for the future by the law of Fate, has received that name from the Greek word τεθειμένα ("fixed"), and has been placed by ancient theologians in the bed and on the throne of Jupiter, who gives life to all the world.

9. Auguries and auspices are not collected from the will of birds who are themselves ignorant of the future (for there is no one so silly as to say they understand it); but God directs the flight of birds, so that the sound of their beaks, or the motion of their feathers, whether quiet or disturbed, indicates the character of the future. For the kindness of the deity, whether it be that men deserve it, or that he is touched by affection for them, likes by these acts to give information of what is impending.

10. Again, those who attend to the prophetic entrails of cattle, which often take all kinds of shapes, learn from them what happens. Of this practice a man called Tages was the inventor, who, as is reported, was certainly seen to rise up out of the earth in the district of Etruria.

11. Men too, when their hearts are in a state of excitement, foretell the future, but then they are speaking under divine inspiration. For the sun, which is, as natural philosophers say, the mind of the world, and which scatters our minds among us as sparks proceeding from itself, when it has inflamed them with more than usual vehemence, renders them conscious of the future. From which the Sibyls often say they are burning and fired by a vast power of flames; and with reference to these cases the sound of voices, various signs, thunder, lightning, thunderbolts, and falling stars, have a great significance.

12. But the belief in dreams would be strong and undoubted if the interpreters of them were never deceived; and sometimes, as Aristotle asserts, they are fixed and stable when the eye of the person, being soundly asleep, turns neither way, but looks straight forward.

13. And because the ignorance of the vulgar often talks loudly, though ignorantly, against these ideas, asking why, if there were any faculty of foreseeing the future, one man should be ignorant that he would be killed in battle, or another that he would meet with some

misfortune, and so on; it will be enough to reply that sometimes a grammarian has spoken incorrectly, or a musician has sung out of tune, or a physician been ignorant of the proper remedy for a disease; but these facts do not disprove the existence of the sciences of grammar, music, or medicine.

14. So that Tully is right in this as well as other sayings of his, when he says, "Signs of future events are shown by the gods; if any one mistakes them he errs, not because of the nature of the gods, but because of the conjectures of men." But lest this discussion, running on this point beyond the goal, as the proverb is, should disgust the reader, we will now return to relate what follows.

II.

§ 1. While Julian, still with the rank of Cæsar only, was at Paris one day, exercising himself in the camp-field, and moving his shield in various directions, the joints by which it was fastened gave way, and the handle alone remained in his hand, which he still held firmly, and when those present were alarmed, thinking it a bad omen, he said, "Let no one be alarmed, I still hold firmly what I had before."

2. And again, when one day after a slight dinner, he was sleeping at Vienne, in the middle of the darkness of the night a figure of unusual splendour appeared to him, and when he was all but awake, repeated to him the following heroic verses, reciting them over and over again; which he believed, so that he felt sure that no ill fortune remained for him:—

> *"When Jove has passed the water-carrier's sign,*
> *And Saturn's light, for five-and-twenty days*
> *Has lightened up the maid; the king divine*
> *Of Asia's land shall enter on the ways*
> *That painful lead to death and Styx's gloomy maze."*

3. Therefore in the mean time he made no change in the existing condition of affairs, but arranged everything that occurred with a quiet and easy mind, gradually strengthening himself, in order to make the increase of his power correspond with the increase of his dignity.

4. And in order, without any hindrance, to conciliate the goodwill of all men, he pretended to adhere to the Christian religion, which in fact he had long since secretly abandoned, though very few were aware of his private opinions, giving up his whole attention to soothsaying and divination, and the other arts which have always been practised by the worshippers of the gods.

5. But to conceal this for a while, on the day of the festival at the beginning of January, which the Christians call Epiphany, he went into their church, and offered solemn public prayer to their God.

III.

§ 1. While these events were proceeding, and spring was coming on, Julian was suddenly smitten with grief and sorrow by unexpected intelligence. For he learnt that the Allemanni had poured forth from the district of Vadomarius, in which quarter, after the treaty which had been made with him, no troubles had been anticipated, and were laying waste the borders of the Tyrol, pouring their predatory hands over the whole frontier, and leaving nothing unravaged.

2. He feared that if this were passed over it might rekindle the flames of war; and so at once sent a count named Libino, with the Celtic and Petulantes legions, who were in winter quarters with him, to put a decided and immediate end to this affair.

3. Libino marched with speed, and arrived at Seckingen; but was seen while at a distance by the barbarians, who had already hidden themselves in the valleys with the intention of giving him battle. His soldiers were inferior in number, but very eager for battle; and he, after haranguing them, rashly attacked the Germans, and at the very beginning of the fight was slain among the first. At his death the confidence of the barbarians increased, while the Romans were excited to avenge their general; and so the conflict proceeded with great obstinacy, but our men were overpowered by numbers, though their loss in killed and wounded was but small.

4. Constantius, as has been related, had made peace with this Vadomarius, and his brother Gundomadus, who was also a king. And when afterwards Gundomadus died, thinking that Vadomarius would be faithful to him, and a silent and vigorous executor of his secret orders (if one may believe what is only report), he gave him directions by letter to harass the countries on his borders, as if he had broken off the treaty of peace, in order to keep Julian, through his fears of him, from ever abandoning the protection of Gaul.

5. In obedience to these directions, it is fair to believe that Vadomarius committed this and other similar actions; being a man from his earliest youth marvellously skilled in artifice and deceit, as he afterwards showed when he enjoyed the dukedom of Phœnice.[115]

6. But now, being discovered, he desisted from his hostilities. For one of his secretaries, whom he had sent to Constantius, was taken prisoner by Julian's outposts, and when he was searched to see if he

was the bearer of anything, a letter was found on him, which contained these words among others, "Your Cæsar is not submissive." But when he wrote to Julian he always addressed him as lord, and emperor, and god.

IV.

§ 1. These affairs were full of danger and doubt; and Julian considering them likely to lead to absolute destruction, bent all his mind to the one object of seizing Vadomarius unawares, through the rapidity of his movements, in order to secure his own safety and that of the provinces. And the plan which he decided on was this.

2. He sent to those districts Philagrius, one of his secretaries, afterwards count of the East, in whose proved prudence and fidelity he could thoroughly rely; and besides a general authority to act as he could upon emergencies, he gave him also a paper signed by himself, which he bade him not to open nor read unless Vadomarius appeared on the western side of the Rhine.

3. Philagrius went as he was ordered, and while he was in that district busying himself with various arrangements, Vadomarius crossed the river, as if he had nothing to fear, in a time of profound peace, and pretending to know of nothing having been done contrary to treaty, when he saw the commander of the troops who were stationed there, made him a short customary speech, and to remove all suspicion, of his own accord promised to come to a banquet to which Philagrius also had been invited.

4. As soon as Philagrius arrived, when he saw the king, he recollected Julian's words, and pretending some serious and urgent business, returned to his lodging, where having read the paper intrusted to him, and learnt what he was to do, he immediately returned and took his seat among the rest.

5. But when the banquet was over he boldly arrested Vadomarius, and gave him to the commander of the forces, to be kept in strict custody in the camp, reading to him the commands he had received; but as nothing was mentioned about Vadomarius's retinue, he ordered them to return to their own country.

6. But the king was afterwards conducted to Julian's camp, and despaired of pardon when he heard that his secretary had been taken, and the letters which he had written to Constantius read; he was however not even reproached by Julian, but merely sent off to Spain, as it was an object of great importance that, while Julian was absent from

Gaul, this ferocious man should not be able to throw into confusion the provinces which had been tranquillized with such great difficulty.

7. Julian, being much elated at this occurrence, since the king, whom he feared to leave behind him while at a distance, had been caught more quickly than he expected, without delay prepared to attack the barbarians who, as we have just related, had slain Count Libino and some of his soldiers in battle.

8. And to prevent any rumour of his approach giving them warning to retire to remoter districts, he passed the Rhine by night with great silence, with some of the most rapid of his auxiliary bands; and so came upon them while fearing nothing of the sort. And he at once attacked them the moment they were first roused by the sound of enemies, and while still examining their swords and javelins; some he slew, some he took prisoners, who sued for mercy and offered to surrender their booty; to the rest who remained and implored peace, and promised to be quiet for the future, he granted peace.

V.

§ 1. While these transactions were carried on in this spirited manner, Julian, considering to what great internal divisions his conduct had given rise, and that nothing is so advantageous for the success of sudden enterprise as celerity of action, saw with his usual sagacity that if he openly avowed his revolt from the emperor, he should be safer; and feeling uncertain of the fidelity of the soldiers, having offered secret propitiatory sacrifices to Bellona, he summoned the army by sound of trumpet to an assembly, and standing on a tribune built of stone, with every appearance of confidence in his manner, he spoke thus with a voice unusually loud:—

2. "I imagine that you, my gallant comrades, exalted by the greatness of your own achievements, have long been silently expecting this meeting, in order to form a previous judgment of, and to take wise measures against the events which may be expected. For soldiers united by glorious actions ought to hear rather than speak; nor ought a commander of proved justice to think anything but what is worthy of praise and approbation. That therefore I may explain to you what I propose, I entreat you to listen favourably to what I will briefly set before you.

3. "From my earliest year, by the will of God, I have been placed among you, with whom I have crushed the incessant inroads of the Franks and Allemanni, and checked the endless licentiousness of their ravages; by our united vigour we have opened the Rhine to the Roman

armies, whenever they choose to cross it; standing immovable against reports, as well as against the violent attacks of powerful nations, because I trusted to the invincibility of your valour.

4. "Gaul, which has beheld our labours, and which, after much slaughter and many periods of protracted and severe disasters, is at last replaced in a healthy state, will for ever bear witness to posterity of our achievements.

5. "But now since, constrained both by the authority of your judgment, and also by the necessity of the case, I have been raised to the rank of emperor, under the favour of God and of you, I aim at still greater things, if fortune should smile on my undertakings. Boasting at least that I have secured to the army, whose equity and mighty exploits are so renowned, a moderate and merciful chief in time of peace, and in war a prudent and wary leader against the combined forces of the barbarians.

6. "In order therefore that by the cordial unanimity of our opinions we may prevent ill fortune by anticipating it, I beg you to follow my counsel, salutary, as I think it, since the state of our affairs corresponds to the purity of my intentions and wishes. And while the legions of Illyricum are occupied by no greater force than usual, let us occupy the further frontier of Dacia; and then take counsel from our success what is to be done next.

7. "But as brave generals, I entreat you to promise with an oath that you will adhere to me with unanimity and fidelity; while I will give my customary careful attention to prevent anything from being done rashly or carelessly; and if any one requires it, will pledge my own unsullied honour that I will never attempt nor think of anything but what is for the common good.

8 "This especially I request and beseech you to observe, that none of you let any impulse of sudden ardour lead you to inflict injury on any private individual; recollecting that our greatest renown is not derived so much from the numberless defeats of the enemy as from the safety of the provinces, and their freedom from injury, which is celebrated as an eminent example of our virtue."

9. The emperor's speech was approved as though it had been the voice of an oracle, and the whole assembly was greatly excited, and being eager for a change, they all with one consent raised a tremendous shout, and beat their shields with a violent crash, calling him a great and noble general, and, as had been proved, a fortunate conqueror and king.

10. And being all ordered solemnly to swear fidelity to him, they put their swords to their throats with terrible curses, and took the oath in the prescribed form, that for him they would undergo every kind of suffering, and even death itself, if necessity should require it; and their officers and all the friends of the prince gave a similar pledge with the same forms.

11. Nebridius the prefect alone, boldly and unshakenly refused, declaring that he could not possibly bind himself by an oath hostile to Constantius, from whom he had received many and great obligations.

12. When these words of his were heard, the soldiers who were nearest to him were greatly enraged, and wished to kill him; but he threw himself at the feet of Julian, who shielded him with his cloak. Presently, when he returned to the palace, Nebridius appeared before him, threw himself at his feet as a suppliant, and entreated him to relieve his fears by giving him his right hand. Julian replied, "Will there be any conspicuous favour reserved for my own friends if you are allowed to touch my hand? However, depart in peace as you will." On receiving this answer, Nebridius retired in safety to his own house in Tuscany.

13. By these preliminary measures, Julian having learnt, as the importance of the affair required, what great influence promptness and being beforehand has in a tumultuous state of affairs, gave the signal to march towards Pannonia, and advancing his standard and his camp, boldly committed himself to fickle fortune.

VI.

A.D. 361.

§ 1. It is fitting now to retrace our steps and to relate briefly what (while these events just related were taking place in Gaul) Constantius, who passed the winter at Antioch, did, whether in peace or war.

2. Besides many others of high rank, some of the most distinguished tribunes generally come to salute an emperor on his arrival from distant lands. And accordingly, when Constantius, on his return from Mesopotamia, received this compliment, a Paphlagonian named Amphilochius, who had been a tribune, and whom suspicion, not very far removed from the truth, hinted at as having, while serving formerly under Constans, sown the seeds of discord between him and his brother, now ventured, with no little audacity, to come forward as if he were to be admitted to pay his duty in this way, but was recognized and refused admittance. Many also raised an outcry against him, crying out that he, as a stubborn rebel, ought not to be permitted to see

another day. But Constantius, on this occasion more merciful than usual, said, "Cease to press upon a man who, indeed, as I believe, is guilty, but who has not been convicted. And remember that if he has done anything of the kind, he, as long as he is in my sight, will be punished by the judgment of his own conscience, which he will not be able to escape." And so he departed.

3. The next day, at the Circensian games, the same man was present as a spectator, just opposite the usual seat of the emperor, when a sudden shout was raised at the moment of the commencement of the expected contest; the barriers, on which he with many others was leaning, were broken, and the whole crowd as well as he were thrown forward into the empty space; and though a few were slightly hurt, he alone was found to be killed, having received some internal injury. At which Constantius rejoiced, prognosticating from this omen protection from his other enemies.

4. About the same time (his wife Eusebia having died some time before) he took another wife, named Faustina. Eusebia's brothers were two men of consular rank, Hypatius and Eusebius. She had been a woman of pre-eminent beauty both of person and character, and for one of her high rank most courteous and humane. And to her favour and justice it was owing, as we have already mentioned, that Julian was saved from danger and declared Cæsar.

5. About the same time Florentius also was rewarded, who had quitted Gaul from fear of a revolution. He was now appointed to succeed Anatolius, the prefect of the prætorium in Illyricum, who had lately died. And in conjunction with Taurus, who was appointed to the same office in Italy, he received the ensigns of this most honourable dignity.

6. Nevertheless, the preparations for both foreign and civil wars went on, the number of the squadrons of cavalry was augmented, and reinforcements for the legions were enlisted with equal zeal, recruits being collected all over the provinces. Also every class and profession was exposed to annoyances, being called upon to furnish arms, clothes, military engines, and even gold and silver and abundant stores of provisions, and various kinds of animals.

7. And because, as the king of Persia had been compelled unwillingly to fall back on account of the difficulties of the winter, it was feared that as soon as the weather became open he would return with greater impetuosity than ever, ambassadors were sent to the kings and satraps across the Tigris, with splendid presents, to advise and entreat them all to join us, and abstain from all designs or plots against us.

8. But the most important object of all was to win over Arsaces and Meribanes, the kings of Armenia and Hiberia, who were conciliated by the gift of magnificent and honourable robes and by presents of all kinds, and who could have done great harm to the Roman interests if at such a crisis they had gone over to the Persians.

9. At this important time, Hermogenes died, and was succeeded in his prefecture by Helpidius, a native of Paphlagonia, a man of mean appearance and no eloquence, but of a frank and truthful disposition, humane and merciful. So much so that once when Constantius ordered an innocent man to be put to the torture before him, he calmly requested to be deprived of his office, and that such commissions might be given to others who would discharge them in a manner more in accordance with the emperor's sentence.

VII.

§ 1. Constantius was perplexed at the danger of the crisis before him, and doubted what to do, being for some time in deep anxiety whether to march against Julian, who was still at a distance, or to drive back the Persians, who were already threatening to cross the Euphrates. And while he was hesitating, and often taking counsel with his generals, he at last decided that he would first finish, or at all events take the edge off, the war which was nearest, so as to leave nothing formidable behind him, and then penetrate through Illyricum and Italy, thinking to catch Julian at the very outset of his enterprise, as he might catch a deer with hounds. For so he used to boast, to appease the fears of those about him.

2. But that his purpose might not appear to cool, and that he might not seem to have neglected any side of the war, he spread formidable rumours of his approach in every direction. And fearing that Africa, which on all occasions seemed to invite usurpers, might be invaded during his absence, as if he had already quitted the eastern frontier, he sent by sea to that country his secretary Gaudentius, whom we have already mentioned as a spy upon the actions of Julian in Gaul.

3. He had two reasons for thinking that this man would be able with prompt obedience to do all that he desired, both because he feared the other side, which he had offended, and also because he was anxious to take this opportunity to gain the favour of Constantius, whom he expected beyond a doubt to see victorious. Indeed no one at that time had any other opinion.

4. When Gaudentius arrived in Africa, recollecting the emperor's orders, he sent letters to Count Cretio, and to the other officers, to in-

struct them what his object was; and having collected a formidable force from all quarters, and having brought over a light division of skirmishers from the two Mauritanias, he watched the coasts opposite to Italy and Gaul with great strictness.

5. Nor was Constantius deceived in the wisdom of this measure. For as long as Gaudentius lived none of the adverse party ever reached that country, although a vast multitude in arms was watching the Sicilian coast between Cape Boeo and Cape Passaro, and ready to cross in a moment if they could find an opportunity.

6. Having made these arrangements as well as the case admitted, in such a way as he thought most for his advantage and having settled other things also of smaller importance, Constantius was warned by messengers and letters from his generals that the Persian army, in one solid body, and led by its haughty king, was now marching close to the banks of the Tigris, though it was as yet uncertain at what point they meant to cross the frontier.

7. And he, feeling the importance of this intelligence, in order, by being near them, to anticipate their intended enterprises, quitted his winter quarters in haste, having called in the infantry and cavalry on which he could rely from all quarters, crossed the Euphrates by a bridge of boats at Capessana, and marched towards Edessa, which was well provisioned and strongly fortified, intending to wait there a short time till he could receive from spies or deserters certain information of the enemy's motions.

VIII.

§ 1. In the mean time, Julian leaving the district of Basle, and having taken all the steps which we have already mentioned, sent Sallustius, whom he had promoted to be a prefect, into Gaul, and appointed Germanianus to succeed Nebridius. At the same time he gave Nevitta the command of the heavy cavalry, being afraid of the old traitor Gumoharius, who, when he was commander of the Scutarii, he heard had secretly betrayed his chief officer, Vetranio. The quæstorship he gave to Jovius, of whom we have spoken when relating the acts of Magnentius, and the treasury he allotted to Mamertinus. Dagalaiphus also was made captain of the household guard, and many others, with whose merits and fidelity he was acquainted, received different commands at his discretion.

2. Being now about to march through the Black Forest, and the country lying on the banks of the Danube, he on a sudden conceived great doubt and fear whether the smallness of his force might not

breed contempt, and encourage the numerous population of the district to resist his advance.

3. To prevent this, he took prudent precautions, and distributing his army into divisions, he sent some under Jovenius and Jovius to advance with all speed by the well-trodden roads of Italy; others under the command of Nevitta, the commander of the cavalry, were to take the inland road of the Tyrol. So that his army, by being scattered over various countries, might cause a belief that its numbers were immense, and might fill all nations with fear. Alexander the Great, and many other skilful generals, had done the same thing when their affairs required it.

4. But he charged them, when they set forth, to march with all speed, as if likely to meet at any moment with an enemy, and carefully to post watches and sentries and outposts at night, so as to be free from the danger of any sudden attack.

IX.

§ 1. These things having been arranged according to the best of his judgment, Julian adhering to the maxim by which he had often forced his way through the countries of the barbarians, and trusting in his continued successes, proceeded in his advance.

2. And when he had reached the spot at which he had been informed that the river was navigable, he embarked on board some boats which good fortune had brought thither in numbers, and passed as secretly as he could down the stream, escaping notice the more because his habits of endurance and fortitude had made him indifferent to delicate food; so that, being contented with meagre and poor fare, he did not care to approach their towns or camps, forming his conduct in this respect according to the celebrated saying of the ancient Cyrus, who, when he was introduced to a host who asked him what he wished to have got ready for supper, answered, "Nothing beyond bread, for that he hoped he should sup by the side of a river."

3. But Fame, which, as they say, having a thousand tongues, always exaggerates the truth, at this time spread abroad a report among all the tribes of Illyricum that Julian, having overthrown a number of kings and nations in Gaul, was coming on flushed with success and with a numerous army.

4. Jovinus, the prefect of the prætorium, being alarmed at this rumour, fled in haste, as if from a foreign enemy; and going by the public conveyances with frequent relays, he crossed the Julian Alps, taking with him also Florentius the prefect.

5. But Count Lucillianus, who at that time had the command of the army in these districts, being at Sirmium, and having received some slight intelligence of Julian's movements, collected the soldiers whom the emergency gave time for being quickly called from their several stations, and proposed to resist his advance.

6. Julian, however, like a firebrand or torch once kindled, hastened quickly to his object; and when, at the waning of the moon, he had reached Bonmunster, which is about nineteen miles from Sirmium,[116] and when, therefore, the main part of the night was dark, he unexpectedly quitted his boats, and at once sent forward Dagalaiphus with his light troops to summon Lucillianus to his presence, and to drag him before him if he resisted.

7. He was asleep, and when he was awakened by the violence of this uproar, and saw himself surrounded by a crowd of strangers, perceiving the state of the case, and being filled with awe at the name of the emperor, he obeyed his orders, though sadly against his will. And though commander of the cavalry, a little while before proud and fierce, he now obeyed the will of another, and mounting a horse which was brought him on a sudden, he was led before Julian, as an ignoble prisoner, and from fear was hardly able to collect his senses.

8. But as soon as he saw the emperor, and was relieved by receiving permission to offer his salutations to his purple robe, he recovered his courage, and feeling safe said, "You have been incautious and rash, O emperor, to trust yourself with but a few troops in the country of another." But Julian, with a sarcastic smile, replied, "Keep these prudent speeches for Constantius. I offered you the ensign of my royal rank to ease you of your fears, and not to take you for my counsellor."

X.

§ 1. So after he had got rid of Lucillianus, thinking no further delay or hesitation admissible, being bold and confident in all emergencies, and on the way, as he presumed, to a city inclined to surrender, he marched on with great speed. When he came near the suburbs, which are very large and much extended, a vast crowd of soldiers and of every class of the population came forth to meet him with lights and flowers and auspicious prayers, and after saluting him as emperor and lord, conducted him to the palace.

2. He, pleased at these favourable omens, and conceiving therefrom a sanguine hope of future success, concluded that the example of so populous and illustrious a metropolis would be followed as a guid-

ing-star by other cities also, and therefore on the very next day exhibited a chariot race, to the great joy of the people. On the third day,
unable to brook any delay, he proceeded by the public roads, and
without any resistance seized upon Succi, and appointed Nevitta governor of the place, as one whom he could trust. It is fitting that I should
now explain the situation of this place Succi.

3. The summits of the mountain chains of Hæmus[117] and
Rhodope, the first of which rises up from the very banks of the Danube, and the other from the southern bank of the river Axius, ending
with swelling ridges at one narrow point, separate the Illyrians and the
Thracians, being on the one side near the inland Dacians and Serdica,
on the other looking towards Thrace and the rich and noble city of
Philippopolis. And, as if Nature had provided for bringing the surrounding nations under the dominion of the Romans, they are of such a
form as to lead to this end. Affording at first only a single exit through
narrow defiles, but at a later period they were opened out with roads of
such size and beauty as to be passable even for waggons. Though still,
when the passes have been blocked up, they have often repelled the
attacks of great generals and mighty armies.

4. The part which looks to Illyricum is of a more gentle ascent,
so as to be climbed almost imperceptibly; but the side opposite to
Thrace is very steep and precipitous, in some places absolutely impassable, and in others hard to climb even where no one seeks to
prevent it. Beneath this lofty chain a spacious level plain extends in
every direction, the upper portion of it reaching even to the Julian
Alps, while the lower portion of it is so open and level as to present no
obstacles all the way to the straits and sea of Marmora.

5. Having arranged these matters as well as the occasion permitted, and having left there the commander of the cavalry, the emperor
returned to Nissa, a considerable town, in order, without any hindrance, to settle everything in the way most suited to his interests.

6. While there he appointed Victor, an historical writer, whom he
had seen at Sirmium, and whom he ordered to follow him from that
city, to be consular governor of the second Pannonia; and he erected in
his honour a brazen statue, as a man to be imitated for his temperance;
and some time after he was appointed prefect of Rome.

7. And now, giving the rein to loftier ideas, and believing it to be
impossible to bring Constantius to terms, he wrote a speech full of bitter invectives to the senate, setting forth many charges of disgrace and
vice against him. And when this harangue, Tertullus still being prefect
of the city, was read in the senate, the gratitude of the nobles, as well

as their splendid boldness, was very conspicuous; for they all cried out with one unanimous feeling, "We expect that you should show reverence to the author of your own greatness."

8. Then he assailed the memory of Constantine also as an innovator and a disturber of established laws and of customs received from ancient times, accusing him of having been the first to promote barbarians to the fasces and robe of the consul. But in this respect he spoke with folly and levity, since, in the face of what he so bitterly reproved, he a very short time afterwards added to Mamertinus, as his colleague in the consulship, Nevitta, a man neither in rank, experience, or reputation at all equal to those on whom Constantine had conferred that illustrious magistracy, but who, on the contrary, was destitute of accomplishments and somewhat rude; and what was less easy to be endured, made a cruel use of his high power.

XI.

§ 1. While Julian was occupied with these and similar thoughts, and was anxious about great and important affairs, a messenger came with terrible and unexpected news of the monstrous attempts of some persons which were likely to hinder his fiery progress, unless by prompt vigilance he could crush them, before they came to a head. I will briefly relate what they were.

2. Under pretence of urgent necessity, but in reality because he still suspected their fidelity to him, he had sent into Gaul two legions belonging to the army of Constantius, with a troop of archers which he had found at Sirmium. They, moving slowly, and dreading the length of the journey and the fierce and continual attacks of the hostile Germans, planned a mutiny, being prompted and encouraged by Nigrinus, a tribune of a squadron of cavalry, a native of Mesopotamia. And having arranged the matter in secret conferences, and kept it close in profound silence, when they arrived at Aquileia, a city important from its situation and wealth, and fortified with strong walls, they suddenly closed the gates in a hostile manner, the native population, by whom the name of Constantius was still beloved, increasing the confusion and the terror. And having blockaded all the approaches, and armed the towers and battlements, they prepared measures to encounter the impending struggle, being in the mean time free and unrestrained. By this daring conduct they roused the Italian natives of the district to espouse the side of Constantius, who was still alive.

XII.

§ 1. When Julian heard of this transaction, being then at Nissa, as he feared nothing unfriendly in his rear, and had read and heard that this city, though often besieged, had never been destroyed or taken, hastened the more eagerly to gain it, either by stratagem, or by some kind of flattery or other, before any more formidable event should arise.

2. Therefore he ordered Jovinus, the captain of his cavalry, who was marching over the Alps, and had entered Noricum, to return with all speed, to remedy by some means or other, the evil which had burst out. And, that nothing might be wanting, he bade him retain all the soldiers who were marching after his court or his standards and passing through that town, and to avail himself of their help to the utmost.

3. When he had made these arrangements, having soon afterwards heard of the death of Constantius, he crossed through Thrace, and entered Constantinople: and having been often assured that the siege would be protracted rather than formidable, he sent Immo with some other counts to conduct it; and removed Jovinus to employ him in other matters of greater importance.

4. Therefore, having surrounded Aquileia with a double line of heavy infantry, the generals all agreed upon trying to induce the garrison to surrender, using alternately threats and caresses; but after many proposals and replies had been interchanged, their obstinacy only increased, and the conferences were abandoned, having proved wholly ineffectual.

5. And because there was now no prospect but that of a battle, both sides refreshed themselves with sleep and food; and at daybreak the trumpets sounded, and the two armies, arrayed for reciprocal slaughter, attacked one another with loud shouts, but with more ferocity than skill.

6. Therefore the besiegers, bearing wooden penthouses over them, and closely woven wicker defences, marched on slowly and cautiously, and attempted to undermine the walls with iron tools: many also bore ladders which had been made of the height of the walls, and came up close to them: when some were dashed down by stones hurled on their heads, others were transfixed by whizzing javelins, and falling back, dragged with them those who were in their rear; and others, from fear of similar mischances, shrank from the attack.

7. The besieged being encouraged by the issue of this first conflict, and hoping for still better success, disregarded the rest of the attacks made on them; and with resolute minds they stationed engines

in suitable positions, and with unwearied toil discharged the duties of watching and of whatever else could tend to their safety.

8. On the other hand, the besiegers, though fearing another combat, and full of anxiety, still out of shame would not appear lazy or cowardly, and as they could make no way by open attacks, they also applied themselves to the various manœuvres employed in sieges. And because there was no ground favourable for working battering-rams or other engines, nor for making mines, since the river Natiso passed under the walls of the city, they contrived a plan worthy to be compared with any effort of ancient skill.

9. With great rapidity they built some wooden towers, higher than the battlements of the enemy, and then fastening their boats together, they placed these towers on them. In them they stationed soldiers, who, with undaunted resolution, laboured to drive down the garrison from the walls; while under them were bodies of light infantry wholly unencumbered, who going forth from the hollow parts of the towers below, threw drawbridges across, which they had put together beforehand, and so tried to cross over to the bottom of the wall while the attention of the garrison was diverted from them; so that while those above them were attacking one another with darts and stones, those who crossed over on the drawbridges might be able without interruption to break down a portion of the wall and so effect an entrance.

10. But once more a clever design failed in its result. For when the towers came close to the walls, they were assailed with brands steeped in pitch, and reeds, and faggots, and every kind of food for flames, all kindled. The towers quickly caught fire, and yielding under the weight of the men who were mounted on them, fell into the river, while some of the soldiers on their summits, even before they fell, had been pierced with javelins hurled from the engines on the walls, and so died.

11. Meanwhile the soldiers at the foot of the wall, being cut off by the destruction of their comrades in the boats, were crushed with huge stones, with the exception of a few, who, in spite of the difficult ground over which their flight lay, escaped by their swiftness of foot. At last, when the contest had been protracted till evening, the usual signal for retreat was given, and the combatants parted to pass the night with very different feelings.

12. The losses of the besiegers, who had suffered greatly, encouraged the defenders of the town with hopes of victory, though they also had to mourn the deaths of some few of their number. Neverthe-

less, the preparations went on rapidly. Rest and food refreshed their bodies during the night; and at dawn of day the conflict was renewed at the trumpet's signal.

13. Some, holding their shields over their heads, in order to fight with more activity; others, in front, bore ladders on their shoulders, and rushed on with eager vehemence, exposing their breasts to wounds from every kind of weapon. Some endeavoured to break down the iron bars of the gates; but were attacked with fire, or crushed under stones hurled from the walls. Some boldly strove to cross the fosses, but fell beneath the sudden sallies of soldiers rushing out from postern gates, or were driven back with severe wounds. For those who sallied forth had an easy retreat within the walls, and the rampart in front of the walls, strengthened with turf, saved those who lay in wait behind it from all danger.

14. Although the garrison excelled in endurance and in the arts of war, without any other aid than that of their walls, still our soldiers, being attacked as they were from a more numerous force, became impatient of the long delay, and moved round and round the suburbs, seeking diligently to discover by what force or what engines they could make their way out of the city.

15. But as, through the greatness of the difficulties in their way, they could not accomplish this, they began to slacken their exertions as to the siege itself, and leaving a few watches and outposts, ravaged the adjacent country, and thus obtained all kinds of supplies, dividing their booty with their comrades. The consequence was, that excessive eating and drinking proved injurious to their health.

16. When, however, Immo and his colleagues reported this to Julian, who was passing the winter at Constantinople, he applied a wise remedy to such a disorder, and sent thither Agilo, the commander of his infantry, an officer in great esteem, that when a man of his rank and reputation appeared there and took the intelligence of the death of Constantius to the army, the siege might be terminated in that way.

17. In the mean while, not to abandon the siege of Aquileia, as all other attempts had proved futile, the generals endeavoured to compel the citizens to surrender by want of water. So they cut the aqueducts; but as the garrison still resisted with undiminished courage, they, with vast valour, diverted the stream of the river. But this again was done in vain; for they reduced the allowance of water to each man; and contented themselves with the scanty supply they could procure from wells.

18. While these affairs were proceeding thus, Agilo arrived, as he had been commanded; and, being protected by a strong body of heavy infantry, came up boldly close to the walls; and in a long and veracious speech, told the citizens of the death of Constantius, and the confirmation of Julian's power; but was reviled and treated as a liar. Nor would any one believe his statement of what had occurred, till on promise of safety he was admitted by himself to the edge of the defences; where, with a solemn oath, he repeated what he had before related.

19. When his story was heard, they all, eager to be released from their protracted sufferings, threw open the gates and rushed out, admitting him in the joy as a captain who brought them peace; and excusing themselves, they gave up Nigrinus as the author of their mad resistance, and a few others; demanding that their punishment should be taken as an atonement for the treason and sufferings of the city.

20. Accordingly, a few days later, the affair was rigorously investigated; Mamertinus, the prefect of the prætorium, sitting as judge; and Nigrinus, as the cause of the war, was burnt alive. After him, Romulus and Sabostius, men who had held high office, being convicted of having sown discord in the empire without any regard to the consequences, were beheaded; and all the rest escaped unpunished, as men who had been driven to hostilities by necessity, and not by their own inclination; this being the decision of the merciful and clement emperor, after a full consideration of justice. These things, however, happened some time afterwards.

21. But Julian, who was still at Nissa, was occupied in the graver cases, being full of fears on both sides. For he was apprehensive lest the defiles of the Julian Alps might be seized and barred against him by some sudden onset of the troops who had been shut up in Aquileia; by which he might lose the provinces beyond, and the supplies which he was daily expecting from that quarter.

22. And he also greatly feared the power of the East; hearing that the soldiers who were scattered over Thrace had been suddenly collected together to act against him, and were advancing towards the frontiers of the Succi, under command of Count Marcianus. But, devising measures suitable to this mass of pressing anxieties, he quickly assembled his Illyrian army, long inured to war, and eager to renew its martial labours under a warlike chief.

23. Nor even at this critical moment did he forget the interests of individuals; but devoted some time to hearing contested causes, especially those concerning municipal bodies, in whose favour he was too

partial, so that he raised several persons who did not deserve such honour to public offices.

24. It was here that he found Symmachus and Maximus, two eminent senators, who had been sent by the nobles as envoys to Constantius, and had returned again. He promoted them with great honour; so that, preferring them to others more deserving, he made Maximus prefect of the eternal city, in order to gratify Rufinus Vulcatius, whose nephew he was. Under his administration the city enjoyed great plenty, and there was an end to the complaints of the common people, which had been so frequent.

25. Afterwards, in order to add security to those of his affairs which were still unsettled, and encourage the confidence of the loyal, he raised Mamertinus, the prefect of the prætorium in Illyricum, and Nevitta to the consulship; though he had so lately assailed the memory of Constantine as the person who had set the example of thus promoting low-born barbarians.

XIII.

§ 1. While Julian was thus carrying out new projects, and alternating between hope and fear, Constantius at Edessa, being made anxious by the various accounts brought him by his spies, was full of perplexity. At one time collecting his army for battle; at another, wishing to lay siege to Bezabde on two sides, if he could find an opportunity; taking at the same time prudent precautions not to leave Mesopotamia unprotected, while about to march into the districts of Armenia.

2. But while still undecided, he was detained by various causes. Sapor also remained on the other side of the Tigris till the sacrifices should become propitious to his moving. For if after crossing the river he found no resistance, he might without difficulty penetrate to the Euphrates. On the other hand, if he wished to keep his soldiers for the civil war, he feared to expose them to the dangers of a siege; having already experienced the strength of the walls and the vigour of the garrison.

3. However, not to lose time, and to avoid inactivity, he sent Arbetio and Agilo, the captains of his infantry and cavalry, with very large forces, to march with all speed; not to provoke the Persians to battle, but to establish forts on the nearest bank of the Tigris, which might be able to reconnoitre, and see in what direction the furious monarch broke forth; and with many counsels given both verbally and

in writing, he charged them to retreat with celerity the moment the enemy's army began to cross the river.

4. While these generals were watching the frontier as they were ordered, and spying out the secret designs of their most crafty enemy, he himself, with the main body of his army, made head against his most pressing foes, as if prepared for battle; and defended the adjacent towns by rapid movements. Meantime spies and deserters continually coming in, related to him opposite stories; being in fact ignorant of what was intended, because among the Persians no one knows what is decided on except a few taciturn and trusty nobles, by whom the god Silence is worshipped.

5. But the emperor was continually sent for by the generals whom I have mentioned, who implored him to send them aid. For they protested that unless the whole strength of the army was collected together, it would be impossible to withstand the onset of the furious Sapor.

6. And while things in this quarter were thus full of anxiety, other messengers arrived in numbers, by whose accurate statements he learnt that Julian had traversed Italy and Illyricum with great rapidity, had occupied the defiles of the Succi, and called in auxiliaries from all quarters, and was now marching through Thrace with a very large force.

7. Constantius, learning this, was overwhelmed with grief, but supported by one comfort, that he had always triumphed over internal commotions. Nevertheless, though the affair made it very difficult for him to decide on a line of action, he chose the best; and sent a body of troops on by public conveyances, in order as quickly as possible to make head against the impending danger.

8. And as that plan was universally approved, the troops went as they were commanded, in the lightest marching order. But the next day, while he was finally arranging these matters, he received intelligence that Sapor, with his whole army, had returned to his own country, because the auspices were unfavourable. So, his fears being removed, he called in all the troops except those who as usual were assigned for the protection of Mesopotamia, and returned to Hierapolis.

9. And still doubting what would be the final result of all his difficulties, when he had collected his army together he convened all the centuries and companies and squadrons by sound of trumpet; and the whole plain being filled with the host, he, standing on a lofty tribune, in order to encourage them the more readily to execute what he should

direct, and being surrounded by a numerous retinue, spoke thus with great appearance of calmness and a studied look of confidence.

10. "Being always anxious never to do or say anything inconsistent with incorruptible honour, like a cautious pilot, who turns his helm this way or that way according to the movement of the waves, I am now constrained, my most affectionate subjects, to confess my errors to you, or rather, if I were to say the plain truth, my humanity, which I did think would be beneficial to our common interests. So now that you may the better understand what is the object of convoking this assembly, listen, I pray you, with impartiality and kindness.

11. "At the time when Magnentius, whom your bravery overcome, was obstinately labouring to throw all things into confusion, I sent Gallus my cousin, who had been lately raised to the rank of Cæsar, to guard the East. But he, having by many wicked and shameful arts departed from justice, was punished by a legal sentence.

12. "Would that Envy had then been contented, that most bitter exciter of troubles! And that we had nothing to grieve us but the single recollection of past sorrows, unaccompanied by any idea of present danger! But now a new circumstance, more grievous than any former one I will venture to say, has taken place, which the gods who aid us will put an end to by means of your innate valour.

13. "Julian, whom, while you were combating the nations which threaten Illyricum on all sides, I appointed to protect Gaul, presuming on the issue of some trifling battles which he has fought against the half-armed Germans, and full of silly elation, has taken a few auxiliary battalions into his noble alliance, men from their natural ferocity and the desperateness of their situation ready for acts of the most mischievous audacity, and has conspired against the public safety, trampling down justice, the parent and nurse of the Roman world. That power I believe, both because I myself have experienced it, and because all antiquity assures me of its might, will, as an avenger of wickedness, soon trample down their pride like so many ashes.

14. "What then remains, except to hasten to encounter the whirlwind thus raised against us? so as by promptitude to crush the fury of this rising war before it comes to maturity and strength? Nor can it be questioned that, with the favour of the supreme deity, by whose everlasting sentence ungrateful men are condemned, the sword which they have wickedly drawn will be turned to their own destruction. Since never having received any provocation, but rather after having been loaded with benefits, they have risen up to threaten innocent men with danger.

15. "For as my mind augurs, and as justice, which will aid upright counsels, promises, I feel sure that when once we come to close quarters, they will be so benumbed with fear as neither to be able to stand the fire of your glancing eyes nor the sound of your battle cry." This speech harmonized well with the feelings of the soldiers. In their rage they brandished their shields, and after answering him in terms of eager good-will, demanded to be led at once against the rebels. Their cordiality changed the emperor's fear into joy; and having dismissed the assembly, as he knew by past experience that Arbetio was most eminently successful in putting an end to intestine wars, he ordered him to advance first by the road which he himself designed to take, with the spearmen and the legion of Mattium,[118] and several battalions of light troops; he also ordered Gomoarius to take with him the Leti, to check the enemy on their arrival among the defiles of the Succi; he was selected for this service because he was unfriendly to Julian on account of some slight he had received from him in Gaul.

XIV.

§ 1. While the fortune of Constantius was now wavering and tottering in this tumult of adverse circumstances, it showed plainly by signs which almost spoke that a very critical moment of his life was at hand. For he was terrified by nocturnal visions, and before he was thoroughly asleep he had seen the shade of his father bringing him a beautiful child; and when he received it and placed it in his bosom, it struck a globe which he had in his right hand to a distance. Now this indicated a change of circumstances, although those who interpreted it gave favourable answers when consulted.

2. After this he confessed to his most intimate friends that, as if he were wholly forsaken, he had ceased to see a secret vision which sometimes he had fancied appeared to him in mournful guise; and he believed that the genius who had been appointed to watch over his safety had abandoned him, as one who was soon to leave the world.

3. For the opinion of theologians is, that all men when they are born (without prejudice to the power of destiny) are connected with a superior power of this kind, who, as it were, guides their actions; but who is seen by very few, and only by those who are endued with great and various virtues.

4. This may be collected both from oracles and from eminent writers. Among whom is the comic poet Menander, in whose works these two verses are found:—

"A spirit is assigned to every man
When born to guide him in the path of life."

5. It may also be gathered from the immortal poetry of Homer, that they were not really the gods of heaven who conversed with his heroes, or stood by them and aided them in their combats; but the familiar genii who belonged to them; to whom also, as their principal support, Pythagoras owes his eminence, and Socrates and Numa Pompilius and the elder Scipio. And, as some fancy, Marius, and Octavianus the first, who took the name of Augustus. And Hermes Trismegistus, and Apollonius of Tyana, and Plotinus, who ventured upon some very mystical discussions of this point; and endeavoured to show by profound reasoning what is the original cause why these genii, being thus connected with the souls of mortals, protect them as if they had been nursed in their own bosoms, as far as they are permitted; and, if they find them pure, preserving the body untainted by any connection with vice, and free from all taint of sin, instruct them in loftier mysteries.

XV.

§ 1. Constantius therefore, having hastened to Antioch, according to his wont, at the first movement of a civil war which he was eager to encounter, as soon as he had made all his preparations, was in amazing haste to march, though many of his court were so unwilling as even to proceed to murmurs. For no one dare openly to remonstrate or object to his plan.

2. He set forth towards the end of autumn; and when he reached the suburb called Hippocephalus, which is about three miles from the town, as soon as it was daylight he saw on his right the corpse of a man who had been murdered, lying with his head torn off from the body, stretched out towards the west—and though alarmed at the omen, which seemed as if the Fates were preparing his end, he went on more resolutely, and came to Tarsus, where he caught a slight fever; and thinking that the motion of his journey would remove the distemper, he went on by bad roads; directing his course by Mopsucrenæ, the farthest station in Cilicia for those who travel from hence, at the foot of Mount Taurus.

3. But when he attempted to proceed the next day he was prevented by the increasing violence of his disorder, and the fever began gradually to inflame his veins, so that his body felt like a little fire, and could scarcely be touched; and as all remedies failed, he began in the last extremity to bewail his death; and while his mental faculties were

still entire, he is said to have indicated Julian as the successor to his power. Presently the last struggle of death came on, and he lost the power of speech. And after long and painful agony he died on the fifth of October, having lived and reigned forty years and a few months.

4. After bewailing his death with groans, lamentations, and mourning, those of the highest rank in the royal palace deliberated what to do or to attempt; and having secretly consulted a few persons about the election of an emperor, at the instigation, as it is said, of Eusebius, who was stimulated by his consciousness of guilt (since Julian was approaching who was prepared to oppose his attempts at innovation), they sent Theolaiphus and Aligildus, who at that time were counts, to him, to announce the death of his kinsman; and to entreat him to lay aside all delay and hasten to take possession of the East, which was prepared to obey him.

5. But fame and an uncertain report whispered that Constantius had left a will, in which, as we have already mentioned, he had named Julian as his heir; and had given commissions and legacies to his friends. But he left his wife in the family way, who subsequently had a daughter, who received the same name, and was afterwards married to Gratianus.

XVI.

§ 1. In accurately distinguishing the virtues and vices of Constantius, it will be well to take the virtues first. Always preserving the dignity of the imperial authority, he proudly and magnanimously disdained popularity. In conferring the higher dignities he was very sparing, and allowed very few changes to be made in the administration of the finances. Nor did he ever encourage the arrogance of the soldiers.

2. Nor under him was any general promoted to the title of most illustrious.[119] For there was also, as we have already mentioned, the title of most perfect.[120] Nor had the governor of a province occasion to court a commander of cavalry; as Constantius never allowed those officers to meddle with civil affairs. But all officers, both military and civil, were according to the respectful usages of old, inferior to that of the prefect of the prætorium, which was the most honourable of all.

3. In taking care of the soldiers he was very cautious: an examiner into their merits, sometimes over-scrupulous, giving dignities about the palace as if with scales. Under him no one who was not well known to him, or who was favoured merely by some sudden impulse, ever received any high appointment in the palace. But only such as had

served ten years in some capacity or other could look for such appointments as master of the ceremonies or treasurer. The successful candidates could always be known beforehand; and it very seldom happened that any military officer was transferred to a civil office; while on the other hand none but veteran soldiers were appointed to command troops.

4. He was a diligent cultivator of learning, but, as his blunted talent was not suited to rhetoric, he devoted himself to versification; in which, however, he did nothing worth speaking of.

5. In his way of life he was economical and temperate, and by moderation in eating and drinking he preserved such robust health that he was rarely ill, though when ill dangerously so. For repeated experience and proof has shown that this is the case with persons who avoid licentiousness and luxury.

6. He was contented with very little sleep, which he took when time and season allowed; and throughout his long life he was so extremely chaste that no suspicion was ever cast on him in this respect, though it is a charge which, even when it can find no ground, malignity is apt to fasten on princes.

7. In riding and throwing the javelin, in shooting with the bow, and in all the accomplishments of military exercises, he was admirably skilful. That he never blew his nose in public, never spat, never was seen to change countenance, and that he never in all his life ate any fruit I pass over, as what has been often related before.

8. Having now briefly enumerated his good qualities with which we have been able to become acquainted, let us now proceed to speak of his vices. In other respects he was equal to average princes, but if he had the slightest reason (even if founded on wholly false information) for suspecting any one of aiming at supreme power, he would at once institute the most rigorous inquiry, trampling down right and wrong alike, and outdo the cruelty of Caligula, Domitian, or Commodus, whose barbarity he rivalled at the very beginning of his reign, when he shamefully put to death his own connections and relations.

9. And his cruelty and morose suspicions, which were directed against everything of the kind, were a cruel addition to the sufferings of the unhappy persons who were accused of sedition or treason.

10. And if anything of the kind got wind, he instituted investigations of a more terrible nature than the law sanctioned, appointing men of known cruelty as judges in such cases; and in punishing offenders he endeavoured to protract their deaths as long as nature would allow, being in such cases more savage than even Gallienus. For he, though

assailed by incessant and real plots of rebels, such as Aureolus, Posthumus, Ingenuus, and Valens who was surnamed the Thessalonian, and many others, often mitigated the penalty of crimes liable to sentence of death; while Constantius caused facts which were really unquestionable to be looked upon as doubtful by the excessive inhumanity of his tortures.

11. In such cases he had a mortal hatred of justice, even though his great object was to be accounted just and merciful: and as sparks flying from a dry wood, by a mere breath of wind are sometimes carried on with unrestrained course to the danger of the country villages around, so he also from the most trivial causes kindled heaps of evils, being very unlike that wise emperor Marcus Aurelius, who, when Cassius in Syria aspired to the supreme power, and when a bundle of letters which he had written to his accomplices, was taken with their bearer, and brought to him, ordered them at once to be burned, while he was still in Illyricum, in order that he might not know who had plotted against him, and so against his will be obliged to consider some persons as his enemies.

12. And, as some right-thinking people are of opinion, it was rather an indication of great virtue in Constantius to have quelled the empire without shedding more blood, than to have revenged himself with such cruelty.

13. As Cicero also teaches us, when in one of his letters to Nepos he accuses Cæsar of cruelty, "For," says he, "felicity is nothing else but success in what is honourable;" or to define it in another way, "Felicity is fortune assisting good counsels, and he who is not guided by such cannot be happy. Therefore in wicked and impious designs such as those of Cæsar there could be no felicity; and in my judgment Camillus when in exile was happier than Manlius at the same time, even if Manlius had been able to make himself king, as he wished."

14. The same is the language of Heraclitus of Ephesus, when he remarks that men of eminent capacity and virtue, through the caprice of fortune, have often been overcome by men destitute of either talent or energy. But that that glory is the best when power, existing with high rank, forces, as it were, its inclinations to be angry and cruel, and oppressive under the yoke, and so erects a glorious trophy in the citadel of its victorious mind.

15. But as in his foreign wars this emperor was unsuccessful and unfortunate, on the other hand in his civil contests he was successful; and in all those domestic calamities he covered himself with the horrid blood of the enemies of the republic and of himself; and yielding to his

elation at these triumphs in a way neither right nor usual, he erected at a vast expense triumphal arches in Gaul and the two Pannonias, to record his triumphs over his own provinces; engraving on them the titles of his exploits ... as long as they should last, to those who read the inscriptions.

16. He was preposterously addicted to listening to his wives, and to the thin voices of his eunuchs, and some of his courtiers, who applauded all his words, and watched everything he said, whether in approval or disapproval, in order to agree with it.

17. The misery of these times was further increased by the insatiable covetousness of his tax-collectors, who brought him more odium than money; and to many persons this seemed the more intolerable, because he never listened to any excuse, never took any measures for relief of the provinces when oppressed by the multiplicity of taxes and imposts; and in addition to all this he was very apt to take back any exemptions which he had granted.

18. He confused the Christian religion, which is plain and simple, with old women's superstitions; in investigating which he preferred perplexing himself to settling its questions with dignity, so that he excited much dissension; which he further encouraged by diffuse wordy explanations: he ruined the establishment of public conveyances by devoting them to the service of crowds of priests, who went to and fro to different synods, as they call the meetings at which they endeavour to settle everything according to their own fancy.

19. As to his personal appearance and stature, he was of a dark complexion with prominent eyes; of keen sight, soft hair, with his cheeks carefully shaved, and bright looking. From his waist to his neck he was rather long, his legs were very short and crooked, which made him a good leaper and runner.

20. When the body of the deceased emperor had been laid out, and placed in a coffin, Jovianus, at that time the chief officer of the guard, was ordered to attend it with royal pomp to Constantinople, to be buried among his relations.

21. While he was proceeding on the vehicle which bore the remains, samples of the military provisions were brought to him as an offering, as is usual in the case of princes; and the public animals were paraded before him; and a concourse of people came out to meet him as was usual; which, with other similar demonstrations, seemed to portend to Jovianus, as the superintendent of his funeral, the attainment of the empire, but an authority only curtailed and shadowy.

Notes

[114] The Quinquennalia (games under which title had been previously instituted in honour of Julius Cæsar and Augustus) were revived by Nero, A.D. 60, again fell into disuse, and were again revived by Domitian.—Cf. Tacit. An. xiv. 20.

[115] V. infra, Leo xxvi. c. 8.

[116] Sirmium was very near the existing town of Peterwaradin.

[117] Now the Balkan.

[118] It is believed that Mattium is the same as Marburg; it is not quite certain.

[119] These and other titles, such as "respectable" (spectabiles), "illustrious" (egregrie, illustres), were invented by the emperors of this century. They none of them appear to have conferred any substantive power.

[120] This office had been first established by Augustus, who created two prefects of the prætorian cohorts, under whose command also all the soldiers in Italy were placed. Commodus raised the number to three, and Constantine to four, whom (when he abolished the prætorian cohort), he made, in fact, governors of provinces. There was one præfectus prætorio for Gaul, one for Italy, one for Illyricum, and one for the East.

BOOK XXII

Egypt; mention of the Nile, the crocodile, the ibis, and the pyramids.—
XVI. Description of the five provinces of Egypt, and of their famous
cities.

I.

A.D. 361.

§ 1. While the variable events of fortune were bringing to pass these events in different parts of the world, Julian, amid the many plans which he was revolving while in Illyricum, was continually consulting the entrails of victims and watching the flight of birds in his eagerness to know the result of what was about to happen.

2. Aprunculus Gallus, an orator and a man of skill as a soothsayer, who was afterwards promoted to be governor of Narbonne, announced these results to him, being taught beforehand by the inspection of a liver, as he affirmed, which he had seen covered with a double skin. And while Julian was fearing that he was inventing stories to correspond with his desires, and was on that account out of humour, he himself beheld a far more favourable omen, which clearly predicted the death of Constantius. For at the same moment that that prince died in Cilicia, the soldier who, as he was going to mount his horse, had supported him with his right hand, fell down, on which Julian at once exclaimed, in the hearing of many persons, that he who had raised him to the summit had fallen.

3. But he did not change his plans, but remained within the border of Dacia, still being harassed with many fears. Nor did he think it prudent to trust to conjectures, which might perhaps turn out contrary to his expectations.

II.

§ 1. But while he was thus in suspense, the ambassadors, Theolaiphus and Aligildus, who had been despatched to him to announce the death of Constantius, suddenly arrived, adding that that prince with his last words had named him as his successor in his dignity.

2. As soon as he learnt this, being delighted at his deliverance from the turmoils of war and its consequent disorders, and fully relying on the prophecies he had received, having besides often experienced the advantages of celerity of action, he issued orders to march to Thrace. Therefore speedily advancing his standards, he passed over the high ground occupied by the Succi, and marched towards the ancient city of Eumolpias, now called Philippopolis, all his army following him with alacrity.

3. For they now saw that the imperial power which they were on their way to seize, in the face of imminent danger, was in a measure beyond their hopes put into their hands by the course of nature. And as report is wont marvellously to exaggerate events, a rumour got abroad that Julian, formidable both by sea and land, had entered Heraclea, called also Perinthus, borne over its unresisting walls on the chariot of Triptolemus, which from its rapid movements the ancients, who loved fables, had stated to be drawn by flying serpents and dragons.

4. When he arrived at Constantinople, people of every age and sex poured forth to meet him, as though he were some one dropped from heaven. On the eleventh of December he was received with respectful duty by the senate, and by the unanimous applause of the citizens, and was escorted into the city by vast troops of soldiers and civilians, marshalled like an army, while all eyes were turned on him, not only with the gaze of curiosity, but with great admiration.

5. For it seemed to them like a dream, that a youth in the flower of his age, of slight body, but renowned for great exploits, after many victories over barbarian kings and nations, having passed from city to city with unparalleled speed, should now, by an accession of wealth and power as rapid as the spread of fire, have become the unresisted master of the world; and the will of God itself having given him the empire, should thus have obtained it without any injury to the state.

III.

§ 1. His first step was to give to Secundus Sallustius, whom he promoted to be prefect of the prætorium, being well assured of his loyalty, a commission to conduct some important investigations, joining with him as colleagues Mamertinus, Arbetio, Agilo, and Nevitta, and also Jovinus, whom he had recently promoted to the command of the cavalry in Illyricum.

2. They all went to Chalcedon, and in the presence of the chiefs and tribunes, the Jovian and Herculian legions, they tried several causes with too much rigour, though there were some in which it was undeniable that the accused were really guilty.

3. They banished Palladius, the master of the ceremonies, to Britain, though there was but a suspicion that he had prejudiced Constantius against Gallus, while he was master of the ceremonies under that prince as Cæsar.

4. They banished Taurus, who had been prefect of the prætorium, to Vercelli, who, to all persons capable of distinguishing between right and wrong, will appear very excusable in respect to the act for which

he was condemned. For his offence was only that, fearing a violent disturbance which had arisen, he fled to the protection of his prince. And the treatment inflicted on him could not be read without great horror, when the preamble of the public accusation began thus:—"In the consulship of Taurus and Florentius, Taurus being brought before the criers ..."

5. Pentadius also was destined for a similar sentence; the charge against him being that, having been sent on a mission by Constantius, he had made notes of the replies given by Gallus when he was examined on several subjects before he was put to death. But as he defended himself with justice, he was at last discharged.

6. With similar iniquity, Florentius, at that time master of the ceremonies, the son of Nigridianus, was banished to Boæ, an island on the coast of Dalmatia. The other Florentius, who had been prefect of the prætorium, and was then consul, being alarmed at the sudden change in the aspect of affairs, in order to save himself from danger, hid himself and his wife for some time, and never returned during Julian's life; still he was, though absent, condemned to death.

7. In the same way, Evagrius, the comptroller of the private demesnes of the emperor, and Saturninus, late superintendent of the palace, and Cyrinus, late secretary, were all banished. But Justice herself seems to have mourned over the death of Ursulus, the treasurer, and to accuse Julian of ingratitude to him. For when, as Cæsar, he was sent to the west, with the intent that he was to be kept in great poverty, and without any power of making presents to any of his soldiers, in order to make them less inclined to favour any enterprise which he might conceive, this same Ursulus gave him letters to the superintendent of the Gallic treasury, desiring him to give the Cæsar whatever he might require.

8. After his death, Julian, feeling that he was exposed to general reproach and execration, thinking that an unpardonable crime could be excused, affirmed that the man had been put to death without his being aware of it, pretending that he had been massacred by the fury of the soldiers, who recollected what he had said (as we mentioned before) when he saw the destruction of Amida.

9. And therefore it seemed to be through fear, or else from a want of understanding what was proper, that he appointed Arbetio, a man always vacillating and arrogant, to preside over these investigations, with others of the chief officers of the legions present for the look of the thing, when he knew that he had been one of the chief

enemies to his safety, as was natural in one who had borne, a distinguished share in the successes of the civil war.

10. And though these transactions which I have mentioned vexed those who wished him well, those which came afterwards were carried out with a proper vigour and severity.

11. It was only a deserved destiny which befel Apodemius, who had been the chief steward, and whose cruel machinations with respect to the deaths of Silvanus and Gallus we have already mentioned, and Paulus, the secretary, surnamed "The Chain," men who are never spoken of without general horror, and who were now sentenced to be burnt alive.

12. They also sentenced to death Eusebius, the chief chamberlain of Constantius, a man equally full of ambition and cruelty, who from the lowest rank had been raised so high as even almost to lord it over the emperor, and who had thus become wholly intolerable; and whom Nemesis, who beholds all human affairs, having often, as the saying is, plucked him by the ear, and warned to conduct himself with more moderation, now, in spite of his struggles, hurled headlong from his high position.

IV.

§ 1. After this Julian directed his whole favour and affection to people of every description about the palace; not acting in this like a philosopher anxious for the discovery of truth.

2. For he might have been praised if he had retained a few who were moderate in their disposition, and of proved honesty and respectability. We must, indeed, confess that the greater part of them had nourished as it were such a seed-bed of all vices, which they spread abroad so as to infect the whole republic with evil desires, and did even more injury by their example than by the impunity which they granted to crimes.

3. Some of them had been fed on the spoils of temples, had smelt out gain on every occasion, and having raised themselves from the lowest poverty to vast riches, had set no bounds to their bribery, their plunder, or their extravagance, being at all times accustomed to seize what belonged to others.

4. From which habit the beginnings of licentious life sprang up, with perjuries, contempt of public opinion, and an insane arrogance, sacrificing good faith to infamous gains.

5. Among which vices, debauchery and unrestrained gluttony grew to a head, and costly banquets superseded triumphs for victories.

The common use of silken robes prevailed, the textile arts were encouraged, and above all was the anxious care about the kitchen. Vast spaces were sought out for ostentatious houses, so vast that if the consul Cincinnatus had possessed as much land, he would have lost the glory of poverty after his dictatorship.

6. To these shameful vices was added the loss of military discipline; the soldier practised songs instead of his battle-cry, and a stone would no longer serve him for a bed, as formerly, but he wanted feathers and yielding mattresses, and goblets heavier than his sword, for he was now ashamed to drink out of earthenware; and he required marble houses, though it is recorded in ancient histories that a Spartan soldier was severely punished for venturing to appear under a roof at all during a campaign.

7. But now the soldier was fierce and rapacious towards his own countrymen, but towards the enemy he was inactive and timid, by courting different parties, and in times of peace he had acquired riches, and was now a judge of gold and precious stones, in a manner wholly contrary to the recollection of very recent times.

8. For it is well known that when, in the time of the Cæsar Maximian, the camp of the king of Persia was plundered; a common soldier, after finding a Persian bag full of pearls, threw the gems away in ignorance of their value, and went away contented with the mere beauty of his bit of dressed leather.

9. In those days it also happened that a barber who had been sent for to cut the emperor's hair, came handsomely dressed; and when Julian saw him, he was amazed, and said, "I did not send for a superintendent, but for a barber." And when he was asked what he made by his business, he answered that he every day made enough to keep twenty persons, and as many horses, and also a large annual income, besides many sources of accidental gain.

10. And Julian, angry at this, expelled all the men of this trade, and the cooks, and all who made similar profits, as of no use to him, telling them, however, to go where they pleased.

V.

§ 1. And although from his earliest childhood he was inclined to the worship of the gods,[121] and gradually, as he grew up, became more attached to it, yet he was influenced by many apprehensions which made him act in things relating to that subject as secretly as he could.

2. But when his fears were terminated, and he found himself at liberty to do what he pleased, he then showed his secret inclinations,

and by plain and positive decrees ordered the temples to be opened, and victims to be brought to the altars for the worship of the gods.

3. And in order to give more effect to his intentions, he ordered the priests of the different Christian sects, with the adherents of each sect, to be admitted into the palace, and in a constitutional spirit expressed his wish that their dissensions being appeased, each without any hindrance might fearlessly follow the religion he preferred.

4. He did this the more resolutely because, as long licence increased their dissensions, he thought he should never have to fear the unanimity of the common people, having found by experience that no wild beasts are so hostile to men as Christian sects in general are to one another. And he often used to say, "Listen to me, to whom the Allemanni and Franks have listened;" imitating in this an expression of the ancient emperor Marcus Aurelius. But he omitted to notice that there was a great difference between himself and his predecessor.

5. For when Marcus was passing through Palestine, on his road to Egypt, he is said, when wearied by the dirt and rebellious spirit of the Jews, to have often exclaimed with sorrow, "O Marcomanni, O Quadi, O Sarmatians, I have at last found others worse than you!"

VI.

§ 1. About the same time many Egyptians, excited by various rumours, arrived at Constantinople; a race given to controversy, and extremely addicted to habits of litigation, covetous, and apt to ask payment of debts due to them over and over again; and also, by way of escaping from making the payments due to them, to accuse the rich of embezzlement, and the tax-gatherers of extortion.

2. These men, collecting into one body, came screeching like so many jackdaws, claiming in a rude manner the attention of the emperor himself, and of the prefects of the prætorium, and demanding the restoration of the contributions which they had been compelled to furnish, justly or unjustly, for the last seventy years.

3. And as they hindered the transaction of any other business, Julian issued an edict in which he ordered them all to go to Chalcedon, promising that he himself also would soon come there, and settle all their business.

4. And when they had gone, an order was given to all the captains of ships which go to and fro, that none of them should venture to take an Egyptian for a passenger. And as this command was carefully observed, their obstinacy in bringing false accusations came to an end, and they all, being disappointed in their object, returned home.

5. After which, as if at the dictation of justice herself, a law was published forbidding any one to exact from any officer the restitution of things which that officer had legally received.

VII.
A.D. 362.
§ 1. At the beginning of the new year, when the consular records had received the names of Mamertinus and Nevitta, the prince humbled himself by walking in their train with other men of high rank; an act which some praised, while others blame it as full of affectation, and mean.

2. Afterwards, when Mamertinus was celebrating the Circensian games, Julian, following an ancient fashion, manumitted some slaves, who were introduced by the consul's officer; but afterwards, being informed that on that day the supreme jurisdiction belonged to another, he fined himself ten pounds of gold as an offender.

3. At the same time he was a continual attendant in the court of justice, settling many actions which were brought in all kinds of cases. One day while he was sitting as judge, the arrival of a certain philosopher from Asia named Maximus, was announced, on which he leapt down from the judgment seat in an unseemly manner, and forgetting himself so far as to run at full speed from the hall, he kissed him, and received him with great reverence, and led him into the palace, appearing by this unseasonable ostentation a seeker of empty glory, and forgetful of those admirable words of Cicero, which describe people like him.

4. "Those very philosophers inscribe their names on the identical books which they write about the contempt of glory, in order that they may be named and extolled in that very thing in which they proclaim their contempt for mention and for praise."[122]

5. Not long afterwards, two of the secretaries who had been banished came to him, boldly promising to point out the hiding-place of Florentius if he would restore them to their rank in the army; but he abused them, and called them informers; adding that it did not become an emperor to be led by underhand information to bring back a man who had concealed himself out of fear of death, and who perhaps would not long be left in his retreat unpardoned.

6. On all these occasions Prætextatus was present, a senator of a noble disposition and of old-fashioned dignity; who at that time had come to Constantinople on his own private affairs, and whom Julian

254

by his own choice selected as governor of Achaia with the rank of pro-consul.

7. Still, while thus diligent in correcting civil evils, Julian did not omit the affairs of the army: continually appointing over the soldiers officers of long-tried worth; repairing the exterior defences of all the cities throughout Thrace, and taking great care that the soldiers on the banks of the Danube, who were exposed to the attacks of the barbarians, and who, as he heard were doing their duty with vigilance and courage, should never be in want of arms, clothes, pay, or provisions.

8. And while superintending these matters he allowed nothing to be done carelessly: and when those about him advised him to attack the Gauls as neighbours who were always deceitful and perfidious, he said he wished for more formidable foes; for that the Gallic merchants were enough for them, who sold them at all times without any distinction of rank.

9. While he gave his attention to these and similar matters, his fame was spreading among foreign nations for courage, temperance, skill in war, and eminent endowments of every kind of virtue, so that he gradually became renowned throughout the whole world.

10. And as the fear of his approach pervaded both neighbouring and distant countries, embassies hastened to him with unusual speed from all quarters at one time; the people beyond the Tigris and the Armenians sued for peace. At another the Indian tribes vied with each other, sending nobles loaded with gifts even from the Maldive Islands and Ceylon; from the south the Moors offered themselves as subjects of the Roman empire; from the north, and also from those hot climates through which the Phasis passes on its way to the sea, and from the people of the Bosphorus, and from other unknown tribes came ambassadors entreating that on the payment of annual duties they might be allowed to live in peace within their native countries.

VIII.

§ 1. The time is now appropriate, in my opinion, since in treating of this mighty prince we are come to speak of these districts, to explain perspicuously what we have learnt by our own eyesight or by reading, about the frontiers of Thrace and the situation of the Black Sea.

2. The lofty mountains of Athos in Macedonia, once made passable for ships by the Persians, and the Eubœan rocky promontory of Caphareus, where Nauplius the father of Palamedes wrecked the Grecian fleet, though far distant from one another, separate the Ægean

from the Thessalian Sea, which, extending as it proceeds, on the right, where it is widest, is full of the Sporades and Cyclades islands, which latter are so called because they lie round Delos, an island celebrated as the birthplace of the gods; on the left it washes Imbros, Tenedos, Lemnos, and Thasos; and when agitated by any gale it beats violently on Lesbos.

3. From thence, with a receding current, it flows past the temple of Apollo Sminthius, and Troas, and Troy, renowned for the adventures of heroes; and on the west it forms the Gulf of Melas, near the head of which is seen Abdera, the abode of Protagoras and Democritus; and the blood-stained seat of the Thracian Diomede; and the valleys through which the Maritza flows on its way to its waves; and Maronea, and Ænus, founded under sad auspices and soon deserted by Æneas, when under the guidance of the gods he hastened onwards to ancient Italy.

4. After this it narrows gradually, and, as if by a kind of natural wish to mingle with its waters, it rushes towards the Black Sea; and taking a portion of it forms a figure like the Greek φ. Then separating the Hellespont from Mount Rhodope, it passes by Cynossema,[123] where Hecuba is supposed to be buried, and Cæla, and Sestos, and Callipolis, and passing by the tombs of Ajax and Achilles, it touches Dardanus and Abydos (where Xerxes, throwing a bridge across, passed over the waters on foot), and Lampsacus, given to Themistocles by the king of Persia; and Parion, founded by Parius the son of Jason.

5. Then curving round in a semicircle and separating the opposite lands more widely in the round gulf of the sea of Marmora, it washes on the east Cyzicus, and Dindyma, the holy seat of the mighty mother Cybele, and Apamia, and Cius, and Astacus afterwards called Nicomedia from the King Nicomedes.

6. On the west it beats against the Chersonese, Ægospotami where Anaxagoras predicted that stones would fall from heaven, and Lysimachia, and the city which Hercules founded and consecrated to the memory of his comrade Perinthus. And in order to preserve the full and complete figure of the letter φ, in the very centre of the circular gulf lies the oblong island of Proconnesus, and also Besbicus.

7. Beyond the upper end of this island the sea again becomes very narrow where it separates Bithynia from Europe, passing by Chalcedon and Chrysopolis, and some other places of no importance.

8. Its left shore is looked down upon by Port Athyras and Selymbria, and Constantinople, formerly called Byzantium, a colony of the

Athenians, and Cape Ceras, having at its extremity a lofty tower to serve as a lighthouse to ships—from which cape also a very cold wind which often arises from that point is called Ceratas.

9. The sea thus broken, and terminated by mingling with the seas at each end, and now becoming very calm, spreads out into wider waters, as far as the eye can reach both in length and breadth. Its entire circuit, if one should measure it as one would measure an island, sailing along its shores, is 23,000 furlongs according to Eratosthenes, Hecatæus, and Ptolemy, and other accurate investigators of subjects of this kind, resembling, by the consent of all geographers, a Scythian bow, held at both ends by its string.

10. When the sun rises from the eastern ocean, it is shut in by the marshes of the Sea of Azov. On the west it is bounded by the Roman provinces. On the north lie many tribes differing in language and manners; its southern side describes a gentle curve.

11. Over this extended space are dispersed many Greek cities, which have for the most part been founded by the people of Miletus, an Athenian colony, long since established in Asia among the other Ionians by Nileus, the son of the famous Codrus, who is said to have devoted himself to his country in the Doric war.

12. The thin extremities of the bow at each end are commanded by the two Bospori, the Thracian and Cimmerian, placed opposite to one another; and they are called Bospori because through them the daughter of Inachus,[124] who was changed (as the poets relate) into a cow, passed into the Ionian sea.

13. The right curve of the Thracian Bosphorus is covered by a side of Bithynia, formerly called Mygdonia, of which province Thynia and Mariandena are districts; as also is Bebrycia, the inhabitants of which were delivered from the cruelty of Amycus by the valour of Pollux; and also the remote spot in which the soothsayer Phineus was terrified by the threatening flight of the Harpies.

14. The shores are curved into several long bays, into which fall the rivers Sangarius, and Phyllis, and Bizes, and Rebas; and opposite to them at the lower end are the Symplegades, two rocks which rise into abrupt peaks, and which in former times were accustomed to dash against one another with a fearful crash, and then rebounding with a sharp spring, to recoil once more against the object already struck. Even a bird could by no speed of its wings pass between these rocks as they pass and meet again without being crushed to death.

15. These rocks, when the Argo, the first of all ships, hastening to Colchis to carry off the golden fleece, had passed unhurt by them,

stood immovable for the future, the power of the whirlwind which used to agitate them being broken; and are now so firmly united that no one who saw them now would believe that they had ever been separated; if all the poems of the ancients did not agree on the point.

16. After this portion of Bithynia, the next provinces are Pontus and Paphlagonia, in which are the noble cities of Heraclea, and Sinope, and Polemonium, and Amisus, and Tios, and Amastris, all originally founded by the energy of the Greeks; and Cerasus, from which Lucullus brought the cherry, and two lofty islands which contain the famous cities of Trapezus and Pityus.

17. Beyond these places is the Acherusian cave, which the natives call Μυχοπόντιον; and the harbour of Acone, and several rivers, the Acheron, the Arcadius, the Iris, the Tibris, and near to that the Parthenius, all of which proceed with a rapid stream into the sea. Close to them is the Thermodon, which rises in Mount Armonius, and flows through the forest of Themiscyra, to which necessity formerly compelled the Amazons to migrate.

18. The Amazons, as may be here explained, after having ravaged their neighbours by bloody inroads, and overpowered them by repeated defeats, began to entertain greater projects; and perceiving their own strength to be superior to their neighbours', and being continually covetous of their possessions, they forced their way through many nations, and attacked the Athenians. But they were routed in a fierce battle, and their flanks being uncovered by cavalry, they all perished.

19. When their destruction became known, the rest, who had been left at home as unwarlike, were reduced to the last extremities; and fearing the attacks of their neighbours, who would now retaliate on them, they removed to the more quiet district of the Thermodon. And after a long time, their posterity again becoming numerous, returned in great force to their native regions, and became in later ages formidable to the people of many nations.

20. Not far from hence is the gentle hill Carambis, on the north, opposite to which, at a distance of 2,500 furlongs, is the Criu-Metopon, a promontory of Taurica. From this spot the whole of the sea-coast, beginning at the river Halys, is like the chord of an arc fastened at both ends.

21. On the frontiers of this district are the Dahæ,[125] the fiercest of all warriors; and the Chalybes, the first people who dug up iron, and wrought it to the use of man. Next to them lies a large plain occupied

by the Byzares, the Saqires, the Tibareni, the Mosynæci, the Macrones and the Philyres, tribes with which we have no intercourse.

22. And at a small distance from them are some monuments of heroes, where Sthenelus, Idmon, and Tiphys are buried, the first being that one of Hercules's comrades who was mortally wounded in the war with the Amazons; the second the soothsayer of the Argonauts; the third the skilful pilot of the crew.

23. After passing by the aforesaid districts, we come to the cave Aulon, and the river of Callichorus, which derives its name from the fact that when Bacchus, having subdued the nations of India in a three years' war, came into those countries, he chose the green and shady banks of this river for the re-establishment of his ancient orgies and dances; and some think that such festivals as these were those called Trieterica.[126]

24. Next to these frontiers come the famous cantons of the Camaritæ, and the Phasis, which with its roaring streams reaches the Colchi, a race descended from the Egyptians; among whom, besides other cities, is one called Phasis from the name of the river; and Dioscurias,[127] still famous, which is said to have been founded by the Spartans Amphitus and Cercius, the charioteers of Castor and Pollux; from whom the nation of Heniochi[128] derives its origin.

25. At a little distance from these are the Achæi, who after some earlier Trojan war, and not that which began about Helen, as some authors have affirmed, were driven into Pontus by foul winds, and, as all around was hostile, so that they could nowhere find a settled abode, they always stationed themselves on the tops of snowy mountains; and, under the pressure of an unfavourable climate they contracted a habit of living on plunder in contempt of all danger; and thus became the most ferocious of all nations. Of the Cercetæ, who lie next to them, nothing is known worth speaking of.

26. Behind them lie the inhabitants of the Cimmerian Bosphorus, living in cities founded by the Milesiani, the chief of which is Panticapæum, which is on the Bog a river of great size, both from its natural waters and the streams which fall into it.

27. Then for a great distance the Amazons stretch as far as the Caspian sea; occupying the banks of the Don, which rises in Mount Caucasus, and proceeds in a winding course, separating Asia from Europe, and falls into the swampy sea of Azov.

28. Near to this is the Rha, on the banks of which grows a vegetable of the same name, which is useful as a remedy for many diseases.

29. Beyond the Don, taking the plain in its width, lie the Sauromatæ, whose land is watered by the never-failing rivers Maræcus, Rhombites, Theophanes, and Totordanes. And there is at a vast distance another nation also known as Sauromatæ, touching the shore at the point where the river Corax falls into the sea.

30. Near to this is the sea of Azov, of great extent, from the abundant sources of which a great body of water pours through the straits of Patares, near the Black Sea; on the right are the islands Phanagorus and Hermonassa, which have been settled by the industry of the Greeks.

31. Round the furthest extremity of this gulf dwell many tribes differing from one another in language and habits; the Jaxamatæ, the Mæotæ, the Jazyges, the Roxolani, the Alani, the Melanchlænæ, the Geloni, and the Agathyrsi, whose land abounds in adamant.

32. And there are others beyond, who are the most remote people of the whole world. On the left side of this gulf lies the Crimea, full of Greek colonies; the people of which are quiet and steady: they practise agriculture, and live on the produce of the land.

33. From them the Tauri, though at no great distance, are separated by several kingdoms, among which are the Arinchi, a most savage tribe, the Sinchi, and the Napæi, whose cruelty, being aggravated by continual licence, is the reason why the sea is called the Inhospitable,[129] from which by the rule of contrary it gets the name of the Euxine, just as the Greeks call a fool εὐήθης, and night εὐθρόνη, and the furies, the Εὐμενίδες.

34. For they propitiated the gods with human victims, sacrificing strangers to Diana, whom they call Oreiloche, and fix the heads of the slain on the walls of their temples, as perpetual monuments of their deeds.

35. In this kingdom of the Tauri lies the uninhabited island of Leuce, which is consecrated to Achilles; and if any ever visit it, as soon as they have examined the traces of antiquity, and the temple and offerings dedicated to the hero, they return the same evening to their ships, as it is said that no one can pass the night there without danger to his life.

36. There is water there, and white birds like kingfishers, the origin of which, and the battles of the Hellespont, we will discuss at a proper time. And there are some cities in this region of which the most eminent are Eupatoria, Dandaca, and Theodosia, and several others which are free from the wickedness of human sacrifices.

37. Up to this we reckon that one of the extremities of the arc extends. We will now follow, as order suggests, the rest of the curve which extends towards the north, along the left side of the Thracian Bosphorus, just reminding the reader that while the bows of all other nations bend along the whole of their material, those of the Scythians and Parthians have a straight rounded line in the centre, from which they curve their spreading horns so as to present the figure of the waning moon.

38. At the very beginning then of this district, where the Rhipæan mountains end, lie the Arimphæi, a just people known for their quiet character, whose land is watered by the rivers Chronius and Bisula; and next to them are the Massagetæ, the Alani, and the Sargetæ, and several other tribes of little note, of whom we know neither the names nor the customs.

39. Then, a long way off, is the bay Carcinites, and a river of the same name, and a grove of Diana, frequented by many votaries in those countries.

40. After that we come to the Dnieper (Borysthenes), which rises in the mountains of the Neuri; a river very large at its first beginning, and which increases by the influx of many other streams, till it falls into the sea with great violence; on its woody banks is the town of Borysthenes, and Cephalonesus, and some altars consecrated to Alexander the Great and Augustus Cæsar.

41. Next, at a great distance, is an island inhabited by the Sindi, a tribe of low-born persons, who upon the overthrow of their lords and masters in Asia, took possession of their wives and properties. Below them is a narrow strip of coast called by the natives the Course of Achilles, having been made memorable in olden time by the exercises of the Thessalian chief, and next to that is the city of Tyros, a colony of the Phœnicians, watered by the river Dniester.

42. But in the middle of the arc which we have described as being of an extended roundness, and which takes an active traveller fifteen days to traverse, are the Europæan Alani, the Costoboci, and the countless tribes of the Scythians, who extend over territories which have no ascertained limit; a small part of whom live on grain. But the rest wander over vast deserts, knowing neither ploughtime nor seedtime; but living in cold and frost, and feeding like great beasts. They place their relations, their homes, and their wretched furniture on waggons covered with bark, and, whenever they choose, they migrate without hindrance, driving off these waggons wherever they like.

43. When one arrives at another point of the circuit where there is a harbour, which bounds the figure of the arc at that extremity, the island Peuce is conspicuous, inhabited by the Troglodytæ, and Peuci, and other inferior tribes, and we come also to Histros, formerly a city of great power, and to Tomi, Apollonia, Anchialos, Odissos, and many others on the Thracian coast.

44. But the Danube, rising near Basle on the borders of the Tyrol, extending over a wider space, and receiving on his way nearly sixty navigable rivers, pours through the Scythian territory by seven mouths into the Black Sea.

45. The first mouth (according to the Greek interpretation of the names) is at the island of Peuce, which we have mentioned; the second is at Naracustoma, the third at Calonstoma, the fourth at Pseudostoma. The Boreonstoma and the Sthenostoma, are much smaller, and the seventh is large and black-looking like a bog.

46. But the whole sea, all around, is full of mists and shoals, and is sweeter than seas in general, because by the evaporation of moisture the air is often thick and dense, and its waters are tempered by the immensity of the rivers which fall into it; and it is full of shifting shallows, because the number of the streams which surround it pour in mud and lumps of soil.

47. And it is well known that fish flock in large shoals to its most remote extremities that they may spawn and rear their young more healthfully, in consequence of the salubrity of the water; while the hollow caverns, which are very numerous there, protect them from voracious monsters. For nothing of the kind is ever seen in this sea, except some small dolphins, and they do no harm.

48. Now the portions of the Black Sea which are exposed to the north wind are so thoroughly frozen that, while the rivers, as it is believed, cannot continue their course beneath the ice, yet neither can the foot of beast or man proceed firmly over the treacherous and shifting ground; a fault which is never found in a pure sea, but only in one of which the waters are mingled with those of rivers. We have digressed more than we had intended, so now let us turn back to what remains to be told.

49. Another circumstance came to raise Julian's present joy, one which indeed had been long expected, but which had been deferred by all manner of delays. For intelligence was brought by Agilo and Jovius, who was afterwards quæstor, that the garrison of Aquileia, weary of the length of the siege, and having heard of the death of Constantius, had opened their gates and come forth, delivering up the

authors of the revolt; and that, after they had been burnt alive, as has been related, the rest had obtained pardon for their offences.

IX.

§ 1. But Julian, elated at his prosperity, began to aspire to greatness beyond what is granted to man: amid continual dangers he had learnt by experience that propitious fortune held out to him, thus peacefully governing the Roman world, a cornucopia as it were of human blessings and all kinds of glory and success: adding this also to his former titles of victory, that while he alone held the reins of empire he was neither disturbed by intestine commotions, nor did any barbarians venture to cross his frontiers; but all nations, eager at all times to find fault with what is past, as mischievous and unjust, were with marvellous unanimity agreed in his praises.

2. Having therefore arranged with profound deliberation all the matters which were required either by the circumstances of the state or by the time, and, having encouraged the soldiers by repeated harangues and by adequate pay to be active in accomplishing all that was to be done, Julian, being in great favour with all men, set out for Antioch, leaving Constantinople, which he had greatly strengthened and enriched; for he had been born there, and loved and protected it as his native city.

3. Then crossing the straits, and passing by Chalcedon and Libyssa, where Hannibal the Carthaginian is buried, he came to Nicomedia; a city of ancient renown, and so adorned at the great expense of former emperors, that from the multitude of its public and private buildings good judges look on it as a quarter, as it were, of the eternal city.

4. When Julian beheld its walls buried in miserable ashes, he showed the anguish of his mind by silent tears, and went slowly on towards the palace; especially lamenting its misfortunes, because the senators who came out to meet him were in poor-looking condition, as well as the people who had formerly been most prosperous; some of them he recognized having been brought up there by the bishop Eusebius, of whom he was a distant relation.

5. Having here made many arrangements for repairing the damage done by an earthquake, he passed through Nisæa to the frontier of Gallo-Græcia, and then turning to the right, he went to Pessinus, to see the ancient temple of Cybele; from which town in the second Punic war, in accordance with the warning of the Sibylline verses, the image of the goddess was removed to Rome by Scipio Nasica.

6. Of its arrival in Italy, with many other matters connected with it, we made mention in recording the acts of the emperor Commodus; but as to what the reason was for the town receiving this name writers differ.

7. For some have declared that the city was so called ἀπὸ τοῦ πεσῖν, from falling; inventing a tale that the statue fell from heaven; others affirm that Ilus, the son of Tros, king of Dardania, gave the place this name, which Theopompus says it received not from this, but from Midas, formerly a most powerful king of Phrygia.

8. Accordingly, having paid his worship to the goddess, and propitiated her with sacrifices and prayers, he returned to Ancyra; and as he was proceeding on this way from thence he was disturbed by a multitude; some violently demanding the restoration of what had been taken from them, others complaining that they had been unjustly attached to different courts; some, regardless of the risk they ran, tried to enrage him against their adversaries, by charging them with treason.

9. But he, a sterner judge than Cassius or Lycurgus, weighed the charges with justice, and gave each his due; never being swayed from the truth, but very severe to calumniators, whom he hated, because he himself, while still a private individual and of low estate, had often experienced the petulant frenzy of many in a way which placed him in great danger.

10. And though there are many other examples of his patience in such matters, it will suffice to relate one here. A certain man laid an information against his enemy, with whom he had a most bitter quarrel, affirming that he had been guilty of outrage and sedition; and when the emperor concealed his own opinion, he renewed the charge for several days, and when at last he was asked who the man was whom he was accusing, he replied, a rich citizen. When the emperor heard this he smiled and said, "What proof led you to the discovery of this conduct of his?" He replied, "The man has had made for himself a purple silk robe."

11. And on this, being ordered to depart in silence, and though unpunished as a low fellow who was accusing one of his own class of too difficult an enterprise to be believed, he nevertheless insisted on the truth of the accusation, till Julian, being wearied by his pertinacity, said to the treasurer, whom he saw near him, "Bid them give this dangerous chatterer some purple shoes to take to his enemy, who, as he gives me to understood, has made himself a robe of that colour; that so he may know how little a worthless piece of cloth can help a man, without the greatest strength."

12. But as such conduct as this is praiseworthy and deserving the imitation of virtuous rulers, so it was a sad thing and deserving of censure, that in his time it was very hard for any one who was accused by any magistrate to obtain justice, however fortified he might be by privileges, or the number of his campaigns, or by a host of friends. So that many persons being alarmed bought off all such annoyances by secret bribes.

13. Therefore, when after a long journey he had reached Pylæ, a place on the frontiers of Cappadocia and Cilicia, he received the ruler of the province, Celsus, already known to him by his Attic studies, with a kiss, and taking him up into his chariot conducted him with him into Tarsus.

14. From hence, desiring to see Antioch, the splendid metropolis of the East, he went thither by the usual stages, and when he came near the city he was received as if he had been a god, with public prayers, so that he marvelled at the voices of the vast multitude, who cried out that he had come to shine like a star on the Eastern regions.

15. It happened that just at that time, the annual period for the celebration of the festival of Adonis, according to the old fashion, came round; the story being, as the poets relate, that Adonis had been loved by Venus, and slain by a boar's tusk, which is an emblem of the fruits of the earth being cut down in their prime. And it appeared a sad thing that when the emperor was now for the first time making his entrance into a splendid city, the abode of princes, wailing lamentations and sounds of mourning should be heard in every direction.

16. And here was seen a proof of his gentle disposition, shown indeed in a trifling, but very remarkable instance. He had long hated a man named Thalassius, an officer in one of the law courts, as having been concerned in plots against his brother Gallus. He prohibited him from paying his salutations to him and presenting himself among the men of rank; which encouraged his enemies against whom he had actions in the courts of law, the next day, when a great crowd was collected in the presence of the emperor, to cry out, "Thalassius, the enemy of your clemency, has violently deprived us of our rights;" and Julian, thinking that this was an opportunity for crushing him, replied, "I acknowledge that I am justly offended with the man whom you mention, and so you ought to keep silence till he has made satisfaction to me who am his principal enemy." And he commanded the prefect who was sitting by him not to hear their business till he himself was recognized by Thalassius, which happened soon afterwards.

X.

§ 1. While wintering at Antioch, according to his wish, he yielded to none of the allurements of pleasure in which all Syria abounds; but under pretence of repose, he devoted himself to judicial affairs, which are not less difficult than those of war, and in which he expended exceeding care, showing exquisite willingness to receive information, and carefully balancing how to assign to every one his due. And by his just sentence the wicked were chastised with moderate punishments, and the innocent were maintained in the undiminished possession of their fortunes.

2. And although in the discussion of causes he was often unreasonable, asking at unsuitable times to what religion each of the litigants adhered, yet none of his decisions were found inconsistent with equity, nor could he ever be accused, either from considerations of religion or of anything else, of having deviated from the strict path of justice.

3. For that is a desirable and right judgment which proceeds from repeated examinations of what is just and unjust. Julian feared anything which might lead him away from such, as a sailor fears dangerous rocks; and he was the better able to attain to correctness, because, knowing the levity of his own impetuous disposition, he used to permit the prefects and his chosen counsellors to check, by timely admonition, his own impulses when they were inclined to stray; and he continually showed that he was vexed if he committed errors, and was desirous of being corrected.

4. And when the advocates in some actions were once applauding him greatly as one who had attained to perfect wisdom, he is said to have exclaimed with much emotion, "I was glad and made it my pride to be praised by those whom I knew to be competent to find fault with me, if I had said or done anything wrong."

5. But it will be sufficient out of the many instances of his clemency which he afforded in judging causes to mention this one, which is not irrelevant to our subject or insignificant. A certain woman being brought before the court, saw that her adversary, formerly one of the officers of the palace, but who had been displaced, was now, contrary to her expectation, re-established and girt in his official dress, complained in a violent manner of this circumstance; and the emperor replied, "Proceed, O woman, if you think that you have been injured in any respect; he is girt as you see in order to go more quickly through the mire; your cause will not suffer from it."

6. And these and similar actions led to the belief, as he was constantly saying, that that ancient justice which Aratus states to have fled to heaven in disgust at the vices of mankind, had returned to earth; only that sometimes he acted according to his own will rather than according to law, making mistakes which somewhat darkened the glorious course of his renown.

7. After many trials he corrected numerous abuses in the laws, cutting away circuitous proceedings, and making the enactments show more plainly what they commanded or forbade. But his forbidding masters of rhetoric and grammar to instruct Christians was a cruel action, and one deserving to be buried in everlasting silence.

XI.

§ 1. At this time, Gaudentius the secretary, whom I have mentioned above as having been sent by Constantius to oppose Julian in Africa, and a man of the name of Julian, who had been a deputy governor, and who was an intemperate partisan of the late emperor, were brought back as prisoners, and put to death.

2. And at the same time, Artemius, who had been Duke of Egypt, and against whom the citizens of Alexandria brought a great mass of heavy accusations, was also put to death, and the son of Marcellus too, who had been commander both of the infantry and of the cavalry, was publicly executed as one who had aspired to the empire by force of arms. Romanus, too, and Vincentius, the tribunes of the first and second battalion of the Scutarii, being convicted of aiming at things beyond their due, were banished.

3. And after a short time, when the death of Artemius was known, the citizens of Alexandria who had feared his return, lest, as he threatened, he should come back among them with power, and avenge himself on many of them for the offences which he had received, now turned all their anger against George, the bishop, by whom they had, so to say, been often attacked with poisonous bites.

4. George having been born in a fuller's shop, as was reported, in Epiphania, a town of Cilicia, and having caused the ruin of many individuals, was, contrary both to his own interest and to that of the commonwealth, ordained bishop of Alexandria, a city which from its own impulses, and without any special cause, is continually agitated by seditious tumults, as the oracles also show.

5. Men of this irritable disposition were readily incensed by George, who accused numbers to the willing ears of Constantius, as being opposed to his authority; and, forgetting his profession, which

ought to give no counsel but what is just and merciful, he adopted all the wicked acts of informers.

6. And among other things he was reported to have maliciously informed Constantius that in that city all the edifices which had been built by Alexander, its founder, at vast public expense, ought properly to be a source of emolument to the treasury.

7. To these wicked suggestions he added this also, which soon afterwards led to his destruction. As he was returning from court, and passing by the superb temple of the Genius, escorted by a large train, as was his custom, he turned his eyes towards the temple, and said, "How long shall this sepulchre stand?" And the multitude, hearing this, was thunderstruck, and fearing that he would seek to destroy this also, laboured to the utmost of their power to effect his ruin by secret plots.

8. When suddenly there came the joyful news that Artemius was dead; on which all the populace, triumphing with unexpected joy, gnashed their teeth, and with horrid outcries set upon George, trampling upon him and kicking him, and tearing him to pieces with every kind of mutilation.

9. With him also, Dracontius, the master of the mint, and a count named Diodorus, were put to death, and dragged with ropes tied to their legs through the street; the one because he had overthrown the altar lately set up in the mint, of which he was governor; the other because while superintending the building of a church, he insolently cut off the curls of the boys, thinking thus to affect the worship of the gods.

10. But the savage populace were not content with this; but having mutilated their bodies, put them on camels and conveyed them to the shore, where they burnt them and threw the ashes into the sea; fearing, as they exclaimed, lest their remains should be collected and a temple raised over them, as the relics of men who, being urged to forsake their religion, had preferred to endure torturing punishments even to a glorious death, and so, by keeping their faith inviolate, earning the appellation of martyrs. In truth the wretched men who underwent such cruel punishment might have been protected by the aid of the Christians, if both parties had not been equally exasperated by hatred of George.

11. When this event reached the emperor's ears, he roused himself to avenge the impious deed; but when about to inflict the extremity of punishment on the guilty, he was appeased by the intercession of those about him, and contented himself with issuing an

edict in which he condemned the crime which had been committed in stern language, and threatening all with the severest vengeance if anything should be attempted for the future contrary to the principles of justice and law.

XII.

§ 1. In the mean time, while preparing the expedition against the Persians, which he had long been meditating with all the vigour of his mind, he resolved firmly to avenge their past victories; hearing from others, and knowing by his own experience, that for nearly sixty years that most ferocious people had stamped upon the East bloody records of massacre and ravage, many of our armies having often been entirely destroyed by them.

2. And he was inflamed with a desire for the war on two grounds: first, because he was weary of peace, and dreaming always of trumpets and battles; and secondly, because, having been in his youth exposed to the attacks of savage nations, the wishes of whose kings and princes were already turning against us, and whom, as was believed, it would be easier to conquer than to reduce to the condition of suppliants, he was eager to add to his other glories the surname of Parthieus.

3. But when his inactive and malicious detractors saw that these preparations were being pressed forward with great speed and energy, they cried out that it was an unworthy and shameful thing for such unseasonable troubles to be caused by the change of a single prince, and laboured with all their zeal to postpone the campaign; and they were in the habit of saying, in the presence of those whom they thought likely to report their words to the emperor, that, unless he conducted himself with moderation during his excess of prosperity, he, like an over-luxuriant crop, would soon be destroyed by his own fertility.

4. And they were continually propagating sayings of this kind, barking in vain at the inflexible prince with secret attacks, as the Pygmies or the clown Thiodamas of Lindus assailed Hercules.

5. But he, as more magnanimous, allowed no delay to take place, nor any diminution in the magnitude of his expedition, but devoted the most energetic care to prepare everything suitable for such an enterprise.

6. He offered repeated victims on the altars of the gods; sometimes sacrificing one hundred bulls, and countless flocks of animals of all kinds, and white birds, which he sought for everywhere by land, and sea; so that every day individual soldiers who had stuffed them-

269

selves like boors with too much meat, or who were senseless from the eagerness with which they had drunk, were placed on the shoulders of passers-by, and carried to their homes through the streets from the public temples where they had indulged in feasts which deserved punishment rather than indulgence. Especially the Petulantes and the Celtic legion, whose audacity at this time had increased to a marvellous degree.

7. And rites and ceremonies were marvellously multiplied with a vastness of expense hitherto unprecedented; and, as it was now allowed without hindrance, every one professed himself skilful in divination, and all, whether illiterate or learned, without any limit or any prescribed order, were permitted to consult the oracles, and to inspect the entrails of victims; and omens from the voice of birds, and every kind of sign of the future, was sought for with an ostentatious variety of proceeding.

8. And while this was going on, as if it were a time of profound peace, Julian, being curious in all such branches of learning, entered on a new path of divination. He proposed to reopen the prophetic springs of the fountain of Castalia, which Hadrian was said to have blocked up with a huge mass of stones, fearing lest, as he himself had attained the sovereignty through obedience to the predictions of these waters, others might learn a similar lesson; and Julian immediately ordered the bodies which had been buried around it to be removed with the same ceremonies as those with which the Athenians had purified the island of Delos.

XIII.

§ 1. About the same time, on the 22nd of October, the splendid temple of Apollo, at Daphne, which that furious and cruel king Antiochus Epiphanes had built with the statue of the god, equal in size to that of Olympian Jupiter, was suddenly burnt down.

2. This terrible accident inflamed the emperor with such anger, that he instantly ordered investigations of unprecedented severity to be instituted, and the chief church of Antioch to be shut up. For he suspected that the Christians had done it out of envy, not being able to bear the sight of the magnificent colonnade which surrounded the temple.

3. But it was reported, though the rumour was most vague, that the temple had been burnt by means of Asclepiades the philosopher, of whom we have made mention while relating the actions of Magnentius. He is said to have come to the suburb in which the temple stood

to pay a visit to Julian, and being accustomed to carry with him wherever he went a small silver statue of the Heavenly Venus, he placed it at the feet of the image of Apollo, and then, according to his custom, having lighted wax tapers in front of it, he went away. At midnight, when no one was there to give any assistance, some sparks flying about stuck to the aged timbers; and from that dry fuel a fire was kindled which burnt everything it could reach, however separated from it by the height of the building.

4. The same year also, just as winter was approaching, there was a fearful scarcity of water, so that some rivers were dried up, and fountains too, which had hitherto abounded with copious springs. But afterwards they all were fully restored.

5. And on the second of December, as evening was coming on, all that remained of Nicomedia was destroyed by an earthquake, and no small portion of Nicæa.

XIV.

§ 1. These events caused great concern to the emperor; but still he did not neglect other affairs of urgency, till the time of entering on his intended campaign should arrive. But in the midst of his important and serious concerns, it appeared superfluous that, without any plausible reason, and out of a mere thirst for popularity, he took measures for producing cheapness; a thing which often proves contrary to expectation and produces scarcity and famine.

2. And when the magistrates of Antioch plainly proved to him that his orders could not be executed, he would not depart from his purpose, being as obstinate as his brother Gallus, but not bloodthirsty. On which account, becoming furious against them, as slanderous and obstinate, he composed a volume of invectives which he called "The Antiochean," or "Misopogon," enumerating in a bitter spirit all the vices of the city, and adding others beyond the truth; and when on this he found that many witticisms were uttered at his expense, he felt compelled to conceal his feelings for a time; but was full of internal rage.

3. For he was ridiculed as a Cercops;[130] again, as a dwarf spreading out his narrow shoulders, wearing a beard like that of a goat, and taking huge strides, as if he had been the brother of Otus and Ephialtes,[131] whose height Horace speaks of as enormous. At another time he was "the victim-killer," instead of the worshipper, in allusion to the numbers of his victims; and this piece of ridicule was seasonable and

deserved, as once out of ostentation he was fond of carrying the sacred vessels before the priests, attended by a train of girls. And although these and similar jests made him very indignant, he nevertheless kept silence, and concealed his emotions, and continued to celebrate the solemn festivals.

4. At last, on the day appointed for the holiday, he ascended Mount Casius, a mountain covered with trees, very lofty, and of a round form; from which at the second crowing of the cock[132] we can see the sun rise. And while he was sacrificing to Jupiter, on a sudden he perceived some one lying on the ground, who, with the voice of a suppliant, implored pardon and his life; and when Julian asked him who he was, he replied, that he was Theodotus, formerly the chief magistrate of Hierapolis, who, when Constantius quitted that city, had escorted him with other men of rank on his way; basely flattering him as sure to be victorious; and he had entreated him with feigned tears and lamentations to send them the head of Julian as that of an ungrateful rebel, in the same way as he recollected the head of Magnentius had been exhibited.

5. When Julian heard this, he said, "I have heard of this before, from the relation of several persons. But go thou home in security, being relieved of all fear by the mercy of the emperor, who, like a wise man, has resolved to diminish the number of his enemies, and is eager to increase that of his friends."

6. When he departed, having fully accomplished the sacrifices, letters were brought to him from the governor of Egypt, who informed him that after a long time he had succeeded in finding a bull Apis, which he had been seeking with great labour, a circumstance which, in the opinion of the inhabitants of those regions, indicates prosperity, abundant crops, and several other kinds of good fortune.

7. On this subject it seems desirable to say a few words. Among the animals which have been consecrated by the reverence of the ancients, Mnevis and Apis are the most eminent. Mnevis, concerning whom there is nothing remarkable related, is consecrated to the sun, Apis to the moon. But the bull Apis is distinguished by several natural marks; and especially by a crescent-shaped figure, like that of a new moon, on his right side. After living his appointed time, he is drowned in the sacred fountain (for he is not allowed to live beyond the time fixed by the sacred authority of their mystical books; nor is a cow brought to him more than once a year, who also must be distinguished with particular marks); then another is sought amid great public mourning; and if one can be found distinguished by all the required

marks, he is led to Memphis, a city of great renown, and especially celebrated for the patronage of the god Æsculapius.

8. And after he has been led into the city by one hundred priests, and conducted into a chamber, he is looked upon as consecrated, and is said to point out by evident means the signs of future events. Some also of those who come to him he repels by unfavourable signs; as it is reported he formally rejected Cæsar Germanicus when he offered him food; thus portending what shortly happened.

XV.

§ 1. Let us then, since the occasion seems to require it, touch briefly on the affairs of Egypt, of which we have already made some mention in our account of the emperors Hadrian and Severus, where we related several things which we had seen.[133]

2. The Egyptian is the most ancient of all nations, except indeed that its superior antiquity is contested by the Scythians: their country is bounded on the south[134] by the greater Syrtes, Cape Ras, and Cape Borion, the Garamantes, and other nations; on the east, by Elephantine, and Meroe, cities of the Ethiopians, the Catadupi, the Red Sea, and the Scenite Arabs, whom we now call Saracens. On the north it joins a vast track of land, where Asia and the Syrian provinces begin; on the west it is bounded by the Sea of Issus, which some call the Parthenian Sea.

3. We will also say a few words concerning that most useful of all rivers, the Nile, which Homer calls the Ægyptus; and after that we will enumerate other things worthy of admiration in these regions.

4. The sources of the Nile, in my opinion, will be as unknown to posterity as they are now. But since poets, who relate fully, and geographers who differ from one another, give various accounts of this hidden matter, I will in a few words set forth such of their opinions as seem to me to border on the truth.

5. Some natural philosophers affirm that in the districts beneath the North Pole, when the severe winters bind up everything, the vast masses of snow congeal; and afterwards, melted by the warmth of the summer, they make the clouds heavy with liquid moisture, which, being driven to the south by the Etesian winds, and dissolved into rain by the heat of the sun, furnish abundant increase to the Nile.

6. Some, again, assert that the inundations of the river at fixed times are caused by the rains in Ethiopia, which fall in great abundance in that country during the hot season; but both these theories

seem inconsistent with the truth—for rain never falls in Ethiopia, or at least only at rare intervals.

7. A more common opinion is, that during the continuance of the wind from the north, called the Precursor, and of the Etesian gales, which last forty-five days without interruption, they drive back the stream and check its speed, so that it becomes swollen with its waves thus dammed back; then, when the wind changes, the force of the breeze drives the waters to and fro, and the river growing rapidly greater, its perennial sources driving it forward, it rises as it advances, and covers everything, spreading over the level plains till it resembles the sea.

8. But King Juba, relying on the text of the Carthaginian books, affirms that the river rises in a mountain situated in Mauritania, which looks on the Atlantic Ocean, and he says, too, that this is proved by the fact that fishes, and herbs, and animals resembling those of the Nile are found in the marshes where the river rises.

9. But the Nile, passing through the districts of Ethiopia, and many different countries which give it their own names, swells its fertilizing stream till it comes to the cataracts. These are abrupt rocks, from which in its precipitous course it falls with such a crash, that the Ati, who used to live in that district, having lost their hearing from the incessant roar, were compelled to migrate to a more quiet region.

10. Then proceeding more gently, and receiving no accession of waters in Egypt, it falls into the sea through seven mouths, each of which is as serviceable as, and resembles, a separate river. And besides the several streams which are derived from its channel, and which fall with others like themselves, there are seven navigable with large waves; named by the ancients the Heracleotic, the Sebennitic, the Bolbitic, the Phatnitic, the Mendesian, the Tanitic, and the Pelusian mouths.

11. This river, rising as I have said, is driven on from the marshes to the cataracts, and forms several islands; some of which are said to be of such extent that the stream is three days in passing them.

12. Among these are two of especial celebrity, Meroe and Delta. The latter derives its name from its triangular form like the Greek letter; but when the sun begins to pass through the sign of Cancer, the river keeps increasing till it passes into Libra; and then, after flowing at a great height for one hundred days, it falls again, and its waters being diminished it exhibits, in a state fit for riding on, fields which just before could only be passed over in boats.

13. If the inundation be too abundant it is mischievous, just as it is unproductive if it be too sparing; for if the flood be excessive, it keeps the ground wet too long; and so delays cultivation; while if it be deficient, it threatens the land with barrenness. No landowner wishes it to rise more than sixteen cubits. If the flood be moderate, then the seed sown in favourable ground sometimes returns seventy fold. The Nile, too, is the only river which does not cause a breeze.

14. Egypt also produces many animals both terrestrial and aquatic, and some which live both on the earth and in the water, and are therefore called amphibious. In the dry districts antelopes and buffaloes are found, and sphinxes, animals of an absurd-looking deformity, and other monsters which it is not worth while to enumerate.

15. Of the terrestrial animals, the crocodile is abundant in every part of the country. This is a most destructive quadruped, accustomed to both elements, having no tongue, and moving only the upper jaw, with teeth like a comb, which obstinately fasten into everything he can reach. He propagates his species by eggs like those of a goose.

16. And as he is armed with claws, if he had only thumbs his enormous strength would suffice to upset large vessels, for he is sometimes ten cubits long. At night he sleeps under water; in the day he feeds in the fields, trusting to the stoutness of his skin, which is so thick that missiles from military engines will scarcely pierce the mail of his back.

17. Savage as these monsters are at all other times, yet as if they had concluded an armistice, they are always quiet, laying aside all their ferocity, during the seven days of festival on which the priests at Memphis celebrate the birthday of Apis.

18. Besides those which die accidentally, some are killed by wounds which they receive in their bellies from the dorsal fins of some fish resembling dolphins, which this river also produces.

19. Some also are killed by means of a little bird called the trochilus, which, while seeking for some picking of small food, and flying gently about the beast while asleep, tickles its cheeks till it comes to the neighbourhood of its throat. And when the hydrus, which is a kind of ichneumon, perceives this, it penetrates into its mouth, which the bird has caused to open, and descends into its stomach, where it devours its entrails, and then comes forth again.

20. But the crocodile, though a bold beast towards those who flee, is very timid when it finds a brave enemy. It has a most acute sight, and for the four months of winter is said to do without food.

21. The hippopotamus, also, is produced in this country; the most sagacious of all animals destitute of reason. He is like a horse, with cloven hoofs, and a short tail. Of his sagacity it will be sufficient to produce two instances.

22. The animal makes his lair among dense beds of reeds of great height, and while keeping quiet watches vigilantly for every opportunity of sallying out to feed on the crops. And when he has gorged himself, and is ready to return, he walks backwards, and makes many tracks, to prevent any enemies from following the straight road and so finding and easily killing him.

23. Again, when he feels lazy from having his stomach swollen by excessive eating, it rolls its thighs and legs on freshly-cut reeds, in order that the blood which is discharged through the wounds thus made may relieve his fat. And then he smears his wounded flesh with clay till the wounds get scarred over.

24. This monster was very rare till it was first exhibited to the Roman people in the ædileship of Scaurus, the father of that Scaurus whom Cicero defended, when he charged the Sardinians to cherish the same opinion as the rest of the world of the authority of that noble family. Since that time, at different periods, many specimens have been brought to Rome, and now they are not to be found in Egypt, having been driven, according to the conjecture of the inhabitants, up to the Blemmyæ[135] by being incessantly pursued by the people.

25. Among the birds of Egypt, the variety of which is countless, is the ibis, a sacred and amiable bird, also valuable, because by heaping up the eggs of serpents in its nest for food it causes these fatal pests to diminish.

26. They also sometimes encounter flocks of winged snakes, which come laden with poison from the marshes of Arabia. These, before they can quit their own region, they overcome in the air, and then devour them. This bird, we are told, produces its young through its mouth.

27. Egypt also produces innumerable quantities of serpents, destructive beyond all other creatures. Basilisks, amphisbænas,[136] scytalæ, acontiæ, dipsades, vipers, and many others. The asp is the largest and most beautiful of all; but that never, of its own accord, quits the Nile.

28. There are also in this country many things exceedingly worthy of observation, of which it is a good time now to mention a few. Everywhere there are temples of great size. There are seven marvellous pyramids, the difficulty of building which, and the length of time

consumed in the work, are recorded by Herodotus. They exceed in height anything ever constructed by human labour, being towers of vast width at the bottom and ending in sharp points.

29. And their shape received this name from the geometricians because they rise in a cone like fire (πῦρ). And huge as they are, as they taper off gradually, they throw no shadow, in accordance with a principle of mechanics.

30. There are also subterranean passages, and winding retreats, which, it is said, men skilful in the ancient mysteries, by means of which they divined the coming of a flood, constructed in different places lest the memory of all their sacred ceremonies should be lost. On the walls, as they cut them out, they have sculptured several kinds of birds and beasts, and countless other figures of animals, which they call hieroglyphics.

31. There is also Syene, where at the time of the summer solstice the rays surrounding upright objects do not allow the shadows to extend beyond the bodies. And if any one fixes a post upright in the ground, or sees a man or a tree standing erect, he will perceive that their shadow is consumed at the extremities of their outlines. This also happens at Meroe, which is the spot in Ethiopia nearest to the equinoctial circle, and where for ninety days the shadows fall in a way just opposite to ours, on account of which the natives of that district are called Antiscii.[137]

32. But as there are many other wonders which would go beyond the plan of our little work, we must leave these to men of lofty genius, and content ourselves with relating a few things about the provinces.

XVI.

§ 1. In former times Egypt is said to have been divided into three provinces: Egypt proper, the Thebais, and Libya, to which in later times two more have been added, Augustamnica, which has been cut off from Egypt proper, and Pentapolis, which has been detached from Libya.

2. Thebais, among many other cities, can boast especially of Hermopolis, Coptos, and Antinous, which Hadrian built in honour of his friend Antinous. As to Thebes, with, its hundred gates, there is no one ignorant of its renown.

3. In Augustamnica, among others, there is the noble city of Pelusium, which is said to have been founded by Peleus, the father of Achilles, who by command of the gods was ordered to purify himself in the lake adjacent to the walls of the city, when, after having slain his

brother Phocus, he was driven about by horrid images of the Furies; and Cassium, where the tomb of the great Pompey is, and Ostracine, and Rhinocolura.

4. In Libya Pentapolis is Cyrene, a city of great antiquity, but now deserted, founded by Battus the Spartan, and Ptolemais, and Arsinoë, known also as Teuchira, and Darnis, and Berenice, called also Hesperides.

5. And in the dry Libya, besides a few other insignificant towns, there are Parætonium, Chærecla, and Neapolis.

6. Egypt proper, which ever since it has been united to the Roman empire has been under the government of a prefect, besides some other towns of smaller importance, is distinguished by Athribis, and Oxyrynchus, and Thmuis, and Memphis.

7. But the greatest of all the cities is Alexandria, ennobled by many circumstances, and especially by the grandeur of its great founder, and the skill of its architect Dinocrates, who, when he was laying the foundation of its extensive and beautiful walls, for want of mortar, which could not be procured at the moment, is said to have marked out its outline with flour; an incident which foreshowed that the city should hereafter abound in supplies of provisions.

8. At Inibis the air is wholesome, the sky pure and undisturbed; and, as the experience of a long series of ages proves, there is scarcely ever a day on which the inhabitants of this city do not see the sun.

9. The shore is shifty and dangerous; and as in former times it exposed sailors to many dangers, Cleopatra erected a lofty tower in the harbour, which was named Pharos, from the spot on which it was built, and which afforded light to vessels by night when coming from the Levant or the Libyan sea along the plain and level coast, without any signs of mountains or towns or eminences to direct them, they were previously often wrecked by striking into the soft and adhesive sand.

10. The same queen, for a well-known and necessary reason, made a causeway seven furlongs in extent, admirable for its size and for the almost incredible rapidity with which it was made. The island of Pharos, where Homer in sublime language relates that Proteus used to amuse himself with his herds of seals, is almost a thousand yards from the shore on which the city stands, and was liable to pay tribute to the Rhodians.

11. And when on one occasion the farmers of this revenue came to make exorbitant demands, she, being a wily woman, on a pretext of it being the season of solemn holidays, led them into the suburbs, and ordered the work to be carried on without ceasing. And so seven fur-

longs were completed in seven days, being raised with the soil of the adjacent shore. Then the queen, driving over it in her chariot, said that the Rhodians were making a blunder in demanding port dues for what was not an island but part of the mainland.

12. Besides this there are many lofty temples, and especially one to Serapis, which, although no words can adequately describe it, we may yet say, from its splendid halls supported by pillars, and its beautiful statues and other embellishments, is so superbly decorated, that next to the Capitol, of which the ever-venerable Rome boasts, the whole world has nothing worthier of admiration.

13. In it were libraries of inestimable value; and the concurrent testimony of ancient records affirm that 70,000 volumes, which had been collected by the anxious care of the Ptolemies, were burnt in the Alexandrian war when the city was sacked in the time of Cæsar the Dictator.

14. Twelve miles from this city is Canopus, which, according to ancient tradition, received its name from the prophet of Menelaus, who was buried there. It is a place exceedingly well supplied with good inns, of a most wholesome climate, with refreshing breezes; so that any one who resides in that district might think himself out of our world while he hears the breezes murmuring through the sunny atmosphere.

15. Alexandria itself was not, like other cities, gradually embellished, but at its very outset it was adorned with spacious roads. But after having been long torn by violent seditions, at last, when Aurelian was emperor, and when the intestine quarrels of its citizens had proceeded to deadly strife, its walls were destroyed, and it lost the largest half of its territory, which was called Bruchion, and had long been the abode of eminent men.

16. There had lived Aristarchus, that illustrious grammarian; and Herodianus, that accurate inquirer into the fine arts; and Saccas Ammonius, the master of Plotinus, and many other writers in various useful branches of literature, among whom Didymus, surnamed Chalcenterus, a man celebrated for his writings on many subjects of science, deserves especial mention; who, in the six books in which he, sometimes incorrectly, attacks Cicero, imitating those malignant farce writers, is justly blamed by the learned as a puppy barking from a distance with puny voice against the mighty roar of the lion.

17. And although, besides those I have mentioned, there were many other men of eminence in ancient times, yet even now there is much learning in the same city; for teachers of various sects flourish,

and many kinds of secret knowledge are explained by geometrical science. Nor is music dead among them, nor harmony. And by a few, observations of the motion of the world and of the stars are still cultivated; while of learned arithmeticians the number is considerable; and besides them there are many skilled in divination.

18. Again, of medicine, the aid of which in our present extravagant and luxurious way of life is incessantly required, the study is carried on with daily increasing eagerness; so that while the employment be of itself creditable, it is sufficient as a recommendation for any medical man to be able to say that he was educated at Alexandria. And this is enough to say on this subject.

19. But if any one in the earnestness of his intellect wishes to apply himself to the various branches of divine knowledge, or to the examination of metaphysics, he will find that the whole world owes this kind of learning to Egypt.

20. Here first, far earlier than in any other country, men arrived at the various cradles (if I may so say) of different religions. Here they still carefully preserve the elements of sacred rites as handed down in their secret volumes.

21. It was in learning derived from Egypt that Pythagoras was educated, which taught him to worship the gods in secret, to establish the principle that in whatever he said or ordered his authority was final, to exhibit his golden thigh at Olympia, and to be continually seen in conversation with an eagle.

22. Here it was that Anaxagoras derived the knowledge which enabled him to predict that stones would fall from heaven, and from the feeling of the mud in a well to foretell impending earthquakes. Solon too derived aid from the apophthegms of the priests of Egypt in the enactment of his just and moderate laws, by which he gave great confirmation to the Roman jurisprudence. From this source too Plato, soaring amid sublime ideas, rivalling Jupiter himself in the magnificence of his voice, acquired his glorious wisdom by a visit to Egypt.

23. The inhabitants of Egypt are generally swarthy and dark complexioned, and of a rather melancholy cast of countenance, thin and dry looking, quick in every motion, fond of controversy, and bitter exactors of their rights. Among them a man is ashamed who has not resisted the payment of tribute, and who does not carry about him wheals which he has received before he could be compelled to pay it. Nor have any tortures been found sufficiently powerful to make the hardened robbers of this country disclose their names unless they do so voluntarily.

24. It is well known, as the ancient annals prove, that all Egypt was formerly under kings who were friendly to us. But after Antony and Cleopatra were defeated in the naval battle at Actium, it became a province under the dominion of Octavianus Augustus. We became masters of the dry Libya by the last will of king Apion. Cyrene and the other cities of Libya Pentapolis we owe to the liberality of Ptolemy. After this long digression, I will now return to my original subject.

Notes

[121] Ammianus uses the phrase "worship of *the gods*," in opposition to Christianity.

[122] Pro Archias Poeta, cap. xxii.

[123] The fable was that Hecuba was turned into a bitch, from which this place was called κονος σῆμα, a dog's tomb.

[124] To—the name Βόσπορος is derived from βοὸς πόρος, the passage of the Cow.

[125] So Virgil calls them Indomitique Dahæ. In the Georgics, also, he speaks of the Chalybes as producers of iron. At Chalybes nudi ferrum.

[126] Or triennial, from τρεῖς, three; and ἔτος, a year.

[127] From Διόσκουροι, the sons of Jupiter, *i.e.*, Castor and Pollux.

[128] From ἡνίοχος, a charioteer.

[129] The old name was Ἄξεινος, inhospitable; turned into εὔξεινος, friendly to strangers—εὐήθης, according to etymology, would mean "of a good disposition:" εὐφρόνη, "the time when people have happy thoughts;" Εὐμενίδες, "deities of propitious might."

[130] A people living in one of the islands near Sicily, and changed by Jupiter as related, Ov. Met. xiv., into monkeys.

[131] Two of the chief giants, Hom. Od. xi.

[132] A time spoken of by Pliny as before the fourth watch.

[133] These books are lost.

[134] We must remark here Ammianus's complete ignorance of comparative geography and the bearings of the different countries of which he speaks. The Syrtes and Cape Ras are due *west*, not south of Egypt, The Ethiopians and Catadupi are on the north; while the Arabs, whom he places in the same line, are on the south-east. The Sea of Issus, on the Levant, which he places on the west, is on the north.

[135] The Blemmyæ were an Ethiopian tribe to the south of Egypt.

[136] These names seem derived from the real or fancied shape of the snakes mentioned: the amphisbæna, from ἀμφὶ and βαίνω, to go both ways, as it

was believed to have a head at each end. The scytalas was like "a staff;" the acontias, like "a javelin;" the dipsas was a thirsty snake.

[137] From ἀντὶ, opposite; and σκιὰ, shadow.

BOOK XXIII

ARGUMENT

I. Julian in vain attempts to restore the temple at Jerusalem, which had been destroyed long before.—II. He orders Arsaces, king of Armenia, to prepare for the war with Persia, and with an army and auxiliary troops of the Scythians crosses the Euphrates.—III. As he marches through Mesopotamia, the princes of the Saracenic tribes of their own accord offer him a golden crown and auxiliary troops—A Roman fleet of eleven hundred ships arrives, and bridges over the Euphrates.—IV. A description of several engines, balistæ, scorpions, or wild-asses, battering-rams, helepoles, and fire-machines.—V. Julian, with all his army, crosses the river Aboras by a bridge of boats at Circesium—He harangues his soldiers.—VI. A description of the eighteen principal provinces of Persia, their cities, and the customs of their inhabitants.

I.

A.D. 363.

§ 1. To pass over minute details, these were the principal events of the year. But Julian, who in his third consulship had taken as his colleague Sallustius, the prefect of Gaul now entered on his fourth year, and by a novel arrangement took as his colleague a private individual; an act of which no one recollected an instance since that of Diocletian and Aristobulus.

2. And although, foreseeing in his anxious mind the various accidents that might happen, he urged on with great diligence all the endless preparations necessary for his expedition, yet distributing his diligence everywhere; and being eager to extend the recollection of his reign by the greatness of his exploits, he proposed to rebuild at a vast expense the once magnificent temple of Jerusalem, which after many deadly contests was with difficulty taken by Vespasian and Titus, who succeeded his father in the conduct of the siege. And he assigned the

task to Alypius of Antioch, who had formerly been proprefect of Britain.

3. But though Alypius applied himself vigorously to the work, and though the governor of the province co-operated with him, fearful balls of fire burst forth with continual eruptions close to the foundations, burning several of the workmen and making the spot altogether inaccessible. And thus the very elements, as if by some fate, repelling the attempt, it was laid aside.

4. About the same time the emperor conferred various honours on the ambassadors who were sent to him from the Eternal City, being men of high rank and established excellence of character. He appointed Apronianus to be prefect of Rome, Octavianus to be proconsul of Africa, Venustus to be viceroy of Spain, and promoted Rufinus Aradius to be count of the East in the room of his uncle Julian, lately deceased.

5. When all this had been carried out as he arranged, he was alarmed by an omen which, as the result showed, indicated an event immediately at hand. Felix, the principal treasurer, having died suddenly of a hemorrhage, and Count Julian having followed him, the populace, looking on their public titles, hailed Julian as Felix and Augustus.

6. Another bad omen had preceded this, for, on the very first day of the year, as the emperor was mounting the steps of the temple of the Genius, one of the priests, the eldest of all, fell without any one striking him and suddenly expired; an event which the bystanders, either out of ignorance or a desire to flatter, affirmed was an omen affecting Sallustius, as the elder consul; but it was soon seen that the death it portended was not to the elder man, but to the higher authority.

7. Besides these several other lesser signs from time to time indicated what was about to happen; for, at the very beginning of the arrangements for the Parthian campaign, news came that there had been an earthquake at Constantinople, which those skilful in divination declared to be an unfavourable omen to a ruler about to invade a foreign country; and therefore advised Julian to abandon his unreasonable enterprise, affirming that these and similar signs can only be disregarded with propriety when one's country is invaded by foreign armies, as then there is one everlasting and invariable law, to defend its safety by every possible means, allowing no relaxation nor delay. News also came by letter that at Rome the Sibylline volumes had been consulted on the subject of the war by Julian's order, and that they had in plain terms warned him not to quit his own territories that year.

II.

§ 1. But in the mean time embassies arrived from several nations promising aid, and they were liberally received and dismissed; the emperor with plausible confidence replying that it by no means became the power of Rome to rely on foreign aid to avenge itself, as it was rather fitting that Rome should give support to its friends and allies if necessity drove them to ask it.

2. He only warned Arsaces, king of Armenia, to collect a strong force, and wait for his orders, as he should soon know which way to march, and what to do. Then, as soon as prudence afforded him an opportunity, hastening to anticipate every rumour of his approach by the occupation of the enemy's country, before spring had well set in, he sent the signal for the advance to all his troops, commanding them to cross the Euphrates.

3. As soon as the order reached them, they hastened to quit their winter quarters; and having crossed the river, according to their orders, they dispersed into their various stations, and awaited the arrival of the emperor. But he, being about to quit Antioch, appointed a citizen of Heliopolis, named Alexander, a man of turbulent and ferocious character, to govern Syria, saying that he indeed had not deserved such a post, but that the Antiochians, being covetous and insolent, required a judge of that kind.

4. When he was about to set forth, escorted by a promiscuous multitude who wished him a fortunate march and a glorious return, praying that he would be merciful and kinder than he had been, he (for the anger which their addresses and reproaches had excited in his breast was not yet appeased) spoke with severity to them, and declared that he would never see them again.

5. For he said that he had determined, after his campaign was over, to return by a shorter road to Tarsus in Cilicia, to winter there: and that he had written to Memorius, the governor of the city, to prepare everything that he might require in that city. This happened not long afterwards; for his body was brought back thither and buried in the suburbs with a very plain funeral, as he himself had commanded.

6. As the weather was now getting warm he set out on the fifth of March, and by the usual stages arrived at Hieropolis; and as he entered the gates of that large city a portico on the left suddenly fell down, and as fifty soldiers were passing under it at that moment it wounded many, crushing them beneath the vast weight of the beams and tiles.

7. Having collected all his troops from thence, he marched with such speed towards Mesopotamia, that before any intelligence of his march could arrive (an object about which he was especially solicitous) he came upon the Assyrians quite unexpectedly. Then having led his whole army and the Scythian auxiliaries across the Euphrates by a bridge of boats, he arrived at Batnæ, a town of Osdroene, and there again a sad omen met him.

8. For when a great crowd of grooms was standing near an enormously high haystack, in order to receive their forage (for in this way those supplies used to be stored in that country), the mass was shaken by the numbers who sought to strip it, and falling down, overwhelmed fifty men.

III.

§ 1. Leaving this place with a heavy heart, he marched with great speed, and arrived at Carrhæ, an ancient town notorious for the disasters of Crassus and the Roman army. From this town two royal roads branch off, both leading into Persia; that on the left hand through Adiabene and along the Tigris, that on the right through the Assyrians and along the Euphrates.

2. There he stayed some days, preparing necessary supplies; and according to the custom of the district he offered sacrifices to the moon, which is religiously worshipped in that region; and it is said that while before the altar, no witness to the action being admitted, he secretly gave his own purple robe to Procopius, and bade him boldly assume the sovereignty if he should hear that he had died among the Parthians.

3. Here while asleep his mind was agitated with dreams, and foresaw some sad event about to happen; on which account he and the interpreters of dreams considering the omens which presented themselves, pronounced that the next day, which was the nineteenth of March, ought to be solemnly observed. But, as was ascertained subsequently, that very same night, while Apronianus was prefect of Rome, the temple of the Palatine Apollo was burnt in the Eternal City; and if aid from all quarters had not come to the rescue the violence of the conflagration would have destroyed even the prophetic volumes of the Sibyl.

4. After these things had happened in this manner, and while Julian was settling his line of march, and making arrangements for supplies of all kinds, his scouts come panting in, and bring him word that some squadrons of the enemy's cavalry have suddenly passed the

frontier in the neighbourhood of the camp, and have driven off a large booty.

5. Indignant at such atrocity and at such an insult, he immediately (as indeed he had previously contemplated) put thirty thousand chosen men under the orders of Procopius, who has been already mentioned, uniting with him in this command Count Sebastian, formerly Duke of Egypt; and he ordered them to act on this side of the Tigris, observing everything vigilantly, so that no danger might arise on any side where it was not expected, for such things had frequently happened. He charged them further, if it could be done, to join King Arsaces; and march with him suddenly through Corduena and Moxoëne, ravaging Chiliocomus, a very fertile district of Media, and other places; and then to rejoin him while still in Assyria, in order to assist him as he might require.

6. Having taken these measures, Julian himself, pretending to march by the line of the Tigris, on which road he had purposely commanded magazines of provisions to be prepared, turned towards the right, and after a quiet night, asked in the morning for the horse which he was accustomed to ride: his name was Babylonius. And when he was brought, being suddenly griped and starting at the pain, he fell down, and rolling about scattered the gold and jewels with which his trappings were decked. Julian, in joy at this omen, cried out, amid the applause of those around, that "Babylon had fallen, and was stripped of all her ornaments."

7. Having delayed a little that he might confirm the omen by the sacrifice of some victims, he advanced to Davana, where he had a garrison-fortress, and where the river Belias rises which falls into the Euphrates. Here he refreshed his men with food and sleep, and the next day reached Callinicus, a strong fortress, and also a great commercial mart, where, on the 27th of March (the day on which at Rome the annual festival in honour of Cybele is celebrated, and the car in which her image is borne is, as it is said, washed in the waters of the Almo), he kept the same feast according to the manner of the ancients, and then, retiring to rest, passed a triumphant, and joyful night.

8. The next day he proceeded along the bank of the river, which other streams began to augment, marching with an armed escort; and at night he rested in a tent where some princes of the Saracenic tribes came as suppliants, bringing him a golden crown, and adoring him as the master of the world and of their own nations: he received them graciously, as people well adapted for surprises in war.

9. And while addressing them a fleet arrived equal to that of the mighty sovereign Xerxes, under the command of the tribune Constantianus, and Count Lucillianus; they threw a bridge over the broadest part of the Euphrates: the fleet consisted of one thousand transports, of various sorts and sizes, bringing large supplies of provisions, and arms, and engines for sieges, and fifty ships of war, and as many more suitable for the construction of bridges.

IV.

§ 1. I am reminded by the circumstances to explain instruments of this kind briefly, as far as my moderate talent may enable me to do, and first I will set forth the figure of the balista.

2. Between two axletrees a strong large iron bar is fastened, like a great rule, round, smooth, and polished; from its centre a square pin projects for some distance, hollowed out into a narrow channel down its middle. This is bound by many ligatures of twisted cords: to it two wooden nuts are accurately fitted, by one of which stands a skilful man who works it, and who fits neatly into the hollow of the pin or pole a wooden arrow with a large point; and as soon as this is done, some strong young men rapidly turn a wheel.

3. When the tip of the arrow's point has reached the extremity of the cords, the arrow is struck by a blow from the balista, and flies out of sight; sometimes even giving forth sparks by its great velocity, and it often happens that before the arrow is seen, it has given a fatal wound.

4. The scorpion, which they now call the wild-ass, is in the following form. Two axletrees of oak or box are cut out and slightly curved, so as to project in small humps, and they are fastened together like a sawing machine, being perforated with large holes on each side; and between them, through the holes, strong ropes are fastened to hold the two parts together, and prevent them from starting asunder.

5. From these ropes thus placed a wooden pin rises in an oblique direction, like the pole of a chariot, and it is so fastened by knotted cords as to be raised or depressed at pleasure. To its top, iron hooks are fastened, from which a sling hangs, made of either cord or iron. Below the pin is a large sack filled with shreds of cloth, fastened by strong ties, and resting on heaped-up turves or mounds of brick. For an engine of this kind, if placed on a stone wall would destroy whatever was beneath it, not by its weight, but by the violence of its concussion.

6. Then when a conflict begins, a round stone is placed on the sling, and four youths on each side, loosening the bar to which the

cords are attached, bend the pin back till it points almost upright into the air; then the worker of the engine, standing by on high ground, frees by a blow with the heavy hammer the bolt which keeps down the whole engine; and the pin being set free by the stroke, and striking against the mass of cloth shreds, hurls forth the stone with such force as to crush whatever it strikes.

7. This engine is called a *tormentum*, because all its parts are twisted (*torquetur*); or a scorpion, because it has an erect sting; but modern times have given it the name of the wild-ass, because when wild asses are hunted, they throw the stones behind them by their kicks so as to pierce the chests of those who pursue them, or to fracture their skulls.

8. Now let us come to the battering ram. A lofty pine or ash is chosen, the top of which is armed with a long and hard head of iron, resembling a ram, which form has given the name to the engine. It is suspended from iron beams running across on each side, like the top of a pair of scales, and is kept in its place by ropes hanging from a third beam. A number of men draw it back as far as there is room, and then again drive it forward to break down whatever opposes it by mighty blows, like a ram which rises up and butts.

9. By the frequent blows of this rebounding thunderbolt, buildings are torn asunder and walls are loosened and thrown down. By this kind of engine, if worked with proper vigour, garrisons are deprived of their defences, and the strongest cities are laid open and sieges rapidly brought to a conclusion.

10. Instead of these rams, which from their common use came to be despised, a machine was framed called in Greek the helepolis, by the frequent use of which Demetrius, the son of king Antigonus, took Rhodes and other cities, and earned the surname of Poliorcetes.

11. It is constructed in this manner. A vast testudo is put together, strengthened with long beams and fastened with iron nails; it is covered with bullocks' hides and wicker-work made of freshly cut twigs, and its top is smeared over with clay to keep off missiles and fiery darts.

12. Along its front very sharp spears with three points are fastened, heavy with iron, like the thunderbolts represented by painters or sculptors, and strong enough with the projecting points to tear to pieces whatever it strikes.

13. A number of soldiers within guide this vast mast with wheels and ropes, urging with vehement impulse against the weaker parts of

the wall, so that, unless repelled by the strength of the garrison above, it breaks down the wall and lays open a great breach.

14. The firebolts, which are a kind of missile, are made thus. They take an arrow of cane, joined together between the point and the reed with jagged iron, and made in the shape of a woman's spindle, with which linen threads are spun; this is cunningly hollowed out in the belly and made with several openings, and in the cavity fire and fuel of some kind is placed.

15. Then if it be shot slowly from a slack bow (for if it be shot with too much speed the fire is extinguished), so as to stick anywhere, it burns obstinately, and if sprinkled with water it creates a still fiercer fire, nor will anything but throwing dust upon it quench it. This is enough to say of mural engines; let us now return to our original subject.

V.

§ 1. Having received the reinforcements of the Saracens which they so cheerfully offered, the emperor advanced with speed, and at the beginning of April entered Circesium, a very secure fortress, and skilfully built, it is surrounded by the two rivers Aboras (or Chaboras) and Euphrates, which make it as it were an island.

2. It had formerly been small and insecure, till Diocletian surrounded it with lofty towers and walls when he was strengthening his inner frontier within the very territories of the barbarians, in order to prevent the Persians from overrunning Syria, as had happened a few years before to the great injury of the province.

3. For it happened one day at Antioch, when the city was in perfect tranquillity, a comic actor being on the stage with his wife, acting some common play, while the people were delighted with his acting, the wife suddenly exclaimed, "Unless I am dreaming, here are the Persians;" and immediately the populace turning round, were put to flight, and driven about in every direction while seeking to escape the darts which were showered upon them; and so the city being burnt and numbers of the citizens slain, who, as is usual in time of peace, were strolling about carelessly, and all the places in the neighbourhood being burnt and laid waste, the enemy loaded with booty returned in safety to their own country after having burnt Mareades alive, who had wickedly guided them to the destruction of his fellow-citizens. This event took place in the time of Gallienus.

4. But Julian, while remaining at Circesium to give time for his army and all its followers to cross the bridge of boats over the Aboras,

received letters with bad news from Sallust, the prefect of Gaul, entreating him to suspend his expedition against the Parthians, and imploring him not in such an unseasonable manner to rush on irrevocable destruction before propitiating the gods.

5. But Julian disregarded his prudent adviser, and advanced boldly; since no human power or virtue can ever avail to prevent events prescribed by the order of the Fates. And immediately, having crossed the river, he ordered the bridge to be taken to pieces, that the soldiers might have no hope of safety by quitting their ranks and returning.

6. Here also a bad omen was seen; the corpse of an officer who had been put to death by the executioner, whom Sallust, the prefect, while in this country had condemned to death, because, after having promised to deliver an additional supply of provisions by an appointed day, he disappointed him through some hindrance. But after the unhappy man had been executed, the very next day there arrived, as he had promised, another fleet heavily laden with corn.

7. Leaving Circesium, we came to Zaitha, the name of the place meaning an olive-tree. Here we saw the tomb of the emperor Gordian, which is visible a long way off, whose actions from his earliest youth, and whose most fortunate campaigns and treacherous murder we related at the proper time,[138] and when, in accordance with his innate piety he had offered due honours to this deified emperor and was on his way to Dura, a town now deserted, he stood without moving on beholding a large body of soldiers.

8. And as he was doubting what their object was, they brought him an enormous lion which had attacked their ranks and had been slain by their javelins. He, elated at this circumstance, which he looked on as an omen of success in his enterprise, advanced with increased exultation; but so uncertain is fortune, the event was quite contrary to his expectation. The death of a king was certainly foreshown, but who was the king was uncertain.

9. For we often read of ambiguous oracles, never understood till the results interpreted them; as, for instance, the Delphic prophecy, which foretold that after crossing the Halys, Crœsus would overthrow a mighty kingdom; and another, which by hints pointed out the sea to the Athenians as the field of combat against the Medes; and another; later than these, but not less ambiguous:—

"O son of Æacus,
I say that you the Romans can subdue."

10. The Etrurian soothsayers who accompanied him, being men skilful in portents, had often warned him against this campaign, but got no credit; so now they produced their books of such signs, and showed that this was an omen of a forbidding character, and unfavourable to a prince who should invade the country of another sovereign however justly.

11. But he spurned the opposition of philosophers, whose authority he ought to have reverenced, though at times they were mistaken, and though they were sometimes obstinate in cases which they did not thoroughly understand. In truth, they brought forward as a plausible argument to secure credit to their knowledge, that in time past, when Cæsar Maximianus was about to fight Narses, king of the Persians, a lion and a huge boar which had been slain were at the same time brought to him, and after subduing that nation he returned in safety; forgetting that the destruction which was now portended was to him who invaded the dominions of another, and that Narses had given the offence by being the first to make an inroad into Armenia, a country under the Roman jurisdiction.

12. On the next day, which was the 7th of April, as the sun was setting, suddenly the air became darkened, and all light wholly disappeared, and after repeated claps of thunder and flashes of lightning, a soldier named Jovianus was struck by the lightning and killed, with two horses which he was leading back from the river to which he had taken them to drink.

13. When this was seen, the interpreters of such things were sent for and questioned, and they with increased boldness affirmed that this event forbade the campaign, demonstrating it to be a monitory lightning (for this term is applied to signs which advise or discourage any line of action). And this, as they said, was to be the more guarded against, because it had killed a soldier of rank, with war-horses; and the books which explain lightnings pronounce that places struck in this manner should not be trodden on, nor even looked upon.

14. On the other hand, the philosophers declared that the brilliancy of this sacred fire thus suddenly presented to the eye had no special meaning, but was merely the course of a fiercer breath descending by some singular power from the sky to the lower parts of the world; and that if any foreknowledge were to be derived from such a circumstance, it was rather an increase of renown which was portended to the emperor now engaged in a glorious enterprise; since it is notorious that flame, if it meet with no obstacle, does of its own nature fly upwards.

15. The bridge then, as has been narrated, having been finished, and all the troops having crossed it, the emperor thought it the most important of all things to address his soldiers who were advancing resolutely, in full reliance on their leader and on themselves. Accordingly, a signal having been given by the trumpets, the centurions, cohorts, and maniples assembled, and he, standing on a mound of earth, and surrounded by a ring of officers of high rank, spoke thus with a cheerful face, being favourably heard with the unanimous good will of all present.

16. "Seeing, my brave soldiers, that you are full of great vigour and alacrity, I have determined to address you, to prove to you by several arguments that the Romans are not, as spiteful grumblers assert, now for the first time invading the kingdom of Persia. For, to say nothing of Lucullus or of Pompey, who, having forced his way through the Albani and Massagetæ, whom we call Alani, penetrated through this nation also so as to reach the Caspian lake; we know that Ventidius, the lieutenant of Antony, gained many victories in these regions.

17. "But to leave those ancient times, I will enumerate other exploits of more recent memory. Trajan, and Verus, and Severus have all gained victories and trophies in this country; and the younger Gordian, whose monument we have just been honouring, would have reaped similar glory, having conquered and routed the king of Persia at Resaina, if he had not been wickedly murdered in this very place by the faction of Philip, the prefect of the prætorium, with the assistance of a few other impious men.

18. "But his shade was not long left to wander unavenged, since, as if Justice herself had laboured in the cause, all those who conspired against him have been put to death with torture. Those men, indeed, ambition prompted to the atrocious deed; but we are exhorted by the miserable fate of cities recently taken, by the unavenged shades of our slaughtered armies, by the heaviness of our losses, and the loss of many camps and fortresses, to the enterprise which we have undertaken. All men uniting in their wishes that we may remedy past evils, and having secured the honour and safety of the republic on this side, may leave posterity reason to speak nobly of us.

19. "By the assistance of the eternal deity, I, your emperor, will be always among you as a leader and a comrade, relying, as I well believe, on favourable omens. But if variable fortune shall defeat me in battle, it will still be sufficient for me to have devoted myself for the welfare of the Roman world, like ancient Curtii and Mucii, and the

illustrious family of the Decii. We have to abolish a most pernicious nation, on whose swords the blood of our kindred is not yet dry.

20. "Our ancestors have before now devoted ages to cause the destruction of enemies who harassed them. Carthage was overthrown after a long and distressing war; and its great conqueror feared to let it survive his victory. After a long and often disastrous siege, Scipio utterly destroyed Numantia. Rome destroyed Fidenæ, that it might not grow up as a rival to the empire; and so entirely laid waste Falisci and Veii, that it is not easy to attach so much faith to ancient records as to believe that those cities ever were powerful.

21. "These transactions I have related to you as one acquainted with ancient history. It follows that all should lay aside, as unworthy of him, the love of plunder, which has often been the insidious bane of the Roman soldier, and that every one should keep steadily to his own troop and his own standard, when the necessity for fighting arises, knowing that should he loiter anywhere he will be hamstrung and left to his fate. I fear nothing of our over-crafty enemies but their tricks and perfidy.

22. "Finally, I promise you all, that when our affairs have met with success, without entrenching myself behind my imperial prerogative, so as to consider all my own decisions and opinions irrefragably just and reasonable because of my authority, I will give, if required, a full explanation of all that I have done, that you may be able to judge whether it has been wise or not.

23. "Therefore, I entreat you, now summon all your courage, in full reliance on your good fortune, sure at all events that I will share all dangers equally with you, and believing that victory ever accompanies justice."

24. When he had ended his harangue with this pleasant peroration, the soldiers, exulting in the glory of their chief, and elated with the hopes of success, lifted up their shields on high, and cried out that they should think nothing dangerous nor difficult under an emperor who imposed more toil on himself than on his common soldiers.

25. And above all the rest his Gallic troops showed this feeling with triumphant shouts, remembering how often while he as their leader was marshalling their ranks, they had seen some nations defeated and others compelled to sue for mercy and peace.

VI.

§ 1. Our history here leads us to a digression explanatory of the situation of Persia. It has been already dilated upon by those who describe different nations, though but few of them have given a correct account; if my story should be a little longer, it will contribute to a better knowledge of the country. For whoever affects excessive conciseness while speaking of things but little known, does not so much consider how to explain matters intelligibly, as how much he may omit.

2. This kingdom, formerly but small, and one which had been known by several names, from causes which we have often mentioned, after the death of Alexander at Babylon received the name of Parthia from Arsaces, a youth of obscure birth, who in his early youth was a leader of banditti, but who gradually improved his condition, and rose to high renown from his illustrious actions.

3. After many splendid and gallant exploits he defeated Nicator Seleucus, the successor of the above-named Alexander, who had received the surname of Nicator[139] from his repeated victories; and having expelled the Macedonian garrisons, he lived for the remainder of his life in peace, like a merciful ruler of willing subjects.

4. At last, after all the neighbouring districts had been brought under his power, either by force or by fear, or by his reputation for justice, he died a peaceful death in middle age, after he had filled all Persia with flourishing cities and well-fortified camps and fortresses, and had made it an object of terror to its neighbours whom previously it used to fear. And he was the first of these kings who had by the unanimous consent of all his countrymen of all ranks, in accordance with the tenets of their religion, had his memory consecrated as one now placed among the stars.

5. And it is from his era that the arrogant sovereigns of that nation have allowed themselves to be entitled brothers of the sun and moon. And, as the title of Augustus is sought for and desired by our emperors, so now the additional dignities first earned by the fortunate auspices of Arsaces are claimed by all the Parthian kings, who were formerly abject and inconsiderable.

6. So that they still worship and honour Arsaces as a god, and down to our day have given him so much honour that, in conferring the royal power, one of his race has been always preferred to any one else. And also in intestine quarrels, such as are common in that nation, every one avoids as sacrilege wounding any descendant of Arsaces, whether in arms or living as a private individual.

7. It is well known that this nation, after subduing many others by force, extended its dominions as far as the Propontis and Thrace; but that it subsequently became diminished and suffered great disasters, owing to the arrogance of its ambitious monarchs, who carried their licentious inroads into distant countries. First, in consequence of the conduct of Cyrus, who crossed the Bosphorus with a fabulous host, but was wholly destroyed by Tomyris, queen of the Scythians, who thus terribly avenged her sons.

8. After him, when Darius, and subsequently Xerxes, changed the use[140] of the elements and invaded Greece, they had nearly all their forces destroyed by land and sea, and could scarcely escape in safety themselves. I say nothing of the wars of Alexander, and of his leaving the sovereignty over the whole nation by will to his successor.

9. Then, a long time after these events, while our republic was under consuls, and was afterwards brought under the power of the Cæsars, that nation was constantly warring with us, sometimes with equal fortune; being at one time defeated, and at another victorious.

10. Now I will in a few words describe the situation and position of the country as well as I can. It is a region of great extent both in length and breadth, entirely surrounding on all sides the famous Persian gulf with its many islands. The mouth of this gulf is so narrow that from Harmozon, the promontory of Carmania, the opposite headland, which the natives call Maces, is easily seen.

11. When the strait between these capes is passed, and the water becomes wider, they are navigable up to the city Teredon, where, after having suffered a great diminution of its waters, the Euphrates falls into the sea. The entire gulf, if measured round the shore, is 20,000 furlongs, being of a circular form as if turned in a lathe. And all round its coasts are towns and villages in great numbers; and the vessels which navigate its waters are likewise very numerous.

12. Having then passed through this strait we come to the gulf of Armenia on the east, the gulf of Cantichus on the south, and on the west to a third, which they call Chalites.[141] These gulfs, after washing many islands, of which but few are known, join the great Indian Ocean, which is the first to receive the glowing rising of the sun, and is itself of an excessive heat.

13. As the pens of geographers delineate it, the whole of the region which we have been speaking of is thus divided. From the north to the Caspian gates it borders on the Cadusii, and on many Scythian tribes, and on the Arimaspi, a fierce one-eyed people. On the west it is bounded by the Armenians, and Mount Niphates, the Asiatic Albani,

the Red Sea, and the Scenite Arabs, whom later times have called the Saracens. To the south it looks towards Mesopotamia, on the east it reaches to the Ganges, which falls into the Southern Ocean after intersecting the countries of the Indians.

14. The principal districts of Persia, under command of the Vitaxæ, that is to say of the generals of the cavalry, and of the king's Satraps, for the many inferior provinces it would be difficult and superfluous to enumerate, are Assyria, Susiana, Media, Persia, Parthia, the greater Carmania, Hyrcania, Margiana, the Bactrians, the Sogdians, the Sacæ, Scythia beyond Mount Emodes, Serica, Aria, the Paropanisadæ, Drangiana, Arachosia, and Gedrosia.

15. Superior to all the rest is that which is the nearest to us, Assyria, both in renown, and extent, and its varied riches and fertility. It was formerly divided among several peoples and tribes, but is now known under one common name as Assyria. It is in that country that amid its abundance of fruits and ordinary crops, there is a lake named Sosingites, near which bitumen is found. In this lake the Tigris is for a while absorbed, flowing beneath its bed, till, at a great distance, it emerges again.

16. Here also is produced naphtha, an article of a pitchy and glutinous character, resembling bitumen: on which if ever so small a bird perches, it finds its flight impeded and speedily dies. It is a species of liquid, and when once it has taken fire, human ingenuity can find no means of extinguishing it except that of heaping dust on it.

17. In the same district is seen an opening in the earth from which a deadly vapour arises, which by its foul odour destroys any animal which comes near it. The evil arises from a deep well, and if that odour spread beyond its wide mouth before it rose higher, it would make all the country around uninhabitable by its fetid effect.

18. There used, as some affirm, to be a similar chasm near Hierapolis in Phrygia; from which a noxious vapour rose in like manner with a fetid smell which never ceased, and destroyed everything within the reach of its influence, except eunuchs; to what this was owing we leave natural philosophers to determine.

19. Also near the temple of the Asbamæan Jupiter, in Cappadocia (in which district that eminent philosopher Apollonius is said to have been born near the town of Tyana), a spring rises from a marsh, which, however swollen with its rising floods, never overflows its banks.

20. Within this circuit is Adiabene, which was formerly called Assyria, but by long custom has received its present name from the

circumstance, that being placed between the two navigable rivers the Ona and the Tigris, it can never be approached by fording; for in Greek we use διαβαίνειν for to "cross:" this was the belief of the ancients.

21. But we say that in this country there are two rivers which never fail, which we ourselves have crossed, the Diabas, and the Adiabas: both having bridges of boats over them; and that Adiabene has received its name from this last, as Homer tells us Egypt received its name from its great river, and India also, and Commagena which was formerly called Euphratensis, as did the country now called Spain, which was formerly called Iberia from the Iberus.[142] And the great Spanish province of Bœtica from the river Bœtis.[143]

22. In this district of Adiabene is the city of Nineveh, named after Ninus, a most mighty sovereign of former times, and the husband of Semiramis, who was formerly queen of Persia, and also the cities of Ecbatana, Arbela, and Gaugamela, where Alexander, after several other battles, gave the crowning defeat to Darius.

23. In Assyria there are many cities, among which one of the most eminent is Apamia, surnamed Mesene, and Teredon, and Apollonia, and Vologesia, and many others of equal importance. But the most splendid and celebrated are these three, Babylon, the walls of which Semiramis cemented with pitch; for its citadel indeed was founded by that most eminent monarch Belus. And Ctesiphon which Vardanes built long ago, and which subsequently King Pacorus enlarged by an immigration of many citizens, fortifying it also with walls, and giving it a name, made it the most splendid place in Persia—next to it Seleucia, the splendid work of Seleucus Nicator.

24. This, however, as we have already related, was stormed by the generals of Verus Cæsar, who carried the image of the Cumæan Apollo to Rome, and placed it in the temple of the Palatine Apollo, where it was formally dedicated to that god by his priests. But it is said that after this statue was carried off, and the city was burnt, the soldiers, searching the temple, found a narrow hole, and when this was opened in the hope of finding something of value in it, from some deep gulf which the secret science of the Chaldæans had closed up, issued a pestilence, loaded with the force of incurable disease, which in the time of Verus and Marcus Antoninus polluted the whole world from the borders of Persia to the Rhine and Gaul with contagion and death.

25. Near to this is the region of the Chaldæans, the nurse of the ancient philosophy, as the Chaldæans themselves affirm; and where

the art of true divination has most especially been conspicuous. This district is watered by the noble rivers already mentioned, by the Marses, by the Royal river, and by that best of all, the Euphrates, which divides into three branches, and is navigable in them all, having many islands, and irrigating the fields around in a manner superior to any industry of cultivators, making them fit both for the plough and for the production of trees.

26. Next to these come the Susians, in whose province there are not many towns; though Susa itself is celebrated as a city which has often been the home of kings, and Arsiana, and Sele, and Aracha. The other towns in this district are unimportant and obscure. Many rivers flow through this region, the chief of which are the Oroates, the Harax, and the Meseus, passing through the narrow sandy plain which separates the Caspian from the Red Sea, and then fall into the sea.

27. On the left, Media is bounded by the Hyrcanian Sea;[144] a country which, before the reign of the elder Cyrus and the rise of Persia, we read was the supreme mistress of all Asia after the Assyrians had been conquered; the greater part of whose cantons had their name changed into one general appellation of Acrapatena, and fell by right of war under the power of the Medes.

28. They are a warlike nation, and the most formidable of all the eastern tribes, next to the Parthians, by whom alone they are conquered. The region which they inhabit is in the form of a square. All the inhabitants of these districts extend over great breadth of country, reaching to the foot of a lofty chain of mountains known by the names of Zagrus, Orontes, and Jasonium.

29. There is another very lofty mountain called Coronus; and those who dwell on its western side abound in corn land and vineyards, being blessed with a most fertile soil, and one enriched by rivers and fountains.

30. They have also green meadows, and breeds of noble horses, on which (as ancient writers relate, and as we ourselves have witnessed) their men when going to battle mount with great exultation. They call them Nesæi.[145]

31. They have also as many cities as Media, and villages as strongly built as towns in other countries, inhabited by large bodies of citizens. In short, it is the richest quarter of the kingdom.

32. In these districts the lands of the Magi are fertile; and it may be as well to give a short account of that sect and their studies, since we have occasion to mention their name. Plato, that most learned deliverer of wise opinions, teaches us that Magiæ is by a mystic name

Machagistia,[146] that is to say, the purest worship of divine beings; of which knowledge in olden times the Bactrian Zoroaster derived much from the secret rites of the Chaldæans; and after him Hystaspes, a very wise monarch, the father of Darius.

33. Who while boldly penetrating into the remoter districts of upper India, came to a certain woody retreat, of which with its tranquil silence the Brahmans, men of sublime genius, were the possessors. From their teaching he learnt the principles of the motion of the world and of the stars, and the pure rites of sacrifice, as far as he could; and of what he learnt he infused some portion into the minds of the Magi, which they have handed down by tradition to later ages, each instructing his own children, and adding to it their own system of divination.

34. From his time, through many ages to the present era, a number of priests of one and the same race has arisen, dedicated to the worship of the gods. And they say, if it can be believed, that they even keep alive in everlasting fires a flame which descended from heaven among them; a small portion of which, as a favourable omen, used to be borne before the kings of Asia.

35. Of this class the number among the ancients was small, and the Persian sovereigns employed their ministry in the solemn performance of divine sacrifices, and it was profanation to approach the altars, or to touch a victim before a Magus with solemn prayers had poured over it a preliminary libation. But becoming gradually more numerous they arrived at the dignity and reputation of a substantial race; inhabiting towns protected by no fortifications, allowed to live by their own laws, and honoured from the regard borne to their religion.

36. It was of this race of Magi that the ancient volumes relate that after the death of Cambyses, seven men seized on the kingdom of Persia, who were put down by Darius, after he obtained the kingdom through the neighing of his horse.

37. In this district a medical oil is prepared with which if an arrow be smeared, and it be shot gently from a loose bow (for it loses its effect in a rapid flight), wherever it sticks it burns steadily, and if any one attempts to quench it with water it only burns more fiercely, nor can it be put out by any means except by throwing dust on it.

38. It is made in this manner. Those skilful in such arts mix common oil with a certain herb, keep it a long time and when the mixture is completed they thicken it with a material derived from some natural source, like a thicker oil. The material being a liquor produced in Persia, and called, as I have already said, naphtha in their native language.

39. In this district there are many cities, the most celebrated of which are Zombis, Patigran, and Gazaca; but the richest and most strongly fortified are Heraclia, Arsacia, Europos, Cyropolis, and Ecbatana, all of which are situated in the Syromedian region at the foot of Mount Jasonius.

40. There are many rivers in this country, the principal of which are the Choaspes, the Gyndes, the Amardus, the Charinda, the Cambyses, and the Cyrus, to which, on account of its size and beauty, the elder Cyrus, that amiable king, gave its present name, abolishing that which it used to bear, when he was proceeding on his expedition against Scythia; his reason being that it was strong, as he accounted himself to be, and that making its way with great violence, as he proposed to do, it falls into the Caspian Sea.

41. Beyond this frontier ancient Persia, stretching towards the south, extends as far as the sea, and is very thickly peopled, being also rich in grain and date-trees, and well supplied with excellent water. Many of its rivers fall into the gulf already mentioned, the chief of which are the Vatrachites, the Rogomanis, the Brisoana, and the Bagrada.

42. Its inland towns are very considerable; it is uncertain why they built nothing remarkable on the sea-coast. Those of most note are Persepolis, Ardea, Obroatis, and Tragonice. The only islands visible from that coast are these:—Tabiana, Fara, and Alexandria.

43. On the borders of this ancient Persia towards the north is Parthia, a country subject to snow and frost; the principal river which intersects that region is the Choatres; the chief towns are Genonia, Mœsia, Charax, Apamia, Artacana, and Hecatompylos; from its frontier along the shores of the Caspian Sea to the Caspian gates is a distance of 1040 furlongs.

44. The inhabitants of all the countries in that district are fierce and warlike, and they are so fond of war and battle that he who is slain in battle is accounted the happiest of men, while those who die a natural death are reproached as degenerate and cowardly.

45. These tribes are bounded on the east and the south by Arabia Felix, so called because it abounds equally in corn, cattle, vines, and every kind of spice: a great portion of that country reaches on the right down to the Red Sea, and on its left extends to the Persian Gulf; so that the inhabitants reap the benefits of both.

46. There are in that country many havens and secure harbours, and well-frequented marts; many spacious and splendid abodes for their kings, and wholesome springs of water naturally warm, and a

great number of rivers and streams; the climate is temperate and healthy, so that if one considers the matter rightly, the natives seem to want nothing to perfect their happiness.

47. There are in it very many cities both on the coast and inland; many fertile hills and valleys. The chief cities are Geapolis, Nascon, Baraba, Nagara, Mephra, Taphra, and Dioscurias. And in both seas it possesses several islands lying off the coast, which it is not worth while to enumerate. But the most important of them is Turgana, in which there is said to be a magnificent temple of Serapis.

48. Beyond the frontier of this nation is the greater Carmania, lying on high ground, and stretching to the Indian Sea; fertile in fruit and timber trees, but neither so productive nor so extensive as Arabia. With rivers it is as well supplied, and in grass and herbage scarcely inferior.

49. The most important rivers are the Sagareus, the Saganis, and the Hydriacus. The cities are not numerous, but admirably supplied with all the necessaries and luxuries of life; the most celebrated of them all are Carmania the metropolis, Portospana, Alexandria, and Hermopolis.

50. Proceeding inland, we next come to the Hyrcanians, who live on the coast of the sea of that name. Here the land is so poor that it kills the seed crops, so that agriculture is not much attended to; but they live by hunting, taking wonderful pleasure in every kind of sport. Thousands of tigers are found among them, and all kinds of wild beasts; we have already mentioned the various devices by which they are caught.

51. Not indeed that they are ignorant of the art of ploughing, and some districts where the soil is fertile are regularly sown; nor are trees wanting to plant in suitable spots: many of the people too support themselves by commerce.

52. In this province are two rivers of universal celebrity the Oxus and the Maxera, which tigers sometimes, when urged by hunger, cross by swimming, and unexpectedly ravage the neighbouring districts. It has also besides other smaller towns some strong cities, two on the sea-shore named Socunda and Saramanna; and some inland, such as Azmorna and Sole, and Hyrcana, of higher reputation than either.

53. Opposite to this tribe, towards the north, live the Abii, a very devout nation, accustomed to trample under foot all worldly things, and whom, as Homer somewhat fabulously says, Jupiter keeps in view from Mount Ida.

54. The regions next to the Hyrcaneans are possessed by the Margiani, whose district is almost wholly surrounded by high hills, by which they are separated from the sea; and although the greater part of this province is deserted from want of water, still there are some towns in it; the best known of which are Jasonium, Antiochia, and Nisæa.

55. Next to them are the Bactrians, a nation formerly very warlike and powerful, and always hostile to the Persians, till they drew all the nations around under their dominion, and united them under their own name; and in old time the Bactrian kings were formidable even to Arsaces.

56. The greater part of their country, like that of the Margiani, is situated far from the sea-shore, but its soil is fertile, and the cattle which feed both on the plains and on the mountains in that district are very large and powerful; of this the camels which Mithridates brought from thence, and which were first seen by the Romans at the siege of Cyzicus, are a proof.

57. Many tribes are subject to the Bactrians, the most considerable of which are the Tochari: their country is like Italy in the number of its rivers, some of which are the Artemis and the Zariaspes, which were formerly joined, and the Ochus and Orchomanes, which also unite and afterwards fall into the Oxus, and increase that large river with their streams.

58. There are also cities in that country, many of them on the border of different rivers, the best of which are Chatra, Charte, Alicodra, Astacea, Menapila, and Bactra itself, which has given its name both to the region and to the people.

59. At the foot of the mountains lie a people called the Sogdians, in whose country are two rivers navigable for large vessels, the Araxates and the Dymas, which, flowing among the hills and through the valleys into the open plain, form the extensive Oxian marsh. In this district the most celebrated towns are Alexandria, Cyreschata, and Drepsa the metropolis.

60. Bordering on these are the Sacæ, a fierce nation dwelling in a gloomy-looking district, only fit for cattle, and on that account destitute of cities. They are at the foot of Mount Ascanimia and Mount Comedus, along the bottom of which, and by a town called the Stone Tower, is the long road much frequented by merchants which leads to China.

61. Around the glens at the bottom of the Imanian and Tapurian mountains, and within the Persian frontier, is a tribe of Scythians, bordering on the Asiatic Sarmatians, and touching the furthest side of the

Allemanni, who, like dwellers in a secluded spot, and made for solitude, are scattered over the regions at long distances from one another, and live on hard and poor food.

62. And various tribes inhabit these districts, which, as I am hastening to other topics, I think superfluous to enumerate. But this is worth knowing, that among these tribes, which are almost unapproachable on account of their excessive ferocity, there are some races of gentle and devout men, as the Jaxartæ and the Galactophagi, whom Homer mentions in his verses:—

Γλακτοφάγων, Ἀβίωντε, δικαιοτάτων ἀνθρώπων.[147]

63. Among the many rivers which flow through this land, either uniting at last with larger streams, or proceeding straight to the sea, the most celebrated are the Rœmnus, the Jaxartes, and the Talicus. There are but three cities there of any note, Aspabota, Chauriana, and Saga.

64. Beyond the districts of the two Scythias, on the eastern side, is a ring of mountains which surround Serica, a country considerable both for its extent and the fertility of its soil. This tribe on their western side border on the Scythians, on the north and the east they look towards snowy deserts; towards the south they extend as far as India and the Ganges. The best known of its mountains are Annib, Nazavicium, Asmira, Emodon, and Opurocarra.

65. The plain, which descends very suddenly from the hills, and is of considerable extent, is watered by two famous rivers, the Œchardes and the Bautis, which is less rapid than the other. The character too of the different districts is very varied. One is extensive and level, the other is on a gentle slope, and therefore very fertile in corn, and cattle, and trees.

66. The most fertile part of the country is inhabited by various tribes, of which the Alitrophagi, the Annibi, the Sisyges, and the Chardi lie to the north, exposed to the frost; towards the east are the Rabannæ, the Asmiræ, and the Essedones, the most powerful of all, who are joined on the west by the Athagoræ, and the Aspacaræ; and on the south by the Betæ, who live on the highest slopes of the mountains. Though they have not many cities they have some of great size and wealth; the most beautiful and renowned of which are Asmira, Essedon, Asparata, and Sera.

67. The Seres themselves live quietly, always avoiding arms and battles; and as ease is pleasant to moderate and quiet men, they give trouble to none of their neighbours. Their climate is agreeable and healthy; the sky serene, the breezes gentle and delicious. They have numbers of shining groves, the trees of which through continued wa-

tering produce a crop like the fleece of a sheep, which the natives make into a delicate wool, and spin into a kind of fine cloth, formerly confined to the use of the nobles, but now procurable by the lowest of the people without distinction.

68. The natives themselves are the most frugal of men, cultivating a peaceful life, and shunning the society of other men. And when strangers cross their river to buy their cloth, or any other of their merchandise, they interchange no conversation, but settle the price of the articles wanted by nods and signs; and they are so moderate that, while selling their own produce, they never buy any foreign wares.

69. Beyond the Seres, towards the north, live the Ariani; their land is intersected by a navigable river called the Arias, which forms a huge lake known by the same name. This district of Asia is full of towns, the most illustrious of which are Bitaxa, Sarmatina, Sotera, Nisibis, and Alexandria, from which last down the river to the Caspian Sea is a distance of fifteen hundred furlongs.

70. Close to their border, living on the slopes of the mountains, are the Paropanisatæ, looking on the east towards India, and on the west towards Mount Caucasus. Their principal river is Ortogordomaris, which rises in Bactria. They have some cities, the principal being Agazaca, Naulibus, and Ortopana, from which if you coast along the shore to the borders of Media which are nearest to the Caspian gates, the distance is two thousand two hundred furlongs.

71. Next to them, among the hills, are the Drangiani, whose chief river is the Arabis, so called because it rises in Arabia; and their two principal towns are Prophthasia and Aniaspe, both wealthy and well known.

72. Next to them is Arachosia, which on the right extends as far as India. It is abundantly watered by a river much smaller than the Indus, that greatest of rivers, which gives its name to the surrounding regions; in fact their river flows out of the Indus, and passes on till it forms the marsh known as Arachotoscrene. Its leading cities are Alexandria, Arbaca, and Choaspa.

73. In the most inland districts of Persia is Gedrosia; which on its right touches the frontier of India, and is fertilized by several rivers, of which the greatest is the Artabius. There the Barbitani mountains end, and from their lowest parts rise several rivers which fall into the Indus, losing their own names in the greatness of that superior stream. They have several islands, and their principal cities are Sedratyra and Gynæcon.

74. We need not detail minutely every portion of the sea-coast on the extremity of Persia, as it would lead us into too long a digression. It will suffice to say that the sea which stretches from the Caspian mountains along the northern side to the straits above mentioned, is nine thousand furlongs in extent; the southern frontier, from the mouth of the Nile to the beginning of Carmania, is fourteen thousand furlongs.

75. In these varied districts of different languages, the races of men are as different as the places. But to describe their persons and customs in general terms, they are nearly all slight in figure, swarthy or rather of a pale livid complexion; fierce-looking, with goat-like eyes, and eyebrows arched in a semicircle and joined, with handsome beards, and long hair. They at all times, even at banquets and festivals, wear swords; a custom which that excellent author Thucydides tells us the Athenians were the first of the Greeks to lay aside.

76. They are generally amazingly addicted to amatory pleasures; each man scarcely contenting himself with a multitude of concubines: from unnatural vices they are free. Each man marries many or few wives, as he can afford them, so that natural affection is lost among them because of the numerous objects of their licence. They are frugal in their banquets, avoiding immoderate indulgence and especially hard drinking, as they would the plague.

77. Nor, except at the king's table, have they any settled time for dining, but each man's stomach serves as his sun-dial; nor does any one eat after he is satisfied.

78. They are marvellously temperate and cautious, so that when sometimes marching among the gardens and vineyards of enemies, they neither desire nor touch anything, from fear of poison or witch-craft.

79. They perform all the secret functions of nature with the most scrupulous secrecy and modesty.

80. But they are so loose in their gait, and move with such correct ease and freedom, that you would think them effeminate, though they are most vigorous warriors; still they are rather crafty than bold, and are most formidable at a distance. They abound in empty words, and speak wildly and fiercely; they talk big, are proud, unmanageable, and threatening alike in prosperity and adversity; they are cunning, arrogant, and cruel, exercising the power of life and death over their slaves, and all low-born plebeians. They flay men alive, both piece-meal, and by stripping off the whole skin. No servant while waiting on

them, or standing at their table, may gape, speak, or spit, so that their mouths are completely shut.

81. Their laws are remarkably severe: the most stringent are against ingratitude and against deserters; some too are abominable, inasmuch as for the crime of one man they condemn all his relations.

82. But as those only are appointed judges who are men of proved experience and uprightness, and of such wisdom as to stand in no need of advice, they laugh at our custom of sometimes appointing men of eloquence and skill in public jurisprudence as guides to ignorant judges. The story that one judge was compelled to sit on the skin of another, who had been condemned for his injustice, is either an ancient fable, or else, if ever there was such a custom, it has become obsolete.

83. In military system and discipline, by continual exercises in the business of the camp, and the adoption of the various manœuvres which they have learnt from us, they have become formidable even to the greatest armies; they trust chiefly to the valour of their cavalry, in which all their nobles and rich men serve. Their infantry are armed like mirmillos,[148] and are as obedient as grooms; and they always follow the cavalry like a band condemned to everlasting slavery, never receiving either pay or gratuity. This nation, besides those whom it has permanently subdued, has also compelled many others to go under the yoke; so brave is it and so skilful in all warlike exercises, that it would be invincible were it not continually weakened by civil and by foreign wars.

84. Most of them wear garments brilliant with various colours, so completely enveloping the body that even though they leave the bosoms and sides of their robes open so as to flutter in the wind, still from their shoes to their head no part of their person is exposed. After conquering Crœsus and subduing Lydia, they learnt also to wear golden armlets and necklaces, and jewels, especially pearls, of which they had great quantities.

85. It only remains for me to say a few words about the origin of this stone. Among the Indians and Persians pearls are found in strong white sea-shells, being created at a regular time by the admixture of dew. For the shells, desiring as it were a kind of copulation, open so as to receive moisture from the nocturnal aspersion. Then becoming big they produce little pearls in triplets, or pairs, or unions, which are so called because the shells when scaled often produce only single pearls, which then are larger.

86. And a proof that this produce arises from and is nourished by some aërial derivation rather than by any fattening power in the sea, is that the drops of morning dew when infused into them make the stones bright and round; while the evening dew makes them crooked and red, and sometimes spotted. They become either small or large in proportion to the quality of the moisture which they imbibe, and other circumstances. When they are shaken, as is often the case by thunder, the shells either become empty, or produce only weak pearls, or such as never come to maturity.

87. Fishing for them is difficult and dangerous, and this circumstance increases their value; because, on account of the snares of the fishermen they are said to avoid the shores most frequented by them, and hide around rocks which are difficult of access and the hiding places of sharks.

88. We are not ignorant that the same species of jewel is also produced and collected in the remote parts of the British sea; though of an inferior value.

Notes

[138] The book containing this account is lost.

[139] From νικάω, to conquer.

[140] As the Greek epigram has it—

Τὸν γαίης καὶ πόντου ἀμειφθείσαισι κελευθοῖς
Ναύτην ἠπείρου, πέζόπορον πελάγους.

Thus translated in Bohn's 'Greek Anthology,' p. 25:—

Him, who reversed the laws great Nature gave,
Sail'd o'er the continent and walk'd the wave,
Three hundred spears from Sparta's iron plain
Have stopp'd. Oh blush, ye mountains and thou main!

[141] The probability is that all these names are corrupt. Ammianus's ignorance of the relative bearings of countries makes it difficult to decide what they ought to be. If the proper reading of the last name be, as Valesius thinks, Sarbaletes, that is the name given by Ptolemy to a part of the Red Sea. A French translator of the last century considers the Gulf of Armenia a portion of the Caspian Sea.

[142] The Ebro.

[143] The Guadalquivir.

[144] Ammianus seems to distinguish between the Hyrcanian and Caspian Sea, which are only different names for the same sea or inland lake.

[145] A name not very unlike Nejid, to this day the most celebrated Arab breed.

[146] There is evidently some corruption here; there is no such Greek word as Machagistia.

[147] Il. xiii. 10.

[148] A kind of gladiator.

BOOK XXIV

I.

A.D. 363.

§ 1. After having ascertained the alacrity of his army, which with ardour and unanimity declared with their customary shout that their fortunate emperor was invincible, Julian thinking it well to put an early end to his enterprise, after a quiet night ordered the trumpets to sound a march; and everything being prepared which the arduous difficulties of the war required, he at daybreak entered the Assyrian territory in high spirits, riding in front of his ranks, and exciting all to discharge the duties of brave men in emulation of his own courage.

2. And as a leader of experience and skill, fearing lest his ignorance of the country might lead to his being surprised by secret ambuscades, he began his march in line of battle. He ordered fifteen hundred skirmishers to precede him a short distance, who were to

march slowly looking out on each side and also in front, to prevent any sudden attack. The infantry in the centre were under his own command, they being the flower and chief strength of the whole army, while on the right were some legions under Nevitta, who was ordered to march along the banks of the Euphrates. The left wing with the cavalry he gave to Arinthæus and Hormisdas, with orders to lead them in close order through the level and easy country of the plain. The rear was brought up by Dagalaiphus and Victor, and the last of all was Secundinus, Duke of Osdruena.

3. Then in order to alarm the enemy by the idea of his superior numbers, should they attack him anywhere, or perceive him from a distance, he opened his ranks so as to spread both horses and men over a larger space, in such a way that the rear was distant from the van nearly ten miles; a manœuvre of great skill which Pyrrhus of Epirus is said to have often put in practice, extending his camp, or his lines, and sometimes on the other hand compressing them all, so as to present an appearance of greater or lesser numbers than the reality, according to the circumstances of the moment.

4. The baggage, the sutlers, all the camp-followers, and every kind of equipment, he placed between the two flanks of troops as they marched, so as not to leave them unprotected and liable to be carried off by any sudden attack, as has often happened. The fleet, although the river was exceedingly winding, was not allowed either to fall behind or to advance before the army.

5. After two days' march we came near a deserted town called Dura, on the bank of the river, where many herds of deer were found, some of which were slain by arrows, and others knocked down with the heavy oars, so that soldiers and sailors all had plenty of food; though the greater part of the animals, being used to swimming, plunged into the rapid stream and could not be stopped till they had reached their well known haunts.

6. Then after an easy march of four days, as evening came on, he embarked a thousand light-armed troops on board his boats, and sent the Count Lucillianus to storm the fortress of Anatha, which, like many other forts in that country, is surrounded by the waters of the Euphrates; Lucillianus having, as he was ordered, placed his ships in suitable places, besieged the island, a cloudy night favouring a secret assault.

7. But as soon as it became light, one of the garrison going out to get water, saw the enemy, and immediately raised an outcry, which roused the awakened garrison to arm in their defence. And presently,

from a high watch-tower, the emperor examined the situation of the fort, and came up with all speed escorted by two vessels, and followed by a considerable squadron laden with engines for the siege.

8. And as he approached the walls, and considered that the contest could not be carried on without great risk, he tried both by conciliatory and threatening language to induce the garrison to surrender; and they, having invited Hormisdas to a conference, were won over by his promises and oaths to rely on the mercy of the Romans.

9. At last, driving before them a crowned ox, which among them is a sign of peace, they descended from the fort as suppliants; the fort was burnt, and Pusæus, its commander, who was afterwards Duke of Egypt, was appointed to the rank of tribune. The rest of the garrison with their families and property were conducted with all kindness to the Syrian city of Chalcis.

10. Among them was found a certain soldier, who formerly, when Maximian invaded Persia, had been left in this district as an invalid, though a very young man, but who was now bent with age, and according to his own account had several wives, as is the custom of that country, and a numerous offspring. He now full of joy, professing to have been a principal cause of the surrender, was led to our camp, calling many of his comrades to witness that he had long foreseen and often foretold that, though nearly a hundred years' old, he should be buried in Roman ground. After this event, the Saracens brought in some skirmishers of the enemy whom they had taken; these were received with joy by the emperor, the Saracens rewarded, and sent back to achieve similar exploits.

11. The next day another disaster took place; a whirlwind arose, and made havoc in many places, throwing down many buildings, tearing in pieces the tents, and throwing the soldiers on their backs or on their faces, the violence of the wind overpowering their steadiness of foot. And the same day another equally perilous occurrence took place. For the river suddenly overflowed its banks, and some of the ships laden with provisions were wrecked, the piers and dams which had been constructed of stone to check and repress the waters being swept away; and whether that was done by treachery or through the weight of the waters could not be known.

12. After having stormed and burnt the chief city, and sent away the prisoners, the army with increased confidence raised triumphant shouts in honour of the emperor, thinking that the gods were evidently making him the object of their peculiar care.

13. And because in these unknown districts they were forced to be on unusual guard against hidden dangers, the troops especially feared the craft and exceeding deceitfulness of the enemy; and therefore the emperor was everywhere, sometimes in front, sometimes with his light-armed battalions protecting the rear, in order to see that no concealed danger threatened it, reconnoitring the dense jungles and valleys, and restraining the distant sallies of his soldiers, sometimes with his natural gentleness, and sometimes with threats.

14. But he allowed the fields of the enemy which were loaded with every kind of produce to be burnt with their crops and cottages, after his men had collected all that they could themselves make use of. And in this way the enemy were terribly injured before they were aware of it; for the soldiers freely used what they had acquired with their own hands, thinking that they had found a fresh field for their valour; and joyful at the abundance of their supplies, they saved what they had in their own boats.

15. But one rash soldier, being intoxicated, and having crossed over to the opposite bank of the river, was taken prisoner before our eyes by the enemy, and was put to death.

II.

§ 1. After this we arrived at a fort called Thilutha, situated in the middle of the river on a very high piece of ground, and fortified by nature as if by the art of man. The inhabitants were invited gently, as was best, to surrender, since the height of their fort made it impregnable; but they refused all terms as yet, though they answered that when the Romans had advanced further so as to occupy the interior of the country, they also as an appendage would come over to the conqueror.

2. Having made this reply they quietly looked down upon our boats as they passed under the very walls without attempting to molest them. When that fort was passed we came to another called Achaiacala, also defended by the river flowing round it, and difficult to scale, where we received a similar answer, and so passed on. The next day we came to another fort which had been deserted because its walls were weak; and we burnt it and proceeded.

3. In the two next days we marched two hundred furlongs, and arrived at a place called Paraxmalcha. We then crossed the river, and seven miles further on we entered the city of Diacira, which we found empty of inhabitants but full of corn and excellent salt, and here we saw a temple placed on the summit of a lofty height. We burnt the city and put a few women to death whom we found there, and having

passed a bituminous spring; we entered the town of Ozogardana, which its inhabitants had deserted for fear of our approaching army; in that town is shown a tribunal of the emperor Trajan.

4. This town also we burnt after we had rested there two days to refresh our bodies. On the second day just at nightfall, the Surena (who is the officer next in rank to the king among the Persians), and a man named Malechus Podosaces, the chief of the Assanite Saracens, who had long ravaged our frontiers with great ferocity, laid a snare for Hormisdas, whom by some means or other they had learnt was about to go forth on a reconnoitring expedition, and only failed because the river being very narrow at that point, was so deep as to be unfordable.

5. And so at daybreak, when the enemy were now in sight, the moment that they were discovered by their glittering helmets and bristling armour, our men sprang up vigorously to the conflict, and dashed at them with great courage; and although the enemy wielded their huge bows with great strength, and the glistening of their weapons increased the alarm of our soldiers, yet their rage, and the compactness of their ranks, kept alive and added fuel to their courage.

6. Animated by their first success, our army advanced to the village of Macepracta, where were seen vestiges of walls half destroyed, which had once been of great extent, and had served to protect Assyria from foreign invasion.

7. At this point a portion of the river is drawn off in large canals which convey it to the interior districts of Babylonia, for the service of the surrounding country and cities. Another branch of the river known as the Nahamalca, which means "the river of kings," passes by Ctesiphon; at the beginning of this stream there is a lofty tower like a lighthouse, by which our infantry passed on a carefully constructed bridge.

8. The cavalry and cattle then took the stream where it was less violent, and swam across obliquely; another body was suddenly attacked by the enemy with a storm of arrows and javelins, but our light-armed auxiliaries as soon as they reached the other side, supported them, and put the enemy to flight, cutting them to pieces as they fled.

9. After having successfully accomplished this exploit, we arrived at the city of Pirisabora, of great size and populousness, and also surrounded with water. But the emperor having ridden all round the walls and reconnoitred its position, began to lay siege to it with great caution, as if he would make the townsmen abandon its defence from mere terror. But after several negotiations and conferences with them, as they would yield neither to promises nor to threats, he set about the

siege in earnest, and surrounded the walls with three lines of soldiers. The whole of the first day the combat was carried on with missiles till nightfall.

10. But the garrison, full of courage and vigour, spreading cloths loose everywhere over the battlements to weaken the attacks of our weapons, and protected by shields strongly woven of osier, made a brave resistance, looking like figures of iron, since they had plates of iron closely fitting over every limb, which covered their whole person with a safe defence.

11. Sometimes also they earnestly invited Hormisdas as a countryman and a prince of royal blood to a conference; but when he came they reviled him with abuse and reproaches as a traitor and deserter; and after a great part of the day had been consumed in this slow disputing, at the beginning of night many kinds of engines were brought against the walls, and we began to fill up the ditches.

12. But before it was quite dawn, the garrison perceived what was being done, with the addition that a violent stroke of a battering-ram had broken down a tower at one corner; so they abandoned the double city wall, and occupied a citadel close to the wall, erected on the level summit of a ragged hill, of which the centre, rising up to a great height in its round circle, resembled an Argive shield, except that in the north it was not quite round, but at that point it was protected by a precipice which ran sheer down into the Euphrates; the walls were built of baked bricks and bitumen, a combination which is well known to be the strongest of all materials.

13. And now the savage soldiery, having traversed the city, which they found empty, were fighting fiercely with the defenders who poured all kinds of missiles on them from the citadel. Being hard pressed by the catapults and balistæ of our men, they also raised on the height huge bows of great power, the extremities of which, rising high on each side, could only be bent slowly; but the string, when loosed by violent exertion of the fingers, sent forth iron-tipped arrows with such force as to inflict fatal wounds on any one whom they struck.

14. Nevertheless, the fight was maintained on both sides with showers of stones thrown by the hand, and as neither gained any ground a fierce contest was protracted from daybreak to nightfall with great obstinacy; and at last they parted without any advantage to either side. The next day the fight was renewed with great violence, and numbers were slain on each side, and still the result was even; when the emperor, being eager amid this reciprocal slaughter to try every chance, being guarded by a solid column, and defended from the ar-

rows of the enemy by their closely packed shields, rushed forward with a rapid charge up to the enemy's gates, which were faced with stout iron.

15. And although he was still in some danger, being hard pressed with stones and bullets and other weapons, still he cheered on his men with frequent war-cries while they were preparing to force in the gates in order to effect an entrance, and did not retreat till he found himself on the point of being entirely overwhelmed by the mass of missiles which were poured down on him.

16. However, he came off safe with only a few of his men slightly wounded; not without feeling some modest shame at being repulsed. For he had read that Scipio Æmilianus, with the historian Polybius, a citizen of Megalopolis in Arcadia, and thirty thousand soldiers, had, by a similar attack, forced the gate of Carthage.

17. But the account given by the old writers may serve to defend this modern attempt; for Æmilianus approached a gate protected by a stone-covered testudo, under which he safely forced his way into the city while the garrison was occupied in demolishing this stone roof. But Julian attacked a place completely exposed, while the whole face of heaven was darkened by the fragments of rock and weapons which were showered upon him, and was even then with great difficulty repulsed and forced to retire.

18. After this hasty and tumultuous assault, as the vast preparations of sheds and mounds which were carried on were attended with much difficulty, through the hindrances offered by the garrison, Julian ordered an engine called helepolis to be constructed with all speed; which, as we have already mentioned, King Demetrius used, and earned the title of Poliorcetes by the number of cities which he took.

19. The garrison, anxiously viewing this engine, which was to exceed the height of their lofty towers, and considering at the same time the determination of the besiegers, suddenly betook themselves to supplications, and spreading over the towers and walls, imploring the pardon and protection of the Romans with outstretched hands.

20. And when they saw that the works of the Romans were suspended, and that those who were constructing them were doing nothing, which seemed a sure token of peace, they requested an opportunity of conferring with Hormisdas.

21. And when this was granted, Mamersides, the commander of the garrison, was let down by a rope, and conducted to the emperor as he desired; and having received a promise of his own life, and of impunity to all his comrades he was allowed to return to the city. And

when he related what had been done, the citizens unanimously agreed to follow his advice and accept the terms; and peace was solemnly made with all the sanctions of religion, the gates were thrown open, and the whole population went forth proclaiming that a protecting genius had shone upon them in the person of the great and merciful Cæsar.

22. The number of those who surrendered was two thousand five hundred, for the rest of the citizens, expecting the siege beforehand, had crossed the river in small boats and abandoned the city. In the citadel a great store of arms and provisions was found; and after they had taken what they required, the conquerors burnt the rest as well as the place itself.

III.

§ 1. The day after these transactions, serious news reached the emperor as he was quietly taking his dinner, that the Surena, the Persian general, had surprised three squadrons of our advanced guard, and slain a few, among whom was one tribune; and had also taken a standard.

2. Immediately Julian became violently exasperated, and flew to the spot with an armed band, placing much hope of success in the rapidity of his movements: he routed the assailants disgracefully, cashiered the other two tribunes as blunderers and cowards, and in imitation of the ancient laws of Rome disbanded ten of the soldiers who had fled, and then condemned them to death.

3. Then, having burnt the city as I have already mentioned, he mounted a tribunal which he had caused to be erected, and having convoked his army, he thanked them, and counted upon their achieving other similar exploits. He also promised them each a hundred pieces of silver; but seeing that they were inclined to murmur, as being disappointed at the smallness of the sum, he became most indignant and said:—

4. "Behold the Persians who abound in wealth of every kind; their riches may enrich you if we only behave gallantly with one unanimous spirit of resolution. But after having been very rich, I assure you that the republic is at this moment in great want, through the conduct of those men who, to increase their own wealth, taught former emperors to return home after buying peace of the barbarians with gold.

5. "The treasury is empty, the cities are exhausted, the finances are stripped bare. I myself have neither treasures, nor, noble as I am by

birth, do I inherit anything from my family but a heart free from all fear. Nor shall I be ashamed to place all my happiness in the cultivation of my mind, while preferring an honourable poverty. For the Fabricii also conducted great wars while poor in estate and rich only in glory.

6. "Of all these things you may have plenty, if, discarding all fear, you act with moderation, obeying the cautious guidance of God and myself, as far as human reason can lead you safely; but if you disobey, and choose to return to your former shameful mutinies, proceed.

7. "As an emperor should do, I by myself, having performed the important duties which belong to me, will die standing, despising a life which any fever may take from me: or else I will abdicate my power, for I have not lived so as to be unable to descend to a private station. I rejoice in, and feel proud of the fact that there are with me many leaders of proved skill and courage, perfect in every kind of military knowledge."

8. By this modest speech of their emperor, thus unmoved alike by prosperity and adversity, the soldiers were for a time appeased, regaining confidence with an expectation of better success; and unanimously promised to be docile and obedient, at the same time extolling Julian's authority and magnanimity to the skies; and, as is their wont when their feelings are genuine and cordial, they showed them by a gentle rattling of their arms.

9. Then they returned to their tents, and refreshed themselves with food, for which they had abundant means, and with sleep during the night. But Julian encouraged his army not by the idea of their families, but by the thoughts of the greatness of the enterprises in which they were embarked: continually making vows—"So might he be able to make the Persians pass under the yoke." "So might he restore the Roman power which had been shaken in those regions,"—in imitation of Trajan, who was accustomed frequently to confirm anything he had said by the imprecations—"So may I see Dacia reduced to the condition of a province; so may I bridge over the Danube and Euphrates,"—using many similar forms of attestation.

10. Then after proceeding fourteen miles further we came to a certain spot where the soil is fertilized by the abundance of water. But as the Persians had learnt that we should advance by this road, they removed the dams and allowed the waters to flood the country.

11. The ground being thereby, for a great distance, reduced to the state of a marsh, the emperor gave the soldiers the next day for rest, and advancing in front himself, constructed a number of little bridges

of bladders, and coracles[149] made of skins, and rafts of palm-tree timber, and thus led his army across, though not without difficulty.

12. In this region many of the fields are planted with vineyards and various kinds of fruit trees; and palm-trees grow there over a great extent of country, reaching as far as Mesene and the ocean, forming great groves. And wherever any one goes he sees continual stocks and suckers of palms, from the fruit of which abundance of honey and wine is made, and the palms themselves are said to be divided into male and female, and it is added that the two sexes can be easily distinguished.

13. They say further that the female trees produce fruit when impregnated by the seeds of the male trees, and even that they feel delight in their mutual love: and that this is clearly shown by the fact that they lean towards one another, and cannot be bent back even by strong winds—and if by any unusual accident a female tree is not impregnated by the male seed, it produces nothing but imperfect fruit, and if they cannot find out with what male tree any female tree is in love, they smear the trunk of some tree with the oil which proceeds from her, and then some other tree naturally conceives a fondness for the odour; and these proofs create some belief in the story of their copulation.

14. The army then, having sated itself with these fruits, passed by several islands, and instead of the scarcity which they apprehended, the fear arose that they would become too fat. At last, after having been attacked by an ambuscade of the enemy's archers, but having avenged themselves well, they came to a spot where the larger portion of the Euphrates is divided into a number of small streams.

IV.

§ 1. In this district a city, which on account of the lowness of its walls, had been deserted by its Jewish inhabitants, was burnt by our angry soldiers. And afterwards the emperor proceeded further on, being elated at the manifest protection, as he deemed it, of the Deity.

2. And when he had reached Maogamalcha, a city of great size and surrounded with strong walls, he pitched his tent, and took anxious care that his camp should not be surprised by any sudden attack of the Persian cavalry; whose courage in the open plains is marvellously dreaded by the surrounding nations.

3. And when he had made his arrangements, he himself, with an escort of a few light troops, went forth on foot to reconnoitre the posi-

tion of a city by a close personal examination; but he fell into a dangerous snare from which he with difficulty escaped with his life.

4. For ten armed Persians stole out by a gate of the town of which he was not aware, and crawled on their hands and knees along the bottom of the hill, till they got within reach so as to fall silently upon our men, and two of them distinguishing the emperor by his superior appearance, made at him with drawn swords; but he encountered them with his shield raised, and protecting himself with that, and fighting with great and noble courage, he ran one of them through the body, while his guards killed the other with repeated blows. The rest, of whom some were wounded, were put to flight, and the two who were slain were stripped of their arms, and the emperor led back his comrades in safety, laden with their spoils, into the camp, where he was received with universal joy.

5. Torquatus took a golden necklace from one of the enemy whom he had slain. Valerius by the aid of a crow defeated a haughty Gaul and earned the surname of Corvinus, and by this glory these heroes were recommended to posterity. We do not envy them, but let this gallant exploit be added to those ancient memorials.

6. The next day a bridge was laid across the river, and the army passed over it, and pitched their camp in a fresh and more healthy place, fortifying it with a double rampart, since, as we have said, the open plains were regarded with apprehension. And then he undertook the siege of the town, thinking it too dangerous to march forward while leaving formidable enemies in his rear.

7. While he was making great exertions to complete his preparations, the Surena, the enemy's general, fell upon the cattle which were feeding in the palm groves, but was repulsed by those of our squadrons who were appointed to that service, and, having lost a few men, he retired.

8. And the inhabitants of two cities which are made islands by the rivers which surround them, fearing to trust in their means of defence, fled for refuge to Ctesiphon, some fleeing through the thick woods, others crossing the neighbouring marshes on canoes formed out of hollowed trees, and thus made a long journey to the principal or indeed the only shelter which existed for them, intending to proceed to still more distant regions.

9. Some of them were overtaken, and on their resistance were put to death by our soldiers, who, traversing various districts in barks and small boats, brought in from time to time many prisoners. For it had been cleverly arranged that, while the infantry was besieging the town,

the squadrons of cavalry should scour the country in small bands in order to bring in booty. And by this system, without doing any injury to the inhabitants of the provinces, the soldiers fed on the bowels of the enemy.

10. And by this time the emperor was besieging with all his might and with a triple line of heavily armed soldiers this town which was fortified with a double wall; and he had great hope of succeeding in his enterprise. But if the attempt was indispensable, the execution was very difficult. For the approach to the town lay everywhere over rocks of great height and abruptness; across which there was no straight road; and dangers of two kinds seemed to render the place inaccessible. In the first place there were towers formidable both for their height and for the number of their garrison; equalling in height the natural mountain on which the citadel was built; and secondly, a sloping plain reached down to the river, which again was protected by stout ramparts.

11. There was a third difficulty not less formidable that the numerous garrison of picked men which defended the place could not be won over by any caresses to surrender, but resisted the enemy as if resolved either to conquer or to perish amid the ashes of their country. The soldiers, who desired to attack at once, and also insisted upon a pitched battle in a fair field, could hardly be restrained, and when the retreat was sounded they burnt with indignation, being eager to make courageous onsets on the enemy.

12. But the wisdom of our leaders overcame the eagerness of mere courage; and the work being distributed, every one set about his allotted task with great alacrity. For on one side high mounds were raised; on another other parties were raising the deep ditches to the level of the ground; in other quarters hollow pitfalls were covered over with long planks; artisans also were placing mural engines soon intended to burst forth with fatal roars.

13. Nevitta and Dagalaiphus superintended the miners and the erection of the vineæ, or penthouses; but the beginning of the actual conflict, and the defence of the machines from fire or from sallies of the garrison, the emperor took to himself. And when all the preparations for taking the city had been completed by this variety of labour, and the soldiers demanded to be led to the assault, a captain named Victor returned, who had explored all the roads as far as Ctesiphon, and now brought word that he had met with no obstacles.

14. At this news all the soldiers became wild with joy, and being more elated and eager for the contest than ever, they waited under arms for the signal.

15. And now on both sides the trumpets sounded with martial clang, and the Roman vanguard, with incessant attacks and threatening cries, assailed the enemy, who were covered from head to foot with thin plates of iron like the feathers of a bird, and who had full confidence that any weapons that fell on this hard iron would recoil; while our close-packed shields with which our men covered themselves as with a testudo, opened loosely so as to adapt themselves to their continual motion. On the other hand the Persians, obstinately clinging to their walls, laboured with all their might to avoid and frustrate our deadly attacks.

16. But when the assailants, pushing the osier fences before them, passed up to the walls, the archers, slingers and others, rolling down huge stones, with firebrands and fire-pots, repelled them to a distance. Then the balistæ, armed with wooden arrows, were bent and loosened with a horrid creak, and poured forth incessant storms of darts. And the scorpions hurled forth round stones under the guidance of the skilful hands of their workers.

17. The combat was repeated and redoubled in violence till the heat increasing up to midday, and the sun burning up everything with its evaporation, recalled from the battle the combatants on both sides, equally intent as they were on the works and on the fray, but thoroughly exhausted by fatigue and dripping with sweat.

18. The same plan was followed the next day, the two parties contending resolutely in various modes of fighting, and again they parted with equal valour, and equal fortune. But in every danger the emperor was foremost among the armed combatants, urging on the destruction of the city lest, by being detained too long before its walls, he should be forced to abandon other objects which he had at heart.

19. But in times of emergency nothing is so unimportant as not occasionally to influence great affairs, even contrary to all expectation. For when, as had often happened, the two sides were fighting slackly, and on the point of giving over, a battering-ram which had just been brought up, being pushed forward awkwardly, struck down a tower which was higher than any of the others, and was very strongly built of baked brick, and its fall brought down all the adjacent portion of the wall with a mighty crash.

20. Then in the variety of incidents which arose, the exertions of the besiegers and the gallantry of the besieged were equally conspicu-

ous with noble exploits. For to our soldiers, inflamed with anger and indignation, nothing appeared difficult. To the garrison, fighting for their safety, nothing seemed dangerous or formidable. At last, when the fierce contest had raged a long time and was still undecided, great slaughter having been made on both sides, the close of day broke it off, and both armies yielded to fatigue.

21. While these matters were thus going on in broad daylight, news was brought to the emperor, who was full of watchful care, that the legionary soldiers to whom the digging of the mines had been intrusted, having hollowed out their subterranean paths and supported them with stout stakes, had now reached the bottom of the foundations of the walls, and were ready to issue forth if he thought fit.

22. When therefore a great part of the night was passed, the brazen trumpets sounded the signal for advancing to battle, and the troops ran to arms; and as had been planned, the wall was attacked on both its faces, in order that while the garrison were running to and fro to repel the danger, and while the noise of the iron tools of the miners digging at the foundations was overpowered by the din of battle, the miners should come forth on a sudden without any one being at the mouth of the mine to resist them.

23. When these plans had all been arranged, and the garrison was fully occupied, the mine was opened, and Exsuperius, a soldier of the Victorian legion, sprung out, followed by a tribune named Magnus, and Jovianus, a secretary, and an intrepid body of common soldiers, who, after slaughtering all the men found in the temple into which the mine opened, went cautiously forward and slew the sentinels, who were occupying themselves after the fashion of their country in singing the praises, the justice, and good fortune of their king.

24. It was believed that Mars himself (if indeed the gods are permitted to mingle with men) aided Luscinus when he forced the camp of the Lucanians. And it was the more believed because in the height of the conflict there was seen an armed figure of enormous size carrying ladders, who the next day, when the roll was called over, though sought for very carefully, could not be found anywhere; when if he had really been a soldier he would have come forward of his own accord from a consciousness of his gallant action. But though on that occasion it was never known who performed that splendid achievement, yet those who now behaved bravely were not unknown, but received obsidional crowns, and were publicly praised according to the ancient fashion.

25. At last the fated city, its numerous entrances being laid open, was entered by the Romans, and the furious troops destroyed all whom they found, without regard to age or sex. Some of the citizens, from dread of impending destruction, threatened on one side with fire, on the other with the sword, weeping threw themselves headlong over the walls, and being crippled in all their limbs, led for a few hours or days a life more miserable than any death till they were finally killed.

26. But Nabdates, the captain of the garrison, was taken alive with eighty of his guards; and when he was brought before the emperor, that magnanimous and merciful prince ordered him to be kept in safety. The booty was divided according to a fair estimate of the merits and labours of the troops. The emperor, who was contented with very little, took for his own share of the victory he had thus gained three pieces of gold and a dumb child who was brought to him, and who by elegant signs and gesticulations explained all he knew, and considered that an acceptable and sufficient prize.

27. But of the virgins who were taken prisoners, and who, as was likely in Persia, where female beauty is remarkable, were exceedingly beautiful, he would neither touch nor even see one; imitating Alexander and Scipio, who refused similar opportunities, in order, after having proved themselves unconquered by toil, not to show themselves the victims of desire.

28. While the battle was going on, an engineer on our side, whose name I do not know, who happened to be standing just behind a scorpion, was knocked down and killed by the recoil of a stone, which the worker of the engine had fitted to the sling carelessly, his whole body being so dislocated and battered that he could not even be recognized.

29. After the town was taken intelligence was brought to the emperor that a troop was lying in ambuscade in some concealed pits around the walls of the town just taken (of which pits there are many in those districts), with the intention of surprising the rear of our army by a sudden attack.

30. A body of picked infantry of tried courage was therefore sent to take the troop prisoners. But as they could neither force their way into the pits, nor induce those concealed in them to come forth to fight, they collected some straw and faggots, and piled them up before the mouths of the caves, and then set them on fire, from which the smoke penetrated into the caverns through the narrow crevice, being the more dense because of the small space through which it was forced, and so suffocated some of them; others the fire compelled to come forth to

instant destruction; and in this manner they were destroyed by sword or by fire, and our men returned with speed to their camp. Thus was this large and populous city, with its powerful garrison, stormed by the Romans, and the city itself reduced to ruins.

31. After this glorious exploit the bridges which led over several rivers were crossed in succession, and we reached two forts, constructed with great strength and skill, where the son of the king endeavoured to prevent Count Victor, who was marching in the van of the army, from crossing the river, having advanced for that purpose from Ctesiphon with a large body of nobles and a considerable armed force; but when he saw the numbers which were following Victor, he retreated.

V.

§ 1. So we advanced and came to some groves, and also to some fields fertile with a great variety of crops, where we found a palace built in the Roman fashion, which, so pleased were we with the circumstance, we left unhurt.

2. There was also in this same place a large round space, enclosed, containing wild beasts, intended for the king's amusement; lions with shaggy manes, tusked boars, and bears of amazing ferocity (as the Persian bears are), and other chosen beasts of vast size. Our cavalry, however, forced the gates of this enclosure, and killed all the beasts with hunting-spears and clouds of arrows.

3. This district is rich and well cultivated: not far off is Coche, which is also called Seleucia; where we fortified a camp with great celerity, and rested there two days to refresh the army with timely supplies of water and provisions. The emperor himself in the meanwhile proceeded with his advanced guard and reconnoitred a deserted city which had been formerly destroyed by the Emperor Verus, where an everlasting spring forms a large tube which communicates with the Tigris. Here we saw, hanging on gallows, many bodies of the relations of the man whom we have spoken of above as having betrayed Pirisabora.

4. Here also Nabdates was burnt alive, he whom I have mentioned above as having been taken with eighty of his garrison while hiding among the ruins of the city which we had taken; because at the beginning of the siege he had secretly promised to betray it, but afterwards had resisted us vigorously, and after having been unexpectedly pardoned had risen to such a pitch of violence as to launch all kinds of abuse against Hormisdas.

5. Then after advancing some distance we heard of a sad disaster: for while three cohorts of the advanced guard, who were in light marching order, were fighting with a Persian division which had made a sally out of the city gates, another body of the enemy cut off and slew our cattle, which were following us on the other side of the river, with a few of our foragers who were straggling about in no great order.

6. The emperor was enraged and indignant at this; he was now near the district of Ctesiphon, and had just reached a lofty and well-fortified castle. He went himself to reconnoitre it, being, as he fancied, concealed, as he rode with a small escort close to the walls; but as from too much eagerness he got within bowshot, he was soon noticed, and was immediately assailed by every kind of missile, and would have been killed by an arrow shot from an engine on the walls, if it had not struck his armour-bearer, who kept close by his side, and he himself, being protected by the closely-packed shields of his guards, fell back, after having been exposed to great danger.

7. At this he was greatly enraged, and determined to lay siege to the fort; but the garrison was very resolute to defend it, believing the place to be nearly inaccessible, and that the king, who was advancing with great speed at the head of a large army, would soon arrive to their assistance.

8. And now, the vineæ and everything else required for the siege being prepared, at the second watch, when the night, which happened to be one of very bright moonlight, made everything visible to the defenders on the battlements, suddenly the whole multitude of the garrison formed into one body, threw open the gates and sallied out, and attacking a division of our men who were not expecting them, slew numbers, among whom one tribune was killed as he was endeavouring to repel the attack.

9. And while this was going on, the Persians, having attacked a portion of our men in the same manner as before from the opposite side of the river, slew some and took others prisoners. And our men, in alarm, and because they believed the enemy had come into the field in very superior numbers, behaved at first with but little spirit; but presently, when they recovered their courage, they flew again to arms, and being roused by the sound of the trumpets, they hastened to the charge with threatening cries, upon which the Persians retired to the garrison without further contest.

10. And the emperor, being terribly angry, reduced those of the cavalry who had shown a want of courage when attacked to serve in the infantry, which is a severer service and one of less honour.

11. Then, being very eager to take a castle where he had incurred so much danger, he devoted all his own labour and care to that end, never himself retiring from the front ranks of his men, in order that by fighting in the van he might be an example of gallantry to his soldiers, and might be also sure to see, and therefore able to reward, every gallant action. And when he had exposed himself a long time to imminent danger, the castle, having been assailed by every kind of manœuvre, weapon, and engine, and by great valour on the part of the besiegers, was at length taken and burnt.

12. After this, in consideration of the great labour of the exploits which they had performed, and which were before them, he granted rest to his army, exhausted with its excessive toil, and distributed among them provisions in abundance. Then a rampart was raised round the camp, with dense rows of palisades, and a deep fosse, as sudden sallies and various formidable manœuvres were dreaded, since they were very near Ctesiphon.

VI.

§ 1. From this place they advanced to a canal known as Naharmalcha, a name which means "The River of Kings." It was then dry. Long ago Trajan, and after him Severus, had caused the soil to be dug out, and had given great attention to constructing this as a canal of great size, so that, being filled with water from the Euphrates, it might enable vessels to pass into the Tigris.

2. And for every object in view it appeared best that this should now be cleaned out, as the Persians, fearing such an operation, had blocked it up with a mass of stones. After it had been cleared and the dams removed, a large body of water was let in, so that our fleet, after a safe voyage of thirty furlongs, passed into the Tigris. There the army at once threw bridges across the river, and passing over to the other side, marched upon Coche.

3. And that after our fatigue we might enjoy seasonable rest, we encamped in an open plain, rich with trees, vines, and cypresses, in the middle of which was a shady and delicious pavilion, having all over it, according to the fashion of the country, pictures of the king slaying wild beasts in the chase; for they never paint or in any way represent anything except different kinds of slaughter and war.

4. Having now finished everything according to his wish, the emperor, rising higher in spirit as his difficulties increased, and building such hopes on Fortune, which had not yet proved unfavourable to him, that he often pushed his boldness to the verge of temerity,

unloaded some of the strongest of the vessels which were carrying provisions and warlike engines, and put on board of them eight hundred armed men; and keeping the main part of the fleet with him, which he divided into three squadrons, he settled that one under the command of Count Victor should start at nightfall, in order to cross the river with speed, and so seize on the bank in possession of the enemy.

5. The generals were greatly alarmed at this plan, and unanimously entreated him to forego it; but as they could not prevail, the signal for sailing was raised, as he commanded, and at once five ships hastened onwards out of sight; and when they drew near to the bank they were attacked with an incessant storm of fire-pots and every kind of contrivance to handle flames, and they would have been burnt soldiers and all if the emperor, being roused, had not with great energy hastened to the spot, shouting out that our men, as they were ordered, had made him a signal that they were now masters of the bank of the river, and ordering the whole fleet to hasten forward with all speed.

6. In consequence of which vigour the ships were saved, and the soldiers, though harassed by the enemy from their commanding ground with stones and every kind of missile, nevertheless after a fierce conflict made good their footing on the high bank of the river, and established themselves immovably.

7. History marvels that Sertorius swam across the Rhone with his arms and his breastplate; but on this occasion, some soldiers, though disordered, fearing to remain behind after the signal for battle was raised, clinging firmly to their shields, which are broad and concave, and guiding them, though without much skill, kept pace with the speed of the vessels through a river full of currents.

8. The Persians resisted this attack with squadrons of cuirassier cavalry in such close order that their bodies dazzled the eye, fitting together, as it seemed, with their brilliant armour; while their horses were all protected with a covering of stout leather. As a reserve to support them several maniples of infantry were stationed, protected by crooked, oblong shields, made of wicker-work and raw hides, behind which they moved in compact order. Behind them were elephants, like so many walking hills, which by every motion of their huge bodies threatened destruction to all who came near them, and our men had been taught to fear them by past experience.

9. On this the emperor, according to the arrangement of the Greek army as mentioned by Homer,[150] allotted the centre space between his two lines to his weakest infantry, lest if they were placed in the front rank, and should then misbehave, they should disorder the

whole of his line; or lest, on the other hand, if posted in the rear, behind all the other centuries, they should flee without shame, since there would be no one to check them: he with his light-armed auxiliaries moving as might be required between the lines.

10. Therefore when the two armies beheld each other, the Romans glittering with their crested helmets, and brandishing their shields, proceeded slowly, their bands playing an anapæstic measure; and after a preliminary skirmish, carried on by the missiles of the front rank, they rushed to battle with such vehemence that the earth trembled beneath them.

11. The battle-shout was raised on all sides, as was usual, the braying trumpets encouraged the eagerness of the men: all fought in close combat with spears and drawn swords, so that the soldiers were free from all danger of arrows the more rapidly they pressed onwards. Meanwhile, Julian, like a gallant comrade, at the same time that he was a skilful general, hasten to support his hardly-pressed battalions with reserves, and to cheer on the laggards.

12. So the front line of the Persians wavered, having been never very fierce; and at last, no longer able to support the heat of their armour, they retreated in haste to their city, which was near: they were pursued by our soldiers, weary as they were with having fought in those torrid plains from daybreak to sunset; and we, pressing close on their heels, drove them, with their choicest generals, Pigranes, the Surena, and Narses, right up to the walls of Ctesiphon, inflicting many wounds on their legs and backs.

13. And we should have forced our entrance into the city if a general named Victor had not, by lifting up his hands and his voice, checked us, being himself pierced through the shoulder with an arrow, and fearing lest if the soldiers allowed themselves to be hurried within the walls without any order, and could then find no means of returning, they might be overwhelmed by the mass of their enemies.

14. Let the poets celebrate the ancient battles of Hector, or extol the valour of the Thessalian Achilles; let past ages tell the praises of Sophanes, and Aminias, and Callimachus, and Cynægirus, those thunderbolts of war in the struggles of the Greeks against Persia; but it is evident by the confession of all men that the gallantry displayed by some of our troops on that day was equal to any of their exploits.

15. After having laid aside their fears, and trampled on the carcases of their enemies, the soldiers, still stained with the blood so justly shed, collected round the tent of the emperor, loading him with praises and thanks, because, while behaving with such bravery that it

was hard to say whether he had been more a general or a soldier, he had conducted the affair with such success that not above seventy of our men had fallen, while nearly two thousand five hundred of the Persians had been slain. And he in his turn addressed by name most of those whose steady courage and gallant actions he had witnessed, presenting them with naval, civic, and military crowns.

16. Thinking that this achievement would surely be followed by other similar successes, he prepared a large sacrifice to Mars the Avenger. Ten most beautiful bulls were brought for the purpose, nine of which, even before they reached the altars, lay down of their own accord with mournful countenances, but the tenth broke his bonds and escaped, and was with difficulty brought back at all; and when sacrificed displayed very unfavourable omens; but when he saw this, Julian became very indignant, and exclaimed, calling Jupiter to witness, that henceforth he would offer no sacrifices to Mars. Nor did he recall his vow, being cut off by a speedy death.

VII.

§ 1. Julian, having discussed with his chief officers the plan for the siege of Ctesiphon, it appeared to some of them that it would be an act of unseasonable temerity to attack that city, both because its situation made it almost impregnable, and also because King Sapor was believed to be hastening to its protection with a formidable army.

2. The better opinion prevailed; and the sagacious emperor being convinced of its wisdom, sent Arinthæus with a division of light infantry, to lay waste the surrounding districts, which were rich both in herds and in crops, with orders also to pursue the enemy with equal energy, for many of them were wandering about, concealed amid overgrown by-ways, and lurking-places known only to themselves. The booty was abundant.

3. But Julian himself, being always eager to extend his conquests, disregarded the advice of those who remonstrated against his advance; and reproaching his chiefs, as men who out of mere laziness and a love of ease advised him to let go the kingdom of Persia when he had almost made himself master of it, left the river on his left hand, and led by unlucky guides, determined to proceed towards the inland parts of the country by forced marches.

4. And he ordered all his ships to be burnt, as if with the fatal torch of Bellona herself, except twelve of the smaller vessels, which he arranged should be carried on waggons, as likely to be of use for building bridges. And he thought this a most excellently conceived

plan, to prevent his fleet if left behind from being of any use to the enemy, or on the other hand to prevent what happened at the outset of the expedition, nearly twenty thousand men being occupied in moving and managing the vessels.

5. Then, as the men began in their alarm to grumble to themselves (as indeed manifest truth pointed out), that the soldiers if hindered from advancing by the height of the mountains or the dryness of the country, would have no means of returning to get water, and when the deserters, on being put to the torture openly confessed that they had made a false report, he ordered all hands to labour to extinguish the flames. But the fire, having got to a great head, had consumed most of them, so that only the twelve could be preserved unhurt, which were set apart to be taken care of.

6. In this way the fleet being unseasonably destroyed, Julian, relying on his army which was now all united, having none of its divisions diverted to other occupations, and so being strong in numbers, advanced inland, the rich district through which he marched supplying him with an abundance of provisions.

7. When this was known, the enemy, with a view to distressing us by want of supplies, burnt up all the grass and the nearly ripe crops; and we, being unable to advance by reason of the conflagration, remained stationary in our camp till the fire was exhausted. And the Persians, insulting us from a distance, sometimes spread themselves widely on purpose, sometimes offered us resistance in a compact body; so that to us who beheld them from a distance it might seem that the reinforcements of the king had come up, and we might imagine that it was on that account that they had ventured on their audacious sallies and unwonted enterprises.

8. Both the emperor and the troops were greatly vexed at this, because they had no means of constructing a bridge, since the ships had been inconsiderately destroyed, nor could any check be offered to the movements of the strange enemy, whom the glistening brilliancy of their arms showed to be close at hand; this armour of theirs being singularly adapted to all the inflections of their body. There was another evil of no small weight, that the reinforcements which we were expecting to arrive under the command of Arsaces and some of our own generals, did not make their appearance, being detained by the causes already mentioned.

VIII.

§ 1. The emperor, to comfort his soldiers who were made anxious by these events, ordered the prisoners who were of slender make, as the Persians usually are, and who were now more than usually emaciated, to be brought before the army; and looking at our men he said, "Behold what those warlike spirits consider men, little ugly dirty goats; and creatures who, as many events have shown, throw away their arms and take to flight before they can come to blows."

2. And when he had said this, and had ordered the prisoners to be removed, he held a consultation on what was to be done; and after many opinions of different kinds had been delivered, the common soldiers inconsiderately crying out that it was best to return by the same way they had advanced, the emperor steadily opposed this idea, and was joined by several officers who contended that this could not be done, since all the forage and crops had been destroyed throughout the plain, and the remains of the villages which had been burnt were all in complete destitution, and could afford no supplies; because also the whole soil was soaked everywhere from the snows of winter, and the rivers had overflowed their banks and were now formidable torrents.

3. There was this further difficulty, that in those districts where the heat and evaporation are great, every place is infested with swarms of flies and gnats, and in such numbers that the light of the sun and of the stars is completely hidden by them.

4. And as human sagacity was of no avail in such a state of affairs, we were long in doubt and perplexity; and raising altars and sacrificing victims we consulted the will of the gods; inquiring whether it was their will that we should return through Assyria, or advancing slowly along the foot of the mountain chain, should surprise and plunder Chiliocomum near Corduena; but neither of these plans was conformable to the omens presented by an inspection of the sacrifices.

5. However it was decided, that since there was no better prospect before us, to seize on Corduena; and on the 16th June we struck our camp, and at daybreak the emperor set forth, when suddenly was seen either smoke or a great cloud of dust; so that many thought it was caused by herds of wild asses, of which there are countless numbers in those regions, and who were now moving in a troop, in order by their compactness to ward off the ferocious attacks of lions.

6. Some, however, fancied that it was caused by the approach of the Saracen chieftains, our allies, who had heard that the emperor was

besieging Ctesiphon in great force: some again affirmed that the Persians were lying in wait for us on our march.

7. Therefore amid all these doubtful opinions, the trumpets sounded a halt, in order to guard against any reverse, and we halted in a grassy valley near a stream, where, packing our shields in close order and in a circular figure, we pitched our camp and rested in safety. Nor, so dark did it continue till evening, could we distinguish what it was that had so long obscured the view.

Notes

[149] Small boats made of wicker and covered with hide; still used in Wales, where they are also called thorricle, truckle, or cobble.

[150] See Il. iv. 297:—

 Ἱππῆας μὲν πρῶπα σὺν ἵπποισιν καὶ ὄχέσφιν
 πεζοὺς δ' εξόπιθεν στῆσεν πολέας τε καὶ ἐσθλούς
 ἕρκος ἔμεν πολέμοιο, κακοὺς δ' εἰς μέσσον ἔλασσεν.

Thus translated by Pope:—

 "The horse and chariots to the front assigned,
 The foot (the strength of war) he placed behind;
 The middle space suspected troops supply,
 Enclosed by both, nor left the power to fly."

BOOK XXV

I.

A.D. 363.

§ 1. The night was dark and starless, and passed by us as nights are passed in times of difficulty and perplexity; no one out of fear daring to sit down, or to close his eyes. But as soon as day broke, brilliant breastplates surrounded with steel fringes, and glittering cuirasses, were seen at a distance, and showed that the king's army was at hand.

2. The soldiers were roused at this sight, and hastened to engage, since only a small stream separated them from the Persians, but were checked by the emperor; a sharp skirmish did indeed take place between our outposts and the Persians, close to the rampart of our camp, in which Machamæus, the captain of one of our squadrons was stricken down: his brother Maurus, afterwards Duke of Phœnicia, flew to his support, and slew the man who had killed Machamæus, and crushed all who came in his way, till he himself was wounded in the shoulder by a javelin; but he still was able by great exertions to bring off his brother, who was now pale with approaching death.

3. Both sides were nearly exhausted with the intolerable violence of the heat and the repeated conflicts, but at last the hostile battalions were driven back in great disorder. Then while we fell back to a greater distance, the Saracens were also compelled to retreat from fear of our infantry, but presently afterwards joining themselves to the Persian host, they attacked us again, with more safety to themselves for the purpose of carrying off the Roman baggage. But when they saw the emperor they again retreated upon their reserve.

4. After leaving this district we reached a village called Hucumbra, where we rested two days, procuring all kinds of provisions and abundance of corn, so that we moved on again after being refreshed beyond our hopes; all that the time would not allow us to take away we burnt.

5. The next day the army was advancing more quietly, when the Persians unexpectedly fell upon our last division, to whom that day the duty fell of bringing up the rear, and would easily have slain all the men, had not our cavalry, which happened to be at hand, the moment that they heard what was going on, hastened up, though scattered over the wide valley, and repulsed this dangerous attack, wounding all who had thus surprised them.

6. In this skirmish fell Adaces, a noble satrap, who had formerly been sent as ambassador to the emperor Constantius, and had been kindly received by him. The soldier who slew him brought his arms to Julian, and received the reward he deserved.

7. The same day one of our corps of cavalry, known as the third legion, was accused of having gradually given way, so that when the legions were on the point of breaking the enemy's line, they nearly broke the spirit of the whole army.

8. And Julian, being justly indignant at this, deprived them of their standards, broke their spears, and condemned all those who were convicted of having misbehaved of marching among the baggage and prisoners; while their captain, the only one of their number who had behaved well, was appointed to the command of another squadron, the tribune of which was convicted of having shamefully left the field.

9. And four other tribunes of companies were also cashiered for similar misconduct; for the emperor was contented with this moderate degree of punishment out of consideration for his impending difficulties.

10. Accordingly, having advanced seventy furlongs with very scanty supplies, the herbage and the corn being all burnt, each man saved for himself just as much of the grain or forage as he could snatch from the flames and carry.

11. And having left this spot, when the army had arrived at the district called Maranx, near daybreak an immense multitude of Persians appeared, with Merenes, the captain of their cavalry, and two sons of the king, and many nobles.

12. All the troops were clothed in steel, in such a way that their bodies were covered with strong plates, so that the hard joints of the armour fitted every limb of their bodies; and on their heads were effigies of human faces so accurately fitted, that their whole persons being covered with metal, the only place where any missiles which fell upon them could stick, was either where there were minute openings to allow of the sight of the eyes penetrating, or where holes for breathing were left at the extremities of the nostrils.

13. Part of them who were prepared to fight with pikes stood immovable, so that you might have fancied they were held in their places by fastenings of brass; and next to them the archers (in which art that nation has always been most skilful from the cradle) bent their supple bows with widely extended arms, so that the strings touched their right breasts, while the arrows lay just upon their left hands; and the whistling arrows flew, let loose with great skill of finger, bearing deadly wounds.

14. Behind them stood the glittering elephants in formidable array, whose grim looks our terrified men could hardly endure; while the

horses were still more alarmed at their growl, odour, and unwonted aspect.

15. Their drivers rode on them, and bore knives with handles fastened to their right hands, remembering the disaster which they had experienced at Nisibis; and if the ferocious animal overpowered his overseer, they pierced the spine where the head is joined to the neck with a vigorous blow, that the beast might not recoil upon their own ranks, as had happened on that occasion, and trample down their own people; for it was found out by Hasdrubal, the brother of Hannibal, that in this way these animals might be very easily deprived of life.

16. The sight of these beasts caused great alarm; and so this most intrepid emperor, attended with a strong body of his armed cohorts and many of his chief officers, as the crisis and the superior numbers of the enemy required, marshalled his troops in the form of a crescent with the wings bending inwards to encounter the enemy.

17. And to hinder the onset of the archers from disordering our columns, by advancing with great speed he baffled the aim of their arrows; and after he had given the formal signal for fighting, the Roman infantry, in close order, beat back the front of the enemy with a vigorous effort.

18. The struggle was fierce, and the clashing of the shields, the din of the men, and the doleful whistle of the javelins, which continued without intermission, covered the plains with blood and corpses, the Persians falling in every direction; and though they were often slack in fighting, being accustomed chiefly to combat at a distance by means of missiles, still now foot to foot they made a stout resistance; and when they found any of their divisions giving way, they retreated like rain before the wind, still with showers of arrows seeking to deter their foes from pursuing them. So the Parthians were defeated by prodigious efforts, till our soldiers, exhausted by the heat of the day, on the signal for retreat being sounded, returned to their camp, encouraged for the future to greater deeds of daring.

19. In this battle, as I have said, the loss of the Persians was very great—ours was very slight. But the most important death in our ranks was that of Vetranio, a gallant soldier who commanded the legion of Zianni.[152]

II.

§ 1. After this there was an armistice for three days, while the men attended to their own wounds or those of their friends, during which we were destitute of supplies, and distressed by intolerable hunger; and since, as all the corn and forage was burnt, both men and cattle were in extreme danger of starvation, a portion of the food which the horses of the tribunes and superior officers were carrying was distributed among the lower classes of the soldiers, who were in extreme want.

2. And the emperor, who had no royal dainties prepared for himself, but who was intending to sup under the props of a small tent on a scanty portion of pulse, such as would often have been despised by a prosperous common soldier, indifferent to his own comfort, distributed what was prepared for him among the poorest of his comrades.

3. He gave a short time to anxious and troubled sleep; and when he awoke, and, as was his custom, began to write something in his tent, in imitation of Julius Cæsar, while the night was still dark, being occupied with the consideration of the writings of some philosophers, he saw, as he told his friends, in mournful guise, the vision of the Genius of the Empire, whom, when he first became emperor, he had seen in Gaul, sorrowfully departing through the curtains of his tent with the cornucopia, which he bore in his hand veiled, as well as his head.

4. And although for a moment he stood stupefied, yet being above all fear, he commended the future to the will of heaven; and leaving his bed, which was made on the ground, he rose, while it was still but little past midnight, and supplicating the deities with sacred rites to avert misfortune, he thought he saw a bright torch, falling, cut a passage through the air and vanish from his sight; and then he was horror-stricken, fearing that the star of Mars had appeared openly threatening him.

5. For this brightness was of the kind which we call διαΐσσοντα, not falling down or reaching the ground. Indeed, he who thinks that solid substances can fall from heaven is rightly accounted profane and mad. But these occurrences take place in many ways, of which it will be enough to enumerate a few.

6. Some think that sparks falling off from the ethereal fire, as they are able to proceed but a short distance, soon become extinguished; or, perhaps, that rays of fire coming against the dense clouds, sparkle from the suddenness of the contact; or that some light attaches itself to a cloud, and taking the form of a star, runs on as long as it is supported by the power of the fire; but being presently exhausted by the magnitude of the space which it traverses, it becomes dissolved into air, passing into that substance from the excessive attrition of which it originally derived its heat.

7. Therefore, without loss of time, before daybreak, he sent for the Etruscan soothsayers, and consulted them what this new kind of star portended; who replied, that he must cautiously avoid attempting any new enterprise at present, showing that it was laid down in the works of Tarquitius,[153] "on divine affairs," that when a light of this kind is seen in heaven, no battle ought to be engaged in, or any similar measure be undertaken.

8. But as he despised this and many other similar warnings, the diviners at least entreated him to delay his march for some hours; but they could not prevail even to this extent, as the emperor was always opposed to the whole science of divination. So at break of day the camp was struck.

III.

§ 1. When we set forward, the Persians, who had learnt by their frequent defeats to shun pitched battles, laid secret ambuscades on our road, and, occupying the hills on each side, continually reconnoitred our battalions as they marched, so that our soldiers, being kept all day on the watch, could neither find time to erect ramparts round their camp, or to fortify themselves with palisades.

2. And while our flanks were strongly guarded, and the army proceeded onward in as good order as the nature of the ground would allow, being formed in squares, though not quite closed up, suddenly news was brought to the emperor, who had gone on unarmed to reconnoitre the ground in front, that our rear was attacked.

3. He, roused to anger by this mishap, without stopping to put on his breastplate, snatched up his shield in a hurry, and while hastening to support his rear, was recalled by fresh news that the van which he had quitted was now exposed to a similar attack.

4. Without a thought of personal danger, he now hastened to strengthen this division, and then, on another side, a troop of Persian cuirassiers attacked his centre, and pouring down with vehemence on his left wing, which began to give way, as our men could hardly bear up against the foul smell and horrid cries of the elephants, they pressed us hard with spears and clouds of arrows.

5. The emperor flew to every part of the field where the danger was hottest; and our light-armed troops dashing out wounded the backs of the Persians, and the hocks of the animals, which were turned the other way.

6. Julian, disregarding all care for his own safety, made signs by waving his hands, and shouted out that the enemy were fleeing in con-

sternation; and cheering on his men to the pursuit, threw himself eagerly into the conflict. His guards called out to him from all sides to beware of the mass of fugitives who were scattered in consternation, as he would beware of the fall of an ill-built roof, when suddenly a cavalry spear, grazing the skin of his arm, pierced his side, and fixed itself in the bottom of his liver.

7. He tried to pull it out with his right hand, and cut the sinews of his fingers with the double-edged point of the weapon; and, falling from his horse, he was borne with speed by the men around him to his tent; and the physician tried to relieve him.

8. Presently, when his pain was somewhat mitigated, so that his apprehensions were relieved, contending against death with great energy, he asked for arms and a horse in order that, by revisiting his troops, who were still engaged, he might restore their confidence, and appear so secure of his own recovery as to have room for anxiety for the safety of others; with the same energy though with a different object, with which the celebrated leader, Epaminondas, when he was mortally wounded at Mantinea, and had been borne out of the battle, asked anxiously for his shield; and when he saw it he died of his wound cheerfully, having been in fear for the loss of his shield, while quite fearless about the loss of his life.

9. But as Julian's strength was inferior to his firmness, and as he was weakened by the loss of blood, he remained without moving: and presently he gave up all hope of life; because, on inquiry, he found that the place where he had fallen was called Phrygia; for he had been assured by an oracle that he was destined to die in Phrygia.

10. When he was brought back to his tent, it was marvellous with what eagerness the soldiers flew to avenge him, agitated with anger and sorrow; and striking their spears against their shields, determined to die if Fate so willed it. And although vast clouds of dust obscured their sight, and the burning heat hindered the activity of their movements, still, as if they were released from all military discipline by the loss of their chief, they rushed unshrinkingly on the enemy's swords.

11. On the other hand the Persians, fighting with increased spirit, shot forth such clouds of arrows, that we could hardly see the shooters through them; while the elephants, slowly marching in front, by the vast size of their bodies, and the formidable appearance of their crests, terrified alike our horses and our men.

12. And far off was heard the clashing of armed men, the groans of the dying, the snorting of the horses, and the clang of swords, till

both sides were weary of inflicting wounds, and the darkness of night put an end to the contest.

13. Fifty nobles and satraps of the Persians, with a vast number of the common soldiers, were slain; and among them, two of their principal generals, Merena and Nohodares. Let the grandiloquence of antiquity marvel at the twenty battles fought by Marcellus in different places; let it add Sicinius Dentatus, adorned with his mass of military crowns; let it further extol Sergius, who is said to have received twenty-three wounds in his different battles, among whose posterity was that last Catiline, who tarnished the glories of his distinguished family by everlasting infamy.

14. But sorrow now overpowered the joy at this success. While the conflict was thus carried on after the withdrawal of the emperor, the right wing of the army was exhausted by its exertions; and Anatolius, at that time the master of the offices, was killed; Sallust the prefect was in imminent danger, and was saved only by the exertions of his attendant, so that at last he escaped, while Sophorius his counsellor was killed; and certain soldiers, who, after great danger, had thrown themselves into a neighbouring fort, were unable to rejoin the main army till three days afterwards.

15. And while these events were taking place, Julian, lying in his tent, thus addressed those who stood around him sorrowing and mourning: "The seasonable moment for my surrendering this life, O comrades, has now arrived, and, like an honest debtor, I exult in preparing to restore what nature reclaims; not in affliction and sorrow, since I have learnt, from the general teaching of philosophers, how much more capable of happiness the mind is than the body; and considering that when the better part is separated from the worse, it is a subject of joy rather than of mourning. Reflecting, also, that there have been instances in which even the gods have given to some persons of extreme piety, death as the best of all rewards.

16. "And I well know that it is intended as a gift of kindness to me, to save me from yielding to arduous difficulties, and from forgetting or losing myself; knowing by experience that all sorrows, while they triumph over the weak, flee before those who endure them manfully.

17. "Nor have I to repent of any actions; nor am I oppressed by the recollection of any grave crime, either when I was kept in the shade, and, as it were, in a corner, or after I arrived at the empire, which, as an honour conferred on me by the gods, I have preserved, as I believe, unstained. In civil affairs I have ruled with moderation and,

whether carrying on offensive or defensive war, have always been under the influence of deliberate reason; prosperity, however, does not
always correspond to the wisdom of man's counsels, since the powers
above reserve to themselves the regulation of results.

18. "But always keeping in mind that the aim of a just sovereign
is the advantage and safety of his subjects, I have been always, as you
know, inclined to peace, eradicating all licentiousness—that great cor-
ruptress of things and manners—by every part of my own conduct;
and I am glad to feel that in whatever instances the republic, like an
imperious mother, has exposed me deliberately to danger, I have stood
firm, inured to brave all fortuitous disturbing events.

19. "Nor am I ashamed to confess that I have long known, from
prophecy, that I should fall by the sword. And therefore do I venerate
the everlasting God that I now die, not by any secret treachery, nor by
a long or severe disease, or like a condemned criminal, but I quit the
world with honour, fairly earned, in the midst of a career of nourishing
glory. For, to any impartial judge, that man is base and cowardly who
seeks to die when he ought not, or who avoids death when it is seasonable for him.

20. "This is enough for me to say, since my strength is failing
me; but I designedly forbear to speak of creating a new emperor, lest I
should unintentionally pass over some worthy man; or, on the other
hand, if I should name one whom I think proper, I should expose him
to danger in the event of some one else being preferred. But, as an
honest child of the republic, I hope that a good sovereign will be found
to succeed me."

21. After having spoken quietly to this effect, he, as it were with
the last effort of his pen, distributed his private property among his
dearest friends, asking for Anatolius, the master of the offices. And
when the prefect Sallust replied that he was now happy, he understood
that he was slain, and bitterly bewailed the death of his friend, though
he had so proudly disregarded his own.

22. And as all around were weeping, he reproved them with still
undiminished authority, saying that it was a humiliating thing to
mourn for an emperor who was just united to heaven and the stars.

23. And as they then became silent, he entered into an intricate
discussion with the philosophers Maximus and Priscus on the sublime
nature of the soul, while the wound of his pierced side was gaping
wide. At last the swelling of his veins began to choke his breath, and
having drank some cold water, which he had asked for, he expired
quietly about midnight, in the thirty-first year of his age. He was born

at Constantinople, and in his childhood lost his father, Constantius, who, after the death of his brother Constantine, perished amid the crowd of competitors for the vacant crown. And at the same early age he lost his mother, Basilina, a woman descended from a long line of noble ancestors.

IV.

§ 1. Julian was a man to be classed with heroic characters, and conspicuous for the brilliancy of his exploits and his innate majesty. For since, as wise men lay it down, there are four cardinal virtues,—temperance, prudence, justice, and fortitude,—with corresponding external accessaries, such as military skill, authority, prosperity, and liberality, he eagerly cultivated them all as if they had been but one.

2. And in the first place, he was of a chastity so inviolate that, after the loss of his wife he never indulged in any sexual pleasures, recollecting what is told in Plato of Sophocles the tragedian, that being asked when he was a very old man whether he still had any commerce with women, he said "No," with this further addition, that "he was glad to say that he had at all times avoided such indulgence as a tyrannous and cruel master."

3. And to strengthen this resolution he often called to mind the words of the lyric poet Bacchylides, whom he used to read with pleasure, and who said that as a fine painter makes a handsome face, so chastity adorns a life that aims at greatness. And even when in the prime of life he so carefully avoided this taint that there was never the least suspicion of his becoming enamoured even of any of his household, as has often happened.

4. And this kind of temperance increased in him, being strengthened by a sparing indulgence in eating and sleeping, to which he rigidly adhered whether abroad or at home. For in time of peace his frugal allowance of food was a marvel to all who knew him, as resembling that of a man always wishing to resume the philosopher's cloak. And in his various campaigns he used commonly only to take a little plain food while standing, as is the custom of soldiers.

5. And when after being fatigued by labour he had refreshed his body with a short rest, as soon as he awoke he would go by himself round all the sentries and outposts; after which he retired to his serious studies.

6. And if any voice could bear witness to his use of the nocturnal lamp, by which he pursued his lucubrations, it would show that there was a vast difference between some emperors and him, who did not

even indulge himself in those pleasures permitted by the necessities of human nature.

7. Of his prudence there were also many proofs, of which it will be sufficient to recount a few. He was profoundly skilled in war, and also in the arts of peace. He was very attentive to courtesy, claiming just so much respect as he considered sufficient to mark the difference between contempt and insolence. He was older in virtue than in years, being eager to acquire all kinds of knowledge. He was a most incorruptible judge, a rigid censor of morals and manners, mild, a despiser of riches, and indeed of all mortal things. Lastly, it was a common saying of his, "That it was beneath a wise man, since he had a soul, to aim at acquiring praise by his body."

8. Of his justice there are many conspicuous proofs: first, because, with all proper regard to circumstances and persons, he inspired awe without being cruel; secondly, because he repressed vice by making examples of a few, and also because he threatened severe punishment more frequently than he employed it.

9. Lastly, to pass over many circumstances, it is certain that he treated with extreme moderation some who were openly convicted of plotting against him, and mitigated the rigour of the punishment to which they were sentenced with genuine humanity.

10. His many battles and constant wars displayed his fortitude, as did his endurance of extreme cold and heat. From a common soldier we require the services of the body, from an emperor those of the mind. But having boldly thrown himself into battle, he would slay a ferocious foe at a single blow; and more than once he by himself checked the retreat of our men at his own personal risk. And when he was putting down the rule of the furious Germans, and also in the scorching sands of Persia, he encouraged his men by fighting in the front ranks of his army.

11. Many well-known facts attest his skill in all that concerns a camp; his storming of cities and castles amid the most formidable dangers; the variety of his tactics for battles, the skill he showed in choosing healthy spots for his camps, the safe principles on which his lines of defence and outposts were managed.

12. So great was his authority, that while he was feared he was also greatly loved as his men's comrade in their perils and dangers. And in the hottest struggles he took notice of cowards for punishment. And while he was yet only Cæsar, he kept his soldiers in order while confronting the barbarians, and destitute of pay as I have mentioned before. And haranguing his discontented troops, the threat which he

used was that he would retire into private life if they continued mutinous.

13. Lastly, this single instance will do as well as many, by haranguing the Gallic legions, who were accustomed to the frozen Rhine, in a simple address, he persuaded them to traverse vast regions and to march through the warm plains of Assyria to the borders of Media.

14. His good fortune was so conspicuous that, riding as it were on the shoulders of Fortune, who was long his faithful guide, he overcame enormous difficulties in his victorious career. And after he quitted the regions of the west, they all remained quiet during his lifetime, as if under the influence of a wand powerful enough to tranquillize the world.

15. Of his liberality there are many and undoubted proofs. Among which are his light exactions of tribute, his remission of the tribute of crowns, and of debts long due, his putting the rights of individuals on an equal footing with those of the treasury, his restoration of their revenues and their lands to different cities, with the exception of such as had been lawfully sold by former princes; and also the fact that he was never covetous of money, which he thought was better kept by its owners, often quoting the saying, "that Alexander the Great, when he was asked where he kept his treasures, kindly answered 'Among my friends.'"

16. Having discussed those of his good qualities which have come within our knowledge, let us now proceed to unfold his faults, though they have been already slightly noticed. He was of an unsteady disposition; but this fault he corrected by an excellent plan, allowing people to set him right when guilty of indiscretion.

17. He was a frequent talker, rarely silent. Too much devoted to divination, so much so as in this particular to equal the emperor Adrian. He was rather a superstitious than a legitimate observer of sacred rites, sacrificing countless numbers of victims; so that it was reckoned that if he had returned from the Parthians there would have been a scarcity of cattle. Like the celebrated case of Marcus Cæsar,[154] about whom it was written, as it is said, "The white cattle to Marcus Cæsar, greeting. If you conquer there is an end of us."

18. He was very fond of the applause of the common people, and an immoderate seeker after praise even in the most trifling matters; often, from a desire of popularity, indulging in conversation with unworthy persons.

19. But in spite of all this he deserved, as he used to say himself, to have it thought that that ancient Justice, whom Aratus says fled to

heaven from disgust with the vices of men, had in his reign returned again to the earth; only that sometimes he acted arbitrarily and inconsistently.

20. For he made some laws which, with but few exceptions, were not offensive, though they very positively enforced or forbade certain actions. Among the exceptions was that cruel one which forbade Christian masters of rhetoric and grammar to teach unless they came over to the worship of the heathen gods.

21. And this other ordinance was equally intolerable, namely one which allowed some persons to be unjustly enrolled in the companies of the municipal guilds, though they were foreigners, or by privilege or birth wholly unconnected with such companies.

22. As to his personal appearance it was this. He was of moderate stature, with soft hair, as if he had carefully dressed it, with a rough beard ending in a point, with beautiful brilliant eyes, which displayed the subtlety of his mind, with handsome eyebrows and a straight nose, a rather large mouth, with a drooping lower lip, a thick and stooping neck, large and broad shoulders. From head to foot he was straight and well proportioned, which made him strong and a good runner.

23. And since his detractors have accused him of provoking new wars, to the injury of the commonwealth, let them know the unquestionable truth, that it was not Julian but Constantius who occasioned the hostility of the Parthians by greedily acquiescing in the falsehoods of Metrodorus, as we have already set forth.

24. In consequence of this conduct our armies were slain, numbers of our soldiers were taken prisoners, cities were rased, fortresses were stormed and destroyed, provinces were exhausted by heavy expenses, and in short the Persians, putting their threats into effect, were led to seek to become masters of everything up to Bithynia and the shores of the Propontis.

25. While the Gallic wars grew more and more violent, the Germans overrunning our territories, and being on the point of forcing the passes of the Alps in order to invade Italy, there was nothing to be seen but tears and consternation, the recollection of the past being bitter, the expectation of the future still more woeful. All these miseries, this youth, being sent into the West with the rank of Cæsar, put an end to with marvellous celerity, treating the kings of those countries as base-born slaves.

26. Then in order to re-establish the prosperity of the east, with similar energy he attacked the Persians, and would have gained in that

country both a triumph and a surname, if the will of heaven had been in accordance with his glorious plans and actions.

27. And as we know by experience that some men are so rash and hasty that if conquered they return to battle, if shipwrecked, to the sea, in short, each to the difficulties by which he has been frequently overcome, so some find fault with this emperor for returning to similar exploits after having been repeatedly victorious.

V.

§ 1. After these events there was no time for lamentation or weeping. For after he had been laid out as well as the circumstances and time permitted, that he might be buried where he himself had formerly proposed, at daybreak the next morning, which was on the 27th of June, while the enemy surrounded us on every side, the generals of the army assembled, and having convened the chief officers of the cavalry and of the legions, deliberated about the election of an emperor.

2. There were great and noisy divisions. Arinthæus and Victor, and the rest of those who had been attached to the court of Constantius, sought for a fit man of their own party. On the other hand, Nevitta and Dagalaiphus, and the nobles of the Gauls, sought for a man among their own ranks.

3. While the matter was thus in dispute, they all unanimously agreed upon Sallustius. And when he pleaded ill health and old age, one of the soldiers of rank observing his real and fixed reluctance said, "And what would you do if the emperor while absent himself, as has often happened, had intrusted you with the conduct of this war? Would you not have postponed all other considerations and applied yourself to extricating the soldiers at once from the difficulties which press on them? Do so now: and then, if we are allowed to reach Mesopotamia, it will be time enough for the united suffrages of both armies to declare a lawful emperor."

4. Amid these little delays in so important a matter, before opinions were justly weighed, a few made an uproar, as often happens in critical circumstances, and Jovian was elected emperor, being the chief officer of the guards, and a man of fair reputation in respect of his father's services. For he was the son of Varronianus, a distinguished count,[155] who had not long since retired from military service to lead a private life.

5. And immediately he was clothed in the imperial robes, and was suddenly led forth out of the tent and passed at a quick pace through the army as it was preparing to march.

6. And as the line extended four miles, those in the van hearing some persons salute Jovian as Augustus, raised the same cry still more loudly, for they were caught by the relationship, so to say, of the name, which differed only by one letter from that of Julian, and so they thought that Julian was recovered and was being led forth with great acclamations as had often been the case. But when the new emperor, who was both taller and less upright, was seen, they suspected what had happened, and gave vent to tears and lamentations.

7. And if any lover of justice should find fault with what was done at this extreme crisis as imprudent, he might still more justly blame sailors who, having lost a skilful pilot when both winds and waves are agitated by a storm, commit the helm of their vessel to some one of their comrades.

8. This affair having been thus settled by a blind sort of decision of Fortune, the standard-bearer of the Jovian legion, which Varronianus had formerly commanded, having had a quarrel with the new emperor while he was a private individual, because he had been a violent disparager of his father, now fearing danger at his hand, since he had risen to a height exceeding any ordinary fortune, fled to the Persians. And having been allowed to tell what he knew, he informed Sapor, who was at hand, that the prince whom he dreaded was dead, and that Jovian, who had hitherto been only an officer of the guards, a man of neither energy nor courage, had been raised by a mob of camp drudges to a kind of shadow of the imperial authority.

9. Sapor hearing this news, which he had always anxiously prayed for, and being elated by this unexpected good fortune, having reinforced the troops who had fought against us with a strong body of the royal cavalry, sent them forward with speed to attack the rear of our army.

VI.

§ 1. And while these arrangements were being made, the victims and entrails were inspected on behalf of Jovian, and it was pronounced that he would ruin everything if he remained in the camp, as he proposed, but that if he quitted it he would have the advantage.

2. And just as we were beginning our march, the Persians attacked us, preceded by their elephants. Both our horses and men were at first disordered by their roaring and formidable onset; but the Jovian

and Herculean legions slew a few of the monsters, and made a gallant resistance to the mounted cuirassiers.

3. Then the legions of the Jovii and Victores coming up to aid their comrades, who were in distress, also slew two elephants and a great number of the enemy's troops. And on our left wing three most gallant men were slain, Julian, Macrobius, and Maximus, all tribunes of the legions which were then the chief of the whole army.

4. When they were buried as well as circumstances permitted, as night was drawing on, and as we were pressing forward with all speed towards a fort called Sumere, the dead body of Anatolius was recognized and buried with a hurried funeral. Here also we were rejoined by sixty soldiers and a party of the guards of the palace, whom we have mentioned as having taken refuge in a fort called Vaccatum.

5. Then on the following day we pitched our camp in a valley in as favourable a spot as the nature of the ground permitted, surrounding it with a rampart like a wall, with sharp stakes fixed all round like so many swords, with the exception of one wide entrance.

6. And when the enemy saw this they attacked us with all kinds of missiles from their thickets, reproaching us also as traitors and murderers of an excellent prince. For they had heard by the vague report of some deserters that Julian had fallen by the weapon of a Roman.

7. And presently, while this was going on, a body of cavalry ventured to force their way in by the Prætorian gate, and to advance almost up to the emperor's tent. But they were vigorously repulsed with the loss of many of their men killed and wounded.

8. Quitting this camp, the next night we reached a place called Charcha, where we were safe, because the artificial mounds of the river had been broken to prevent the Saracens from overrunning Armenia, so that no one was able to harass our lines as they had done before.

9. Then on the 1st of July we marched thirty furlongs more, and came to a city called Dura, where our baggage-horses were so jaded, that their drivers, being mostly recruits, marched on foot till they were hemmed in by a troop of Saracens; and they would all have been killed if some squadrons of our light cavalry had not gone to their assistance in their distress.

10. We were exposed to the hostility of these Saracens because Julian had forbidden that the presents and gratuities, to which they had been accustomed, should be given to them; and when they complained to him, they were only told that a warlike and vigilant emperor had iron, not gold.

11. Here, owing to the obstinate hostility of the Persians, we lost four days. For when we advanced they followed us, compelling us to retrace our steps by their incessant attacks. When we halted gradually to fight, they retired, tormenting us by their long delay. And now (for when men are in great fear even falsehoods please them) a report being spread that we were at no great distance from our own frontier, the army raised an impatient shout, and demanded to be at once led across the Tigris.

12. But the emperor and his officers opposed this demand, and showed them that the river, now just at the time of the rising of the Dogstar, was much flooded, entreated them not to trust themselves to its dangerous currents, reminding them that most of them could not swim, and adding likewise that the enemy had occupied the banks of the river, swoln as it was at many parts.

13. But when the demand was repeated over and over again in the camp, and the soldiers with shouts and great eagerness began to threaten violence, the order was given very unwillingly that the Gauls, mingled with the northern Germans, should lead the way into the river, in order that if they were carried away by the violence of the stream the obstinacy of the rest might be shaken; or on the other hand, if they accomplished the passage in safety the rest might attempt it with more confidence.

14. And men were selected suited to such an enterprise, who from their childhood had been accustomed in their native land to cross the greatest rivers. And when the darkness of night presented an opportunity for making the attempt unperceived, as if they had just escaped from a prison, they reached the opposite bank sooner than could have been expected; and having beaten down and slain numbers of the Persians whom, though they had been placed there to guard the passage, their fancied security had lulled into a gentle slumber, they held up their hands, and shook their cloaks so as to give the concerted signal that their bold attempt had succeeded.

15. And when the signal was seen, the soldiers became eager to cross, and could only be restrained by the promise of the engineers to make them bridges by means of bladders and the hides of slaughtered animals.

VII.

§ 1. While these vain attempts were going on, king Sapor, both while at a distance, and also when he approached, received from his scouts and from our deserters a true account of the gallant exploits of our men, of the disgraceful slaughter of his own troops, and also of his elephants in greater numbers than he ever remembered to have lost before. And he heard also that the Roman army, being hardened by its continual labours since the death of its glorious chief, did not now think so much, as they said, of safety as of revenge; and were resolved to extricate themselves from their difficulties either by a complete victory or by a glorious death.

2. He looked on this news as formidable, being aware by experience that our troops who were scattered over these provinces could easily be assembled, and knowing also that his own troops after their heavy losses were in a state of the greatest alarm; he also heard that we had in Mesopotamia an army little inferior in numbers to that before him.

3. And besides all this, his courage was damped by the fact of five hundred men having crossed that swollen river by swimming in perfect safety, and having slain his guards, and so emboldening the rest of their comrades to similar hardihood.

4. In the mean time, as the violence of the stream prevented any bridges from being constructed, and as everything which could be eaten was consumed, we passed two days in great misery, and the starving soldiers began to be furious with rage, thinking it better to perish by the sword than by hunger, that most degrading death.

5. But the eternal providence of God was on our side, and beyond our hopes the Persians made the first overtures, sending the Surena and another noble as ambassadors to treat for peace, and they themselves being in a state of despondency, as the Romans, having proved superior in almost every battle, weakened them daily.

6. But the conditions which they proposed were difficult and intricate, since they pretended that, out of regard for humanity, their merciful monarch was willing to permit the remains of our army to return home, provided the Cæsar, with his officers, would satisfy his demands.

7. In reply, we sent as ambassadors on our part, Arinthæus and Sallustius; and while the proper terms were being discussed with great deliberation, we passed four more days in great suffering from want of provisions, more painful than any kind of torture.

8. And in this truce, if before the ambassadors were sent, the emperor, being disabused, had retired slowly from the territories of the enemy, he would have reached the forts of Corduena, a rich region belonging to us, only one hundred miles from the spot where these transactions were being carried on.

351

9. But Sapor obstinately demanded (to use his own language) the restoration of those territories which had been taken from him by Maximian; but as was seen in the progress of the negotiation, he in reality required, as the price of our redemption, five provinces on the other side of the Tigris,—Arzanena, Moxœna, Zabdicena, Rehemena, and Corduena, with fifteen fortresses, besides Nisibis, and Singara, and the important fortress called the camp of the Moors.

10. And though it would have been better to fight ten battles than to give up one of them, still a set of flatterers harassed our pusillanimous emperor with harping on the dreaded name of Procopius, and affirmed that unless we quickly recrossed the river, that chieftain, as soon as he heard of the death of Julian, would easily bring about a revolution which no one could resist, by means of the fresh troops which he had under his command.

11. Jovian, being wrought upon by the constant reiteration of these evil counsels, without further delay gave up everything that was demanded, with this abatement, which he obtained with difficulty, that the inhabitants of Nisibis and Singara should not be given up to the Persians as well as the cities themselves; and that the Roman garrisons in the forts about to be surrendered should be permitted to retire to fortresses of our own.

12. To which another mischievous and unfair condition was added, that after this treaty was concluded we were not to be at liberty to assist Arsaces against the Persians, if he implored our aid, though he had always been our friend and trusty ally. And this was insisted on by Sapor for two reasons, in order that the man might be punished who had laid waste Chiliocomum at the emperor's command, and also that facility might be given for invading Armenia without a check. In consequence of this it fell out subsequently that Arsaces was taken prisoner, and that, amid different dissensions and disturbances, the Parthians laid violent hands on the greater portion of Armenia, where it borders on Media, and on the town of Artaxata.

13. This ignoble treaty being made, that nothing might be done during the armistice, in contravention of its terms, some men of rank were given as hostages on each side: on ours, Remora, Victor, and Bellovædius, tribunes of distinguished legions: and on that of the enemy, one of their chief nobles named Bineses, and three other satraps of note.

14. So peace was made for thirty years, and ratified by solemn oaths; and we, returning by another line of march, because the parts

near the river were rugged and difficult, suffered severely for want of water and provisions.

VIII.

§ 1. The peace which had been granted on pretence of humanity was turned to the ruin of many who were so exhausted by want of food as to be at the last gasp, and who in consequence could only creep along, and were either carried away by the current of the river from not being able to swim, or if able to overcome the force of the stream so far as to reach the bank, were either slain like sheep by the Saracens or Persians (because, as we stated some time back, the Germans had driven them out), or sent to a distance to be sold for slaves.

2. But when the trumpets openly gave the signal for crossing the river, it was dreadful to see with what ardour every individual hastened to rush into this danger, preferring himself to all his comrades, in the desire of avoiding the many dangers and distresses behind him. Some tried to guide the beasts who were swimming about at random, with hurdles hurriedly put together; others, seated on bladders, and others, being driven by necessity to all kinds of expedients, sought to pass through the opposing waves by crossing them obliquely.

3. The emperor himself with a few others crossed over in the small boats, which we said were saved when the fleet was burnt, and then sent the same vessels backwards and forwards till our whole body was brought across. And at length all of us, except such as were drowned, reached the opposite bank of the river, being saved amid our difficulties by the favour of the Supreme Deity.

4. While we were still oppressed with the fear of impending disasters, we learnt from information brought in by our outposts that the Persians were throwing a bridge over the river some way off, at a point out of our sight, in order that while all ideas of war were put an end to on our side by the ratification of the treaty of peace, they might come upon our invalids as they proceeded carelessly onwards, and on the animals exhausted with fatigue. But when they found their purpose discovered, they relinquished their base design.

5. Being now relieved from this suspicion, we hastened on by rapid marches, and approached Hatra, an ancient town in the middle of a desert, which had been long since abandoned, though at different times those warlike emperors, Trajan and Severus, had attacked it with a view to its destruction, but had been almost destroyed with their armies, as we have related in our history of their exploits.

6. And as we now learnt that over the vast plain before us for seventy miles in that arid region no water could be found but such as was brackish and fetid, and no kind of food but southernwood, wormwood, dracontium, and other bitter herbs, we filled the vessels which we had with sweet water, and having slain the camels and the rest of the beasts of burden, we thus sought to insure some kind of supplies, though not very wholesome.

7. For six days the army marched, till at last even grass, the last comfort of extreme necessity, could not be found; when Cassianus, Duke of Mesopotamia, and the tribune Mauricius, who had been sent forward with this object, came to a fort called Ur, and brought some food from the supplies which the army under Procopius and Sebastian, by living sparingly, had managed to preserve.

8. From this place another person of the name of Procopius, a secretary, and Memoridus, a military tribune, was sent forward to Illyricum and Gaul to announce the death of Julian, and the subsequent promotion of Jovian to the rank of emperor.

9. And Jovian deputed them to present his father-in-law Lucillianus (who, after giving up military service, had retired to the tranquillity of private life, and who was at that time dwelling at Sirmium) with a commission as captain of the forces of cavalry and infantry, and to urge him at the same time to hasten to Milan, to support him there in any difficulties which might arise, or (what he feared most) to oppose any attempts which might be made to bring about a revolution.

10. And he also gave them still more secret letters, in which he warned Lucillianus to bring him some picked men of tried energy and fidelity, of whose aid he might avail himself according as affairs should turn out.

11. He also made a wise choice, and selected Malarichus, who was at that time in Italy on his own private affairs, sending him the ensigns of office that he might succeed Jovinus as commander of the forces in Gaul, in which appointment he had an eye on two important objects; first, to remove a general of especial merit who was an object of suspicion on that very account, and also by the promotion to so high a position of a man whose hopes were not set on anything so lofty to bind him to exert all his zeal in supporting the doubtful position of the maker of his fortunes.

12. And the officers who went to perform these commands were also enjoined to extol the emperor's conduct, and wherever they went to agree in reporting that the Parthian campaign had been brought to

an honourable termination; they were also charged to prosecute their journey with all speed by night and day, delivering as they went letters from the new emperor to all the governors of provinces and commanders of the forces on their road; and when they had secretly learnt the opinions of them all, to return to him with all speed, in order that when he knew what was being done in the distant provinces, he might be able to frame well-digested and wise plans for strengthening himself in his government.

13. But Fame (being alway the most rapid bearer of bad news), outstripping these couriers, flew through the different provinces and nations; and above all others struck the citizens of Nisibis with bitter sorrow when they heard that their city was surrendered to Sapor, whose anger and enmity they dreaded, from recollecting the havoc and slaughter which he had made in his frequent attempts to take the place.

14. For it was clear that the whole eastern empire would have fallen under the power of Persia long before if it had not been for the resistance which this city, strong in its admirable position and its mighty walls, had been able to offer. But miserable as they now were, and although they were filled with a still greater fear of what might befall them hereafter, they were supported by this slender hope, that, either from his own inclination or from being won over by their prayers, the emperor might consent to keep their city in its existing state, as the strongest bulwark of the east.

15. While different reports were flying about of what had taken place, the scanty supplies which I have spoken of as having been brought, were consumed, and necessity might have driven the men to eat one another, if the flesh of the animals slain had not lasted them a little longer; but the consequence of our destitute condition was, that the arms and baggage were thrown away; for we were so worn out with this terrible famine, that whenever a single bushel of corn was found (which seldom happened), it was sold for ten pieces of gold at the least.

16. Marching on from thence, we come to Thilsaphata where Sebastian and Procopius, with the tribunes and chief officers of the legions which had been placed under their command for the protection of Mesopotamia, came to meet the emperor as the solemn occasion required, and being kindly received, accompanied us on our march.

17. After this, proceeding with all possible speed, we rejoiced when we saw Nisibis, where the emperor pitched a standing camp outside the walls; and being most earnestly entreated by the whole population to come to lodge in the palace according to the custom of

his predecessors, he positively refused, being ashamed that an impregnable city should be surrendered to an enraged enemy while he was within its walls.

18. But as the evening was getting dark, Jovian, the chief secretary, was seized while at supper, the man who at the siege of the city Maogamalcha we have spoken of as escaping with others by a subterranean passage, and being led to an out-of-the-way place, was thrown headlong down a dry well, and overwhelmed with a heap of stones which were thrown down upon him, because after the death of Julian he also had been named by a few persons as fit to be made emperor; and after the election of his namesake had not behaved with any modesty, but had been heard to utter secret whispers concerning the business, and had from time to time invited some of the leading soldiers to entertainments.

IX.

§ 1. The next day Bineses, one of the Persians of whom we have spoken as the most distinguished among them, hastening to execute the commission of his king, demanded from Jovian the immediate performance of his promise; and by his permission he entered the city of Nisibis, and raised the standard of his nation on the citadel, announcing to the citizens a miserable emigration from their native place.

2. Immediately they were all commanded to expatriate themselves, in vain stretching forth their hands in entreaty not to be compelled to depart, affirming that they by themselves, without drawing on the public resources for either provisions or soldiers, were sufficient to defend their own home in full confidence that Justice would be on their side while fighting for the place of their birth, as they had often found her to be before. Both nobles and common people joined in this supplication; but they spoke in vain as to the winds, the emperor fearing the crime of perjury, as he pretended, though in reality the object of his fear was very different.

3. Then a man of the name of Sabinus, eminent among his fellow-citizens both for his fortune and birth, replied with great fluency that Constantius too was at one time defeated by the Persians in the terrible strife of fierce war, that afterwards he fled with a small body of comrades to the unguarded station of Hibita, where he lived on a scanty and uncertain supply of bread which was brought him by an old woman from the country; and yet that to the end of his life he lost no territory; while Jovian, at the very beginning of his reign, was yielding

up the wall of his provinces, by the protection of which barrier they had hitherto remained safe from the earliest ages.

4. But as he could not prevail on the emperor, who persisted obstinately in alleging the obligation of his oath, presently, when Jovian, who had for some time refused the crown which was offered to him, accepted it under a show of compulsion, an advocate, named Silvanus, exclaimed boldly, "May you, O emperor, be so crowned in the rest of your cities." But Jovian was offended at his words, and ordered the whole body of citizens to quit the city within three days, in despair as they were at the existing state of affairs.

5. Accordingly, men were appointed to compel obedience to this order, with threats of death to every one who delayed his departure; and the whole city was a scene of mourning and lamentation, and in every quarter nothing was heard but one universal wail, matrons tearing their hair when about to be driven from their homes, in which they had been born and brought up, the mother who had lost her children, or the wife her husband, about to be torn from the place rendered sacred by their shades, clinging to their doorposts, embracing their thresholds, and pouring forth floods of tears.

6. Every road was crowded, each person straggling away as he could. Many, too, loaded themselves with as much of their property as they thought they could carry, while leaving behind them abundant and costly furniture, for this they could not remove for want of beasts of burden.

7. Thou in this place, O fortune of the Roman world, art justly an object of accusation, who, while storms were agitating the republic, didst strike the helm from the hand of a wise sovereign, to intrust it to an inexperienced youth, whom, as he was not previously known for any remarkable actions in his previous life, it is not fair either to blame or praise.

8. But it sunk into the heart of all good citizens, that while, out of fear of a rival claimant of his power, and constantly fancying some one in Gaul or in Illyricum might have formed ambitious designs, he was hastening to outstrip the intelligence of his approach, he should have committed, under pretence of reverence for an oath, an act so unworthy of his imperial power as to abandon Nisibis, which ever since the time of Mithridates had been the chief hindrance to the encroachments of the Persians in the East.

9. For never before since the foundation of Rome, if one consults all its annals, I believe has any portion of our territories been surrendered by emperor or consul to an enemy. Nor is there an instance of a

triumph having been celebrated for the recovery of anything that had been lost, but only for the increase of our dominions.

10. On this principle, a triumph was refused to Publius Scipio for the recovery of Spain, to Fulvius for the acquisition of Capua after a long struggle, and to Opimius after many battles with various results, because the people of Fregellæ, who at that time were our implacable enemies, had been compelled to surrender.

11. For ancient records teach us that disgraceful treaties, made under the pressure of extreme necessity, even after the parties to them have sworn to their observance in set terms, have nevertheless been soon dissolved by the renewal of war; as in the olden time, after the legions had been made to pass under the yoke at the Caudine Forks, in Samnium; and also when an infamous peace was contemplated by Albinus in Numidia; and when Mancinus, the author of a peace which was concluded in disgraceful haste, was surrendered to the people of Numantia.

12. Accordingly, when the citizens had been withdrawn, the city surrendered, and the tribune Constantius had been sent to deliver up to the Persian nobles the fortresses and districts agreed upon, Procopius was sent forward with the remains of Julian, to bury them in the suburbs of Tarsus, according to his directions while alive. He departed, I say, to fulfil this commission, and as soon as the body was buried, he quitted Tarsus, and though sought for with great diligence, he could not be found anywhere, till long afterwards he was suddenly seen at Constantinople invested with the purple.

X.

§ 1. These transactions having been thus concluded, after a long march we arrived at Antioch, where for several days in succession many terrible omens were seen, as if the gods were offended, since those who were skilled in the interpretation of prodigies foretold that impending events would be melancholy.

2. For the statue of Maximian Cæsar, which was placed in the vestibule of the palace, suddenly lost the brazen globe, formed after the figure of the heavens, which it bore in its hand. Also the beams in the council chamber sounded with an ominous creak; comets were seen in the daytime, respecting the nature of which natural philosophers differ.

3. For some think they have received the name because they scatter fire wreathed like hair[156] by a number of stars being collected into one mass; others think that they derive their fire from the dry

evaporation of the earth rising gradually to a greater height; some fancy that the sunbeams as they rapidly pass, being prevented by dense clouds from descending lower, by infusing their brilliancy into a dense body show a light which, as it were, seems spotted with stars to the eyes of mortals. Some again have a fixed opinion that this kind of light is visible when some cloud, rising to a greater height than usual, becomes illuminated by its proximity to the eternal fires; or, that at all events there are some stars like the rest, of which the special times of their rising and setting are not understood by man. There are many other suggestions about comets which have been put forth by men skilled in mundane philosophy, but I must pass over them, as my subject calls me in another direction.

4. The emperor remained a short time at Antioch, distracted by many important cares, but desirous above all things to proceed. And so, sparing neither man nor beast, he started from that city in the depth of winter, though, as I have stated, many omens warned him from such a course, and made his entrance into Tarsus, a noble city of Cilicia, the origin of which I have already related.

5. Being in excessive haste to depart from thence, he ordered decorations for the tomb of Julian, which was placed in the suburb, in the road leading to the defiles of Mount Taurus. Though a sound judgment would have decided that the ashes of such a prince ought not to lie within sight of the Cydnus, however beautiful and clear that river is, but, to perpetuate the glory of his achievements, ought rather to be placed where they might be washed by the Tiber as it passes through the Eternal City and winds round the monuments of the ancient gods.

6. Then quitting Tarsus, he reached by forced marches Tyana, a town of Cappadocia, where Procopius the secretary and Memoridus the tribune met him on their return, and related to him all that occurred; beginning, as the order of events required, at the moment when Lucillianus (who had entered Milan with the tribunes Seniauchus and Valentinian, whom he had brought with him, as soon as it was known that Malarichus had refused to accept the post which was offered to him) hastened on with all speed to Rheims.

7. There, as if it had been a time of profound tranquillity, he went quite beside the mark, as we say, and while things were still in a very unsettled state, he most unseasonably devoted his attention to scrutinizing the accounts of the commissary, who, being conscious of fraud and guilt, fled to the standards of the soldiers, and pretended that while Julian was still alive some one of the common people had attempted a revolution. By this false report the army became so greatly

excited that they put Lucillianus and Seniauchus to death. For Valentinian, who soon afterwards became emperor, had been concealed by his host Primitivus in a safe place, overwhelmed with fear and not knowing which way to flee.

8. This disastrous intelligence was accompanied by one piece of favourable news,—that the soldiers who had been sent by Jovian were approaching (men known in the camp as the heads of the classes), who brought word that the Gallic army had cordially embraced the cause of Jovian.

9. When this was known, the command of the second class of the Scutarii was given to Valentinian, who had returned with those men; and Vitalianus, who had been a soldier of the Heruli, was placed among the body-guards, and afterwards, when raised to the rank of count, met with very ill success in Illyricum. And at the same time Arinthæus was despatched into Gaul with letters for Jovinus, with an injunction to maintain his ground and act with resolution and constancy; and he was further charged to make an example of the author of the disturbance which had taken place, and to send the ringleaders of the sedition as prisoners to the court.

10. When these matters had been arranged as seemed most expedient, the Gallic soldiers obtained an audience of the emperor at Aspuna, a small town of Galatia, and having been admitted into the council chamber, after the message which they brought had been listened to with approval, they received rewards and were ordered to return to their standards.

A.D. 364.

11. When the emperor had made his entry into Ancyra, everything necessary for his procession having been prepared as well as the time permitted, Jovian entered on the consulship, and took as his colleague his son Varronianus, who was as yet quite a child, and whose cries as he obstinately resisted being borne in the curule chair, according to the ancient fashion, was an omen of what shortly happened.

12. Here also the appointed termination of life carried off Jovian with rapidity. For when he had reached Dadastana, a place on the borders of Bithynia and Galatia, he was found dead in the night; and many uncertain reports were spread concerning his death.

13. It was said that he had been unable to bear the unwholesome smell of the fresh mortar with which his bedchamber had been plastered. Also that his head had swollen in consequence of a great fire of coals, and that this had been the cause of his death; others said that he

had died of a surfeit from over eating. He was in the thirty-third year of his age. And though he and Scipio Æmilianus both died in the same manner, we have not found out that any investigation into the death of either ever took place.

14. Jovian was slow in his movements, of a cheerful countenance, with blue eyes; very tall, so much so that it was long before any of the royal robes could be found to fit him. He was anxious to imitate Constantius, often occupying himself with serious business till after midday, and being fond of jesting with his friends in public.

15. He was given to the study of the Christian law, sometimes doing it marked honour; he was tolerably learned in it, very well inclined to its professors, and disposed to promote them to be judges, as was seen in some of his appointments. He was fond of eating, addicted to wine and women, though he would perhaps have corrected these propensities from a sense of what was due to the imperial dignity.

16. It was said that his father, Varronianus, through the warning of a dream, had long since foreseen what happened, and had foretold it to two of his most faithful friends, with the addition that he himself also should become consul. But though part of his prophecy became true, he could not procure the fulfilment of the rest. For though he heard of his son's high fortune, he died before he could see him.

17. And because the old man had it foretold to him in his sleep that the highest office was destined for his name, his grandson Varronianus, while still an infant, was made consul with his father Jovian, as we have related above.

Notes

[151] Primicerius: he was the third officer of the guard; the first being the lower; the second, the tribune—answering, as one might say, to our major.

[152] The Zianni were an Armenian tribe. The legion belonged to the Thracian establishment.

[153] Tarquitius was an ancient Etruscan soothsayer, who had written on the subject of his art.

[154] That is Marcus Aurelius.

[155] It must be remembered that throughout Ammianus's history a count is always spoken of as of higher rank than a duke.

[156] From κόμη, hair.

BOOK XXVI

I.

A.D. 364.

§ 1. Having narrated with exceeding care the series of transactions in my own immediate recollection, it is necessary now to quit the track of notorious events, in order to avoid the dangers often found in connection with truth; and also to avoid exposing ourselves to unreasonable critics of our work, who would make an outcry as if they had been personally injured, if anything should be passed over which the emperor has said at dinner, if any cause should be overlooked for which the common soldiers were assembled round their standards, or if there were not inserted a mention of every insignificant fort, however little such things ought to have room in a varied description of different districts. Or if the name of every one who filled the office of urban prætor be not given, and many other things quite impertinent to the proper idea of a history, which duly touches on prominent occurrences, and does not stoop to investigate petty details or secret motives, which any one who wishes to know may as well hope to be able to count those little indivisible bodies flying through space, which we call atoms.

2. Some of the ancients, fearing this kind of criticism, though they composed accounts of various actions in a beautiful style, forbore to publish them, as Tully, a witness of authority, mentions in a letter to Cornelius Nepos. However, let us, despising the ignorance of people in general, proceed with the remainder of our narrative.

3. The course of events being terminated so mournfully, by the death of two emperors at such brief intervals, the army, having paid the last honours to the dead body which was sent to Constantinople to be interred among the other emperors, advanced towards Nicæa, which is the metropolis of Bithynia, where the chief civil and military authorities applied themselves to an anxious consideration of the state of affairs, and as some of them were full of vain hopes, they sought for a ruler of dignity and proved wisdom.

4. In reports, and the concealed whispers of a few persons, the name of Equitius was ventilated, who was at that time tribune of the first class of the Scutarii; but he was disapproved by the most influential leaders as being rough and boorish; and their inclinations rather tended towards Januarius, a kinsman of Julian, who was the chief commissary of the camp in Illyricum.

5. However, he also was rejected because he was at a distance; and, as a man well qualified and at hand, Valentinian was elected by the unanimous consent of all men, and the manifest favour of the De-

ity. He was the tribune of the second class of the Scutarii, and had been left at Ancyra, it having been arranged that he should follow afterwards. And, because no one denied that this was for the advantage of the republic, messengers were sent to beg him to come with all speed; and for ten days the empire was without a ruler, which the soothsayer Marcus, by an inspection of entrails at Rome, announced to be the case at that moment in Asia.

6. But in the meanwhile, to prevent any attempt to overturn what had been thus settled, or any movement on the part of the fickle soldiers to set aside the election in favour of some one on the spot, Equitius and Leo, who was acting as commissary under Dagalaiphus the commander of the cavalry, and who afterwards incurred great odium as master of the offices,[157] strove with great prudence and vigilance to establish, to the best of their power, what had been the decision of the whole army, they being also natives of Pannonia, and partisans of the emperor elect.

7. When Valentinian arrived in answer to the summons he had received, either in obedience to omens which guided him in the prosecution of the affair, as was generally thought, or to repeated warnings conveyed in dreams, he would not come into public or be seen by any one for two days, because he wished to avoid the bissextile day of February which came at that time, and which he knew to have been often an unfortunate day for the Roman empire: of this day I will here give a plain explanation.

8. The ancients who were skilled in the motions of the world and the stars, among whom the most eminent are Meton, Euctemon, Hipparchus, and Archimedes, define it as the period of the revolving year when the sun, in accordance with the laws which regulate the heavens, having gone through the zodiac, in three hundred and sixty-five days and nights, returns to the same point: as, for instance, when, after having moved on from the second degree of the Ram, it returns again to it after having completed its circuit.

9. But the exact period of a year extends over the number of days above mentioned and six hours more. And so the correct commencement of the next year will not begin till after midday and ends in the evening. The third year begins at the first watch, and lasts till the sixth hour of the night. The fourth begins at daybreak.

10. Now as the beginning of each year varies, one commencing at the sixth hour of the day, another at the same hour of the night, to prevent the calculation from throwing all science into confusion by its perplexing diversity, and the months of autumn from sometimes being

found to come in the spring, it has been settled that those six hours which in a period of four years amount to twenty-four shall be put together so as to make one day and night.

11. And after much consideration it has been so arranged with the concurrence of many learned men, that thus the revolutions of the year may come to one regular end, removed from all vagueness and uncertainty, so that the theory of the heavens may not be clouded by any error, and that the months may retain their appointed position.

12. Before their dominions had reached any wide extent, the Romans were for a long time ignorant of this fact, and having been for many years involved in obscure difficulties, they were in deeper darkness and error than ever, when they gave the priests the power of intercalating, which they, in profligate subservience to the interests of the farmers of the revenue, or people engaged in lawsuits, effected by making additions or subtractions at their own pleasure.

13. And from this mode of proceeding many other expedients were adopted, all of which were fallacious, and which I think it superfluous now to enumerate. But when they were given up, Octavianus Augustus, in imitation of the Greeks, corrected these disorderly arrangements and put an end to these fluctuations, after great deliberation fixing the duration of the year at twelve months and six hours, during which the sun with its perpetual movement runs through the whole twelve signs, and concludes the period of a whole year.

14. This rule of the bissextile year, Rome, which is destined to endure to the end of time, established with the aid of the heavenly Deity. Now let us return to our history.

II.

§ 1. When this day, so little fit in the opinion of many for beginning any great affair, had passed, at the approach of evening, by the advice of the prefect Sallust, an order was issued by general consent, and with the penalty of death attached to any neglect of it, that no one of higher authority, or suspected of aiming at any objects of ambition, should appear in public the next morning.

2. And when, while the numbers who allowed their own empty wishes to torment them were weary of the slowness of time, the night ended at last, and daylight appeared, the soldiers were all assembled in one body, and Valentinian advanced into the open space, and mounting a tribunal of some height which had been erected on purpose, he was declared ruler of the empire as a man of due wisdom by this as-

sembly, bearing the likeness of a comitia, with the unanimous acclamations of all present.

3. Presently he was clothed with the imperial robe, and crowned, and saluted as Augustus with all the delight which the pleasure of this novelty could engender; and then he began to harangue the multitude in a premeditated speech. But as he put forth his arm to speak more freely, a great murmur arose, the centuries and maniples beginning to raise an uproar, and the whole mass of the cohorts presently urging that a second emperor should be at once elected.

4. And though some people fancied that this cry was raised by a few corrupt men in order to gain the favour of those who had been passed over, it appeared that that was a mistake, for the cry that was raised did not resemble a purchased clamour, but rather the unanimous voice of the whole multitude all animated with the same wish, because recent examples had taught them to fear the instability of this high fortune. Presently the murmurs of the furious and uproarious army appeared likely to give rise to a complete tumult, and men began to fear that the audacity of the soldiers might break out into some atrocious act.

5. And as Valentinian feared this above everything, he raised his hand firmly with the vigour of an emperor full of confidence, and venturing to rebuke some as obstinate and seditious, he delivered the speech he had intended without interruption.

6. "I exult, O ye gallant defenders of our provinces, and boast and always shall boast that your valour has conferred on me, who neither expected nor desired such an honour, the government of the Roman empire, as the fittest man to discharge its duties. That which was in your hands before an emperor was elected, you have completed beneficially and gloriously, by raising to this summit of honour a man whom you know by experience to have lived from his earliest youth to his present age with honour and integrity. Now then I entreat you to listen with quietness to a few plain observations which I think will be for the public advantage.

7. "So numerous are the matters for the consideration of an emperor, that I neither deny nor even doubt that it is a desirable thing that he should have a colleague of equal power to deal with every contingency. And I myself, as a man, do also fear the great accumulation of cares which must be mine, and the various changes of events. But still we must use every exertion to insure concord, by which even the smallest affairs give strength. And that is easily secured if, your patience concurring with your equity, you willingly grant me what

belongs to me in this matter. For Fortune, the ally of all good counsels, will I trust aid me, while to the very utmost of my ability and power, I diligently search for a wise and temperate partner. For as wise men lay it down, not only in the case of empire where the dangers are frequent and vast, but also in matters of private and everyday life, a man ought rather to take a stranger into his friendship after he has had opportunities of judging him to be wise, than to ascertain his wisdom after he has made him his friend.

8. "This, in hopes of a happier fortune, I promise. Do you, retaining your steadiness of conduct and loyalty, recruit the vigour of your minds and bodies while rest in your winter quarters allows you to do so. And you shall soon receive what is your due on my nomination as emperor."

9. Having finished this speech, to which his unexpected authority gave weight, the emperor by it brought all over to his opinion. And even those who a few minutes before with loud voices demanded something different, now, following his advice, surrounded him with the eagles and standards, and, forming a splendid and formidable escort of all classes and ranks of the army, conducted him to the palace.

III.

§ 1. While the decisions of Fate were rapidly bringing these events to pass in the East, Apronianus, the governor of Rome, an upright and severe judge, among the grave cases by which that prefecture is continually oppressed, was labouring with most particular solicitude to suppress the magicians, who were now getting scarce, and who, having been taken prisoners, had been, after being put to the question, manifestly convicted by the evidence of their accomplices of having injured some persons. These he put to death, hoping thus, by the punishment of a few, to drive the rest, if any were still concealed, out of the city through fear of similar treatment.

2. And he is said to have acted thus energetically because having been promoted by Julian while he was still in Syria, he had lost one eye on his journey to take possession of his office, and he suspected that this was owing to his having been the object of some nefarious practices; therefore with just but unusual indignation he exerted great industry in searching out these and similar crimes. This made him appear cruel to some persons, because the populace were continually pouring in crowds into the amphitheatre while he was conducting the examination of some of the greatest criminals.

3. At last, after many punishments of this kind had been inflicted, he condemned to death the charioteer Hilarinus, who was convicted on his own confession of having intrusted his son, who was but a very young boy, to a sorcerer to be taught some secret mysteries forbidden by the laws, in order that he might avail himself of unlawful assistance without the privity of any one. But, as the executioner held him but loosely he suddenly escaped and fled to a Christian altar, and had to be dragged from it, when he was immediately beheaded.

4. But soon ample precautions were taken against the recurrence of this and similar offences, and there were none or very few who ventured afterwards to insult the rigour of the public law by practising these iniquities. But at a later period long impunity nourished atrocious crimes; and licentiousness increased to such a pitch that a certain senator followed the example of Hilarinus, and was convicted of having almost articled by a regular contract one of his slaves to a teacher of the black art, to be instructed in his impious mysteries, though he escaped punishment by an enormous bribe, as common report went.

5. And, as it was said, having thus procured an acquittal, though he ought to have been ashamed even to have such an accusation, he took no pains to efface the stain, but as if, among a lot of infamous persons, he were the only one absolutely innocent, he used to ride on a handsomely caparisoned horse through the streets, and is still always attended by a troop of slaves, as if by a new and curious fashion he were desirous to attract particular observation, just as Duilius in ancient times after his glorious naval victory became so arrogant as to cause a flute-player to precede him with soft airs when he returned to his house after any dinner-party.

6. Under this same Apronianus all necessaries were so abundant in Rome that not the slightest murmur because of any scarcity of supplies was ever heard, which is very common at Rome.

IV.

§ 1. But in Bithynia, Valentinian, as we have already mentioned, having been declared emperor, having fixed the next day but one for beginning his march, assembled his chief officers, and, as if the course which he preferred was to follow their advice, inquired whom they recommended him to take for his colleague; and when no one made him any answer, Dagalaiphus, who at that time was commander of the cavalry, boldly answered "If, O excellent emperor, you love your own kindred, you have a brother; if you love the republic, then seek the fittest man to invest."

2. Valentinian was offended with this speech, but kept silence, and dissembled his displeasure and his intentions. And having made a rapid journey he reached Nicomedia on the first of March, where he appointed his brother Valens master of the horse with the rank of tribune.

3. And after that, when he reached Constantinople, revolving many considerations in his mind, and considering that he himself was already overwhelmed with the magnitude of pressing business, he thought that the emergency would admit of no delay; and on the 28th of March he led Valens into the suburbs, where, with the consent of all men (and indeed no one dared to object), he declared him emperor, had him clothed in the imperial robes, and crowned with a diadem, and then brought him back in the same carriage with himself as the legitimate partner of his power, though in fact he was to be more like an obedient servant, as the remainder of my narrative will show.

4. After these matters had been thus settled without any interruption, the two emperors suffered a long time from a violent fever; but when out of danger (as they were more active in the investigation of evils than in removing them) they intrusted the commission to investigate the secret causes of this malady to Ursatius the master of the offices, a fierce Dalmatian, and to Juventius Siscianus the quæstor, their real motive, as was constantly reported, being to bring the memory of Julian and that of his friends into odium, as if their illness had been owing to their secret malpractices. But this insinuation was easily disposed of, since not a word could be adduced to justify any imputation of such treason.

5. At this time the trumpet as it were gave signal for war throughout the whole Roman world; and the barbarian tribes on our frontier were moved to make incursion on those territories which lay nearest to them. The Allemanni laid waste Gaul and Rhætia at the same time. The Sarmatians and Quadi ravaged Pannonia. The Picts, Scots, Saxons, and Atacotti harassed the Britons with incessant invasions; the Austoriani and other Moorish tribes attacked Africa with more than usual violence. Predatory bands of the Goths plundered Thrace.

6. The king of the Persians poured troops into Armenia, exerting all his power to reduce that people again into subjection to his authority; without any just cause, arguing, that after the death of Julian, with whom he had made a treaty of peace, there was nothing that ought to hinder him from recovering those lands which he could prove to have belonged in former times to his ancestors.

V.

A.D. 365.

§ 1. So after the winter had passed off quietly, the two emperors in perfect harmony, one having been formally elected, and the other having been admitted to share that honour, though chiefly in appearance, having traversed Thrace, arrived at Nissa, where in the suburb which is known as Mediana, and is three miles from the city, they divided the counts between them as if they were going to separate.

2. To the share of Valentinian, by whose will everything was settled, there fell Jovinus, who had lately been promoted by Julian to be the commander of the forces in Gaul, and Dagalaiphus, on whom Jovian had conferred a similar rank; while Victor was appointed to follow Valens to the east: and he also had originally been promoted by the decision of Julian; and to him was given Ariathæus as a colleague. For Lupicinus, who in like manner had sometime before been appointed by Jovian to command the cavalry, was defending the eastern districts.

3. At the same time Equitius received the command of the army of Illyricum, with the rank not of general but of count; and Serenianus, who sometime before had retired from the service, now, being a citizen of Pannonia, returned to it, and joined Valens as commander of the cohort of his guards. This was the way in which these affairs were settled, and in which the troops were divided.

4. After this, when the two brothers entered Sirmium, they divided their courts also, and Valentinian as the chief took Milan, while Valens retired to Constantinople.

5. Sallust, with the authority of prefect, governed the East, Mamertinus Italy with Africa and Illyricum, and Germanianus the provinces of Gaul.

6. It was in the cities of Milan and Constantinople that the emperors first assumed the consular robes. But the whole year was one of heavy disaster to the Roman state.

7. For the Allemanni burst through the limits of Germany, and the cause of their unusual ferocity was this. They had sent ambassadors to the court, and according to custom they were entitled to regular fixed presents, but received gifts of inferior value; which, in great indignation, they threw away as utterly beneath them. For this they were roughly treated by Ursatius, a man of a passionate and cruel temper, who at that time was master of the offices; and when they returned and related, with considerable exaggeration, how they had been treated,

they roused the anger of their savage countrymen as if they had been despised and insulted in their persons.

8. About the same time, or not much later, Procopius attempted a revolution in the east; and both these occurrences were announced to Valentinian on the same day, the 1st of November, as he was on the point of making his entry into Paris.

9. He instantly sent Dagalaiphus to make head against the Allemanni, who, when they had laid waste the land nearest to them, had departed to a distance without bloodshed. But with respect to the measures necessary to crush the attempt of Procopius before it gained any strength, he was greatly perplexed, being made especially anxious by his ignorance whether Valens were alive or dead, that Procopius thus attempted to make himself master of the empire.

10. For Equitius, as soon as he heard the account of the tribune Antonius, who was in command of the army in the interior of Dacia, before he was able to ascertain the real truth of everything, brought the emperor a plain statement of what had taken place.

11. On this Valentinian promoted Equitius to the command of a division, and resolved on retiring to Illyricum to prevent a rebel who was already formidable from overrunning Thrace and then carrying an hostile invasion into Pannonia. For he was greatly terrified by recollecting recent events, considering how, not long before, Julian, despising an emperor who had been invariably successful in every civil war, before he was expected or looked for, passed on from city to city with incredible rapidity.

12. But his eager desire to return was cooled by the advice of those about him, who counselled and implored him not to expose Gaul to the barbarians, who were threatening it; nor to abandon on such a pretence provinces which were in need of great support. And then prayers were seconded by embassies from several important cities which entreated him not in a doubtful and disastrous crisis to leave them wholly undefended, when by his presence he might at once deliver them from the greatest dangers, by the mere terror which his mighty name would strike into the Germans.

13. At last, having given much deliberation to what might be most advisable, he adopted the opinion of the majority, and replied that Procopius was the foe only of himself and his brother, but the Allemanni were the enemies of the whole Roman world; and so he determined in the mean time not to move beyond the frontier of Gaul.

14. And advancing to Rheims, being also anxious that Africa should not be suddenly invaded, he appointed Neotherius, who at that

time was only a secretary, but who afterwards became a consul, to go to the protection of that country; and with him Masaucio, an officer of the domestic guard, being induced to add him by the consideration that he was well acquainted with the disturbed parts, since he had been brought up there under his father Cretion, who was formerly Count of Africa; he added further, Gaudentius, a commander of the Scutarii, a man whom he had long known, and on whose fidelity he placed entire confidence.

15. Because therefore these sad disturbances arose on both sides at one and the same time, we will here arrange our account of each separately in suitable order; relating first what took place in the East, and afterwards the war with the barbarians; since the chief events both in the West and the East occurred in the same months; lest, by any other plan, if we skipped over in haste from place to place, we should present only a confused account of everything, and so involve our whole narrative in perplexity and disorder.

VI.

§ 1. Procopius was born and bred in Cilicia, of a noble family, and occupied an advantageous position from his youth, as being a relation of Julian who afterwards became emperor. He was very strict in his way of life and morals, reserved and silent; but both as secretary, and afterwards as tribune distinguishing himself by his services in war, and rising gradually to the highest rank. After the death of Constantius, in the changes that ensued, he, being a kinsman of the emperor, began to entertain higher aims, especially after he was admitted to the order of counts; and it became evident that if ever he were sufficiently powerful, he would be a disturber of the public peace.

2. When Julian invaded Persia he left him in Mesopotamia, in command of a strong division of troops, giving him Sebastian for his colleague with equal power; and he was enjoined (as an uncertain rumour whispered, for no certain authority for the statement could be produced) to be guided by the course of events, and if he should find the republic in a languid state, and in need of further aid, to cause himself without delay to be saluted as emperor.

3. Procopius executed his commission in a courteous and prudent manner; and soon afterwards heard of the mortal wound and death of Julian, and of the elevation of Jovian to the supreme authority; while at the same time an ungrounded report had got abroad that Julian with his last breath had declared that it was his will that the helm of the state should be intrusted to Procopius. He therefore, fearing that in conse-

quence of this report he might be put to death uncondemned, withdrew from public observation; being especially alarmed after the execution of Jovian, the principal secretary, who, as he heard, had been cruelly put to death with torture, because after the death of Julian he had been named by a few soldiers as one worthy to succeed to the sovereignty, and on that account was suspected of meditating a revolution.

4. And because he was aware that he was sought for with great care, he withdrew into a most remote and secret district, seeking to avoid giving offence to any one. Then, finding that his hiding-place was still sought out by Jovian with increased diligence, he grew weary of living like a wild beast (since he was not only driven from high rank to a low station, but was often in distress even for food, and deprived of all human society); so at last, under the pressure of extreme necessity, he returned by secret roads into the district of Chalcedon.

5. Where, since that appeared a safer retreat, he concealed himself in the house of a trusty friend, a man of the name of Strategius, who from being an officer about the palace had risen to be a senator; crossing over at times to Constantinople whenever he could do so without being perceived; as was subsequently learnt from the evidence of this same Strategius after repeated investigations had been made into the conduct of all who were accomplices in his enterprise.

6. Accordingly, like a skilful scout, since hardship and want had so altered his countenance that no one knew him, he collected the reports that were flying about, spread by many who, as the present is always grievous, accused Valens of being inflamed with a passion for seizing what belonged to others.

7. An additional stimulus to his ferocity was the emperor's father-in-law, Petronius, who, from the command of the Martensian cohort, had been suddenly promoted to be a patrician. He was a man deformed both in mind and appearance, and cruelly eager to plunder every person without distinction; torturing all, guilty and innocent, and then binding them with fourfold bonds; exacting debts due as far back as the time of the emperor Aurelian, and grieving if any one escaped without loss.

8. And his natural cruelty was inflamed by this additional incentive, that as he was enriched by the sufferings of others, he was inexorable, cruel, hard hearted, and unfeeling, incapable either of doing justice or of listening to reason. He was more hated than even Cleander, who, as we read, while prefect in the time of Commodus, oppressed people of all ranks with his foolish arrogance; and more tyrannical than Plautian, who was prefect under Severus, and who with

more than mortal pride would have thrown everything into confusion, if he had not been murdered out of revenge.

9. The cruelties which in the time of Valens, who acted under the influence of Petronius, closed many houses both of poor men and nobles, and the fear of still worse impending, sank deep into the hearts of both the provincials and soldiers, who groaned under the same burdens; and though the prayers breathed were silent and secret, yet some change of the existing state of things by the interposition of the supreme Deity was unanimously prayed for.

10. This state of affairs came home to the knowledge of Procopius, and he, thinking that if Fate were at all propitious, he might easily rise to the highest power, lay in wait like a wild beast which prepares to make its spring the moment it sees anything to seize.

11. And while he was eagerly maturing his plans, the following chance gave him an opportunity which proved most seasonable. After the winter was past, Valens hastened into Syria; and when he had reached the borders of Bithynia he learnt from the accounts of the generals that the nation of the Goths, who up to that time had never come into collision with us, and who were therefore very fierce and untractable, were all with one consent preparing for an invasion of our Thracian frontier. When he heard this, in order to proceed on his own journey without hindrance, he ordered a sufficient force of cavalry and infantry to be sent into the districts in which the inroads of these barbarians were apprehended.

12. Therefore, as the emperor was now at a distance, Procopius, being wearied by his protracted sufferings, and thinking even a cruel death preferable to a longer endurance of them, precipitately plunged into danger; and not fearing the last extremities, but being wrought up almost to madness, he undertook a most audacious enterprise. His desire was to win over the legions known as the Divitenses and the younger Tungricani, who were under orders to march through Thrace for the coming campaign, and, according to custom, would stop two days at Constantinople on their way; and for this object he intended to employ some of them whom he knew, thinking it safer to rely on the fidelity of a few, and dangerous and difficult to harangue the whole body.

13. Those whom he selected as emissaries, being secured by the hope of great rewards, promised with a solemn oath to do everything he desired; and undertook also for the good-will of their comrades, among whom they had great influence from their long and distinguished service.

374

14. As was settled between them, when day broke, Procopius, agitated by all kinds of thoughts and plans, repaired to the Baths of Anastasia, so called from the sister of Constantine, where he knew these legions were stationed; and being assured by his emissaries that in an assembly which had been held during the preceding night all the men had declared their adherence to his party, he received from them a promise of safety, and was gladly admitted to their assembly; where, however, though treated with all honour by the throng of mercenary soldiers, he found himself detained almost as a hostage; for they, like the prætorians who after the death of Pertinax had accepted Julian as their emperor because he bid highest, now undertook the cause of Procopius in the hope of great gain to themselves from the unlucky reign he was planning.

15. Procopius therefore stood among them, looking pale and ghost-like; and as a proper royal robe could not be found, he wore a tunic spangled with gold, like that of an officer of the palace, and the lower part of his dress like that of a boy at school; and purple shoes; he also bore a spear, and carried a small piece of purple cloth in his right hand, so that one might fancy that some theatrical figure or dramatic personification had suddenly come upon the stage.

16. Being thus ridiculously put forward as if in mockery of all honours, he addressed the authors of his elevation with servile flattery, promising them vast riches and high rank as the first-fruits of his promotion; and then he advanced into the streets, escorted by a multitude of armed men; and with raised standards he prepared to proceed, surrounded by a horrid din of shields clashing with a mournful clang, as the soldiers, fearing lest they might be injured by stones or tiles from the housetops, joined them together above their heads in close order.

17. As he thus advanced boldly the people showed him neither aversion nor favour; but he was encouraged by the love of sudden novelty, which is implanted in the minds of most of the common people, and was further excited by the knowledge that all men unanimously detested Petronius, who, as I have said before, was accumulating riches by all kinds of violence, reviving actions that had long been buried, and oppressing all ranks with the exaction of forgotten debts.

18. Therefore when Procopius ascended the tribunal, and when, as all seemed thunderstruck and bewildered, even the gloomy silence was terrible, thinking (or, indeed, expecting) that he had only found a shorter way to death, trembling so as to be unable to speak, he stood for some time in silence. Presently when he began, with a broken and

languid voice, to say a few words, in which he spoke of his relationship to the imperial family, he was met at first with but a faint murmur of applause from those whom he had bribed; but presently he was hailed by the tumultuous clamours of the populace in general as emperor, and hurried off to the senate-house, where he found none of the nobles, but only a small number of the rabble of the city; and so he went on with speed, but in an ignoble style, to the palace.

19. One might marvel that this ridiculous beginning, so improvidently and rashly engaged in, should have led to melancholy disasters for the republic, if one were ignorant of previous history, and imagined that this was the first time any such thing had happened. But, in truth, it was in a similar manner that Andriscus of Adramyttium, a man of the very lowest class, assuming the name of Philip, added a third calamitous war to the previous Macedonian wars. Again, while the emperor Macrinus was at Antioch, it was then that Antoninus Heliogabalus issued forth from Emessa. Thus also Alexander, and his mother Mamæa, were put to death by the unexpected enterprise of Maximinus. And in Africa the elder Gordian was raised to the imperial authority, till, being overwhelmed with agony at the dangers which threatened him, he put an end to his life by hanging himself.

VII.

§ 1. So the dealers in cheap luxuries, and those who were about the palace, or who had ceased to serve, and all who, having been in the ranks of the army, had retired to a more tranquil life, now embarked in this unusual and doubtful enterprise, some against their will, and others willingly. Some, however, thinking anything better than the present state of affairs, escaped secretly from the city, and hastened with all speed to the emperor's camp.

2. They were all outstripped by the amazing celerity of Sophronius, at that time a secretary, afterwards prefect of Constantinople, who reached Valens as he was just about to set out from Cæsarea in Cappadocia, in order, now that the hot weather of Cilicia was over, to go to Antioch; and having related to him all that had taken place, brought him, though wholly amazed and bewildered at so doubtful and perplexing a crisis, back into Galatia to encounter the danger before it had risen to a head.

3. While Valens was pushing forward with all speed, Procopius was using all his energy day and night, producing different persons who with cunning boldness pretended that they had arrived, some from

the east, some from Gaul, and who reported that Valentinian was dead, and that everything was easy for the new and favoured emperor.

4. And because enterprises suddenly and wantonly attempted are often strengthened by promptness of action, and in order to neglect nothing, Nebridius, who had been recently promoted through the influence of Petronius to be prefect of the prætorium in the place of Sallust, and Cæsarius, the prefect of Constantinople, were at once thrown into prison; and Phronemius was intrusted with the government of the city, with the customary powers; and Euphrasius was made master of the offices, both being Gauls, and men of known accomplishments and good character. The government of the camp was intrusted to Gomoarius and Agilo, who were recalled to military service with that object—a very ill-judged appointment, as was seen by the result.

5. Now because Count Julius, who was commanding the forces in Thrace, was feared as likely to employ the troops at the nearest stations to crush the rebels if he received information of what was being done, a vigorous measure was adopted; and he was summoned to Constantinople by letter, which Nebridius, while still in prison, was compelled to write, as if he had been appointed by Valens to conduct some serious measures in connection with the movements of the barbarians; and as soon as he arrived he was seized and kept in close custody. By this cunning artifice the warlike tribes of Thrace were brought over without bloodshed, and proved a great assistance to this disorderly enterprise.

6. After this success, Araxius, by a court intrigue, was made prefect of the prætorium, as if at the recommendation of Agilo, his son-in-law. Many others were admitted to various posts in the palace, and to the government of provinces; some against their will, others voluntarily, and even giving bribes for their promotion.

7. And, as often happens in times of intestine commotion, some men, from the very dregs of the populace, rose to a high position, led by desperate boldness and insane expectations; while, on the contrary, others of noble birth fell from the highest elevation down to exile and death.

8. When by these and similar acts the party of Procopius seemed firmly established, the next thing was to assemble a sufficient military force; and that was easily managed, though sometimes, in times of public disorder, a failure here has hindered great enterprises, and even some which had a lawful origin.

9. The divisions of cavalry and infantry which were passing through Thrace were easily gained over, and being kindly and liberally treated, were collected into one body, and at once presented the appearance of an army; and being excited by magnificent promises, they swore with solemn oaths fidelity to Procopius, promising to defend him with unswerving loyalty.

10. For a most seasonable opportunity of gaining them over was found; because he carried in his arms the little daughter of Constantius, whose memory was still held in reverence, himself also claiming relationship with Julian. He also availed himself of another seasonable incident, namely, that it was while Faustina, the mother of the child, was present that he had received the insignia of the imperial rites.

11. He employed also another expedient (though it required great promptitude); he chose some persons, as stupid as they were rash, whom he sent to Illyricum, relying on no support except their own impudence; but also well furnished with pieces of gold stamped with the head of the new emperor, and with other means suited to win over the multitude. But these men were arrested by Equitius, who was the commander of the forces in that country, and were put to death by various methods.

12. And then, fearing similar attempts by Procopius, he blocked up the three narrowest entrances into the northern province; one through Dacia, along the course of the different rivers; another, and that the most frequented, through the Succi; and the third through Macedonia, which is known as the Acontisma. And in consequence of these precautions the usurper was deprived of all hope of becoming master of Illyricum, and lost one great resource for carrying on the war.

13. In the mean time Valens, overwhelmed with the strange nature of this intelligence, and being already on his return through Gallo-Græcia, after he had heard what had happened at Constantinople, advanced with great diffidence and alarm; and as his sudden fears deprived him of his usual prudence, he fell into such despondency that he thought of laying aside his imperial robes as too heavy a burden; and in truth he would have done so if those about him had not hindered him from adopting so dishonourable a resolution. So, being encouraged by the opinions of braver men, he ordered two legions, known as the Jovian and the Victorian, to advance in front to storm the rebel camp.

14. And when they approached, Procopius, who had returned from Nicæa, to which city he had lately gone with the legion of Divit-

enses and a promiscuous body of deserters, which he had collected in a few days, hastened to Mygdus on the Sangarius.

15. And when the legions, being now prepared for battle, assembled there, and while both sides were exchanging missiles as if wishing to provoke an attack, Procopius advanced by himself into the middle, and under the guidance of favourable fortune, he remarked in the opposite ranks a man named Vitalianus (it is uncertain whether he had known him before), and having given him his hand and embraced him, he said, while both armies were equally astonished.

16. "And is this the end of the ancient fidelity of the Roman armies, and of the oaths taken under the strictest obligations of religion! Have you decided, O gallant men, to use your swords in defence of strangers, and that a degenerate Pannonian should undermine and upset everything, and so enjoy a sovereign power which he never even ventured to picture to himself in his prayers, while we lament over your ill-fortune and our own. Follow rather the race of your own noble princes which is now in arms, not with the view of seizing what does not belong to it, but with the hope of recovering its ancestral possessions and hereditary dignities."

17. All were propitiated by this conciliatory speech, and those who had come with the intention of fighting now readily lowered their standards and eagles, and of their own accord came over to him; instead of uttering their fearful yells, they unanimously saluted Procopius emperor, and escorted him to his camp, calling Jupiter to witness, after their military fashion, that Procopius should prove invincible.

VIII.

§ 1. Another fortunate circumstance occurred to swell the prosperity of the rebels. A tribune named Rumitalca, who had joined the partisans of Procopius, having been intrusted with the guard of the palace, digested a plan, and after mingling with the soldiers, passed over by sea to the town formerly known as Drepanum, but now as Helenopolis, and thence marched upon Nicæa, and made himself master of it before any one dreamt of such a step.

2. Valens sent Vadomarius, who had formerly been duke and king of the Allemanni, with a body of troops experienced in that kind of work, to besiege Nicæa, and proceeded himself to Nicomedia; and passing on from that city, he pressed the siege of Chalcedon with all his might; but the citizens poured reproaches on him from the walls,

calling him Sabaiarius, or beer-drinker. Now Sabai is a drink made of barley or other grain, and is used only by poor people in Illyricum.

3. At last, being worn out by the scarcity of supplies and the exceeding obstinacy of the garrison, he was preparing to raise the siege, when the garrison who were shut up in Nicæa suddenly opened the gates and issued forth, destroying a great portion of the works of the besiegers, and under the command of the faithful Rumitalca hastened on eagerly in the hope of cutting off Valens, who had not yet quitted the suburb of Chalcedon. And they would have succeeded in their attempt if he had not learnt the imminence of his danger from some rumour, and eluded the enemy who were pressing on his track, by departing with all speed by a road lying between the lake Sunon and the winding course of the river Gallus. And through this circumstance Bithynia also fell into the hands of Procopius.

4. When Valens had returned by forced marches from this city to Ancyra, and had learnt that Lupicinus was approaching with no inconsiderable force from the East, he began to entertain better hopes, and sent Arinthæus as his most approved general to encounter the enemy.

5. And when Arinthæus reached Dadastana, where we have mentioned that Jovian died, he suddenly saw in his front, Hyperechius, who had previously been only a subaltern, but who now, as a trusty friend, had received from Procopius the command of the auxiliary forces. And thinking it no credit to defeat in battle a man of no renown, relying on his authority and on his lofty personal stature, he shouted out a command to the enemy themselves to take and bind their commander; they obeyed, and so this mere shadow of a general was arrested by the hands of his own men.

6. In the interim, a man of the name of Venustus, who had been an officer of the treasury under Valens, and who had some time before been sent to Nicomedia, to distribute pay to the soldiers who were scattered over the East, when he heard of this disaster, perceived that the time was unfavourable for the execution of his commission, and repaired in haste to Cyzicus with the money which he had with him.

7. There, as it happened, he met Serenianus, who was at that time the count of the guards, and who had been sent to protect the treasury, and who now, with a garrison collected in a hurry, had undertaken the defence of the city, which was impregnable in its walls, and celebrated also for many ancient monuments, though Procopius, in order, now that he had got possession of Bithynia, to make himself master of the Hellespont, had sent a strong force to besiege it.

8. The siege went on slowly; often numbers of the besiegers were wounded by arrows and bullets, and other missiles; and by the skill of the garrison a barrier of the strongest iron chain was thrown across the mouth of the harbour, fastened strongly to the land on each side, to prevent the ships of the enemy, which were armed with beaks, from forcing their way in.

9. This boom, however, after great exertions on the part of both soldiers and generals, who were all exhausted by the fierce nature of the struggle, a tribune of the name of Aliso, an experienced and skilful warrior, cut through in the following manner:—He fastened together three vessels, and placed upon them a kind of testudo, thus,—on the benches stood a body of armed men, united together by their shields, which joined above their heads; behind them was another row, who stooped, so as to be lower; a third rank bent lower still, so as to form a regular gradation; so that the last row of all, resting on their haunches, gave the whole formation the appearance of an arch. This kind of machine is employed in contests under the walls of towns, in order that while the blows of missiles and stones fall on the slippery descent they may pass off like so much rain.

10. Aliso then, being for a while defended from the shower of missiles, by his own vast strength held a log under this chain, while with a mighty blow of his axe he cut it through, so that being driven asunder, it left the broad entrance open, and thus the city was laid open unprotected to the assault of the enemy. And on this account, when, after the death of the originator of all this confusion, cruel vengeance was taken on the members of his party, the same tribune, from a recollection of his gallant action, was granted his life and allowed to retain his commission, and a long time afterwards fell in Isauria in a conflict with a band of ravagers.

11. When Cyzicus was thus opened to him, Procopius hastened thither, and pardoned all who had opposed him, except Serenianus, whom he put in irons, and sent to Nicæa, to be kept in close confinement.

12. And immediately he appointed the young Hormisdas (the son of the former Prince Hormisdas) proconsul intrusting him in the ancient fashion with the command both in civil and military affairs. He conducted himself, as his natural disposition prompted him, with moderation, but was almost seized by the soldiers whom Valens had sent by the difficult passes of Phrygia; he saved himself, however, by great energy, embarking on board a vessel which he kept in readiness for any emergency, carrying off also his wife, who followed him, and was

nearly taken prisoner, had he not protected her under a shower of arrows. She was a lady of high family and great wealth, whose modesty and the glorious destiny reserved for her subsequently saved her husband from great dangers.

13. In consequence of this victory Procopius was elated beyond measure, and not knowing that a man, however happy, if Fortune turns her wheel may become most miserable before evening, he ordered the house of Arbetio, which he had previously spared as that of one of his own partisans, to be rifled, and it was full of furniture of countless value. The reason of his indignation against Arbetio was, that though he had summoned him several times to come to him, he had deferred his audience, pleading old age and sickness.

14. And this presumptuous man might, from the uncertainty in human affairs, have feared some great change; but though without any resistance he could have overrun the provinces of the East with the willing consent of the natives themselves, who, from weariness of the severe rule under which they then were, were eager for any change whatever, he indolently lingered, hoping to gain over some cities of Asia Minor, and to collect some men who were skilful in procuring gold, and who would be of use to him in future battles, which he expected would be both numerous and severe.

15. Thus he was allowing himself to grow blunt, like a rusty sword; just as formerly Pescennius Niger, when repeatedly urged by the Roman people to come to their aid at a time of great extremity, lost a great deal of time in Syria, and at last was defeated by Severus in the Gulf of Issus (which is a town in Cilicia, where Alexander conquered Darius), and was put to death by a common soldier in a suburb of Antioch.

IX.

A.D. 366.

§ 1. These events took place in the depth of winter, in the consulship of Valentinian and Valens. But this high office of consul was transferred to Gratian, who was as yet only a private individual, and to Dagalaiphus. And then, having collected his forces at the approach of spring, Valens, having united Lupicinus's troops, which were a numerous body, to his own, marched with all speed towards Pessinus, which was formerly reckoned a town of Phrygia, but was now considered to belong to Galatia.

2. Having speedily secured it with a garrison, to prevent any unforeseen danger from arising in that district, he proceeded along the

foot of Mount Olympus by very difficult passes to Lycia, intending to attack Gomoarius, who was loitering in that province.

3. Many vehemently opposed this project from this consideration, that his enemy, as has been already mentioned, always bore with him on a litter the little daughter of Constantius, with her mother Faustina, both when marching and when preparing for battle, thus exciting the soldiers to fight more resolutely for the imperial family, with which, as he told them, he himself was connected. So formerly, when the Macedonians were on the point of engaging in battle with the Illyrians, they placed their king, who was still an infant,[158] in his cradle behind the line of battle, and the fear lest he should be taken prisoner made them exert themselves the more so as to defeat their enemies.

4. To counteract this crafty manœuvre the emperor, in the critical state of his affairs, devised a sagacious remedy, and summoned Arbetio, formerly consul, but who was now living in privacy, to join him, in order that the fierce minds of the soldiers might be awed by the presence of a general who had served under Constantine. And it happened as he expected.

5. For when that officer, who was older in years than all around him, and superior in rank, showed his venerable gray hairs to the numbers who were inclined to violate their oaths, and accused Procopius as a public robber, and addressing the soldiers who followed his guilty leadership as his own sons and the partners of his former toils, entreated them rather to follow him as a parent known to them before as a successful leader than obey a profligate spendthrift who ought to be abandoned, and who would soon fall.

6. And when Gomoarius heard this, though he might have escaped from the enemy and returned in safety to the place from whence he came, yet, availing himself of the proximity of the emperor's camp, he passed over under the guise of a prisoner, as if he had been surrounded by the sudden advance of a superior force.

7. Encouraged by this, Valens quickly moved his camp to Phrygia, and engaged the enemy near Nacolia, and the battle was doubtful till Agilo, the leader of Procopius's forces, betrayed his side by a sudden desertion of his ranks; and he was followed by many who, brandishing their javelins and their swords, crossed over to the emperor, bearing their standards and their shields reversed, which is the most manifest sign of defection.

8. When this unexpected event took place, Procopius abandoning all hope of safety, dismounted, and sought a hiding-place on foot in the groves and hills. He was followed by Florentius and the tribune

Barchalbas, who having been known ever since the time of Constantine in all the terrible wars which had taken place, was now driven into treason by necessity not by inclination.

9. So when the greater part of the night was passed, as the moon, which had risen in the evening, by continuing her light till dawn increased their fear, Procopius, finding it impossible to escape, and having no resources, as is often the case in moments of extreme danger, began to blame his mournful and disastrous fortune. And being overwhelmed with care, he was on a sudden taken and bound by his own comrades, and, at daybreak led to the camp, and brought, silent and downcast, before the emperor. He was immediately beheaded; and his death put an end to the increasing disturbances of civil war. His fate resembled that of Perpenna of old, who, after Sertorius had been slain at a banquet, enjoyed the power for a short time, but was dragged out of the thicket where he was concealed, and brought to Pompey, by whose orders he was put to death.

10. Giving way to equal indignation against Florentius and Barchalbas, though they delivered up Procopius, he instantly ordered them also to be slain, without listening to reason. For if they had betrayed their legitimate prince, Justice herself would pronounce them justly slain; but if he whom they betrayed was a rebel and an enemy to the tranquillity of the state, as was alleged, then they ought to have received an ample reward for so memorable an action.

11. Procopius perished at the age of forty years and ten months. He was of a goodly appearance, tall, inclined to stoop, always looking on the ground as he walked, and in his reserved and melancholy manners like Crassus, whom Lucillius and Cicero record never to have smiled but once in his life; and what is very remarkable, as long as he lived he never shed blood.

X.

§ 1. About the same time, his kinsman Marcellus, an officer of the guard, who commanded the garrison of Nicæa, hearing of the treachery of the soldiers and the death of Procopius, attacked Serenianus, who was confined in the palace, unexpectedly at midnight, and put him to death. And his death was the safety of many.

2. For if he, a man of rude manners, bitter temper, and a love of injuring people, had survived Valens's victory, having also great influence with Valens from the similarity of his disposition and the proximity of their birthplaces, he would have studied the secret incli-

nations of a prince always inclined to cruelty, and would have shed the blood of many innocent persons.

3. Having killed him, Marcellus by a rapid march seized on Chalcedon, and with the aid of a few people, whom the lowness of their condition and despair urged to crime, obtained a shadow of authority which proved fatal to him, being deceived by two circumstances, because he thought that the three thousand Goths who, after their kings had been conciliated, had been sent to aid Procopius, who had prevailed on them to support him by pleading his relationship to Constantine, would at a small cost be easily won over to support him, and also because he was ignorant of what had happened in Illyricum.

4. While these alarming events were taking place, Equitius, having learnt by trustworthy reports from his scouts that the whole stress of the war was now to be found in Asia, passed through the Succi, and made a vigorous attempt to take Philippopolis, the ancient Eumolpias,[159] which was occupied by a garrison of the enemy. It was a city in a most favourable position, and likely to prove an obstacle to his approach if left in his rear, and if he, while conducting reinforcements to Valens (for he was not yet acquainted with what had happened at Nacolia), should be compelled to hasten to the district around Mount Hæmus.

5. But when, a few days later, he heard of the foolish usurpation of Marcellus, he sent against him a body of bold and active troops, who seized him as a mischievous slave, and threw him into prison. From which, some days afterwards, he was brought forth, scourged severely with his accomplices, and put to death, having deserved favour by no action of his life except that he had slain Serenianus, a man as cruel as Phalaris, and faithful only in barbarity, which he displayed on the slightest pretext.

6. The war being now at an end by the death of the leader, many were treated with much greater severity than their errors or faults required, especially the defenders of Philippopolis, who would not surrender the city or themselves till they saw the head of Procopius, which was conveyed to Gaul.

7. Some, however, by the influence of intercessors, received mercy, the most eminent of whom was Araxius, who, when the crisis was at its height, had applied for and obtained the office of prefect. He, by the intercession of his son-in-law Agilo, was punished only by banishment to an island, from which he soon afterwards escaped.

8. But Euphrasius and Phronemius were sent to the west to be at the disposal of Valentinian. Euphrasius was acquitted, but Phronemius was transported to the Chersonesus, being punished more severely than the other, though their case was the same, because he had been a favourite with the late emperor Julian, whose memorable virtues the two brothers now on the throne joined in disparaging, though they were neither like nor equal to him.

9. To these severities other grievances of greater importance, and more to be dreaded than any sufferings in battle, were added. For the executioner, and the rack, and bloody modes of torture, now attacked men of every rank, class, or fortune, without distinction. Peace seemed as a pretext for establishing a detestable tribunal, while all men cursed the ill-omened victory that had been gained as worse than the most deadly war.

10. For amid arms and trumpets the equality of every one's chance makes danger seem lighter; and often the might of martial valour obtains what it aims at; or else a sudden death, if it befalls a man, is attended by no feeling of ignominy, but brings an end to life and to suffering at the same time. When, however, laws and statutes are put forth as pretexts for wicked counsels, and judges, affecting the equity of Cato or Cassius, sit on the bench, though in fact everything is done at the discretion of over-arrogant power, on the whim of which every man's life or death depends, the mischief is fatal and incurable.

11. For at this time any one might go to the palace on any pretext, and if he were inflamed with a desire of appropriating the goods of others, though the person he accused might be notoriously innocent, he was received by the emperor as a friend to be trusted and deserving to be enriched at the expense of others.

12. For the emperor was quick to inflict injury, always ready to listen to informers, admitting the most deadly accusations, and exulting unrestrainedly in the diversity of punishments devised; ignorant of the expression of Tully, which teaches us that those men are unhappy who think themselves privileged to do everything.

13. This implacability, unworthy of a just cause, and disgracing his victory, exposed many innocent men to the torturers, crushing them beneath the rack, or slaying them by the stroke of the fierce executioner. Men who, if nature had permitted, would rather have lost ten lives in battle than be thus tortured while guiltless of all crime, having their estates confiscated, as if guilty of treason, and their bodies mutilated before death, which is the most bitter kind of death.

14. At last, when his ferocity was exhausted by his cruelties, men of the highest rank were still exposed to proscription, banishment, and other punishments which, though severe, appear lighter to some people. And in order to enrich some one else, men of noble birth, and perhaps still more richly endowed with virtues, were stripped of their patrimony and driven into exile, where they were exhausted with misery, perhaps being even reduced to subsist by beggary. Nor was any limit put to the cruelties which were inflicted till both the prince and those about him were satiated with plunder and bloodshed.

15. While the usurper, whose various acts and death we have been relating, was still alive, on the 21st of July, in the first consulship of Valentinian and his brother, fearful dangers suddenly overspread the whole world, such as are related in no ancient fables or histories.

16. For a little before sunrise there was a terrible earthquake, preceded by incessant and furious lightning. The sea was driven backwards, so as to recede from the land, and the very depths were uncovered, so that many marine animals were left sticking in the mud. And the depths of its valleys and the recesses of the hills, which from the very first origin of all things had been lying beneath the boundless waters, now beheld the beams of the sun.

17. Many ships were stranded on the dry shore, while people straggling about the shoal water picked up fishes and things of that kind in their hands. In another quarter the waves, as if raging against the violence with which they had been driven back, rose, and swelling over the boiling shallows, beat upon the islands and the extended coasts of the mainland, levelling cities and houses wherever they encountered them. All the elements were in furious discord, and the whole face of the world seemed turned upside down, revealing the most extraordinary sights.

18. For the vast waves subsided when it was least expected, and thus drowned many thousand men. Even ships were swallowed up in the furious currents of the returning tide, and were seen to sink when the fury of the sea was exhausted; and the bodies of those who perished by shipwreck floated about on their backs or faces.

19. Other vessels of great size were driven on shore by the violence of the wind, and cast upon the housetops, as happened at Alexandria; and some were even driven two miles inland, of which we ourselves saw one in Laconia, near the town of Mothone, which was lying and rotting where it had been driven.

Notes

[157] Master of the Offices—v. Bohn's 'Gibbon,' ii., 223.

[158] The young king's name was Eropus, v. Justin, vii. 122.

[159] Called also *Trimontium*, from standing on three hills; the modern name is *Philippopoli*. See Smith's 'Anc. Geography,' p. 333.

BOOK XXVII

ARGUMENT

I. The Allemanni having defeated the Romans, put the counts Charietto and Severianus to death.—II. Jovinus, the commander of the cavalry in Gaul, surprises and routs two divisions of the Allemanni; defeats a third army in the country of the Catalauni, the enemy losing six thousand killed and four thousand wounded.—III. About the three prefects of the city, Symmachus, Lampadius, and Juventius—The quarrels of Damasus and Ursinus about the bishopric of Rome.—IV. The people and the six provinces of Thrace are described, and the chief cities in each province.—V. The emperor Valens attacks the Goths, who had sent Procopius' auxiliary troops to be employed against him, and after three years makes peace with them.—VI. Valentinian, with the consent of the army, makes his son Gratian emperor; and, after investing the boy with the purple, exhorts him to behave bravely, and recommends him to the soldiers.—VII. The passionate temper, ferocity, and cruelty of the emperor Valentinian.—VIII. Count Theodosius defeats the Picts, Attacotti, and Scots, who were ravaging Britain with impunity, after having slain the duke and count of that province, and makes them restore their plunder.—IX. The Moorish tribes ravage Africa—Valens checks the predatory incursions of the Isaurians—Concerning the office of city prefect.—X. The emperor Valentinian crosses the Rhine, and in a battle, attended with heavy loss to both sides, defeats and routs the Allemanni, who had taken refuge in their highest mountains.—XI. On the high family, wealth, dignity, and character of Probus.—XII. The Romans and Persians quarrel about the possession of Armenia and Iberia.

I.

A.D. 367.

§ 1. While these events which we have related were taking place with various consequences in the east, the Allemanni, after the many disasters and defeats which they had received in their frequent contests with the emperor Julian, at length, having recruited their strength, though not to a degree equal to their former condition, for the reason which has been already set forth, crossed the frontier of Gaul in formidable numbers. And immediately after the beginning of the year, while winter was still in its greatest severity in those frozen districts, a vast multitude poured forth in a solid column, plundering all the places around in the most licentious manner.

2. Their first division was met by Charietto, who at that time had the authority of count in both the German provinces, and who marched against them with his most active troops, having with him as a colleague count Severianus, a man of great age and feeble health, who had the legions Divitenses and Tungricana under his command, near Cabillonum (Châlons).[160]

3. Then having formed the whole force into one solid body, and having with great rapidity thrown a bridge over a small stream, the Romans assailed the barbarians from a distance with arrows and light javelins, which they shot back at us with great vigour.

4. But when the battalions met and fought with drawn swords, our line was shaken by the vehement onset of the enemy, and could neither resist nor do any valorous deeds by way of attack, but were all put to flight as soon as they saw Severianus struck down from his horse and severely wounded by an arrow.

5. Charietto, too, while labouring by the exposure of his own person, and with bitter reproaches, to encourage his men, who were giving way, and while by the gallantry with which he maintained his own position he strove to efface the disgrace they were incurring, was slain by a mortal wound from a javelin.

6. And after his death the standard of the Eruli and of the Batavi was lost, and the barbarians raised it on high, insulting it, dancing round it, but after a fierce struggle it was recovered.

II.

A.D. 367.

§ 1. The news of this disaster was received with great sorrow, and Dagalaiphus was sent from Paris to restore affairs to order. But as he delayed some time, and made excuses, alleging that he was unable to attack the barbarians, who were dispersed over various districts, and as he was soon after sent for to receive the consulship with Gratian, who was still only a private individual, Jovinus was appointed commander of the cavalry; and he being well provided and fully prepared, attacked the fortress of Churpeigne, protecting both his wings and

flanks with great care. And at this place he fell on the barbarians unexpectedly, before they could arm themselves, and in a very short time
utterly destroyed them.

2. Then leading on the soldiers while exulting in the glory of this
easy victory, to defeat the other divisions, and advancing slowly, he
learnt from the faithful report of his scouts that a band of ravagers,
after having plundered the villages around, were resting on the bank of
the river. And as he approached, while his army was concealed by the
lowness of the ground and the thickness of the trees, he saw some of
them bathing, some adorning their hair after their fashion, and some
carousing.

3. And seizing this favourable opportunity, he suddenly bade the
trumpet give the signal, and burst into the camp of the marauders. On
the other hand, the Germans could do nothing but pour forth useless
threats and shouts, not being allowed time to collect their scattered
arms, or to form in any strength, so vigorously were they pressed by
the conquerors. Thus numbers of them fell pierced with javelins and
swords, and many took to flight, and were saved by the winding and
narrow paths.

4. After this success, which was won by valour and good fortune,
Jovinus struck his camp without delay, and led on his soldiers with
increased confidence (sending out a body of careful scouts in advance)
against the third division. And arriving at Châlons by forced marches,
he there formed the whole body ready for battle.

5. And having constructed a rampart with seasonable haste, and
refreshed his men with food and sleep as well as the time permitted, at
daybreak he arranged his army in an open plain, extending his line
with admirable skill, in order that by occupying an extensive space of
ground the Romans might appear to be equal in number to the enemy:
being in fact inferior in that respect though equal in strength.

6. Accordingly, when the trumpet gave the signal and the battle
began to rage at close quarters, the Germans stood amazed, alarmed at
the well-known appearance of the shining standards. But though they
were checked for a moment, they presently recovered themselves, and
the conflict was protracted till the close of the day, when our valorous
troops would have reaped the fruit of their gallantry without any loss if
it had not been for Balchobaudes, a tribune of the legions, who being
as sluggish as he was boastful, at the approach of evening retreated in
disorder to the camp. And if the rest of the cohorts had followed his
example and had also retired, the affair would have turned out so ruin-

ous that not one of our men would have been left alive to tell what had happened.

7. But our soldiers, persisting with energy and courage, showed such a superiority in personal strength that they wounded four thousand of the enemy and slew six thousand, while they did not themselves lose more than twelve hundred killed and two hundred wounded.

8. At the approach of night the battle terminated, and our weary men having recruited their strength, a little before dawn our skilful general led forth his army in a square, and found that the barbarians had availed themselves of the darkness to escape. And having no fear there of ambuscade, he pursued them over the open plain, trampling on the dying and the dead, many of whom had perished from the effect of the severity of the cold on their wounds.

9. After he had advanced some way further, without finding any of the enemy he returned, and then he learnt that the king of the hostile army had been taken prisoner, with a few followers, by the Ascarii,[161] whom he himself had sent by another road to plunder the tents of the Allemanni, and they had hanged him. But the general being angry at this, ordered the punishment of the tribune who had ventured on such an act without consulting his superior officer, and he would have condemned him if he had not been able to establish by manifest proof that the atrocious act had been committed by the violent impulse of the soldiers.

10. After this, when he returned to Paris with the glory of this success, the emperor met him with joy, and appointed him to be consul the next year, being additionally rejoiced because at the very same time he received the head of Procopius, which had been sent to him by Valens.

11. Besides these events, many other battles of inferior interest and importance took place in Gaul, which it would be superfluous to recount, since they brought no results worth mentioning, and it is not fit to spin out history with petty details.

III.

§ 1. At this time, or a little before, a new kind of prodigy appeared in the corn district of Tuscany; those who were skilful in interpreting such things being wholly ignorant of what it portended. For in the town of Pistoja, at about the third hour of the day, in the sight of many persons, an ass mounted the tribunal, where he was heard to bray loudly. All the bystanders were amazed, as were all those who heard of the occurrence from the report of others, as no one could conjecture what was to happen.

2. But soon afterwards the events showed what was portended, for a man of the name of Terence, a person of low birth and a baker by trade, as a reward for having given information against Orsitus, who had formerly been prefect, which led to his being convicted of peculation, was intrusted with the government of this same province. And becoming elated and confident, he threw affairs into great disorder, till he was convicted of fraud on transactions relating to some shipmasters, as was reported, and was executed while Claudius was prefect of Rome.

3. But some time before this happened Symmachus succeeded Apronianus; a man deserving to be named among the most eminent examples of learning and moderation; under whose government the most sacred city enjoyed peace and plenty in an unusual degree; being also adorned with a magnificent and solid bridge which he constructed, and opened amid the great joy of his ungrateful fellow-citizens, as the result very plainly showed.

4. For they some years afterwards burnt his beautiful house on the other side of the Tiber, being enraged because some worthless plebeian had invented a story, which there was no evidence or witness to support, that he had said that he would prefer putting out the limekilns with his own wine, to selling the lime at the price expected of him.

5. After him the prefect of the city was Lampadius, who had been prefect of the prætorium, a man of such boundless arrogance, that he grew very indignant if he were not praised even when he spat, as if he did that with more grace than any one else; but still a man of justice, virtue, and economy.

6. When as prætor he was celebrating some splendid games, and giving abundant largesses, being unable to bear the tumult of the populace, which was often urgent to have gifts distributed to those who were unworthy, in order to show his liberality and his contempt for the multitude, he sent for a crowd of beggars from the Vatican, and enriched them with great presents.

7. But, not to digress too much, it will be sufficient to record one instance of his vanity, which, though of no great importance, may serve as a warning to judges. In every quarter of the city which had been adorned at the expense of different emperors he inscribed his own name, and that, not as if he were the restorer of old works, but their founder. This same fault is said to have characterized the emperor

Trajan, from which the people in jest named him "The Pellitory of the wall."

8. While he was prefect he was disturbed by frequent commotions, the most formidable being when a vast mob of the lowest of the people collected, and with firebrands and torches would have burnt his house near the baths of Constantine, if they had not been driven away by the prompt assistance of his friends and neighbours, who pelted them with stones and tiles from the tops of the houses.

9. And he himself, being alarmed at a sedition, which on this occasion had become so violent, retired to the Mulvian bridge (which the elder Scaurus is said to have built), and waited there till the discontent subsided, which indeed had been excited by a substantial grievance.

10. For when he began to construct some new buildings, he ordered the cost to be defrayed, not from the customary sources of revenue, but if iron, or lead, or copper, or anything of that kind was required, he sent officers who, pretending to try the different articles, did in fact seize them without paying any price for them. This so enraged the poor, since they suffered repealed losses from such a practice, that it was all he could do to escape from them by a rapid retreat.

11. His successor had formerly been a quæstor of the palace, his name was Juventius, a man of integrity and prudence, a Pannonian by birth. His administration was tranquil and undisturbed, and the people enjoyed plenty under it. Yet he also was alarmed by fierce seditions raised by the discontented populace, which arose from the following occurrence.

12. Damasus and Ursinus, being both immoderately eager to obtain the bishopric, formed parties and carried on the conflict with great asperity, the partisans of each carrying their violence to actual battle, in which men were wounded and killed. And as Juventius was unable to put an end to, or even to soften these disorders, he was at last by their violence compelled to withdraw to the suburbs.

13. Ultimately Damasus got the best of the strife by the strenuous efforts of his partisans. It is certain that on one day one hundred and thirty-seven dead bodies were found in the Basilica of Sicininus, which is a Christian church.[162] And the populace who had been thus roused to a state of ferocity were with great difficulty restored to order.

14. I do not deny, when I consider the ostentation that reigns at Rome, that those who desire such rank and power may be justified in labouring with all possible exertion and vehemence to obtain their wishes; since after they have succeeded, they will be secure for the

future, being enriched by offerings from matrons, riding in carriages, dressing splendidly, and feasting luxuriously, so that their entertainments surpass even royal banquets.

15. And they might be really happy if, despising the vastness of the city, which they excite against themselves by their vices, they were to live in imitation of some of the priests in the provinces, whom the most rigid abstinence in eating and drinking, and plainness of apparel, and eyes always cast on the ground, recommend to the everlasting Deity and his true worshippers as pure and sober-minded men. This is a sufficient digression on this subject: let us now return to our narrative.

IV.

§1. While the events above mentioned were taking place in Gaul and Italy, a new campaign was being prepared in Thrace. For Valens, acting on the decision of his brother, by whose will he was entirely governed, marched against the Goths, having a just cause of complaint against them, because at the beginning of the late civil war they had sent assistance to Procopius. It will here be desirable to say a few words of the origin of this people, and the situation of their country.

2. The description of Thrace would be easy if the pens of ancient authors agreed on the subject; but as the obscurity and variety of their accounts is of but little assistance to a work which professes to tell the truth, it will be sufficient for us to record what we remember to have seen ourselves.

3. The undying authority of Homer informs us that these countries were formerly extended over an immense space of tranquil plains and high rising grounds; since that poet represents both the north and the west wind as blowing from thence;[163] a statement which is either fabulous, or else which shows that the extensive district inhabited by all those savage tribes was formerly included under the single name of Thrace.

4. Part of this region was inhabited by the Scordisci, who now live at a great distance from these provinces; a race formerly savage and uncivilized, as ancient history proves, sacrificing their prisoners to Bellona and Mars, and drinking with eagerness human blood out of skulls. Their ferocity engaged the Roman republic in many wars; and on one occasion led to the destruction of an entire army with its general.[164]

5. But we see that the country now, the district being in the form of a crescent, resembles a splendid theatre; it is bounded on the west

by mountains, on the abrupt summit of which are the thickly wooded passes of the Succi, which separate Thrace from Dacia.

6. On the left, or northern side, the heights of the Balkan form the boundary, as in one part does the Danube also, where it touches the Roman territory: a river with many cities, fortresses, and castles on its banks.

7. On the right, or southern side, lies Mount Rhodope; on the east, the country is bounded by a strait, which becomes more rapid from being swollen by the waters of the Euxine sea, and proceeds onwards with its tides towards the Ægean, separating the continents of Europe and Asia by a narrow space.

8. At a confined corner on the eastward it joins the frontier of Macedonia by a strait and precipitous defile named Acontisma; near to which are the valley and station of Arethusa, where one may see the tomb of Euripides, illustrious for his sublime tragedies; and Stagira, where we are told that Aristotle, who as Cicero says pours from his mouth a golden stream, was born.

9. In ancient times, tribes of barbarians occupied these countries, differing from each other in customs and language. The most formidable of which, from their exceeding ferocity, were the Odrysæans, men so accustomed to shed human blood, that when they could not find enemies enough, they would, at their feasts, when they had eaten and drunk to satiety, stab their own bodies as if they belonged to others.

10. But as the republic grew in strength while the authority of the consular form of government prevailed, Marcus Didius, with great perseverance, attacked these tribes which had previously been deemed invincible, and had roved about without any regard either to divine or human laws. Drusus compelled them to confine themselves to their own territories; Minucius defeated them in a great battle on the river Maritza, which flows down from the lofty mountains of the Odrysæans; and after those exploits, the rest of the tribes were almost destroyed in a terrible battle by Appius Claudius the proconsul. And the Roman fleets made themselves masters of the towns on the Bosporus, and on the coast of the Sea of Marmora.

11. After these generals came Lucullus; who was the first of all our commanders who fought with the warlike nation of the Bessi: and with similar vigour he crushed the mountaineers of the district of the Balkan, in spite of their obstinate resistance. And while he was in that country the whole of Thrace was brought under the power of our ancestors, and in this way, after many doubtful campaigns, six provinces were added to the republic.

12. Of these provinces the first one comes to, that which borders on the Illyrians, is called by the especial name of Thrace; its chief cities are Philippopolis, the ancient Eumolpias, and Beræa; both splendid cities. Next to this the province of the Balkan boasts of Hadrianople, which used to be called Uscudama, and Anchialos, both great cities. Nest comes Mysia, in which is Marcianopolis, so named from the sister of the emperor Trajan, also Dorostorus, and Nicopolis, Odyssus.

13. Next comes Scythia, in which the chief towns are Dionysiopolis, Tomis, and Calatis. The last of all is Europa; which besides many municipal towns has two principal cities, Apri and Perinthus, which in later times has received the name of Heraclea. Beyond this is Rhodope, in which are the cities of Maximianopolis, Maronea, and Ænus, after founding and leaving which, it was thought Æneas proceeded onwards to Italy, of which, after long wanderings, he became master, expecting by the auspices to enjoy there perpetual prosperity.

14. But it is certain, as the invariable accounts of all writers represent, that these tribes were nearly all agricultural, and, that living on the high mountains in these regions above mentioned, they are superior to us in health, vigour, and length of life; and they believe that this superiority arises from the fact, that in their food they for the most part abstain from all that is hot; also that the constant dews besprinkle their persons with a cold and bracing moisture, and that they enjoy the freshness of a purer atmosphere; and that they are the first of all tribes to feel the rays of the morning sun, which are instinct with life, before they become tainted with any of the foulness arising from human things. Having discussed this matter let us now return to our original narrative.

V.

§ 1. After Procopius had been overpowered in Phrygia, and all material for domestic discords had thus been removed, Victor, the commander of the cavalry, was sent to the Goths to inquire, without disguise, why a nation friendly to the Romans, and bound to it by treaties of equitable peace, had given the support of its arms to a man who was waging war against their lawful emperor. And they, to excuse their conduct by a valid defence, produced the letters from the abovementioned Procopius, in which he alleged that he had assumed the sovereignty as his due, as the nearest relation to Constantine's family; and they asserted that this was a fair excuse for their error.

2. When Victor reported this allegation of theirs, Valens disregarding it as a frivolous excuse, marched against them, they having

already got information of his approach. And at the beginning of spring he assembled his army in a great body, and pitched his camp near a fortress named Daphne, where having made a bridge of boats he crossed the Danube without meeting any resistance.

3. And being now full of elation and confidence, as while traversing the country in every direction he met with no enemy to be either defeated or even alarmed by his advance; they having all been so terrified at the approach of so formidable a host, that they had fled to the high mountains of the Serri, which were inaccessible to all except those who knew the country.

4. Therefore, that he might not waste the whole summer, and return without having effected anything, he sent forward Arinthæus, the captain of the infantry, with some light forces, who seized on a portion of their families, which were overtaken as they were wandering over the plains before coming to the steep and winding defiles of the mountains. And having obtained this advantage, which chance put in his way, he returned with his men without having suffered any loss, and indeed without having inflicted any.

5. The next year he attempted with equal vigour again to invade the country of the enemy; but being checked in his advance by the inundations of the Danube, which covered a wide extent of country, he remained near the town of Capri, where he pitched a camp in which he remained till the autumn. And from thence, as he was prevented from undertaking any operations on account of the magnitude of the floods, he retired to Marcianopolis into winter quarters.

6. With similar perseverance he again invaded the land of the barbarians a third year, having crossed the river by a bridge of boats at Nivors; and by a rapid march he attacked the Gruthungi, a warlike and very remote tribe, and after some trivial skirmishes, he defeated Athanaric, at that time the most powerful man of the tribe, who dared to resist him with what he fancied an adequate force, but was compelled to flee for his life. And then he returned himself with his army to Marcianopolis to spend the winter there, as the cold was but slight in that district.

7. After many various events in the campaigns of three years, there arose at last some very strong reasons in the minds of the barbarians for terminating the war. In the first place, because the fear of the enemy was increased by the continued stay made by the emperor in that country. Secondly, because as all their commerce was cut off they began to feel great want of necessaries. So that they sent several embassies with submissive entreaties for pardon and peace.

8. The emperor was as yet inexperienced, but still he was a very just observer of events, till having been captivated by the pernicious allurements of flattery, he subsequently involved the republic in an ever-to-be-lamented disaster; and now taking counsel for the common good, he determined that it was right to grant them peace.

9. And in his turn he sent to them Victor and Arinthæus, who at that time were the commanders of his infantry and cavalry; and when they sent him letters truly stating that the Goths were willing to agree to the conditions which they had proposed, he appointed a suitable place for finally settling the terms of the peace. And since Athanaric alleged that he was bound by a most dreadful oath, and also forbidden by the strict commands of his father ever to set foot on the Roman territory, and as he could not be brought to do so, while, on the other hand, it would be unbecoming and degrading for the emperor to cross over to him, it was decided by negotiation that some boats should be rowed into the middle of the river, on which the emperor should embark with an armed guard, and that there also the chief of the enemy should meet him with his people, and conclude a peace as had been arranged.

10. When this had been arranged, and hostages had been given, Valens returned to Constantinople, whither afterwards Athanaric fled, when he was driven from his native land by a faction among his kinsmen; and he died in that city, and was buried with splendid ceremony according to the Roman fashion.

VI.

§ 1. In the mean time, Valentinian being attacked with a violent sickness and at the point of death, at a secret entertainment of the Gauls who were present in the emperor's army, Rusticus Julianus, at that time master of the records, was proposed as the future emperor; a man as greedy of human blood as a wild beast, seeming to be smitten with some frenzy, as had been shown while governing Africa as proconsul.

2. For in his prefecture of the city, a post which he was filling when he died, fearing a change in the tyranny through the exercise of which he, as if in a dearth of worthy men, had been raised to that dignity, he was compelled to appear more gentle and merciful.

3. Against his partisans others with higher aims were exerting themselves in favour of Severus, who at that time was captain of the infantry, as a man very fit for such a dignity, who, although rough and

unpopular, seemed yet more tolerable than the other, and worthy of being preferred to him by any means that could be devised.

4. But all these plans were formed to no purpose; for in the meantime, the emperor, through the variety of remedies applied, recovered, and would scarcely believe that his life had been saved with difficulty. And he proposed to invest his son Gratian, who was now on the point of arriving at manhood, with the ensigns of the imperial authority.

5. And when everything was prepared, and the consent of the soldiers secured, in order that all men might willingly accept the new emperor, immediately upon the arrival of Gratian, Valentinian advancing into the open space, mounted the tribune, and surrounded by a splendid circle of nobles and princes, and holding the boy by his right hand, showed him to them all, and in the following formal harangue recommended their intended sovereign to the army.

6. "This imperial robe which I wear is a happy indication of your good will towards me when you adjudged me superior to many illustrious men. Now, with you as the partners of my counsels and the favourers of my wishes, I will proceed to a seasonable work of affection, relying on the protecting promises of God, to whose eternal assistance it is owing that the Roman state stands and ever shall stand unshaken.

7. "Listen, I beseech you, O most gallant men, with willing minds to my desire, recollecting that these things which the laws of natural affection sanction, we have in this instance not only wished to accomplish with your perfect cognizance, but we have also desired to have them confirmed by you as what is proper for us and likely to prove beneficial.

8. This, my grown-up son Gratian, to whom all of you bear affection as a common pledge, who has long lived among your own children, I am, for the sake of securing the public tranquillity on all sides, about to take as my colleague in the imperial authority, if the propitious will of the ruler of heaven and of your dignity, shall co-operate with a parent's affection. He has not been trained by a rigid education from his very cradle as we ourselves have; nor has he been equally taught to endure hardships; nor is he as yet, as you see, able to endure the toils of war; but in his disposition he is not unworthy of the glorious reputation of his family, or the mighty deeds of his ancestors, and, I venture to say, he is likely to grow up equal to still greater actions.

9. "For as I often think when contemplating, as I am wont to do, his manners and passions though not yet come to maturity, he is so furnished with the liberal sciences, and in all accomplishments and graces, that even now, while only entering on manhood, he will be able to form an accurate judgment of virtuous and vicious actions. He will so conduct himself that virtuous men may see that they are appreciated; he will be eager in the performance of noble actions; he will never desert the military standards and eagles; he will cheerfully bear heat, snow, frost, and thirst; he will, if necessity should arise, never shrink from fighting in defence of his country; he will expose his life to save his comrades from danger, and (and this is the highest and greatest work of piety) he will love the republic as his own paternal and ancestral home."

10. Before he had finished his speech, every soldier hastened to anticipate his comrades as well as his position permitted him, in showing that these words of the emperor met with their cheerful assent. And so, as partakers in his joy, and as convinced of the advantage of his proposal, they declared Gratian emperor, mingling the propitious clashing of their arms with the loud roar of the trumpets.

11. When Valentinian saw this, his confidence increased; he adorned his son with a crown and with the robes befitting his now supreme rank, and kissed him; and then thus addressed him, brilliant as he appeared, and giving careful attention to all his words:—

12. "You wear now," said he, "my Gratian, the imperial robe, as we have all desired, which has been conferred on you with favourable auspices by my will and that of our comrades. Therefore now, considering the weight of the affairs which press upon us, gird yourself up as the colleague of your father and your uncle; and accustom yourself to pass fearlessly with the infantry over the Danube and the Rhine, which are made passable by the frost, to keep close to your soldiers, to devote your blood and your very life with all skill and deliberation for the safety of those under your command; to think nothing unworthy of your attention which concerns any portion of the Roman empire.

13. "This is enough by way of admonition to you at the present moment, at other times I will not fail to give further advice. Now you who remain, the defenders of the state, I entreat, I beseech you to preserve with a steady affection and loyalty your youthful emperor thus intrusted to your fidelity."

14. These words of the emperor were accepted and ratified with all possible solemnity; Eupraxius, a native of Mauritania Cæsariensis, at that time master of the records, led the way by the exclamation,

"The family of Gratian deserves this." And being at once promoted to be quæstor, he set an example of judicious confidence worthy of being imitated by all wise men; especially as he in no wise departed from the habits of his fearless nature, but was at all times a man of consistency and obedient to the laws, which, as we have remarked, speak to all men with one and the same voice under the most varied circumstances. He at this time was the more steady in adhering to the side of justice which he always espoused, because on one occasion when he had given good advice, the emperor had attacked him with violence and threats.

15. After this, the whole assembly broke out into praises of both emperors, the elder and the new one; and especially of the boy, whose brilliant eyes, engaging countenance and person, and apparent sweetness of disposition, recommended him to their favour. And these qualities would have rendered him an emperor worthy to be compared to the most excellent princes of former times, if fate had permitted, and his relations who even then began to overshadow his virtue, before it was firmly rooted, with their own wicked actions.

16. But in this affair, Valentinian went beyond the custom which had been established for several generations, in making his brother and his son, not Cæsar, but emperors; acting indeed in this respect with great kindness. Nor had any one yet ever created a colleague with powers equal to his own, except the emperor Marcus Aurelius, who made his adopted brother Verus his colleague in the empire without any inferiority of power.

VII.

A.D. 368.

§ 1. After these transactions had been thus settled to the delight both of the prince and of the soldiers, but a few days intervened; and then Avitianus, who had been deputy, accused Mamertinus, the prefect of the prætorium, of peculation, on his return from the city whither he had gone to correct some abuses.

2. And in consequence of this accusation he was replaced by Rufinus, a man accomplished in every respect, who had attained the dignity of an honourable old age, though it is true that he never let slip any opportunity of making money when he thought he could do so secretly.

3. He now availed himself of his access to the emperor to obtain permission for Orfitus, who had been prefect of the city, but who was

now banished, to receive back his property which had been confiscated, and return home.

4. And although Valentinian was a man of undisguised ferocity, he nevertheless, at the beginning of his reign, in order to lessen the opinion of his cruelty, took all possible pains to restrain the fierce impetuosity of his disposition. But this defect increasing gradually, from having been checked for some time, presently broke out more unrestrained to the ruin of many persons; and his severity was increased by the vehemence of his anger. For wise men define passion as a lasting ulcer of the mind, and sometimes an incurable one, usually engendered from a weakness of the intellect; and they have a plausible argument for asserting this in the fact that people in bad health are more passionate than those who are well; women, than men; old men, than youths; and people in bad circumstances than the prosperous.

5. About this time, among the deaths of many persons of low degree, that of Diocles, who had previously been a treasurer of Illyricum, was especially remarked; the emperor having had him burnt alive for some very slight offence, as was also the execution of Diodorus, who had previously had an honourable employment in the provinces, and also that of three officers of the vicar prefect of Italy, who were all put to death with great cruelty because the count of Italy had complained to the emperor that Diodorus had, though in a constitutional manner, implored the aid of the law against him; and that the officers, by command of the judge, served a summons on him as he was setting out on a journey, commanding him to answer to the action according to law. And the Christians at Milan to this day cherish their memory, and call the place where they were buried, the tomb of the innocents.

6. Afterwards, in the affair of a certain Pannonian, named Maxentius, on account of the execution of a sentence very properly commanded by the judge to be carried out immediately, he ordered all the magistrates of these towns to be put to death, when Eupraxius, who at that time was quæstor, interposed, saying, "Be more sparing, O most pious of emperors, for those whom you command to be put to death as criminals, the Christian religion honours as martyrs, that is as persons acceptable to the deity."

7. And the prefect Florentius, imitating the salutary boldness of Eupraxius, when he heard that the emperor was in a similar manner very angry about some trifling and pardonable matter, and that he had ordered the execution of three of the magistrates in each of several cities, said to him, "And what is to be done if any town has not got so

many magistrates? It will be necessary to suspend the execution there till there are a sufficient number for the purpose."

8. And besides this cruel conduct there was another circumstance horrible even to speak of, that if any one came before him protesting against being judged by a powerful enemy, and requiring that some other judge might hear his case, he always refused it; and however just the arguments of the man might be, he remitted his cause to the decision of the very judge whom he feared. And there was another very bad thing much spoken of; namely, that when it was urged that any debtor was in such absolute want as to be unable to pay anything, he used to pronounce sentence of death on him.

9. But some princes do these and other similar actions with the more lofty arrogance, because they never allow their friends any opportunity of setting them right in any mistake they make, either in a plan or in its execution; while they terrify their enemies by the greatness of their power. There can be no question of mistake or error raised before men who consider whatever they choose to do to be in itself the greatest of virtues.

VIII.

§ 1. Valentinian having left Amiens, and being on his way to Treves in great haste, received the disastrous intelligence that Britain was reduced by the ravages of the united barbarians to the lowest extremity of distress; that Nectaridus, the count of the sea-coast, had been slain in battle, and the duke Fullofaudes had been taken prisoner by the enemy in an ambuscade.

2. This news struck him with great consternation, and he immediately sent Severus, the count of the domestic guards, to put an end to all these disasters if he could find a desirable opportunity. Severus was soon recalled, and Jovinus, who then went to that country, sent forward Provertuides with great expedition to ask for the aid of a powerful army; for they both affirmed that the imminence of the danger required such a reinforcement.

3. Last of all, on account of the many formidable reports which a continual stream of messengers brought from that island, Theodosius was appointed to proceed thither, and ordered to make great haste. He was an officer already distinguished for his prowess in war, and having collected a numerous force of cavalry and infantry, he proceeded to assume the command in full confidence.

4. And since when I was compiling my account of the acts of the emperor Constantine, I explained as well as I could the movement of

the sea in those parts at its ebb and flow, and the situation of Britain, I look upon it as superfluous to return to what has been once described; as the Ulysses of Homer when among the Phæacians hesitated to repeat his adventures by reason of the sufferings they brought to mind.

5. It will be sufficient here to mention that at that time the Picts, who were divided into two nations, the Dicalidones and the Vecturiones, and likewise the Attacotti, a very warlike people, and the Scots were all roving over different parts of the country and committing great ravages. While the Franks and the Saxons who are on the frontiers of the Gauls were ravaging their country wherever they could effect an entrance by sea or land, plundering and burning, and murdering all the prisoners they could take.

6. To put a stop to these evils, if a favourable fortune should afford an opportunity, the new and energetic general repaired to that island situated at the extreme corner of the earth; and when he had reached the coast of Boulogne, which is separated from the opposite coast by a very narrow strait of the sea, which there rises and falls in a strange manner, being raised by violent tides, and then again sinking to a perfect level like a plain, without doing any injury to the sailors. From Boulogne he crossed the strait in a leisurely manner, and reached Richborough, a very tranquil station on the opposite coast.

7. And when the Batavi, and Heruli, and the Jovian and Victorian legions who followed from the same place, had also arrived, he then, relying on their number and power, landed and marched towards Londinium, an ancient town which has since been named Augusta; and dividing his army into several detachments, he attacked the predatory and straggling bands of the enemy who were loaded with the weight of their plunder, and having speedily routed them while driving prisoners in chains and cattle before them, he deprived them of their booty which they had carried off from these miserable tributaries of Rome.

8. To whom he restored the whole except a small portion which he allotted to his own weary soldiers; and then joyful and triumphant he made his entry into the city which had just before been overwhelmed by disasters, but was now suddenly re-established almost before it could have hoped for deliverance.

9. This success encouraged him to deeds of greater daring, and after considering what counsels might be the safest, he hesitated, being full of doubts as to the future, and convinced by the confession of his prisoners and the information given him by deserters, that so vast a multitude, composed of various nations, all incredibly savage, could only be vanquished by secret stratagems and unexpected attacks.

10. Then, by the publication of several edicts, in which he promised them impunity, he invited deserters and others who were
straggling about the country on furlough, to repair to his camp. At this
summons numbers came in, and he, though eager to advance, being
detained by anxious cares, requested to have Civilis sent to him, to
govern Britain, with the rank of proprefect, a man of quick temper, but
just and upright; and he asked at the same time for Dulcitius, a general
eminent for his military skill.

IX.

§ 1. These were the events which occurred in Britain. But in another quarter, from the very beginning of Valentinian's reign, Africa
had been overrun by the fury of the barbarians, intent on bloodshed
and rapine, which they sought to carry on by audacious incursions.
Their licentiousness was encouraged by the indolence and general
covetousness of the soldiers, and especially by the conduct of Count
Romanus.

2. Who, foreseeing what was likely to happen, and being very
skilful in transferring to others the odium which he himself deserved,
was detested by men in general for the savageness of his temper, and
also because it seemed as if his object was to outrun even our enemies
in ravaging the provinces. He greatly relied on his relationship to Remigius, at that time master of the offices, who sent all kinds of false
and confused statements of the condition of the country, so that the
emperor, cautious and wary as he plumed himself on being, was long
kept in ignorance of the terrible sufferings of the Africans.

3. I will explain with great diligence the complete series of all
the transactions which took place in those regions, the death of Ruricius the governor, and of his lieutenants, and all the other mournful
events which took place, when the proper opportunity arrives.

4. And since we are able here to speak freely, let us openly say
what we think, that this emperor was the first of all our princes who
raised the arrogance of the soldiers to so great a height, to the great
injury of the state, by increasing their rank, dignity, and riches. And
(which was a lamentable thing, both on public and private accounts)
while he punished the errors of the common soldiers with unrelenting
severity, he spared the officers, who, as if complete licence were given
to their misconduct, proceeded to all possible lengths of rapacity and
cruelty for the acquisition of riches, and acting as if they thought that
the fortunes of all persons depended directly on their nod.

5. The framers of our ancient laws had sought to repress their pride and power, sometimes even condemning the innocent to death, as is often done in cases when, from the multitude concerned in some atrocity, some innocent men, owing to their ill luck, suffer for the whole. And this has occasionally extended even to the case of private persons.

6. But in Isauria the banditti formed into bodies and roamed through the villages, laying waste and plundering the towns and wealthy country houses; and by the magnitude of their ravages they also greatly distressed Pamphylia and Cilicia. And when Musonius, who at that time was the deputy of Asia Minor, having previously been a master of rhetoric at Athens, had heard that they were spreading massacre and rapine in every direction, being filled with grief at the evil of which he had just heard, and perceiving that the soldiers were rusting in luxury and inactivity, he took with him a few light-armed troops, called Diogmitæ, and resolved to attack the first body of plunderers he could find. His way led through a narrow and most difficult defile, and thus he fell into an ambuscade, which he had no chance of escaping, and was slain, with all the men under his command.

7. The robber bands became elated at this advantage, and roamed over the whole country with increased boldness, slaying many, till at last our army was aroused, and drove them to take refuge amid the recesses of the rocks and mountains they inhabit. And then, as they were not allowed to rest, and were cut off from all means of obtaining necessary supplies, they at last begged for a truce, as a prelude to peace, being led to this step by the advice of the people of Germanico-polis, whose opinions always had as much weight with them as standard-bearers have with an army. And after giving hostages as they were desired, they remained for a long time quiet, without venturing on any hostilities.

8. While these events were taking place, Prætextatus was administering the prefecture of the city in a noble manner, exhibiting numerous instances of integrity and probity, virtues for which he had been eminent from his earliest youth; and thus he obtained what rarely happens to any one, that while he was feared, he did not at the same time lose the affection of his fellow-citizens, which is seldom strongly felt for those whom they fear as judges.

9. By his authority, impartiality, and just decisions, a tumult was appeased, which the quarrels of the Christians had excited, and after Ursinus was expelled complete tranquillity was restored, which best corresponded to the wishes of the Roman people; while the glory of

their illustrious governor, who performed so many useful actions, continually increased.

10. For he also removed all the balconies, which the ancient laws of Rome had forbidden to be constructed, and separated from the sacred temples the walls of private houses which had been improperly joined to them; and established one uniform and proper weight in every quarter, for by no other means could he check the covetousness of those who made their scales after their own pleasure. And in the adjudication of lawsuits he exceeded all men in obtaining that praise which Cicero mentions in his panegyric of Brutus, that while he did nothing with a view to please anybody, everything which he did pleased everybody.

X.

§ 1. About the same time, when Valentinian had gone forth on an expedition very cautiously as he fancied, a prince of the Allemanni, by name Rando, who had been for some time preparing for the execution of a plan which he had conceived, with a body of light-armed troops equipped only for a predatory expedition, surprised and stormed Mayence, which was wholly destitute of a garrison.

2. And as he arrived at the time when a great solemnity of the Christian religion was being celebrated, he found no obstacle whatever in carrying off a vast multitude of both men and women as prisoners, with no small quantity of goods as booty.

3. After this, for a short interval a sudden hope of brighter fortune shone upon the affairs of Rome. For as king Vithicabius, the son of Vadomarius, a bold and warlike man, though in appearance effeminate and diseased, was continually raising up the troubles of war against us, great pains were taken to have him removed by some means or other.

4. And because after many attempts it was found impossible to defeat him or to procure his betrayal, his most confidential servant was tampered with by one of our men, and by his hand he lost his life; and after his death, all hostile attacks upon us were laid aside for a while. But his murderer, fearing punishment if the truth should get abroad, without delay took refuge in the Roman territory.

5. After this an expedition on a larger scale than usual was projected with great care and diligence against the Allemanni, to consist of a great variety of troops: the public safety imperatively required such a measure, since the treacherous movements of that easily recruited nation were regarded with continual apprehension, while our

soldiers were the more irritated, because, on account of the constant suspicion which their character awakened, at one time abject and suppliant, at another arrogant and threatening, they were never allowed to rest in peace.

6. Accordingly, a vast force was collected from all quarters, well furnished with arms and supplies of provisions, and the count Sebastian having been sent for with the Illyrian and Italian legions which he commanded, as soon as the weather got warm, Valentinian, accompanied by Gratian, crossed the Rhine without resistance. Having divided the whole army into four divisions, he himself marched with the centre, while Jovinus and Severus, the two captains of the camp, commanded the divisions on each side, thus protecting the army from any sudden attack.

7. And immediately under the guidance of men who knew the roads, all the approaches having been reconnoitred, the army advanced slowly through a most extensive district, the soldiers by the slowness of their march being all the more excited to wish for battle, and gnashing their teeth in a threatening manner, as if they had already found the barbarians. And as, after many days had passed, no one could be found who offered any resistance, the troops applied the devouring flame to all the houses and all the crops which were standing, with the exception of such supplies for their own magazines as the doubtful events of war compelled them to collect and store up.

8. After this the emperor advanced further, with no great speed, till he arrived at a place called Solicinium, where he halted, as if he had suddenly come upon some barrier, being informed by the accurate report of his advanced guard that the barbarians were seen at a distance.

9. They, seeing no way of preserving their safety unless they defended themselves by a speedy battle, trusting in their acquaintance with the country, with one consent occupied a lofty hill, abrupt and inaccessible in its rugged heights on every side except the north, where the ascent was gentle and easy. Our standards were fixed in the usual manner, and the cry, "To arms!" was raised; and the soldiers, by the command of the emperor and his generals, rested in quiet obedience, waiting for the raising of the emperor's banner as the signal for engaging in battle.

10. And because little or no time could be spared for deliberation, since on one side the impatience of the soldiers was formidable, and on the other the Allemanni were shouting out their horrid yells all around, the necessity for rapid operations led to the plan that Sebastian

with his division should seize the northern side of the hill, where we have said the ascent was gentle, in which position it was expected that, if fortune favoured him, he would be able easily to destroy the flying barbarians. And when he, as had been arranged, had moved forward first, while Gratian was kept behind with the Jovian legion, that young prince being as yet of an age unfit for battle or for hard toil, Valentinian, like a deliberate and prudent general, took off his helmet, and reviewed his centuries and maniples, and not having informed any of the nobles of his secret intentions, and having sent back his numerous body of guards, went forward himself with a very small escort, whose courage and fidelity he could trust, to reconnoitre the foot of the hill, declaring (as he was always apt to think highly of his own skill) that it must be possible to find another path which led to the summit besides that which the advanced guard had reported.

11. He then, as he advanced by a devious track over ground strange to him, and across pathless swamps, was very nearly being killed by the sudden attack of a band placed in an ambuscade on his flank, and being driven to extremities, only escaped by spurring his horse to a gallop in a different direction over a deep swamp, so at last, after being in the most imminent danger, he rejoined his legions. But so great had been his peril that his chamberlain, who was carrying his helmet, which was adorned with gold and precious stones, disappeared, helmet and all, while the man's body could never be found, so that it could be known positively whether he were alive or dead.

12. Then, when the men had been refreshed by rest, and the signal for battle was raised, and the clang of warlike trumpets roused their courage, two youths of prominent valour, eager to be the first to encounter the danger, dashed on with fearless impetuosity before the line of their comrades. One was of the band of Scutarii, by name Salvius, the other, Lupicinus, belonging to the Gentiles. They raised a terrible shout, brandished their spears, and when they reached the foot of the rocks, in spite of the efforts of the Allemanni to repel them, pushed steadily on to the higher ground; while behind them came the main body of the army, which following their lead over places rough with brambles and rugged, at last, after vast exertions, reached the very summit of the heights.

13. Then again, with great spirit on both sides, the conflict raged with spears and swords. On our side the soldiers were more skilful in the art of war; on the other side the barbarians, ferocious but incautious, closed with them in the mighty fray; while our army extending itself, outflanked them on both sides with its overlapping wings, the

410

enemy's alarm being increased by our shouts, the neighing of the horses, and the clang of trumpets.

14. Nevertheless they resisted with indomitable courage, and the battle was for some time undecided; both sides exerted themselves to the utmost, and death was scattered almost equally.

15. At last the barbarians were beaten down by the ardour of the Romans, and being disordered and broken, were thrown into complete confusion; and as they began to retreat they were assailed with great effect by the spears and javelins of their enemies. Soon the retreat became a flight, and panting and exhausted, they exposed their backs and the back sinews of their legs and thighs to their pursuers. After many had been slain, those who fled fell into the ambuscade laid for them by Sebastian, who was posted with his reserve at the back of the mountain, and who now fell unexpectedly on their flank, and slew numbers of them, while the rest who escaped concealed themselves in the recesses of the woods.

16. In this battle we also suffered no inconsiderable loss. Among those who fell was Valerian, the first officer of the domestic guards, and one of the Scutarii, named Natuspardo, a warrior of such preeminent courage that he might be compared to the ancient Sicinius or Sergius.

17. After these transactions, accompanied with this diversity of fortune, the army went into winter quarters, and the emperor returned to Treves.

XI.

§ 1. About this time, Vulcatius Rufinus died, while filling the office of prefect of the prætorium, and Probus was summoned from Rome to succeed him, a man well known to the whole Roman world for the eminence of his family, and his influence, as well as for his vast riches, for he possessed a patrimonial inheritance which was scattered over the whole empire; whether acquired justly or unjustly it is not for us to decide.

2. A certain good fortune, as the poets would represent it, attended him from his birth, and bore him on her rapid wings, exhibiting him sometimes as a man of beneficent character, promoting the interests of his friends, though often also a formidable intriguer, and cruel and mischievous in the gratification of his enmities. As long as he lived he had great power, owing to the magnificence of his gifts and to his frequent possession of office, and yet he was at times timid towards the bold, though domineering over the timid; so that when full

of self-confidence he appeared to be spouting in the tragic buskin, and when he was afraid he seemed more abased than the most abject character in comedy.

3. And as fishes, when removed from their natural element, cannot live long on the land, so he began to pine when not in some post of authority which he was driven to be solicitous for by the squabbles of his troops of clients, whose boundless cupidity prevented their ever being innocent, and who thrust their patron forward into affairs of state in order to be able to perpetrate all sorts of crimes with impunity.

4. For it must be confessed that though he was a man of such magnanimity that he never desired any dependent or servant of his to do an unlawful thing, yet if he found that any one of them had committed a crime, he laid aside all consideration of justice, would not allow the case to be inquired into, but defended the man without the slightest regard for right or wrong. Now this is a fault expressly condemned by Cicero, who thus speaks: "For what difference is there between one who has advised an action, and one who approves of it after it is performed? or what difference does it make whether I wished it be done, or am glad that it is done?"

5. He was a man of a suspicious temper, self-relying, often wearing a bitter smile, and sometimes caressing a man the more effectually to injure him.

6. This vice is a very conspicuous one in dispositions of that kind, and mostly so when it is thought possible to conceal it. He was also so implacable and obstinate in his enmities, that if he ever resolved to injure any one he would never be diverted from his purpose by any entreaties, nor be led to pardon any faults, so that his ears seemed to be stopped not with wax but with lead.

7. Even when at the very summit of wealth and dignity he was always anxious and watchful, and therefore he was continually subject to trifling illnesses.

8. Such was the course of events which took place in the western provinces of the empire.

XII.

§ 1. The King of Persia, the aged Sapor, who from the very commencement of his reign had been addicted to the love of plunder, after the death of the Emperor Julian, and the disgraceful treaty of peace subsequently made, for a short time seemed with his people to be friendly to us; but presently he trampled under foot the agreement which he had made with Jovian, and poured a body of troops into Armenia to annex that country to his own dominions, as if the whole of the former arrangements had been abolished.

2. At first he contented himself with various tricks, intrigues, and deceits, inflicting some trifling injuries on the nation which unanimously resisted him, tampering with some of the nobles and satraps, and making sudden inroads into the districts belonging to others.

3. Afterwards by a system of artful cajolery fortified by perjury, he got their king Arsaces into his hands, having invited him to a banquet, when he ordered him to be seized and conducted to a secret chamber behind, where his eyes were put out, and he was loaded with silver chains, which in that country is looked upon as a solace under punishment for men of rank, trifling though it be; then he removed him from his country to a fortress called Agabana, where he applied to him the torture, and finally put him to death.

4. After this, in order that his perfidy might leave nothing unpolluted, having expelled Sauromaces, whom the authority of the Romans had made governor of Hiberia, he conferred the government of that district on a man of the name of Aspacuras, even giving him a diadem, to mark the insult offered to the decision of our emperors.

5. And after these infamous actions he committed the charge of Armenia to an eunuch named Cylaces, and to Artabannes, a couple of deserters whom he had received some time before (one of them having been prefect of that nation, and the other commander in-chief); and he enjoined them to use every exertion to destroy the town of Artogerassa, a place defended by strong walls and a sufficient garrison, in which were the treasures, and the wife and son of Arsaces.

6. These generals commenced the siege as they were ordered. And as it is a fortress placed on a very rugged mountain height, it was inaccessible at that time, while the ground was covered with snow and frost: and so Cylaces being an eunuch, and, as such, suited to feminine manœuvres, taking Artabannes with him, approached the walls; after having received a promise of safety, and he and his companion had been admitted into the city, he sought by a mixture of advice and threats to persuade the garrison and the queen to pacify the wrath of the implacable Sapor by a speedy surrender.

7. And after many arguments had been urged on both sides, the woman bewailing the sad fortune of her husband, these men, who had been most active in wishing to compel her to surrender, pitying her distress, changed their views; and conceiving a hope of higher preferment, they in secret conferences arranged that at an appointed hour of the night the gates should be suddenly thrown open, and a strong de-

tachment should sally forth and fall upon the ramparts of the enemy's camp, surprising it with sudden slaughter; the traitors promising that, to prevent any knowledge of what was going on, they would come forward to meet them.

8. Having ratified this agreement with an oath, they quitted the town, and led the besiegers to acquiesce in inaction by representing that the besieged had required two days to deliberate on what course they ought to pursue. Then in the middle of the night, when they were all soundly asleep in fancied security, the gates of the city were thrown open, and a strong body of young men poured forth with great speed, creeping on with noiseless steps and drawn swords, till they entered the camp of the unsuspecting enemy, where they slew numbers of sleeping men, without meeting with any resistance.

8. This unexpected treachery of his officers, and the loss thus inflicted on the Persians, caused a terrible quarrel between us and Sapor; and another cause for his anger was added, as the Emperor Valens received Para, the son of Arsaces, who at his mother's instigation had quitted the fortress with a small escort, and had desired him to stay at Neo-Cæsarea, a most celebrated city on the Black Sea, where he was treated with great liberality and high respect. Cylaces and Artabannes, being allured by this humanity of Valens, sent envoys to him to ask for assistance, and to request that Para might be given them for their king.

10. However, for the moment assistance was refused them; but Para was conducted by the general Terentius back to Armenia, where he was to rule that nation without any of the insignia of royalty; which was a very wise regulation, in order that we might not be accused of breaking our treaty of peace.

11. When this arrangement became known, Sapor was enraged beyond all bounds, and collecting a vast army, entered Armenia and ravaged it with the most ferocious devastation. Para was terrified at his approach, as were also Cylaces and Artabannes, and, as they saw no other resource, fled into the recesses of the lofty mountains which separate our frontiers from Lazica; where they hid in the depths of the woods and among the defiles of the hills for five months, eluding the various attempts of the king to discover them.

12. And Sapor, when he saw that he was losing his labour in the middle of winter, burnt all the fruit trees, and all the fortified castles and camps, of which he had become master by force or treachery, and also burnt Artogerassa, which had long been blockaded by his whole army, and after many battles was taken through the exhaustion of the

garrison; and he carried off from thence the wife of Arsaces and all his treasures.

13. For these reasons, Arinthæus was sent into these districts with the rank of count, to aid the Armenians if the Persians should attempt to harass them by a second campaign.

14. At the same time, Sapor, with extraordinary cunning, being either humble or arrogant as best suited him, under pretence of an intended alliance, sent secret messengers to Para to reproach him as neglectful of his own dignity, since, with the appearance of royal majesty, he was really the slave of Cylaces and Artabannes. On which Para, with great precipitation, cajoled them with caresses till he got them in his power, and slew them, sending their heads to Sapor in proof of his obedience.

15. When the death of these men became generally known, it caused such dismay that Armenia would have been ruined without striking a blow in its own defence, if the Persians had not been so alarmed at the approach of Arinthæus that they forbore to invade it again, contenting themselves with sending ambassadors to the emperor, demanding of him not to defend that nation, according to the agreement made between them and Jovian.

16. Their ambassadors were rejected, and Sauromaces, who, as we have said before, had been expelled from the kingdom of Hiberia, was sent back with twelve legions under the command of Terentius; and when he reached the river Cyrus, Aspacuras entreated him that they might both reign as partners, being cousins; alleging that he could not withdraw nor cross over to the side of the Romans, because his son Ultra was as a hostage in the hands of the Persians.

17. The emperor learning this, in order by wisdom and prudence to put an end to the difficulties arising out of this affair, acquiesced in the division of Hiberia, allowing the Cyrus to be the boundary of the two divisions: Sauromaces to have the portion next to the Armenians and Lazians, and Aspacuras the districts which border on Albania and Persia.

18. Sapor, indignant at this, exclaimed that he was unworthily treated, because we had assisted Armenia contrary to our treaty, and because the embassy had failed which he had sent to procure redress, and because the kingdom of Hiberia was divided without his consent or privity; and so, shutting as it were, the gates of friendship, he sought assistance among the neighbouring nations, and prepared his own army in order, with the return of fine weather, to overturn all the ar-

rangements which the Romans had made with a view to their own interests.

Notes

[160] Cabillonum is Châlons-sur-Soane, in Burgundy; Catalauni is Châlons-sur-Marne, in Champagne.

[161] These seem to have been a tribe of the *Batavi*; but some editors give, as a various reading, *Hastarii*, which may be translated, a detachment of lancers.

[162] Probably the church of Santa Maria Maggiore; but see note in Gibbon, ch. xxv. (vol. iii. p. 91, Bohn).

[163] See Iliad, ix. 5:—

Βορέης καὶ ζέφυρος τώτε Θρήκηθεν ἄητον
Ἐλθοντ' ἐξοπίνης.

Thus translated by Pope:—

"As from its cloudy dungeon, issuing forth
A double tempest of the west and north
Swells o'er the sea from Thracia's frozen shore,
Heaps waves on waves, and bids th' Ægean roar."

[164] The contents of the sixty-third book of Livy record that C. Porcius Cato lost his whole army in a campaign against the Scordisci, who were a Pannonian tribe; but neither Livy nor any other writer, except Ammianus, mentions that Cato himself was killed.

BOOK XXVIII

I.

A.D. 368.

§ 1. While the perfidy of the king was exciting these unexpected troubles in Persia, as we have related above, and while war was reviving in the east, sixteen years and rather more after the death of Nepotianus, Bellona, raging through the eternal city, destroyed everything, proceeding from trifling beginnings to the most lamentable disasters. Would that they could be buried in everlasting silence, lest perhaps similar things may some day be again attempted, which will do more harm by the general example thus set than even by the misery they occasion.

2. And although after a careful consideration of different circumstances, a reasonable fear would restrain me from giving a minute account of the bloody deeds now perpetrated, yet, relying on the moderation of the present age, I will briefly touch upon the things most deserving of record, nor shall I regret giving a concise account of the fears which the events that happened at a former period caused me.

3. In the first Median war, when the Persians had ravaged Asia, they laid siege to Miletus with a vast host, threatening the garrison with torture and death, and at last reduced the citizens to such straits, that they all, being overwhelmed with the magnitude of their distresses, slew their nearest relations, cast all their furniture and movables into the fire, and then threw themselves in rivalry with one another on the common funeral pile of their perishing country.

4. A short time afterwards, Phrynichus made this event the subject of a tragedy which he exhibited on the stage at Athens; and after he had been for a short time listened to with complacency, when amid all its fine language the tragedy became more and more distressing, it was condemned by the indignation of the people, who thought that it was insulting to produce this as the subject of a dramatic poem, and that it had been prompted not by a wish to console, but only to remind them to their own disgrace of the sufferings which that beautiful city had endured without receiving any aid from its founder and parent. For Miletus was a colony of the Athenians, and had been established there among the other Ionian states by Neleus, the son of that Codrus who is said to have devoted himself for his country in the Dorian war.

5. Let us now return to our subject. Maximinus, formerly deputy prefect of Rome, was born in a very obscure rank of life at Sopianæ, a town of Valeria; his father being only a clerk in the president's office, descended from the posterity of those Carpi whom Diocletian removed from their ancient homes and transferred to Pannonia.

6. After a slight study of the liberal sciences, and some small practice at the bar, he was promoted to be governor of Corsica, then of Sardinia, and at last of Tuscany. From hence, as his successor loitered a long while on his road, he proceeded to superintend the supplying of the eternal city with provisions, still retaining the government of the province; and three different considerations rendered him cautious on his first entrance into office, namely:—

7. In the first place, because he bore in mind the prediction of his father, a man pre-eminently skilful in interpreting what was portended by birds from whom auguries were taken, or by the note of such birds as spoke. And he had warned him that though he would rise to su-

preme authority, he would perish by the axe of the executioner; secondly, because he had fallen in with a Sardinian (whom he himself subsequently put to death by treachery, as report generally affirmed) who was a man skilled in raising up evil spirits, and in gathering presages from ghosts; and as long as that Sardinian lived, he, fearing to be betrayed, was more tractable and mild; lastly, because while he was slowly making his way through inferior appointments, like a serpent that glides underground, he was not yet of power sufficient to perpetrate any extensive destruction or executions.

8. But the origin of his arriving at more extensive power lay in the following transaction: Chilo, who had been deputy, and his wife, named Maxima, complained to Olybrius, at that time prefect of the city, asserting that their lives had been attacked by poison, and with such earnestness that the men whom they suspected were at once arrested and thrown into prison. These were Sericus, a musician, Asbolius, a wrestling master, and Campensis, a soothsayer.

9. But as the affair began to cool on account of the long-continued violence of some illness with which Olybrius was attacked, the persons who had laid the complaint, becoming impatient of delay, presented a petition in which they asked to have the investigation of their charge referred to the superintendent of the corn-market; and, from a desire for a speedy decision, this request was granted.

10. Now, therefore, that he had an opportunity of doing injury, Maximin displayed the innate ferocity which was implanted in his cruel heart, just as wild beasts exhibited in the amphitheatre often do when at length released from their cages. And, as this affair was represented first in various ways, as if in a kind of prelude, and some persons with their sides lacerated named certain nobles, as if by means of their clients and other low-born persons known as criminals and informers, they had employed various artifices for injuring them. This infernal delegate, carrying his investigations to an extravagant length, presented a malicious report to the emperor, in which he told him that such atrocious crimes as many people had committed at Rome could not be investigated nor punished without the severest penalties.

11. When the emperor learnt this he was exasperated beyond measure, being rather a furious than a rigorous enemy to vice; and accordingly, by one single edict applying to causes of this kind, which in his arrogance he treated as if they partook of treason, he commanded that all those whom the equity of the ancient law and the judgment of the gods had exempted from examination by torture, should, if the case seemed to require it, be put to the rack.

12. And in order that the authority to be established, by being doubled and raised to greater distinction, might be able to heap up greater calamities, he appointed Maximin proprefect at Rome, and gave him as colleague in the prosecution of these inquiries, which were being prepared for the ruin of many persons, a secretary named Leo, who was afterwards master of the ceremonies. He was by birth a Pannonian, and by occupation originally a brigand, as savage as a wild beast, and insatiable of human blood.

13. The accession of a colleague so much like himself, inflamed the cruel and malignant disposition of Maximin, which was further encouraged by the commission which conferred this dignity on them; so that, flinging himself about in his exultation, he seemed rather to dance than to walk, while he studied to imitate the Brachmans who, according to some accounts, move in the air amid the altars.

14. And now the trumpets of intestine discords sounded, while all men stood amazed at the atrocity of the things which were done. Among which, besides many other cruel and inhuman actions so various and so numerous that it is impossible for me to relate them all, the death of Marinus, the celebrated advocate, was especially remarkable. He was condemned to death on a charge which was not even attempted to be supported by evidence, of having endeavoured by wicked acts to compass a marriage with Hispanilla.

15. And since I think that perhaps some persons may read this history who, after careful investigation, will object to it that such and such a thing was done before another; or again that this or that circumstance has been omitted, I consider that I have inserted enough, because it is not every event which has been brought about by base people that is worth recording; nor, if it were necessary to relate them all, would there be materials for such an account, not even if the public records themselves were examined, when so many atrocious deeds were common, and when this new frenzy was throwing everything into confusion without the slightest restraint; and when what was feared was evidently not a judicial trial but a total cessation of all justice.

16. At this time, Cethegus, a senator, who was accused of adultery, was beheaded, and a young man of noble birth, named Alypius, who had been banished for some trivial misconduct, with some other persons of low descent, were all publicly executed; while every one appeared in their sufferings to see a representation of what they themselves might expect, and dreamt of nothing but tortures, prisons, and dark dungeons.

17. At the same time also, the affair of Hymetius, a man of very eminent character, took place, of which the circumstances were as follows. When he was governing Africa as proconsul, and the Carthaginians were in extreme distress for want of food, he supplied them with corn out of the granaries destined for the Roman people; and shortly afterwards, when there was a fine harvest, he without delay fully replaced what he had thus consumed.

18. But as at the time of the scarcity ten bushels had been sold to those who were in want for a piece of gold, while he now bought thirty for the same sum, he sent the profit derived from the difference in price to the emperor's treasury. Therefore, Valentinian, suspecting that there was not as much sent as there ought to have been as the proceeds of this traffic, confiscated a portion of his property.

19. And to aggravate the severity of this infliction, another circumstance happened about the same time which equally tended to his ruin. Amantius was a soothsayer of pre-eminent celebrity at that period, and having been accused by some secret informer of being employed by this same Hymetius to offer a sacrifice for some evil purpose, he was brought before a court of justice and put to the rack; but in spite of all his tortures, he denied the charge with steadfast resolution.

20. And as he denied it, some secret papers were brought from his house, among which was found a letter in the handwriting of Hymetius, in which he asked Amantius to propitiate the gods by some solemn sacrifices to engage them to make the disposition of the emperor favourable to him; and at the end of the letter were found some reproachful terms applied to the emperor as avaricious and cruel.

21. Valentinian learnt these facts from the report of some informers, who exaggerated the offence given, and with very unnecessary vigour ordered an inquiry to be made into the affair; and because Frontinus, the assessor of Hymetius, was accused of having been the instrument of drawing up this letter, he was scourged with rods till he confessed, and then he was condemned to exile in Britain. But Amantius was subsequently convicted of some capital crimes and was executed.

22. After these transactions, Hymetius was conducted to the town of Otricoli, to be examined by Ampelius, the prefect of the city, and deputy of Maximin; and when he was on the point of being condemned, as was manifest to every one, he judiciously seized an opportunity that was afforded to him of appealing to the protection of

the emperor, and being protected by his name, he came off for the time in safety.

23. The emperor, however, when he was consulted on the matter, remitted it to the senate, who examined into the whole affair with justice, and banished him to Boæ, a village in Dalmatia, for which they were visited with the wrath of the emperor, who was exceedingly enraged when he heard that a man whom in his own mind he had condemned to death had been let off with a milder punishment.

24. These and similar transactions led every one to fear that the treatment thus experienced by a few was intended for all: and that these evils should not, by being concealed, grow greater and greater till they reached an intolerable height, the nobles sent a deputation consisting of Prætextatus, formerly a prefect of the city, Venustus, formerly deputy, and Minervius, who had been a consular governor, to entreat the emperor not to allow the punishments to exceed the offences, and not to permit any senator to be exposed to the torture in an unprecedented and unlawful manner.

25. But when these envoys were admitted into the council chamber, Valentinian denied that he had ever given such orders, and insisted that the charges made against him were calumnies. He was, however, refuted with great moderation by the prætor Eupraxius; and in consequence of this freedom, the cruel injunction that had been issued, and which had surpassed all previous examples of cruelty, was amended.

26. About the same time, Lollianus, a youth of tender age, the son of Lampadius, who had been prefect, being accused before Maximin, who investigated his case with great care, and being convicted of having copied out a book on the subject of the unlawful acts (though, as his age made it likely, without any definite plan of using it), was, it seemed, on the point of being sentenced to banishment, when, at the suggestion of his father, he appealed to the emperor; and being by his order brought to court, it appeared that he had, as the proverb has it, gone from the frying-pan into the fire, as he was now handed over to Phalangius, the consular governor of Bætica, and put to death by the hand of the executioner.

27. There were also Tarratius Bassus, who afterwards became prefect of the city, his brother Camenius, a man of the name of Marcian, and Eusapius, all men of great eminence, who were prosecuted on the ground of having protected the charioteer Auchenius, and being his accomplices in the act of poisoning. The evidence was very doubtful, and they were acquitted by the decision of Victorinus, as

general report asserted; Victorinus being a most intimate friend of Maximin.

28. Women too were equally exposed to similar treatment. For many of this sex also, and of noble birth, were put to death on being convicted of adultery or unchastity. The most notorious cases were those of Claritas and Flaviana; the first of whom, when conducted to death, was stripped of the clothes which she wore, not even being permitted to retain enough to cover her with bare decency; and for this the executioner also was convicted of having committed a great crime, and burnt to death.

29. Paphius and Cornelius, both senators, confessed that they had polluted themselves by the wicked practice of poisoning, and were put to death by the sentence of Maximin; and by a similar sentence the master of the mint was executed. He also condemned Sericus and Asbolius, who have been mentioned before; and because while exhorting them to name any others who occurred to them, he had promised them with an oath that they should not themselves be punished either by fire or sword, he had them slain by violent blows from balls of lead. After this he also burnt alive Campensis the soothsayer, not having in his case bound himself by any oath or promise.

30. Here it is in my opinion convenient to explain the cause which brought Aginatius headlong to destruction, a man ennobled by a long race of ancestors, as unvarying tradition affirms, though no proof of his ancestral renown was ever substantiated.

31. Maximin, full of pride and arrogance, and being then also prefect of the corn-market, and having many encouragements to audacity, proceeded so far as to show his contempt for Probus, the most illustrious of all the nobles, and who was governing the provinces with the authority of prefect of the prætorium.

32. Aginatius, being indignant at this, and feeling it a hardship that in the trial of causes Olybrius had preferred Maximin to himself, while he was actually deputy at Rome, secretly informed Probus in private letters that the arrogant and foolish man who had thus set himself against his lofty merits, might easily be put down if he thought fit.

33. These letters, as some affirm, Probus sent to Maximin, hardened as he was in wickedness, because he feared his influence with the emperor; letting none but the bearer know the business. And when he had read them, the cruel Maximin became furious, and henceforth set all his engines at work to destroy Aginatius, like a serpent that had been bruised by some one whom it knew.

34. There was another still more powerful cause for intriguing against him, which ultimately became his destruction. For he charged Victorinus, who was dead, and from whom he had received a very considerable legacy, with having while alive made money of the decrees of Maximin; and with similar maliciousness he had also threatened his wife Anepsia with a lawsuit.

35. Anepsia, alarmed at this, and to support herself by the aid of Maximin, pretended that her husband in a will which he had recently made, had left him three thousand pounds weight of silver. He, full of covetousness, for this too was one of his vices, demanded half the inheritance, and afterwards, not being contented with that, as if it were hardly sufficient, he contrived another device which he looked upon as both honourable and safe; and not to lose his hold of the handle thus put in his way for obtaining a large estate, he demanded the daughter of Anepsia, who was the stepdaughter of Victorinus, as a wife for his son; and this marriage was quickly arranged with the consent of the woman.

36. Through these and other atrocities equally lamentable, which threw a gloom over the whole of the eternal city, this man, never to be named without a groan, grew by the ruin of numerous other persons, and began to stretch out his hands beyond the limits of lawsuits and trials: for it is said that he had a small cord always suspended from a remote window of the prætorium, the end of which had a loop which was easily drawn tight, by means of which he received secret informations supported by no evidence or testimony, but capable of being used to the ruin of many innocent persons. And he used often to send his officers, Mucianus and Barbarus, men fit for any deceit or treachery, secretly out of his house.

37. Who then, as if bewailing some hardship which as they pretended had fallen upon them, and exaggerating the cruelty of the judge, with constant repetition assured those who really lay under execution that there was no remedy by which they could save themselves except that of advancing heavy accusation against men of high rank; because if such men were involved in such accusations, they themselves would easily procure an acquittal.

38. In this way, Maximin's implacable temper overwhelmed those yet in his power; numbers were thrown into prison, and persons of the highest rank were seen with anxious faces and in mourning attire. Nor ought any one of them to be blamed for bowing down to the ground in saluting this monster, when they heard him vociferating with

the tone of a wild beast, that no one could ever be acquitted unless he choose.

39. For sayings like that, when instantly followed by their natural result, would have terrified even men like Numa, Pompilius, or Cato. In fact things went on in such a way that some persons never had their eyes dried of the tears caused by the misfortunes of others, as often happens in such unsettled and dangerous times.

40. And the iron-hearted judge, continually disregarding all law and justice, had but one thing about him which made him endurable; for sometimes he was prevailed upon by entreaties to spare some one, though this too is affirmed to be nearly a vice in the following passage of Cicero. "If anger be implacable, it is the extreme of severity; if it yield to entreaties, it is the extreme of levity; though in times of misfortune even levity is to be preferred to cruelty."

41. After these events, Leo arrived, and was received as his successor, and Maximin was summoned to the emperor's court and promoted to the office of prefect of the prætorium, where he was as cruel as ever, having indeed greater power of inflicting injury, like a basilisk serpent.

42. Just at this time, or not long before, the brooms with which the senate-house of the nobles was swept out were seen to flower, and this portended that some persons of the very lowest class would be raised to high rank and power.

43. Though it is now time to return to the course of our regular history, yet without neglecting the proper order of time, we must dwell on a few incidents, which through the iniquity of the deputy prefects of the city, were done most unjustly, being in fact done at the word and will of Maximin by those same officers, who seemed to look on themselves as the mere servants of his pleasure.

44. After him came Ursicinus, a man of a more merciful disposition, who, wishing to act cautiously and in conformity to the constitution, confronted a man named Esaias with some others who were in prison on a charge of adultery with Rufina; who had attempted to establish a charge of treason against Marcellus her husband, formerly in a situation of high trust. But this act led to his being despised as a dawdler, and a person little fit to carry out such designs with proper resolution, and so he was removed from his place of deputy.

45. He was succeeded by Simplicius of Emona, who had been a schoolmaster, but was now the assessor of Maximin. After receiving this appointment, he did not grow more proud or arrogant, but assumed a supercilious look, which gave a repulsive expression to his

countenance. His language was studiously moderate, while he meditated the most rigorous proceedings against many persons. And first of all he put Rufina to death with all the partners of her adultery, and all who were privy to it, concerning whom Ursicinus, as we have related, had already made a report. Then he put numbers of others to death, without any distinction between the innocent and the guilty.

46. Running a race of bloodshed with Maximin, as if he had, as it were, been his leader, he sought to surpass him in destroying the noblest families, imitating Busiris and Antæus of old, and Phalaris, so that he seemed to want nothing but the bull of Agrigentum.

47. After these and other similar transactions had taken place, a certain matron named Hesychia, who was accused of having attempted some crime, becoming greatly alarmed, and being of a fierce and resolute disposition, killed herself in the house of the officer to whom she was given in custody, by muffling her face in a bed of feathers, and stopping up her nostrils and so becoming suffocated.

48. To all these calamities another of no less severity was added. For Eumenius and Abienus, two men of the highest class, having been accused, during Maximin's term of office, of adultery with Fausiana, a woman of rank, after the death of Victorinus, under whose protection they were safe, being alarmed at the arrival of Simplicius, who was as full of audacity and threats as Maximin, withdrew to some secret hiding place.

49. But after Fausiana had been condemned they were recorded among the accused, and were summoned by public edict to appear, but they only hid themselves the more carefully. And Abrenus was for a very long time concealed in the house of Anepsia. But as it continually happens that unexpected accidents come to aggravate the distresses of those who are already miserable, a slave of Anepsia named Apaudulus, being angry because his wife had been flogged, went by night to Simplicius, and gave information of the whole affair, and officers were sent to drag them both from their place of concealment.

50. The charge against Abrenus was strengthened by another charge which was brought against him, of having seduced Anepsia, and he was condemned to death. But Anepsia herself, to get some hope of saving her life by at least procuring the delay of her execution, affirmed that she had been assailed by unlawful arts, and had been ravished in the house of Aginatius.

51. Simplicius with loud indignation reported to the emperor all that had taken place, and as Maximin, who was now at court, hated Aginatius for the reason which we have already explained, and having

his rage increased against him at the same time that his power was augmented, entreated with great urgency that he might be sentenced to death; and such a favour was readily granted to this furious and influential exciter of the emperor's severity.

52. Then fearing the exceeding unpopularity which would fall upon him if a man of patrician family should perish by the sentence of Simplicius, who was his new assessor and friend, he kept the imperial edict for the execution by him for a short time, wavering and doubting whom to pitch upon as a trusty and efficient perpetrator of so atrocious a deed.

53. At length, as like usually finds like, a certain Gaul of the name of Doryphorianus was discovered, a man daring even to madness; and as he promised to accomplish the matter in a short time, he obtained for him the post of deputy, and gave him the emperor's letter with an additional rescript; instructing the man, who though savage had no experience in such matters, how, if he used sufficient speed, he would meet with no obstacle to his slaying Aginatius; though, if there were any delay, he would be very likely to escape.

54. Doryphorianus, as he was commanded, hastened to Rome by rapid journeys; and while beginning to discharge the duties of his new office, he exerted great industry to discover how he could put a senator of eminent family to death without any assistance. And when he learnt that he had been some time before found in his own house where he was still kept in custody, he determined to have him brought before him as the chief of all the criminals, with Anepsia, in the middle of the night; an hour at which men's minds are especially apt to be bewildered by terror; as, among many other instances, the Ajax of Homer[165] shows us, when he expresses a wish rather to die by daylight, than to suffer the additional terrors of the night.

55. And as the judge, I should rather call him the infamous robber, intent only on the service he had promised to perform, carried everything to excess, having ordered Aginatius to be brought in, he also commanded the introduction of a troop of executioners; and while the chains rattled with a mournful sound, he tortured the slaves who were already exhausted by their long confinement, till they died, in order to extract from them matter affecting the life of their master; a proceeding which in a trial for adultery our merciful laws expressly forbids.

56. At last, when the tortures which were all but mortal had wrung some hints from the maid-servant, without any careful examination of the truth of her words, Aginatius was at once sentenced to be

led to execution, and without being allowed to say a word in his defence, though with loud outcries he appealed to and invoked the names
of the emperors, he was carried off and put to death, and Anepsia was
executed by a similar sentence. The eternal city was filled with mourning for these executions which were perpetrated either by Maximin
himself when he was present in the city, or by his emissaries when he
was at a distance.

57. But the avenging Furies of those who had been murdered
were preparing retribution. For, as I will afterwards relate at the proper
season, this same Maximin giving way to his intolerable pride when
Gratian was emperor, was put to death by the sword of the executioner; and Simplicius also was beheaded in Illyricum. Doryphorianus
too was condemned to death, and thrown into the Tullian prison, but
was taken from thence by the emperor at his mother's suggestion, and
when he was brought back to his own country was put to death with
terrible torments. Let us now return to the point at which we left our
history. Such, however, was the state of affairs in the city of Rome.

II.

A.D. 369.

§ 1. Valentinian having several great and useful projects in his
head, began to fortify the entire banks of the Rhine, from its beginning
in the Tyrol to the straits of the ocean,[166] with vast works; raising lofty
castles and fortresses, and a perfect range of towers in every suitable
place, so as to protect the whole frontier of Gaul; and sometimes, by
constructing works on the other side of the river, he almost trenched
upon the territories of the enemy.

2. At last considering that one fortress, of which he himself had
laid the very foundations, though sufficiently high and safe, yet, being
built on the very edge of the river Neckar, was liable to be gradually
undermined by the violent beating of its waters, he formed a plan to
divert the river itself into another channel; and, having sought out
some workmen who were skilful in such works and collected a strong
military force, he began that arduous labour.

3. Day after day large masses of oaken beams were fastened together, and thrown into the channel, and by them huge piles were
continually fixed and unfixed, being all thrown into disorder by the
rising of the stream, and afterwards they were broken and carried away
by the current.

4. However, the resolute diligence of the emperor and the labour
of the obedient soldiery prevailed; though the troops were often up to

their chins in the water while at work; and at last, though not without considerable risk, the fixed camp was protected against all danger from the violence of the current, and is still safe and strong.

5. Joyful and exulting in this success, the emperor, perceiving that the weather and the season of the year did not allow him any other occupation, like a good and active prince began to apply his attention to the general affairs of the republic. And thinking the time very proper for completing one work which he had been meditating, he began with all speed to raise a fortification on the other side of the Rhine, on Mount Piri, a spot which belongs to the barbarians. And as rapidity of action was one great means of executing this design with safety, he sent orders to the Duke Arator, through Syagrius, who was then a secretary, but who afterwards became prefect and consul, to attempt to make himself master of this height in the dead of the night.

6. The duke at once crossed over with the secretary, as he was commanded; and was beginning to employ the soldiers whom he had brought with him to dig out the foundations, when he received a successor, Hermogenes. At the very same moment there arrived some nobles of the Allemanni, fathers of the hostages, whom, in accordance with our treaty, we were detaining as important pledges for the long continuance of the peace.

7. And they, with bended knees entreated him not to let the Romans, with an improvident disregard of all safety (they whose fortune their everlasting good faith had raised to the skies), now be misled by a base error to trample all former agreements under foot, and attempt an act unworthy of them.

8. But since it was to no purpose that they used these and similar arguments, as they were not listened to, and finding that they had no chance of a conciliatory answer, they reluctantly returned, bewailing the loss of their sons; and when they were gone, from a secret hiding-place in a neighbouring hill a troop of barbarians sprang forth, waiting, as far as was understood, for the answer which was to be given to the nobles; and attacking our half-naked soldiers, who were carrying loads of earth, drew their swords and quickly slew them, and with them the two generals.

9. Nor was any one left to relate what had happened, except Syagrius, who, after they were all destroyed returned to the court, where by the sentence of his offended emperor he was dismissed the service; on which he retired to his own home; being judged by the severe decision of the prince to have deserved this sentence because he was the only one who escaped.

10. Meanwhile the wicked fury of bands of robbers raged through Gaul to the injury of many persons; since they occupied the most frequented roads, and without any hesitation seized upon everything valuable which came in their way. Besides many other persons who were the victims of these treacherous attacks, Constantianus, the tribune of the stable, was attacked by a secret ambuscade and slain; he was a relation of Valentinian, and the brother of Cerealis and Justina.

11. In other countries, as if the Furies were stirring up similar evils to afflict us on every side, the Maratocupreni, those most cruel banditti, spread their ravages in every direction. They were the natives of a town of the same name in Syria, near Apamea; very numerous, marvellously skilful in every kind of deceit, and an object of universal fear, because, under the character of merchants or soldiers of high rank, they spread themselves quietly over the country, and then pillaged all the wealthy houses, villages, and towns which came in their way.

12. Nor could any one guard against their unexpected attacks; since they fell not upon any previously selected victim, but in places in various parts, and at great distances, and carried their devastations wherever the wind led them. For which reason the Saxons were feared beyond all other enemies, because of the suddenness of their attacks. They then, in bands of sworn comrades, destroyed the riches of many persons; and being under the impulse of absolute fury, they committed the most mournful slaughters, being not less greedy of blood than of booty. Nevertheless, that I may not, by entering into too minute details, impede the progress of my history, it will be sufficient to relate one destructive device of theirs.

13. A body of these wicked men assembled in one place, pretending to be the retinue of a receiver of the revenue, or of the governor of the province. In the darkness of the evening they entered the city, while the crier made a mournful proclamation, and attacked with swords the house of one of the nobles, as if he had been proscribed and sentenced to death. They seized all his valuable furniture, because his servants, being utterly bewildered by the suddenness of the danger, did not defend the house; they slew several of them, and then before the return of daylight withdrew with great speed.

14. But being loaded with a great quantity of plunder, since from their love of booty they had left nothing behind, they were intercepted by a movement of the emperor's troop, and were cut off and all slain to a man. And their children, who were at the time very young, were also destroyed to prevent their growing up in the likeness of their fathers;

and their houses which they had built with great splendour at the expense of the misery of others, were all pulled down. These things happened in the order in which they have been related.

III.

§ 1. But Theodosius, a general of very famous reputation, departed in high spirits from Augusta, which the ancients used to call Londinium, with an army which he had collected with great energy and skill; bringing a mighty aid to the embarrassed and disturbed fortunes of the Britons. His plan was to seek everywhere favourable situations for laying ambuscades for the barbarians; and to impose no duties on his troops of the performance of which he did not himself cheerfully set the example.

2. And in this way, while he performed the duties of a gallant soldier, and showed at the same time the prudence of an illustrious general, he routed and vanquished the various tribes in whom their past security had engendered an insolence which led them to attack the Roman territories; and he entirely restored the cities and the fortresses which through the manifold disasters of the time had been injured or destroyed, though they had been originally founded to secure the tranquillity of the country.

3. But while he was pursuing this career, a great crime was planned which was likely to have resulted in serious danger, if it had not been crushed at the very beginning.

4. A certain man named Valentine, in Valeria of Pannonia, a man of a proud spirit, the brother-in-law of Maximin, that wicked and cruel deputy, who afterwards became prefect, having been banished to Britain for some grave crime, and being a restless and mischievous beast, was eager for any kind of revolution or mischief, began to plot with great insolence against Theodosius, whom he looked upon as the only person with power to resist his wicked enterprise.

5. But while both openly and privily taking many precautions, as his pride and covetousness increased, he began to tamper with the exiles and the soldiers, promising them rewards sufficient to tempt them as far at least as the circumstances and his enterprise would permit.

6. But when the time for putting his attempt into execution drew near, the duke, who had received from some trustworthy quarter information of what was going on, being always a man inclined to a bold line of conduct, and resolutely bent on chastising crimes when detected, seized Valentine with a few of his accomplices who were most deeply implicated, and handed them over to the general Dulcitius to be

put to death. But at the same time conjecturing the future, through that knowledge of the soldiers in which he surpassed other men, he forbade the institution of any examination into the conspiracy generally, lest if the fear of such an investigation should affect many, fresh troubles might revive in the province.

7. After this he turned his attention to make many necessary amendments, feeling wholly free from any danger in such attempts, since it was plain that all his enterprises were attended by a propitious fortune. So he restored cities and fortresses, as we have already mentioned, and established stations and outposts on our frontiers; and he so completely recovered the province which had yielded subjection to the enemy, that through his agency it was again brought under the authority of its legitimate ruler, and from that time forth was called Valentia, by desire of the emperor, as a memorial of his success.

8. The Areans, a class of men instituted in former times, and of whom we have already made some mention in recording the acts of Constans, had now gradually fallen into bad practices, for which he removed them from their stations; in fact they had been undeniably convicted of yielding to the temptation of the great rewards which were given and promised to them, so as to have continually betrayed to the barbarians what was done among us. For their business was to traverse vast districts, and report to our generals the warlike movements of the neighbouring nations.

9. In this manner the affairs which I have already mentioned, and others like them, having been settled, he was summoned to the court, and leaving the provinces in a state of exultation, like another Furius Camillus or Papirius Cursor, he was celebrated everywhere for his numerous and important victories. He was accompanied by a large crowd of well-wishers to the coast, and crossing over with a fair wind, arrived at the emperor's camp, where he was received with joy and high praise, and appointed to succeed Valens Jovinus, who was commander of the cavalry.

IV.

§ 1. I have thus made a long and extensive digression from the affairs of the city, being constrained by the abundance of events which took place abroad; and now I will return to give a cursory sketch of them, beginning with the tranquil and moderate exercise of the prefect's authority by Olybrius, who never forgot the rights of humanity, but was continually anxious and careful that no word or deed of his should ever be harsh or cruel. He was a merciless punisher of calumnies; he restrained the exactions of the treasury wherever he could; he was a careful discriminator of right and wrong; an equitable judge, and very gentle towards those placed under his authority.

2. But all these good qualities were clouded by one vice which, though not injurious to the commonwealth, was very discreditable to a judge of high rank; namely, that his private life was one of great luxury, devoted to theatrical exhibitions, and to amours, though not such as were either infamous or incestuous.

3. After him Ampelius succeeded to the government of the city; he also was a man addicted to pleasure, a native of Antioch, and one who from having been master of the offices was twice promoted to a proconsulship, and sometime afterwards to that supreme rank, the prefecture. In other respects he was a cheerful man, and one admirably suited to win the favour of the people; though sometimes over-severe, without being as firm in his purposes as might have been wished. Had he been, he would have corrected, though perhaps not effectually, the gluttonous and debauched habits which prevailed; but, as it was, by his laxity of conduct, he lost a glory which otherwise might have been enduring.

4. For he had determined that no wine-shop should be opened before the fourth hour of the day; and that none of the common people, before a certain fixed hour, should either warm water or expose dressed meat for sale; and that no one of respectable rank should be seen eating in public.

5. Since these unseemly practices, and others still worse, owing to long neglect and connivance, had grown so frequent that even Epimenides of Crete, if, according to the fabulous story, he could have risen from the dead and returned to our times, would have been unable by himself to purify Rome; such deep stains of incurable vices overwhelmed it.

6. And in the first place we will speak of the faults of the nobles, as we have already repeatedly done as far as our space permitted; and then we will proceed to the faults of the common people, touching, however, only briefly and rapidly on either.

7. Some men, conspicuous for the illustriousness of their ancestry as they think, gave themselves immoderate airs, and call themselves Reburri, and Fabunii, and Pagonii, and Geriones, Dalii, Tarracii, or Perrasii, and other finely-sounding appellations, indicating the antiquity of their family.

8. Some also are magnificent in silken robes, as if they were being led to execution, or, to speak without words of so unfavourable an

omen, as if after the army had passed they were bringing up the rear, and are followed by a vast troop of servants, with a din like that of a company of soldiers.

9. Such men when, while followed by fifty servants apiece, they have entered the baths, cry out with threatening voice, "Where are my people?" And if they suddenly find out that any unknown female slave has appeared, or any worn-out courtesan who has long been subservient to the pleasures of the townspeople, they run up, as if to win a race, and patting and caressing her with disgusting and unseemly blandishments, they extol her, as the Parthians might praise Semiramis, Egypt her Cleopatra, the Carians Artemisia, or the Palmyrene citizens Zenobia. And men do this, whose ancestor, even though a senator, would have been branded with a mark of infamy because he dared, at an unbecoming time, to kiss his wife in the presence of their common daughter.

10. Some of these, when any one meets and begins to salute them, toss their heads like bulls preparing to butt, offering their flatterers their knees or hands to kiss, thinking that quite enough for their perfect happiness; while they deem it sufficient attention and civility to a stranger who may happen to have laid them under some obligation to ask him what warm or cold bath he frequents, or what house he lives in.

11. And while they are so solemn, looking upon themselves as especial cultivators of virtue, if they learn that any one has brought intelligence that any fine horses or skilful coachmen are coming from any place, they rush with as much haste to see them, examine them, and put questions concerning them, as their ancestors showed on beholding the twin-brothers Tyndaridæ,[167] when they filled the whole city with joy by the announcement of that ancient victory.

12. A number of idle chatterers frequent their houses, and, with various pretended modes of adulation, applaud every word uttered by men of such high fortune; resembling the parasites in a comedy, for as they puff up bragging soldiers, attributing to them, as rivals of the heroes of old, sieges of cities, and battles, and the death of thousands of enemies, so these men admire the construction of the lofty pillars, and the walls inlaid with stones of carefully chosen colours, and extol these grandees with superhuman praises.

13. Sometimes scales are sent for at their entertainments to weigh the fish, or the birds, or the dormice which are set on the table; and then the size of them is dwelt on over and over again, to the great weariness of those present, as something never seen before; especially

when near thirty secretaries stand by, with tablets and memorandum books, to record all these circumstances; so that nothing seems to be wanting but a schoolmaster.

14. Some of them, hating learning as they hate poison, read Juvenal and Marius Maximus[168] with tolerably careful study; though, in their profound laziness, they never touch any other volumes; why, it does not belong to my poor judgment to decide.

15. For, in consideration of their great glories and long pedigrees, they ought to read a great variety of books; in which, for instance, they might learn that Socrates, when condemned to death and thrown into prison, asked some one who was playing a song of the Greek poet Stesichorus with great skill, to teach him also to do that, while it was still in his power; and when the musician asked him of what use this skill could be to him, as he was to die the next day, he answered, "that I may know something more before I die."

16. And there are among them some who are such severe judges of offences, that if a slave is too long in bringing them hot water, they will order him to be scourged with three hundred stripes; but should he intentionally have killed a man, while numbers insist that he ought to be unhesitatingly condemned as guilty, his master will exclaim, "What can the poor wretch do? what can one expect from a good-for-nothing fellow like that?" But should any one else venture to do anything of the kind, he would be corrected.

17. Their ideas of civility are such that a stranger had better kill a man's brother than send an excuse to them if he be asked to dinner; for a senator fancies that he has suffered a terrible grievance, equal to the loss of his entire patrimony, if any guest be absent, whom, after repeated deliberations, he has once invited.

18. Some of them, if they have gone any distance to see their estates in the country, or to hunt at a meeting collected for their amusement by others, think they have equalled the marches of Alexander the Great, or of Cæsar; or if they have gone in some painted boats from Lake Avernus to Pozzuoli or Cajeta, especially if they have ventured on such an exploit in warm weather. Where if, amid their golden fans, a fly should perch on the silken fringes, or if a slender ray of the sun should have pierced through a hole in their awning, they complain that they were not born among the Cimmerians.

19. Then, when they come from the bath of Silvanus, or the waters of Mamæa, which are so good for the health, after they come out of the water, and have wiped themselves with cloths of the finest linen, they open the presses, and take out of them robes so delicate as to be

transparent, selecting them with care, till they have got enough to clothe eleven persons; and at length, after they have picked out all they choose, they wrap themselves up in them, and take the rings which they had given to their attendants to hold, that they might not be injured by the damp; and then they depart when their fingers are properly cooled.

20. Again, if any one having lately quitted the military service of the emperor, has retired to his home.[169] ...

21. Some of them, though not many, wish to avoid the name of gamblers, and prefer to be called dice-players; the difference being much the same as that between a thief and a robber. But this must be confessed that, while all friendships at Rome are rather cool, those alone which are engendered by dice are sociable and intimate, as if they had been formed amid glorious exertions, and were firmly cemented by exceeding affection; to which it is owing that some of this class of gamblers live in such harmony that you might think them the brothers Quintilii.[170] And so you may sometimes see a man of base extraction, who knows all the secrets of the dice, as grave as Porcius Cato when he met with a repulse which he had never expected nor dreamt of, when a candidate for the prætorship, with affected solemnity and a serious face, because at some grand entertainment or assembly some man of proconsular rank has been preferred to himself.

22. Some lay siege to wealthy men, whether old or young, childless or unmarried, or even with wives and children (for with such an object no distinction is ever regarded by them), seeking by most marvellous tricks to allure them to make their wills; and then if, after observing all the forms of law, they bequeath to these persons what they have to leave, being won over by them to this compliance, they speedily die.[171]

23. Another person, perhaps only in some subordinate office, struts along with his head up, looking with so slight and passing a glance upon those with whom he was previously acquainted, that you might fancy it must be Marcus Marcellus just returned from the capture of Syracuse.

24. Many among them deny the existence of a superior Power in heaven, and yet neither appear in public, nor dine, nor think that they can bathe with any prudence, before they have carefully consulted an almanac, and learnt where (for example) the planet Mercury is, or in what portion of Cancer the moon is as she passes through the heavens.

25. Another man, if he perceives his creditor to be importunate in demanding a debt, flies to a charioteer who is bold enough to venture

on any audacious enterprise, and takes care that he shall be harassed with dread of persecution as a poisoner; from which he cannot be released without giving bail and incurring a very heavy expense. One may add to this, that he includes under this head a debtor who is only so through the engagements into which he has entered to avoid a prosecution, as if he were a real debtor, and that he never lets him go till he has obtained the discharge of the debt.

26. On the other side, a wife, who, as the old proverb has it, hammers on the same anvil day and night, to compel her husband to make his will, and then the husband is equally urgent that his wife shall do the same. And men learned in the law are procured on each side, the one in the bedchamber, and his opponent in the dining-room, to draw up counter-documents. And under their employ are placed ambiguous interpreters of the contracts of their victims, who, on the one side, promise with great liberality high offices, and the funerals of wealthy matrons; and from these they proceed to the obsequies of the husbands, giving hints that everything necessary ought to be prepared; and[172] ... as Cicero says, "Nor in the affairs of men do they understand anything good, except what is profitable; and they love those friends most (as they would prefer sheep) from whom they expect to derive the greatest advantage."[173]

27. And when they borrow anything, they are so humble and cringing, you would think you were at a comedy, and seeing Micon or Laches; when they are constrained to repay what they have borrowed, they become so turgid and bombastic that you would take them for those descendants of Hercules, Cresphontes and Temenus. This is enough to say of the senatorial order.

28. And let us come to the idle and lazy common people, among whom some, who have not even got shoes boast of high-sounding names; calling themselves Cimessores, Statarii, Semicupæ, Serapina, or Cicimbricus, or Gluturiorus, Trulla, Lucanicus, Pordaca, or Salsula,[174] with numbers of other similar appellations. These men spend their whole lives in drinking, and gambling, and brothels, and pleasures, and public spectacles; and to them the Circus Maximus is their temple, their home, their public assembly; in fact, their whole hope and desire.[175]

29. And you may see in the forum, and roads, and streets, and places of meeting, knots of people collected, quarrelling violently with one another, and objecting to one another, and splitting themselves into violent parties.

30. Among whom those who have lived long, having influence by reason of their age, their gray hairs and wrinkles, are continually crying out that the republic cannot stand, if in the contest which is about to take place, the skilful charioteer, whom some individual backs, is not foremost in the race, and does not dextrously shave the turning-post with the trace-horses.

31. And when there is so much ruinous carelessness, when the wished-for day of the equestrian games dawns, before the sun has visibly risen, they all rush out with headlong haste, as if with their speed they would outstrip the very chariots which are going to race; while as to the event of the contest they are all torn asunder by opposite wishes, and the greater part of them, through their anxiety, pass sleepless nights.

32. From hence, if you go to some cheap theatre, the actors on the stage are driven off by hisses, if they have not taken the precaution to conciliate the lowest of the people by gifts of money. And if there should be no noise, then, in imitation of the people in the Tauric Chersonese, they raise an outcry that the strangers ought to be expelled (on whose assistance they have always relied for their principal support), using foul and ridiculous expressions; such as are greatly at variance with the pursuits and inclinations of that populace of old, whose many facetious and elegant expressions are recorded by tradition and by history.

33. For these clever gentlemen have now devised a new method of expressing applause, which is, at every spectacle to cry out to those who appear at the end, whether they are couriers, huntsmen, or charioteers—in short, to the whole body of actors, and to the magistrates, whether of great or small importance, and even to nations, "It is to your school that he ought to go." But what he is to learn there no one can explain.

34. Among these men are many chiefly addicted to fattening themselves up by gluttony, who, following the scent of any delicate food, and the shrill voices of the women who, from cockcrow, cry out with a shrill scream, like so many peacocks, and gliding over the ground on tiptoe, get an entrance into the halls, biting their nails while the dishes are getting cool. Others fix their eyes intently on the tainted meat which is being cooked, that you might fancy Democritus, with a number of anatomists, was gazing into the entrails of sacrificed victims, in order to teach posterity how best to relieve internal pains.

35. For the present this is enough to say of the affairs of the city; now let us return to other events which various circumstances brought to pass in the provinces.

V.

§ 1. In the third consulship of the emperors a vast multitude of Saxons burst forth, and having crossed the difficult passage of the ocean, made towards the Roman frontier by rapid marches, having before often battened on the slaughter of our men. The first storm of this invasion fell upon the count Nannenus, who was in command in that district, being a veteran general of great merit and experience.

2. He now engaged in battle with a host which fought as if resolved on death; but when he found that he had lost many of his men, and that he himself, having been wounded, would be unequal to a succession of battles, he sent word to the emperor of what was necessary, and prevailed on him to send Severus, the commander of the infantry, to aid him at this crisis.

3. That general brought with him a sufficient body of troops, and when he arrived in the country he so arrayed his men that he terrified the barbarians, and threw them into such disorder, even before any battle took place, that they did not venture to engage him, but, panic-stricken at the brilliant appearance of the standards and eagles, they implored pardon and peace.

4. The question of granting it to them was long discussed, with variety of opinion, between the Roman commanders; but at last, as it seemed for the advantage of the republic, a truce was granted, and after they had agreed to the conditions proposed, one of which was that they should furnish a number of young men suitable for military service, the Saxons were permitted to withdraw, but without their baggage, and to return to their own country.

5. But when they, being now freed from all fear, were preparing to return, some of our infantry were sent forward, who secretly laid an ambuscade in a certain hidden defile, from which they would easily be able to attack them as they passed. But the matter turned out very differently from what was expected.

6. For some of our men being roused by the noise of the Saxons, sprang from their ambush unseasonably; and being suddenly seen, while they were hastening to establish themselves, the barbarians, with a terrible yell, put them to flight. Presently, however, they halted in a solid body, and being now driven to extremities, were compelled to fight, though their strength was far from great. The slaughter was

great, and they would have been all cut off to a man, had not a column of cuirassier cavalry, which had been similarly placed in ambuscade at a place where the road divided, in order there also to attack the barbarians in their passage, been roused by the uproar, and come up suddenly.

7. Then the battle raged more fiercely, and with dauntless breasts the Romans pressed forward on all sides, and with drawn swords hemmed in their enemies, and slew them; nor did any of them ever return home, for not one survived the slaughter. And although an impartial judge will blame the action as treacherous and disgraceful, still if he weighs all the circumstances, he will not regret that a mischievous band of robbers was at length destroyed when such an opportunity presented itself.

8. After these affairs had been consummated thus successfully, Valentinian revolving in his mind a great variety of opinions, was filled with anxious solicitude, considering and contemplating different measures for breaking the pride of the Allemanni and their king Macrianus, who were incessantly and furiously disturbing the republic with their restless movements.

9. For that ferocious nation, though from its earliest origin diminished by various disasters, yet continually revives, so that it might be considered as having been free from attacks for many ages. At last, after the emperor had considered and approved of one plan after another, it was finally determined to excite the Burgundians to attack them, the Burgundians being a warlike people, with an immense population of active youths, and therefore formidable to all their neighbours.

10. And the emperor sent repeated letters to their chiefs by some silent and trustworthy messengers, to urge them to attack the Allemanni at a certain fixed time, and promising that he likewise would cross the Rhine with the Roman legions, and attack their forces when in disorder, and seeking to escape the unexpected attack of the Burgundians.

11. The letters of the emperor were received with joy, for two reasons: first, because for many ages the Burgundians had looked upon themselves as descended from the Romans; and secondly, because they had continual quarrels with the Allemanni about their salt-pits and their borders. So they sent against them some picked battalions, which, before the Roman soldiers could be collected, advanced as far as the banks of the Rhine, and, while the emperor was engaged in the

construction of some fortresses, caused the greatest alarm to our people.

12. Therefore, after waiting for some time, Valentinian having failed to come on the appointed day as promised, and finding that none of his engagements were performed, they sent ambassadors to the court, requesting assistance to enable them to return in safety to their own land, and to save them from exposing their rear unprotected to their enemies.

13. But when they perceived that their request was virtually refused by the excuses and pleas for delay with which it was received, they departed from the court in sorrow and indignation; and when the chiefs of the Burgundians received their report, they were very furious, thinking they had been mocked; and so they slew all their prisoners and returned to their native land.

14. Among them their king is called by one general name of "Hendinos," and according to a very ancient custom of theirs, is deposed from his authority if under his government the state meets with any disaster in war; or if the earth fails to produce a good crop; in the same way as the Egyptians are accustomed to attribute calamities of that kind to their rulers. The chief priest among the Burgundians is called "the Sinistus." But he is irremovable and not exposed to any such dangers as the kings.

15. Taking advantage of this favourable opportunity, Theodosius, the commander of the cavalry, passed through the Tyrol and attacked the Allemanni, who, out of fear of the Burgundians, had dispersed into their villages. He slew a great number, and took some prisoners, whom by the emperor's command he sent to Italy, where some fertile districts around the Po were assigned to them, which they still inhabit as tributaries.

VI.

§ 1. Let us now migrate, as it were, to another quarter of the world, and proceed to relate the distresses of Tripoli, a province of Africa; distresses which, in my opinion, even Justice herself must have lamented, and which burst out rapidly like flames. I will now give an account both of them and of their causes.

2. The Asturians are barbarians lying on the frontier of this province, a people always in readiness for rapid invasions, accustomed to live on plunder and bloodshed; and who, after having been quiet for a while, now relapsed into their natural state of disquiet, alleging the following as the serious cause for their movements.

3. One of their countrymen, by name Stachao, while freely traversing our territories, as in time of peace, did some things forbidden by the laws; the most flagrant of his illegal acts being that he endeavoured, by every kind of deceit and intrigue, to betray the province, as was shown by the most undeniable evidence, for which crime he was burnt to death.

4. To avenge his death, the Asturians, claiming him as their clansman, and affirming that he had been unjustly condemned, burst forth from their own territory like so many mad wild beasts during the reign of Jovian, but fearing to approach close to Leptis, which was a city with a numerous population, and fortified by strong walls, they occupied the district around it, which is very fertile, for three days: and having slain the agricultural population on it, whom terror at their sudden inroad had deprived of all spirit, or had driven to take refuge in caves, and burnt a great quantity of furniture which could not be carried off, they returned home, loaded with vast plunder, taking with them as prisoner a man named Silva, the principal noble of Leptis, whom they found with his family at his country house.

5. The people of Leptis being terrified at this sudden disaster, not wishing to incur the further calamities with which the arrogance of the barbarians threatened them, implored the protection of Count Romanus, who had recently been promoted to the government of Africa. But when he came at the head of an army, and received their request to come to their immediate assistance in their distress, he declared that he would not move a step further unless abundant magazines and four thousand camels were provided for his troops.

6. At this answer the wretched citizens were stupefied, and declared to him, that after the devastations and conflagrations to which they had been exposed, it was impossible for them to make such exertions, even for the reparation of the cruel disasters which they had suffered; and, after waiting forty days there with vain pretences and excuses, the count retired without attempting any enterprise.

7. The people of Tripoli, disappointed in their hopes, and dreading the worst extremities, at their next council day, appointed Severus and Flaccianus ambassadors to carry to Valentinian some golden images of victory in honour of his accession to the empire, and to state fully and boldly to him the miserable distress of the province.

8. When this step became known, Romanus sent a swift horseman as a messenger to the master of the offices, Remigius, his own kinsman and his partner in plunder, bidding him take care, that by the

emperor's decision, the investigation into this matter should be committed to the deputy and himself.

9. The ambassadors arrived at the court, and having obtained access to the emperor, they, in a set speech, laid all their distresses before him, and presented him with a decree of their council in which the whole affair was fully set forth. When the emperor had read it, he neither trusted the report of the master of the offices, framed to defend the misconduct of the count, nor, on the other hand, did he place confidence in these men who made a contrary report; but promised a full investigation into the affair, which however was deferred in the manner in which high authorities are wont to let such matters give place to their more pleasant occupations and amusements.

10. While waiting in suspense and protracted anxiety for some relief from the emperor's camp, the citizens of Tripoli were again attacked by troops of the same barbarians, now elated with additional confidence by their past successes. They ravaged the whole territory of Leptis and also that of Œa, spreading total ruin and desolation everywhere, and, at last, retired loaded with an enormous quantity of spoil, and having slain many of our officers, the most distinguished of whom were Rusticianus, one of the priests, and the ædile, Nicasius.

11. This invasion was prevented from being repelled by the fact, that at the entreaty of the ambassadors, the conduct of the military affairs, which had at first been intrusted to Ruricius, the president, had been subsequently transferred to Count Romanus.

12. So now a new messenger was sent to Gaul with an account of this fresh disaster; and his intelligence roused the emperor to great anger. So Palladius, his secretary, who had also the rank of tribune, was sent at once to liquidate the pay due to the soldiers, who were dispersed over Africa, and to examine into all that had taken place in Tripoli, he being an officer whose report could be trusted.

13. But while all these delays took place from the continual deliberations held on the case, and while the people of Tripoli were still waiting for the answer, the Asturians, now still more insolent after their double success, like birds of prey whose ferocity has been sharpened by the taste of blood, flew once more to attack them; and having slain every one who did not flee from the danger, they carried off all the spoil which they had previously left behind, cutting down all the trees and vines.

14. Then a certain citizen named Mychon, a man of high station and great influence, was taken prisoner in the district outside of the city; but before they could bind him he gave them the slip, and be-

cause an attack of gout rendered him unable to effect his escape, he threw himself down a dry well, from which he was drawn up by the barbarians with his ribs broken, and was conducted near to the gates of the city, where he was ransomed by the affection of his wife, and was drawn up to the battlements of the wall by a rope; but two days afterwards he died.

15. These events encouraged the pertinacity of the invaders, so that they advanced and attacked the very walls of Leptis, which resounded with the mournful wailings of the women, who were terrified in an extraordinary manner and quite bewildered, because they had never before been blockaded by an enemy. And after the city had been besieged for eight days continuously, during which many of the besiegers were wounded, while they made no progress, they retired much discouraged to their own country.

16. In consequence of these events, the citizens, being still doubtful of their safety, and desirous of trying every possible resource, before the ambassadors who had been first sent had returned, sent Jovinus and Pancratius to lay before the emperor a faithful account of the sufferings which they had endured, and which they themselves had seen: these envoys found the former ambassadors, Severus and Flaccianus, at Carthage; and on asking them what they had done, they learnt that they had been referred for a hearing to the deputy and the count. And immediately after this Severus was attacked by a dangerous illness and died; but notwithstanding what they had heard, the new ambassadors proceeded on their journey to the court.

17. After this, when Palladius arrived in Africa, the count, who knew on what account he had come, and who had been warned before to take measures for his own safety, sent orders to the principal officers of the army by certain persons who were in his secrets, to pay over to him, as being a person of great influence, and being the person most nearly connected with the principal nobles of the palace, the chief part of the money for the soldiers' pay which he had brought over, and they obeyed him.

18. So he, having been thus suddenly enriched, reached Leptis; and that he might arrive at a knowledge of the truth, he took with him to the districts that had been laid waste, Erecthius and Aristomenes, two citizens of great eloquence and reputation, who freely unfolded to him the distress which their fellow-citizens and the inhabitants of the adjacent districts had suffered. They showed him everything openly; and so he returned after seeing the lamentable desolation of the province: and reproaching Romanus for his inactivity, he threatened to

report to the emperor an accurate statement of everything which he had seen.

19. He, inflamed with anger and indignation, retorted that he also should soon make a report, that the man who had been sent as an incorruptible secretary had converted to his own uses all the money which had been sent out as a donation to the soldiers.

20. The consequence was that Palladius, being hampered by the consciousness of his flagitious conduct, proceeded from henceforth in harmony with Romanus, and when he returned to court, he deceived Valentinian with atrocious falsehoods, affirming that the citizens of Tripoli complained without reason. Therefore he was sent back to Africa a second time with Jovinus, the last of all the ambassadors (for Pancratius had died at Treves), in order that he, in conjunction with the deputy, might inquire into everything connected with the second embassy. And besides this, the emperor ordered the tongues of Erecthius and Aristomenes to be cut out, because this same Palladius had intimated that they made some malignant and disloyal statements.

21. The secretary, following the deputy, as had been arranged, came to Tripoli. When his arrival was known, Romanus sent one of his servants thither with all speed, and Cæcilius, his assessor, who was a native of the province; and by their agency (whether they employed bribery or deceit is doubtful) all the citizens were won over to accuse Jovinus, vigorously asserting that he had never issued any of the commands which he had reported to the emperor; carrying their iniquity to such a pitch, that Jovinus himself was compelled by them to confess, to his own great danger, that he had made a false report to the emperor.

22. When these events were learnt from Palladius on his return, Valentinian, being always inclined to severe measures, commanded the execution of Jovinus as the author of such a report, and of Cælestinus, Concordius, and Lucius, as privy to it, and partners in it. He also commanded Ruricius, the president, to be put to death for falsehood; the charge against him being aggravated by the circumstance that his report contained some violent and intemperate expressions.

23. Ruricius was executed at Sitifis; the rest were condemned at Utica by the sentence of the deputy Crescens. But before the death of the ambassadors, Flaccianus, while being examined by the deputy and the count, and while resolutely defending his own safety, was assailed with abuse, and then attacked with loud outcries and violence by the angry soldiers, and was nearly killed; the charge which they made against him being that the cause which had prevented the people of

Tripoli from being defended was, that they had refused to furnish necessaries for the use of any expedition.

24. On this account he was thrown into prison, till the emperor could be consulted on his case, and should decide what ought to be done; but his gaolers were tampered with, as was believed, and he escaped from prison and fled to Rome, where he concealed himself for some time, till his death.

25. In consequence of this memorable catastrophe, Tripoli, which had been often harassed by external and domestic calamities, brought forward no further accusations against those who had left it undefended, knowing that the eternal eye of justice was awake, as well as the avenging furies of the ambassadors and the president. And a long time afterwards the following event took place:—Palladius, having been dismissed from the military service, and stript of all that nourished his pride, retired into private life.

26. And when Theodosius, that magnificent commander of armies, came into Africa to put down Firmus, who was entertaining some pernicious designs, and, as he was ordered, began to examine the movable effects of Romanus, he found among his papers a letter of a certain person named Meterius, containing this passage: "Meterius, to his lord and patron, Romanus;" and at the end of the letter many expressions unconnected with its general subject. "Palladius, who has been cashiered, salutes you. He who says he was cashiered for no other reason than that in the case of the people of Tripoli he made a false report to the sacred ears."

27. When this letter was sent to the court and read, Meterius was arrested by order of Valentinian, and confessed that the letter was his writing. Therefore Palladius also was ordered to appear, and reflecting on all the crimes he had committed, while at a halting place on the road, he watched an opportunity afforded him by the absence of his guards, as soon as it got dark (for, as it was a festival of the Christian religion, they passed the whole night in the church), and hanged himself.

28. The news of this propitious event—the death of the principal cause of their sad troubles—being known, Erecthius and Aristomenes, who when they first heard that their tongues were ordered to be cut out for sedition, had escaped, now issued from their hiding-places. And when the emperor Gratian was informed of the wicked deceit that had been practised (for by this time Valentinian was dead), their fears vanished, and they were sent to have their cause heard before Hesperus the proconsul and Flavian the deputy, men whose justice was sup-

ported by the righteous authority of the emperor, and who, after putting Cæcilius to the torture, learnt from his clear confession that he himself had persuaded the citizens to bring false accusations against the ambassadors. These actions were followed by a report which gave the fullest possible account of all that had taken place, to which no answer was given.

29. And that the whole story might want nothing of tragic interest, the following occurrence also took place after the curtain had fallen. Romanus went to court, taking with him Cæcilius, with the intent to accuse the judges as having been unduly biassed in favour of the province; and being received graciously by Merobaudes, he demanded that some more necessary witnesses should be summoned. And when they had come to Milan, and had shown by proofs which seemed correct, though these were false, that they had been falsely accused, they were acquitted, and returned home. Valentinian was still alive, when after these events which we have related, Remigius also retired from public life, and afterwards hanged himself, as we shall relate in the proper place.

Notes

[165] See the Iliad, XVIII. 1. 645, where Ajax prays:—
"Lord of earth and air,
O King! O Father, hear my humble prayer!
Dispel this cloud, the light of heaven restore;
Give me to see, and Ajax asks no more!
If Greece must perish, we thy will obey,
But let us perish in the face of day."
Pope's *Trans.*, 1. 727, etc.

[166] See Gibbon, vol. III. p. 97 (Bohn's edition).

[167] This is an allusion to the story of Castor and Pollux bringing news of the victory gained at the battle of Regillus to Domitius (B.C. 496). The legend adds that they stroked his black beard, which immediately became red; from which he and his posterity derived the surname of Ænobarbus.—See Dion. Hal. vi. 13.

[168] Marius Maximus was an author who wrote an account of the lives of the Cæsars.

[169] § 20 is mutilated, so that no sense can be extracted from the remainder of it.

[170] Two brothers who had been colleagues in several important offices, and who were at last put to death together by Commodus.

[171] The end of § 22 is also mutilated.

[172] This passage, again, seems hopelessly mutilated.

[173] Cicero, de Amicitia, c. xxi.

[174] These are not in reality noble names, but names derived from low occupa-tions. Trulla is a dish; Salsula, belonging to pickles, &c.

[175] Compare Juvenal's description of the circumspect in his time:—

"Atque duas tantum resarexius optat
Panem et Circenses."

BOOK XXIX

I.

A.D. 371.

§ 1. At the conclusion of the winter, Sapor, king of Persia, being full of cruelty and arrogance from the confidence engendered by his former battles, having completed his army to its full number, and greatly strengthened it, sent out a force of cuirassiers, archers, and mercenary troops, to make an invasion of our territories.

2. Against this force, Count Trajan and Vadomarius, the ex-king of the Allemanni, advanced with a mighty army, having been enjoined by the emperor to remember his orders to act on the defensive rather than on the offensive against the Persians.

3. When they arrived at Vagabanta, a place well suited for the manœuvres of the legions, they supported against their will a rapid charge which was made upon them by the squadrons of the enemy, and retreated with the design not to be the first to slay any of the hostile soldiers, and not to be looked upon as guilty of having broken the treaty. At last, under the pressure of extreme necessity, they came to an engagement with the barbarians, and after having slain a great number of them, were victorious.

4. During the cessation of regular operations which ensued, several slight skirmishes occurred through the impatience of both armies, which ended with different results; and at last the summer ended, and a truce was agreed to by common consent, and the two armies separated, though the generals were violently inflamed against each other. The king of Parthia, intending to pass the winter at Ctesiphon, returned to his own home, and the Roman emperor went to Antioch; and while he tarried there, in complete security from foreign enemies, he had very nearly perished through domestic treachery, as shall be related in the coming narrative.

5. A certain Procopius, a restless man, at all times covetous and fond of disturbances, had persuaded Anatolius and Spudasius, officers about the palace, who had been ordered to restore what they had appropriated from the treasury, to bring a plot against the Count Fortunatianus, who was especially obnoxious as being represented to be the principal demander of this restitution. He, being a man of naturally harsh temper, was thereupon inflamed almost to insanity, and exercising the authority of the office which he filled, he delivered up to trial before the tribunal of the prefect a person of the lowest birth, named Palladius, for being a poisoner in the train of Anatolius and Spudasius; Heliodorus, also an interpreter of the Fates from the events which happened at any one's birth; with the intent that they should be compelled by torture to relate all that they knew.

6. And when they came with rigid scrutiny to inquire into what had been done or attempted, Palladius boldly exclaimed, that the matters now under investigation were trivial, and such as might well be passed over; that he himself, if he might be allowed to speak, could bring forward some circumstances both formidable and more important, which, having been prepared with great exertion, would throw everything into confusion, if they were not provided against beforehand. Being ordered to explain without fear all he knew, he made a deposition at great length, affirming that Fidustius the president, and Pergamius and Irenæus, had secretly learnt, by the detestable arts of

450

magic, the name of the person who should become emperor after Valens.

7. Fidustius was at once arrested (for he happened by chance be on the spot), and being brought secretly before the emperor, when confronted with the informer, he did not attempt by any denial to throw a doubt on what was already revealed, but laid open the whole of this wretched plot; confessing in plain words, that he himself, with Hilarius and Patricius, men skilled in the art of soothsaying, of whom Hilarius had filled high offices in the palace, had held consultations about the future possessors of the empire; that by secret arts they had searched into the Fates, which had revealed to them the name of an excellent emperor, admonishing them at the same time that a miserable end awaited the investigators of these omens.[176]

8. And while they were hesitating, unable to decide who at that moment was superior to all other men in vigour of mind, Theodorus appeared to excel all the rest, a man who had already arrived at the second class of secretaries. And in truth he deserved the opinion which they entertained of him; for he was descended from an ancient and illustrious family in Gaul; he had been liberally educated from his earliest childhood; he was eminent for modesty, prudence, humanity, courtesy, and literature. He always appeared superior to the post or place which he was filling, and was equally popular among high and low, and he was nearly the only man whose tongue was never unbridled, but who always reflected on what he was going to say, yet without ever being restrained by any fear of danger.

9. Fidustius, who had been tortured so severely that he was at the point of death, added further, that all that he had now stated he had communicated to Theodorus by the intervention of Eucærius, a man of great literary accomplishments, and of very high reputation; indeed, he had a little time before governed Asia with the title of proprefect.

10. Eucærius was now thrown into prison; and when a report of all that had taken place was, as usual, laid before the emperor, his amazing ferocity burst out more unrestrainedly than ever, like a burning firebrand, being fed by the base adulation of many persons, and especially of Modestus, at that time prefect of the prætorium.

11. He, being every day alarmed at the prospect of a successor, addressed himself to the task of conciliating Valens, who was of a rustic and rather simple character, by tickling him with all kinds of disguised flattery and caresses, calling his uncouth language and rude expressions "flowers of Ciceronian eloquence." Indeed, to raise his

vanity higher, he would have promised to raise him up to the stars if he had desired it.

12. So Theodorus also was ordered to be arrested with all speed at Constantinople, to which city he had repaired on some private business, and to be brought to the court. And while he was on his way back, in consequence of various informations and trials which were carried on day and night, numbers of people were dragged away from the most widely separated countries—men eminent for their birth and high authority.

13. The public prisons, being now completely filled, could no longer contain the crowds which were confined in them, while private houses were equally crammed to suffocation, for nearly every one was a prisoner, and every man shuddered to think when it might be his turn or that of his nearest relations.

14. At last Theodorus himself arrived, in deep mourning, and half dead through fear. And while he was kept concealed in some obscure place in the vicinity, and all things were being got ready for his intended examination, the trumpet of civil discord suddenly sounded.

15. And because that man who knowingly passes over facts appears to be an equally unfaithful historian with him who invents circumstances which never happened, we do not deny (what, in fact, is quite undoubted) that the safety of Valens had often before been attacked by secret machinations, and was now in the greatest possible danger. And that a sword, as one may say, was presented to his throat by the officers of the army, and only averted by Fate, which was reserving him for lamentable misfortunes in Thrace.

16. For one day as he was taking a gentle nap in the afternoon, in a shady spot between Antioch and Seleucia, he was attacked by Sallust, at that time an officer of the Scutarii; and on various other occasions he was plotted against by many other persons, from whose treacherous designs he only escaped because the precise moment of his death had been determined at his birth by Destiny.

17. As sometimes happened in the times of the emperors Commodus and Severus, whose safety was continually assailed with extreme violence, so that after many various dangers at the hands of their countrymen, the one was dangerously wounded by a dagger in the amphitheatre, as he entered it for the purpose of witnessing an entertainment, by a senator named Quintianus, a man of wicked ambition. The other, when extremely old, was assailed as he was lying in his bedchamber, by a centurion of the name of Saturninus, who was

instigated to the act by Plautian the prefect, and would have been killed if his youthful son had not come to his assistance.

18. Valens, therefore, was to be excused for taking every precaution to defend his life, which traitors were endeavouring to take. But it was an unpardonable fault in him that, through tyrannical pride, he, with haste and with inconsiderate and malicious persecution, inflicted the same severities on the innocent as on the guilty, making no distinction between their deserts; so that while the judges were still doubting about their guilt, the emperor had made up his mind about their punishment, and men learnt that they were condemned before they knew that they were suspected.

19. But his obstinate resolution was strengthened since it received a spur from his own avarice, and that also of those who at that time were about the palace, and were constantly seeking new sources of gain; while if on any rare occasion any mention was made of humanity, they styled it slackness; and by their bloodthirsty flatteries perverted the resolution of a man who bore men's lives on the tip of his tongue, guiding it in the worst direction, and assailing everything with unseemly confusion, while seeking to accomplish the total ruin of the most opulent houses.

20. For Valens was a man who was especially exposed and open to the approaches of treacherous advisers, being tainted with two vices of a most mischievous character: one, that when he was ashamed of being angry, that very shame only rendered him the more intolerably furious; and secondly, that the stories which, with the easiness of access of a private individual, he heard in secret whispers, he took at once to be true and certain, because his haughty idea of the imperial dignity did not permit him to examine whether they were true or not.

21. The consequence was that, under an appearance of clemency, numbers of innocent men were driven from their homes, and sent into exile: and their property was confiscated to the public treasury, and then seized by himself for his private uses; so that the owners, after their condemnation, had no means of subsistence but such as they could beg; and were worn out with the distresses of the most miserable poverty. For fear of which that wise old poet Theognis advises a man to rush even into the sea.[177]

22. And even if any one should grant that these sentences were in some instances right, yet it surely was an odious severity; and from this conduct of his it was remarked that the maxim was sound which says, "that there is no sentence more cruel than that which, while seeming to spare, is still harsh."

23. Therefore all the chief magistrates and the prefect of the prætorium, to whom the conduct of these investigations was committed, having been assembled together, the racks were got ready, and the weights, and lead, and scourges, and other engines of torture. And all places resounded with the horrors of the cruel voice of the executioners, and the cries uttered amid the clanking of chains: "Hold him!" "Shut him up!" "Squeeze him!" "Hide him!" and other yells uttered by the ministers of those hateful duties.

24. And since we saw numbers condemned to death after having endured cruel torture, everything being thrown into complete confusion as if in perfect darkness, because the complete recollection of everything which then took place has in some degree escaped me, I will mention briefly what I do remember.

25. Among the first who were summoned before the bench, was Pergamius, who, as we have already mentioned, was betrayed by Palladius, who accused him of having arrived at a foreknowledge of certain events through wicked incantations. As he was a man of exceeding eloquence, and very likely to say dangerous things, and after some very trivial interrogatories had been put to him, seeing that the judges were hesitating what questions to put first and what last, he began himself to harangue them boldly, and shouting out the names with a loud voice and without any cessation, he named several thousand persons as accomplices with himself, demanding that people should be brought forward to be accused of great crimes from every part of the empire, up to the very shores of the great Atlantic. The task that he thus seemed to be putting together for them was too arduous; so they condemned him to death; and afterwards put whole troops of others to death, till they came to the case of Theodorus, which was regarded, after the manner of the Olympian games, as a crowning of the whole.

26. The same day, among other circumstances, this melancholy event took place, that Salia, who a little while before had been the chief treasurer in Thrace, when he was about to be brought out of his prison to have his cause heard, and was putting on his shoes, as if suddenly overwhelmed by the dread of his impending destruction, died in the hands of his gaolers.

27. So when the court was opened, and when the judges exhibited the decrees of the law, though, in accordance with the desire of the emperor, they moderated the severity of the charges brought before them, one general alarm seized all people. For Valens had now so wholly departed from justice, and had become so accomplished in the infliction of injury, that he was like a wild beast in an amphitheatre;

454

and if any one who had been brought before the court escaped, he grew furious beyond all restraint.

28. Presently Patricius and Hilarius were brought before the court, and were ordered to enumerate the whole series of their actions: and as they differed a little at the beginning of their statement, they were both put to the torture, and presently the tripod which they had used was brought in;[178] and they, being reduced now to the greatest extremity, gave a true account of the whole affair from the very beginning. And first Hilarius spoke as follows:—

29. "We did construct, most noble judges, under most unhappy auspices, this little unfortunate tripod which you see, in the likeness of that at Delphi, making it of laurel twigs: and having consecrated it with imprecations of mysterious verses, and with many decorations and repeated ceremonies, in all proper order, we at last moved it; and the manner in which we moved it as often as we consulted it upon any secret affair, was as follows:—

30. "It was placed in the middle of a building, carefully purified on all sides by Arabian perfumes; and a plain round dish was placed upon it, made of different metals. On the outer side of which the four-and-twenty letters of the alphabet were engraved with great skill, being separated from one another by distances measured with great precision.

31. "Then a person clothed in linen garments, and shod with slippers of linen, with a small linen cap on his head, bearing in his hand sprigs of vervain as a plant of good omen, in set verses, propitiated the deity who presides over foreknowledge, and thus took his station by this dish, according to all the rules of the ceremony. Then over the tripod he balanced a ring which he held suspended by a flaxen thread of extreme fineness, and which had also been consecrated with mystic ceremonies. And as this ring touched and bounded off from the different letters which still preserved their distances distinct, he made with these letters, by the order in which he touched them, verses in the heroic metre, corresponding to the questions which we had asked; the verses being also perfect in metre and rhythm; like the answers of the Pythia which are so celebrated, or those given by the oracles of the Branchidæ.

32. "Then, when we asked who should succeed the present emperor, since it was said that it would be a person of universal accomplishments, the ring bounded up, and touched the two syllables ΘΕΟ; and then as it added another letter, some one of the bystanders exclaimed that Theodorus was pointed out by the inevitable decrees of

Fate. We asked no further questions concerning the matter: for it seemed quite plain to us that he was the man who was intended."

33. And when he had with this exactness laid the knowledge of this affair open to the eyes of the judges, he added with great benevolence, that Theodorus knew nothing of the matter. When after this they were asked whether the oracles which they had consulted had given them any foreknowledge of their present sufferings, they repeated these well-known verses which clearly pronounce that this employment of investigating those high secrets would cost them their lives. Nevertheless, they added, that the Furies equally threatened the judges themselves, and also the emperor, breathing only slaughter and conflagration against them. It will be enough to quote the three final verses.

"Οὐ μὰν νηποινίγε σὸν ἔσσεται αἷμα, καὶ αὐτοῖς
Τισφόνη βαρύμηνις ἐφοπλίζει κανιὸν οἶτον
Ἐν πεδίοισι Μίμαντος ἀλαλεμένοισιν ἄρηα."

"Thy blood shall not fall unaveng'd on earth:
The fierce Tisiphone still keeps her eye
Fixed on thy slayers; arming evil fate
Against them when arrayed on Mima's plain
They seek to stem the tide of horrid war."

When he had read these verses they were both tortured with great severity, and carried away dead.

34. Afterwards, that the whole workshop where the wickedness had been wrought might be disclosed to the world, a great number of men of rank were brought in, among whom were some of the original promoters of the whole business. And when each, regarding nothing but his own personal safety, sought to turn the destruction which menaced himself in some other quarter, by the permission of the judges, Theodorus began to address them. First of all, he humbled himself with entreaties for pardon; then being compelled to answer more precisely to the charges alleged, he proved that he, after having been informed of the whole affair by Eucærius, was prevented by him from repeating it to the emperor, as he had often attempted to do: since Eucærius affirmed that what did not spring from a lawless desire of reigning, but from some fixed law of inevitable fate, would surely come to pass.

35. Eucærius, when cruelly tortured, confirmed this statement by his own confession. His own letters were employed to convict Theodorus, letters which he had written to Hilarius full of indirect hints, which showed that he had conceived a sure hope of such events from

the prophecies of the soothsayers; and was not inclined to delay, but was looking for an opportunity of attaining the object of his desires.

36. After the establishment of these facts, the prisoners were removed; and Eutropius, who at that time was governing Asia with the rank of proconsul, having been involved in the accusation as having been a partisan of theirs, was nevertheless acquitted; being exculpated by Pasiphilus the philosopher, who, though cruelly tortured to make him implicate Eutropius by a wicked lie, could not be moved from his vigorous resolution and fortitude.

37. To that was added the philosopher Simonides, a young man, but the most rigidly virtuous of all men in our time. An information had been laid against him as having been made aware of what was going on by Fidustius, as he saw that his cause depended, not on its truth, but on the will of one man, avowed that he had known all that was alleged, but had forborne to mention it out of regard for his character for constancy.

38. When all these matters had been minutely inquired into, the emperor, in answer to the question addressed to him by the judges, ordered them all to be condemned and at once executed: and it was not without shuddering that the vast populace beheld the mournful spectacle; filling the whole air with lamentations (since they looked on the misery of each individual as threatening the whole community with a similar fate) when the whole number of accused persons, except Simonides, were executed in a melancholy manner. Simonides being reserved to be burnt alive by the express command of the savage judge, who was enraged at his dignified constancy.

39. And he, abandoning life as an imperious mistress, and defying the sudden destruction thus coming on him, was burnt without giving any sign of shrinking; imitating, in his death, the philosopher Peregrinus, surnamed Proteus, who having determined to quit the world, at the quinquennial games of Olympia, in the sight of all Greece, mounted a funeral pile which he had built himself, and was there burnt alive.

40. After his death, on the ensuing days a vast multitude of almost all ranks, whose names it would be too arduous a task to enumerate, being convicted by calumnious accusations, were despatched by the executioners, after having been first exhausted by every description of torture. Some were put to death without a moment's breathing-time or delay, while the question was still being asked whether they deserved to be punished at all; in fact, men were slaughtered like sheep in all directions.

41. After this, innumerable quantities of papers, and many heaps of volumes were collected, and burnt under the eyes of the judges, having been taken out of various houses as unlawful books; in order to lessen the unpopularity arising from so many executions, though in fact, the greater part of them were books teaching various kinds of liberal accomplishments, or books of law.

42. Not long afterwards, Maximus, the celebrated philosopher, a man of vast reputation for learning, from whose eloquent discourses the emperor Julian derived his great learning and wisdom, being accused of having been acquainted with the verses of the oracle mentioned above, and confessing that he had known something of them, but that he had not divulged what he knew, as being bound to keep silence out of consideration for his promise; but adding that he had of his own accord predicted that those who had consulted the oracle would perish by public execution, was conducted to Ephesus, his native place, and there beheaded. And thus by his own forfeiture of life, he found that the injustice of a judge is the worst of all crimes.

43. Diogenes, too, a man of noble family, great forensic eloquence and pre-eminent courtesy, who had some time before been governor of Bithynia, being entangled in the toils of wicked falsehood, was put to death in order to afford a pretext for seizing on his ample patrimony.

44. Alypius also, who had been governor of Britain, a man of most delightful mildness of temper, and who had lived a tranquil and retired life (since even against such as him did Injustice stretch forth her hands), was involved in the greatest misfortune; and was accused with Hierocles his son, a youth of most amiable disposition of having been guilty of poisoning, on the unsupported information of a low fellow named Diogenes, who had been tortured with extreme severity to force him to make confessions which might please the emperor, or rather, which might please his accuser. When his limbs could no longer endure their punishment, he was burnt alive; and Alypius, after having had his property confiscated, was condemned to banishment, though by an extraordinary piece of good fortune he received back his son after he had been condemned, and had actually been led out to suffer a miserable death.

II.

§ 1. During all this time, Palladius, the original cause of these miseries, whom we have already spoken of as having been arrested by Fortunatianus, being, from the lowness of his original condition, a man ready to fall into every kind of wickedness, by heaping one murder on another diffused mourning and lamentation over the whole empire.

2. For being allowed to name any persons he chose, without distinction of rank, as men contaminated by the practice of forbidden arts, like a huntsman who has learnt to mark the secret tracks of wild beasts, he enclosed many victims within his wretched toils, some as being polluted with a knowledge of poisonings, others as accomplices of those who were guilty of treason.

3. And that wives too might not have leisure to weep over the miseries of their husbands, officers were sent at once to seal up the house of any one who was condemned, and who, while examining all the furniture, slipped in among it old women's incantations, or ridiculous love-tokens, contrived to bring destruction on the innocent; and then, when these things were mentioned before the bench, where neither law, nor religion, nor equity were present to separate truth from falsehood, those whom they thus accused, though utterly void of offence, without any distinction, youths, and decrepit old men, without being heard in their defence, found their property confiscated, and were hurried off to execution in litters.

4. One of the consequences in the eastern provinces was, that from fear of similar treatment, people burnt all their libraries; so great was the terror which seized upon all ranks. For, to cut my story short, at that time all of us crawled about as if in Cimmerian darkness, in the same kind of dread as the guest of Dionysius of Sicily; who, while feasting at a banquet more irksome than famine itself, saw a sword suspended over his head by a single horsehair.

5. There was a man named Bassianus, of most noble family, a secretary, and eminently distinguished for his military services, who, on a charge of having entertained ambitious projects, and of having sought oracles concerning their issue, though he declared he had only consulted the oracles to know the sex of his next child, was saved indeed from death by the great interest made for him by his relations who protected him; but he was stripped of all his splendid inheritance.

6. Amid all this destruction and ruin, Heliodorus, that hellish colleague of Palladius in bringing about these miseries (being what the common people call a mathematician), having been admitted into the secret conferences of the imperial palace, and been tempted by every

kind of caress and cajolery to relate all he knew or could invent, was putting forth his fatal stings.

7. For he was carefully feasted on the most delicate food, and furnished with large sums of money to give to his concubines; and he strutted about in every direction with a pompous, haughty countenance, and was universally dreaded. Being the more confident and arrogant, because as he was high chamberlain, he could go constantly and openly to the brothels, in which, as he desired, he was freely entertained, while revealing the edicts of the "parental guardian of the state," which were destined to be disastrous to many.

8. And through his means, as an advocate at the bar, Valens was instructed beforehand in what would most contribute to success—what to place in the first part of his speech, and with what figures, and what inventions to work up splendid passages.

9. And as it would take a long time to enumerate all the devices of that villain, I will mention this one only, which, in its rash boldness, assailed the very pillars of the patrician dignity. As I have said before, he was raised to exceeding arrogance by being admitted to the secret conferences of the princes; and being, from the lowness of his birth, a man ready for any wickedness, he laid an information against that illustrious pair of consuls, the brothers Eusebius and Hypatius, relations of the former emperor Constantius, as having conceived desires of a higher fortune, and formed projects and entered into enterprises for the attainment of supreme power. Adding, in order to procure additional credit for this falsehood, that Eusebius had had a set of imperial robes prepared for him.

10. And when the story had been swallowed willingly, Valens raging and threatening, a prince who never ought to have had any power at all, because he thought that everything, even injustice, was in his power, was incessantly active in causing the production, even from the most distant countries, of all those whom the lawless accuser in profound security had insisted ought to be produced; and further commanded a prosecution to be instituted on the criminal charge.

11. And when equity had long been tossed to and fro by knotty difficulties, while that abandoned profligate persisted with unyielding obstinacy in maintaining the truth of his assertions, while the severest tortures were unable to wring any confession from the prisoners, and when every circumstance proved that those eminent men were free from all consciousness of anything of the kind, still the false accuser was treated with the same respect as he had previously received. But though the prisoners were sentenced to exile and a heavy fine, a short

time afterwards they were recalled from banishment, restored to their former rank and dignity, and their fine repaid.

12. Still after all these shameful transactions, the prince did not proceed with any more moderation or decency than before; never considering that in a wise government it is well not to be too keen in hunting out offences, even as a means of inflicting distress upon one's enemies; and that nothing is so unbecoming as to display a bitterness of disposition in connection with supreme authority.

13. But when Heliodorus died, whether of sickness or through some deliberate violence is uncertain (I should not like to say, and I wish that the facts themselves were equally silent), many men of rank in mourning robes, among whom were these two brothers of consular rank, by the express command of the emperor, attended his funeral when he was borne to his grave by the undertakers.

14. At that time, and in that place, the whole vileness and stupidity of the ruler of the empire was publicly displayed. When he was entreated to abstain from abandoning himself to inconsolable grief, he remained obstinately inflexible, as if he had stopped his ears with wax to pass the rocks of the Sirens.

15. But at last, being overcome by the pertinacious entreaties of his court, he ordered some persons to go on foot, bareheaded, and with their hands folded, to the burial-place of this wretched gladiator to do him honour. One shudders now to recollect the decree by which so many men of high rank were humiliated, especially some of consular dignity, after all their truncheons and robes of honour, and all the worldly parade of having their names recorded in the annals of their nation.

16. Among them all, our friend Hypatius was most conspicuous, recommended as he was to every one by the beauty of the virtues which he had practised from his youth; being a man of quiet and gentle wisdom, preserving an undeviating honesty combined with the greatest courtesy of manner, so that he conferred a fresh lustre on the glory of his ancestors, and was an ornament to his posterity, by the memorable actions which he performed in the office of prefect, to which he was twice appointed.

17. At the same time, this circumstance came to crown the other splendid actions of Valens, that, while in the case of others he gave way to such furious violence, that he was even vexed when the severity of their punishment was terminated by death, yet he pardoned Pollentianus, the tribune, a man stained with such enormous wickedness, that at that very time he was convicted on his own confession of

having cut out the womb of a living woman and taken from it her child, in order to summon forth spirits from the shades below, and to consult them about a change in the empire. He looked on this wretch with the eye of friendship, in spite of the murmurs of the whole bench of senators, and discharged him in safety, suffering him to retain not only his life, but his vast riches and full rank in the army.

18. O most glorious learning, granted by the express gift of heaven to happy mortals, thou who hast often refined even vicious natures! How many faults in the darkness of that age wouldst thou have corrected if Valens had ever been taught by thee that, according to the definition of wise men, empire is nothing else but the care of the safety of others; and that it is the duty of a good emperor to restrain power, to resist any desire to possess all things, and all implacability of passion, and to know, as the dictator Cæsar used to say, "That the recollection of cruelty was an instrument to make old age miserable!" And therefore that it behoves any one who is about to pass a sentence affecting the life and existence of a man, who is a portion of the world, and makes up the complement of living creatures, to hesitate long and much, and never to give way to intemperate haste in a case in which what is done is irrevocable. According to that example well known to all antiquity.

19. When Dolabella was proconsul in Asia, a matron at Smyrna confessed that she had poisoned her son and her husband, because she had discovered that they had murdered a son whom she had had by a former husband. Her case was adjourned—the council to whom it had been referred being in doubt how to draw a line between just revenge and unprovoked crime; and so she was remitted to the judgment of the Areopagus, those severe Athenian judges, who are said to have decided disputes even among the gods. They, when they had heard the case, ordered the woman and her accuser to appear before them again in a hundred years, to avoid either acquitting a poisoner, or punishing one who had been the avenger of her kindred. So that is never to be thought too slow which is the last of all things.

20. After all the acts of various iniquity already mentioned, and after even the free persons who were allowed to survive had been thus shamefully branded, the eye of Justice which never sleeps, that unceasing witness and avenger of events, became more attentive and vigilant. For the avenging Furies of those who had been put to death, working on the everlasting deity with their just complaints, kindled the torches of war, to confirm the truth of the oracle, which had given warning that no crime can be perpetrated with impunity.

21. While the affairs thus narrated were taking place, Antioch was exposed to great distress through domestic dissension, though not molested by any attacks on the side of Parthia. But the horrid troop of Furies, which after having caused all sorts of miseries there, had quitted that city, now settled on the neck of the whole of Asia, as will be seen in what follows.

22. A certain native of Trent, by name Festus, a man of the lowest obscurity of birth, being a relation of Maximin, and one who had assumed the manly robe at the same time with himself, was cherished by him as a companion, and by the will of the Fates had now crossed over to the east, and having there become governor of Syria, and master of the records, he set a very good and respectable example of lenity. From this he was promoted to govern Asia with the rank of proconsul, being thus, as the saying is, borne on with a fair wind to glory.

23. And hearing that Maximin caused the destruction of every virtuous man, he began from this time to denounce his actions as mischievous and disgraceful. But when he saw that, in consequence of the removal of those persons whom he had impiously put to death, that wicked man had arrived at the dignity of prefect, he began to be excited to similar conduct and similar hopes. And suddenly changing his character like an actor, he applied himself to the study of doing injury, and went about with fixed and severe eyes, trusting that he also should soon become a prefect, if he only polluted himself with the blood of innocent men.

24. And although there are many and various instances in which, to put the best construction on them, he acted with great harshness, still it will be sufficient to enumerate a few, which are notorious and commonly spoken of, seeming to be done in rivalry of the deeds which were committed at Rome; for the principle of good and bad actions is the same everywhere, even if the importance of the circumstances be unequal.

25. There was a philosopher named Cæranius, a man of no inconsiderable merit, whom he put to death with the most cruel tortures, and without any one coming forward to avenge him, because, when writing familiarly to his wife, he had put a postscript in Greek, "σὺ δὲ νόει, καὶ στέφε τὴν πύλην."—"Do you take care and adorn the gate," which is a common expression to let the hearer know that something of importance is to be done.

26. There was a certain simple old woman who was wont to cure intermittent fever by a gentle incantation, whom he put to death as a

witch, after she had been summoned, with his consent, to his daughter, and had cured her.

27. There was a certain citizen of high respectability, among whose papers, when they were searched by the officers on some business or other, was found the nativity of some one of the name of Valens. He, when asked on what account he had troubled himself about the star of the emperor, had repelled the accusation by declaring that it was his own brother Valens whose nativity was thus found, and when he promised to bring abundant proof that he had long been dead, the judges would not wait for evidence of the truth of his assertion, but put him to the torture and cruelly slew him.

28. A young man was seen in the bath to put the fingers of each hand alternately against the marble and against his own chest, and then to repeat the names of the seven vowels, fancying that a remedy for a pain in the stomach. For this he was brought before the court, put to the torture, and then beheaded.

III.

§ 1. These events, and the account of Gaul to which I am now about to proceed, will cause some interruption to the narration of occurrences in the metropolis. Among many terrible circumstances, I find that Maximin was still prefect, who by the wide extent of his power was a cruel prompter to the emperor, who combined the most unrestrained licence with unbounded power. Whoever, therefore, considers what I have related, must also reflect on the other facts which have been passed over, and, like a prudent man, he will pardon me if I do not record everything which the wickedness of certain counsels has occasioned by exaggerating every accusation?

2. For while severity, the foe of all right principles, increased, Valentinian, being a man of a naturally ferocious disposition, when Maximin arrived, having no one to give him good advice or to restrain him, proceeded, as if hurried on by a storm of winds and waves, to all kinds of cruel actions; so that when angry, his voice, his countenance, his gait, and his complexion, were continually changing. And of this passionate intemperance there are many undoubted instances, of which it will be sufficient to recount a few.

3. A certain grown-up youth, of those called pages, having been appointed to take care of a Spartan hound which had been brought out for hunting, let him loose before the appointed moment, because the animal, in its efforts to escape, leaped upon him and bit him; and for this he was beaten to death and buried the same day.

4. The master of a workshop, who had brought the emperor an offering of a breastplate most exquisitely polished, and who was therefore in expectation of a reward, was ordered by him to be put to death because the steel was of less weight than he considered requisite.... There was a certain native, of Epirus, a priest of the Christian religion.[179] ...

5. Constantianus, the master of the stables, having ventured to change a few of the horses, to select which he had been despatched to Sardinia, was, by his order, stoned to death. Athanasius, a very popular character, being suspected by him of some levity in the language he held among the common people, was sentenced to be burnt alive if he ever did anything of the kind again; and not long afterwards, being accused of having practised magic, he was actually burnt, no pardon being given even to one whose devices had often afforded the emperor great amusement.

6. Africanus was an advocate of great diligence, residing in Rome; he had had the government of one province, and aspired to that of another. But when Theodosius, the commander of the cavalry, supported his petition for such an office, the emperor answered him somewhat rudely, "Away with you, O count, and change the head of the man who wishes to have his province changed." And by this sentence a man of great eloquence perished, only because, like many others, he wished for higher preferment.

7. Claudian and Sallust were officers of the Jovian legion, who had gradually risen to the rank of tribunes; but they were accused by some man of the most despicable baseness of having said something in favour of Procopius when he aimed at the imperial power. And when a diligent investigation into this charge had proved ineffectual, the emperor gave orders to the captains of the cavalry who had been employed in it, to condemn Claudian to banishment, and to pass sentence of death upon Sallust, promising that he would reprieve him as he was being led to execution. The sentence was passed, as he commanded; but Sallust was not reprieved, nor was Claudian recalled from exile till after the death of Valentinian.... After they had been exposed to frequent tortures.

8. Nevertheless after so many persons had been put to the question, some of whom had even expired under the severity of their tortures, still no traces of the alleged crimes could be discovered. In this affair some of the body-guards, who had been sent to arrest certain persons, were, in a most unusual manner, beaten to death.

9. The mind shudders at the idea of recapitulating all that took place, and, indeed, dreads to do so, lest we should appear to make a business of pointing out the vices of an emperor who, in other respects, had many good qualities. But this one circumstance may not be passed over in silence nor suppressed, that he kept two ferocious she-bears who were used to eat men; and they had names, Golden Camel and Innocence, and these beasts he took such care of that he had their dens close to his bedchamber; and appointed over them trusty keepers who were bound to take especial care that the odious fury of these monsters should never be checked. At last he had Innocence set free, after he had seen the burial of many corpses which she had torn to pieces, giving her the range of the forests as a reward for her services.[180]

IV.

§ 1. These actions are the most undeniable proof of his habits and real character; but even the most obstinate disparager of his disposition cannot deny him the praise of great ability, which never forgot the interests of the state; especially when it is recollected, that perhaps it is a greater and more beneficial, as well as difficult, task to control the barbarians by means of an army, than to repulse them. And when ... If any one of the enemy moved, he was seen from the watch-towers and immediately overwhelmed.

2. But among many other subjects of anxiety, the first and most important thing of all which was agitated, was to seize alive, either by force or by trickery, as Julian had formerly taken Vadomarius, Macrianus, the king, who, through all the changes which had taken place, had obtained a considerable increase of power, and was rising up against our people with full-grown strength: and after all the measures had been taken which seemed required by the affair itself and the time, and when it had been learnt by information collected from deserters when the aforesaid monarch could be seized before he expected anything of the kind, the emperor threw a bridge of boats across the Rhine with as much secrecy as was possible, lest any one should interpose any obstacle to such a work.

3. Severus, who was the commander of the infantry, led the van of the army towards Wiesbaden; and then, reflecting on his scanty numbers, halted in consternation; being afraid lest, as he should be quite unequal to resist them, he should be overwhelmed by the mass of the hostile army if it attacked him.

4. And because he suspected that the dealers who brought slaves for sale, whom he found at that place by chance, would be likely to repair with speed to the king to tell him what they had seen, he stripped them of all their merchandise, and then put them all to death.

5. Our generals were now encouraged by the arrival of more troops; and speedily contrived a temporary camp, because none of the baggage-beasts had arrived, nor had any one a proper tent, except the emperor, for whom one was constructed of carpets and tapestry. Then waiting a short time on account of the darkness of the night, at day-break the army quitted the camp and proceeded onwards; being led by guides well acquainted with the country. The cavalry, under Theodosius, its captain, was appointed to lead the way ... was inconvenienced by the great noise made by his men; whom his repeated commands could not restrain from rapine and incendiarism. For the guards of the enemy being roused by the crackling of the flames, and suspecting what had happened, put the king on a light carriage and carrying him off with great speed, hid him among the defiles of the neighbouring mountains.

6. Valentinian being defrauded of the glory of taking him, and that neither through any fault of his own or of his generals, but through the insubordination of his soldiers, which was often the cause of great misfortunes to the Roman state, laid waste all the enemy's country for fifty miles with fire and sword; and then returned dejected to Treves.

7. Where like a lion raging for the loss of a deer or a goat and champing with empty jaws, while fear was breaking and dividing the enemy, he proceeded to command the Bucenobantes, who are a tribe of the Allemanni opposite to Mayence, to elect Fraomarius as their king in place of Macrianus. And, shortly afterwards, when a fresh invasion had entirely desolated that canton, he removed him to Britain, where he gave him the authority of a tribune, and placed a number of the Allemanni under his command, forming for him a division strong both in its numbers and the excellence of its appointments. He also gave two other nobles of the same nation, by name Bitheridus and Hortarius, commands in his army; of whom Hortarius, being betrayed by the information of Florentius, Duke of Germany, who accused him of having written letters to Macrianus and the chieftains of the barbarians, containing language unfavourable to the republic, was put to the torture, and having been compelled to confess the truth, was condemned to be burnt alive.

V.

§ 1. After this ... it seems best to relate these matters in one connected narrative, lest the introduction of other affairs wholly unconnected with them, and which took place at a distance, should lead to confusion, and prevent the reader from acquiring a correct knowledge of these numerous and intricate affairs.

2. Nubel, who had been the most powerful chieftain among the Mauritanian nations, died, and left several sons, some legitimate, others born of concubines, of whom Zamma, a great favourite of the Count Romanus, was slain by his brother Firmus; and this deed gave rise to civil discords, and wars. For the count being exceedingly eager to avenge his death, made formidable preparations for the destruction of his treacherous enemy. And as continual reports declared, most exceeding pains were taken in the palace, that the despatches of Romanus, which contained many most unfavourable statements respecting Firmus, should be received and read by the prince; while many circumstances strengthened their credibility. And, on the other hand, that those documents which Firmus frequently, for the sake of his own safety, endeavoured to lay before the emperor by the agency of his friends, should be kept from his sight as long as possible, Remigius, a friend and relation of Romanus, and who was at that time master of the offices, availed himself of other more important affairs which claimed the emperor's attention to declare that Firmus's papers were all unimportant and superfluous, only to be read at a perfectly favourable opportunity.

3. But when Firmus perceived that these intrigues were going on to keep his defence out of sight, trembling for fear of the worst if all his excuses should be passed over, and he himself be condemned as disaffected and mischievous, and so be put to death, he revolted from the emperor's authority, and aided ... in devastation.[181]

4. Therefore, to prevent an implacable enemy from gaining strength by such an increase of force, Theodosius, the commander of the cavalry, was sent with a small body of the emperor's guards to crush him at once. Theodosius was an officer whose virtues and successes were at that time conspicuous above those of all other men: he resembled those ancient heroes, Domitius Corbulo, and Lusius; the first of whom was distinguished by a great number of gallant achievements in the time of Nero, and the latter of equal reputation under Trajan.

5. Theodosius marched from Arles with favourable auspices, and having crossed the sea with the fleet under his command so rapidly

that no report of his approach could arrive before himself, he reached the coast of Mauritania Sitifensis; that portion of the coast being called, by the natives, Igilgitanum. There, by accident, he met Romanus, and addressing him kindly, sent him to arrange the stations of the sentries and the outposts, without reproaching him for any of the matters for which he was liable to blame.

6. And when he had gone to the other province, Mauritania Cæsariensis, he sent Gildo, the brother of Firmus and Maximus, to assist Vincentius, who, as the deputy of Romanus, was the partner of his disloyal schemes and thefts.

7. Accordingly, as soon as his soldiers arrived, who had been delayed by the length of the sea voyage, he hastened to Sitifis; and gave orders to the body-guards to keep Romanus and his attendants under surveillance. He himself remained in the city, full of embarrassment and anxiety, working many plans in his mind, while devising by what means or contrivances he could conduct his soldiers who were accustomed to a cold climate through a country parched up with heat; or how he could catch an enemy always on the alert and appearing when least expected, and who relied more on surprises and ambuscades than a pitched battle.

8. When news of these facts reached Firmus, first through vague reports, and subsequently by precise information, he, terrified at the approach of a general of tried valour, sent envoys and letters to him, confessing all he had done, and imploring pardon; asserting that it was not of his own accord that he had been driven on to an action which he knew to be criminal, but that he had been goaded on by unjust treatment of a flagitious character, as he undertook to show.

9. When his letters had been read, and when peace was promised him, and hostages received from him, Theodosius proceeded to the Pancharian station to review the legions to which the protection of Africa was intrusted, and who had been ordered to assemble to meet him at that place. There he encouraged the hopes of them all by confident yet prudent language; and then returned to Sitifis, having reinforced his troops with some native soldiers; and, not being inclined to admit of any delay, he hastened to regain his camp.

10. Among many other admirable qualities which he displayed, his popularity was immensely increased by an order which he issued, forbidding the army to demand supplies from the inhabitants of the province; and asserting, with a captivating confidence, that the harvests and granaries of the enemy were the magazines of the valour of our soldiers.

11. Having arranged these matters in a way which caused great joy to the landowners, he advanced to Tubusuptum, a town near Mons Ferratus, where he rejected a second embassy of Firmus, because it had not brought with it the hostages, as had been provided before. From this place, having made as careful an examination of everything as the time and place permitted, he proceeded by rapid marches to the Tyndenses and Massisenses; tribes equipped with light arms, under the command of Mascizel and Dius, brothers of Firmus.

12. When the enemy, being quick and active in all their movements, came in sight, after a fierce skirmish by a rapid interchange of missiles, both sides engaged in a furious contest; and amid the groans of the wounded and dying were heard also the wailing and lamentations of barbarian prisoners. When the battle was over, the territory for a great distance was ravaged and wasted by fire.

13. Among the havoc thus caused, the destruction of the farm of Petra, which was razed to the ground, and which had been originally built by Salmaces, its owner, a brother of Firmus, in such a manner as to resemble a town, was especially remarkable. The conqueror was elated at this success, and with incredible speed proceeded to occupy the town of Lamforctense, which was situated among the tribes already mentioned; here he caused large stores of provisions to be accumulated, in order that if, in his advance into the inland districts, he should find a scarcity of supplies, he might order them to be brought from this town, which would be at no great distance.

14. In the mean time Mascizel, having recruited his forces by auxiliaries which he had procured from the tribes on the borders, ventured on a pitched battle with our army, in which his men were routed, and a great portion of them slain, while he himself was with difficulty saved from death by the speed of his horse.

15. Firmus, being weakened by the losses he had sustained in two battles, and in great perplexity, in order to leave no expedient untried, sent some priests of the Christian religion with the hostages, as ambassadors to implore peace. They were received kindly, and having promised supplies of food for our soldiers, as they were commissioned to do, they brought back a propitious answer. And then, sending before him a present, Firmus himself went with confidence to meet the Roman general, mounted on a horse fitted for any emergency. When he came near Theodosius, he was awe-struck at the brilliancy of the standards, and the terrible countenance of the general himself; and leapt from his horse, and with neck bowed down almost to the ground, he,

with tears, laid all the blame on his own rashness, and entreated pardon and peace.

16. He was received with a kiss, since such treatment of him appeared advantageous to the republic; and being now full of joyful hope, he supplied the army with provisions in abundance; and having left some of his own relations as hostages, he departed in order, as he promised, to restore those prisoners whom he had taken at the first beginning of these disturbances. And two days afterwards, without any delay, he restored the town of Icosium (of the founders of which we have already spoken), also the military standards, the crown belonging to the priest, and all the other things which he had taken, as he had been commanded to do.

17. Leaving this place, our general, advancing by long marches, reached Tiposa, where, with great elation, he gave answers to the envoys of the Mazices, who had combined with Firmus, and now in a suppliant tone implored pardon, replying to their entreaties that he would at once march against them as perfidious enemies.

18. When he had thus cowed them by the fear of impending danger, and had commanded them to return to their own country, he proceeded onwards to Cæsarea, a city formerly of great wealth and importance, of the origin of which we have given a full account in our description of Africa. When he reached it, and saw that nearly the whole of it had been destroyed by extensive conflagrations, and that the flint stones of the streets were covered with ashes, he ordered the first and second legions to be stationed there for a time, that they might clear away the heaps of cinders and ashes, and keep guard there to prevent a fresh attack of the barbarians from repeating this devastation.

19. When accurate intelligence of these events had arrived, the governors of the province and the tribune Vincentius issued forth from the places of concealment in which they had been lying, and came with speed and confidence to the general. He saw and received them with joy, and, while still at Cæsarea, having accurately inquired into every circumstance, he found that Firmus, while assuming the disguise of an ally and a suppliant, was secretly planning how, like a sudden tempest, to overwhelm his army while unprepared for any such danger.

20. On this he quitted Cæsarea, and went to the town of Sugabarritanum, which is on the slope of Mount Transcellensis. There he found the cavalry of the fourth cohort of archers, who had revolted to the rebels, and in order to show himself content with lenient punish-

ments, he degraded them all to the lowest class of the service, and ordered them, and a portion of the infantry of the Constantian legion, to come to Tigaviæ with their tribunes, one of whom was the man who, for want of a diadem, had placed a neck-chain on the head of Firmus.

21. While these events were proceeding, Gildo and Maximus returned, and brought with them Bellenes, one of the princes of the Mazices, and Fericius, prefect of that nation, both of whom had espoused the faction of the disturber of the public peace, leading them forth in chains.

22. When this order had been executed, Theodosius himself came forth from his camp at daybreak, and on seeing those men surrounded by his army, said, "What, my trusty comrades, do you think ought to be done to these nefarious traitors?" And then, in compliance with the acclamations of the whole army, who demanded that their treason should be expiated by their blood, he, according to the ancient fashion, handed over those of them who had served in the Constantian legion to the soldiers to be put to death by them. The officers of the archers he sentenced to lose their hands, and the rest he condemned to death, in imitation of Curio, that most vigorous and severe general, who by this kind of punishment crushed the ferocity of the Dardanians, when it was reviving like the Lernæan hydra.

23. But malignant detractors, though they praise the ancient deed, vituperate this one as terrible and inhuman, affirming that the Dardanians[182] were implacable enemies, and therefore justly suffered the punishment inflicted on them; but that those soldiers, who belonged to our own standards, ought to have been corrected with more lenity, for falling into one single error. But we will remind these cavillers, of what perhaps they know already, namely, that this cohort was not only an enemy by its own conduct, but also by the example which it set to others.

24. He also commanded Bellenes and Fericius, who have been mentioned above, and whom Gildo brought with him, to be put to death; and likewise Curandius, a tribune of the archers, because he had always been backward in engaging the enemy himself, and had never been willing to encourage his men to fight. And he did this in recollection of the principle laid down by Cicero, that "salutary vigour is better than an empty appearance of clemency."

25. Leaving Sugabarri, he came to a town called Gallonatis, surrounded by a strong wall, and a secure place of refuge for the Moors, which, as such, he destroyed with his battering-rams. And having slain all the inhabitants, and levelled the walls, he advanced along the foot

of Mount Ancorarius to the fortress of Tingetanum, where the Mazices were all collected in one solid body. He at once attacked them, and they encountered him with arrows and missiles of all kinds as thick as hail.

26. The battle proceeded for some time vigorously on both sides, till at last the Mazices, though a hardy and warlike race, being unable to withstand the fury of our men and the shock of their arms, after sustaining heavy loss, fled in every direction in disgraceful panic; and as they fled they were put to the sword in great numbers, with the exception only of those who, contriving to make their escape, afterwards, by their humble supplications, obtained the pardon which the times permitted to be granted to them.

27. Their leader Suggena, who succeeded Romanus, was sent into Mauritania Sitifensis to establish other garrisons necessary to prevent that province from being overrun; and he himself, elated by his recent achievements, marched against the nation of the Musones, who, from a consciousness of the ravages and murders of which they had been guilty, had joined the party of Firmus, hoping that he would soon obtain the chief authority.

28. Having advanced some distance, he found, near the town of Addense, that a number of tribes, who, though differing from each other in manners and language, were all animated with one feeling, in fomenting the outbreaks of terrible wars, being urged on and encouraged by the hope of great rewards from a sister of Firmus, named Cyria; who being very rich, and full of feminine resolution, was resolved to make a great effort to help her brother.

29. Therefore Theodosius, fearing to become involved in a war to which his forces were unequal, and that if he with his small force (for he had but three thousand five hundred men) should engage with an immense multitude, he should lose his whole army, at first hesitating between the shame of retreating and his wish to fight, gradually fell back a little; but presently was compelled by the overpowering mass of the barbarians to retire altogether.

30. The barbarians were exceedingly elated at this event, and pursued him with great obstinacy.... Being compelled by necessity to fight, he would have lost all his army and his own life, had not these tumultuous tribes, the moment they saw a troop of the Mazican auxiliaries, with a few Roman soldiers in their front, fancied that a numerous division was advancing to charge them, and in consequence taking to flight, opened to our men a way of escape which was previously shut against them.

31. Theodosius now drew off his army in safety; and when he had reached a town called Mazucanum, he found there a number of deserters, some of whom he burnt alive, and others he mutilated after the fashion of the archers whose hands had been cut off. He then proceeded towards Tipata, which he reached in the course of February.

32. There he stayed some time deliberating, like that old delayer, Fabius, on the circumstances around him, desiring to subdue the enemy, who was not only warlike, but so active as usually to keep out of bowshot, rather by manœuvres and skill than by hazardous engagements.

33. Still he from time to time sent out envoys, skilled in the arts of persuasion, to the surrounding tribes, the Basuræ, the Cautauriani, the Anastomates, the Cafaves, the Davares, and other people in their neighbourhood, trying to bring them over to our alliance, either by presents, threats, or by promises of pardon for past violence ... seeking by delays and intrigues to crush an enemy who offered so stout a resistance to his attacks, just as Pompey in times past had subdued Mithridates.

34. On this account Firmus, avoiding immediate destruction, although he was strengthened by a large body of troops, abandoned the army which he had collected by a lavish expenditure of money, and as the darkness of night afforded a chance of concealment, he fled to the Caprarian mountains, which were at a great distance, and from their precipitous character inaccessible.

35. On his clandestine departure, his army also dispersed, being broken up into small detachments without any leader, and thus afforded our men an opportunity of attacking their camp. That was soon plundered, and all who resisted were put to the sword, or else taken prisoners; and then, having devastated the greater portion of the country, our wise general appointed prefects of tried loyalty as governors of the different tribes through which he passed.

36. The traitor was thrown into consternation by the unexpected boldness of his pursuit, and with the escort of only a few servants, hoping to secure his safety by the rapidity of his movements, in order to have nothing to impede his flight, threw away all the valuable baggage which he had taken with him. His wife, exhausted with continual toil....

37. Theodosius ... showing mercy to none of them, having refreshed his soldiers by a supply of better food, and gratified them by a distribution of pay, defeated the Capracienses and Abanni, who were the next tribes to them, in some unimportant skirmishes, and then ad-

vanced with great speed to the town of ... and having received certain intelligence that the barbarians had already occupied the hills, and were spread over the precipitous and broken ground to a great height, so that they were quite inaccessible to any but natives who were intimately acquainted with the whole country, he retired, giving the enemy an opportunity by a truce, short as it was, to receive an important reinforcement from the Ethiopians in the neighbourhood.

38. Then having assembled all their united forces, they rushed on to battle with threatening shouts, and an utter disregard of their individual safety, compelling him to retreat, full of consternation at the apparently countless numbers of their army. But soon the courage of his men revived, and he returned, bringing with him vast supplies, and with his troops in a dense column, and brandishing their shields with formidable gestures, he again engaged the enemy in close combat.

39. The barbarians rattled their arms in a savage manner, and our battalions, with equal rage, pushed on, they also rattling their shields against their knees. Still the general, like a cautious and prudent warrior, aware of the scantiness of his numbers, advanced boldly with his army in battle array, till he came to a point, at which he turned off, though still preserving an undaunted front, towards the city of Contensis, where Firmus had placed the prisoners whom he had taken from us, as in a remote and safe fortress. He recovered them all, and inflicted severe punishment, according to his custom, on the traitors among the prisoners, and also on the guards of Firmus.

40. While he was thus successful, through the protection of the Supreme Deity, he received correct intelligence from one of his scouts that Firmus had fled to the tribe of the Isaflenses. He at once entered their territory to require that he should be given up, with his brother Mazuca, and the rest of his relations: and on being refused, he declared war against the nation.

41. And after a fierce battle, in which the barbarians displayed extraordinary courage and ferocity, he threw his army into a solid circle; and then the Isaflenses were so completely overpowered by the weight of our battalions pressing on them that numbers were slain; and Firmus himself, gallantly as he behaved, after exposing himself to imminent danger by the rashness of his courage, put spurs to his horse, and fled; his horse being accustomed to make his way with great speed over the most rocky and precipitous paths. But his brother Mazuca was taken prisoner, mortally wounded.

42. It was intended to send him to Cæsarea, where he had left behind him many records of his atrocious cruelties; but his wounds

reopened, and he died. So his head was cut off, and (his body being left behind) was conveyed to that city, where it was received with great joy by all who saw it.

43. After this our noble general inflicted most severe punishment, as justice required, on the whole nation of the Isaflenses, which had resisted till it was thus subdued in war. And he burnt alive one of the most influential of the citizens, named Evasius, and his son Florus, and several others, who were convicted on undeniable evidence of having aided the great disturber of tranquillity by their secret counsels.

44. From thence Theodosius proceeded into the interior, and with great resolution attacked the tribe of the Jubileni, to which he heard that Nubel, the father of Firmus, belonged; but presently he halted, being checked by the height of the mountains, and their winding defiles. And though he had once attacked the enemy, and opened himself a further road by slaying a great number of them, still, fearing the high precipices as places pre-eminently adapted for ambuscades, he withdrew, and led back his army in safety to a fortress called Audiense, where the Jesalenses, a warlike tribe, came over to him, voluntarily promising to furnish him with reinforcements and provisions.

45. Our noble general, exulting in this and similarly glorious achievements, now made the greatest efforts to overtake the original disturber of tranquillity himself, and therefore having halted for some time near a fortress named Medianum, he planned various schemes through which he hoped to procure that Firmus should be given up to him.

46. And while he was directing anxious thoughts and deep sagacity to this object, he heard that he had again gone back to the Isaflenses; on which, as before, without any delay, he marched against them with all possible speed. Their king, whose name was Igmazen, a man of great reputation in that country, and celebrated also for his riches, advanced with boldness to meet him, and addressed him thus, "To what country do you belong, and with what object have you come hither? Answer me." Theodosius, with firm mind and stern looks, replied, "I am a lieutenant of Valentinian, the master of the whole world, sent hither to destroy a murderous robber; and unless you at once surrender him, as the invincible emperor has commanded, you also, and the nation of which you are king, will be entirely destroyed." Igmazen, on receiving this answer, heaped a number of insulting epithets on our general, and then retired full of rage and indignation.

47. And the next morning at daybreak the two armies, breathing terrible threats against each other, advanced to engage in battle: nearly

twenty thousand barbarians constituted the front of their army, with very large reserves posted behind, out of sight, with the intention that they should steal forward gradually, and hem in our battalions with their vast and unexpected numbers. These were also supported by a great number of auxiliaries of the Jesalenian tribes, whom we have mentioned as having promised reinforcements and supplies to ourselves.

48. On the other side, the Roman army, though scanty in numbers, nevertheless being full of natural courage, and elated by their past victories, formed into dense columns, and joining their shields firmly together, in the fashion of a testudo, planted their feet firmly in steady resistance; and from sunrise to the close of day the battle was protracted. A little before evening Firmus was seen mounted on a tall horse, expanding his scarlet cloak in order to attract the notice of his soldiers, whom he was exciting with a loud voice at once to deliver up Theodosius, calling him a ferocious and cruel man—an inventor of merciless punishments—as the only means of delivering themselves from the miseries which he was causing them.

49. This unexpected address only provoked some of our men to fight with more vigour than ever, but there were others whom it seduced to desert our ranks. Therefore when the stillness of night arrived, and the country became enveloped in thick darkness, Theodosius returned to the fortress of Duodiense, and, recognizing those soldiers who had been persuaded by fear and Firmus's speech to quit the fight, he put them all to death by different modes of execution; of some he cut off the right hands, others he burnt alive.

50. And conducting himself with ceaseless care and vigilance, he routed a division of the barbarians who, though afraid to show themselves by day, ventured, after the moon had set, to make an attempt upon his camp: some of those who advanced further than their comrades he took prisoners. Departing from this place, he made a forced march through by-roads to attack the Jesalensians, who had shown themselves disloyal and unfaithful. He could not obtain any supplies from their country, but he ravaged it, and reduced it to complete desolation. Then he passed through the towns of Mauritania and Cæsarensis, and returned to Sitifis, where he put to the torture Castor and Martinianus, who had been the accomplices of Romanus in his rapine and other crimes, and afterwards burnt them.

51. After this the war with the Isaflenses was renewed; and in the first conflict, after the barbarians had been routed with heavy loss, their king Igmazen, who had hitherto been accustomed to be victori-

ous, agitated by fears of the present calamity, and thinking that all his alliances would be destroyed, and that he should have no hope left in life if he continued to resist, with all the cunning and secrecy that he could, fled by himself from the battle; and reaching Theodosius, besought him in a suppliant manner to desire Masilla, the chief magistrate of the Mazices, to come to him.

52. When that noble had been sent to him as he requested, he employed him as his agent to advise the general, as a man by nature constant and resolute in his plans, that the way to accomplish his purpose would be to press his countrymen with great vigour, and, by incessant fighting, strike terror into them; as, though they were keen partisans of Firmus, they were nevertheless wearied out by repeated disasters.

53. Theodosius adopted this advice, and, by battle after battle, so completely broke the spirits of the Isaflenses, that they fell away like sheep, and Firmus again secretly escaped, and hiding himself for a long time in out-of-the-way places and retreats, till at last, while deliberating on a further flight, he was seized by Igmazen, and put in confinement.

54. And since he had learnt from Masilla the plans which had been agitated in secret, he at last came to reflect that in so extreme a necessity there was but one remedy remaining, and he determined to trample under foot the love of life by a voluntary death; and having designedly filled himself with wine till he became stupefied, when, in the silence of the night, his keepers were sunk in profound slumber, he, fully awake from dread of the misfortune impending over him, left his bed with noiseless steps, and crawling on his hands and feet, conveyed himself to a distance, and then, having found a rope which chance provided for the end of his life, he fastened it to a nail which was fixed in the wall, and hanging himself, escaped the protracted sufferings of torture.

55. Igmazen was vexed at this, lamenting that he was thus robbed of his glory, because it had not been granted to him to conduct this rebel alive to the Roman camp; and so, having received a pledge of the state for his own safety, through the intervention of Masilla, he placed the body of the dead man on a camel, and when he arrived at the camp of the Roman army, which was pitched near the fortress of Subicarense, he transferred it to a pack-horse, and offered it to Theodosius, who received it with exultation.

56. And Theodosius having assembled a crowd of soldiers and citizens, and having asked them whether they recognized the face of

the corpse, learnt by their answers that there was no question at all that it was the man; after this he stayed there a short time, and then returned to Sitifis in great triumph, where he was received with joyful acclamations of the people of every age and rank.

VI.

§ 1. While Theodosius was thus exerting himself, and toiling in Mauritania and Africa, the nation of the Quadi was roused to make a sudden movement. It was a nation now not very formidable, but one which had formerly enjoyed vast renown for its warlike genius and power, as its achievements prove, some of which were distinguished for the rapidity, as well as for the greatness, of their success; instances are:—Aquileia, which was besieged by them and the Marcomanni; Opitergium, which was destroyed by them, and many other bloody successes which were gained in that rapid campaign when the Julian Alps were passed, and that illustrious emperor Marcus, of whom we have already spoken, was hardly able to offer them any resistance. And indeed they had, for barbarians, just ground of complaint.

2. For Valentinian, who from the beginning of his reign had been full of a resolution to fortify his frontier, which was a glorious decision, but one carried too far in this case, ordered a fortress capable of containing a strong garrison to be constructed on the south side of the river Danube, in the very territories of the Quadi, as if they were subject to the Roman authority. The natives, being very indignant at this, and anxious for their own rights and safety, at first contented themselves with trying to avert the evil by an embassy and expostulations.

3. But Maximin, always eager for any wickedness, and unable to bridle his natural arrogance, which was now increased by the pride which he felt in his rank as prefect, reproached Equitius, who at that time was the commander of the forces in Illyricum, as careless and inactive, because the work, which it was ordered should be carried on with all speed, was not yet finished. And he added, as a man guided only by zeal for the common good, that if the rank of Duke of Valeria were only conferred on his own little son, Marcellianus, the fortification would be soon completed without any more pretexts for delay. Both his wishes were presently granted.

4. Marcellianus received the promotion thus suggested, and set out to take possession of his government; and when he reached it, being full of untimely arrogance, as might be expected from the son of such a father, without attempting to conciliate those whom false dreams of gain had caused to quit their native land, he applied himself

to the work which had been recently begun, and had only been suspended to afford an opportunity for the inhabitants to present petitions against it.

5. Lastly, when their king Gabinius requested, in a most moderate tone, that no innovations might be made, he as if intending to assent to his petition, with feigned courtesy invited him and some other persons to a banquet; and then as he was departing after the entertainment, unsuspicious of treachery, he caused him, in infamous violation of the sacred rights of hospitality, to be murdered.

6. The report of so atrocious an act was speedily spread abroad, and roused the indignation of the Quadi and other surrounding tribes, who, bewailing the death of the king, collected together and sent forth predatory bands, which crossed the Danube; and when no hostilities were looked for, attacked the people who were occupied in the fields about the harvest; and having slain the greater portion of them, carried off all the survivors to their own country with a great booty of different kinds of cattle.

7. And at that time an inexpiable atrocity was very near being committed, which would have been reckoned among the most disgraceful disasters which ever happened to the Roman state, for the daughter of Constantius had a narrow escape of being taken prisoner as she was at dinner in a hotel called the Pistrensian, when on her way to be married to Gratian: and she was only saved by the promptitude of Messala the governor of the province, who, aided by the favour of the propitious Deity, placed her in a carriage belonging to him as governor, and conducted her back with all possible speed to Sirmium, a distance of about twenty-six miles.

8. By this fortunate chance the royal virgin was delivered from the peril of miserable slavery; and if she had been taken and her captors had refused to ransom her, it would have been the cause of terrible disasters to the republic. After this the Quadi in conjunction with the Sarmatians, extended their ravages further (since both these tribes were addicted beyond measure to plunder and robbery), carrying off, men, women, and cattle, and exulting in the ashes of burnt villas, and in the misery of the murdered inhabitants, whom they fell upon unexpectedly and slaughtered without mercy.

9. All the neighbouring districts were filled with apprehension of similar evils, and Probus, the prefect of the prætorium, who was at that time at Sirmium, a man wholly unexperienced in war, being panic-struck with the calamitous appearance of these new occurrences, and scarcely able to raise his eyes for fear, was for a long time wavering in

doubt what to do. At first he prepared some swift horses and resolved to fly the next night; but afterwards, taking advice from some one who gave him safer counsel, he stayed where he was, but without doing anything.

10. For he had been assured that all those who were within the walls of the city would immediately follow him, with the intention of concealing themselves in suitable hiding-places; and if that had been done, the city, left without defenders, would have fallen into the hands of the enemy.

11. Presently, after his terror had been a little moderated, he applied himself with some activity to do what was most pressing; he cleared out the fosses which were choked up with ruins; he repaired the greater portion of the walls which, through the security engendered by a long peace, had been neglected, and had fallen into decay, and raised them again to the height of lofty towers, devoting himself zealously to the work of building. In this way the work was speedily completed, because he found that the sums which some time before had been collected for the erection of a theatre were sufficient for the purpose he was now pressing forward. And to this prudent measure he added another of like precaution, in summoning a cohort of archer cavalry from the nearest station, that it might be at hand to resist a siege should any take place.

12. By these barriers, as they may be called, the barbarians were forced to abandon their design of besieging the city, since they were not skilful in contests of this kind, and were also hampered by the burden of their booty; accordingly they turned aside to pursue Equitius. And when, from the information given them by their prisoners, they learnt that he had retired to the most remote part of Valeria, they hastened thither by forced marches, gnashing their teeth, and determined on his death, because they believed that it was through his means their innocent king had been circumvented.

13. And as they were hastening onwards with impetuous and vengeful speed, they were met by two legions, the Pannonian and the Mœsian, both of approved valour, who, if they had acted in harmony, must unquestionably have come off victorious. But while they were hastening onward to attack the barbarians separately, a quarrel arose between them on the subject of their honour and dignity, which impeded all their operations.

14. And when intelligence of this dissension reached the Sarmatians, who are a most sagacious people, they, without waiting for any regular signal of battle, attacked the Mœsians first; and while the sol-

diers, being surprised and in disorder, were slowly making ready their arms, many of them were killed; on which the barbarians with increased confidence attacked the Pannonians, and broke their line also; and when the line of battle was once disordered, they redoubled their efforts, and would have destroyed almost all of them, if some had not saved themselves from the danger of death by a precipitate flight.

15. Amid these calamitous inflictions of adverse fortune, Theodosius the younger, Duke of Mœsia, then in the first bloom of youth, but afterwards a prince of the highest reputation, in many encounters defeated and vanquished the Free Sarmatians (so called to distinguish them from their rebellious slaves), who had invaded our frontier on the other side, till he exhausted them by his repeated victories; and with such vigour did he crush the assembled crowds combined to resist his arms, that he glutted the very birds and beasts with the blood of the vast numbers justly slain.

16. Those who remained having lost all their pride and spirit, fearing lest a general of such evident promptitude and courage should rout or destroy these invading battalions on the very edge of his frontier, or lay ambuscades for them in the recesses of the woods, made from time to time many vain attempts to escape, and at last, discarding all confidence in battle, they begged indulgence and pardon for their past hostility. And being thoroughly subdued, they did nothing for some time contrary to the treaty of peace, being more especially terrified because a strong force of Gallic soldiers had come to the defence of Illyricum.

17. While these events were agitating the empire, and while Claudius was prefect of the Eternal City, the Tiber, which intersects its walls, and which, after receiving the waters of many drains and copious streams, falls into the Tyrrhenian Sea, overflowed its banks, in consequence of an abundance of rain, and extending to a size beyond that of a river, overwhelmed almost everything with its flood.

18. All those parts of the city which lie in the plain were under water, and nothing reared its head above but the hills and other spots of rising ground, which seemed like islands, out of the reach of present danger. And, as the vastness of the inundation permitted of no departure in any direction to save the multitude from dying of famine, great quantities of provisions were brought in barges and boats. But when the bad weather abated, and the river which had burst its bounds returned to its accustomed channel, the citizens discarded all fear, and apprehended no inconvenience for the future.

19. Claudius, as a prefect, conducted himself very quietly, nor was any sedition in his time provoked by any real grievance. He also repaired many ancient buildings; and among his improvements he built a large colonnade contiguous to the bath of Agrippa, and gave it the name of The Colonnade of Success, because a temple bearing that title is close to it.

Notes

[176] For an account of this incantation, see Gibbon, Bohn's edition vol. iii., p. 75, note.

[177] The lines of Theognis are—

Ἄνδρ᾽ ἀγαθὸν πενίη πάντων δάμνησι μάλιστα
Καὶ γήρως πολιοῦ, Κύρνε, καὶ ἠπιάλου
Ἥν δὴ χρὴ φεύγοντα καὶ ἐς μεγακήτεα πόντον
Ῥίπτειν, καὶ πετρῶν Κύρνε, κατ᾽ ἠλιβάτων."

Which may be thus translated:—

"Want crushes a brave man far worse than age,
O Cyrnus! or than fever's fiery rage;
Flee, should thy flight beneath the greedy wave,
Or from steep rocks but ope a milder grave."

[178] For the purposes of divination.

[179] This sentence is so mutilated as to be unintelligible, but is filled up by conjecture, founded on a knowledge of the facts, thus: "who was executed because he had not given up Octavian, who had been formerly proconsul of Africa, and who had taken refuge in his house when accused of some crime."

[180] The end of this chapter also is lost, as are one or two passages in the beginning of Chapter IV.

[181] Manuscript imperfect.

[182] The Dardanians were a Thracian tribe.

BOOK XXX

I.

A.D. 374.

§ 1. While all these difficulties and disturbances had been caused by the perfidy of the Duke Marcellianus, in treacherously murdering the king of the Quadi, a terrible crime was committed in the East, where Para, king of Armenia was also murdered by secret treachery; the original cause of which wicked action we have ascertained to be this:—

2. Some men of perverse temperament, who delighted in public misfortune, had concocted a number of accusations against this prince for acts which they imputed to him even when scarcely grown up, and had exaggerated them to Valens. Among these men was the Duke Terentius, a man who always walked about with a downcast melancholy look, and throughout his life was an unwearied sower of discord.

3. He, having formed a combination with a few people of Para's nation, whom a consciousness of their own crimes had filled with fear, was continually harping in his letters to the court on the deaths of Cylax and Artabannes; adding also that this same young king was full of haughtiness in all his conduct, and that he behaved with excessive cruelty to his subjects.

4. In consequence of these letters, Para, as if it were intended that he should become a partaker in a treaty of which existing circumstances required ratification, was invited to court with all the ceremony to which he was entitled as a king, and then was detained at Tarsus in Cilicia, with a show of honour, without being able to procure permission to approach the emperor's camp, or to learn why his arrival had been so eagerly pressed; since on this point all around him preserved a rigid silence. At last, however, by means of private information, he learnt that Terentius was endeavouring by letter to persuade the Roman sovereign to send without delay another king to Armenia; lest, out of hatred to Para, and a knowledge of what they had to expect if he returned among them, his nation, which at present was friendly to us, should revolt to the Persians, who had long been eager to reduce them under their power either by violence, fear, or flattery.

5. Para, reflecting on this warning, foreboded grievous mischief for himself; and being a man of forethought and contrivance, as he could not perceive any means of safety, except by a speedy departure, by the advice of his most trusty friends he collected a body of 300 persons who had accompanied him from his own country, and with horses selected for especial speed, acting as men are wont to do under the pressure of great terror and perplexity, that is to say, with more boldness than prudence; late one afternoon he started boldly forth at the head of his escort, formed in one solid body.

6. And when the governor of the province, having received information from the officer who kept the gate, came with prompt energy and found him in the suburb, he earnestly entreated him to remain; but finding that he could not prevail upon him, he quitted him, for fear of his own life.

7. And not long afterwards Para, with his escort, turned back upon the legion which was pursuing him and on the point of overtaking him, and pouring arrows upon them as thick as sparks of fire, though designedly missing them, he put them to flight, filling them, tribune and all, with complete consternation, so that they returned to the city with greater speed than they left it.

8. After this, Para being released from all fear, continued his laborious and rapid journey for two days and two nights, till he reached the Euphrates; where, for want of boats, he was unable to pass the river, which at that place is full of strong currents and too deep to be forded. His men, not being skilful swimmers, were afraid to trust themselves to the stream, and he himself showed more hesitation than any of them; indeed he would have halted there altogether, if while every one was suggesting one plan or another, he had not at last hit upon the following expedient, which seemed the safest in this emergency.

9. They took a number of little beds which they found in the neighbouring houses, and supported them each on two bladders, of which there were plenty at hand in the vineyards. And then he and his nobles placed themselves each on a bed, leading their horses after them, and so floated down and across the stream; by which contrivance, after extreme danger, they at last reached the opposite bank.

10. All the rest swam their horses, and though they were terribly tossed about and often almost sunk by the eddying stream, still, though much exhausted by their wetting, they also reached the opposite bank; when having rested for a short time and refreshed themselves, they proceeded on their way, travelling further than on the previous days.

11. When this transaction became known, the emperor being greatly moved at the king's flight, fearing he would break off his alliance, sent Daniel and Barzimeres to bring him back; the one being a count, the other the tribune of the Scutarii, and he placed under their command a thousand archers prepared for a rapid march by the lightness of their equipment.

12. These officers, trusting to their acquaintance with the country, and feeling sure that Para, as a stranger who was not accustomed to it, would take a roundabout way, sought to cut him off by marking a short cut through some valleys; and having divided their forces, they blockaded the two nearest roads, which were three miles from one another, in order that whichever Para took he might be caught before he expected it. But he escaped their manœuvre in this way:—

13. A traveller who happened to be hastening towards the western bank of the river, saw that the two roads were filled with armed soldiers, and accordingly quitted this road in order to avoid them, and made his way by an almost invisible path, which lay between them, overgrown with bushes and brambles, and fell in with the Armenians, who were by this time greatly fatigued. He was brought before the king, and, being admitted by him to a private conference, related to him secretly what he had seen, and was detained in safety.

14. And presently, without anything being done to give an idea that they were alarmed, a horseman was sent secretly to the road on the right side to prepare a resting-place and some food. And when he had been gone a little time, another was sent to the left with directions to move with great rapidity, and do the same thing; neither horseman being aware that the other had been sent in a different direction.

15. And after this arrangement had been thus cleverly made, the king himself, with his escort, retraced his steps through the jungle by which the traveller had come, taking him for his guide, and passing through this overgrown path, which was almost too narrow for a loaded horse, he left the Roman soldiers behind him and so escaped. Meanwhile our troops, who had made prisoners of the soldiers who had been thus sent out to impose upon them, waited a long time, while watching for the king, and stretching out their hands, as one may say, to seize the game which they expected would rush into them. And while they were thus waiting for the arrival of Para, he reached his kingdom in safety, where he was received with great joy by his countrymen, and still remained unshaken in his fidelity to us, burying in silence the injuries which he had received.

16. After this, Daniel and Barzimeres, having been thus balked of their prey, returned to Tarsus, and were loaded with bitter reproaches as inactive and blundering officers. But like venomous serpents whose first spring has failed, they only whetted their deadly fangs, in order at the first opportunity to inflict all the injury in their power on the king who had thus escaped them.

17. And, with a view to palliate the effect of their own mistake, or rather of the defeat their hopes, which the deeper sagacity of the king had contrived, they began to fill the emperor's ears, which were at all times most ready to receive all kinds of reports with false accusations against Para; pretending that he was skilled in Circean incantations, so as to be able to transform people, or to afflict them with sickness in a marvellous manner, adding, moreover, that it was by means of arts of this kind that he had rendered himself invisible, and

that if allowed to continue changing his shape, he would cause them great trouble, if permitted to live to boast of having deceived them.

18. In this manner the hatred which Valens had conceived against him was increased to an incredible degree; and plan after plan was laid to take his life, either by force or stratagem; and orders to that effect were transmitted by secret letters to Trajan, who at that time was in Armenia, in chief command of the forces in that kingdom.

19. Trajan, accordingly, began to surround Para with treacherous blandishments—at one time showing him some letters of Valens, which appeared to indicate that he was favourably disposed towards the king—at another, partaking cheerfully of his entertainments, he at last, with great apparent respect (but in pursuance of a deliberate plot), invited him to supper. Para, fearing no hostility, came, and was placed in the seat of honour at the feast.

20. Exquisite delicacies were set before him, and the splendid palace resounded with the music of lyres and lutes. Presently, when the wine had circulated freely, the master of the feast quitted it for a moment, under pretence of some natural want, and immediately a ferocious barbarian of the troop they call Supræ[183] was sent in, brandishing a drawn sword, and with a terribly ferocious countenance, to murder the youth, against whose escape ample precautions had now been taken.

21. As soon as he saw him, the king, who as it happened was on the further side of the couch, jumped up and drew his dagger to defend his life by every means in his power, but was stabbed in the breast, and fell like a miserable victim, being shamefully cut to pieces with repeated blows.

22. By this foul contrivance was his credulity shamefully deceived at a feast which is respected even on the coast of the Euxine Sea, under the eye of the Deity of Hospitality; and the blood of a stranger and a guest was sprinkled on the splendid tablecloths, and, by its foaming gore, filled the guests with loathing, who at once dispersed in great horror. If the dead can feel sorrow or indignation, then let that illustrious Fabricius Luscinus groan at the evidence of this deed, knowing with what greatness of mind he himself repelled Demochares (or, as some call him, Nicias), the king's servant, who in a secret conference offered to poison Pyrrhus, at that time desolating Italy with cruel wars, and wrote to the king, bidding him beware of his immediate attendants: such great reverence in the first ages of antiquity was there for the rights of hospitality even when claimed by an enemy.

23. But this modern, strange, and shameful act was excused by the precedent afforded by the death of Sertorius; though the emperor's flatterers were perhaps ignorant that, as Demosthenes—the everlasting glory of Greece—affirms, an unlawful and wicked action cannot be defended by its resemblance to another crime, or by the fact that that crime met with impunity.

II.

§ 1. These are the transactions which especially attracted notice in Armenia; but Sapor, after the last defeat which his troops had experienced, having heard of the death of Para, whom he had been earnestly labouring to win to his own alliance, was terribly grieved; and, as the activity of our army increased his apprehensions, he began to dread still greater disasters to himself.

2. He therefore sent Arsaces as his ambassador to the emperor, to advise him utterly to destroy Armenia as a perpetual cause of trouble; or, if that plan should be decided against, asking that an end might be put to the division of Hiberia into two provinces, that the Roman garrison might be withdrawn, and that Aspacuras, whom he himself had made the sovereign of the nation, might be permitted to reign with undivided authority.

3. To this proposal, Valens replied, that he could not change the resolutions which had been agreed to by both of them; and, indeed, that he should maintain them with zealous care. Towards the end of the winter, letters were received from the king of a tenor very contrary to this noble determination of Valens, full of vain and arrogant boasting. For in them Sapor affirmed that it was impossible for the seeds of discord to be radically extirpated, unless those who had been witnesses of the peace which had been made with Julian were all collected, some of whom he knew to be already dead.

4. After this, the matter becoming a source of greater anxiety, the emperor, who was more skilful in choosing between different plans than in devising them himself, thinking that it would be beneficial to the state in general, ordered Victor, the commander of the cavalry, and Urbicius, the Duke of Mesopotamia, to march with all speed to Persia, bearing a positive and plain answer to the proposals of Sapor: namely, that he, who boasted of being a just man, and one contented with his own, was acting wickedly in coveting Armenia, after a promise had been made to its inhabitants, that they should be allowed to live according to their own laws. And unless the soldiers who had been left as auxiliaries to Sauromaces returned without hindrance at the begin-

ning of the ensuing year, as had been agreed, he would compel Sapor by force to perform what he might at present do with a good grace.

5. And this embassy would in all respects have been a just and honourable one, if the ambassadors had not, contrary to their instructions, accepted some small districts in this same Armenia which were offered them. When the ambassadors returned, the Surena (the magistrate who enjoys an authority second only to that of the king) came with them, offering the said districts to the emperor which our ambassadors had ventured to take.

6. He was received with liberality and magnificence; but dismissed without obtaining what he requested. And then, great preparations were made for war, in order that, as soon as the severity of the winter was over, the emperor might invade Persia with three armies; and with this object he began with all speed to bargain for the services of some Scythian auxiliaries.

7. Sapor not having succeeded in obtaining what his vain hopes had led him to reckon on, and being exasperated in an extraordinary degree, because he had learnt that our emperor was preparing for an expedition, nevertheless stifled his wrath, and gave the Surena a commission to endeavour to recover by force of arms (if any one should resist him) the territories which Count Victor and Urbicius had accepted, and to press hostilities with the utmost rigour against those soldiers who had been destined to aid Sauromaces.

8. His orders were at once carried out. Nor was it found possible to prevent or resist their execution, because a new cause of alarm suddenly came on the republic; as the entire nation of the Goths suddenly burst into Thrace. The calamities which we experienced from that event shall be related succinctly in their proper places.

9. These were the occurrences which took place in the East. And while they were proceeding, as has been related, the unfailing arm of justice avenged the losses we had sustained in Africa, and the slaughter of the ambassadors of Tripoli, whose shades were still wandering about unavenged. For Justice, though a late, is yet a scrupulous and unerring discriminator between right and wrong.

10. Remigius, whom we have already spoken of as favouring Count Romanus, who had laid waste these provinces after Leo had succeeded him as master of the offices, retired from office and from public life, and devoted himself to rural pursuits in his own native district near Mayence.

11. And while he was living there in security, Maximin, the prefect of the prætorium, despising him because of his return to a tranquil

life, as he was accustomed to attack everything like a terrible pestilence, set to work to do him injury by every means in his power. And, in order to hunt out all his secrets, he seized Cæsarius who had formerly been a servant of his, and afterwards had become a secretary of the emperor, and put him to the question, torturing him with great severity to learn from him what Remigius had done, and how much he had received to induce him to countenance the wicked actions of Romanus.

12. But when Remigius heard this in his retreat, to which, as has been said, he had retired; being oppressed by the consciousness of his acts, or perhaps letting the dread of false accusation overpower his reason, he hanged himself.

III.

§ 1. The next year Gratian took Equitius as his colleague in the consulship; and Valentinian, after desolating some cantons of the Allemanni, was building a fortress near Basle, which the natives of the country call Robur, when a report was brought to him from the prefect Probus with an account of the disasters which had taken place in Illyricum.

2. He read them with a very careful examination, as became a prudent general; and then being filled with anxious thoughts, he sent his secretary, Paternianus, to that country, to inquire minutely into the whole details of the affair. And, as he soon received from him a true account of all that had taken place, he prepared to repair thither himself with all speed, in order to overwhelm with the first crash of his arms (such was his idea) the barbarians who had dared to pollute our frontier.

3. But, because, as it was now the end of autumn, there were many serious difficulties in the way, all the nobles in the palace pressed him earnestly to allow the time between that and the beginning of spring to be spent in embassies and conferences. Reminding him, in the first place, that the roads were all impassable through frost—that it was impossible to find herbage to feed the cattle, or anything else that would be useful. In the next place, they dwelt on the ferocity of the chieftains who lay nearest to Gaul, and especially of Macrianus whom they greatly dreaded, as it was quite certain that he was no friend to us, and was inclined to attack even the fortified cities.

4. By recapitulating these arguments, and adding others of great weight, they brought the emperor to adopt a wiser plan; and immediately (as was best for the commonwealth) King Macrianus was invited

in courteous terms to come to Mayence; and the event proved that he also was well inclined to make a treaty. When he arrived, however, it was marvellous how proud and arrogant he was, as if he were to be the supreme arbiter of the peace. And on a day appointed for a conference he came, carrying himself very loftily, to the very brink of the Rhine, and escorted by a number of his countrymen, who made a great clang with their shields.

5. On the other hand, the emperor, having embarked in a boat, such as is used on that river, and likewise escorted by a strong force, came with great confidence up to the eastern bank, being conspicuous through the brilliancy of his glittering standards; and when the frantic gestures and murmurs of the barbarians had been quieted, a long discussion took place on both sides, and at last a firm friendship was agreed on, and ratified with an oath.

6. When this was over, the king, who had been the cause of all these troubles, retired, quite pacified, and destined to prove an ally to us for the future; indeed, he afterwards, to the very end of his life, gave proof of his constancy and resolution to preserve his agreement with us, by many noble and gallant actions.

7. But subsequently he died in the country of the Franks, which he had invaded and ravaged in a most destructive manner, till at last he was cut off by the manœuvres of Mellobaudes, the warlike king of that nation, and slain. After the treaty had thus been solemnly ratified, Valentinian retired into winter quarters, at Treves.

IV.

§ 1. These were the events which took place in Gaul and the northern countries. But in the east, while all our foreign affairs were quiet, great domestic evils were increasing in consequence of the conduct of the friends and relations of Valens, who had more regard to expediency than honesty; for they laboured with the utmost diligence to bring about the recall from his post a judge of rigid probity, who was fond of deciding lawsuits equitably, out of a fear lest, as in the times of Julian, when Innocence was allowed a fair opportunity of defending itself, the pride of the powerful nobles, which was accustomed to roam at large with unrestrained licence, might again be broken down.

2. With these and similar objects a great number of persons conspired together, being led by Modestus, the prefect of the prætorium, who was a complete slave to the wishes of the emperor's eunuchs, and who, under a specious countenance, concealed a rough disposition

which had never been polished by any study of ancient virtue or literature, and who was continually asserting that to look into the minute
details of private actions was beneath the dignity of the emperor. He
thinking, as he said, that the examination of such matters had been imposed on the nobles to lower their dignity, abstained from all such
matters himself, and opened the doors to plunder; which doors are now
daily more and more opened by the depravity of the judges and advocates, who are all of the same mind, and who sell the interests of the
poor to the military commanders, or the persons of influence within
the palace, by which conduct they themselves have gained riches and
high rank.

3. This profession of forensic oratory the wisdom of Plato de-
fines to be πολιτικῆς μορίου εἴδωλον, "the shadow of a fraction of the
art of government," or a fourth part of the art of flattery. But Epicurus
calls it κακοτεχνία, reckoning it among the wicked arts. Tisias, who
has Gorgias of Leontinum on his side, calls the orator an artist of persuasion.

4. And while such has been the opinion formed of this art by the
ancients, the craft of some of the Eastern people has put it forward so
as to make it an object of hatred to good men, on which account an
orator it is sometimes restricted to a limited time for speaking.[184]
Therefore, after saying a few words about its unworthy character, as I
found by experience while in those countries, I will return to my original subject.

5. The tribunals, in former times, when good taste prevailed,
were greatly adorned by our advocates, when orators of spirited eloquence—laborious and accomplished scholars—shone pre-eminent in
genius, honesty, fluency, and every kind of embellishment of language. As Demosthenes, who, as we learn from the Athenian records,
whenever he was going to speak, drew together a vast concourse of
people from the whole of Greece, who assembled for the sake of hearing him; and Callistratus, who, when summing up his noble pleading
on the subject of Oropus in Eubœa, produced such an impression that
that same Demosthenes quitted the academy, at the time when Plato
was at its head, to become his follower. And Hyperides, and Æschines,
and Andocides, and Dinarchus, and Antiphon the Rhamnusian, who is
the first man spoken of in ancient history as having received a fee for
pleading a cause.

6. And similarly among the Romans, the Rutilii, and Galbæ, and
Scauri, men of eminent reputation for purity of life and manners, and
for frugality; and in the succeeding generations, many men of censo-

493

rian and consular rank, and even many who had celebrated triumphs, such as the Crassi, the Antonii, the Philipii, the Scævolæ, and numbers of others, after having commanded armies with glory, gained victories, and raised trophies, became eminent also for their civil services to the State, and won fresh laurels by their noble contests at the bar, thus reaping the highest honour and glory.

7. And after them Cicero, the most excellent of them all, who repeatedly saved many who were in distress from the scorching flames of judgment by the stream of his imperious eloquence, used to affirm "that if men could not be defended without their advocate incurring blame, they certainly could not be carelessly defended without his being guilty of crime."

8. But now throughout all the regions of the East one may see the most violent and rapacious classes of men hovering about the courts of law, and besieging the houses of the rich like Spartan or Cretan hounds, cunningly pursuing different traces, in order to create the occasion of a lawsuit.

9. Of these the chief is that tribe of men who, sowing every variety of strife and contest in thousands of actions, wear out the doorposts of widows and the thresholds of orphans, and create bitter hatred among friends, relations, or connections, who have any disagreement, if they can only find the least pretext for a quarrel. And in these men, the progress of age does not cool their vices as it does those of others, but only hardens and strengthens them. And amid all their plunder they are insatiable and yet poor, whetting the edge of their genius in order by their crafty orations to catch the ear of the judges, though the very title of those magistrates is derived from the name of Justice.

10. In the pertinacity of these men rashness assumes the disguise of freedom—headlong audacity seeks to be taken for constancy, and an empty fluency of language usurps the name of eloquence—by which perverse arts, as Cicero tells us, it is a shame for the holy gravity of a judge be deceived. For he says, "And as nothing in a republic ought to be so incorruptible as a suffrage or a sentence, I do not understand why the man who corrupts such things with money is to be esteemed worthy of punishment, while he who perverts them by eloquence receives commendation. In fact, the latter appears to me to do the most harm, it being worse to corrupt a judge by a speech than by a bribe, inasmuch as no one can corrupt a wise man with a bribe, though it is possible that he may with eloquence."

11. There is a second class of those men who, professing the science of the law, especially the interpretation of conflicting and

obsolete statutes, as if they had a bridle placed in their mouths, keep a resolute silence, in which they rather resemble their shadows than themselves. These, like those men who cast nativities or interpret the oracles of the sibyl, compose their countenances to a sort of gravity, and then make money of their supine drowsiness.

12. And that they may appear to have a more profound knowledge of the laws, they speak of Trebatius,[185] and Cascellius, and Alfenus, and of the laws of the Aurunci and Sicani, which have long become obsolete, and have been buried ages ago with the mother of Evander. And if you should pretend to have deliberately murdered your mother, they will promise you that there are many cases recorded in abstruse works which will secure your acquittal, if you are rich enough to pay for it.

13. There is a third class of these men, who, to arrive at distinction in a turbulent profession, sharpen their mercenary mouths to mystify the truth, and by prostituting their countenances and their vile barking, work their way with the public. These men, whenever the judge is embarrassed and perplexed, entangle the matter before him with further difficulties, and take pains to prevent any arrangement, carefully involving every suit in knotty subtleties. When these courts, however, go on rightly, they are temples of equity; but when they are perverted they are hidden and treacherous pitfalls, and if any person falls into them, he will not escape till after many years have elapsed, and till he himself has been sucked dry to his very marrow.

14. There is a fourth and last class, impudent, saucy, and ignorant, consisting of those men who, having left school too early, run about the corners of cities, giving more time to farces than to the study of actions and defences, wearing out the doors of the rich, and hunting for the luxuries of banquets and rich food.

15. And when they have given themselves up to gains, and to the task of hunting for money by every means, they incite men, on any small pretence whatever, to go to law; and if they are permitted to defend a cause, which but seldom happens, it is not till they are before the judge, while the pleadings are being recited, that they begin to inquire into the cause of the client, or even into his name; and then they so overflow with a heap of unarranged phrases and circumlocutions, that from the noise and jabber of the vile medley you would fancy you were listening to Thersites.

16. But when it happens that they have no single allegation they can establish, they then resort to an unbridled licence of abuse; for which conduct they are continually brought to trial themselves, and

convicted, when they have poured ceaseless abuse upon people of honour; and some of these men are so ignorant that they do not appear ever to have read any books.

17. And if in a company of learned men the name of any ancient author is ever mentioned, they fancy it to be some foreign name of a fish or other eatable. And if any stranger asks (we will say) for Marcianus, as one with whom he is as yet unacquainted, they all at once pretend that their name is Marcianus.

18. Nor do they pay the slightest attention to what is right; but as if they had been sold to and become the property of Avarice, they know nothing but a boundless licence in asking. And if they catch any one in their toils, they entangle him in a thousand meshes, pretending sickness by way of protracting the consultations. And to produce an useless recital of some well-known law, they prepare seven costly methods of introducing it, thus weaving infinite complications and delays.

19. And when at last days and months and years have been passed in these proceedings, and the parties to the suit are exhausted, and the whole matter in dispute is worn out with age, then these men, as if they were the very heads of their profession, often introduce sham advocates along with themselves. And when they have arrived within the bar, and the fortune or safety of some one is at stake, and they ought to labour to ward off the sword of the executioner from some innocent man, or calamity and ruin, then, with wrinkled brows, and arms thrown about with actor-like gestures, so that they want nothing but the flute of Gracchus at their back,[186] then they keep silence for some time on both sides; and at last, after a scene of premeditated collusion, some plausible preamble is pronounced by that one of them who is most confident in his power of speaking, and who promises an oration which shall rival the beauties of the oration for Cluentius[187] or for Ctesiphon.[188] And then, when all are eager for him to make an end, he concludes his preamble with a statement that the chief advocates have as yet only had three years since the commencement of the suit to prepare themselves to conduct it; and so obtains an adjournment, as if they had to wrestle with the ancient Antæus, while still they resolutely demand the pay due for their arduous labours.

20. And yet, in spite of all these things, advocates are not without some inconveniences, which are hard to be endured by one who would live uprightly. For being allured by small gains, they quarrel bitterly among themselves, and offend numbers by the insane ferocity of their

evil speaking, which they pour forth when they are unable to maintain the weakness of the case intrusted to them by any sound reasoning.

21. And sometimes the judges prefer persons who have been instructed in the quibbles of Philistion or Æsop, to those who come from the school of Aristides the Just, or of Cato—men who, having bought public offices for large sums of money, proceed like troublesome creditors to hunt out every one's fortune, and so shake booty for themselves out of the laps of others.

22. Finally, the profession of a lawyer, besides other things, has in it this, which is most especially formidable and serious (and this quality is almost innate in all litigants), namely that when, through one or other out of a thousand accidents, they have lost their action, they fancy that everything which turned out wrong was owing to the conduct of their counsel, and they usually attribute the loss of every suit to him, and are angry, not with the weakness of their case or (as they often might be) with the partiality of the judge, but only with their advocate. Let us now return to the affairs from which we have thus digressed.

V.

A.D. 375.

§ 1. At the beginning of the spring Valentinian quitted Treves, and proceeded by rapid marches along the usual high roads. And as he approached the districts to which he was hastening, he was met by ambassadors from the Sarmatians, who threw themselves at his feet, and, with prayers, breathing no wish but for peace, entreated him to be favourable and merciful to them, assuring him that he would not find any of their countrymen implicated in or privy to any evil action.

2. And when they had frequently repeated this assertion, he, after careful deliberation, made answer to them, that these matters must be diligently inquired into by an accurate investigation in the district where they were said to have happened, and if they had happened, then they must be punished. After this, when he had reached Carnuntum, a city of the Illyrians, now indeed in a desolate and ruinous state, but still very convenient for the general of an army, he from thence sallied out whenever either chance or skill afforded him an opportunity; and by the possession of this post in their neighbourhood, he checked the inroads of the barbarians.

3. And although he alarmed all people in that district, since it was expected that, as a man of active and impetuous feelings, he would speedily command the judges to be condemned through whose

perfidy or desertion the empire had been left undefended on the side of the Pannonians, yet when he did arrive he was so lukewarm in the business that he neither inquired into the death of the king Gabricius, nor did he make any accurate investigation into the calamities which the republic had sustained, with a view to learning through whose misconduct or negligence these events had taken place; so that in fact, in proportion as he was severe in punishing his common soldiers, he was remiss in correcting (even by harsh words) those of higher rank.

4. The only person whom he pursued with any especial hatred was Probus; whom from the first moment that he saw him he never ceased to threaten, and to whom he never softened; and the causes of this animosity against him were not obscure nor trivial. When Probus first obtained the rank of prefect of the prætorium, the power of which he was continually labouring to extend by all kinds of means (I wish I could say by all lawful means), he forgot the lessons which he might have learnt from his illustrious descent, and devoted himself more to flattery than to modesty.

5. For reflecting on the resolution of the emperor, who considered nothing but how he might amass money from all quarters, without any distinction between just and unjust actions; he never attempted to lead back the misguided prince into the path of equity, as mild and wise rulers often have done; but rather followed his lead through all his winding and tortuous paths.

6. And to this conduct were owing the heavy distresses which afflicted the emperor's subjects; the ruinous titles, privileges, and exemptions, which alike ate up the fortunes of poor and rich; under different pretexts which were produced, each more powerful than the other, as the fruit of a long experience in injuring. Lastly, the burdens of all tributes and taxes were augmented in a manifold degree; and drove some of the highest nobles from fear of the worst to emigrate from their homes; some also after being drained to the utmost by the cruelty of the revenue officers, as they really had nothing more to give, were thrown into prison, of which they became permanent inmates. And some, becoming weary of life and light, sought a release from their miseries by hanging themselves.

7. Unvarying report made known the treacherous and inhuman character of these transactions; but Valentinian, as if his ears had been stopped with wax, was ignorant of the report, being eager to acquire money indiscriminately, even from the most trivial sources, and thinking only of what was presented to him; though he would perhaps have spared the Pannonian provinces, if he had earlier known of these mel-

ancholy sources of gain with which he became acquainted when it was too late, owing to the following occurrence:—

8. Following the example of the inhabitants of other provinces, the people of Epirus were compelled by the prefect to send envoys to thank him, and a certain philosopher named Iphicles, a man of tried courage and magnanimity (who was very unwilling to undertake the commission), was elected to discharge that duty.

9. And when he saw the emperor, having been recognized by him and questioned as to the cause of his arrival, he answered in Greek; and, like a philosopher who professed himself a votary of truth, when the prince inquired more precisely, if those who had sent him did really think well of the prefect, he replied, that they had sent him against their will, and with bitter groans.

10. The emperor, stricken by this speech as by an arrow, now investigated his actions like a sagacious beast, inquiring of him, in his own language, about different persons whom he knew: for instance, where was this man or that man (mentioning some one of high reputation and honour, or some very rich man, or some other person well known as having filled some high office). And when he learnt that this man had been hanged, that that one had been banished beyond the seas, and that a third had killed himself or had expired under torture, he became furiously angry, while Leo, who was at that time master of the offices, added fuel to his passion—O shameful villany! Leo, it should be borne in mind, was at this very time secretly aiming at the prefecture; and had he obtained that office and authority, he would undoubtedly have governed with such audacity, that the administration of Probus would in comparison have been extolled as a model of justice and humanity.

11. So the emperor remained at Carnuntum; and during the three summer months he occupied himself uninterruptedly in preparing arms and magazines, in the hope that chance might afford him a good opportunity of making use of them; intending to take a favourable season for attacking the Quadi, who had lately caused an atrocious disturbance; since in their chief town, Faustinus, the nephew of Juventius, the prefect of the prætorium, who had attained the rank of military secretary, was tortured and then put to death by the executioners, under the very eyes of Probus; having been accused of slaying an ass in some magical operation, as his enemies asserted; but he himself said it was to use for strengthening his hair, which was beginning to fall off.

12. Another charge was also maliciously brought against him, namely, that when a person of the name of Nigrinus had in jest asked

him to make him a secretary, he replied in ridicule of the man and his petition, "Make me emperor if you wish to obtain that." And because some gave an unfair interpretation to this jest, Faustinus himself, and Nigrinus, and several other persons were put to death.

13. Accordingly, having sent forward Merobaudes with a strong force of infantry under his command, and Sebastian for his colleague, to ravage the districts of the barbarians with fire and sword, Valentinian speedily moved his camp to Buda; and having with great rapidity made a bridge of boats in order to guard against any sudden mishap, he crossed the river in another place and entered the territories of the Quadi, who from their precipitous mountains were watching for his approach; the main body of their nation, in their perplexity and uncertainty of what might happen, had taken refuge with their families in those hills; but were overwhelmed with consternation when they unexpectedly saw the imperial standards in their country.

14. Valentinian advanced with as much rapidity as he could, slaughtering every one of whatever age whom his sudden inroad surprised straggling about the country, and after burning all their dwellings, he returned safe without having experienced the slightest loss. And then, as autumn was now on the wane, he stopped awhile at Buda, seeking where best to fix his winter quarters in a region subject to very rigorous frost. And he could not find any suitable place except Sabaria, though that town was at the time in a very bad state of defence, having been ruined by frequent sieges.

15. Accordingly when he reached this place, though it was one of great consequence to him, he remained there but a very short time; and having left it, he marched along the bank of the river, which he strengthened with several forts and castles, and manned them with adequate garrisons. He then proceeded to Bregitio; and in that town, after settling down there in quiet, his Destiny, by numerous prodigies, portended to him his approaching fate.

16. For a very few days before some of those comets, which ever give token of the ruins of lofty fortunes, and of which we have already explained the origin, appeared in the heavens. Also, a short time before, a thunderbolt fell at Sirmium, accompanied with a terrific clap of thunder, and set fire to a portion of the palace and senate-house: and much about the same time an owl settled on the top of the royal baths at Sabaria, and pouring forth a funeral strain, withstood all the attempts to slay it with arrows or stones, however truly aimed, and though numbers of people shot at it in diligent rivalry.

17. And again, when the emperor was quitting the city to return to the camp, he set out to leave it by the same gate by which he had entered it, with the object of obtaining an augury that he should speedily return to Gaul. But the spot through neglect had become choked up with ruins; and when they were cleaning it out they found that the door, which had originally closed the entrance, had fallen down: and a great multitude of people, though labouring with all their might, were unable to remove it; so that after waiting the greater part of the day there, he was obliged at last to go out by another gate.

18. And on the night preceding the day on which he died, he saw in a dream, such as often visits a man in his sleep, his absent wife sitting by, with dishevelled hair, and clad in a mourning robe; which some people fancied was Fortune, who was about in this sad apparel to take her leave of him.

19. After this, when he came forth in the morning, his brow was contracted, and his countenance somewhat melancholy; and when his horse was brought to him, it would not let him mount, but reared up its forefeet over the shoulders of the equerry who was holding it. Valentinian, according to the usual bent of his savage temper, grew immoderately furious, and ordered the equerry's hand to be cut off, which had, he said, pushed him aside when mounting a horse he was used to: and the innocent youth would have perished under torture if Cerealis, the principal master of the horse, had not delayed the barbarous infliction at his own risk.

VI.

§ 1. After this event ambassadors arrived from the Quadi, with humble supplications, entreating peace, and oblivion of the past: and that there might be no obstacle to their obtaining this, they promised to furnish a body of recruits, and some other things which would be of use to the Roman state.

2. And after they had been received, and had obtained permission to return with the grant of an armistice which they had solicited (but in truth, our want of supplies and the unfavourable season of the year prevented us from harassing them any longer), they were, by the influence of Equitius, who became security for their good behaviour, admitted into the council-chamber. When introduced they seemed quite overcome by fear, bowing down to the ground; and on being ordered to unfold their message, they urged all the customary pretences and excuses, confirming them by an oath; assuring the council that whatever offence had been committed against any of our people, had

not been done by the consent of the nobles of the nation, but only by some foreign banditti who dwelt on the borders of the river; they added further, as a fact quite sufficient to establish the truth of their allegations, that the fortress which had been begun to be built both unjustly and unreasonably, had inflamed the savage temper of those rude men to a great pitch of ferocity.

3. By this speech the emperor was excited to most vehement wrath; and as he began to reply to it he grew more indignant, reproaching the whole nation in bitter language, as unmindful of kindness, and ungrateful. But after a time he became pacified, and inclined to a milder view of the case, when suddenly, as if he had been stricken from heaven, his breathing and his voice ceased, and his countenance appeared bloodshot, and in a moment the blood burst forth, and a deadly sweat broke forth over his whole body; and to save him from falling down in the sight of a number of low-born persons, he was led by his servants into one of the private chambers in the interior of the palace.

4. When he was placed on his bed, breathing with difficulty, though the vigour of his intellect was not as yet at all diminished, he recognized those who stood around, having been collected by the chamberlains with great promptitude, to prevent any of them being suspected of having murdered him. And as on account of the fever which was racking his bowels it was necessary to open a vein, yet no surgeon could be found, because he had dispersed them all over different districts to cure the soldiers among whom a dangerous pestilence was raging.

5. At last, however, one was procured; but though he punctured a vein over and over again, he could not produce a single drop of blood, while all the time his bowels were burning with the intensity of his fever; or (as some fancied) because his limbs were wholly dried up in consequence of some of the passages, which we now call hæmorrhoidal, were closed up and crusted over through the severity of the cold.

6. The emperor, from the exceeding violence of his agony, felt that the moment of his death was at hand; and attempted to say something, and to give some orders, as was indicated by a sobbing, which shook his whole frame, a gnashing of the teeth, and a series of violent gestures with his arms, resembling those of boxers with the cæstus: at last he became exhausted, and covered all over with livid spots, and after a severe struggle he expired, in the fifty-fifth year of his age, having reigned twelve years all but a hundred days.

VII.

§ 1. This is a seasonable opportunity to do as we have often done before, namely, to retrace from the original appearance of the father of this emperor down to the time of his own death, all his actions, just touching on them cursorily with a brief mention, not omitting to distinguish between his vices and his virtues, both of which his lofty position held up to the world; being a condition which naturally reveals the inward disposition of every man.

2. The elder Gratian was born at Cibalæ, a town of Pannonia, of a mean family; and from his childhood he received the surname of Funarius, because, while still very young, while he was carrying about a rope (funem) for sale, he resisted the attempt of five soldiers who laboured with all their might to take it from him: thus rivalling Milo of Crotona, from whom no amount of strength could ever wrest an apple, whether he held it in his right or his left hand.

3. Therefore, on account of his exceeding personal strength, and his skill in wrestling after the military fashion, he became well known to many persons, was promoted to the rank of an officer of the guard, then to the post of tribune: after this he was made count, and sent to command the forces in Africa: but there he was suspected of theft; and having quitted that province, he was some time afterwards sent to command the army in Britain, with the same authority which he had enjoyed in Africa. At length he received an honourable discharge from military service, and returned home; and while living there in quiet, he suddenly had all his property confiscated by Constantius, on the ground that, when the civil discord was at its height, he was said to have received Magnentius as a guest when passing through his land to carry his designs into execution.

4. The merits of Gratian brought Valentinian into notice from his early youth; and, indeed, he was further aided by his own eminent qualities; so that he received the ornaments of the imperial majesty at Nicæa; when he also made his brother Valens his colleague, as one bound to him not only by his relationship as a brother, but also by the most perfect agreement—Valens, as we shall show at a suitable time, being made up almost equally of vices and of virtues.

5. Therefore Valentinian, after having experienced many dangers and much distress as a private individual, as soon as he began to reign went to visit the towns and cities which were situated on the rivers; and repaired to Gaul, which was exposed to the inroads of the Allemanni, who had begun to recover their courage and to reassume an imposing attitude since they had heard of the death of the Emperor

503

Julian—the only prince whom they had feared since the time of Constans.

6. And Valentinian was deservedly dreaded by them because he took care to keep up the numbers of his army by strong reinforcements, and because also he fortified both banks of the Rhine with lofty fortresses and castles, to prevent the enemy from ever passing over into our territory without being perceived.

7. We may pass over many circumstances, and many acts which he performed with the authority of an emperor whose power was fully established, and many of the reforms which he either effected himself, or caused to be carried out by his vigorous lieutenants. But we must record how, after he had raised his son Gratian to a partnership in the imperial authority, he contrived the secret murder of Vithigabius, the king of the Allemanni, and the son of Vadomarius, a young man in the flower of youth, who was actively stirring up the surrounding nations to tumults and wars; doing this because he found it impossible to procure his death openly. How also he fought a battle against the Allemanni near Solicinium, where he was nearly circumvented and slain by the manœuvres of the enemy; but where at last he utterly destroyed their whole army with the exception of a few who saved themselves by the aid of the darkness which assisted the rapidity of their flight.

8. Amid all these prudent actions he also turned his attention to the Saxons who had lately broken out with extreme ferocity, making attacks in every direction where they were least expected, and had now penetrated into the inland districts, from which they were returning enriched by a vast booty. He destroyed them utterly by a device which was indeed treacherous, but most advantageous; and he recovered by force all the booty which the defeated robbers were carrying off.

9. Nor did he disregard the condition of the Britons, who were unable to make head against the vast hosts of their enemies, who were overrunning their country; he revived their hopes of better fortune, and re-established liberty and steady tranquillity among them; routing their invaders so completely that scarcely any of them returned to their own country.

10. With similar vigour he crushed Valentinus the Pannonian exile (who was labouring to disturb the general tranquillity in that province), before his enterprise could become dangerous. He also delivered Africa from great dangers at a time when it was thrown into confusion by an unexpected disaster: when Firmus, unable to bear the greediness and arrogance of the soldiers, was exciting the people of

Mauritania to every kind of discord and disturbance. With similar resolution would he have avenged the disasters sustained in Illyricum, had he not left that important duty uncompleted, in consequence of being thus cut off by a premature death.

11. And although these various achievements, which we have here recorded, were consummated by the assistance of his admirable generals, yet it is very notorious that he himself also performed many considerable exploits; being a man fertile in resources, and of long experience and great skill in military affairs: and certainly it would have been an admirable crown to his great actions if he had been able to take King Macrianus alive, who at that time was a very formidable sovereign; nevertheless he exerted great energy in attempting to do so, after he heard that he had escaped from the Burgundians, whom he himself had led against the Allemanni; and the certainty of his escape was to him a cause of great sorrow and indignation.

VIII.

§ 1. Thus have I rapidly run over the different actions of this prince. Now, relying on the certainty that posterity, inasmuch as it is free both from fear and from base flattery, is usually an honest judge of all past transactions, I will rapidly run over his vices, intending afterwards to relate his good qualities.

2. Sometimes he put on an affectation of clemency, though the bent of his natural disposition inclined him more to cruelty: forgetful forsooth, that by a man who governs a vast empire extremes of every kind are to be avoided as rocks by a mariner.

3. Nor indeed was he ever found to be contented with moderate punishments, but was continually commanding cruel tortures to be multiplied; so that many, after undergoing this murderous kind of examination, were brought to death's door. And he was so eager to inflict injury, that he never once saved any one who had been condemned to death, by a milder sentence, though even the most inhuman of emperors have sometimes done so.

4. And yet he might have reflected on many examples in former ages; and he might have imitated the many models of humanity and of piety which he could have found both among natives of the empire and among those of foreign extraction (and humanity and piety are defined by philosophers to be qualities nearly akin). Of such instances it will suffice to enumerate these which follow:—Artaxerxes, that very powerful king of Persia, to whom the great length of one of his limbs caused the name of Longhand to be given, wishing, through the natural

lenity of his disposition, to reprove the varieties of punishment in which his nation, always cruel, had hitherto delighted, punished some criminals by taking off their turbans instead of their heads: and instead of the old royal fashion of cutting off people's ears for their offences, he used to cut the tassels which hang from their caps. And this moderation and lenity made him so popular and respected that all the Grecian writers vie with each other in celebrating his many admirable actions.

5. Again, when Prænestinus was prætor, and was brought before the court of justice, because, in the Samnite war, when ordered to march with all speed to reinforce the army, he had been very dilatory in his movements, Papirius Cursor, who at that time was dictator, ordered the lictor to get ready his axe; and when the prætor, having discarded all hope of being able to clear himself, seemed utterly stupefied at the order, he commanded the lictor to cut down a shrub close by; and having in this jocular manner reproved him, he let him go: without himself incurring any disrespect by so doing, since all knew him for a man who, by his own unassisted vigour, had brought long and dangerous wars to a happy termination; and had been the only man reckoned able to resist Alexander the Great if that prince had invaded Italy.

6. Valentinian, perhaps, was ignorant of these models; and as he never considered that the mercy of the emperor is always the best comfort of persons in distress, he increased all punishments by his free use of both fire and sword: punishments which the merciful disposition of our ancestors looked upon as the very last resource in the most imminent dangers—as we may learn from the beautiful sentiment of Isocrates, who continually insists that we ought rather to pardon a king who is sometimes defeated in war, than one who is ignorant of justice.

7. And it was under the influence of this saying of his that I imagine Cicero uttered that admirable sentence, in his defence of Oppius: "That indeed to have greatly contributed to the safety of one other person was an honour to many; but that to have had no share in injuring others had never been thought discreditable to any one."

8. A desire of increasing his riches without any regard to right and wrong, and of hunting out every kind of source of gain, even at the cost of other people's lives, raged in this emperor to a most excessive degree, and never flagged. Some, indeed, attempted to excuse it by pleading the example of the Emperor Aurelian; affirming that as he, after the death of Gallienus and the lamentable disasters which the republic suffered at that time, finding his treasury totally exhausted, fell

upon the rich like a torrent, so Valentinian also, after the losses which he sustained in his Parthian campaign, being reduced to want by the greatness of his expenses, in order to procure reinforcements for his army and pay for his troops, mingled with his severity a desire of collecting excessive wealth. Pretending not to know that there are some things which, although strictly speaking lawful, still ought not to be done. In this he was very unlike the celebrated Themistocles of old times, who, when strolling carelessly about after he had destroyed the Persian host in the battle of Salamis, and seeing a number of golden armlets and chains lying on the ground, said to one of his companions who was by—"You may take up these things because you are not Themistocles," thinking it became a magnanimous general to spurn any idea of personal gain.

9. Many examples of similar moderation abound in the Roman generals; and without stopping to enumerate them, since such acts are not indications of perfect virtue (for indeed it is no great glory to abstain from carrying off other persons' property), I will just mention one single instance of the forbearance of people in general in this respect in ancient times:—When Marius and Cinna had given the Roman populace leave to plunder the wealthy houses of certain persons whom they had proscribed, the minds of the mob, who, however uncivilized they might be, were accustomed to respect the rights of men, refused to touch the produce of other men's labours; so that in fact no one could be found so needy or so base as to be willing to profit by the miseries of the state.

10. Besides these things the aforesaid emperor was a prey in his inmost heart to a devouring envy; and as he knew that most vices put on a semblance of virtue, he used to be fond of repeating, that severity is the inseparable companion of lawful power. And as magistrates of the highest rank are in the habit of thinking everything permitted to them, and are always inclined to depress those who oppose them, and to humiliate those who are above them, so he hated all who were well dressed, or learned, or opulent, or high born; and he was always disparaging the brave, that he might appear to be the only person eminent for virtue. And this is a vice which, as we read, was very flagrant in the Emperor Hadrian.

11. This same emperor used to be continually abusing the timid, calling them sordid and base, and people who deserved to be depressed below the very lowest of the low; and yet he himself often grew pale, in the most abject manner, with groundless fears, and often

from the bottom of his soul was terrified at things which had no existence at all.

12. Remigius, the master of the ceremonies, knowing this, and also that Valentinian was used to get into furious passions at every trifling incident, spread a report, among other things, that some of the barbarians were in motion; and the emperor, when he heard this, became at once so broken-spirited through fear that he became as gentle and merciful as Antoninus Pius.

13. He never intentionally appointed unjust judges but if he learned that those whom he had once promoted were acting cruelly, he boasted that he had discovered new Lycurguses and Cassiuses, those ancient pillars of justice; and he used to be continually exhorting them by his letters severely to chastise even the slightest errors.

14. Nor had those who were under accusations, if any misfortune fell upon them, any refuge in the kindness of the prince; which ought to be, as it were, a desirable haven to those tossed about in a stormy sea. For, as wise men teach us, "The advantage and safety of the subject is the true end of just government."

IX.

§ 1. It is natural for us, after discussing these topics, if we would act fairly, now to come to his virtuous and laudable actions; since if he had tempered his vices fairly with them he would have been a second Trajan or Marcus Aurelius. Towards the people of the provinces he was very considerate, lightening the burden of their tributes throughout the empire. He also exerted himself in a very beneficial manner in building towns and strengthening the frontiers. He was a strict observer of military discipline, erring only in this respect, that while he punished even slight misconduct on the part of the common soldiers, he allowed the crimes of the officers of rank and of the generals to proceed to greater and greater lengths, and shut his ears against every complaint that was uttered against them. And this partiality of his was the cause of the murmurs in Britain, and the disasters in Africa, and the devastation of Illyricum.

2. He was, both at home and abroad, a strict observer of modesty and chastity, keeping his conscience wholly free from all taint of impurity or obscenity, and in consequence he bridled the wantonness of the imperial court as with a strong rein; and he was the more easily able to do this because he had never shown any indulgence to his own relations, whom he either kept in obscurity, or (if he promoted them at all) raised to a very moderate rank, with the exception of his brother,

whom, in deference to the necessities of the times, he made his partner in the imperial dignity.

3. He was very scrupulous in giving high rank to any one; nor, as long as he was emperor, did any one of the moneyed interest become ruler of a province, nor was any government sold, unless it was at the beginning of his reign, when wicked actions were sometimes committed in the hope that the new prince would be too much occupied to punish them.

4. In waging war, and in defending himself from attacks, he was prudent and very skilful, like a veteran of great experience in military affairs. He was a very wise admirer of all that was good, and dissuader from all that was bad; and a very accurate observer of all the details of military service. He wrote with elegance, and described everything with great neatness and skill in composition. He was an inventor of new arms. He had an excellent memory, and a fluent, easy style of speaking, which at times bordered closely upon eloquence. He was a lover of elegant simplicity, and was fond, not so much of profuse banquets, as of entertainments directed by good taste.

5. Lastly, he was especially remarkable during his reign for his moderation in this particular, that he kept a middle course between the different sects of religion; and never troubled any one, nor issued any orders in favour of one kind of worship or another; nor did he promulgate any threatening edicts to bow down the necks of his subjects to the form of worship to which he himself was inclined; but he left these parties just as he found them, without making any alterations.

6. His body was muscular and strong: the brightness of his hair—the brilliancy of his complexion, with his blue eyes, which always looked askance with a stern aspect—the beauty of his figure—his lofty stature, and the admirable harmony of all his features—filled up the dignity and beauty of an appearance which bespoke a monarch.

X.

§ 1. After the last honours had been paid to the emperor, and his body had been prepared for burial, in order to be sent to Constantinople to be there entombed among the remains of former emperors, the campaign which was in preparation was suspended, and people began to be anxious as to what part would be taken by the Gallic cohorts, who were not always steady in loyalty to the lawful emperor, but looked upon themselves as the disposers of power, and were regarded by others as very likely to venture on some new enterprise at so favourable a moment. This circumstance also was likely to aid any attempt that might be made at a revolution, that Gratian, who knew nothing of what had taken place, was still at Treves, where his father, when about to set out on his own expedition, had desired him to wait.

2. While affairs were in this state of uncertainty, and when every one shared the same fears, looking on themselves as all in the same boat, and sure to be partners in danger, if danger should arise, at last it was decided by the advice of the principal nobles to take up the bridge which had been necessarily made when they meditated invading the territories of the enemy, in order that, in compliance with the commands given by Valentinian while alive, Merobaudes might be at once summoned to the camp.

3. He, being a man of great cunning and penetration, divined what had happened (perhaps indeed he had been informed of it by the messenger who brought him his summons), and suspecting that the Gallic troops were likely to break the existing concord, he pretended that a token which had been agreed upon had been sent to him that he was to return with the messenger to watch the banks of the Rhine; since the fury of the barbarians was again menacing hostilities, and (in compliance with a secret injunction which he received, at the same time) he removed to a distance. Sebastian also as yet was ignorant of the death of the emperor; and he being an orderly and quietly disposed man, but very popular among the soldiers, required on that account to be strictly watched.

4. Accordingly when Merobaudes had returned, the chief men took careful counsel as to what was to be done; and at last it was arranged that the child Valentinian, the son of the deceased emperor, at that time a boy of four years old, should be associated in the imperial power. He was at present a hundred miles off, living with his mother, Justina, in a small town called Murocincta.

5. This decision was ratified by the unanimous consent of all parties; and Cerealis, his uncle, was sent with speed to Murocincta, where he placed the royal child on a litter, and so conducted him to the camp. On the sixth day after his father's death, he was declared lawful emperor, and saluted as Augustus with the usual solemnities.

6. And although at the time many persons thought that Gratian would be indignant that any one else had been appointed emperor without his permission, yet afterwards, when all fear and anxiety was removed, they lived in greater security, because he, wise and kind-hearted man as he was, loved his young relative with exceeding affection, and brought him up with great care.

Notes

[183] No one has succeeded in explaining this word. Some editors wish to read Suræ, explaining that as "men picked out for their great strength," by a reference to Juvenal, xvi. 14—Grandes magna adsubsellia Suræ. Wagner proposes to read Scurræ, a name sometimes given to the guards in this age.

[184] As at Athens, where the orators were only allowed to speak as long as an hour-glass, filled with water, was running down.

[185] All these men are spoken of by Horace as distinguished lawyers in his time.

[186] See Cicero, de Oratore iii. 60.

[187] The Speech of Cicero pro Cœlio Cluentio.

[188] The celebrated speech of Demosthenes, more usually known as that of De Coronâ.

BOOK XXXI

ARGUMENT

I. Omens announcing the death of the Emperor Valens, and a disaster to be inflicted by the Gauls.—II. A description of the abodes and customs of the Huns, the Alani, and other tribes, natives of Asiatic Scythia.—III. The Huns, either by arms or by treaties, unite the Alani on the Don to themselves; invade the Goths, and drive them from their country.—IV. The chief division of the Goths, surnamed the Thuringians, having been expelled from their homes, by permission of Valens are conducted by the Romans into Thrace, on condition of promising obedience and a supply of auxiliary troops. The Gruthungi also, who form the other division of the Goths, secretly cross the Danube by a bridge of boats.—V. The Thuringians being in great distress from hunger and the want of supplies, under the command of their generals Alavivus and Fritigern, revolt from Valens, and defeat Lupicinus and his army.—VI. Why Sueridus and Colias, nobles of the Gothic nation, after having been received in a friendly manner, revolted; and after slaying the people of Hadrianopolis, united themselves to Fritigern, and then turned to ravage Thrace.—VII. Profuturus, Trajan, and Richomeres fought a drawn battle against the Goths.—VIII. The Goths being hemmed in among the defiles at the bottom of the Balkan, after the Romans by returning had let them escape, invaded Thrace, plundering, massacring, ravishing, and burning, and slay Barzimeres, the tribune of the Scutarii.—IX. Frigeridus, Gratian's general, routs Farnobius at the head of a large body of Goths and Taifalæ; sparing the rest, and giving them some lands around the Po.—X. The Lentiensian Alemanni are defeated in battle by the generals of the emperor Gratian, and their king Priamis is slain. Afterwards, having yielded and furnished Gratian with a body of recruits, they are allowed to return to their own country.—XI. Sebastian surprises the Goths at Berœa as they are returning home loaded with plunder, and defeats them with great slaughter; a few saved themselves by flight. Gratian hastens to his uncle Valens, to carry him aid against the Goths.—XII. Valens, before the arrival of Gratian resolves to fight the Goths.—XIII. All the Goths unite together, that is to say, the Thuringians, under their king Fritigern. The Gruthungi, under their dukes Alatheus and Salaces, encounter the Romans in a pitched battle, rout their cavalry, and then falling on the infantry when deprived of the support of their horse, and huddled together in a dense body, they defeat them with enormous loss, and put them to flight. Valens is slain, but his body cannot be found.—XIV. The virtues and vices of Valens.—XV. The victorious Goths besiege Hadrianopolis, where Valens had left his treasures and his insignia of imperial rank, with the prefect and the members of his council; but after trying every means to take the city, without success, they at last retire.—XVI. The Goths, having by bribes won over the forces of the Huns and of the Alani to join them, make an attack upon Constantinople without success. The device by which Julius, the commander of the forces beyond Mount Taurus, delivered the eastern provinces from the Goths.

I.

A.D. 375.

§ 1. In the mean time the swift wheel of Fortune, which continually alternates adversity with prosperity, was giving Bellona the Furies for her allies, and arming her for war; and now transferred our disasters to the East, as many presages and portents foreshowed by undoubted signs.

2. For after many true prophecies uttered by diviners and augurs, dogs were seen to recoil from howling wolves, and the birds of night constantly uttered querulous and mournful cries; and lurid sunrises made the mornings dark. Also, at Antioch, among the tumults and squabbles of the populace, it had come to be a custom for any one who fancied himself ill treated to cry out in a licentious manner, "May Valens be burnt alive!" And the voices of the criers were constantly heard ordering wood to be carried to warm the baths of Valens, which had been built under the supertendence of the emperor himself.

3. All which circumstances all but pointed out in express words that the end of the emperor's life was at hand. Besides all these things, the ghost of the king of Armenia, and the miserable shades of those who had lately been put to death in the affair of Theodorus, agitated numbers of people with terrible alarms, appearing to them in their sleep, and shrieking out verses of horrible import.[189]

4. ... and its death indicated an extensive and general calamity arising from public losses and deaths. Last of all, when the ancient

walls of Chalcedon were thrown down in order to build a bath at Constantinople, and the stones were torn asunder, on one squared stone which was hidden in the very centre of the walls these Greek verses were found engraved, which gave a full revelation of what was to happen:—

"Ἀλλ' ὅποταν νύμφαι δροσερῇ κατὰ ἄστυ χορείῃ
Τεπόμεναι στρέψωνται εὔστεέφας κατ' ἀγυιὰς
Καὶ τεῖχος λούτροιο πολύστονον ἔσσεται ἄλκαὶ
Δὴ τότε μύρια φῦλα πολυσπερέων ἀνθρώπων
Ἴστρου καλλιρόοιο πόρον περάοντα σὺν αἰχμῇ
Καὶ Σκυθικὴν ὀλέσει χώῃην καὶ Μυσίδα γαῖαν
Παιονίης δ' ἐπιβάντα σὺν σὺν ἐλπίσι μαινομένῃσιν
Αὐτόου καὶ βιότο ο τέλος καὶ δῆρις εφεξει."

Translation.

"But when young wives and damsels blithe, in dances that delight,
Shall glide along the city streets, with garlands gaily bright;
And when these walls, with sad regrets, shall fall to raise a bath,
Then shall the Huns in multitude break forth with might and wrath.
By force of arms the barrier-stream of Ister they shall cross,
O'er Scythic ground and Mœsian lands spreading dismay and loss:
They shall Pannonian horsemen brave, and Gallic soldiers slay,
And nought but loss of life and breath their course shall ever stay."

II.

§ 1. The following circumstances were the original cause of all the destruction and various calamities which the fury of Mars roused up, throwing everything into confusion by his usual ruinous violence: the people called Huns, slightly mentioned in the ancient records, live beyond the Sea of Azov, on the border of the Frozen Ocean, and are a race savage beyond all parallel.

2. At the very moment of their birth the cheeks of their infant children are deeply marked by an iron, in order that the usual vigour of their hair, instead of growing at the proper season, may be withered by the wrinkled scars; and accordingly they grow up without beards, and consequently without any beauty, like eunuchs, though they all have closely-knit and strong limbs, and plump necks; they are of great size, and low legged, so that you might fancy them two-legged beasts, or the stout figures which are hewn out in a rude manner with an axe on the posts at the end of bridges.

3. They are certainly in the shape of men, however uncouth, but are so hardy that they neither require fire nor well-flavoured food, but

live on the roots of such herbs as they get in the fields, or on the half-raw flesh of any animal, which they merely warm rapidly by placing it between their own thighs and the backs of their horses.

4. They never shelter themselves under roofed houses, but avoid them as people ordinarily avoid sepulchres as things not fitted for common use. Nor is there even to be found among them a cabin thatched with reed; but they wander about, roaming over the mountains and the woods and accustom themselves to bear frost and hunger and thirst from their very cradles. And even when abroad they never enter a house unless under the compulsion of some extreme necessity; nor, indeed, do they think people under roofs as safe as others.

5. They wear linen clothes, or else garments made of the skins of field-mice: nor do they wear a different dress out of doors from that which they wear at home; but after a tunic is once put round their necks, however it becomes worn, it is never taken off or changed till, from long decay, it becomes actually so ragged as to fall to pieces.

6. They cover their heads with round caps, and their shaggy legs with the skins of kids; their shoes are not made on any lasts, but are so unshapely as to hinder them from walking with a free gait. And for this reason they are not well suited to infantry battles, but are nearly always on horseback, their horses being ill-shaped, but hardy; and sometimes they even sit upon them like women if they want to do anything more conveniently. There is not a person in the whole nation who cannot remain on his horse day and night. On horseback they buy and sell, they take their meat and drink, and there they recline on the narrow neck of their steed, and yield to sleep so deep as to indulge in every variety of dream.

7. And when any deliberation is to take place on any weighty matter, they all hold their common council on horseback. They are not under the authority of a king, but are contented with the irregular government of their nobles, and under their lead they force their way through all obstacles.

8. Sometimes when provoked, they fight; and when they go into battle, they form in a solid body, and utter all kinds of terrific yells. They are very quick in their operations, of exceeding speed, and fond of surprising their enemies. With a view to this, they suddenly disperse, then reunite, and again, after having inflicted vast loss upon the enemy, scatter themselves over the whole plain in irregular formations: always avoiding a fort or an entrenchment.

9. And in one respect you may pronounce them the most formidable of all warriors, for when at a distance they use missiles of

various kinds tipped with sharpened bones instead of the usual points of javelins, and these bones are admirably fastened into the shaft of the javelin or arrow; but when they are at close quarters they fight with the sword, without any regard for their own safety; and often while their antagonists are warding off their blows they entangle them with twisted cords, so that, their hands being fettered, they lose all power of either riding or walking.

10. None of them plough, or even touch a plough-handle: for they have no settled abode, but are homeless and lawless, perpetually wandering with their waggons, which they make their homes; in fact they seem to be people always in flight. Their wives live in these waggons, and there weave their miserable garments; and here too they sleep with their husbands, and bring up their children till they reach the age of puberty; nor, if asked, can any one of them tell you where he was born, as he was conceived in one place, born in another at a great distance, and brought up in another still more remote.

11. In truces they are treacherous and inconstant, being liable to change their minds at every breeze of every fresh hope which presents itself, giving themselves up wholly to the impulse and inclination of the moment; and, like brute beasts, they are utterly ignorant of the distinction between right and wrong. They express themselves with great ambiguity and obscurity; have no respect for any religion or superstition whatever; are immoderately covetous of gold; and are so fickle and irascible, that they very often on the same day that they quarrel with their companions without any provocation, again become reconciled to them without any mediator.

12. This active and indomitable race, being excited by an unrestrainable desire of plundering the possessions of others, went on ravaging and slaughtering all the nations in their neighbourhood till they reached the Alani, who were formerly called the Massagetæ; and from what country these Alani come, or what territories they inhabit (since my subject has led me thus far), it is expedient now to explain: after showing the confusion existing in the accounts of the geographers, who ... at last have found out ... of truth.

13. The Danube, which is greatly increased by other rivers falling into it, passes through the territory of the Sauromatæ, which extends as far as the river Don, the boundary between Asia and Europe. On the other side of this river the Alani inhabit the enormous deserts of Scythia, deriving their own name from the mountains around; and they, like the Persians, having gradually subdued all the bordering nations by repeated victories, have united them to them-

selves, and comprehended them under their own name. Of these other tribes the Neuri inhabit the inland districts, being near the highest mountain chains, which are both precipitous and covered with the everlasting frost of the north. Next to them are the Budini and the Geloni, a race of exceeding ferocity, who flay the enemies they have slain in battle, and make of their skins clothes for themselves and trappings for their horses. Next to the Geloni are the Agathyrsi, who dye both their bodies and their hair of a blue colour, the lower classes using spots few in number and small—the nobles broad spots, close and thick, and of a deeper hue.

15. Next to these are the Melanchænæ and the Anthropophagi, who roam about upon different tracts of land and live on human flesh. And these men are so avoided on account of their horrid food, that all the tribes which were their neighbours have removed to a distance from them. And in this way the whole of that region to the north-east, till you come to the Chinese, is uninhabited.

16. On the other side the Alani again extend to the east, near the territories of the Amazons, and are scattered among many populous and wealthy nations, stretching to the parts of Asia which, as I am told, extend up to the Ganges, a river which passes through the country of the Indians, and falls into the Southern Ocean.

17. Then the Alani, being thus divided among the two quarters of the globe (the various tribes which make up the whole nation it is not worth while to enumerate), although widely separated, wander, like the Nomades, over enormous districts. But in the progress of time all these tribes came to be united under one generic appellation, and are called Alani....

18. They have no cottages, and never use the plough, but live solely on meat and plenty of milk, mounted on their waggons, which they cover with a curved awning made of the bark of trees, and then drive them through their boundless deserts. And when they come to any pasture-land, they pitch their waggons in a circle, and live like a herd of beasts, eating up all the forage—carrying, as it were, their cities with them in their waggons. In them the husbands sleep with their wives—in them their children are born and brought up; these waggons, in short, are their perpetual habitation, and wherever they fix them, that place they look upon as their home.

19. They drive before them their flocks and herds to their pasturage; and, above all other cattle, they are especially careful of their horses. The fields in that country are always green, and are interspersed with patches of fruit trees, so that, wherever they go, there is

no dearth either of food for themselves or fodder for their cattle. And this is caused by the moisture of the soil, and the number of the rivers which flow through these districts.

20. All their old people, and especially all the weaker sex, keep close to the waggons, and occupy themselves in the lighter employments. But the young men, who from their earliest childhood are trained to the use of horses, think it beneath them to walk. They are also all trained by careful discipline of various sorts to become skilful warriors. And this is the reason why the Persians, who are originally of Scythian extraction, are very skilful in war.

21. Nearly all the Alani are men of great stature and beauty; their hair is somewhat yellow, their eyes are terribly fierce; the lightness of their armour renders them rapid in their movements; and they are in every respect equal to the Huns, only more civilized in their food and their manner of life. They plunder and hunt as far as the Sea of Azov and the Cimmerian Bosphorus, ravaging also Armenia and Media.

22. And as ease is a delightful thing to men of a quiet and placid disposition, so danger and war are a pleasure to the Alani, and among them that man is called happy who has lost his life in battle. For those who grow old, or who go out of the world from accidental sicknesses, they pursue with bitter reproaches as degenerate and cowardly. Nor is there anything of which they boast with more pride than of having killed a man: and the most glorious spoils they esteem the scalps which they have torn from the heads of those whom they have slain, which they put as trappings and ornaments on their war horses.

23. Not is there any temple or shrine seen in their country, nor even any cabin thatched with straw, their only idea of religion being to plunge a naked sword into the ground with barbaric ceremonies, and then they worship that with great respect, as Mars, the presiding deity of the regions over which they wander.

24. They presage the future in a most remarkable manner; for they collect a number of straight twigs of osier, then with certain secret incantations they separate them from one another on particular days; and from them they learn clearly what is about to happen.

25. They have no idea of slavery, inasmuch as they themselves are all born of noble families; and those whom even now they appoint to be judges are always men of proved experience and skill in war. But now let us return to the subject which we proposed to ourselves.

III.

§ 1. Therefore the Huns, after having traversed the territories of the Alani, and especially of that tribe of them who border on the Grut-hungi, and who are called Tanaitæ, and having slain many of them and acquired much plunder, they made a treaty of friendship and alliance with those who remained. And when they had united them to them-selves, with increased boldness they made a sudden incursion into the extensive and fertile districts of Ermenrichus, a very warlike prince, and one whom his numerous gallant actions of every kind had ren-dered formidable to all the neighbouring nations.

2. He was astonished at the violence of this sudden tempest, and although, like a prince whose power was well established he long at-tempted to hold his ground, he was at last overpowered by a dread of the evils impending over his country, which were exaggerated by common report, till he terminated his fear of great danger by a volun-tary death.

3. After his death Vithimiris was made king. He for some time maintained a resistance to the Alani, relying on the aid of other tribes of the Huns, whom by large promises of pay he had won over to his party; but, after having suffered many losses, he was defeated by supe-rior numbers and slain in battle. He left an infant son named Viderichus, of whom Alatheus and Saphrax undertook the guardian-ship, both generals of great experience and proved courage. And when they, yielding to the difficulties of the crisis, had given up all hope of being able to make an effectual resistance, they retired with caution till they came to the river Dniester, which lies between the Danube and the Dnieper, and flows through a vast extent of country.

4. When Athanaric, the chief magistrate of the Thuringians (against whom, as I have already mentioned, Valens had begun to wage war, to punish him for having sent assistance to Procopius), had become informed of these unexpected occurrences, he prepared to maintain his ground, with a resolution to rise up in strength should he be assailed as the others had been.

5. At last he pitched his camp at a distance in a very favourable spot near the banks of the Dniester and the valleys of the Gruthungi, and sent Muderic, who afterwards became Duke of the Arabian fron-tier, with Lagarimanus and others of the nobles, with orders to advance for twenty miles, to reconnoitre the approach of the enemy while in the mean time he himself, without delay, marshalled his troops in line of battle.

6. However, things turned out in a manner very contrary to his expectations. For the Huns (being very sagacious in conjectures) sus-

pecting that there must be a considerable multitude further off, contrived to pass beyond those they had seen, and arranged themselves to
take their rest where there was nothing at hand to disturb them; and
then, when the moon dispelled the darkness of night, they forded the
river, which was the best plan that presented itself, and fearing lest the
piquets at the outposts might give the alarm to the distant camp, they
made all possible speed and advanced with the hope of surprising
Athanaric himself.

7. He was stupefied at the suddenness of their onset, and after
losing many of his men, was compelled to flee for refuge to the precipitous mountains in the neighbourhood, where, being wholly
bewildered with the strangeness of this occurrence, and the fear of
greater evils to come, he began to fortify with lofty walls all the territory between the banks of the river Pruth and the Danube, where it
passes through the lands of the Taifali, and he completed this line of
fortification with great diligence, thinking that by this step he should
secure his own personal safety.

8. While this important work was going on, the Huns kept pressing on his traces with great speed, and they would have overtaken and
destroyed him if they had not been forced to abandon the pursuit from
being impeded by the great quantity of their booty. In the mean time a
report spread extensively through the other nations of the Goths, that a
race of men, hitherto unknown, had suddenly descended like a whirlwind from the lofty mountains, as if they had risen from some secret
recess of the earth, and were ravaging and destroying everything
which came in their way. And then the greater part of the population
which, because of their want of necessaries had deserted Athanaric,
resolved to flee and to seek a home remote from all knowledge of the
barbarians; and after a long deliberation where to fix their abode, they
resolved that a retreat into Thrace was the most suitable for these two
reasons: first of all, because it is a district most fertile in grass; and
also because, by the great breadth of the Danube, it is wholly separated
from the barbarians, who were already exposed to the thunderbolts of
foreign warfare. And the whole population of the tribe adopted this
resolution unanimously.

IV.

A.D. 376.

§ 1. Accordingly, under the command of their leader Alavivus, they occupied the banks of the Danube; and having sent ambassadors to Valens, they humbly entreated to be received by him as his subjects, promising to live quietly, and to furnish a body of auxiliary troops if any necessity for such a force should arise.

2. While these events were passing in foreign countries, a terrible rumour arose that the tribes of the north were planning new and unprecedented attacks upon us: and that over the whole region which extends from the country of the Marcomanni and Quadi to Pontus, a barbarian host composed of different distant nations, which had suddenly been driven by force from their own country, was now, with all their families, wandering about in different directions on the banks of the river Danube.

3. At first this intelligence was lightly treated by our people, because they were not in the habit of hearing of any wars in those remote districts till they were terminated either by victory or by treaty.

4. But presently, as the belief in these occurrences grew stronger, being confirmed, too, by the arrival of the foreign ambassadors, who, with prayers and earnest entreaties, begged that the people thus driven from their homes and now encamped on the other side of the river, might be kindly received by us, the affair seemed a cause of joy rather than of fear, according to the skilful flatterers who were always extolling and exaggerating the good fortune of the emperor; congratulating him that an embassy had come from the furthest corners of the earth unexpectedly, offering him a large body of recruits; and that, by combining the strength of his own nation with these foreign forces, he would have an army absolutely invincible; observing further that, by the yearly payment for military reinforcements which came in every year from the provinces, a vast treasure of gold might be accumulated in his coffers.

5. Full of this hope he sent forth several officers to bring this ferocious people and their waggons into our territory. And such great pains were taken to gratify this nation which was destined to overthrow the empire of Rome, that not one was left behind, not even of those who were stricken with mortal disease. Moreover, having obtained permission of the emperor to cross the Danube and to cultivate some districts in Thrace, they crossed the stream day and night, without ceasing, embarking in troops on board ships and rafts, and canoes made of the hollow trunks of trees, in which enterprise, as the Danube

is the most difficult of all rivers to navigate, and was at that time swollen with continual rains, a great many were drowned, who, because they were too numerous for the vessels, tried to swim across, and in spite of all their exertions were swept away by the stream.

6. In this way, through the turbulent zeal of violent people, the ruin of the Roman empire was brought on. This, at all events, is neither obscure nor uncertain, that the unhappy officers who were intrusted with the charge of conducting the multitude of the barbarians across the river, though they repeatedly endeavoured to calculate their numbers, at last abandoned the attempt as hopeless: and the man who would wish to ascertain the number might as well (as the most illustrious of poets[190] says) attempt to count the waves in the African sea, or the grains of sand tossed about by the zephyr.

7. Let, however, the ancient annals be accredited which record that the Persian host which was led into Greece, was, while encamped on the shores of the Hellespont, and making a new and artificial sea,[191] numbered in battalions at Doriscus; a computation which has been unanimously regarded by all posterity as fabulous.

8. But after the innumerable multitudes of different nations, diffused over all our provinces, and spreading themselves over the vast expanse of our plains, who filled all the champaign country and all the mountain ranges, are considered, the credibility of the ancient accounts is confirmed by this modern instance. And first of all Fritigern was received with Alavivus; and the emperor assigned them a temporary provision for their immediate support, and ordered lands to be assigned them to cultivate.

9. At that time the defences of our provinces were much exposed, and the armies of barbarians spread over them like the lava of Mount Etna. The imminence of our danger manifestly called for generals already illustrious for their past achievements in war: but nevertheless, as if some unpropitious deity had made the selection, the men who were sought out for the chief military appointments were of tainted character. The chief among them were Lupicinus and Maximus, the one being Count of Thrace, the other a leader notoriously wicked—and both men of great ignorance and rashness.

10. And their treacherous covetousness was the cause of all our disasters. For (to pass over other matters in which the officers aforesaid, or others with their unblushing connivance, displayed the greatest profligacy in their injurious treatment of the foreigners dwelling in our territory, against whom no crime could be alleged) this one melancholy and unprecedented piece of conduct (which, even if they were to

choose their own judges, must appear wholly unpardonable) must be mentioned.

11. When the barbarians who had been conducted across the river were in great distress from want of provisions, those detested generals conceived the idea of a most disgraceful traffic: and having collected hounds from all quarters with the most insatiable rapacity, they exchanged them for an equal number of slaves, among whom were several sons of men of noble birth.

12. About this time also, Vitheric, the king of the Gruthungi, with Alatheus and Saphrax, by whose influence he was mainly guided, and also with Farnobius, approached the bank of the Danube, and sent envoys to the emperor to entreat that he also might be received with the same kindness that Alavivus and Fritigern had experienced.

13. But when, as seemed best for the interests of the state, these ambassadors had been rejected, and were in great anxiety as to what they should do, Athanaric, fearing similar treatment, departed; recollecting that long ago when he was discussing a treaty of alliance with Valens, he had treated that emperor with contempt, in affirming that he was bound by a religious obligation never to set his foot on the Roman territory; and that by this excuse he had compelled the emperor to conclude a peace in the middle of the war. And he, fearing that the grudge which Valens bore him for this conduct was still lasting, withdrew with all his forces to Caucalandes, a place which, from the height of its mountains and the thickness of its woods, is completely inaccessible; and from which he had lately driven out the Sarmatians.

V.

§ 1. But the Thuringians, though they had some time since received permission to cross the river, were still wandering up and down the banks, being hindered by a twofold obstacle; first, that in consequence of the mischievous dissimulation of the said generals they were not supplied with the necessary provisions; and also because they were designedly detained that they might the more easily be plundered under the wicked semblance of traffic.

2. And when they ascertained these facts, they began to grumble, and proposed to resist the evils which they apprehended from the treachery of these men by open force; and Lupicinus, who feared that they would resist, brought up his troops close to them, in order to compel them to be gone with all possible rapidity.

3. The Gruthungi seized this as a favourable opportunity, and seeing that the Roman soldiers were occupied in another quarter, and

that the vessels which used to go up and down, to prevent them from crossing, were now stationary, crossed the river on roughly-made rafts, and pitched their camp at a great distance from Fritigern.

4. But he, by his innate foresight, provided against everything that could happen, and marching on slowly as well in obedience to the commands he had received as to allow time for other powerful kings to join him, came by slow marches to Marcianopolis, arriving later than he was expected. And here another atrocious occurrence took place, which kindled the torches of the Furies for general calamity.

5. Alavivus and Fritigern were invited to a banquet; while Lupicinus drew up his soldiers against the chief host of the barbarians, and so kept them at a distance from the walls of the town; though they with humble perseverance implored admission in order so to procure necessary provisions, professing themselves loyal and obedient subjects. At last a serious strife arose between the citizens and the strangers who were thus refused admittance, which gradually led to a regular battle. And the barbarians, being excited to an unusual pitch of ferocity when they saw their relations treated as enemies, began to plunder the soldiers whom they had slain.

6. But when Lupicinus, of whom we have already spoken, learnt by secret intelligence that this was taking place, while he was engaged in an extravagant entertainment, surrounded by buffoons, and almost overcome by wine and sleep, he, fearing the issue, put to death all the guards who, partly as a compliment and partly as a guard to the chiefs, were on duty before the general's tent.

7. The people who were still around the walls heard of this with great indignation, and rising up by degrees into a resolution to avenge their kings, who, as they fancied, were being detained as prisoners, broke out with furious threats. And Fritigern, being a man of great readiness of resource, and fearing that perhaps he might be detained with the rest as a hostage, exclaimed that there would be a terrible and destructive conflict if he were not allowed to go forth with his companions in order to pacify the multitude, who he said had broken out in this tumult from believing that their leaders had been trepanned and murdered under show of courtesy. Having obtained permission, they all went forth, and were received with cheers and great delight; they then mounted their horses and fled, in order to kindle wars in many quarters.

8. When Fame, ever the malignant nurse of bad news, bruited this abroad, the whole nation of the Thuringians became suddenly inflamed with a desire for war; and among many preparations which

seemed to betoken danger, the standards of war were raised according to custom, and the trumpets poured forth sounds of evil omen; while the predatory bands collected in troops plundering and burning villages, and throwing everything that came in their way into alarm by their fearful devastations.

9. Against these hosts, Lupicinus, having collected his forces with the greatest possible rapidity, advanced with more rashness than prudence, and halted in battle array nine miles from the city. The barbarians, perceiving this, charged our battalions before we expected them, and dashing upon the shields with which they covered their bodies, they cut down all who fell in their way with their swords and spears; and urged on by their bloodthirsty fury, they continued the slaughter, till they had taken our standards, and the tribunes and the greater part of the soldiers had fallen, with the exception of the unhappy general, who could find nothing to do but, while all the rest were fighting, to betake himself to flight, and return full gallop to the city. And then the enemies, clothing themselves in the arms of the Romans whom they had slain, pushed on their devastating march without hindrance.

10. And since, after recounting various other exploits, we have now come to this portion of our subject, we call upon our readers (if we shall ever have any) not to expect a minute detail of everything that took place, or of the number of the slain, which indeed it would be utterly impossible to give. It will be sufficient to abstain from concealing any part of the truth by a lie, and to give the general outline of what took place: since a faithful honesty of narration is always proper if one would hand events down to the recollection of posterity.

11. Those who are ignorant of antiquity declare that the republic was never so overwhelmed with the darkness of adverse fortune; but they are deceived in consequence of the stupor into which they are thrown by these calamities, which are still fresh in their memory. For if the events of former ages, or even of those immediately preceding our own times are considered, it will be plain that such melancholy events have often happened, of which I will bring to mind several instances.

12. The Teutones and the Cimbri came suddenly from the remote shores of the ocean, and overran Italy; but, after having inflicted enormous disasters on the Roman republic, they were at last overcome by our illustrious generals, and being wholly vanquished, learnt by their ultimate destruction what martial valour, combined with skill, can effect.

13. Again, in the reign of the Emperor Marcus Aurelius, the insane fury of a number of different nations combined together, after fearful wars ... would have left but a small part of them.

14. But, soon after these calamitous losses, the state was re-established in all its former strength and prosperity; because the soberness of our ancestry had not yet become infected with the luxury and softness of a more effeminate way of life, and had not learnt to indulge in splendid banquets, or the criminal acquisition of riches. But both the highest classes and the lowest living in harmony, and imbued with one unanimous spirit, eagerly embraced a glorious death in the cause of the republic as a tranquil and quiet haven.

15. The great multitudes of the Scythian nations, having burst through the Bosphorus, and made their way to the shores of the Sea of Azov with 2000 ships, inflicted fearful losses on us by land and sea; but also lost a great portion of their own men, and so at last returned to their own country.

16. Those great generals, the Decii, father and son, fell fighting against the barbarians. The cities of Pamphylia were besieged, many islands were laid waste; Macedon was ravaged with fire and sword. An enormous host for a long time blockaded Thessalonica and Cyzicus. Arabia also was taken; and so at the same time was Nicopolis, which had been built by the Emperor Trajan as a monument of his victory over the Dacians.

17. After many fearful losses had been both sustained and inflicted Philippopolis was destroyed, and, unless our annals speak falsely, 100,000 men were slaughtered within its walls. Foreign enemies roved unrestrained over Epirus, and Thessaly, and the whole of Greece; but after that glorious general Claudius had been taken as a colleague in the empire (though again lost to us by an honourable death), the enemy was routed by Aurelian, an untiring leader, and a severe avenger of injuries; and after that they remained quiet for a long time without attempting anything, except that some bands of robbers now and then ranged the districts in their own neighbourhood, always, however, to their own injury. And now I will return to the main history from which I have digressed.

VI.

§ 1. When this series of occurrences had been made generally known by frequent messengers, Sueridus and Colias, two nobles of the Goths, who had some time before been friendly received with their people, and had been sent to Hadrianople to pass the winter in that city, thinking their own safety the most important of all objects, looked on all the events which were taking place with great indifference.

2. But, on a sudden, letters having arrived from the emperor, in which they were ordered to cross over to the province of the Hellespont, they asked, in a very modest manner, to be provided with money to defray the expenses of their march, as well as provisions, and to be allowed a respite of two days. But the chief magistrate of the city was indignant at this request, being also out of humour with them on account of some injury which had been done to property of his own in the suburbs, and collected a great mob of the lowest of the people, with a body of armourers, of whom there is a great number in that place, and led them forth armed to hasten the departure of the Goths. And ordering the trumpeters to sound an alarm, he menaced them with destruction unless they at once departed with all speed, as they had been ordered.

3. The Goths, bewildered by this unexpected calamity, and alarmed at this outbreak of the citizens, which looked more as if caused by a sudden impulse than by any deliberate purpose, stood without moving. And being assailed beyond all endurance by reproaches and manifestations of ill will, and also by occasional missiles, they at last broke out into open revolt; having slain several of those who had at first attacked them with too much petulance, and having put the rest to flight, and wounded many with all kinds of weapons, they stripped their corpses and armed themselves with the spoils in the Roman fashion; and then, seeing Fritigern near them, they united themselves to him as obedient allies, and blockaded the city. They remained some time, maintaining this difficult position and making promiscuous attacks, during which they lost some of their number by their own audacity, without being able to avenge them; while many were slain by arrows and large stones hurled from slings.

4. Then Fritigern, perceiving that his men, who were unaccustomed to sieges, were struggling in vain, and sustaining heavy losses, advised his army to leave a force sufficient to maintain the blockade, and to depart with the rest, acknowledging their failure, and saying that "He did not war with stone walls." Advising them also to lay waste all the fertile regions around without any distinction, and to plunder those places which were not defended by any garrisons.

5. His counsel was approved, as his troops knew that he was always a very able commander in bringing their plans to success; and then they dispersed over the whole district of Thrace, advancing cautiously; while those who came of their own accord to surrender, or

those whom they had taken prisoners, pointed out to them the richest towns, and especially those where it was said that supplies of provisions could be found. And in addition to their natural confidence they were greatly encouraged by this circumstance, that a multitude of that nation came in daily to join them who had formerly been sold as slaves by the merchants, with many others whom, when at their first passage of the river they were suffering from severe want, they had bartered for a little bad wine or morsels of bread.

6. To these were added no inconsiderable number of men skilled in tracing out veins of gold, but who were unable to endure the heavy burden of their taxes; and who, having been received with the cheerful consent of all, they were of great use to them while traversing strange districts—showing them the secret stores of grain, the retreats of men, and other hiding-places of divers kinds.

7. Nor while these men led them on as their guides did anything remain untouched by them, except what was inaccessible or wholly out of the way; for without any distinction of age or sex they went forward destroying everything in one vast slaughter and conflagration: tearing infants even from their mother's breast and slaying them; ravishing their mothers; slaughtering women's husbands before the eyes of those whom they thus made widows; while boys of tender and of adult age were dragged over the corpses of their parents.

8. Lastly, numbers of old men, crying out that they had lived long enough, having lost all their wealth, together with beautiful women, had their hands bound behind their back, and were driven into banishment, bewailing the ashes of their native homes.

VII.

A.D. 377.

§ 1. This news from Thrace was received with great sorrow, and caused the Emperor Valens much anxiety.[192] He instantly sent Victor, the commander of the cavalry, into Persia, to make such arrangements in Armenia as were required by the impending danger. While he himself prepared at once to quit Antioch and go to Constantinople, sending before him Profuturus and Trajan, both officers of rank and ambition, but of no great skill in war.

2. When they arrived at the place where it seemed most expedient to combat this hostile multitude in detail and by ambuscades and surprises, they very injudiciously adopted the ill-considered plan of opposing the legions which had arrived from Armenia to barbarians who were still raging like madmen. Though the legions had repeatedly

proved equal to the dangers of a pitched battle and regular warfare, they were not suited to encounter an innumerable host which occupied all the chains of the lofty hills, and also all the plains.

3. Our men had never yet experienced what can be effected by indomitable rage united with despair, and so having driven back the enemy beyond the abrupt precipices of the Balkan, they seized upon the rugged defiles in order to hem in the barbarians on ground from which they would be unable to find any exit, and where it seemed they might be overcome by famine. They themselves intended to await the arrival of Frigeridus, the duke, who was hastening towards them with the auxiliaries from Pannonia and other countries, and whom, at the request of Valens, Gratian had commanded to march to the camp to aid those who were menaced with total destruction.

4. After him, Richomeres, at that time count of the domestics, who also, by the command of Gratian, had moved forwards from Gaul, hastened towards Thrace,[193] bringing with him some cohorts, which were cohorts in name, though the greater portion of them had already deserted (if we would believe some people), by the persuasion of Merobaudes, fearing lest Gaul, now divested of all the troops, would be ravaged without check after the barbarians had forced the passage of the Rhine.

5. But Frigeridus was prevented from moving by the gout, or at all events (as some of his malicious detractors represented it), he pleaded sickness as an excuse for not being present in the struggles which were expected, and so Richomeres, being unanimously called to the chief command, with Profuturus and Trajan for his colleagues, advanced towards the town of Salices—at no great distance from which was a countless host of barbarians, arranged in a circle, with a great multitude of waggons for a rampart around them, behind which, as if protected by a spacious wall, they enjoyed ease and an abundance of booty.

6. Filled with hopes of success, the Roman generals—resolved on some gallant enterprise should fortune afford them an opportunity—were carefully watching the movements of the Goths! having formed the design—if they moved their camp in any other direction, which they were very much in the habit of doing—to fall upon their rear, making no doubt that they should slay many of them, and recover a great portion of their spoil.

7. When the barbarians learnt this, probably through the information of some deserter, from whom they obtained a knowledge of our operations, they remained for some time in the same place; but at last,

being influenced by fear of the opposing army, and of the reinforcements which might be expected to throng to them, they assembled, by
a preconcerted signal, the predatory bands dispersed in different districts, and which, the moment they received the orders of their leaders,
returned like firebrands, with the swiftness of birds, to their "encampment of chariots" (as they call it), and thus gave their countrymen
confidence to attempt greater enterprises.

8. After this there was no cessation of hostilities between the two
parties except what was afforded by a few short truces; for after those
men had returned to the camp whom necessity had forced to quit it, the
whole body which was crowded within the circuit of the encampment,
being full of fierce discontent, excitement, and a most ferocious spirit,
and now reduced to the greatest extremities, were eager for bloodshed:
nor did their chiefs, who were present with them, resist their desire;
and as the resolution to give battle was taken when the sun was sinking, and when the approach of night invited the sullen and
discontented troops to rest, they took some food quietly, but remained
all night sleepless.

9. On the other hand the Romans, knowing what was going on,
kept themselves also awake, fearing the enemy and their insane leaders
as so many furious wild beasts: nevertheless, with fearless minds they
awaited the result, which, though they acknowledged it to be doubtful
in respect of their inferiority in number, they still trusted would be
propitious because of the superior justice of their cause.

10. Therefore the next day, as soon as it was light, the signal for
taking arms having been given by the trumpets on both sides, the barbarians, after having, in accordance with their usual custom, taken an
oath to remain faithful to their standards, attempted to gain the higher
ground, in order that from it they might descend down the steep like
wheels, overwhelming their enemy by the vigour of their attack. When
this was seen, our soldiers all flocked to their proper regiments, and
then stood firm, neither turning aside nor in any instance even leaving
their ranks to rush forward.

11. Therefore when the armies on both sides, advancing more
cautiously, at last halted and stood immovable, the warriors, with mutual sternness, surveying each other with fierce looks. The Romans in
every part of their line sang warlike songs, with a voice rising from a
lower to a higher key, which they call barritus,[194] and so encouraged
themselves to gallant exertions. But the barbarians, with dissonant
clamour, shouted out the praises of their ancestors, and amid their
various discordant cries, tried occasional light skirmishes.

12. And now each army began to assail the other with javelins and other similar missiles; and then with threatening shouts rushed on to close combat, and packing their shields together like a testudo, they came foot to foot with their foes. The barbarians, active, and easily rallied, hurled huge bludgeons, burnt at one end, against our men, and vigorously thrust their swords against the opposing breasts of the Romans, till they broke our left wing; but as it recoiled, it fell back on a strong body of reserve which was vigorously brought up on their flank, and supported them just as they were on the very point of destruction.

13. Therefore, while the battle raged with vast slaughter, each individual soldier rushing fiercely on the dense ranks of the enemy, the arrows and javelins flew like hail; the blows of swords were equally rapid; while the cavalry, too, pressed on, cutting down all who fled with terrible and mighty wounds on their backs; as also on both sides did the infantry, slaughtering and hamstringing those who had fallen down, and through fear were unable to fly.

14. And when the whole place was filled with corpses, some also lay among them still half alive, vainly cherishing a hope of life, some of them having been pierced with bullets hurled from slings, others with arrows barbed with iron. Some again had their heads cloven in half with blows of swords, so that one side of their heads hung down on each shoulder in a most horrible manner.

15. Meanwhile, stubborn as the conflict was, neither party was wearied, but they still fought on with equal valour and equal fortune, nor did any one relax in his sternness as long as his courage could give him strength for exertion. But at last the day yielded to the evening, and put an end to the deadly contest: the barbarians all withdrew, in no order, each taking his own path, and our men returned sorrowfully to their tents.

16. Then having paid the honours of burial to some among the dead, as well as the time and place permitted, the rest of the corpses were left as a banquet to the ill-omened birds, which at that time were accustomed to feed on carcases—as is even now shown by the places which are still white with bones. It is quite certain that the Romans, who were comparatively few, and contending with vastly superior numbers, suffered serious losses, while at the same time the barbarians did not escape without much lamentable slaughter.

VIII.

§ 1. Upon the melancholy termination of this battle, our men sought a retreat in the neighbouring city of Marcianopolis. The Goths, of their own accord, fell back behind the ramparts formed by their waggons, and for seven days they never once ventured to come forth or show themselves. So our soldiers, seizing the opportunity, raised a barrier, and shut in some other vast multitudes of the barbarians among the defiles of the Balkan, in hope, forsooth, that this destructive host being thus hemmed in between the Danube and the desert, and having no road by which to escape, must perish by famine, since everything which could serve to sustain life had been conveyed into the fortified cities, and these cities were safe from any attempt of the barbarians to besiege them, since they were wholly ignorant of the use of warlike engines.

2. After this Richomeres returned to Gaul, to convey reinforcements to that country, where a fresh war of greater importance than ever, was anticipated. These events took place in the fourth consulship of Gratian, and the first of Merobaudes, towards the autumn of the year.

3. In the mean time Valens, having heard of the miserable result of these wars and devastations, gave Saturninus the command of the cavalry, and sent him to carry aid to Trajan and Profuturus.

4. At that time, throughout the whole countries of Scythia and Mœsia, everything which could be eaten had been consumed; and so, urged equally by their natural ferocity and by hunger, the barbarians made desperate efforts to force their way out of the position in which they were enclosed but though they made frequent attempts, they were constantly overwhelmed by the vigour of our men, who made an effectual resistance by the aid of the rugged ground which they occupied; and at last, being reduced to the extremity of distress, they allured some of the Huns and Alani to their alliance by the hope of extensive plunder.

5. When this was known, Saturninus (for by this time he had arrived and was busy in arranging the outposts and military stations in the country) gradually collected his men, and was preparing to retreat, in pursuance of a sufficiently well-devised plan, lest the multitude of barbarians by some sudden movement (like a river which had burst its barriers by the violence of a flood) should easily overthrow his whole force, which had now been for some time watching the place from which danger was suspected.

6. The moment that, by the seasonable retreat of our men, the passage of these defiles was opened, the barbarians, in no regular order, but wherever each individual could find a passage, rushed forth without hindrance to spread confusion among us; and raging with a desire for devastation and plunder, spread themselves with impunity over the whole region of Thrace, from the districts watered by the Danube, to Mount Rhodope and the strait which separates the Ægean from the Black Sea, spreading ravage, slaughter, bloodshed, and conflagration, and throwing everything into the foulest disorder by all sorts of acts of violence committed even on the free-born.

7. Then one might see, with grief, actions equally horrible to behold and to speak of: women panic-stricken, beaten with cracking scourges; some even in pregnancy, whose very offspring, before they were born, had to endure countless horrors: here were seen children twining round their mothers; there one might hear the lamentations of noble youths and maidens all seized and doomed to captivity.

8. Again, grown-up virgins and chaste matrons were dragged along with countenances disfigured by bitter weeping, wishing to avoid the violation of their modesty by any death however agonizing. Here some wealthy nobleman was dragged along like a wild beast, complaining, of fortune as merciless and blind, who in a brief moment had stripped him of his riches, of his beloved relations, and his home; had made him see his house reduced to ashes, and had reduced him to expect either to be torn limb from limb himself, or else to be exposed to scourging and torture, as the slave of a ferocious conqueror.

9. But the barbarians, like beasts who had broken loose from their cages, pouring unrestrainedly over the vast extent of country, marched upon a town called Dibaltum, where they found Barzimeres, a tribune of the Scutarii, with his battalion, and some of the Cornuti legion, and several other bodies of infantry pitching a camp, like a veteran general of great experience as he was.

10. Instantly (as the only means of avoiding immediate destruction) he ordered the trumpet to give the signal for battle; and strengthening his flanks, rushed forward with his little army in perfect order. And he made so gallant a struggle, that the barbarians would have obtained no advantage over him, if a strong body of cavalry had not come round upon him from behind, while his men were panting and weary with their exertions: so at last he fell, but not without having inflicted great slaughter on the barbarians, though the vastness of their numbers made their losses less observed.

IX.

§ 1. After this affair had terminated, the Goths, being uncertain what next to do, went in quest of Frigeridus, with the resolution to destroy him wherever they could find him, as a formidable obstacle to their success; and having rested for a while to refresh themselves with sleep and better food than usual, they then pursued him like so many wild beasts, having learnt that by Gratian's order he had returned into Thrace, and had pitched his camp near Beræa, intending to wait there to see how affairs would turn out.

2. They hastened accordingly, that by a rapid march they might carry out their proposed plan; but Frigeridus, who knew as well how to command as to preserve his troops, either suspected their plans, or else obtained accurate information respecting them from the scouts whom he had sent out; and therefore returned over the mountains and through the thick forests into Illyricum; being full of joy at the success which an unexpected chance threw in his way.

3. For as he was retreating, and moving on steadily with his force in a solid column, he came upon Farnobius, one of the chieftains of the Goths, who was roaming about at random with a large predatory band, and a body of the Taifali, with whom he had lately made an alliance, and who (if it is worth mentioning), when our soldiers were all dispersed for fear of the strange nations which were threatening them, had taken advantage of their dispersion to cross the river, in order to plunder the country thus left without defenders.

4. When their troops thus suddenly came in sight, our general with great prudence prepared to bring on a battle at close quarters, and, in spite of their ferocious threats, at once attacked the combined leaders of the two nations; and would have slain them all, not leaving a single one of them to convey news of their disaster, if, after Farnobius, hitherto the much-dreaded cause of all these troubles, had been slain, with a great number of his men, he had not voluntarily spared the rest on their own earnest supplication; and then he distributed those to whom he had thus granted their lives in the districts around the Italian towns of Modena, Reggio, and Parma, which he allotted to them to cultivate.

5. It is said that this nation of the Taifali was so profligate, and so immersed in the foulest obscenities of life, that they indulged in all kinds of unnatural lusts, exhausting the vigour both of youth and manhood in the most polluted defilements of debauchery. But if any adult caught a boar or slew a bear single-handed, he was then exempted from all compulsion of submitting to such ignominious pollution.

X.

§ 1. It was when autumn was passing into winter that terrible whirlwinds swept over Thrace; and as if the Furies were throwing everything into confusion, awful storms extended even into distant regions.

2. And now the people of the Allemanni, belonging to the district of Lintz, who border on the Tyrol, having by treacherous incursions violated the treaty which had been made with them some time before, began to make attempts upon our frontier; and this calamity had the following lamentable beginning.

3. One of this nation who was serving among the guards of the emperor, returned home at the call of some private business of his own; and being a very talkative person, when he was continually asked what was doing in the palace, he told them that Valens, his uncle, had sent for Gratian to conduct the campaign in the East, in order that by their combined forces they might drive back the inhabitants of the countries on our eastern frontier, who had all conspired for the overthrow of the Roman state.

4. The people of Lintz greedily swallowed this intelligence, looking on it as if it concerned themselves also as neighbours, being so rapid and active in their movements; and so they assembled, in predatory bands, and when the Rhine was sufficiently frozen over to be passable, in the month of February.... The Celtæ, with the Petulantes legion, repulsed them, but not without considerable loss.

5. These Germans, though thus compelled to retreat, being aware that the greater part of our army had been despatched into Illyricum, where the emperor was about to follow to assume the command, became more bold than ever, and conceived the idea of greater enterprises. Having collected the inhabitants of all the adjacent countries into one body, and with 40,000 armed men, or 70,000, as some, who seek to enhance the renown of the emperor, have boasted, they with great arrogance and confidence burst into our territories.

6. Gratian, when he heard of this event, was greatly alarmed, and recalling the cohorts which he had sent on before into Pannonia, and collecting others whom he had prudently retained in Gaul, he committed the affair to the conduct of Nannienus, a leader of great prudence and skill, joining with him as his colleague with equal power, Mellobaudes, the count-commander of the domestics and king of the Franks, a man of great courage and renown in war.[195]

7. Nannienus took into his consideration the variable chances of fortune, and therefore voted for acting slowly and with caution, while Mellobaudes, hurried away by a fierce desire for fighting, according to his usual custom, was eager at once to march against the enemy; and would not brook delay.

8. Presently a horrid shout was raised by the enemy, and the trumpeters on our side also gave the signal for battle, upon which a fierce engagement began near Colmar. On both sides numbers fell beneath the blows of arrows and hurled javelins.

9. But while the battle was raging, the multitude of the enemy appeared so countless, that our soldiers, avoiding a conflict with them on the open field, dispersed as best they could among the different narrow paths overgrown with trees; but they afterwards stood their ground firmly, and by the boldness of their carriage and the dazzling splendour of their arms, when seen from a distance, made the barbarians fear that the emperor himself was at hand.

10. And they suddenly turned their backs, still offering occasional resistance, to leave no chance for safety untried; but at last they were routed with such slaughter that of their whole number not above 9,000, as was reckoned, escaped, and these owed their safety to the thickness of the woods. Among the many bold and gallant men who perished was their king, Priarius, who had been the principal cause of this ruinous war.

11. Gratian was greatly delighted and encouraged by this success; and intending now to proceed to the East, he secretly crossed the Rhine, and turned his march to the left, being full of sanguine hopes, and resolving, if fortune should only favour his enterprise, to destroy the whole of this treacherous and turbulent nation.

12. And as intelligence of this design was conveyed to the people of Lintz by repeated messengers, they, who had already been reduced to great weakness by the almost entire destruction of their forces, and were now greatly alarmed at the expected approach of the emperor, hesitated what to do, and as neither by resistance, nor by anything which they could do or devise, did they perceive any possibility of obtaining ever so brief a respite, they withdrew with speed to their hills, which were almost inaccessible from the steepness of their precipices, and reaching the most inaccessible rocks by a winding path, they conveyed thither their riches and their families, and prepared to defend them with all their might.

13. Having deliberated on this difficulty, our general selected 500 men of proved experience in war out of each legion, to station op-

posite to the entrances to this wall of rock. And they, being further encouraged by the fact that the emperor himself was continually seen actively employed among the front rank, endeavoured to scale the precipices, not doubting but that if they could once set foot upon the rocks they should instantly catch the barbarians, like so much game, without any conflict; and so an engagement was commenced towards the approach of noon, and lasted even to the darkness of night.

14. Both sides experienced heavy losses. Our men slew numbers, and fell in numbers; and the armour of the emperor's body-guard, glittering with gold and brilliant colours, was crushed beneath the weight of the heavy missiles hurled upon them.

15. Gratian held a long deliberation with his chief officers; and it seemed to them fruitless and mischievous to contend with unreasonable obstinacy against these rugged and overhanging rocks; at last (as is usual in such affairs), after various opinions had been delivered, it was determined, without making any more active efforts, to blockade the barbarians and reduce them by famine; since against all active enterprises the character of the ground which they occupied was a sufficient defence.

16. But the Germans still held out with unflinching obstinacy, and being thoroughly acquainted with the country, retreated to other mountains still more lofty than those which they occupied at first. Thither also the emperor turned with his army, with the same energy as before, seeking for a path which might lead him to the heights.

17. And when the barbarians saw him thus with unwearied perseverance intent upon their destruction, they surrendered; and having by humble supplication obtained mercy, they furnished a reinforcement of the flower of their youth to be mingled with our recruits, and were permitted to retire in safety to their native land.

18. It is beyond all belief how much vigour and rapidity of action Gratian, by the favour of the eternal Deity, displayed in gaining this seasonable and beneficial victory, which broke the power of the Western tribes at a time when he was preparing to hasten in another direction. He was indeed a young prince of admirable disposition, eloquent, moderate, warlike, and merciful, rivalling the most admirable of his predecessors, even while the down of youth was still upon his cheeks; the only drawback to his character being that he was sometimes drawn into ridiculous actions, when, in consequence of temptations held out by his minions and favourites, he imitated the vain pursuits of Cæsar Commodus; but he was never bloodthirsty.

19. For as that prince, because he had been accustomed to slay numbers of wild beasts with his javelins in the sight of the people, and prided himself beyond measure on the skill with which he slew a hundred lions let loose at the same time in the amphitheatre with different missiles, and without ever having to repeat his shot; so Gratian, in the enclosures called preserves, slew wild beasts with his arrows, neglecting much serious business for this amusement, and this at a time when if Marcus Antoninus had resumed the empire he would have found it hard, without colleagues of equal genius to his own, and without the most serious deliberation of counsel, to remedy the grievous disasters of the republic.

20. Therefore having made all the arrangements which the time would permit for the affairs of Gaul, and having punished the traitor of the Scutarii who had betrayed to the barbarians the intelligence that the emperor was about to depart with all speed for Illyricum, Gratianus quitted the army, and passing through the fortress known as that of Arbor Felix, he proceeded by forced marches to carry his assistance to those who needed it.

21. About this time, while Frigeridus was with great wisdom devising many schemes likely to prove of advantage to the general safety, and was preparing to fortify the defiles of the Succi, to prevent the enemy (who, by the rapidity of their movements and their fondness for sallies, were always threatening the northern provinces like a torrent) from extending their inroads any further he was superseded by a count named Maurus, a man cruel, ferocious, fickle, and untrustworthy. This man, as we have related in our account of preceding transactions being one of Julian's body-guard to whom the defence of the palace was expressly committed, while that prince was doubting about accepting the imperial authority, took the chain from his own neck and offered it to him for a diadem.

22. Thus, in the most critical aspect of our difficulties, a cautious and energetic general was removed, when, even if he had previously retired into private life, he ought, from the greatness of the affairs which required his superintendence, to have been brought back again to the camp.

XI.

A.D. 378.

§ 1. About the same time Valens quitted Antioch, and, after a long journey, came to Constantinople, where he stayed a few days, being made anxious by a trifling sedition among the citizens. He in-

trusted the command of the infantry, which had previously been committed to Trajan, to Sebastian, who at his request had been lately sent
to him from Italy, being a general of well-known vigilance; and he
himself went to Melanthias, a country palace belonging to the emperors, where he conciliated the soldiers by giving them their pay,
furnishing them with provisions, and frequently addressing them in
courteous speeches.

2. Having left this place, he proceeded according to the stages he
had marked out, and came to a station named Nice, where he learnt
from intelligence brought by his scouts, that the barbarians, who had
collected a rich booty, were returning loaded with it from the districts
about Mount Rhodope, and were now near Hadrianople. They, hearing
of the approach of the emperor with a numerous force, were hastening
to join their countrymen, who were in strong positions around Beræa
and Nicopolis; and immediately (as the ripeness of the opportunity
thus thrown in his way required) the emperor ordered Sebastian to hasten on with three hundred picked soldiers of each legion, to do
something (as he promised) of signal advantage to the commonweal.

3. Sebastian pushed on by forced marches, and came in sight of
the enemy near Hadrianople; but as the gates were barred against him,
he was unable to approach nearer, since the garrison feared that he had
been taken prisoner by the enemy, and won over by them: so that
something to the injury of the city might happen, like what had formerly taken place in the case of Count Actus, who had been cunningly
taken prisoner by the soldiers of Magnentius, and who thus caused the
opening of the passes of the Julian Alps.

4. At last, though late, they recognized Sebastian, and allowed
him to enter the city. He, then, as well as he could, refreshed the troops
under his command with food and rest, and next morning secretly issued forth, and towards evening, being partially concealed by the
rising ground and some trees, he suddenly caught sight of the predatory bands of the Goths near the river Maritza, where, favoured by the
darkness of night, he charged them while in disorder and unprepared,
routing them so completely that, with the exception of a few whom
swiftness of foot saved from death, the whole body were slain, and he
recovered such an enormous quantity of booty, that neither the city,
nor the extensive plains around could contain it.

5. Fritigern was greatly alarmed; and fearing lest this general,
who as we have often heard succeeded in all his undertakings, should
surprise and utterly destroy his different detachments, which were
scattered at random over the country, intent only on plunder, he called

in all his men near the town of Cabyle, and at once made off, in order to gain the open country, where he would not be liable to be straitened for want of provisions, or harassed by secret ambuscades.

6. While these events were proceeding in Thrace, Gratian having sent letters to inform his uncle of the energy with which he had overcome the Allemanni, and forwarded his baggage by land, himself, with a picked band of his quickest troops, crossed the Danube, reached Bononia, and afterwards Sirmium, where he halted four days. He then descended the river to the Camp of Mars, where he was laid up by an intermittent fever, and, being suddenly assailed by the Alani, lost a few of his followers.

XII.

§ 1. At this time Valens was disturbed by a twofold anxiety, having learned that the people of Lintz had been defeated, and also because Sebastian, in the letters which he sent from time to time, exaggerated what had taken place by his pompous language. Therefore he advanced from Melanthias, being eager by some glorious exploit to equal his youthful nephew, by whose virtue he was greatly excited. He was at the head of a numerous force, neither unwarlike nor contemptible, and had united with them many veteran bands, among whom were several officers of high rank, especially Trajan, who a little while before had been commander of the forces.

2. And as by means of spies and observation it was ascertained that the enemy were intending to blockade the different roads by which the necessary supplies must come, with strong divisions, he sent a sufficient force to prevent this, despatching a body of the archers of the infantry and a squadron of cavalry, with all speed, to occupy the narrow passes in the neighbourhood.

3. Three days afterwards, when the barbarians, who were advancing slowly, because they feared an attack in the unfavourable ground which they were traversing, arrived within fifteen miles from the station of Nice, which was the aim of their march, the emperor, with wanton impetuosity, resolved on attacking them instantly, because those who had been sent forward to reconnoitre (what led to such a mistake is unknown) affirmed that their entire body did not exceed ten thousand men.

4. Marching on with his army in battle array, he came near the suburb of Hadrianople, where he pitched his camp, strengthening it with a rampart of palisades, and then impatiently waited for Gratian. While here, Richomeres, Count of the Domestici, arrived, who had

been sent on by that emperor with letters announcing his immediate approach.

5. And imploring Valens to wait a little while for him that he might share his danger, and not rashly face the danger before him single handed, he took counsel with his officers as to what was best to be done.

6. Some, following the advice of Sebastian, recommended with urgency that he should at once go forth to battle; while Victor, master-general of the cavalry, a Sarmatian by birth, but a man of slow and cautious temper, recommended him to wait for his imperial colleague, and this advice was supported by several other officers, who suggested that the reinforcement of the Gallic army would be likely to awe the fiery arrogance of the barbarians.

7. However, the fatal obstinacy of the emperor prevailed, fortified by the flattery of some of the princes, who advised him to hasten with all speed, so that Gratian might have no share in a victory which, as they fancied, was already almost gained.

8. And while all necessary preparations were being made for the battle, a presbyter of the Christian religion (as he called himself), having been sent by Fritigern as his ambassador, came, with some colleagues of low rank, to the emperor's camp; and having been received with courtesy, he presented a letter from that chieftain, openly requesting that the emperor would grant to him and to his followers, who were now exiles from their native homes, from which they had been driven by the rapid invasions of savage nations, Thrace, with all its flocks and all its crops, for a habitation. And if Valens would consent to this, Fritigern would agree to a perpetual peace.

9. In addition to this message, the same Christian, as one acquainted with his commander's secrets, and well trusted, produced other secret letters from his chieftain who, being full of craft and every resource of deceit, informed Valens, as one who was hereafter to be his friend and ally, that he had no other means to appease the ferocity of his countrymen, or to induce them to accept conditions advantageous to the Roman state, unless from time to time he showed them an army under arms close at hand, and by frightening them with the name of the emperor, recalled them from their mischievous eagerness for fighting. The ambassadors retired unsuccessful, having been looked on as suspicious characters by the emperor.

10. When the day broke which the annals mark as the fifth of the Ides of August, the Roman standards were advanced with haste, the baggage having been placed close to the walls of Hadrianople, under a

sufficient guard of soldiers of the legions; the treasures and the chief insignia of the emperor's rank were within the walls, with the prefect and the principal members of the council.

11. Then, having traversed the broken ground which divided the two armies, as the burning day was progressing towards noon, at last, after marching eight miles, our men came in sight of the waggons of the enemy, which had been stated by the scouts to be all arranged in a circle. According to their custom, the barbarian host raised a fierce and hideous yell, while the Roman generals marshalled their line of battle. The right wing of the cavalry was placed in front; the chief portion of the infantry was kept in reserve.

12. But the left wing of the cavalry, of which a considerable number were still straggling on the road, were advancing with speed, though with great difficulty; and while this wing was deploying, not as yet meeting with any obstacle, the barbarians being alarmed at the terrible clang of their arms and the threatening crash of their shields (since a large portion of their own army was still at a distance, under Alatheus and Saphrax, and, though sent for, had not yet arrived), again sent ambassadors to ask for peace.

13. The emperor was offended at the lowness of their rank, and replied, that if they wished to make a lasting treaty, they must send him nobles of sufficient dignity. They designedly delayed, in order by the fallacious truce which subsisted during the negotiation to give time for their cavalry to return, whom they looked upon as close at hand; and for our soldiers, already suffering from the summer heat, to become parched and exhausted by the conflagration of the vast plain; as the enemy had, with this object, set fire to the crops by means of burning faggots and fuel. To this evil another was added, that both men and cattle were suffering from extreme hunger.

14. In the meantime Fritigern, being skilful in divining the future, and fearing a doubtful struggle, of his own head sent one of his men as a herald, requesting that some nobles and picked men should at once be sent to him as hostages for his safety, when he himself would fearlessly bring us both military aid and supplies.

15. The proposition of this formidable chief was received with praise and approbation, and the tribune Equitius, a relation of Valens, who was at that time high steward of the palace, was appointed, with general consent, to go with all speed to the barbarians as a hostage. But he refused, because he had once been taken prisoner by the enemy, and had escaped from Dibaltum, so that he feared their vengeful anger; upon this Richomeres voluntarily offered himself, and willingly

undertook to go, thinking it a bold action, and one becoming a brave man; and so he set out, bearing vouchers of his rank and high birth.

16. And as he was on his way towards the enemy's camp, the accompanying archers and Scutarii, who on that occasion were under the command of Bacurius, a native of Iberia, and of Cassio, yielded, while on their march, to an indiscreet impetuosity, and on approaching the enemy, first attacked them rashly, and then by a cowardly flight disgraced the beginning of the campaign.

17. This ill-timed attack frustrated the willing services of Richomeres, as he was not permitted to proceed; in the mean time the cavalry of the Goths had returned with Alatheus and Saphrax, and with them a battalion of Alani; these descending from the mountains like a thunderbolt, spread confusion and slaughter among all whom in their rapid charge they came across.

XIII.

§ 1. And while arms and missiles of all kinds were meeting in fierce conflict, and Bellona, blowing her mournful trumpet, was raging more fiercely than usual, to inflict disaster on the Romans, our men began to retreat; but presently, roused by the reproaches of their officers, they made a fresh stand, and the battle increased like a conflagration, terrifying our soldiers, numbers of whom were pierced by strokes from the javelins hurled at them, and from arrows.

2. Then the two lines of battle dashed against each other, like the beaks (or rams) of ships, and thrusting with all their might, were tossed to and fro, like the waves of the sea. Our left wing had advanced actually up to the waggons, with the intent to push on still further if they were properly supported; but they were deserted by the rest of the cavalry, and so pressed upon by the superior numbers of the enemy, that they were overwhelmed and beaten down, like the ruin of a vast rampart. Presently our infantry also was left unsupported, while the different companies became so huddled together that a soldier could hardly draw his sword, or withdraw his hand after he had once stretched it out. And by this time such clouds of dust arose that it was scarcely possible to see the sky, which resounded with horrible cries; and in consequence, the darts, which were bearing death on every side, reached their mark, and fell with deadly effect, because no one could see them beforehand so as to guard against them.

3. But when the barbarians, rushing on with their enormous host, beat down our horses and men, and left no spot to which our ranks could fall back to deploy, while they were so closely packed that it

was impossible to escape by forcing a way through them, our men at last began to despise death, and again took to their swords and slew all they encountered, while with mutual blows of battle-axes, helmets and breastplates were dashed in pieces.

4. Then you might see the barbarian towering in his fierceness, hissing or shouting, fall with his legs pierced through, or his right hand cut off, sword and all, or his side transfixed, and still, in the last gasp of life, casting round him defiant glances. The plain was covered with carcases, strewing the mutual ruin of the combatants; while the groans of the dying, or of men fearfully wounded, were intense, and caused great dismay all around.

5. Amidst all this great tumult and confusion, our infantry were exhausted by toil and danger, till at last they had neither strength left to fight, nor spirits to plan anything; their spears were broken by the frequent collisions, so that they were forced to content themselves with their drawn swords, which they thrust into the dense battalions of the enemy, disregarding their own safety, and seeing that every possibility of escape was cut off from them.

6. The ground, covered with streams of blood, made their feet slip, so that all that they endeavoured to do was to sell their lives as dearly as possible; and with such vehemence did they resist their enemies who pressed on them, that some were even killed by their own weapons. At last one black pool of blood disfigured everything, and wherever the eye turned, it could see nothing but piled-up heaps of dead, and lifeless corpses trampled on without mercy.

7. The sun being now high in the heavens, having traversed the sign of Leo, and reached the abode of the heavenly Virgo, scorched the Romans, who were emaciated by hunger, worn out with toil, and scarcely able to support even the weight of their armour. At last our columns were entirely beaten back by the overpowering weight of the barbarians, and so they took to disorderly flight, which is the only resource in extremity, each man trying to save himself as well as he could.

8. While they were all flying and scattering themselves over roads with which they were unacquainted, the emperor, bewildered with terrible fear, made his way over heaps of dead, and fled to the battalions of the Lancearii and the Mattiarii, who, till the superior numbers of the enemy became wholly irresistible, stood firm and immovable. As soon as he saw him. Trajan exclaimed that all hope was lost, unless the emperor, thus deserted by his guards, could be protected by the aid of his foreign allies.

9. When this exclamation was heard, a count named Victor hastened to bring up with all speed the Batavians, who were placed in the reserve, and who ought to have been near at hand, to the emperor's assistance; but as none of them could be found, he too retreated, and in a similar manner Richomeres and Saturninus saved themselves from danger.

10. So now, with rage flashing in their eyes, the barbarians pursued our men, who were in a state of torpor, the warmth of their veins having deserted them. Many were slain without knowing who smote them; some were overwhelmed by the mere weight of the crowd which pressed upon them; and some were slain by wounds inflicted by their own comrades. The barbarians spared neither those who yielded nor those who resisted.

11. Besides these, many half slain lay blocking up the roads, unable to endure the torture of their wounds; and heaps of dead horses were piled up and filled the plain with their carcases. At last a dark moonless night put an end to the irremediable disaster which cost the Roman state so dear.

12. Just when it first became dark, the emperor being among a crowd of common soldiers, as it was believed—for no one said either that he had seen him, or been near him—was mortally wounded with an arrow, and, very shortly after, died, though his body was never found. For as some of the enemy loitered for a long time about the field in order to plunder the dead, none of the defeated army or of the inhabitants ventured to go to them.

13. A similar fate befell the Cæsar Decius, when fighting vigorously against the barbarians; for he was thrown by his horse falling, which he had been unable to hold, and was plunged into a swamp, out of which he could never emerge, nor could his body be found.

14. Others report that Valens did not die immediately, but that he was borne by a small body of picked soldiers and eunuchs to a cabin in the neighbourhood, which was strongly built, with two stories; and that while these unskilful hands were tending his wounds, the cottage was surrounded by the enemy, though they did not know who was in it; still, however, he was saved from the disgrace of being made a prisoner.

15. For when his pursuers, while vainly attempting to force the barred doors, were assailed with arrows from the roof, they, not to lose by so inconvenient a delay the opportunity of collecting plunder, gathered some faggots and stubble, and setting fire to them, burnt down the building, with those who were in it.

16. But one of the soldiers dropped from the windows, and, being taken prisoner by the barbarians, revealed to them what had taken place, which caused them great concern, because they looked upon themselves as defrauded of great glory in not having taken the ruler of the Roman state alive. This same young man afterwards secretly returned to our people, and gave this account of the affair.

17. When Spain had been recovered after a similar disaster, we are told that one of the Scipios was lost in a fire, the tower in which he had taken refuge having been burnt. At all events it is certain that neither Scipio nor Valens enjoyed that last honour of the dead—a regular funeral.

18. Many illustrious men fell in this disastrous defeat, and among them one of the most remarkable was Trajan, and another was Sebastian; there perished also thirty-five tribunes who had no particular command, many captains of battalions, and Valerianus and Equitius, one of whom was master of the horse and the other high steward. Potentius, too, tribune of the promoted officers, fell in the flower of his age, a man respected by all persons of virtue, and recommended by the merits of his father, Ursicinus, who had formerly been commander of the forces, as well as by his own. Scarcely onethird of the whole army escaped.

19. Nor, except the battle of Cannæ, is so destructive a slaughter recorded in our annals; though, even in the times of their prosperity, the Romans have more than once had to deplore the uncertainty of war, and have for a time succumbed to evil Fortune; while the wellknown dirges of the Greeks have bewailed many disastrous battles.

XIV.

§ 1. Such was the death of Valens, when he was about fifty years old, and had reigned rather less than fourteen years. We will now describe his virtues, which were known to many, and his vices.

2. He was a faithful and steady friend—a severe chastiser of ambition—a rigid upholder of both military and civil discipline—always careful that no one should assume importance on account of any relationship to himself; slow both in conferring office, and in taking it away; a very just ruler of the provinces, all of which he protected from injury, as if each had been his own house; devoting singular care to the lessening the burdens of the state, and never permitting any increase of taxation. He was very moderate in the exaction of debts due to the state, but a vehement and implacable foe to all thieves, and to every

one convicted of peculations; nor in affairs of this kind was the East, by its own confession, ever better treated under any other emperor.

3. Besides all this, he was liberal with due regard to moderation, of which quality there are many examples, one of which it will be sufficient to mention here:—As in palaces there are always some persons covetous of the possessions of others, if any one petitioned for lapsed property, or anything else which it was usual to apply for, he made a proper distinction between just and unjust claims, and when he gave it to the petitioner, while reserving full liberty to any one to raise objections, he often associated the successful candidate with three or four partners, in order that those covetous suitors might conduct themselves with more moderation, when they saw the profits for which they were so eager diminished by this device.

4. Of the edifices, which in the different cities and towns he either repaired or built from their foundations, I will say nothing (to avoid prolixity), allowing those things to speak for themselves. These qualities, in my opinion, deserve the imitation of all good men. Now let us enumerate his vices.

5. He was an immoderate coveter of great wealth; impatient of labour, he affected an extreme severity, and was too much inclined to cruelty; his behaviour was rude and rough; and he was little imbued with skill either in war or in the liberal arts. He willingly sought profit and advantage in the miseries of others, and was more than ever intolerable in straining ordinary offences into sedition or treason; he cruelly encompassed the death or ruin of wealthy nobles.

6. This also was unendurable, that while he wished to have it appear that all actions and suits were decided according to the law, and while the investigation of such affairs was delegated to judges especially selected as the most proper to decide them, he still would not allow any decision to be given which was contrary to his own pleasure. He was also insulting, passionate, and always willing to listen to all informers, without the least distinction as to whether the charges which they advanced were true or false. And this vice is one very much to be dreaded, even in private affairs of everyday occurrence.

7. He was dilatory and sluggish; of a swarthy complexion; had a cast in one eye, a blemish, however, which was not visible at a distance; his limbs were well set; his figure was neither tall nor short; he was knock-kneed, and rather pot-bellied.

8. This is enough to say about Valens: and the recollection of his contemporaries will fully testify that this account is a true one. But we must not omit to mention that when he had learnt that the oracle of the

tripod, which we have related to have been moved by Patricius and Hilanus, contained those three prophetic lines, the last of which is,—

"Ἐν πεδίοισι Μίμαντος ἀλαλκομένοισιν ἄρηα."

"Repelling murd'rous war in Mimas' plain;"

—he, being void of accomplishments and illiterate, despised them at first; but as his calamities increased, he became filled with abject fear, and, from a recollection of this same prophecy, began to dread the very name of Asia, where he had been informed by learned men that both Homer and Cicero had spoken of the Mountain of Mimas over the town of Erythræ.

9. Lastly,—after his death, and the departure of the enemy, it is said that a monument was found near the spot where he is believed to have died, with a stone fixed into it inscribed with Greek characters, indicating that some ancient noble of the name of Mimas was buried there.

XV.

§ 1. After this disastrous battle, when night had veiled the earth in darkness, those who survived fled, some to the right, some to the left, or wherever fear guided them, each man seeking refuge among his relations, as no one could think of anything but himself, while all fancied the lances of the enemy sticking in their backs. And far off were heard the miserable wailings of those who were left behind—the sobs of the dying, and the agonizing groans of the wounded.

2. But when daylight returned, the conquerors, like wild beasts rendered still more savage by the blood they had tasted, and allured by the temptations of groundless hope, marched in a dense column upon Hadrianople, resolved to run any risk in order to take it, having been informed by traitors and deserters that the principal officers of State, the insignia of the imperial authority, and the treasures of Valens had all been placed there for safety, as in an impregnable fortress.

3. And to prevent the ardour of the soldiers from being cooled by delay, the whole city was blockaded by the fourth hour; and the siege from that time was carried on with great vigour, the besiegers, from their innate ferocity, pressing in to complete its destruction, while, on the other hand, the garrison was stimulated to great exertions by their natural courage.

4. And while the vast number of soldiers and grooms, who were prohibited from entering the city with their beasts, kept close to the walls and to the houses which joined them, and fought gallantly, considering the disadvantages under which they laboured from the

lowness of the ground which they occupied, and baffled the rage of their assailants till the ninth hour of the day, on a sudden three hundred of our infantry, of those who were nearest the battlements, formed themselves into a solid body, and deserted to the barbarians, who seized upon them with avidity, and (it is not known on what account) at once slaughtered them all. And from that time forth it was remarked that no one, even in the extremity of despair, adopted any similar conduct.

5. Now while all these misfortunes were at their height, suddenly there came a violent thunderstorm, and rain pouring down from the black clouds dispersed the bands of soldiers who were raging around; and they returned to their camp, which was measured out in a circle by their waggons; and being more elated and haughty than ever, they sent threatening letters to our men ... and an ambassador ... on condition of safety to him.

6. But as the messenger did not dare to enter the city, the letters were at last brought in by a certain Christian; and when they had been read and considered with all proper attention, the rest of the day and the whole of the night was devoted to preparing for defence. For inside the city the gates were blocked up with huge stones; the weak parts of the walls were strengthened, and engines to hurl javelins or stones were fixed on all convenient places, and a sufficient supply of water was also provided; for the day before some of the combatants had been distressed almost to death by thirst.

7. On the other hand the Goths, considering the difficulty and uncertainty of all warlike transactions, and becoming anxious at seeing their bravest warriors wounded and slain, and their strength gradually diminished, devised and adopted a crafty counsel, which, however, was revealed to us by Justice herself.

8. They seduced some picked soldiers of our army, who had revolted to them the day before, to pretend to escape back to their former comrades, and thus gain admittance within the walls; and after they had effected their entrance, they were secretly to set fire to some part of the city, so that the conflagration might serve as a secret signal, and while the garrison and citizens were occupied in extinguishing it, the walls might be left undefended, and so be easily stormed.

9. The traitors did as they were commanded; and when they came near the ditch they stretched out their hands, and with entreaties requested to be admitted into the city as Romans. When they were admitted, however (since no suspicion existed to hinder their admission), and were questioned as to the plans of the enemy, they varied in their

tale: and in consequence they were put to the torture, and having formally confessed what they had undertaken to do, they were all beheaded.

10. Accordingly, every resource of war having been prepared, the barbarians, at the third watch discarding all fear from past failures, rushed in enormous numbers against the blocked-up entrances of the city, their officers urging them with great obstinacy. But the provincials and imperial guards, with the rest of the garrison, rose with fearless courage to repel them, and their missiles of every kind, even when shot at random among so vast a crowd, could not fall harmless. Our men perceived that the barbarians were using the same weapons which we ourselves had shot at them: and accordingly an order was given that the strings which fastened the iron points to the javelins and arrows should be cut before they were hurled or shot; so that while flying they should preserve their efficacy, but when they pierced a body or fell on the ground they should come asunder.

11. While affairs were in this critical state an unexpected accident had a considerable influence on the result. A scorpion, a military engine which in ordinary language is also known as the wild-ass, being stationed opposite the dense array of the enemy, hurled forth a huge stone, which, although it fell harmless on the ground, yet by the mere sight of it terrified them so greatly, that in alarm at the strange spectacle they all fell back and endeavoured to retreat.

12. But their officers ordering the trumpets to sound a charge, the battle was renewed; and the Romans, as before, got the advantage, not a single javelin or bullet hurled by a slinger failing of its effect. For the troops of the generals who led the vanguard, and who were inflamed by the desire of possessing themselves of the treasures which Valens had so wickedly acquired, were followed closely by others who were vain of exposing themselves to as much danger as those of greater renown. And some were wounded almost to death: others were struck down, crushed by huge weights, or pierced through their breasts with javelins; some who carried ladders and attempted to scale the walls on different sides were buried under their own burthens, being beaten down by stones which were hurled upon them, and by fragments of pillars and cylinders.

13. And yet, horrible as the sight of this bloodshed was, so great was their ardour that no one relaxed in his gallant exertions till the evening, being encouraged by seeing many of the garrison also fall by various wounds. So, without rest or relaxation, both the besiegers and the besieged fought with unwearied courage.

14. And now no kind of order was observed by the enemy, but they fought in detached bands and in skirmishes (which is the sign of the extremity of despair); and at last, when evening came on, they all returned to their tents, sorrowfully, each man accusing his neighbour of inconsiderate rashness, because they had not taken the advice of Fritigern, and avoided the labours and dangers of a siege.

XVI.

§ 1. After the battle, the soldiers devoted the whole night (which, as it was summer, was not long) to tending the wounded with all the remedies known to their nations, and when daylight returned they began to discuss various plans, doubting what to do. And after many plans had been proposed and objected to, they at last decided to occupy Perinthus, and then, every place where they could hear that any treasures were stored up, the deserters and fugitives having given them all the information they required, so that they learnt what was in every house, to say nothing of what was in every city. Adopting this resolution unanimously, which they thought the best, they advanced by slow marches, ravaging and burning everything as they passed.

2. But those who had been besieged in Hadrianople, after the barbarians had departed, as soon as scouts of approved fidelity had reported that the whole place was free from enemies, issued forth at midnight, and avoiding the public causeways, took out-of-way roads through the woods, and withdrew, some to Philippopolis, and from thence to Serdica, others to Macedonia; with all the wealth which they had saved undiminished, and pressing on with the greatest exertion and celerity, as if they were likely to find Valens in those regions, since they were wholly ignorant that he had perished in battle, or else certainly (as is rather believed) burnt to death in the cottage.

3. Meanwhile the Goths, combining with the Huns and Alani, both brave and warlike tribes, and inured to toil and hardship, whom Fritigern had with great ability won over to his side by the temptation of great rewards—fixed their camp near Perinthus; but recollecting their previous losses, they did not venture to come close to the city, or make any attempt to take it; they, however, devastated and entirely stripped the fertile territory surrounding it, slaying or making prisoners of the inhabitants.

4. From hence they marched with speed to Constantinople in battle array, from fear of ambuscades; being eager to make themselves masters of its ample riches, and resolved to try every means to take that illustrious city. But while giving way to extravagant pride, and

beating almost against the barriers of the gates, they were repulsed in this instance by the Deity.

5. A body of Saracens (a nation of whose origin and manners we have already given a full account in several places), being more suited for sallies and skirmishes than for pitched battles, had been lately introduced into the city; and, as soon as they saw the barbarian host, they sallied out boldly from the city to attack it. There was a stubborn fight for some time; and at last both armies parted on equal terms.

6. But a strange and unprecedented incident gave the final advantage to the eastern warriors; for one of them with long hair, naked—with the exception of a covering round his waist—shouting a hoarse and melancholy cry, drew his dagger and plunged into the middle of the Gothic host, and after he had slain an enemy, put his lips to his throat, and sucked his blood. The barbarians were terrified at this marvellous prodigy, and from that time forth, when they proceeded on any enterprise, displayed none of their former and usual ferocity, but advanced with hesitating steps.

7. As time went on their ardour damped, and they began to take into consideration the vast circuit of the walls (which was the greater on account of the large space occupied by mansions with gardens within it), the inaccessible beauties of the city, and the immensity of its population; also the vicinity of the strait which divides the Black Sea from the Ægean. Then after destroying the works which they had constructed, having sustained greater losses than they had inflicted, they raised the siege, and roamed at random over the northern provinces, which they traversed without restraint as far as the Julian Alps, which the ancients used to call the Venetian Alps.

8. At this time the energy and promptitude of Julius, the commander of the forces on the other side of Mount Taurus, was particularly distinguished; for when he learnt what had happened in Thrace, he sent secret letters to all the governors of the different cities and forts, who were all Romans (which at this time is not very common), requesting them, on one and the same day, as at a concerted signal, to put to death all the Goths who had previously been admitted into the places under their charge; first luring them into the suburbs, in expectation of receiving the pay which had been promised to them. This wise plan was carried out without any disturbance or any delay; and thus the Eastern provinces were delivered from great dangers.

9. Thus have I, a Greek by birth, and formerly a soldier, related all the events from the accession of Nerva to the death of Valens, to the best of my abilities; professing above all things to tell the truth,

which, as I believe, I have never knowingly perverted, either by silence or by falsehood. Let better men in the flower of their age, and of eminent accomplishments, relate the subsequent events. But if it should please them to undertake the task, I warn them to sharpen their tongues to a loftier style.

Notes

[189] The text is unusually mutilated here. It has been proposed to insert: "A little goat with its throat cut was found dead in the street."

[190] Virg. Georg., II. 106.

[191] Ammianus here alludes to the canal out through Mount Athos.

[192] See Gibbon, vol. ii., p. 215 (Bohn's edition).

[193] See Gibbon, vol. iii., p. 229 (Bohn).

[194] Barritus is the word used for the trumpeting of an elephant.

[195] See Gibbon, vol. iii., p. 181 (Bohn).

Also from Benediction Books ...
Wandering Between Two Worlds: Essays on Faith and Art
Anita Mathias
Benediction Books, 2007
152 pages
ISBN: 0955373700

Available from www.amazon.com, www.amazon.co.uk

In these wide-ranging lyrical essays, Anita Mathias writes, in lush, lovely prose, of her naughty Catholic childhood in Jamshedpur, India; her large, eccentric family in Mangalore, a sea-coast town converted by the Portuguese in the sixteenth century; her rebellion and atheism as a teenager in her Himalayan boarding school, run by German missionary nuns, St. Mary's Convent, Nainital; and her abrupt religious conversion after which she entered Mother Teresa's convent in Calcutta as a novice. Later rich, elegant essays explore the dualities of her life as a writer, mother, and Christian in the United States-- Domesticity and Art, Writing and Prayer, and the experience of being "an alien and stranger" as an immigrant in America, sensing the need for roots.

About the Author

Anita Mathias is the author of *Wandering Between Two Worlds: Essays on Faith and Art.* She has a B.A. and M.A. in English from Somerville College, Oxford University, and an M.A. in Creative Writing from the Ohio State University, USA. Anita won a National Endowment of the Arts fellowship in Creative Nonfiction in 1997. She lives in Oxford, England with her husband, Roy, and her daughters, Zoe and Irene.

Visit Anita's website
    http://www.anitamathias.com,
and Anita's blog
    http://dreamingbeneaththespires.blogspot.com, (Dreaming Beneath the Spires).

The Church That Had Too Much
Anita Mathias
Benediction Books, 2010
52 pages
ISBN: 9781849026567

Available from www.amazon.com, www.amazon.co.uk

The Church That Had Too Much was very well-intentioned. She wanted to love God, she wanted to love people, but she was both hampered by her muchness and the abundance of her possessions, and beset by ambition, power struggles and snobbery. Read about the surprising way The Church That Had Too Much began to resolve her problems in this deceptively simple and enchanting fable.

About the Author

Anita Mathias is the author of *Wandering Between Two Worlds: Essays on Faith and Art.* She has a B.A. and M.A. in English from Somerville College, Oxford University, and an M.A. in Creative Writing from the Ohio State University, USA. Anita won a National Endowment of the Arts fellowship in Creative Nonfiction in 1997. She lives in Oxford, England with her husband, Roy, and her daughters, Zoe and Irene.

Visit Anita's website
    http://www.anitamathias.com,
and Anita's blog
    http://dreamingbeneaththespires.blogspot.com (Dreaming Beneath the Spires).

www.ingramcontent.com/pod-product-compliance
Lightning Source LLC
Chambersburg PA
CBHW030522100426

42813CB00001B/126